Administration of
PHYSICAL EDUCATION
& ATHLETIC PROGRAMS

To my wife
Jackie

and my children
Diana, Richard, Nancy, and **Jerry**

Administration of
PHYSICAL EDUCATION
& ATHLETIC PROGRAMS

CHARLES A. BUCHER, A.B., M.A., Ed.D.

Professor and Director, School of Health, Physical Education,
Recreation and Dance, The University of Nevada at Las Vegas,
Las Vegas, Nevada; Consultant to the President's Council
on Physical Fitness and Sports

EIGHTH EDITION

with **372** illustrations

The C. V. Mosby Company

ST. LOUIS • TORONTO • LONDON   1983

A TRADITION OF PUBLISHING EXCELLENCE

Editor: Nancy K. Roberson
Assistant editor: Michelle Turenne
Editing supervisor: Elaine Steinborn
Manuscript editor: Dale Woolery
Book design: Nancy Steinmeyer
Cover design: Diane Beasley
Production: Suzanne Soehngen, Carolyn Biby

Cover photo from H. Armstrong Roberts, Inc.

EIGHTH EDITION

The C.V. Mosby Company
11830 Westline Industrial Drive, St. Louis, Missouri 63141

Library of Congress Cataloging in Publication Data

Bucher, Charles Augustus, 1912-
    Administration of physical education and
athletic programs.

    Bibilography: p.
    Includes index.
    1. Physical education and training—Administra-
tion.   2. Recreational leadership.   I. Title.
GV343.5.B77 1983   375'.6137   82-6479
ISBN 0-8016-0852-X   AACR2

GW/VH/VH 9 8 7 6 5 4 3 2 1   02/C/237

Preface

Administration of Physical Education and Athletic Programs is widely used in colleges and universities, not only throughout the United States, but also in many other countries of the world. Administrators of physical education and athletic programs also have used it as a reference in many of their programs. As this eighth edition comes off the press the text has been used for 28 years and keeps growing in popularity and use with each revision. Why? The answer, according to professional physical educators and athletic directors, is that each revision reflects the latest in concepts and information, maintaining its position as the most authoritative text in the field.

The eighth edition of *Administration of Physical Education and Athletic Programs* has been completely revised to include the many new concepts and practices that have become part of the theory behind and the management of the best programs in this and other countries. Administration is rapidly changing, involving faculty, staff, and members of various organizations. Therefore it is imperative that administrators and practitioners alike know and understand the role they can and should play in the management process.

Many new concepts and practices are included in this revision. The expansion of girls' and women's athletics has made it imperative to treat this subject at length in a separate chapter. The chapter on the administration of programs for the handicapped has been expanded to include organizational structures, instructional strategies, individual education programs, and facilities and equipment. Also receiving attention are community-based programs for the elderly, adult fitness, and recreation. Safety programs and the number of sport injuries are examined, with more space given to the roles of athletic trainers and health specialists. Examples are presented as to how physical educators and athletic directors can gain greater community support. New ways to raise money to support physical education and athletic programs are cited. The step-by-step process for developing programs and the importance of using such new materials as the *Basic Stuff Series I and II* and *Mastery Learning* are outlined. Administrative procedures to avoid lawsuits are indicated. New concepts such as teacher burnout, health-related fitness, affirmative action, use of certified and noncertified personnel, and product liability are dealt with at length. New administrative forms and hundreds of illustrations help to clarify many of the administrative principles discussed.

The eighth edition of *Administration of Physical Education and Athletic Programs* focuses particularly on the student who is preparing for a career in physical education or athletics. At the same time it takes into consideration the administrator who is directing and administering programs in the field.

Special thanks are due Carmen B. Smith for typing the manuscript for this edition.

Charles A. Bucher

Contents

PART ONE

Administrative theory and the management process

1

Administration and the management process

Instructional objectives and competencies to be achieved

After reading this chapter the student should be able to—

■ Define the terms *administration* and *management*.
■ Understand the purpose of administration and administrative theory in conducting physical education and athletic programs.
■ Describe and contrast the traditional view and the new perspective view of administration.
■ Appreciate the advantages and the problems concerned with a democratic and participatory administration.
■ Discuss a modern philosophy of administration.
■ Identify the factors and qualifications essential for an effective physical education and athletic administrator.
■ Enumerate the major duties of an administrator of a physical education program and of an athletic program.
■ Outline the preparation necessary to be an effective administrator.
■ Explain why a study of administration is important to the physical educator.

By analyzing several definitions of administration, a reader will be better able to understand what a text in administration is designed to cover. Some of the definitions proposed by experts in this field represent analyses of the administrative process based on research; others have been formulated as a result of experience as an administrator or of observation of administrators at work.

Based on Hemphill, Griffiths, and Frederickson's* research, Jenson and Clark† propose the following as a definition of administration: "The administrative

process is the way an organization, through working with people, makes decisions and initiates actions to achieve its purposes and goals." Halpin,* after analyzing administration in education, industry, and government, states that administration refers to a human activity involving a minimum of four components: (1) the *functions or tasks* to be performed, (2) the *formal organization* within which administration must operate, (3) the *work group* or groups with which administration must be concerned, and (4) the *leader* or leaders within the organization. Administration has also been defined as a means of bringing about effective cooperative activity to achieve the purposes of an enterprise.

*Hemphill, J., Griffiths, D., and Frederickson, N.: Administrative performance and personality, New York, 1962, Bureau of Publications, Teachers' College, Columbia University. (This study is sometimes referred to as the "Development of Criteria of Success in School Administration" project.)
†Jenson, T.J., and Clark, D.L.: Educational administration, New York, 1964, The Center for Applied Research in Education, Inc. (The Library of Education.)

*Halpin, A.W.: A paradigm for research on administrative behavior. In Campbell, R.F., and Gregg, R.T., editors: Administrative behavior in education, New York, 1957, Harper & Row, Publishers, p. 161.

Fig. 1-1. Dancers preparing for a concert at Longwood College.
Photo by Barbara Stonikinis.

The following definition of *administration* is proposed:

Administration is concerned with the functions and responsibilities essential to the achievement of established goals through associated effort. It is also concerned with that group of individuals who are responsible for directing, guiding, coordinating, and inspiring the associated efforts of individual members, so that the purposes for which an organization has been established may be accomplished in the most effective and efficient manner possible.

The definition of *management* as used in this text is one credited to Laurence A. Appley in his book *Management in Action:*

Management is guiding human and physical resources into a dynamic, hard hitting organizational unit that attains its objectives to the satisfaction of those served, and with a high degree of morale and sense of attainment on the part of those served.

Parkhouse and Lapin,* in their book *The Woman in Athletic Administration,* state that "successful management is working toward the achievement of objectives with and through people."

In light of the definitions of *administration* and *management,* the term *administration* will be used, because it encompasses the management function. In some instances the term *administrative management* will be used.

---

*Parkhouse, B.L., and Lapin, J.: The woman in athletic administration, Santa Monica, Calif., 1980, Goodyear Publishing Co., Inc.

The scope of administrative management in physical education and athletics

It has been estimated that there are more than 5 million individuals in the United States today performing administrative work as their main function. This number is large, but as the technology and the specialized functions of this country advance, more individuals will be needed to perform the myriad administrative duties characteristic of the thousands of organizations in society. There are many more administrative positions in physical education and athletics than there are in schools and colleges. This, of course, runs into several thousands of positions. There are many large educational institutions with several persons who assist in the administration of physical education and athletic programs. Also, there are many agencies such as health spas, industrial fitness programs, senior citizen centers, YMCAs, and Boys' Clubs, which also have administrative positions. Administration offers many career opportunities for both women and men.

In these administrative positions physical educators, athletic directors, and others perform many administrative and managerial duties such as staffing, budgeting, coordinating, planning, communicating, reporting, and scheduling. It is essential that individuals who perform administrative work know the many aspects of this particular field. If they are not aware of certain basic facts and acceptable administrative procedures, they may make many errors. This could result in loss of efficiency, production, and staff morale and in poor human relations. Administration is rapidly becoming a science with a body of specialized knowledge that should be known by all who would administer wisely and effectively.

A new perspective of administration

The role of administration has changed markedly in recent years. First, administration has become more of a science. Today individuals who desire to prepare for administration or management roles pursue college majors or graduate study in this discipline and do considerable work in such areas as the behavioral

sciences, as well as serving an internship to become oriented to the various administrative functions associated with their profession, just as physicians serve internships in hospitals to better understand the many medical problems they will have to face in their field. Such experiences as these enable administrators to predict outcomes that will ensue from administrative actions.

Second, the administrator who has special training in the field is more likely to be selected to fill an administrative position than the person who has no such training. For example, one of the fastest growing kinds of public administration is the city manager plan, the city manager being a person who is selected because of special training in public administration. Also, the person selected today to be a superintendent of schools is most likely an individual who has majored in educational administration. What is true in these cases will also be true in physical education and athletics in the future. Individuals need special preparation and expertise to perform administrative and managerial tasks efficiently.

Third, administrators have a greater responsibility to their staff members, faculty, and other members of the organization than was true many years ago. Today administrators serve the members of their organizations by trying to help all members accomplish their goals, that is, administrators try to obtain the money, provide the facilities and equipment, and mobilize the administrative and community support to get the job done. In other words, the administrator is an implementer, an obstacle clearer, the person who tries to help the various people in the organization to achieve their goals, recognizing that as their goals are achieved so are the organization's goals achieved. As each individual achieves, so does the organization and the administration.

SOME DIFFERENCES BETWEEN THE OLD AND THE NEW ADMINISTRATOR

Scott* has pointed out some of the differences between the old and the new administrator. These include the following:

*Scott, P.M.: The new administrator; a point of view, Journal of Physical Education and Recreation **50:**40, Jaunary, 1979.

Fig. 1-2. Research is a very important part of physical education and athletics.

Courtesy Office of Public Relations, Smith College, Northampton, Mass.

Selection of personnel. Traditionally the chairperson had the greatest and sometimes the only voice in hiring new personnel. Today a search committee is usually appointed to select personnel.

Evaluation of personnel. Traditionally the chairperson decided questions of promotion, tenure, rank, salary, and dismissal. Today personnel evaluation is frequently the function of faculty and staff members.

Faculty governance. Traditionally the chairperson had most to say about how the organization was to be governed. Today staff and faculty members have considerable influence on faculty governance.

Budget determination. Traditionally the chairperson decided how the money was to be spent. Today staff or faculty members have a say, particularly with respect to the priorities and guidelines in funding, although the chairperson administers the funds.

Curriculum. Traditionally curriculum has been a faculty responsibility; however, administrators have provided much of the curriculum leadership. Today faculty members guard their curriculum rights very carefully and do not want any interference from the administration.

Scott further explains some of the reasons for this change in the attitude toward administrators and administration. She lists three primary reasons for the change: (1) *individual determination*—the growing recognition of the importance and dignity of the individual; (2) *impact of unions*—staff and faculty members now frequently look to unions for strength in determining their rights in an organization; and (3) *financial exigencies*—a growing concern among faculty and staff members that although there is decreased support for education resulting in loss of faculty, at the same time, there is usually no loss in the number of administrators, and at times there is an increase in such positions.

Two additional factors that have resulted in a

Fig. 1-3. The great number of people running marathons is one indication of the increased interest in physical education.

Photograph by Philip Yunger. Courtesy President's Council on Physical Fitness and Sports.

change in the attitude toward administration are management by objectives and accountability, and the emphasis on group dynamics.

MANAGEMENT BY OBJECTIVES AND ACCOUNTABILITY

The stress on accountability today has not excluded the role of the administrator. Staff and faculty members are requesting that administrators be evaluated along with themselves. One trend that provides for accountability by administrators is *management by objectives* (MBO). This represents a system or plan that outlines the various tasks an administrator performs. Each task is then translated into an objective for the organization and for the administration to accomplish. Administrators are then evaluated regarding the degree to which they achieve these stated objectives.

GROUP DYNAMICS

Administrators are involved with many tasks that involve the various members of their organization. Therefore it is very important that they be knowledgeable about group dynamics, as well as about individual behavior. A need exists for considerable group interaction under the new style of administration that is expected in more and more organizations. To be successful, groups within an organization need to have common goals, a differentiation of roles, and shared values. For desirable change to take place, therefore, administration must be recognized as a social process that involves the interaction of people. Administrators must recognize the importance of and be able to work within the framework of this social process.

THE NEW PERSPECTIVE OF ADMINISTRATION AND PHYSICAL EDUCATION AND ATHLETICS

The administration of physical education and athletic programs is directly affected by the new perspective of administration. The person who seeks to hold an administrative role in such programs must recognize the importance of each individual in the organization and help in actively promoting each individual's participation. The administrator should recognize the need to help each person in the organization to develop and grow and become a force in helping the organization to achieve its goals. The administrator must be interested in working for the department, division, or school and in performing the many tasks involved in the organization.

If prospective administrators of physical education and athletic programs are thinking about positions that have power over other individuals, places to force personal ideas on other members of the organization, or offices that provide opportunities for making unilateral decisions, then they should not go into administration because they are doomed to failure. The formula for success, on the other hand, is to generate power, adopt ideas, and make decisions with the members of the organization. The power of the organization is important, not the power of the individual.

The new perspective of administration also has implications for staff and faculty members. Because they now share in the many administrative tasks to be performed, they must also assume the responsibility that goes with such a role. This means such things as being knowledgeable about the issues being considered, participating in the discussions, and making informed decisions. Not to accept such responsibilities is to cause irreparable harm to the organization of which one is a member.

Administrative leadership

Being the head of a department, division, or school of physical education and being the leader of these organizations are two different things. The head can be a person who takes care of the clerical details and occupies the main office in a department or division, but he or she may not necessarily be the leader of the organization. The administrative leader of an organization is one who helps and influences others in a certain direction as problems are solved and goals are achieved. In a school, college, business, or agency, the persons influenced are teachers, pupils, clerks, parents, custodians, and any person involved with the organization.

Knezevich* categorizes three kinds of leadership: (1) *symbolic leadership,* which is primarily a personality attribute; (2) *formal leadership,* which would be the use of a title, status, or position denoting a leadership role in a formal organization; and, (3) *functional leadership,* or the role performed in an organized group. Knezevich points out that leadership is a social process involving working with people. Personality traits will not in themselves result in leadership. Furthermore, conferring a title does not necessarily provide leadership. Instead, the existing situation and the ability of the person to lead in that situation are critical. As a general rule, people will contribute most with leaders who are creative and imaginative.

The question of what makes a leader is a provocative one. Much research has been done in recent years concerning what constitutes the administrative leader. Years ago it was felt that combinations of personality characteristics or traits were the ingredients that determined who was a leader. However,

*Knezevich, S.J.: Administration of public education, New York, 1975, Harper & Row, Publishers.

Fig. 1-4. Programs for adult fitness are growing rapidly.

Courtesy Dow Health and Physical Education Center, Hope College, Holland, Mich.

research such as that of Gouldner* indicates that: "At this time there is no reliable evidence concerning the existence of universal leadership traits."

Other studies have provided further information regarding leadership. Stogdill† states as a result of his research that "the qualities, characteristics, and skills required in a leader are determined to a large extent by the demands of the situation in which he is to function as a leader." In other words, a physical education administrative leader in one situation may not necessarily be a leader in another situation. Different styles of leadership are needed to meet the needs of different settings and situations. Administration therefore is a social process.

Certain traits and attributes that influence leader behavior have been identified. For example, Pierce and Merrill* in examining research on leadership, found that such qualities as popularity, originality, adaptability, judgment, ambition, persistence, emotional stability, social and economic status, and communicative skills were very important for persons to possess if they hoped to lead. The traits found to be most significant were popularity, originality, and judgment.

*Gouldner, A.W., editor: Studies in leadership, New York, 1950, Harper & Row, Publishers, p. 34.

†Stogdill, R.M.: Personal factors associated with leadership; a survey of the literature, Journal of Psychology **25**:63, 1948.

*Pierce, T.M., and Merrill, E.C., Jr.: The individual and administrative behavior. In Campbell, R.F., and Gregg, R.T., editors: Administrative behavior in education, New York, 1957, Harper & Row, Publishers, p. 331.

Goldman* examined the research on leadership and suggested that certain factors are significant. When these factors are related to physical education administrative leaders, the following guidelines are worth considering:

1. The administrators of physical education programs who possess such traits as ambition, ability to relate well to others, emotional stability, communicative skill, and judgment have greater potential for success in leadership than persons who do not possess these traits.
2. The administrators of physical education programs who desire to be leaders of their organization must have a clear understanding of the goals of the organization. The direction in which they desire to lead the organization must be within the broad framework of the goals and objectives of the school district and consonant with the needs of the community they serve.
3. The administrators of physical education programs who desire to be leaders of their organizations must understand each of the persons who work with them, including their personal and professional needs.
4. The administrators of physical education programs who desire to be leaders of their organizations need to establish a climate within which the organization goals, personal needs of each staff member, and their own personality traits, can operate harmoniously.

THEORIES OF ADMINISTRATION AND STYLES OF LEADERSHIP

Theories of administration exist by which organizations are led by the persons holding executive positions. In some cases, these theories have been referred to as styles of leadership. In determining which is the best theory or style of leadership it is important to evaluate each in terms of administrative theory.

Value of administrative theory for physical education and athletics

Many physical education programs are administered by persons who have practical experience. They have learned administration and management through

*Goldman, S.: The school principal, New York, 1966, The Center for Applied Research in Education, Inc. (The Library of Education), pp. 88-89.

their own experience and understanding. Practical experience, although valuable, is not sufficient by itself. It is also important to know the research findings of academicians who have studied administration and management and who, through their research, can provide insights into such areas as the structure of organizations, the role of leadership, and the human relations aspects that affect the achievement of goals. Most valuable is a combination of experience and an understanding and application of scientifically sound administration theory. Physical and athletic educators, therefore, will enhance their productivity in the administrative management process if they understand administration from both a theoretical and a practical point of view.

Traditional theories

The traditional theories of administrative philosophy have usually had authoritarian, democratic, or laissez-faire orientations. Other theories of administration or styles of leadership involve the combination of all three traditional theories (the three-dimensional theory) and the systems theory. These orientations may be considered traditional, because they do not allow for the leader who may be part democratic, part authoritarian, and part laissez-faire, depending on the situation. The traditional philosophy views leaders as absolutes, which of course is unrealistic, because the nature of the human personality is seldom so extreme.

Authoritarian theory. The authoritarian philosophy usually implies a one-person leadership with decision making imposed by the leader on group members.

Democratic or equalitarian theory. The democratic or equlitarian philosophy implies a leader who submits important matters to group discussion and involves group members in decision making.

Laissez-faire theory. The laissez-faire philosophy implies a leader who gives guidance but leaves decision making to group members.

Three-dimensional theory. Johnson of Southeastern Louisiana University has proposed a three-dimensional concept of administrative philosophy that suggests a leader may have tendencies toward all three traditional orientations. In illustrating his three-

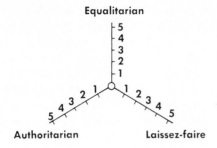

Equalitarian

Authoritarian   Laissez-faire

Fig. 1-5. A three-dimensional concept of administrative philosophy.

Courtesy Dr. Marion Lee Johnson, Southeastern Louisiana University and The Physical Educator **28:**39, 1971.

dimensional philosophy, he assigns point values to the traditional leadership patterns. The maximum number 5 indicates leadership entirely in one orientation. Thus a classic authoritarian administrator would be denoted as $5:0:0$ (leadership patterns are denoted in alphabetical order from left to right). The democratic leader would be denoted as $0:5:0$, and the purely laissez-faire leader would be denoted as $0:0:5$.

Because most leadership is not one-sided, an administrator who is strongly authoritarian, but occasionally employs democratic procedures, might be denoted by $4:1:0$ values. Numerous combinations may be achieved by using a three-dimensional model.

Systems theory. The systems theory of administration has stemmed from the rapid growth of technology and management in recent years. By borrowing techniques from the business world, administrators have constructed models that bring together the many facets of an organization. The systems theory is defined as a method designed to collect data on interrelated and interacting components that, when working in an integrated manner, help accomplish a predetermined goal or goals. The application of this strategy is called a systems theory of administration.

The recommended democratic or participatory theory

In the recommended democratic or participatory theory of administration and style of leadership the administration recognizes certain steps in the democratic process when the staff members of an organization work together to accomplish group goals. Some of the steps that are considered follow.

1. Goals are developed through the group process; they are set and attainable, challenging, and adapted to the capacities of the members.

2. Good morale is developed among all staff members. This is essential to constructive group action. A climate of openness is established in group deliberations. All members feel a sense of belonging and recognize their important contributions in the undertaking. A feeling of oneness pervades the entire group.

3. Group planning is accomplished in a clearly defined manner. A stated procedure is followed. It is a cooperative undertaking, based on known needs, and flexible enough to allow for unforeseen developments. The fulfillment of plans bring satisfaction and a feeling of success to all who participated in their formulation and accomplishment. All members share in recognition for a completed job.

4. In staff meetings and group discussions, the administration applies democratic principles. Each member's contribution is encouraged and respected. Differences of opinion are based on principles rather than on personalities. The organization's objectives must be continually kept in mind. All members are encouraged to facilitate the group process by accepting responsibility, alleviating conflict, making contributions, respecting the opinions of others, abiding by the will of the majority, and promoting good group morale.

5. There is periodic evaluation of progress. The group evaluates itself from time to time on accomplishments in terms of the organization's goals and the effectiveness of the group process. Each individual evaluates his or her own role as a member of the organization with respect to contributions made to the group process and the accomplishments of the group.

The problem of divided opinion. In a democratic organization, it is assumed that the wishes of the majority prevail. A question often arises in this connection: Is the majority always right? Very often an important issue will be determined by one vote. Students of history remember that during post–Civil War days one vote kept Andrew Johnson from being removed from office. Every individual can recall similar situations within organizations when like results have occurred. Is this a weakness of democracy? Should important problems, plans, and issues be decided by such a small difference of opinion?

It seems that the reasoning behind such a dilemma is clear. All who believe in democracy recognize the importance of having as much unanimity of thinking as possible. However, they also recognize that it is much better to have a majority make a decision than to have it made by one person who is an autocrat.

The problem of subjective personal opinion as opposed to scientific fact. In many democratic discussions it appears to some individuals that scientific evidence should dictate policies and that personal opinions must not become involved. On complicated issues, situations develop where certain individuals are acquainted with scientific data that define the issue. Therefore, they conclude that discussion, voting, or other devices are useless, because the course of action is clearly indicated by fact.

The answer to such a problem seems to be that there will be acceptance if individuals know and recognize the facts. Generally, acceptance fails to materialize when evidence is not conclusive or when it has not been properly publicized. The democratic process can contribute immeasurably to such enlightenment. Through discussion, facts can be presented and understanding reached. Individuals with reasonable intelligence will accept scientific fact against personal opinion, if the presentation is clear and the evidence is convincing. William Gerard Hamilton during the late eighteenth century stated: "Two things are always to be observed; whether what is said is true in itself, or being so, is applicable. In general, things are partly true, and partly not; in part applicable, and in part not. You are careful therefore to distinguish; and to show how far this is true and applies, and how far not." The democratic process is the most effective method yet devised to show what is true and applies.

The problem of standards. A question often raised in connection with the democratic process is: What does it do to standards of performance? Some people believe that by allowing majority opinion and decisions to prevail, standards of performance are lowered to a middle level. The individuals who have a low set of standards tend to pull down those with high standards. In effect, this results in a compromise on middle ground.

The answer to this problem is difficult. A democracy rests on the worth of the individual. It has faith in the individual, the goals the individual will set, and the standards the individual wants to follow. The challenge presents itself to those whose standards are high to bring the rest up to their level, rather than to allow themselves to be relegated to a lower one. Such a process may take time. Results are not always immediate in a democracy. Nevertheless, the principles on which it is based are sound. By employing freedom of discussion and assembly, it is possible to educate and to elevate standards.

The problem of time. Democratic discussions, with their need for deliberation and agreement, take time. Such delay often creates problems, sometimes with serious consequences. There is often much delay between the need for action, decision, and execution. Democracy is based on the necessity for individuals to see the need for a course of action, deliberate on it, and finally see that the decision they have made is put into effect.

This difficulty often hinders progress. However, it does not necessarily have to be this way. The federal government acts rapidly in cases of emergency. For example, it did not take long for Congress to declare war after the attack on Pearl Harbor or to vote the necessary supplies and help once our country was at war. Delay occurs when there is misunderstanding, when a situation is not meaningful, and when the course of action is confusing. Perhaps it is wise in many cases to have this time lag. Hasty action can also result in many mistakes.

The problem of uninterested and noninformed individuals. Another problem frequently arising in democratic deliberations is that some individuals who participate in group discussions are not interested or competent to discuss intelligently and constructively

Fig. 1-6. Girls' and women's physical education and athletic programs are expanding.

Courtesy Cramer Products, Inc., Gardner, Kan.

the subject at hand. Such a situation may be helpful as an educational device. As individuals become better informed on various topics, they contribute more. Many minds are better than one or two. Any group should welcome as much help as possible in solving problems.

The problem of authority. The democratic process is often criticized because it results in confusion and poor direction. The authority for certain acts is not clearly established. Furthermore, it is conducive to a conflict of ideas, which results in indecisiveness.

It seems important to recognize the part democratic principles play in such a problem. A democratic organization vests in its members the right to help determine policies, purpose, and methods. They want a "say" in these important factors that vitally affect their lives. At the same time, however, they vest authority for execution of policy and purpose in administrators who are responsible to the group for their actions. Any democratically run organization has to recognize clearly the definite lines that exist between

policy formation and execution. If an individual has been placed in an administrative position, the authority to perform the duties effectively must also be granted. In a sense, all individuals have authority in their respective positions. Authority goes with the job and not with the individual. This is true from the top to the bottom of the organization. There is no "final authority" except as it exists in the entire membership. All organizations that are to be efficient and effective must clearly recognize these principles on which the functioning of an organization rests.

APPLYING ADMINISTRATIVE THEORY

Administration is not something that is hit or miss, trial and error, or a matter of expediency. Instead, a theory of administration is emerging. A study of this administrative theory enhances one's ability to act wisely in specific situations, and because theory is practical, it provides an accurate picture of how human beings work. Administrative theory also helps identify problems that need to be solved for an effective working organization to exist.

Textbooks and the professional literature on administration indicate a search for a substance of administration and for a framework of theory that would make the substance a meaningful whole. The traditional emphasis has been on the form rather than on the substance. Organizations such as the National Conference of Professors of Educational Administration, the Cooperative Program in Educational Administration, and the University Council for Educational Administration are helping to give impetus to this new movement and thereby make administration much more of a science than it has been in the past. Administration is becoming more scientific and thereby characterized by more objectivity, reliability, and a systematic structure of substance.

The traditional view of administration revolved around the idea that administration existed to carry out the policies that had been developed by the duly constituted policy-forming group, such as a board of education. Modern administration not only carries out policy but also plays an important role in developing policy, applying the knowledge and expertise that come from training and experience.

A study of the history of administration shows that policy-forming groups, such as boards of education, were once held accountable for how the schools were administered, whereas the modern approach delegates administrative responsibilities to the trained school administrator. The old concept of leadership in administration was a passive leadership that remained in the background while the policy-forming group provided the strength and skill needed to run the schools. Under the modern view of administration, however, strong administrative leadership is a requirement so that technical and expert judgments can be made to help the schools to achieve their objectives more effectively. The traditional view of administration claimed the best way to prepare to administer was to practice administering: experience was seen to be the best teacher. The modern view of administration, however, recognizes the value of experience but at the same time maintains there exists a body of knowledge or theory that, when mastered, can help

the administration play a more effective role in the organization with which it is associated.

According to Jenson and Clark,* new perspectives of administration are the result of six phenomena:

1. Administration is a science and the administrator is a professional person.
2. An intensive study of administration includes such phenomena as behaviors, social interactions, and human relationships.
3. Application of theory and model constructs are included in the study of administration.
4. Administration is differentiated into two dimensions: content and process.
5. New forces shape new perspectives in administration: new technologies, population trends, value systems, knowledge explosion, ideological conflicts, and so on.
6. Interest of scholars and researchers in the scientific study of the field of administration is increasing.

A philosophy of administration for physical education and athletics

Human beings represent the most important consideration in the world. The real worth of a field of endeavor, organization, or idea is found in what it does for human beings. The most important and worthwhile thing that can be said about a particular vocation, organization, or movement is that it contributes to human betterment.

People have goals that represent a variety of human objectives. They include the need for health and security for oneself and one's family, the desire to obtain an education and to be employed in a worthwhile and gainful occupation, and the right to worship freely and to enjoy recreation.

People do not miraculously work together. They do not spontaneously band together and strive to accomplish common objectives. Because many groups of people have common goals, however, through associated effort they help each other achieve goals that would be impossible for them to accomplish alone. No one person can establish a school for

---

*Jenson and Clark, op. cit., p. 37.

Fig. 1-7. Student at Thornwood High School, South Holland, Ill., performing on the rings.

his or her children's education, for example, but through the cooperative effort and support of many people, a school is made possible. Thus individuals have similar goals that they will work together to attain.

Organizations, to function effectively, need machinery to help them run efficiently, to organize and execute their affairs, and to keep them operating smoothly, so that the goals for which they have been created will be achieved. This machinery is administration. It is the framework of organizations. It is the part that helps organizations implement the purposes for which they have been established.

Administration, therefore, exists to help people achieve the goals they desire to live happy, productive, healthful, and meaningful lives. It is not an end in itself; rather, it is a means to an end—the welfare of the people for whom the organization exists. Administration exists for people, not people for administration. Administration can justify itself only as it serves the people who make up the organization, helping them to achieve the goals they have as human beings.

It can be seen, then, that in an organization, where the associated efforts of many individuals are necessary, it is essential to have human beings cooperate and work together happily and purposefully to achieve an organization's goals. This is accomplished through direction, and administration gives this direction.

To a considerable degree, the actions of human beings in society are determined through their association with formal organizations. Formal organizations have leaders and purposes. They depend on cooperative efforts of individuals to achieve the objectives that have been set. Many times organizations have failed when their administrators have lacked leadership ability, when there has been a lack of cooperative effort among members, or when the objectives have not been essential and good for society.

Administration determines whether an organization is going to progress, operate efficiently, achieve its objectives, and have a group of individuals within its framework who are happy, cooperative, and productive. Administration involves directing, guiding, and integrating the efforts of human beings so that specific aims may be accomplished. It refers particularly to a group of individuals, often called executives, who have as their major responsibility this direction, guidance, integration, and achievement.

Administration is especially concerned with achievement—proof that the organization is attaining its goals. Achieving these results satisfactorily requires an understanding of human relationships and the ability to foresee the future and plan for any eventuality, and it demands the capacity to coordinate human personalities. Good administration ensures that the associated efforts of individuals are productive. To accomplish this, administrators must possess attributes that elicit the most creative efforts of the members of the organization.

Administration also requires close supervision of the facilities, materials, supplies, and equipment essential to the life of the organization. It implies a logical formulation of policies and the effective operation of the organization.

Major administrative duties
POSDCORB

Gulick and Urwick* have used the acronym POSD-CORB to outline the functions of an administrator. POSDCORB refers to the functional elements of (1) planning, (2) organizing, (3) staffing, (4) directing, (5) coordinating, (6) reporting, and (7) budgeting. This is based on Henri Fayol's work, *Industrial and General Administration.* An organization of duties under these major headings is apropos to this section, although the semantics of the subject in some cases is not appropriate to modern administration.

Planning

Planning is the process of outlining the work to be performed logically and purposefully, together with the methods to be used in the performance of this work. The total plan will result in the accomplishment of the purposes for which the organization is established. Of course this requires a clear conception of the aims of the organization.

*Gulick, L., and Urwick, L., editors: Papers on the science of administration, New York, 1937, Institute of Public Administration.

To accomplish this planning, the administrator must have vision to look into the future and to prepare for what is seen. He or she must see the influences that will affect the organization and the requirements that will have to be met.

Organizing

Organizing refers to the development of the formal structure of the organization, whereby the various administrative coordinating centers and subdivisions of work are arranged in an integrated manner, with clearly defined lines of authority. The purpose behind this structure is the effective accomplishment of established objectives. Organizational charts aid in clarifying such organization.

The structure should be set up to avoid red tape and provide for the clear assignment of every necessary duty to a responsible individual. Whenever possible, standards should be established for acceptable performance for each duty assignment.

The coordinating centers of authority are developed and organized chiefly on the basis of the work to be done by the organization, services performed, individuals available in the light of incentives offered, and efficiency of operation. A single administrator cannot perform all the functions necessary, except in the smallest organizations. Hence responsibility must be assigned to others logically. These individuals occupy positions along the line, each position being broken down in terms of its own area of specialization. The higher up the line one goes, the more general the responsibility; the lower down the line one goes, the more specific the responsibility.

Staffing

The administrative duty of staffing refers to the entire personnel function of selection, assignment, training, and providing and maintaining favorable working conditions for all members of the organization. The administrator must have a thorough knowledge of staff members. He or she must select with care and ensure that each subdivision in the organization has a competent leader and that each employee is assigned to the job where he or she can be of greatest service. Personnel should possess energy, initiative, and loyalty. The duties of each position

Fig. 1-8. Girls' and women's volleyball are growing in popularity as shown here at Northland College, Ashland, Wis.

must be clearly outlined. All members of the organization must be encouraged to use their own initiative. They should be rewarded fairly for their services. The mistakes and blunders of employees must be brought to their attention and dealt with accordingly. Vested interests of individual employees must not be allowed to endanger the general interests of all. The conditions of work should be made as pleasant and as nearly ideal as possible. Both physical and social factors should be provided for. Services rendered by personnel increase as the conditions under which they work improve.

Directing

Directing (leading is a more appropriate term) is a responsibility that falls to the administrator as the leader. He or she must direct the operations of the organization. This means making distinct and precise decisions and embodying them in instructions that will ensure their completion. The administrator must direct the work in an impersonal manner, avoid becoming involved in too many details, and see that the organization's purpose is fulfilled according to established principles. Executives have a duty to see that the quantity and quality of performance of each employee are maintained.

The administrator is a leader. Success is determined by the ability to guide others successfully toward established goals. Individuals of weak responsibility and limited capability cannot perform this function successfully. The good administrator must be superior in determination, persistence, endurance, and courage. He or she must clearly understand the organization's purposes and keep them in mind while guiding the way. Through direction, it is essential that he or she instill faith in cooperation, in success, in the achievement of personal ambitions, and in the integrity of the leadership.

Coordinating

Coordinating means interrelating all the various phases of work within an organization; therefore the organization's structure must clearly provide close relationships and competent leadership in the coordinating centers of activity. The administrator must meet regularly with chief assistants to make arrangements for unity of effort, so that obstacles to coordinated work can be eliminated. Coordination can be effective only if there is faith in the enterprise and in the need for coordinated effort. Faith is the motivating factor that stimulates human beings to continue rendering service to accomplish goals.

There should also be coordination with administrative units outside the organization where such responsibilities are necessary.

Reporting

Reporting is the administrative duty of supplying information to administrators or executives higher up on the line of authority or to other groups to whom one is responsible. It also means that subordinates must be kept informed through regular reports, research, and continual observation. In this respect the administrator is a point of intercommunication. In addition to accepting the responsibility for reporting to higher authority, the administrator must continually know what is going on in the area under his or her jurisdiction. Members of the organization must be informed on many topics of general interest, such as goals to be achieved, progress being made, strong and weak points, and new areas proposed for development.

Budgeting

Budgeting refers to financial planning and accounting. It is the duty of the administrator to allocate to various subdivisions the general funds allotted to the organization. This must be done in an equitable and just manner. In carrying out this function, the administrator must keep the organization's purposes in mind and apportion the available money to those areas or projects that will help most in achieving these purposes. It also means that controls must be established to ensure that certain limits will be observed, so-called budget padding will be kept to a minimum, and complete integrity in the handling of all the budgetary aspects of the organization will be maintained. PPBS (planning, programming, budgeting system) is being implemented increasingly in school systems throughout the country.

OTHER APPROACHES TO MANAGEMENT FUNCTIONS

Parkhouse and Lapin* list five functions or duties that are essential for the successful manager of athletics. According to the authors these managerial functions are interrelated and very important to successful administration. They are the following:

Planning. The wise administrator spends considerable time in planning how the organization and program can best meet its goals and objectives.

Decision making and problem solving. Informed decisions are necessary. Issues must be faced intelligently, rationally, objectively. The problem-solving approach is helpful in arriving at informed decisions.

Organization. The administrator should be able to organize and structure the organization so that personnel fit the existing job functions. Clear lines of authority and responsibility are essential.

Controlling and reappraising. There needs to be some accounting, some determination of whether set goals and objectives are being met. Then it is important to consider corrective action if these goals are not being met.

Communication. The administrator should be able to convey his or her correct viewpoint and ideas without them being garbled to others. Clear communication is necessary to gain mutual respect and trust for oneself, one's position, and one's organization.

Two professors of physical education and former athletic directors perceive the following as management functions of the athletic director*:

Planning and budgeting—setting goals and planning for the achievement of these goals and carrying out the budgeting process from formulation to adoption.

Organizing, staffing, coordinating, and communicating—identifying positions within the organization and determining the duties and responsibilities of each.

Direction and delegation—facing problems and making decisions, putting well-thought through plans into action, and working through staff in achieving goals.

Controlling and reporting—measuring performance and guiding actions toward goals and then reporting progress.

Innovation—implementing new programs, ideas, and methods such as in coaching.

Representation—representing the athletic program to outside organizations, groups, and individuals.

*Parkhouse and Lapin, op. cit.

*Fuoss, D.E., and Troppmann, R.J.: Creative management techniques in interscholastic athletics, New York, 1977, John Wiley & Sons.

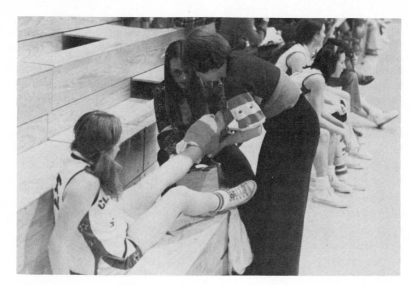

Fig. 1-9. Athletic trainer caring for an athletic injury in women's sport competition.

Courtesy Cramer Products, Inc., Gardner, Kan.

Qualifications of administrators

Tead, in his classic *The Art of Leadership** points out what he considers the qualifications leaders should have. Such qualities apply equally well to administrators and managers. They are the following:

Physical and nervous energy	Technical mastery
Sense of purpose and direction	Decisiveness
Enthusiasm	Intelligence
Friendliness and affection	Be a good teacher
Integrity	Faith

Although the qualities of an administrator need to be considered in relation to the qualities of the persons in the organization he or she is attempting to lead, nevertheless certain leadership characteristics are necessary for a successful administrator. Identifying these qualities is essential to help determine whether one should go into this important field. This identification also helps evaluate the type of administration that exists in one's own organization, whether one is an administrator or not.

The qualifications of an administrator are many. Some (conceptual skills, integrity, ability to instill good human relations, ability to make decisions,

*Tead, O.: The art of leadership, New York, 1935, Whittlesey House.

health and fitness for the job, willingness to accept responsibility, understanding of work, command of administrative skills, and intellectual capacity) are discussed in the following sections. There has been no attempt to list these in order of importance.

Conceptual skills. Conceptual skills include the abilities to see the organization as a whole, to originate ideas, to sense problems, and to work out solutions to these problems that will benefit the organization and establish the right priorities and organizational direction. Proper conceptual skills reduce the risk factor to a minimum.

A research project involving a self-analysis of nearly 1000 executives, all of whom were presidents of industrial organizations, pointed up the following important considerations for the person who wants to be a good administrator: using time effectively, motivating others, building a team, setting the direction, finding expert advice, making crisis decisions, negotiating, and effective self-improvement. Personal improvement, especially directed along lines involving public speaking, planning work, memory skills, conference leadership, writing, producing better ideas, and reading, was also considered necessary.

Some individuals have qualities that, perhaps, have been developed through training and experience and that peculiarly adapt them to administrative work.

These individuals are able to analyze situations objectively, to clarify generalizations, and to administer constructively rather than exploitively. Such persons are sensitive to the important part human relations play in the successful functioning of any organization. These individuals think in imaginative terms. They are able to see into the future and plan a course of action with an open mind. They recognize problems in order of importance, are able to analyze a situation, develop various plans of action, and reach logical conclusions. They have the ability to organize.

Integrity. One of the most important qualifications of any administrator is integrity. Whether or not a leader can inspire staff members, have their cooperation, and achieve the purposes of the organization will depend to a great degree on his or her integrity. Everyone likes to feel confident that an administrator is honest and sincere, keeps promises, and can be trusted with confidential information. Such confidence cannot emanate from administrators unless they have integrity. Failure to fulfill this one qualification will result in low morale and an inefficient organization.

Human relations skills. Human relations skills include the administrator's ability to develop good working relationships among staff members, to get along with people, and to provide a working climate where individuals will not only produce but will also grow on the job.

A former president of the American Alliance for Health, Physical Education, Recreation, and Dance (AAHPERD) suggested the following as considerations for administrators: be friendly and considerate, be alert to the opinons of others, be careful what you say and how you say it, be honest and fair, be wise enough to weigh and decide, tolerate human failings and inefficiency, acquire humility, and plan well for staff meetings.

The ability to get along with associates in work is an essential qualification for an administrator. Only through cooperative effort is it possible for an organization to achieve its goals. This cooperative effort is greatest when those responsible for the coordination of human efforts have the welfare of the various members of the organization at heart. This means that an administrator must be able to coordinate the abilities of many individuals. This is done in many ways. Some of these methods include setting a good example, inspiring confidence, selecting proper incentives, possessing poise, making the right decisions in tense moments, having an impersonal attitude, cooperating and helping others when necessary, and developing and practicing ethical standards. The administrator must be adept at the art of persuasion, which takes into consideration such important items as the points of view, interests, and other factors characterizing those to be persuaded.

There is little associated effort without leadership. The administrator must be a leader and possess the attributes and qualities that people expect if they are to achieve the purposes for which the organization has been established.

Ability to make decisions. The administrator must be able to make decisions when necessary. This requires the ability to discern what is important and what is reasonable, what is in the best interests of the organization and what has the best chance for success, and then to foresee future developments as a result of the decision.

Decision is essential to accomplish objectives at the most opportune time. The administrator should have the capacity and be willing to make a decision. Otherwise, lethargy, suspense, and poor morale are created. The administrator who procrastinates, is afraid of making the wrong decision, thinks only of his or her own welfare, and is oblivious to the organization's needs should never hold an administrative position.

Health and fitness for the job. Good health and physical fitness are essentials for the administrator. They often have a bearing on making the right decisions. Socrates said that people in a state of bad health often made the wrong decisions in regard to affairs of state. Jennings, the famous biologist, pointed out that the body can attend to only one thing at a time. Therefore, if attention is focused on a pain in the chest, a stomach ailment, or a nervous condition, it is difficult to focus it on the functions that an administrator must perform. Poor physical or mental health may be a cause of poor administration.

Vitality and endurance are essential to the administrator. They affect one's manner, personality, attractiveness, and disposition. Administrative duties often require long hours of tedious work under the most trying conditions. Failure to have the necessary strength and endurance under such conditions could mean the inability to perform tasks that are essential to the welfare of the organization. Members of an organization have confidence in those administrators who watch over their interests at all times. It is possible for an administrator to retain this confidence continuously only if he or she is in good health and physically fit to perform arduous duties.

Willingness to accept responsibility. Every administrator must be willing to accept responsibility. The administrator performs duties that influence the welfare of many individuals. Plans have to be fulfilled if the purposes of the organization are to be accomplished. Action is required to ensure production and render services. The person who accepts an administrative job is morally bound to assume the responsibility that goes with that position. A good administrator will experience a feeling of dissatisfaction whenever he or she fails to meet responsibilities.

Understanding of work. The administrator will benefit from having a thorough understanding of the specialized work in which the organization is engaged. If it concerns a particular industry, it will be an advantage to know the production process from the ground up. If it is government, knowledge of related legislative, executive, and judicial aspects will help. If it is education, familiarity with that particular field will be an asset. If it is a specialized field within education, it is necessary to have a knowledge of the particular specialty and also the part it plays in the total educational process. It is difficult to guide purposefully unless the individual knows his or her particular educational specialty and how it relates to other subject-matter areas. One often reads about the Congressman who was once a page in the Senate, the railroad executive who was a yard worker, the bank president who started as a bookkeeper, and the superintendent of schools who started as a teacher. The technical knowledge and understanding

of the total functioning of an organization are best gained through firsthand experience. An administrator will find that detailed knowledge of an organization's work is invaluable in successfully guiding its operations.

Command of technical skills. Technical skills in many ways are similar to the first qualification listed—conceptual skills. There is one essential difference. Conceptual skills refer more to the "know how" and temperament of the individual, whereas technical skills refer to the application of this knowledge and ability. An individual who possesses these skills can plan and budget his or her time and effort and also the time and work of others in the most effective way possible. Time is not spent on details when more important work should be done. Tasks are performed in a relaxed, efficient, calm, and logical manner. Work is accomplished in conformance with established standards. Duties are effectively executed, including those involving excess pressure and time.

It has been said that there are three conditions that rapidly burn out an administrator: performing his or her own duties in a tense, highly emotional manner; handling too many details; and being part of an organization not considerate of its administrators.

Intellectual capacity. Intellectual capacity in itself will not guarantee a good administrator. In fact, the so-called intellectual often makes a very poor administrator. Such traits as absent-mindedness and tardiness, characteristic of some intellectual persons, are often not compatible with acceptance of responsibility. Intellectuals sometimes cannot make decisions because they visualize so many sides of an issue. Furthermore, such an individual is often not interested in people but in books, figures, or other data. This makes a poor leader, because lack of interest in human beings results in poor followership.

However, one should not gain from this discussion that intellectual capacity can be disregarded. To be a good administrator one must be intellectually competent. One should be able to think and reason logically, to apply knowledge effectively, to communicate efficiently, and to possess other abilities closely allied to the intellectual process. There have been many so-called "brains" who failed miserably as adminis-

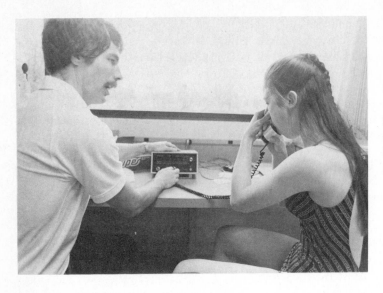

Fig. 1-10. Research project in physical education taking place at the Dow Health and Physical Education Center, Hope College, Holland, Mich.

trators, whereas most good administrators have at least average intellectual capacities.

•   •   •

Space has not permitted a discussion of all the qualifications of the administrator. Others, such as courage and initiative, are also important. There is in addition the ability to be an ambassador for the organization. Liaison work with higher echelon groups in the organization and also with outside groups is important. It is necessary at times to stand up and fight for one's own department or division. To a great degree this will determine whether it is respected and has equal status with other administrative divisions.

The preparation of administrators

The modern view of administration is that a professional preparation program for the person who desires to enter administration should include such essentials as taking foundation work in cognate fields, knowing himself or herself as an individual and as a potential administrator, having technical and conceptual understanding of the community, recognizing the importance of instruction, studying and practicing decision making, and realizing the importance of human relations. Finally, there should be on-the-job

learning experience closely supervised by an experienced professor.

Scott* has stated the type of preparation she feels administrators need to become skilled in management practices and to be able to perform satisfactorily in light of the new perspective of administration. Some areas she feels should occupy an important place in such preparation are the following:

A sound background in business practices. Included in this background should be an emphasis on budgeting and financial management.
Administrative use of computers. Today's administrator-manager needs to understand computer programmers.
Collective bargaining. Unionism is spreading. To cope with unions it is important for today's administrator to be conversant with collective bargaining and the skills needed in the negotiation process.
Public relations. Physical education and athletics need people who can articulate their positions eloquently, both verbally and in written form.
School law. The prevalence of litigation involving professional programs is such that the administrator needs to be well informed about such things as liability, negligence, and product liability.
Interpersonal relations. Intensive work and study in

---

*Scott, op. cit.

personal relations is one of the most important requisites for an effective administrator-manager.

Some universities, as a part of the training and professional preparation of administrators, include a course in sensitivity training or human awareness. The purpose of these courses is to learn through an analysis of one's own and other people's experiences. In human awareness training, participants work together in small groups in an attempt to better understand themselves and other people. This group is frequently called a *T group,* and the leader is called a trainer. His or her role is to help the group learn from its experiences. The group does not have a definite structure, and the leader initially stresses that the participants themselves will be the forces that determine how individual behavior is influenced. The leader also stresses that the data for learning will be the behavior of the group members.

Culbertson* suggested several types of content, all of which are pertinent to physical education administrators, that are needed in the preparation of administrators.

Content should include a study of concept and theories that relate to individual, group, and organization *decision making.* The relationship of such items as basic research, computer technology, and value systems to decision making would also be considered.

A study of *communication*—one-way, two-way, and group, as well as organizational communication—should be included. Mass communications and opinion change should also be considered.

A study of the *dynamics of change* in relation to individuals, groups, and organizations should be made. A study should also be made of barriers to change, how change can be effected, the leadership needed, conflicts, and related topics.

Content should include *building morale* in a modern organization. Special attention should be given to motivation, interpersonal relations, values, organizational loyalty, and perception.

---

*Culbertson, J.: The preparation of administrators. In Behavioral science and educational administration, the Sixty-Third Yearbook of the National Society for the Study of Education, Chicago, 1964, University of Chicago Press.

THE EQUAL OPPORTUNITY MOVEMENT AND WOMEN IN ADMINISTRATION

The equal opportunity movement is primarily responsible for making the public aware of the inferior position of women in many areas, including civil rights, jobs, and salaries. Women have always been active in physical education, athletics, and education. Women, however, have not yet attained equality. Although more women administrators have been hired in recent years, further action should be taken; for example, the following:

1. Female applicants for administrative positions should be actively sought.
2. All discriminatory personnel policies should be eliminated.
3. Female students should be encouraged to become professionals and advised of their administrative career potential.
4. Policy changes should be made in every organization to permit the successful entrance of women into administrative positions.

The importance of administration

A study of administration is important for all physical educators. Some significant reasons why physical educators should understand administration follow.

1. *The way in which organizations are administered determines the course of human lives.* Human beings are affected by administration. It affects the type of program offered, the climate in which the program takes place, the goals that are sought, and the health and happiness of members of the organization.

2. *Administration provides an understanding and appreciation of the underlying principles of the science of this field.* Methods, techniques, and procedures used by the administration can be evaluated more accurately and objectively by staff members if they possess administrative understanding. Also, sound administration will be better appreciated and unsound practices more easily recognized.

3. *A study of administration will help decide whether a person wishes to select administration as a career.* Increased understanding and appreciation of the administrative process will help one evaluate

his or her personal qualifications and possible success.

4. *Most physical educators perform some types of administrative work, and therefore an understanding of administration will contribute to better performance.* Administration is not restricted to one group of individuals. Most staff members have reports to complete, equipment to order, evaluations to make, and other duties to perform that are administrative in nature. An understanding of the science of administration will assist in carrying out these assignments.

5. *Administration is fundamental to associated effort.* Goals are reached, ideas are implemented, and an esprit de corps is developed with planning and cooperative action. A knowledge of administration facilitates the achievement of such aims.

6. *An understanding of administration helps assure continuity.* A fundamental purpose of administration is to carry on what has proved successful rather than to destroy the old and attempt a new and untried path. An appreciation of this concept by all members of an organization will help to ensure the preservation of the best traditional practices that exist in the organization.

7. *A knowledge of administration helps further good human relations.* An understanding of sound administrative principles will assure the cooperation of the members of the organization and produce the greatest efficiency and productivity.

Administration is rapidly becoming a science, and the study of this science is essential to everyone. It can result in a better-ordered society through more efficiently run organizations. Every individual belongs to formal organizations. Through a democratic approach to administration, the individual can aid in carrying on what has proved to be good in the past and in steering a course that will ensure progress in the future.

SELF-ASSESSMENT TESTS

These tests are to assist students in determining if material and competencies presented in this chapter have been mastered:

1. Without consulting the text, describe what is meant by the terms *administrative theory, administration,* and *management* and how they relate to physical education and athletic programs.

2. Take a sheet of paper and divide it into two halves as indicated here. On the left half list the characteristics of traditional administration and on the right the characteristics of the new perspective of administration.

Characteristics of traditional administration	Characteristics of the new perspective of administration

3. Assume you are an administrator who believes in the participatory theory of administration. Describe how you would implement this theory as the administrative leader of a program of physical education and athletics.

4. Discuss your philosophy of administration.

5. You are superintendent of schools of a large school system interviewing applicants for the position of director of physical education and athletics. What qualifications would you look for among the many applicants who apply for the position?

6. List what you consider to be the major duties performed by an administrator of a physical education and athletic program.

7. You aspire to be the administrator of a large physical education and athletic program. To ensure that you will be well prepared to assume such a position, what type of preparation will you seek?

8. Defend the following statement: "More women should be hired as the administrators of physical education and athletic programs."

9. A classmate indicates that a study of administration will not be of any use to him as a physical educator. Prepare a rebuttal to your classmate's statement.

SELECTED REFERENCES

American Alliance for Health, Physical Education, and Recreation: HPER omnibus, Washington, D.C., 1976, The Alliance.

American Alliance for Health, Physical Education, and Recreation: Celeste Ulrich: to seek and find, Washington, D.C., 1976, The Alliance.

American Association of School Administrators: Profiles of the administrative team, Washington, D.C., 1971, The Association.

Annarino, A., et al.: Curriculum theory and design in physical education, ed. 2, St. Louis, 1980, The C.V. Mosby Co.

Bannon, J.J.: Leisure resources; its comprehensive planning, Englewood Cliffs, N.J., 1976, Prentice-Hall, Inc.

Barnett, M.L.: The administrator as helper: quest for instructional excellence, Journal of Physical Education and Recreation **50:**42, January, 1979.

Brickman, W.: 1972 educational developments and issues, Intellest 101, 1973.

Broyles, J.F., and Hay, R.D.: Administration of athletic programs—a managerial approach, Englewood Cliffs, N.J., 1979, Prentice-Hall, Inc.

Bucher, C.A.: Foundations of physical education, ed. 9, St. Louis, 1983, The C.V. Mosby Co.

Bucher, C.A., and Koenig, C.: Methods and materials for secondary school physical education, ed. 6, St. Louis, 1983, The C.V. Mosby Co.

Bucher, C.A., and Thaxton, N.: Physical education and sport: change and challenge, St. Louis, 1981, The C.V. Mosby Co.

Castetter, W.B.: The personnel function in educational administration, New York, 1971, Macmillan, Inc.

Deatherage, D., and Reid, C.P.: Administration of women's competitive sports, Dubuque, Iowa, 1977, Wm. C. Brown Group.

Duryea, E.D., et al.: Faculty unions and collective bargaining, San Francisco, 1973, Jossey-Bass, Inc., Publishers.

Ehrle, E.B.: Observations on the nature of deaning: the emerging role of dean in academic planning, Journal of Physical Education and Recreation **50:**44, January, 1979.

Field, D.: Accountability for the physical educator, Journal of Health, Physical Education, and Recreation **44:**37, 1973.

Foley, J.F.: Critical duties of administrators of health, physical education, and recreation, Physical Education Newsletter, May 1, 1976.

Fuoss, D.B., and Troppmann, R.J.: Creative management techniques in interscholastic athletics, New York, 1977, John Wiley & Sons.

Glines, D.: Why innovative schools don't remain innovative, NASSP Bulletin **57:**1, 1973.

Griffiths, D.E.: The school superintendent, New York, 1966, The Center for Applied Research in Education, Inc. (The Library of Education).

Gulick, L., and Urwick, L., editors: Papers on the science of administration, New York, 1937, Institute of Public Administration.

Halpin, A.W., editor: Administrative theory in education, New York, 1958, Macmillan, Inc.

Hoffman, J.: Superintendent without a ticket, School Management **17:**33, 1973.

Ilowit, and Soupios, M.: There's got to be a better way, Journal of Physical Education and Recreation **50:**38, January, 1979.

Jennings, F.: Tomorrow's curriculum; future imperfect, Educational Horizons, p. 34, 1972.

Kerr, C.: Administration in an era of change and conflict, Educational Record **54:**38, 1973.

McGlynn, G.H., editor: Issues in physical education and sports, Palo Alto, Calif., 1974, National Press Books.

Morphet, E.L., et al.: Educational organization and administration, Englewood Cliffs, N.J., 1967, Prentice-Hall, Inc.

Netcher, J.R.: A management model for competency-based HPER programs, St. Louis, 1977, The C.V. Mosby Co.

Parkhouse, B.L., and Lapin, J.: The woman in athletic administration, Santa Monica, Calif., 1980, Goodyear Publishing Co., Inc.

Scott, P.M.: The new administrator: a point of view, Journal of Physical Education and Recreation **50:**40, January, 1979.

Shane, H.: Reassessment of educational issues, Phi Delta Kappan **54:**4, 1973.

Simon, H.A.: Administrative behavior, New York, 1957, The Free Press.

Tead, O.: The art of leadership, New York, 1935, Whittlesey House.

Thompson, J.D., editor: Approaches to organizational design, Pittsburgh, 1966, University of Pittsburgh Press.

Thomson, S.: Secondary school administration today, The North Central Association Quarterly, p. 265, 1973.

Urwick, L.: The elements of administration, New York, 1943, Harper & Row, Publishers, Inc.

Whaling, T.: Managing the school system; a performance improvement approach, NASSP Bulletin **56:**32, 1972.

Wood, Charles L.: The secondary school principal—manager and supervisor, Boston, 1979, Allyn & Bacon, Inc.

Zeigler, E.F., and Spaeth, M.J.: Administrative theory and practice in physical education and athletics, Englewood Cliffs, N.J., 1975, Prentice-Hall, Inc.

Zeigler, E.F.: The case for management theory and practice in sport and physical education, Journal of Physical Education and Recreation **50:**36, January, 1979.

2

Administrative organization and structures to achieve objectives of physical education and athletics

Instructional objectives and competencies to be achieved

After reading this chapter the student should be able to —

■ Discuss how and why administrative organization and structure are important to the effectiveness of physical education and athletic programs.
■ Identify the objectives of physical education and athletics for which the administrative organization and structure exist.
■ Outline the principles that should be followed in establishing an effective administrative structure for physical education and athletic programs.
■ Describe a formal and an informal type of administrative organization and structure and provide the rationale for each.
■ Outline the factors that need to be considered to develop a functional administrative structure.
■ Describe the organization and structure of physical education and athletic programs that exist in elementary and secondary schools, colleges and universities, and other organizations.
■ Prepare an administrative organization chart for a physical education and athletic program.

Schools, colleges, and other organizations do not function efficiently without some element that holds them together and gives them direction so they can achieve the goals for which they exist. This element is administration. It is the glue that binds the various units cohesively and provides the control and leadership needed to achieve success. To accomplish these functions the administration needs a structure that provides an efficient way of operating and carrying out the various responsibilities existing within the organization. The structure shows the roles various members of the organization play in achieving established goals. It shows to whom each member reports and is responsible in carrying out duties. It portrays a plan of administrative action for getting the job done.

The primary purpose of administrative structure in physical education and athletics is to make it possible to achieve their goals and objectives. Unless the structure performs this function as efficiently as possible, it is a failure and should be abandoned. The structure is a means to an end, not an end in itself. Because this is true, it follows that the goals or objectives of physical education and athletics must be clear in the mind of the administration before establishing the structure of the organization. Therefore the first task is to clarify what goals are being sought for physical education and athletics.

Physical education objectives to be achieved

A study of human beings reveals four general directions or phases in which growth and development take place: physical development, motor or skill develop-

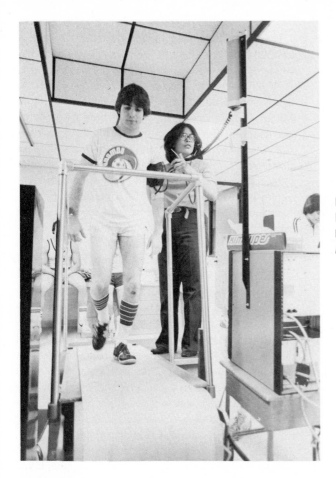

Fig. 2-1. Testing to see if physical development has taken place at the Dow Health and Physical Education Center, Hope College, Holland, Mich.

ment, cognitive development, and social development. Physical education contributes to each of these phases.

THE PHYSICAL DEVELOPMENT OBJECTIVE

The physical development objective deals with the program of activities that builds physical power in an individual through the development of the various organ systems of the body. It results in the ability to sustain adaptive effort, the ability to recover, and the ability to resist fatigue. The value of this objective is based on the fact that an individual will be more active, have better performance, and be healthier if the organ systems of the body are adequately developed and functioning properly.

Muscular activity plays a major role in the development of the organ systems of the body, including the digestive, circulatory, excretory, heat regulatory, respiratory, and other systems. These systems are stimulated and developed through such activities as hanging, climbing, running, throwing, leaping, carrying, and jumping. Health is also related to muscular activity; therefore activities that bring into play all of the fundamental big muscle groups in the body should be vigorously engaged in regularly, so that the various organ systems are sufficiently stimulated.

Vigorous muscular activity produces several beneficial results. The developed heart provides better nourishment to the entire body. It beats more slowly and pumps more blood per stroke, delivering more food to the cells and more efficiently removing waste products. During exercise, the developed heart's speed increases more slowly and has a longer rest period between beats. After exercise it returns to normal much more rapidly. The individual who exercises regularly is able to perform work longer with less expenditure of energy and with much more efficiency than the individual who does not. This trained condition is necessary for a vigorous and abundant life.

THE MOTOR DEVELOPMENT OBJECTIVE

The motor development objective is to perform physical movement proficiently, gracefully, and esthetically, using as little energy as possible. This has implications for one's work, play, and anything else that requires physical movement. The word *motor* involves the relationship of a nerve or nerve fiber that connects the central nervous system, or a ganglion, with a muscle. Movement results as a consequence of the impulse it transmits. The impulse it delivers is known as the motor impulse.

Effective motor movement depends on a harmonious working together of a muscular and nervous systems. It results in greater distance between fatigue and peak performance; it is found in activities involving running, hanging, jumping, dodging, leaping, kicking, bending, twisting, carrying, and throwing; and it will enable one to perform daily work efficiently without reaching the point of exhaustion so quickly.

In physical education activities, the function of efficient body movement, or neuromuscular skill, is to provide the individual with the ability to perform proficiently, which results in greater enjoyment of participation. The objective of physical education is to develop in each individual as many physical skills as possible, so that interests will be wide and varied.

Physical skills are not developed in one lesson. It takes years to acquire coordination, and the most important period for development is during the formative years of a child's growth, when he or she attempts to synchronize the muscular and nervous systems for such movements as creeping, walking, running, and jumping. A study of kinesiology shows that many muscles of the body are used in even the simplest of coordinated movements. Therefore, to obtain efficient motor movement or skill in many activities, it is necessary to start training early in life and to continue into adulthood.

THE COGNITIVE DEVELOPMENT OBJECTIVE

The cognitive development objective involves the accumulation of a body of knowledge and the ability to think and interpret.

Physical activities must be learned; hence, thinking results in an acquisition of knowledge. The coordination involved in various movements must be mastered and adapted to one's activities, whether walking, running, or wielding a tennis racquet. In all these movements one must think and coordinate muscular and nervous systems. Movement education, for example, is designed to provide an awareness of movement principles, such as the role of gravity, so that participants may better understand how to move efficiently.

The individual should also acquire a knowledge of rules, techniques, and strategies involved in physical activities. Basketball can be used as an example. In this sport a person should know the rules, the strategy in offense and defense, the various types of passes, the difference between screening and blocking, and finally the values that are derived from playing this sport. Techniques learned through experience result in knowledge that is also acquired. For example, a ball travels faster and more accurately if one steps with a pass, and time is saved when the pass is made from the same position in which it is received. Furthermore, a knowledge of leadership, courage, self-reliance, assistance to others, safety, and adaptation to group patterns is important.

Knowledge concerning health should play an important part in the program. All individuals should know about their bodies, the importance of sanitation, factors in disease prevention, the importance of exercise, the need for a well-balanced diet, values of good health attitudes and habits, and the community and school agencies that provide health services. This knowledge contributes to physical prowess and to general health. Through the accumulation of a knowledge of these facts, activities take on a new meaning and health practices are associated with definite purposes. This helps each individual to live a healthier and more purposeful life.

THE SOCIAL DEVELOPMENT OBJECTIVE

The social development objective is to help an individual make personal adjustments, group adjust-

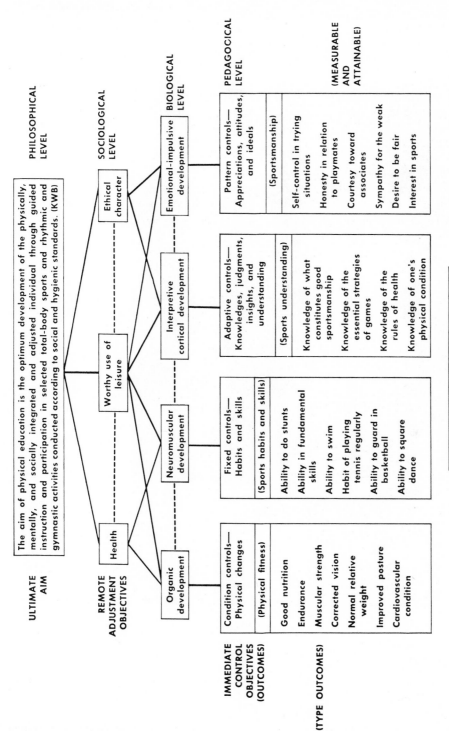

Fig. 2-2. Bookwalter's Objectives of Physical Education.

From Bookwalter, K.W.: Physical education in the secondary schools, Washington, D.C., The Center for Applied Research in Education, Inc.

Fig. 2-3. Physical fitness clinic conducted by a representative of the President's Council on Physical Fitness and Sports, which has been responsible for many changes in physical education programs.

ments, and adjustments as a member of society. Physical education activities offer valuable opportunities for making these adjustments, if there is proper leadership.

Social action is a result of certain hereditary traits and learned behavior. Interests, hungers, desires, ideals, attitudes, and emotional drives are involved in everything we do. A child wants to play because of the drive for physical activity. A man will steal food because of the hunger drive. The responses to all these desires, drives, and hungers may be either social or antisocial. Play activities are one of the oldest and most fundamental drives in human nature. Therefore, by providing individuals with satisfying experiences in activities in which they have a natural desire to engage, physical education presents the opportunity to develop desirable social traits. The key is qualified leadership.

All human beings should experience success, which can be realized through play. Through successful experience in play activities, a person develops self-confidence and finds happiness in achievement. Physical education can provide this satisfying experience by offering a variety of activities and developing the skills necessary for successful achievement.

In a democratic society all individuals should develop a sense of group consciousness and cooperative living, one of the most important objectives of the physical education program. Therefore, in various play activities, the following factors should be stressed: aid for the less-skilled and weaker players, respect for the rights of others, subordination of one's desires to the will of the group, and realization that cooperative living is essential to the success of society. The individual should be helped to feel that he or she belongs to the group and has the responsibility of directing his or her actions in its behalf. The rules of sportsmanship should be developed and practiced in all activities offered in the program. Courtesy, sympathy, truthfulness, fairness, honesty, respect for authority, and abiding by the rules help promote social efficiency. The necessity for good leadership and the ability to follow should also be stressed as important to the interests of society.

The objectives of athletics

Although athletics in many cases is theoretically a part of the total physical education program and has the same general objectives as those already discussed for physical education, at the same time athletics has additional goals that relate directly to the achievement of a high degree of skill and competitive success. In certain situations, some physical educators feel that the goals of some athletic programs are not compatible with the goals of physical education.

Broyles and Hay* summarize the various objectives of today's athletic programs. They are presented here in adapted form:

1. Having a winning team to please spectators
2. Developing character in the players
3. Enhancing the athletic program's image and position
4. Increasing the size of the athletic program
5. Having a profitable enterprise
6. Establishing a leadership position in athletics
7. Surviving as an athletic program
8. Being well represented in the entertainment market
9. Enhancing the quality of life for Americans
10. Satisfying needs of such people as spectators, owners, employees, athletes, managers, community, society, and government

The National Association for Girls and Women in Sport (NAGWS)† has listed certain basic beliefs regarding sports and athletics that in essence would translate into objectives. They are the following:

1. Sports are an integral part of the culture in which we live.
2. Sports programs are a part of the total educational experience of the participant when conducted in educational institutions.
3. Opportunities for instruction and participation in sports appropriate to her skill level should be included in the experience of every girl.

*Broyles, J.F.: and Hay, R.D.: Administration of athletic programs—a managerial approach, Englewood Cliffs, N.J., 1979, Prentice-Hall, Inc.
†Division of Girls and Women's Sports, AAHPERD: Philosophy and standards for girls and women's sports, Washington, D.C., 1973, AAHPERD.

4. Sports skills and sports participation are valuable social and recreational tools which may be used to enrich lives of women in our society.
5. Competition and cooperation may be demonstrated in all sports programs, although the type and intensity of the competition and cooperation will vary with the degree or level of skill of the participants.
6. An understanding of the relationship between competition and cooperation and the utilization of both within the accepted framework of our society is one of the desirable outcomes of sports participation.
7. Physical activity is important in the maintenance of the general health of the participant.
8. Participation in sports contributes to the development of self-confidence and to the establishment of desirable interpersonal relationships.

The Kent School District, Kent, Washington, has listed goals for their athletic program. Some of these are presented here in the following adapted form:

1. To promote physical excellence and an appreciation of competition.
2. To achieve for the participant such goals as self-assurance, an understanding of group loyalty and responsibility, an outlet for expression of emotions, the ability to coordinate various aspects of self (social, emotional, physical, and intellectual) into action, the qualities of good citizenship and other valuable personal qualities, and leadership ability.
3. To provide opportunities for students to engage in activities voluntarily.
4. To release personal energies in constructive ways.
5. To provide a unifying force for school and community.
6. To provide activities that meet students' needs and interests.
7. To provide activities that will help students to live a balanced life.

Developing an administrative structure that will enable objectives of physical education and athletics to be accomplished

After the goals and objectives have been identified for physical education and athletic programs, an administrative structure should then be developed that will contribute to the achievement of these goals.

Planning, developing, and organizing the structure for a physical education program are important administrative responsibilities. Efficient organization and structure result in the proper delegation of authority, effective assignment of responsibilities to staff members, adequate communication among the various administrative units of the organization, and a high degree of morale among staff members. All of these factors determine whether or not the organization's goals are achieved.

PRINCIPLES AND GUIDELINES FOR ADMINISTRATIVE ORGANIZATION AND STRUCTURE

Experts in many areas have developed principles to aid in effective administrative organization. Some of the most significant principles are given here.

1. *The administrative structure of an organization should clarify the delegation of authority and responsibility.* For the goals of the organization to be met efficiently and successfully, the administration must delegate some of its powers to responsible agents. These powers should be clearly defined to avoid overlapping authority.

2. *Administrative work may be most effectively organized by function.* This "doctrine of unity" maintains that all personnel engaged in a particular type of work should function under a single authority.

3. *Span of control should be considered in organizational structure.* The number of subordinates who can be supervised adequately by one individual determines the span of control.

4. *Successful administration depends on communication.* Communication is essential to effective administration, because it helps avoid duplication and waste and promotes cooperation among departments.

5. *Coordination and cooperation among various departments in an organization are essential to effective administration.* Coordination of departments keeps them well informed and working together in a complementary manner.

6. *The administrator must be an effective leader.* An effective leader appreciates both the goals of the organization and the personnel working for the organization. Both are essential.

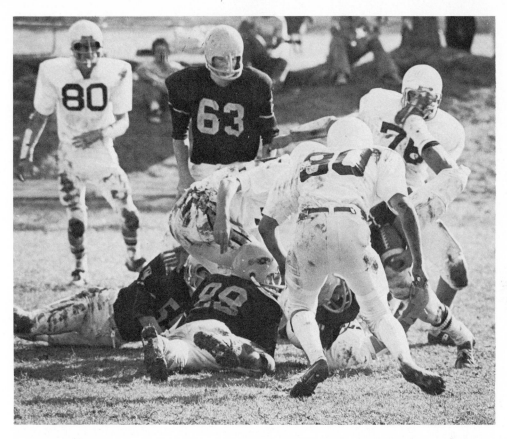

Fig. 2-4. Athletic programs strive to promote physical excellence in various sports.
Courtesy Cramer Products, Inc., Gardner, Kan.

7. *Staff specialization aids effective administration.* To achieve their objectives, organizations must perform many different tasks that require the abilities of various area specialists.

8. *Authority must be commensurate with responsibilities, and lines of authority must be clearly drawn.* An organization chart is a useful way to illustrate the lines of authority. These lines should be unambiguous.

9. *Organization and social purpose cannot be separated.* The structure of an organization is a means and not an end in itself.

10. *There is no single correct form of organization.* Such things as size, personnel, and funds available determine what is the best organization for a particular situation.

Broyles and Hay* indicate there are four fundamental steps in organizing the structure of an athletic program. They are presented here in adapted form:

1. Determine the organizational and personal objectives.
2. Study and analyze the managerial and operative functions necessary for the achievement of the objectives.
3. Arrange managerial and operative functions logically and meaningfully so they will result in efficient administration.
4. Delegate to personnel within the organization the authority, responsibility, and accountability needed to perform specialized functions necessary to accomplish organizational and personal objectives.

*Broyles and Hay, op. cit.

Fig. 2-5. Coeducational basketball at the Methuen Public Schools, Methuen, Mass.

Fig. 2-6. Varsity hockey is a contact sport. The College of Dupage, Glen Ellyn, Ill., varsity hockey team celebrates winning the state championship and receiving a bid to the national tournament.

Translating the administrative structure into graphic form (organization charts)

Once the type of administrative structure desired has been determined, the next step is to prepare it in graphic form so it can be easily understood by members of the organization and by other interested individuals. As Parkhouse and Lapin* state regarding the woman in athletic administration: "An organization chart is an essential tool to an administrator. First, she must make a complete statement of the organization's objectives. Second, she develops a list of jobs and functions. Third, she determines whether each job is considered a line or staff position."

Charts are frequently used to illustrate and clarify the structure of an organization. These charts clearly depict the administrative setup of an organization and the key administrative positions and their functions. They are used to orient new staff members to their responsibilities and to their place in the total structure of the organization. They can also serve as a public relations medium and as a way to evaluate personnel performance. Finally, they are important in establishing accountability for the performance of specific duties of administrative personnel in an organization.

The procedure for developing an organization chart consists of six steps according to Petersen and associates.†

1. *Identify the objectives of the organization.* These objectives determine the structure that needs to be developed. Therefore, goals must be identified first.

2. *Arrange objectives into meaningful functional units.* This step requires assessing the organization with its differentiated parts and units and organizing it to effect a harmonious and integrated whole. If this step is successfully accomplished, it reduces friction and brings about a closely coordinated, smoothly functioning organization.

3. *Arrange the identified functional units into appropriate administrative units, such as departments.*
This step varies in each organization but should represent the most effective relationships for achieving the goals of the organization.

4. *Prepare a model of the structure of the organization and give it a trial run.* To make sure that the model represents the best administrative structure for the organization, it should be used initially on a trial basis.

5. *Revise the model in light of input received.* Views from personnel within and without the organization should be sought and the model revised where necessary to achieve the most satisfactory structure possible.

6. *Evaluate final design and assign persons who work within the organization to appropriate functional units.* As a result of this final step, each member of the organization can see how he or she fits into the total plan.

TYPES OF ORGANIZATION CHARTS

Two of the several types of organization charts available are discussed here—the line and staff chart and the circular pattern of organizational structure.

Line and staff chart

The most common type of organization chart is a line and staff chart (p. 40). A person in a line position has direct responsibility and authority for a specific objective or objectives of an organization. For example, an assistant director of physical education would be in a line position, with direct responsibility for duties assigned by the director. In turn, the assistant director would report directly to the director. A person in a staff position has an indirect relationship to a specific objective or objectives of an organization. An example would be a ticket manager in the athletic administration of a college program. Staff personnel do not have authority over line personnel. Line positions are related to and derive authority from the chief administrator. Staff positions are usually indicated by broken lines and line positions by solid lines.

Circular pattern of organizational structure

The circular pattern of organizational structure has met with some success in recent years in physical education. Its basic concepts, however, have not been

---

*Parkhouse and Lapin, op. cit.

†Petersen, E., et al.: Business organization and management, Homewood, Ill., 1962, Richard D. Irwin, Inc.

widely applied. The model seen in Fig. 2-7 can be explained as follows:

1. The innermost circles represent a general function; the functions become more specialized as the circles radiate outward.
2. The accepted flow of responsibility is indicated by the solid lines.
3. Each program has full access to the resource bank of the organization.
4. The support services contribute to all functions of health, physical education, recreation, and intramural programs.
5. Committees that encompass the total organization should be established in such areas as cirriculum, bylaws, administration, and staff appraisal.

FORMAL AND INFORMAL ORGANIZATION AND STRUCTURE

Organizational theory and structure require that, first, there must be a need for an organization to exist and, second, the organization must know the goals it is trying to achieve. To accomplish these objectives, a structure should be provided that enables the administration to organize, direct, plan, motivate, and evaluate. These tasks can be performed through either a formal or an informal organization.

Formal organization

A formal organization is based on a hierarchal job organization, with tasks assigned by superior to subordinate, an organization seen in most organization charts with their job-task hierarchy and communications network. Such an organization is concerned first with the positions to be filled and tasks to be accomplished and then with the persons to be assigned to these positions and tasks. Clearly delineated lines of authority and formal rules and regulations are earmarks of formal organization, as are dependence, obedience, discipline, reward, and chain of command.

Formal organization is used because it provides a clear picture of the positions that exist and the tasks to be performed. It represents a way to get things done by the use of authority. It places subordinates in a position where they must do what they are instructed to do; therefore things get done. It assumes that the control of behavior is accomplished through rational

judgment, and that the administrator is the person most qualified to solve problems. It assumes that people should be instruments of production. It is strictly authoritarian.

Informal organization

Informal organization realizes that many relationships exist which cannot be illustrated in an organization chart. In other words, things get done outside the formal relationships that a chart reflects. It assumes that relationships occur in many informal settings where ideas are generated, productivity is enhanced, and high morale is developed.

Those who advocate informal organization contend this is how things are actually accomplished and thus oppose the formal, authoritarian type of organization. They also maintain that people who have rank in an organization do not always behave rationally nor do they have complete access to reliable information at all times. These advocates of informal organization also say that members of an organization are not merely instruments of production but instead have desires, values, needs, and aspirations that must be taken into consideration.

Modern theories of organization and structure indicate a shift away from the formal organization and structure to the informal type with a greater human relations perspective. These modern theories are based on the fact that although most persons agree that some type of organizational framework is usually needed, at the same time most individuals are capable of some self-direction.

One aspect of informal organization is the formation of subgroups that do not appear on organization charts. For example, employee unions represent an important group with whom administrators must work. In some organizations there are committees, commissions, and task forces that also represent influential subgroups. The administration, therefore, must understand and appreciate what a staff member wants from his or her position, whether it is high wages, security, good working conditions, interesting work, or some other condition.

Modern theories of management are moving more and more toward a participatory philosophy, where both staff members and administrators are involved

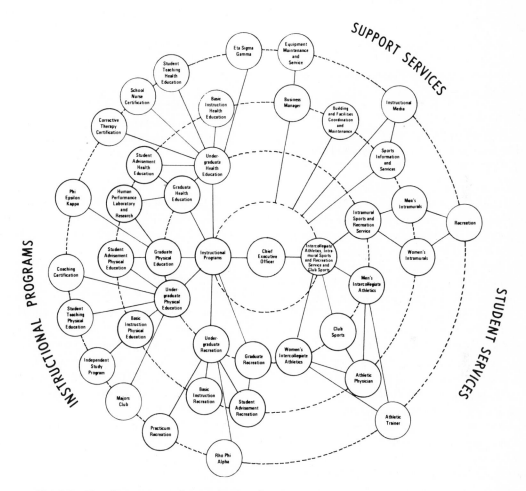

Fig. 2-7. Circular pattern of organizational structure.

Courtesy Dr. Martin McIntyre, State University of New York at Buffalo and the AAHPERD, Journal of Health, Physical Education, and Recreation **44**:28, 1973.

in many organizational decisions. Employees will better identify with an organization if they are involved in the decision-making process.

Administrative structures for physical education and athletic programs

The administrative structures currently used for physical education and athletic programs in many elementary and secondary schools, colleges and universites, and community organizations are discussed on the following pages.

THE ORGANIZATION AND STRUCTURE OF PHYSICAL EDUCATION AND ATHLETICS IN ELEMENTARY AND SECONDARY SCHOOLS

The school district is the basic administrative unit for the operation of elementary and secondary schools and is a quasi-municipal corporation established by the state. This basic educational unit ranges through the United States from a one-teacher rural system to a large metropolitan system serving thousands of pupils. A system may be an independent governmental unit or part of a state government, county, or other local administrative unit. The governing body of the system is the school board. The chief administrative officer is the superintendent of schools.

The board of education* is the legal administrative authority created by the state legislature for each school district. The responsibility of the board is to act on behalf of the residents of the district it represents. It has the duty of appraising and planning the educational program on a local basis. It selects executive personnel and performs duties essential to the successful operation of the schools within the district. The board develops policies that are legal and in the interest of the people it serves. It devises financial means within the legal framework to support the cost of the educational plan. It keeps its constituents informed of the effectiveness and needs of the total program.

*The term *board of education* is used in this discussion although *school committee, community-school boards,* and *board of directors* are used in some sections of the country.

The key administrative personnel in a school system usually consist of the superintendent of schools, assistant superintendent, clerk of the board, principal, supervisor, and director.

Superintendent of schools

Within a large school system is a superintendent who has overall charge of the school program. Associate or assistant superintendents are in charge of technical detail, management, or various phases of the program, such as secondary education. There is also a superintendent's position associated with smaller schools. These officers are known as district superintendents. They are responsible for many schools extending over a wide geographical area.

The superintendent's job is to carry out the educational policies of the state and the board of education. The superintendent acts as the leader in educational matters in the community and also provides the board of education with the professional advice it needs as a lay organization.

Assistant superintendent for business services or school business administrator

The business administrator serves as director of business affairs and of operation and maintenance of buildings and grounds, usually directly supervising the business office staff, the building service and maintenance staff, and indirectly supervising the custodial staff. He or she may perform the duties of the superintendent as directed in the superintendent's absence.

Assistant superintendent or director of instructional services

The director of instruction directly supervises the divisions of elementary education, secondary education, adult education, health and physical education, music education, vocational and practical arts, summer school education, and inservice training of teachers. He or she is involved in developing curriculum materials, organizing and supervising instruction, and teaching. The director of instruction may perform the duties of the superintendent of schools as directed in the superintendent's absence.

Fig. 2-8. Cross-country running as a physical activity.

Courtesy Regis High School, New York.

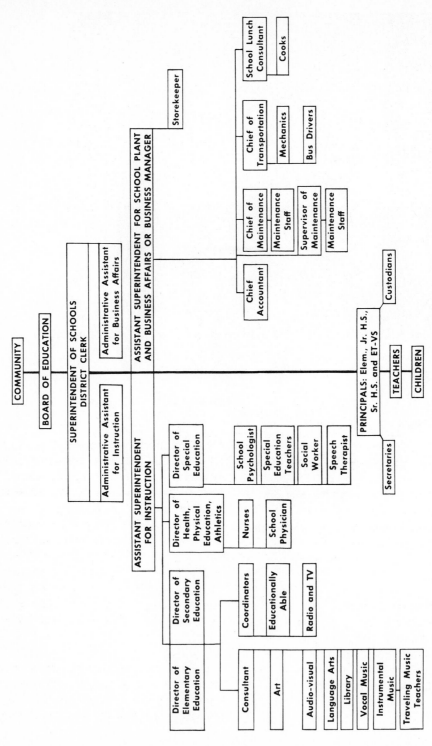

Fig. 2-9. The operational organization chart clarifies channels of communication for the employees of the school district. The superintendent administers school district policies through assistant superintendents, and they in turn utilize intermediate staff members in the process.

Fig. 2-10. School board meeting in Mamaroneck, N.Y.

Assistant superintendent or director of personnel services

The director of personnel supervises both professional and nonprofessional employees and recruits and interviews candidates for positions. He or she is usually responsible for all pupil personnel services, guidance and psychological services, handicapped children and special services, as well as attendance and adjustment, including pupil accounting.

Clerk of the board

The clerk of the board of education is usually under the direction of the superintendent of schools. He or she has custody of the seal of the board, notifies members of the board of regular and special meetings, and has charge of files and records of the board. The clerk sees that all files and records are properly maintained, presents a periodic financial statement, and supervises accounting for tuition pupils.

Principal

The position of principal is similar to that of the superintendent. It differs mainly in the extent of responsibility. Whereas the superintendent is usually in charge of all the schools within a particular community, the principal is in charge of one particular school. The duties of the principal include executing educational policy as outlined by the superintendent, appraising the educational offering, making periodic reports on various aspects of the program, directing the instructional program, promoting good relationships between the community and the school, and supervising the maintenance of the physical plant.

Supervisor

The supervisor is generally responsible for improving instruction in a specific subject area, although sometimes a supervisor is responsible for the entire elementary or secondary instructional program.

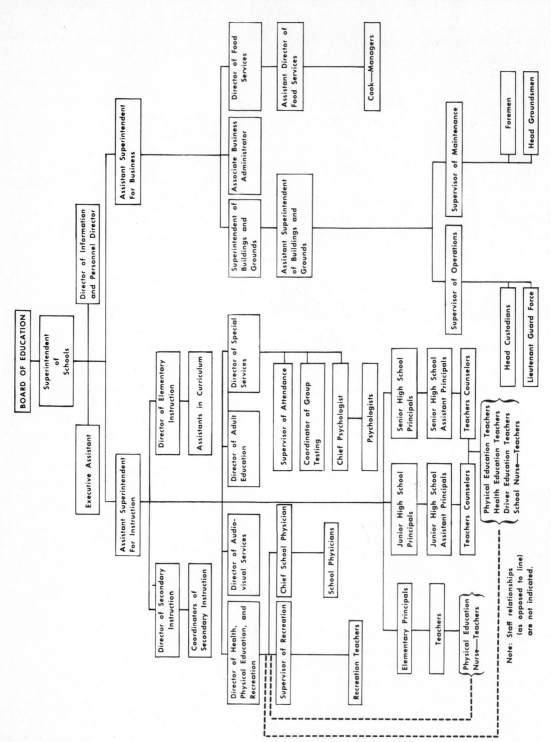

Fig. 2-11. An organization chart for a public school system.

Director

The director is responsible for functions of a specific subject-matter area or a particular educational level. The responsibilities have administrative and supervisory implications.

Director of physical education and athletics. In most cases at the secondary school level the positions of director of physical education and director of athletics are consolidated into one position. There are communities, however, where the two responsibilities are separated into two positions.

The director of physical education and athletics provides leadership, programs, facilities, and other essentials in these special areas. Specific responsibilities include the following:

1. Implement standards established by the state department of education and the local board of education.
2. Interview possible candidates for positions in the special areas and make recommendations for these positions.
3. Work closely with the assistant superintendent in charge of business affairs, assistant superintendent in charge of instruction, and subject matter and classroom teachers.
4. Coordinate areas of physical education and athletics.
5. Supervise inside and outside physical education facilities, equipment, and supplies concerned with special areas—this responsibility includes maintenance, safety, and replacement operations.
6. Maintain liaison with community groups—this responsibility includes such duties as holding educational meetings to interpret and improve the program, scheduling school facilities for community groups, and serving on various community committees for youth needs.
7. Prepare periodic reports regarding areas of activity.
8. Coordinate school civil defense activities in some school systems.
9. Serve on the school health council.
10. Supervise total physical education program (class, adapted, intramurals, extramurals, and varsity interscholastic or intercollegiate athletics).
11. Administer schedules, practice and game facilities, insurance, and equipment.
12. Maintain liaison with county, district, and state professional groups.
13. Upgrade program in general.

High school athletic councils

In some high schools athletic councils are formed to serve in an advisory capacity to boards of education and the administrative officers of the school. Membership includes such personnel as principals, athletic directors, physical education directors, students, athletic trainers, and coaches. These councils perform such functions as make and recommend policy, consider athletic problems, approve awards, determine eligibility regulations, approve budgets, and see that the athletic program is administered according to acceptable educational standards.

THE ORGANIZATION AND STRUCTURE OF PHYSICAL EDUCATION IN COLLEGES AND UNIVERSITIES

A college or university is characterized by a governing board, usually known as a board of trustees, which is granted extensive powers of control by legislative enactment or by its charter. The governing board of a college usually delegates many of its powers to the administration and faculty of the institution. The administrative officers, usually headed by a president, are commonly organized into such principal areas of administration as academic, student personnel services, business, and public relations. The members of the faculty are usually organized into colleges, schools, divisions, and departments of instruction and research. In large institutions one frequently finds a university senate that is the voice of the faculty and serves as a liaison between faculty and administration. The area of physical education can have school, division, or department status. The duties of a dean, director, or chairperson correspond in many ways to a principal, director, or chairperson in a high school.

Physical education is organized as one administrative unit for men and women in a majority of colleges and universities in the United States. The administrative unit may be either a college, school, division, or department; the administrator in charge of the physical education program may be called a dean, director, supervisor, or chairperson. In many institutions of higher learning this administrator is responsible directly to the president or to a dean, but in a few instances, he or she is responsible to the director of

Fig. 2-12. Intercollegiate girls' basketball at Tuskegee Institute, Ala.

athletics. (In some colleges, athletics are included as part of the same administrative setup with the rest of the physical education program.) In some cases the duties of the athletic director and the administrator of the physical education program are assigned to the same person. Many colleges and universities have intramural athletic directors, and in most of these institutions intramural athletics are a part of the physical education program.

The various departments of physical education throughout the country have many different plans of organization. Several years ago it was common to see such titles as Department of Physical Culture or Hygiene. The term *physical training* was also used as a descriptive term for the work performed in this special area.

Today, one also sees a variety of titles associated with physical education, such as the ''Physical Education Department,'' ''Department of Ergonomics and Physical Education,'' the ''Department of Biokinetics,'' ''Health and Physical Education Department,'' and the ''Health, Physical Education, and Recreation Division.'' Camping and safety may also be included.

The titles given also show to some degree the particular work performed within these phases of the total program. In some schools and colleges physical education is organized into a separate unit with the various physical activities—intramural, extramural, and interschool or intercollegiate athletics—comprising this division. In other schools and colleges, health and physical education are combined in one administrative unit. In some cases, although the word *health* is used, there is little evidence of particular specialized health work. This is also true when the word *recreation* is used in the title.

The duties of the head of a physical education department may include coordinating the activities within the particular administrative unit, requisitioning supplies and equipment, preparing schedules, making budgets, holding meetings, teaching classes, coaching, hiring and dismissing personnel, developing community relations, supervising the intramural, extramural, and intercollegiate athletic programs, evaluating and appraising the required class program, representing the department at meetings, and reporting to superiors.

Professional programs in physical education are a part of the physical education program at both the undergraduate and the graduate levels. Physical education and health *education* are frequently combined into the same administrative unit, but health *services,* as a general rule, are not organized as part of the physical education unit. Physical education is commonly responsible for the administration of recreation programs for both students and faculty.

Surveys conducted indicate that most 2-year colleges require 2 hours weekly for ½ unit credit in physical education. Objectives in most cases stress the students' competence in maintaining good health and balanced personal adjustment. Some colleges are seriously attempting to meet these objectives, but others have not yet developed their programs sufficiently to accomplish this task. Athletics appear to be an especially strong point of physical education at the junior college level because of the great student and public interest. Some colleges provide broad programs of team competition in many sports, whereas others are limited.

Many 2-year colleges are offering a certificate in the field of parks and recreation. The person holding this associate degree can be involved in planning, organizing, and conducting recreational activities in such settings as hospitals, military bases, industrial organizations, and local agencies. However, unless these persons continue their education, their administrative and supervisory responsibilities will be minimal.

Most 2-year colleges have a health service program for their students, but instruction in personal and community health is less usual than instruction in physical education. Where a health course is offered, it is usually a 1-semester course for 2 credits.

Interviews with deans of instruction, faculty, and students of 2-year colleges indicate that they prefer to have one department chairperson in charge of both the health and physical education programs. The department chairperson usually is responsible to the dean of students or dean of instruction.

Physical education programs in colleges and in schools are commonly organized into four component parts: (1) the required class or basic instruction program, (2) the adapted or program for the handicapped, (3) the intramural and extramural athletics program, and (4) the varsity interschool or intercollegiate athletics program. (Elementary schools usually do not have intramural and extramural athletics programs in the primary grades or varsity interscholastic athletics in either primary or intermediate grades.)

The *required class* or *basic instruction program* provides physical education for all students and teaches them the rules, strategies, and skills in the various activities that make up the program.

The *adapted program* meets the needs of individuals who are temporarily or permanently unable to take part in the regular physical education program because of some physical inadequacy, functional defect capable of being improved through exercise, or other deficiency.

The *intramural and extramural athletics program* is voluntary physical education for all students within one or a few schools or colleges that includes competitive leagues and tournaments and play and sports days and acts as a laboratory period for the required class program. In the intramural program, activities are conducted for students of only one school or college, whereas in the extramural program, students from more than one school or college participate.

The *varsity interschool* or *intercollegiate athletics program* is designed for the skilled individuals in one school or college who compete with skilled individuals from another school or college in selected physical education activities.

THE ORGANIZATION AND STRUCTURE OF ATHLETICS IN COLLEGES AND UNIVERSITIES

Because athletic programs are organized and administratively structured differently in colleges and universities than in high schools, the organization of athletics in colleges and universities requires further elaboration and discussion.

The athletic director

The athletic director in colleges and universities is responsible for the administration of the athletic program. In large institutions this is a full-time position, whereas in small institutions it may include other responsibilities involved with physical education and coaching.

Some of the key duties of many athletic directors include the following:

1. Scheduling athletic contests and preparing contracts
2. Arranging for team travel
3. Supervising the coaching staff
4. Making arrangements for home athletic contests
5. Representing the institution at athletic association and league meetings
6. Securing officials
7. Checking and preparing eligibility player lists
8. Attending to the public relations aspects of athletic department
9. Preparing the athletic budget
10. Overseeing facility supervision and maintenance
11. Making arrangements for student managers

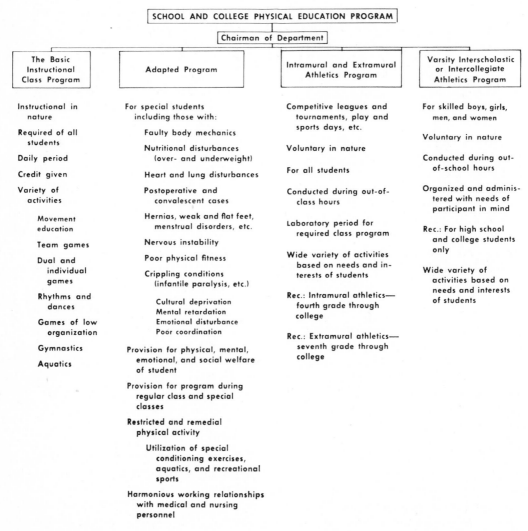

Fig. 2-13. Organization chart for school and college physical education program.

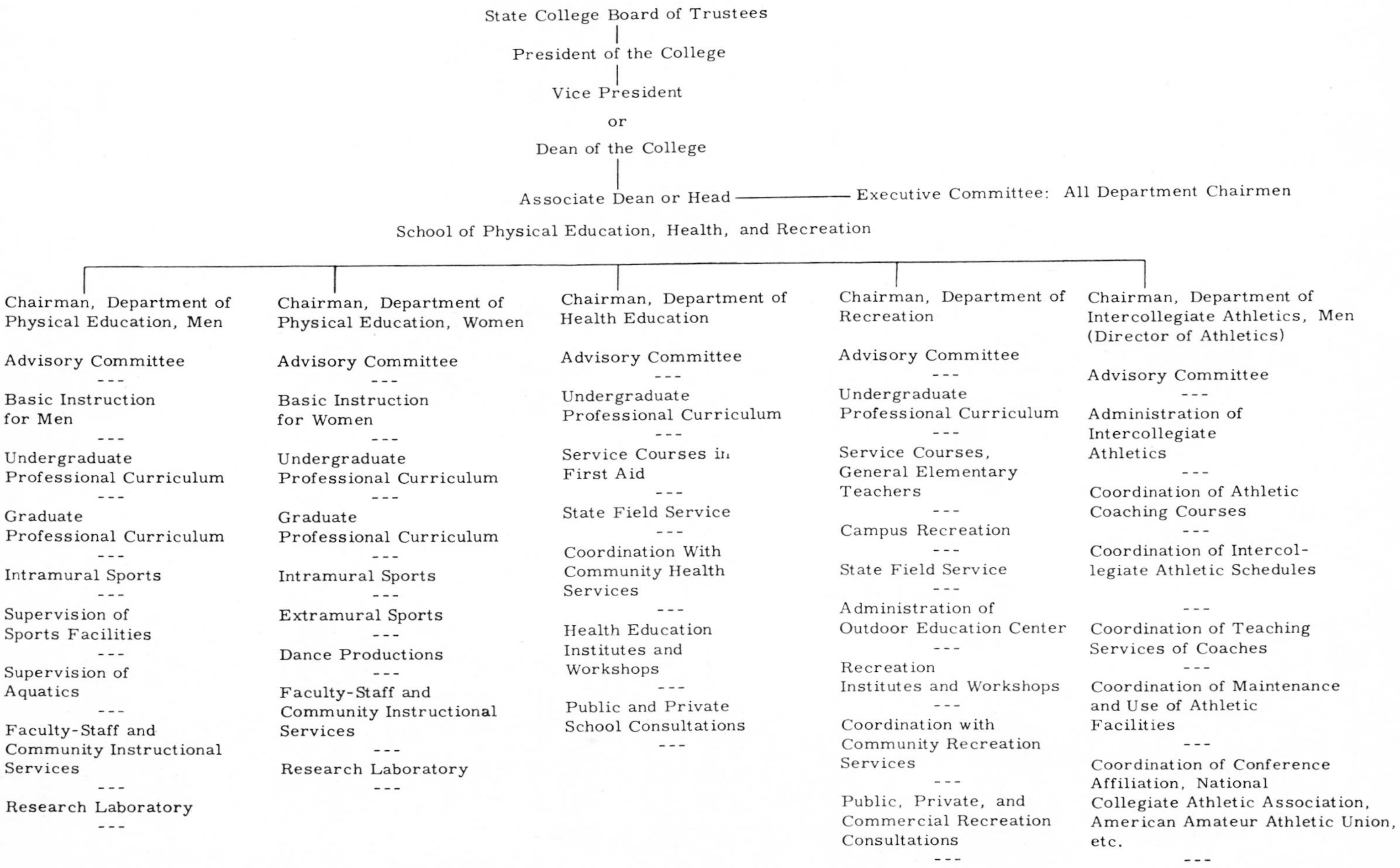

State College Board of Trustees

President of the College

Vice President
or
Dean of the College

Associate Dean or Head ——————— Executive Committee: All Department Chairmen

School of Physical Education, Health, and Recreation

Chairman, Department of Physical Education, Men	Chairman, Department of Physical Education, Women	Chairman, Department of Health Education	Chairman, Department of Recreation	Chairman, Department of Intercollegiate Athletics, Men (Director of Athletics)
Advisory Committee	Advisory Committee	Advisory Committee	Advisory Committee	Advisory Committee
Basic Instruction for Men	Basic Instruction for Women	Undergraduate Professional Curriculum	Undergraduate Professional Curriculum	Administration of Intercollegiate Athletics
Undergraduate Professional Curriculum	Undergraduate Professional Curriculum	Service Courses in First Aid	Service Courses, General Elementary Teachers	Coordination of Athletic Coaching Courses
Graduate Professional Curriculum	Graduate Professional Curriculum	State Field Service	Campus Recreation	Coordination of Intercollegiate Athletic Schedules
Intramural Sports	Intramural Sports	Coordination With Community Health Services	State Field Service	Coordination of Teaching Services of Coaches
Supervision of Sports Facilities	Extramural Sports	Health Education Institutes and Workshops	Administration of Outdoor Education Center	Coordination of Maintenance and Use of Athletic Facilities
Supervision of Aquatics	Dance Productions	Public and Private School Consultations	Recreation Institutes and Workshops	Coordination of Conference Affiliation, National Collegiate Athletic Association, American Amateur Athletic Union, etc.
Faculty-Staff and Community Instructional Services	Faculty-Staff and Community Instructional Services		Coordination with Community Recreation Services	
Research Laboratory	Research Laboratory		Public, Private, and Commercial Recreation Consultations	

Fig. 2-14. Organization chart for school of physical education, health, and recreation. Developed by Don Adee.

Faculty athletic committee

Most colleges with athletic programs of significant size also have a faculty athletic committee. This committee serves in an advisory capacity to the president of the institution. In some cases, there are two such committees, one for women's athletics and one for men's athletics. The membership of such committees frequently includes representatives from the faculty, administration, students, coaches, athletes, and alumni. The athletic director is usually a nonvoting member. The faculty athletic committee is involved in such functions as approving athletic budgets, developing eligibility standards, approving financial awards, authorizing schedules, acting on problems that arise, developing athletic policies, investigating Title IX infractions, reviewing the scholarship program, and deciding to what extent certain sports should be added or eliminated.

Faculty representative

Many colleges and universities have faculty athletic representatives. These are members of the faculty who represent the college or university at national association meetings such as the NAIA and the NCAA, as well as the conference to which the institution belongs. This faculty representative also is used in many institutions to check the eligibility of players in various sports, to attend faculty athletic committee meetings as a nonvoting member, and to give periodic reports to the faculty athletic committee.

Currently being discussed in some institutions of higher learning is the question of who should represent the women's athletic programs. Should the faculty representative be a man or woman? Most women feel strongly that a woman faculty representative should represent women's athletic programs.

Structure of the college or university athletic department

According to Parkhouse and Lapin* there are four basic types of structure for athletic departments.

The first combines both men and women in one department. A man is usually the athletic director and a woman is an associate or assistant athletic director.

*Parkhouse and Lapin, op. cit.

In some cases the woman is called coordinator of women's athletics.

The second provides separate structures for men's and women's athletics. Each has its own athletic director, staff, and support services.

The third is used, for example, at Bowling Green State University and provides that the athletic director is in charge of three revenue-producing sports: football, basketball, and ice hockey. An associate director is the business manager. Another associate director is a woman who is in charge of all non-revenue-producing sports—both men's and women's.

The fourth is found at Stanford University and brings together what were originally separate departments of physical education, intramurals, club sports, recreation, and athletics. All of these are combined into a single department.

THE ORGANIZATION AND STRUCTURE OF PHYSICAL EDUCATION IN INDUSTRY, HEALTH CLUBS, AND ORGANIZATIONS OTHER THAN SCHOOLS AND COLLEGES

Physical education programs exist in settings other than schools and colleges. With the current interest in health and physical fitness, these settings are growing in number. The administrative structure for such programs varies with each organization. In executive fitness programs in industry, for example, the physical education program may be structured so that it is responsible to the medical supervisor, president, or another officer in the organization. In health clubs, the physical education program is often directly under the supervision of the owner or manager of the establishment. In correctional institutions, the physical education program is usually under the direct supervision of the warden.

Because there is such a wide variation in the administration structure of physical education programs in these organizations, it is impossible to describe a standard organization and structure. In a school or college, there is some similarity in the type of administrative structure that exists and the personnel who are identified with the structure. However, in health clubs, industry, and many other organizations the unique makeup and desires of each organization determine the administrative structure.

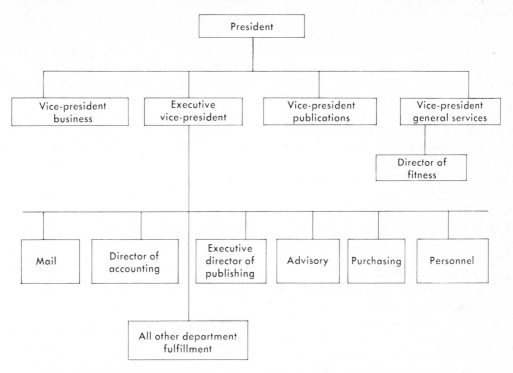

Fig. 2-15. Administration structure of an industrial organization showing role of fitness director.

These physical education programs other than in schools and colleges are designed for the members of or clientele served by the organization. A few are conducted for profit, such as health clubs, whereas most are conducted for the benefit of the members, such as for the employees in industry.

These programs provide various activities, including stress testing to determine exercise tolerance, prescriptive exercises to develop and maintain physical fitness, a variety of sports and physical education activities, highly organized sports competition, and other forms of activitiy.

Equipment and facilities may include sophisticated Nautilus and Universal exercise equipment, and such facilities as gymnasiums, exercise rooms, swimming pools, playfields, tennis courts, and jogging tracks.

The physical education personnel involved in these programs include people trained in such physical education specialities as exercise physiology, biomechanics, athletic administration, coaching, athletic training, and sports writing and public relations.

Considerations for a functional and efficient organization and structure

Developing a functional structure means delegating authority, resolving organizational conflicts, making meaningful decisions, and forming sound policies.

Delegating authority

The wise administrator delegates responsibilities and with them the authority to make the necessary decisions for carrying out such responsibilities.

Most administrators are overwhelmed with their assigned duties. In many cases it is humanly impossible for one person to discharge all of these duties. Therefore it is important to delegate some to qualified persons who can perform them efficiently.

There should be a clear understanding between the administrator and the person to whom the duties are being delegated. The latter must be willing to assume such responsibilities and must know exactly what he or she is responsible for.

In physical education programs the director of physical education or chairperson often delegates to others responsibilities for the adapted program, intramurals, extramurals, and varsity sports. The director of athletics frequently delegates authority to the athletic trainer and to the coaches.

The administrator should recognize that in delegating responsibilities, however, he or she is still responsible for the overall functioning of the unit, such as a school division, department, or program.

Resolving organizational conflicts

Within programs and departments conflicts do occur. Wherever human beings are involved, conflicts develop around such human needs as security, status, esteem, or self-actualization. When certain needs are not satisfied, conflict may arise. Persons have basic needs that can represent physical needs, such as the need for proper bodily comfort, psychological needs, such as a feeling of belonging and recognition, or social needs, such as the desire to work with a certain group of people.

Organizational conflicts, as far as possible, should be solved effectively by the administrator. This means creating an environment in which employees want to work and where there is a place to achieve self-esteem and self-actualization. It means providing opportunities for personal growth. It means keeping channels of communication open at all times both to stifle rumors and to learn about employee complaints. It means making work as interesting as possible to guard against monotony. It means involving employees in decisions that affect their well-being.

Organizational conflicts are kept to a minimum if the administration is aware of human needs and tries to satisfy these needs as far as possible.

Making and implementing meaningful decisions and assessing the results

Decision making in the administrative process requires that certain steps be followed. The traditional problem-solving approach includes the recognition of the problem, identifying the alternatives, gathering and organizing facts, weighing alternatives, and

finally arriving at a decision. Administration should not stop at the point of arriving at a decision; it is essential to go on to the stages that involve implementation and assessment. The sequential stages of this process are well stated by Burr and associates.*

1. *Deliberating.* The problem is discussed, facts on the problem are gathered, and the problem is carefully analyzed.
2. *Decision making.* As a result of the deliberation a decision is made. Alternatives are carefully weighed, and a choice is made based on the facts.
3. *Programming.* After the decision is made, the program is developed so that it is ready for implementation. Questions are asked and actions taken with regard to the resources that are available, the planning that needs to be done, the budget, equipment, and material requirements that exist, and the needs in regard to staff and so on. In other words, information is researched that will provide a successful program and the right direction, in light of the decision that was made.
4. *Stimulating.* After the programming has been developed, it is set into operation. This requires the involvement of people, arousing interest, obtaining commitments, and initiating action. Motivation needs to be encouraged and attitudes developed in this process.
5. *Coordinating.* To effectively implement a program requires the coordination of staff efforts, material resources, proper communication, and other essentials that will assure that the program will be successfully launched.
6. *Appraising.* The last stage in the continuum is evaluating and appraising all stages of the process and the results obtained. It attempts to analyze where the process was successful or where it failed and the reasons for the success or failure. The information gathered will be used in future endeavors.

Forming sound policies

Policies are essential to the efficient administration of any department, school, business, or other organization. Without them, there is little to guide the activities and conduct of the establishment in the pursuit of its goals. With well-reasoned policies, the organization can function efficiently and effectively, and its members will better understand what is expected of them.

*Burr, J.B., et al.: Elementary school administration, Boston, 1963, Allyn & Bacon, Inc., pp. 398-402.

Policies are guides to action. Policies reflect procedures that, when they are adhered to, fulfill the best interests of the organization and the purposes for which it exists. If properly selected and developed, policies enable each member of an organization to know what duties are to be performed, the type of behavior that will result in the greatest productivity for the establishment, how best the department goals can be accomplished, and the procedure by which accountability can be established and evaluated.

The efficient administration of a physical education department requires the establishment of sound policies if it is to achieve its goals. During a school survey several years ago, the office of a director of physical education was visited. When he was asked to supply the policies under which the department was administered, the director replied that no policies existed. Instead, the administrator indicated that he dealt with each problem as it occurred. There were no set guidelines established in advance—no written policies. As a result, chaos reigned in this program. Each faculty member had his or her own way of handling such things as student excuses from class, testing the skill level of boys and girls, and transporting players to athletic events.

The policies of the federal government are reflected in the laws of the land. They are developed in Congress and, after judicial and executive review and approval, become established policies by which the citizens and organizations of this country are guided. As a result, each person and organization knows whether heroin can be ''pushed'' or whether people of another race can be discriminated against. Just as the national government has policies to guide the actions of its citizens and organizations, so also do the state and municipal divisions of government.

State and local systems of education also have established policies that provide guidelines for such important administrative considerations as the number of days school will be in session, what children and youth must attend school, and for whom educational programs are to be provided. Similarly, just as governmental organizations and their subdivisions establish policies to guide the workings of their organizations, so should the physical education department have policies to guide its actions and help achieve its objectives.

Administrative policies are statements of procedures that represent the legalistic framework under which the organization operates. As such, they are not changed frequently, but have some sense of permanence. Therefore they are not developed on short notice or hastily written.

On the other hand, rules and regulations, as compared with policies, are usually more specific and are formulated to carry out the policy that has been established. For example, an established policy of a school might be that all athletes will be transported to interschool contests by school-owned transportation. Rules and regulations then could be established for such purposes as spelling out the nature and type of such transportation, the students who must comply with the policy, and when and how they will comply. Generally, rules and regulations can be changed much more readily than policies. In fact, some administrators develop rules and regulations instead of policies so that they can be changed more easily.

Although policies are considered and formulated carefully, they should be reviewed periodically in light of any new developments that occur. For example, at present some schools are providing faculty and students with new freedoms, rights, and privileges that make some existing policies outdated and obsolete. Therefore change is needed.

How policy is developed. Policy emanates as a result of many phenomena. For example, the Constitution of the United States sets forth various conditions that affect policy development in organizations throughout the country. Educators, for example, must comply with such conditions as equal rights for all in the public schools, separation of church and state, various conditions inherent in the democratic process, and those included in Title IX.

Because education is a state responsibility, the state government also issues policies that must be adhered to by local education authorities. These policies include such items as the number of days schools must be in session, and certification qualifications, subject requirements, and minimum salary schedules for teachers. Within the framework of these policies or guidelines established by federal and state agencies, however, local education authorities, for example, boards of education, are permitted freedom to develop their own policies. Thus they establish policies on whether students can drive their automobiles to school and whether teachers can have sabbatical leaves. The department of physical education can develop policies within the framework of the higher echelons of authority previously mentioned. Sometimes local policies conflict with state policies with the result that local policies are declared invalid.

Policy is developed in many ways in physical education departments. In some organizations it is done autocratically with an administrator or two establishing policy unilaterally. The process is devoid of deliberations and suggestions from the members of the organization. The trend now, however, it toward greater involvement of staff members in developing policy.

As a general rule, the cliché "many heads are better than one" is true in policy development. Policies must be carefully researched and thought through before being written. Therefore it is usually better to involve many people who look at educational problems affecting policies from many different angles.

Although staff members may participate in policy development, it should be recognized that the formulation and development of policy is different from the execution of the policy. Execution of policy is usually an administrative responsibility and should be recognized as such.

Writing policies. Before policies are written, much research must be done to determine what goes into the substance of that policy. This can be done in several ways. One method is for the director of physical education to appoint a committee to research carefully and to recommend policy to the administration.

When the committee has been formed to recommend policy, it will want to investigate the facts thoroughly. It may decide to research the state policies regarding this problem, what other organizations are doing, what policies already exist, the stand taken by selected national professional and athletic associations, views of other administrators, the position of the American Civil Liberties Union, and other sources of information. After gathering all these facts, the committee will want to consider them care-

fully and then make a recommendation. If the recommendation is approved, the director of physical education may then recommend it to his or her superior for approval, who in turn, if he or she agrees, may recommend it to the board or other group for its final approval as the policy governing the organization.

The policy that finally emanates from the committee should be written clearly and concisely. There should be no ambiguities or possibilities of misinterpretation of what is intended by the policy statement. The statement of policy formulated by the committee should in turn be reviewed carefully by the staff members and administration to further determine that the statement says clearly what the organization's position is on this particular issue.

When policy is needed. Only the most important items facing the department of physical education should have policy statements. Policies on trivial matters should not be carried on the books, because confusion and failure to adhere to many of the policies can result when they are not known or understood. Furthermore, with too many policies, the important ones may be obscured by the proliferation of those less important. It is usually better to have only a few carefully researched policies that cover major administrative functions. The other matters, if they need attention, can be covered by rules and regulations or in some other manner.

SELF-ASSESSMENT TESTS

These tests are to assist students in determining if material and competencies presented in this chapter have been mastered:

1. You have been asked by the chief administrator of an organization to identify the objectives that physical education and athletics will be able to achieve for the members of that organization and to show how the administrative structure you have recommended will help achieve these objectives. Prepare a written statement for the chief administrator of the organization that answers his or her questions.

2. Write an essay on the topic: "Developing and Organizing the Structure for a Physical Education Program and for an Athletic Program Is an Important Administrative Responsibility."

3. Cite at least six principles that should be observed in developing an effective administrative organization, and show how each of the following elements are essential to a sound administrative structure: delegation of authority, span of control, communication, and staff specialization.

4. You are an outside consultant with expertise in administrative organization and structure who has been hired by an organization with a physical education and athletic program to give advice as to whether it should have a formal or informal administrative structure. What advice would you give to this organization? Defend your decision.

5. Prepare a model for the administrative structure of a physical education or an athletic program in an organization of your choice, and show why it is a sound administrative structure.

6. Draw a structural organization chart for your college, showing the various administrative divisions. Discuss the responsibilities of each of the divisions.

7. How would the administrative organization and structure you recommended in item 4 provide for each of the following: *delegating authority* to the heads of the instructional program, the program for the handicapped, intramurals and extramurals, and varsity athletics; *resolving a conflict* between the director of athletics and the director of intramurals; *determining budget allocations* for athletics; and *formulating policies* regarding Title IX.

SELECTED REFERENCES

American Alliance for Health, Physical Education, and Recreation: HPER omnibus, Washington, D.C., 1976, The Alliance.

American Alliance for Health, Physical Education, and Recreation, Celeste Ulrich: to seek and find, Washington, D.C., 1976, The Alliance.

American Association for Health, Physical Education, and Recreation: Organizational patterns for instruction in physical education, Washington, D.C., 1971, The Association.

Annarino, A.A., et al.: Curriculum theory and design in physical education, ed. 2, St. Louis, 1980, The C.V. Mosby Co.

Avedisian, C.T.: PPBS planning, programming, budgeting systems, Journal of Health, Physical Education, and Recreation **43:**37, 1972.

Barnett, M.L.: The administrator as helper: quest for instructional excellence, Journal of Physical Education and Recreation **50:**42, January, 1979.

Broyles, J.F., and Hay, R.D.: Administration of athletic programs—a managerial approach, Englewood Cliffs, N.J., 1979, Prentice-Hall, Inc.

Bucher, C.A.: Physical education for life, St. Louis, 1969, McGraw-Hill Book Co.

Bucher, C.A.: Foundations of physical education, ed. 9, St. Louis, 1983, The C.V. Mosby Co.

Bucher, C.A., and Dupee, R.K., Jr.: Athletics in schools and colleges, Washington, D.C., 1965, The Center For Applied Research in Education, Inc. (The Library of Education).

Bucher, C.A., and Koenig, C.: Methods and materials for secondary school physical education, ed. 6, St. Louis, 1983, The C.V. Mosby Co.

Bucher, C.A., and Thaxton, N.: Physical education and sport: change and challenge, St. Louis, 1981, The C.V. Mosby Co.

Deatherage, D., and Reid, C.P.: Administration of women's competitive sports, Dubuque, Iowa, 1977, Wm C. Brown Group.

Dowell, L.J.: Strategies for teaching physical education, Englewood Cliffs, N.J., 1975, Prentice-Hall, Inc.

Ehrle, E.B.: Observations on the nature of deaning: the emerging role of dean in academic planning, Journal of Physical Education and Recreation **50:**44, January, 1979.

Fuoss, D.E., and Troppmann, R.J.: Creative management techniques in interscholastic athletics, New York, 1977, John Wiley & Sons, Inc.

Hall, J.T., et al.: Administration: principles, theory and practice, with applications to physical education, Pacific Palisades, Calif., 1973, Goodyear Publishing Co., Inc.

Ilowit, R., and Soupios, M.: There's got to be a better way, Journal of Physical Education and Recreation **50:**38, January, 1979.

Morphet, E.L., Johns, R.L., and Reller, T.L.: Educational administration, Englewood Cliffs, N.J., 1967, Prentice-Hall, Inc.

Netcher, J.R.: A management model for competency-based HPER programs, St. Louis, 1977, The C.V. Mosby Co.

Parkhouse, B.L., and Lapin, J.: The woman in athletic administration, Santa Monica, Calif., 1980, Goodyear Publishing Co., Inc.

Scott, P.M.: The new administrator: a point of view, Journal of Physical Education and Recreation **50:**40, January, 1979.

Tanner, D.: Using behavioral objectives in the classroom, New York, 1972, Macmillan, Inc.

Taylor, S.: Educational leadership: a male domain? Phi Delta Kappan **55:**124, 1973.

Ulrich, C.: She can play as good as any boy, Phi Delta Kappan **55:**113, 1973.

Whaling, T.: Managing the school system; a performance improvement approach, Education Digest **38:**18, 1973.

Wheeler, R.H., and Hooley, A.M.: Physical education for the handicapped, Philadelphia, 1976, Lea & Febiger.

Wood, C.L.: The secondary school principal—manager and supervisor, Boston, 1979, Allyn & Bacon, Inc.

Zeigler, E.F.: The case for management theory and practice in sport and physical education, Journal of Physical Education and Recreation **50:**36, January, 1979.

PART TWO

Administration of physical education and athletic programs

3

Physical education instructional programs

Instructional objectives and competencies to be achieved

After reading this chapter the student should be able to —

- Provide a description of the nature, scope, purpose, and worth of instructional programs in physical education.
- Describe Basic Stuff Series I and II and discuss the implications for physical education.
- Outline the component parts of preschool, elementary school, secondary school, and college and university physical education instructional programs.
- Describe instructional strategies for physical education programs as a result of Title IX legislation.
- Justify the need for certain administrative procedures, such as scheduling, time allotment for classes, size of classes, instructional loads, class management, uniforms, taking roll, selecting physical education activities, grouping, and areas of student involvement.
- Understand the professional nature of selected administrative problems in instructional programs such as having physical education required or elective, substitutions, credit, class attendance, excuses, instruction by specialist or classroom teacher, dressing and showering, records, and evaluation.

Physical education instructional programs are the foundation on which the rest of the component parts rest. Years ago the basic instructional program was graphically represented as the base of an isosceles triangle. The parts above the base were the adapted, intramural, and extramural programs, and the apex of the triangle was the varsity athletic program. What the isosceles triangle symbolized is still true today. To have a sound physical education program it is essential to have a firm and solid base.

The instructional program in physical education is the place to teach skills, strategies, understandings, and essential knowledge concerning the relation of physical activity to physical, mental, emotional, and social development. It is also a place to get participants to achieve an optimum state of physical fitness.

Skills should be taught from a scientific approach, so that the various biomechanical factors that affect movement are understood clearly by the participant. Demonstrations, super-8 films, loop films, models, slide films, videotapes, posters, and other visual aids and materials can help in instruction. In schools, team teaching and differentiated staffing enable the master teacher of specific skills to be utilized more extensively than in the past.

The material presented throughout the school life of the student should be sequential in development and progressive in application. Just as a student advances in mathematics from simple arithmetic to algebra, geometry, and calculus, so in physical education the individual should progress from basic skills and materials to more complex skills and strategies. A physical fitness program should also be developmental, starting with the individual's present state of fitness and gradually moving to a higher level of fitness.

Performance objectives should be established for individual student achievement. When boys and girls advance from one grade to another, they should have achieved certain objectives in various physical education activities, just as they master various levels of skills and understandings in other subjects.

Physical education should involve more than physical activity. As the participant understands more fully the importance of sports and activities in life, what happens to the human body during exercise, the relation of physical activity to one's biological, psychological, and sociological development, the history of various activities, and the role of physical activity in the cultures of the world, physical education acquires more intellectual respectability and meaning.

Just as textbooks are used in other courses in the educational system, so should physical education in a school program use a textbook, with regular assignments given. Textbooks should not only contain material on physical skills but should also cover the subject matter of physical education.

Records that follow a student from grade to grade should be kept throughout his or her school life. These records will indicate the degree to which the objectives have been achieved by the student, his or her physical status, skill achievement, knowledge about the field, and social conduct, all of which help interpret what physical education has done for the student and what still needs to be done. There should also be homework in physical education to help master subject matter, improve skills, and achieve physical fitness.

The basic instructional physical education period cannot be conducted in a ''hit-or-miss'' fashion. It must be planned in accordance with the needs and interests of the individuals it serves.

Selected new developments in physical education instructional programs

Many new and exciting developments in instructional programs should receive administrative consideration by physical educators. These developments receive only brief attention here, for they are discussed at greater length in Chapter 11.

BASIC STUFF SERIES I AND II

Basic Stuff Series I and II, developed by physical education leaders, represent knowledge and information presented in a conceptual approach format for elementary and secondary school students. They cover facts in exercise physiology, motor development, motor learning, kinesiology, psychosocial aspects of physical education, and humanities in physical education, and then relate these facts to the age groups of early childhood, childhood, and adolescence. Basic Stuff Series I and II represent valuable information for getting at the ''why'' of physical education in the form of concepts that have meaning for elementary and secondary school students. The series, when implemented nationwide, will help gain much academic respect for physical education. It represents an important innovation in physical education instructional programs.

HEALTH-RELATED PHYSICAL FITNESS

The AAHPERD through its Task Force on Youth Fitness has stressed the need for health-related physical fitness. Health-related fitness places an emphasis on cardiovascular function, body composition, strength, and flexibility. These components also represent the ingredients for performance-related physical fitness. The basic instructional program should give consideration to the development of health-related physical fitness for all students in schools and colleges. Performance-related physical fitness should also be considered for students who are interested in achieving high performance in physical education and athletic activities.

THE ''WELLNESS'' MOVEMENT

The emphasis today on the ''wellness'' movement has implications for the basic instructional program in physical education. The trend today is toward seeing how humans can stay well and fit. Self-help medicine is one answer. Students need to follow a personal health regimen and adopt a life-style that stresses fitness. Thus physical activity and physical fitness as part of the instructional program of physical education have an increased value and importance for students.

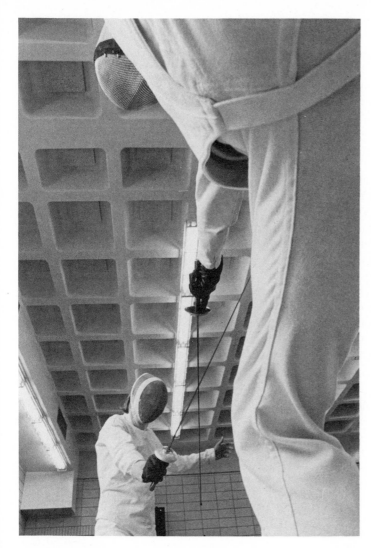

Fig. 3-1. Fencing is one activity that the physical education program provides at Florissant Valley Community College in St. Louis.

Photograph by LeMoyne Coates.

MASTERY LEARNING

Mastery learning is based on the assumption that nearly all students can master material if they are given sufficient time and if the material is presented in an understandable way. The procedure followed in places where it has proved successful is that first the material is presented to an entire group of students. Then an evaluation is conducted and students who have not mastered the material are given a second chance. The material is presented again but in a different way and in a more understandable manner.

Mastery learning operates under the assumption that there are no failures—everyone succeeds. The instructional physical education program should take this new development into consideration.

MOVEMENT EDUCATION
(see also pp. 60-65)

Movement education has proven to be of value in elementary school physical education programs. Therefore physical educators should seriously consider it for instructional programs for elementary school children. It is discussed in more detail in a later section of this chapter.

TITLE IX AND PUBLIC LAW 94-142

The implications of Title IX for the instructional physical education program are discussed later in this chapter. PL 94-142 is considered at length in the following chapter.

HUMANISTIC EDUCATION

Change is needed to humanize our schools and colleges so that students feel a sense of identity and belonging and are actively involved in the decision-making processes that affect them. Physical education instructional programs need to be concerned with humanization and involvement processes.

OLYMPIC CURRICULUM

The education committee of the United States Olympic Committee has prepared booklets designed to incorporate the ideals associated with the Olympic Games into the curriculum of several subjects in the elementary schools, junior high schools, and senior high schools of the nation. One subject in which these Olympic concepts can be taught is physical education. The physical educator will want to review and consider using this material.

NEW GAMES

New Games represents an innovative approach being used by some physical educators. It is based on such concepts as "Any game can be a new game," "Anyone can play," "Creating a new game is part of the fun," "We play for the fun of it," "It is the process of finding a game that we all want to play," and "We learn about play by playing." The New Games organization holds training sessions for individuals who are interested in learning more about this movement.

LIFETIME SPORTS

Considerable emphasis is being placed today on the importance of including lifetime sports in a physical education instructional program. Lifetime sports refers to sports such as tennis, golf, and swimming that can be engaged in throughout a person's entire life. A significant part of the physical education in-

structional program should be devoted to these activities.

HIGH ADVENTURE LEISURE ACTIVITIES

Many people today are engaging in high adventure activities such as skydiving, hang-gliding, and rock climbing. The risks involved in participating in such activities appeal to some individuals who want to be challenged, desire a thrill, and seek excitement. It is questionable whether such activities should be a part of any school physical education curriculum. If they are a part of a college instructional program, there should be considerable stress on participants knowing the fundamentals of the activity and on their being fit to cope successfully with these activities.

DANCE

Dance is becoming very popular and rewarding in instructional programs of physical education. Although administrators in some institutions are unsure about whether dance should be located with the arts or with physical education, no one questions dancing as an important part of the physical education program. Dancing is one of the oldest arts and should be included in programs from the primary grades through college. The dance program in many schools and colleges includes fundamental rhythms, folk dances, athletic or gymnastic dancing, social or ballroom dancing, modern dancing, and tap dancing.

School and college physical education programs

Physical education programs in schools and colleges have had a prominent place in educational systems since the turn of the century. These programs exist at the preschool, elementary school, junior high school, senior high school, and college and university educational levels.

PRESCHOOL PHYSICAL EDUCATION PROGRAMS

The concept of early schooling is no longer regarded as a custodial or compensatory undertaking. Instead it is viewed as a necessary provision for the normal growth and development of children. This change has come about because of research on the growth and development of children from birth to

6 years, as well as the change in family life, as indicated by such developments as working mothers. Research by such professionals as psychologists and sociologists has indicated that the early years are crucial for the child intellectually, physically, and socially. In light of such developments, play schools and nursery schools have gained wide popularity.

Preschool educational programs involve indoor and outdoor play-learning activities. Physical education activities include the development of fundamental movement skills, fitness and self-testing activities, music and rhythmic activities, and rhymes and story plays. The program of selected physical activities helps the child develop a positive self-concept, develop social skills, enhance physical fitness, and improve cognitive and sensorimotor skills.

Research maintains there is a relationship between perception and motor development and that perception is related to cognition; therefore physical movement experiences play a part in cognitive development.

Preschool programs are becoming an important part of educational systems in this country, and physical education is playing an important role in such programs.

ELEMENTARY SCHOOL PHYSICAL EDUCATION PROGRAMS

The elementary schools of the nation are stressing movement education. Experts do not agree on a single definition for movement education. They do agree, however, that movement education depends on physical factors in the environment and on the individual's ability to react intellectually and physically to these factors. Movement education attempts to help the student become mentally and physically aware of his or her bodily movements. It is based on a conceptual approach to human movement. Through movement education, the individual develops his or her own techniques for dealing with the environmental factors of force, time, space, and flow as they relate to various movement problems.

Movement education employs the problem-solving approach. Each skill to be explored presents a challenge to the student. Learning results as the student accepts and solves increasingly more difficult problems. For this reason, the natural movements of child-

hood are considered to be the first challenges that should be presented to the student.

Traditional physical education emphasizes the learning of specific skills through demonstration, drill, and practice. Movement education emphasizes learning skill patterns through individual exploration of the body's movement potential. Traditional physical education stresses the teacher's standard of performance. Movement education stresses the individual child's standard of performance.

Concepts of movement pertinent to elementary school physical education program*

Certain concepts relating to movement must be understood by both teachers and students to accomplish a meaningful study of basic movement. The concepts are aspects of Laban's four components of movement, which are (1) Where does the body move? (spatial awareness), (2) What can the body do? (body awareness), (3) How does the body move? (qualities of movement), and (4) With whom or what does the body move? (relationships). The concept of spatial awareness, as an example, is discussed here with objectives and suggested problems for study.

Spatial awareness. Spatial awareness includes the type of space in which the body moves, as well as the direction, level, and pathway that the body takes in movement.

Space. All movement takes place in space. There are two kinds of space—personal and general. Personal space is the largest space available to a person in a stationary position. This includes the space a person can reach by stretching, bending, and twisting. General space includes all the area in which one person or several people can move. It might be in the gymnasium, the swimming pool, or the hallway.

The amount of space available and the number of people in a particular space affect movement possibilities. Understanding the concepts of personal space and general space is crucial to the student's future growth in movement. Rarely is this understanding reached in a single lesson; therefore, this concept should be reinforced often.

---

*Adapted from Bucher, C.A., and Thaxton, N.: Physical education for children: movement foundations and experiences, New York, 1979, Macmillan, Inc.

Fig. 3-2. Dance is becoming very popular and rewarding in physical education.

Courtesy State University College, Potsdam, New York.

The objectives of a program to teach spatial awareness are as follows:

1. To establish verbal cues to begin and to stop movement in a particular area.
2. To establish awareness of personal space and general space.
3. To establish safety awareness while moving in personal and general space by encouraging no touching and no collisions.

Suggested problems for studying personal and general space would be for the teacher to instruct the children to:

1. Explore space around the body by reaching in all directions with different parts of the body.
2. Keep the feet in one position on the floor and reach for something circling around them.
3. Move the rest of the body around in their personal space, using the hands as the base. How many different ways can the body move around the hands?
4. Move into general space, bouncing a ball, and maintain control, so that they do not run into anyone or let the ball hit anyone.
5. Run anywhere in the room until they hear the signal to stop. They should not touch anyone or anything while moving. Change the style of locomotion, that is, gallop, slide, hop, and so on.

Direction. With an understanding of personal and general space, the student can now apply directional changes while moving in space. Direction refers to movements forward, backward, sideways, upward, downward, diagonally, or any combination of these. The ability to move in a variety of directions is vital to success in such areas as sports, dance, and gymnastics.

The objective in teaching the concept of direction is to have the students understand directional terminology. They should understand all of the directions listed in the preceding paragraph.

Suggested problems for studying direction are as follows:

1. In what direction can they walk? Can they walk in another direction?
2. Can they walk forward? Backward? Sideways?
3. Each time the drum beats, change directions and use different locomotor skills.
4. Move a ball around in all directions within their personal space. Keep passing the ball from hand to hand.

Level. The body moves on varying horizontal planes. These may be high, medium, or low. Levels exist in personal and general space and in all locomotor and axial (nonlocomotor) movements.

Fig. 3-3. Kindergarten children performing Chinese ribbon dance at physical education demonstration at Oak View Elementary School in Fairfax, Va.

The objectives of teaching the concept of level are the following:

1. To differentiate among high, medium, and low levels.
2. To be able to change levels.
3. To combine level changes while using directions and space.

Suggested problems for studying level are as follows:

1. How low can the body go? How high can the body go?
2. Can the child move at a medium level while running, skipping, and so on?
3. Can the child move sideways while walking at a medium level?
4. Move with hands low and toes high.
5. Move with one hand low and the other hand high.
6. Can the student change from high to medium, to low level while running, skipping, jumping, in a forward direction?

Pathways. A pathway is a line of movement from one place to another in a given space. It might be the movement of the entire body in a general space (example: to run from home to first base in a softball game), or the movement of a part of the body in a

personal space (example: a level (horizontal) swing of the bat with the arms).

The objectives for teaching the concept of pathways are the following:

1. To create student awareness of alternative pathways in which they can move, that is, direct and indirect pathways.
2. To develop the ability of the body to move through many pathways.
3. To have the students identify and move on specific pathways.

Suggested problems for studying pathways are as follows:

1. What is the shortest pathway to the wall?
2. Can the students travel in a zigzag path? Circular path?
3. Can the students walk the letter "A" or the number "6"?
4. What is the longest pathway that can be taken to return to the starting personal space from the other end of the gym?
5. In what pathways can the arm move? What other parts of the body can move in different pathways, and what are the pathways?

Fig. 3-4. Elementary school physical education class participating in hoop activities at the Hudson Falls Central School, Hudson Falls, N.Y.

Fig. 3-5. Elementary school children developing body awareness in movement education program.

Courtesy the AAHPERD and Charles Holbrook.

Guidelines for elementary school physical education programs

Elementary schools also are stressing perceptual motor development and, in addition, an interdisciplinary approach whereby the subject matter of physical education is integrated with certain other subjects such as music, science, and art.

Some general guidelines that should be recognized in elementary school physical education programs follow:

1. The program should meet the needs of all children, including the handicapped, slow learners, culturally deprived, gifted, and normal.
2. The program should stress movement education, perceptual-motor development, and interdisciplinary analysis.
3. The program should include a variety of experiences that will help the child form a sound foundation on which to build more complex skills, strategies, and techniques.
4. The program should provide developmental and progressive experiences.
5. The program should stress such factors as creativity, self-expression, positive self-concept, social development, and safety.

The various aspects of the physical education program for elementary school, including the characteristics of children at various ages, opportunities they need, and types of activities that meet these needs and characteristics, have been developed by a group of experts (Tables 3-1 and 3-2). *Of course, the emphasis on movement education should infiltrate the various activities listed. Growth is a continuous process, and children differ in their stages of growth. Therefore any classification into groups must recognize that the report is only a convenient device to try to give a general picture of activities that suit the changing needs of children, each child holding to a path that is his or hers alone.*

SECONDARY SCHOOL PHYSICAL EDUCATION PROGRAMS

The junior high schools and the senior high schools of the nation should build on the physical education provided at the elementary school level. Some general guidelines that represent important considerations in secondary school physical education programs follow:

1. Most of the guidelines set for the elementary school also have merit in developing programs for secondary schools.
2. The program should be based on the developmental tasks of secondary school students.
3. The program should consist of a variety of activities, including gymnastics, self-testing activities, rhythm and dance, aquatics, dual and individual sports, team sports, movement skills, and physical fitness activities.
4. The program should provide an understanding of the human body and the impact of physical activity on its various organic systems. Basic Stuff Series I and II should be used.
5. The program should teach skills progressively and eliminate excessive repetition of activities.
6. Title IX regulations should be adhered to.
7. Handicapped students should be provided a program in the least restrictive environment.
8. The program should encourage vigorous physical activity and develop an optimum state of physical fitness.

In addition, the following points should be stressed:

The physical education class is a place to teach the skills, strategy, appreciation, understanding, knowledge, rules, regulations, and other material and information that are part of the program. It is not a place for free play, intramurals, and varsity competition. It is a place for instruction. Every minute of the class period should be devoted to teaching boys and girls the skills and subject matter of physical education.

Instruction should be basic and interesting. Skills should be broken down into simple components and taught so that each individual may understand clearly what he or she is expected to accomplish and how it should be done. Utilization of demonstrations, loop films, models, slide films, posters, and other visual aids and materials can help to make the instruction more meaningful and interesting.

Instruction should be progressive. There should be a definite progression from simple to complex skills. Just as a student progresses in mathematics from simple arithmetic to algebra, geometry, and calculus, so in physical education the pupil should progress from basic skills and materials to more complex and involved skills and strategies.

Table 3-1. Early childhood—5 to 8 years of age—kindergarten through third grade*

What they are like	What they need OPPORTUNITIES	What to do
Their large muscles (trunk, legs, and arms) are more developed than the smaller muscles (hands and feet)	To experience many kinds of vigorous activities that involve many parts of the body	Activities such as hanging, running, jumping, climbing, dodging, or throwing at an object, such as beanbag toss, jacks, bouncing balls, hopscotch, O'Leary
	To engage in many developmental activities for small muscles	Movement activities involving space, time, flow, tempo; activities to explore various body movements; rhythm activities
They have a short attention span	To engage in many activities of short duration	Choice of activity where a child can change frequently, and activities that can be started quickly, such as Magic Carpet, Pincho, Hill Dill, and stunts
	To develop body awareness	
	To develop a favorable self-concept	
	To develop fundamental movement activities	
They are individualistic and possessive	To play alone and with small groups	Individual activities, such as throwing, catching, bouncing, kicking, climbing, stunts, running, hopping, skipping, building blocks, jumping; dance activities that allow for expression of self, such as clowns, aviators, firemen, tops, airplanes; sport skills and activities; swimming and water safety, apparatus, stunts and tumbling; creative rhythms, movement exploration
	To play as an individual in larger groups	
They are dramatic, imaginative, and imitative	To create and explore	Invent dance and game activities, such as cowboys, circus, Christmas toys; work activities, such as pounding, sawing, raking, and hauling; other play activities, such as farmers, postmen, grocers, elevators, bicycles, leaves, scarecrows
	To identify themselves with people and things	
They are active, energetic, and responsive to rhythmic sounds	To respond to rhythmic sounds such as drums, rattles, voice and nursery rhythms, songs, and music	Running, skipping, walking, jumping, galloping, dodging, swimming; singing and folk games, such as Oats, Peas, Beans, and Barley Grow; Farmer in the Dell; Dixie Polka
They are curious	To explore and handle materials with many types of play	Using materials such as balls, ropes, stilts, parachutes, beanbags, bars, ladders, trees, blocks; games and activities such as hiking, Run-Sheep-Run, Huckle-Buckle Beanstalk. Basic Stuff Series I and II should be used at this level.
They want chances to act on their own and are annoyed at conformity	To make choices, to help make rules, to share and evaluate group experiences	Variety of activities with minimum of rules, such as Center Base, Exchange, Midnight, and Red Light; make-up activities, dances, and games
They are continuing to broaden social contacts and relationships	To cooperate in play and dance, to organize many of their own groups	Group games, such as simple forms of dodge ball, kickball; dance and rhythmic activities, such as Gustaf's Skoal, Dance of Greeting, Bow Balinda
They seem to be in perpetual motion	To play many types of vigorous activities	Running, jumping, skipping, galloping, rolling, fitness routines and activities

*From Report of National Conference on Physical Education for Children of Elementary School Age: Physical education for children of elementary school age, Chicago, 1951, The Athletic Institute, Inc. Adapted and updated by author, 1982.

Table 3-2. Middle childhood—9 to 11 years of age—fourth through sixth grades*

What they are like	What they need OPPORTUNITIES	What to do
They grow steadily in muscles, bone, heart, and lungs	To engage in strenuous activity that regularly taxes these organs to the limits of healthy fatigue	Running, jumping, climbing, and hard play; movement experiences and body mechanics; fitness routines; tumbling, apparatus and stunts
They enjoy rough and tumble activities	To participate in activities that use the elements of roughness	Bumping, pushing, contact activities, such as King of the Ring, Poison Pen, Indian wrestle, hand wrestle, Beater Goes 'Round
Sex differences begin to appear with girls taller and more mature than boys; sex antagonisms may appear	To enjoy their roles as boys and girls, to have wholesome boy-girl relationships in activities	Activities such as folk dances, mixers, squares; swimming and water safety, relays, sport skills and activities; group games, such as volleyball-type games, Newcomb or fist ball, softball; others may be enjoyed separately or together
They respond differently in varying situations	To participate in wide range of activities and organizations using many kinds of materials	Individual, dual, or small and large group activities, such as swimming, tumbling, stilts, track, catch, handball, relays, folk dances, mixers, and simple square dances, such as Csebogar, Captain Jinks, Life on the Ocean Wave
They have a strong sense of rivalry and crave recognition	To succeed in activities that stress cooperative play along with activities that give individual satisfaction	Self-testing activities, such as track events, stunts, chinning, sit-ups, push-ups, ball-throwing, for distance and accuracy; group and team play, such as Newcomb, kickball, Circle or Square Soccer, End Ball, Club Snatch, Progressive Dodge Ball
They may show increasing independence and desire to help	To plan, lead, and check progress. To be involved in planning their own program	Assist with officiating, serve as squad leaders, act as scorers, help with equipment, elect captains, help with younger children and each other
They want to be liked by their own classmates, to belong; they have a strong loyalty to teams, groups, or "gangs"	To belong to groups, to be on many kinds of teams. To engage in a wide range of activities	Group games, such as bounce volleyball, line soccer, keep away, hit pin kickball, net ball; partner play such as deck tennis (ring toss), tennis, aerial darts, horseshoes
They want approval, but not at the expense of their group relationships	To gain respect and approval of others	Participate in activities in which they achieve in the eyes of their group. Basic Stuff Series I and II should be used at this educational level.

*From Report of National Conference on Physical Education for Children of Elementary School Age: Physical education for children of elementary school age, Chicago, 1951, The Athletic Institute, Inc. Adapted and updated by author, 1982.

Fig. 3-6. A child can develop self-confidence and find happiness in achievement through successful experience in play activities such as the one shown here at the Hudson Falls Central School, Hudson Falls, N.Y.

Fig. 3-7. Physical education at Palm Harbor Junior High School, Palm Harbor, Fla.

Fig. 3-8. Physical education at Palm Harbor Junior High School, Palm Harbor, Fla.

Instruction should involve definite standards. Students should be expected to reach individualized standards of achievement in the class program. A reasonable amount of skill—whether it is in swimming, tennis, or another activity—should be mastered, depending on individual differences. Laxity and indifference to achievement should not be tolerated any more in physical education than in any other subject area in the curriculum. When boys and girls graduate from high school they should have met definite standards that indicate that they are *physically educated.*

Instruction should involve more than physical activity. All physical education classes do not have to be held in the gymnasium where physical activity predominates. A reasonable proportion of class time, perhaps as much as 10% to 20%, can be devoted to discussions, lectures, independent study, Basic Stuff Series I and II, working on learning packages, and meaningful classroom activity. Outstanding coaches often have chalk talks for their players, in which they study rules and regulations, strategies, execution of skills, and other materials essential to playing the game effectively. This same principle can be applied to the physical education class period. There is a subject matter content that the student needs to know and understand. Physical activity should not be conducted in a vacuum; if it is, it has no meaning and will not be applied when the student leaves the class and school. As the student understands more fully the importance of sports and activities in life, what happens to the body during exercise, the history of the various activities in which he or she engages, and the role of physical activity in the culture of the world, the class takes on new meaning and physical education takes on new respect and prestige.

There should be records. The instructor should keep adequate records to provide tangible evidence of the degree to which objectives are being met by the students. This means that data on physical fitness, skill achievement, knowledge of rules and other information, and social conduct—such as sportsmanship—should be a part of the record.

There should be homework. It is just as reasonable to assign homework in physical education as in general science. Much subject matter is to be learned, and many skills are to be mastered. If teachers would require their students to work on various activity skills and knowledge outside of class, there would be more time in class for meaningful teaching.

Each student should have a health examination before participating in the physical education program. An annual health examination should be regarded as a minimum essential to determining the amount and nature of physical activity that best meets each student's needs.

The teaching load of physical educators should be determined not only by the number of instructional class periods assigned but also by the total number of activities handled by the teacher both in class and outside of class. To do efficient work a teacher should have a normal work load—not an overload. Some professional standards have established that class instruction should not exceed 5 hours, or the equivalent of five class periods each day.

Program for grades seven and eight. Facilities, time, pupils, and teacher load are some of the factors that determine the basic physical education instructional program for grades seven and eight. The absence or presence of a swimming pool, for example, would influence the type of program offered.

Boys and girls in grades seven and eight are growing rapidly, often exhibiting awkwardness and lack of coordination. Muscles, bones, heart, and lungs are experienceing the growth spurt. Some boys surpass some girls in strength and speed, and interests in different physical activities are common. There is keen interest in competitive activities, and this motivating factor may create the desire to continue participating beyond fatigue to exhaustion. The enjoyment of organized sports is common. The students develop loyalty to groups, have a desire for peer group approval, and a strong desire for recognition. Emotions are easily aroused.

Boys and girls in the seventh and eighth grades need to have opportunities to participate in activities in which they can experience success—activities that do not emphasize their frequent awkwardness, that provide vigorous activity, that provide for group participation, and that challenge their interest and physical capabilities.

A description of students' characteristics and needs

Fig. 3-9. Girls at Franklin High School in Los Angeles developing skill in tennis.
Los Angeles Unified School District, Student Auxiliary Services Branch.
Courtesy Gwen R. Waters.

at the seventh and eighth grade levels together with physical education activities suited to these needs is taken from the report of the National Conference on Physical Education (Table 3-3).

Program for grades nine through twelve. During grades nine through twelve, when students are 14 to 17 years of age, students display distinct physical growth and development characteristics. Girls are about 2 years ahead of boys in skeletal growth. Some girls reach adult height at about 14 years of age, whereas others continue to grow for several years beyond this age. Some boys attain adult height at about 16 years of age, and others continue their growth to 20 years of age or later.

In regard to muscular development, the "awkward age" is ending, and there is a definite improvement in coordination. Posture is improving and control and grace are evident, especially in those who have participated in rhythmic activities such as dancing, swimming, and sports.

In respect to organic development, the heart increases in size, raising a question about very strenuous competitive sports, because the heart and arteries may be disproportionate in size. The puberty cycle is completed in most students. There may be a period of glandular instability with fluctuations in energy level. Some characteristic ailments at this age include headache, nosebleed, nervousness, palpitation, and acne.

The boy or girl of 14 through 17 years of age may have reached physiological adulthood but needs many new experiences for fuller social and emotional development. He or she is emotional and is seeking a feeling of belonging. This attempt to adjust may result in some emotional instability. The desire to conform to the standards of the peer group is often greater than the desire to conform to adult standards. However, there are cases of "hero worship," and in such cases adults have considerable influence on youth. This age group is capable of competing in highly organized games. Groups and "cliques" evolve in accordance with interests and physical maturation. Both sexes are interested in being physically attractive. As a result, good grooming increases. Appetite is good at this age. Various sexual manifestations during these years may cause undue self-consciousness. Because girls mature before boys, girls are, as a rule, more interested in boys than boys are in girls.

There is a need for adult guidance that allows considerable freedom and choice on the part of youth. Family life is important and plays a steadying influence on young people at a time when life is becoming more and more complex. Boys and girls need wholesome activity and experiences where excess emotions and energy can be properly channeled. Certain physical education activities require separate participation on the part of boys and girls. However, there is a need for many experiences where boys and girls play together. Coeducational activities should be adapted to both sexes so that no physiological or physical harm results. Social dancing is important. Also, at this age students are interested in and receive much satisfaction from sports. Although individual differences determine the amount of sleep needed, most can profit from 8 to 10 hours. A need exists for a planned afterschool program adapted to the needs of youths and that includes active recreation and manipulative or contemplative activities.

The activities that best meet the needs of the secondary school student are varied. Highly organized team games occupy an increasingly important place at the junior high school level and even more at the senior high school level. The junior and early senior high school programs should be mainly exploratory, offering a wide variety of activities with the team games modified and presented as leadup activities. Toward the end of senior high school, students should have the opportunity to select and specialize in certain activities that will have a carryover value after formal education ceases. Furthermore, to improve skills in selected activities, many of the team games and other activities should be offered more intensively and in larger blocks of time as the student approaches the end of secondary school.

As a general rule, boys and girls in both junior and senior high school can profit greatly from rhythmic activities such as square, folk, and social dancing; team sports such as soccer, field hockey, softball, baseball, touch football, volleyball, and speedball; individual activities such as track and field, tennis, racquetball, paddle tennis, badminton, hiking, handball, bowling, archery, and fly casting; many forms of

Table 3-3. Later childhood–early adolescence—12 to 13 years of age—seventh and eighth grades*

What they are like	What they need OPPORTUNITIES	What to do
This is a period of rapid physical growth that is frequently uneven in various parts of the body; awkwardness and inability to coordinate sometimes occur	To develop skill and coordination and to take part in activities that do not call attention to their awkwardness or put them in embarrassing situations To develop a favorable body image	Movement experiences and body mechanics Skills in various activities, such as batting, throwing, catching, kicking, dribbling, and serving, as used in softball, soccer, volleyball, basketball; skills in body controls, such as how to walk, run, stand, sit relax; individual activities, such as rope jumping, horseshoes, target throw, jumping, skating, hiking, skiing, and swimming
Muscles, heart, lungs, and bones share liberally in the growth spurt	Vigorous activity to stimulate each of these organs to attain its fullest development	Activities conducted as vigorously as possible with respect for individual reaction; fitness routines and activities

Boys and girls are showing differences in interests and in abilities: boys may tend to surpass girls in strength and speed; girls may be more interested than boys in dance forms	To participate in some activities in separate groups and some together based largely on individual choice	Activities recommended in groupings as follows:
		Group sports
		  Soccer
		  Touch football
		  Softball
		  Basketball
		  Volleyball
		Individual, dual, and group sports
		  Track
		  Badminton
		  Tennis
		  Swimming
		  Outing activities
		Formal dancing
		  Square
		  Social
		  Creative
		  Folk

Interest in members of one's own sex broadens to include an interest in members of opposite sex	To have coeducational activities in small and large groups	Activities such as square, social, and creative dance, tennis, swimming, and outing activities, volleyball, table tennis, badminton
Great loyalty to groups as clubs, gangs, and teams, and group acceptance	To belong to various teams and to plan and develop their own groups	Many teams in all team games, such as class teams, homerooms, and clubs
Strong desire for individual recognition and the urge to be free of adult restrictions	To take part in activities of their own choosing, to be leaders and captains of groups, to create and modify games, and to evaluate progress To develop a favorable body image To be involved in planning program To be able to choose some activities	Squad-leader directed activities as: a. Testing skills—sit-up, push-up b. Officiating in games c. Assigning positions on teams Basic Stuff Series I & II

*From Report of National Conference on Physical Education for Children of Elementary School Age: Physical education for children of elementary school age, Chicago, 1951, The Athletic Institute, Inc. Adapted and updated by author, 1982.

Table 3-3. Later childhood–early adolescence—12 to 13 years of age—seventh and eighth grades—cont'd

What they are like	*What they need* OPPORTUNITIES	*What to do*
Emotions are easily aroused and swayed	To be frequently in situations requiring practice of fair play, when winning or losing To participate in policy decisions affecting their physical education program	Wide variety of activities requiring individual decisions and scoring as in: a. High and broad jumps b. Ball-throwing events c. Running against time d. Stunts and tumbling, as jump stick, Indian wrestle, pull-up, sit-up Independent study Officiating at games as umpiring in softball, timing in races and relays
The interest span lengthens; they may want to continue in activities beyond fatigue to exhaustion	To participate in activities modified to overcome fatiguing factors as time, speed, distance, and pressures to win; to learn when to stop	Games that involve skills of major sports as: Line Soccer (soccer), Keep Away (basketball), End Ball (basketball), Touch Football (football), Newcomb (volleyball), Long Base (softball) Modifications of standard games involve changing fatiguing factors, as: a. Shortening playing periods in vigorous sports: shorter halves in soccer, shorter quarters in basketball b. Frequent time-outs c. Restricting space: Three-Court Soccer, Six-Court Basketball, One-Basket Basketball
There is a keen interest in competitive activities	To compete in a variety of activities that involve a wide range of skills and organization	Self-testing types with competition against self, as tumbling, track events; skill tests as throwing for baskets, pitching at a target; games not highly organized, as Bombardment, End Ball, Ten Trips, Kick Over, Fist Ball
The enjoyment of organized team sports is keen	To give every boy and girl an opportunity to be a participating member on the types of teams that challenge his or her interest and ability	Wide variety of team sports, such as soccer, volleyball, softball, basketball, field ball; many teams in each sport organized on such bases as skill and ability, age-height-weight, squads

Fig. 3-10. Secondary school students engaging in relay race at Morris Brown College, Atlanta.

Courtesy President's Council on Physical Fitness and Sports.

gymnastics such as tumbling, stunts, and apparatus activities; and various forms of games and relays. These activities will comprise the major portion of the program at the secondary level. Of course, the activities are adapted to boys and to girls as they are played separately or on a coeducational basis.

Innovative ideas in secondary school physical education*

Many innovative instructional programs are being used in physical education at the secondary school level. These include programs stressing personalized and individualized learning; those emphasizing performance objectives, competency packages, and goal setting; those concerning themselves with career and leadership opportunities; those including electives; those stressing flexibility in scheduling; and those

*For a detailed discussion of these innovative ideas see Bucher, C.A., and Keonig, C.R.: Methods and materials for secondary school physical education, ed. 6, St. Louis, 1983, The C.V. Mosby Co.

concentrating on such specialized types of experiences as cycling, exercise physiology, and the environment.

COLLEGE AND UNIVERSITY PHYSICAL EDUCATION PROGRAMS

Colleges and universities should provide instruction in physical education that meets the following criteria:

1. The program should be available to all students.
2. The program should not be a repetition of the high school program, but should offer more advanced work in physical education.
3. The program should include innovative features to meet the needs of students and at the same time be interesting and challenging to them.
4. The program should not allow ROTC, band, athletics, or other activities to be a substitute for physical education.
5. The program should provide electives.
6. The program should stress knowledge and understanding of the value of physical activity.

Fig. 3-11. High school girl performing on the bar at Ridgewood High School, Norridge, Ill.

7. The program should stress the study and practice of the science and art of movement.
8. The program should stress lifetime skills.
9. The program should be conducted by qualified faculty members.

A survey of the status of required physical education in colleges and universities in the United States indicates that many institutions require physical education for students. Also, many institutions have made physical education voluntary for students. A few have a requirement for students only in certain departments or schools. The majority of the institutions requiring physical education indicate that the requirement is for a 2-year period. The survey indicates the trend is toward more emphasis on recreation and fitness activities and on coeducational classes.

The college and university physical education program is the end of formal physical education for many students. The age range of individuals in colleges and universities is wide, incorporating those from 16 to 60 years of age. However, most college students are in their late teens or early twenties. These individuals have matured in many ways. They are entering the period of greatest physical efficiency. They have developed the various organ systems of the body. They possess strength, stamina, and coordination, so the program does not have to be restricted for the average college population. College and university students have many interests. They want to prepare themselves for successful vocations, an objective that requires the physical educator to show how the physical education program can contribute to success in their work. College students are interested in the

Fig. 3-12. Player executing a penalty throw from penalty line while other players wait outside 9-meter line.

Courtesy Jim Beech.

opposite sex. They want to develop socially. This has implications for a broad coeducational program, as does Title IX. They are interested in developing skills that they can use and enjoy throughout life.

In formulating a program at the college and university level, one needs to remember that many students enter with limited activity backgrounds. Therefore the program should be broad and varied at the start, with opportunities to elect activities later. There should be considerable opportunity for instruction and practice in those activities in which a student desires to specialize. As much individual attention as possible should be given to ensure necessary skill development.

Most colleges offer physical education twice a week for 2 years. Some colleges and universities require only that the allotted time be put in, whereas others state that certain standards of achievement must be met. Both requirements are important to realize the objectives of physical education.

The program of activities should be based on the interests and needs of students and the facilities and staff available. Some colleges have introduced "Foundations" courses, getting at the subject matter of physical education. An important place for coeducation exists at the college level in such activities as tennis, dancing, swimming, badminton, volleyball, golf, softball, racquetball, aquatics, dance, bowling, table tennis, skating, archery, horseback riding, mountaineering, orienteering, snow skiing, skydiving, judo, hiking, tumbling, and camping.

In college physical education programs, physical achievement tests should be used to assess student needs and assure progress. Special help and prescribed programs should be offered to help physically underdeveloped students. Another suggestion has been made to institute a requirement that all students demonstrate proficiency in swimming and physical fitness.

The growth of the 2-year college has been significant. In many respects the activities for the 2-year college are the same as those for the 4-year institution. However, because many community college students end their education after 2 years of study, there is a need to develop skills to enrich their leisure

time and to stimulate a desire to keep themselves fit throughout their lifetime.

Most of the 2-year colleges require students to take physical education both years. Most of the programs require 2 hours each week and stress the successful completion of the service program as a requirement for graduation. Activities required in one California junior college include aquatics, archery, badminton, bowling, fencing, folk and square dance, golf, ice skating, modern dance, sailing, social dance, tennis, tumbling, gymnastics, trampoline, and volleyball.

Factors relating to one or more educational levels

Certain factors relate to one or more educational levels (elementary, secondary, college). Some of the more pertinent factors include interrelationships of elementary, secondary, and college and university programs; teaching methods—ways of presenting material; teaching aids and materials; teaching styles; class management; implications of Title IX for instructional strategies; and implications of Public Law 94-142 for instructional strategies.

INTERRELATIONSHIPS OF ELEMENTARY, SECONDARY, AND COLLEGE AND UNIVERSITY PROGRAMS

The physical education programs at the elementary, secondary, and college levels should be interrelated. Continuity and progression should characterize the program from the time the student enters school until graduation. Overall planning is essential to ensure that each student becomes physically educated and to guarantee that duplication of effort, waste of time, omissions, and shortages do not occur.

Continuity and progression do not exist today in many of the school systems of the United States. To a great degree each institutional level is autonomous, setting up its own program with little regard for what has preceded and what will follow. Many are concerned only with their own little niche and not with the overall program. If the focus of attention is on the student—the consumer of the product—then program planning will provide the student with a continu-

Fig. 3-13. Self-defense tactics; a controversial activity according to some physical educators.

Courtesy State University College at Potsdam, N.Y.

ous program, developed in light of his or her needs and interests, from the time he or she starts school until graduation. There should also be consideration given to adult years. Directors of physical education for the entire community should shoulder this responsibility and ensure that such a program exists. Some communities have directors over all the school and community physical education and recreation programs, ensuring a continuous program for community residents.

TEACHING METHODS—WAYS OF PRESENTING MATERIAL*

Some of the many ways used to present material to students in the instructional program of physical education include the following:

Lecture—to present information, usually cognitive, such as facts (rules, history, etiquette) or concepts (physical laws, physiological effects of exercise). It is also used to discuss the application, analysis, synthesis, or evaluation of ideas and concepts.

Verbal explanation—to explain the nature of a single concept or to analyze a single skill having immediate relevance to activity of the class period.

Demonstration—to present information visually by giving psychomotor examples of activity. Auditory stimuli may also be involved.

Practice-drill (combined with reinforcement feedback)—to provide for the acquisition and improvement of skills that are essential components of games and activities.

Task (individualized approach)—to provide the student with an independent learning opportunity for acquisition of skill, for discovery of concepts, or for developing solutions to problems.

Reciprocal teaching (partner or small group approach)—to provide independent learning experiences in all three domains of learning.

Guided discovery—to allow students opportunities to discover for themselves appropriate solutions to a given series of sequential problems.

Problem solving—to provide students with independent opportunities to find for themselves one or more solutions to problems provided them in various learning experiences.

---

*For a complete discussion of these methods see Bucher and Keonig, op. cit.

Contract—to provide a self-directed learning experience in an area of personal interest to the student wherein the element of success is generally assured.

Independent study—to provide an elective, self-directed learning opportunity (usually at secondary or college levels)

Question-answer—to promote cognitive processes and to provide information on physical education activities.

Evaluation—to provide self-evaluation opportunities for students through various in-class and out-of-class experiences.

Audiovisual teaching—to supplement the learning process through interesting methods of presenting materials. This method relies on auditory and visual channels for sensory input.

TEACHING AIDS AND MATERIALS

When selecting audiovisual aids or other resources and materials, physical educators should consider the following principles that make using these aids effective and valuable:

Materials should be carefully selected and screened. The teacher should preview the materials to make sure they are appropriate for the unit and age level of the students and that they present information in an interesting and stimulating manner.

Proper preparation of materials should be made. The teacher should check all equipment that may be necessary for the presentation of materials to make sure that it is in operating condition. Record players and movie projectors, in particular, need to be carefully checked before they are used.

The presentation of materials should be planned and integrated into the lesson. Students should be properly introduced to the materials so that they know what to expect and so that they understand their relationship to the unit of study.

Materials should be presented to the students in a proper learning situation. Students should be located so that all may hear, see, and learn from the material being presented to them. They should realize that they will be held responsible for the information being presented.

Materials should be varied. Different types of materials should be chosen for presentation to stimulate the varying interests of the students. A teacher using films or slide films exclusively does not take full advantage of supplementary materials available for widespread appeal.

Use of supplementary materials should be limited. The teacher should place a reasonable limit on the use of extra teaching materials to maintain a balance between supplementary learnings and those gained from regular instructional materials.

Care should be taken to avoid excessive expenses. A reasonable part of the instructional budget should be set aside for supplementary materials. This amount should be in accordance with the emphasis placed on this phase of the teaching program.

Records and evaluations of materials should be maintained. All supplementary materials should be carefully evaluated and records kept on file for future reference. This should save the unnecessary expense involved in reordering or duplicating materials and in maintaining outdated materials.

By following these principles the teacher is able to supplement learnings with materials that are valuable and interesting to the students.

Various types of materials, activities, and personnel that can be used in the instructional process include the following:

Reading materials: textbooks, magazines, booklets, pamphlets

Audiovisual aids: motion pictures, slide films, learning loops, television, videotape, phonographs and audiotape records, records

Special aids: charts, photographic materials, bulletin boards, magnetic boards

Professional personnel: from professional associations and organizations

Community activities: recreational activities, PTA-sponsored events

Clinics: special games and programs put on by visiting teams, teaching organizations, community organizations

TEACHING STYLES

Teaching style is an expression of the educator's individuality in relation to a stated philosophy and the program objectives and is being given much attention in today's educational programs. An educator's teaching style is also reflected in the method of teaching and in class organization and management.

Many styles of teaching have been identified. Probably the ones that have received the most attention are the seven distinct styles of teaching identified by Mosston* that encompass the entire continuum from teacher-centered to student-centered behavior: Command Style, Task Style, Reciprocal Style, Small Group Style, Individual Program Style, Guided Discovery Style, and Problem Style. It is generally concluded that no one style should be used all the time. Each style has its own advantages and disadvantages under specified conditions. Therefore each style should be used in light of such factors as student readiness, goals to be achieved, available equipment, and subject matter.

The teacher-centered physical educator is often described as being autocratic. This educator's philosophy of physical education is stated in terms of a personal relationship to the profession and a personal conception of the goals of the profession in relation to teaching. The educator will evaluate the basketball unit as a success if the dribble, the hook shot, and foul shooting have been taught to the class so that the students can perform to a common standard. Satisfaction to the autocratic physical educator is based not so much on student success as teacher accomplishment in terms of teacher-centered objectives. The teacher-centered physical educator is somewhat of a perfectionist and expects all students will be able to perform a certain skill in the same way. The educator does not seem to realize that all students do not have the ability to meet a single standard of performance. He or she is also a rather rigid individual, and the students are motivated more by fear of failure than by an inner desire to succeed.

The student-centered physical educator is sometimes thought of as a democratic teacher. This educator's philosophy is stated in terms of the relationship of physical education to general education. The program objectives are stated in terms of student needs and interests, and evaluation is based on how well the program has succeeded in meeting these needs and interests. This teacher is especially cognizant of differences in student ability and avoids setting common criteria for skill performance. The student-

---

*Mosston, M.: Teaching physical education, Columbus, Ohio, 1966, Charles E. Merrill Publishing Co.

Fig. 3-14. Athletes put forth great effort in many of their contests.

Courtesy President's Council on Physical Fitness and Sports.

centered physical educator is usually flexible and will adapt a lesson if it is not accomplishing its purpose. This educator welcomes innovations because of the belief that the latest techniques and methods will help students. He or she also attempts to teach students to think for themselves, to be creative, to express themselves, and to ask questions.

CLASS MANAGEMENT

Good management does not just happen. It requires careful thought, good judgment, and planning before the class begins to have a group of participants act in an orderly manner, accomplish the tasks that have been established, and have an enjoyable, satisfying, and worthwhile experience. The leader who is in charge of a class where these optimal conditions exist has spent considerable time planning the details of the class from start to finish.

The following are reasons for good organization that should be recognized by every teacher and administrator:

1. It gives meaning and purpose to instruction and to the activities.

2. It results in efficiency, the right emphasis, and the best use of the time available.

3. It more fully ensures that the needs and interests of the participants will be satisfied.

4. It more fully ensures progression and continuity in the program.

5. It provides for measurement and progress toward objectives.

6. It ensures participant's health and safety.

7. It encourages program adaptations to each individual's needs and interests.

8. It reduces errors and omissions.

9. It helps to conserve the instructor's time and strength and aids in giving the instructor a sense of accomplishment.

Here are some guides for the teacher and administrator:

1. There should be long-term planning—for the semester and the year—as well as daily, weekly, and seasonal planning.

2. A definite time schedule should be planned for each period, considering time to be devoted to showering and dressing, taking roll, class activity, and other essentials.

3. The activity should be carefully planned so that it proceeds with precision and dispatch, with a minimum amount of standing around and a maximum amount of activity for each student.

4. The setting for the class should be safe and healthful. The equipment should be safe, and line markings, arrangements for activities, and other essential details attended to.

5. Procedures to be followed in the locker room should be established to provide for traffic, valuables, clothes, and dressing and showering.

6. The instructor should always be punctual for class meetings.

7. Participants should be encouraged and motivated to do their best.

8. A planned program of measurement and evaluation should be provided to determine progress being made by participants and the effectiveness of teaching.

9. The instructor should wear suitable clothing.

10. The instructor should have a good command of the subject, recognizing the values of demonstrations, visual aids, and other techniques to promote learning.

11. Desirable attitudes and understandings toward physical fitness, skill learning, good sportsmanship, and other concepts inherent in physical education should be stressed at all times.

IMPLICATIONS OF TITLE IX FOR INSTRUCTIONAL STRATEGIES

Today's relevant physical education program must take into account the passage of an important law by the national government, namely, Title IX. On May 27, 1975, the President of the United States signed into law Title IX of the Education Amendments Act of 1972, which prohibits sex discrimination in educational programs that are federally assisted. The effective date of the regulation was July 21, 1975.

Title IX affects nearly all public elementary, secondary, and postsecondary educational institutions. This includes the nation's 16,000 public school systems and nearly 2700 postsecondary institutions. As a first step the regulations provide that educators should perform a searching self-examination of policies and practices in their institutions and take whatever remedial action is needed to bring their institutions into compliance with the federal law.

Reason for Title IX. The main reason for the enactment of Title IX was such testimony before Congressional and other committees as the following:

Girls were frequently denied the opportunity to enroll in traditionally male courses and activities.

Girls and women were frequently denied equal opportunity, such as the case cited where a program for girls was inferior to that provided for boys and another case in which rules in one state prevented the best tennis player (a girl) in a high school from competing on the school's tennis team.

A national survey conducted by the National Education

Association showed that although women constituted a majority of all public school teachers, they accounted for only 3.5% of the junior high school principals and 3% of the senior high school principals.

A study by the National Center for Educational Statistics revealed that women college faculty members received average salaries considerably lower than those of their male counterparts.

Implications for physical education instructional programs

Physical education classes must be organized on a coeducational basis. This regulation does not mean that activities must be taught coeducationally. Within classes, students may be grouped by sex for such contact sports as wrestling, basketball, and football. Also, within physical education classes, students may be grouped on an ability basis even though such grouping results in a single-sex grouping. However, sex must *not* be the criterion for grouping. It must be something other than sex. Furthermore, if an evaluation standard has an adverse impact on one sex, such as a standard of accomplishment in a physical fitness test, different evaluation requirements may be used.

Schools and colleges must provide equal oppor- *tunities for both sexes.* This is true in respect to such items as facilities, equipment and supplies, practice and games, medical and training services, coaching and academic tutoring opportunities, travel and per diem allowances, and housing and dining facilities.

Equal opportunity means that the activities offered must reflect the interests and abilities of students of both sexes.

Adequate facilities and equipment must be available for both sexes in every sport. Furthermore, one sex cannot dominate the facilities or the new equipment.

Also, adequate time for practice and games must be provided for both sexes. Again, one sex cannot dominate.

Schools and colleges must spend funds in an equitable manner. Although equal aggregate expenditures are not required, an educational institution cannot discriminate on the basis of sex in providing proper equipment and supplies.

Title IX takes precedence over all state and local laws and conference regulations that might be in conflict with this federal regulation.

If an institution receives federal aid, it must be in

Fig. 3-15. Coeducational volleyball at Hampton Institute, Hampton, Va.

compliance with Title IX, even though its athletic or physical education program does not directly receive any of this aid.

There can be no discrimination in respect to personnel standards. No discrimination can exist in respect to personnel standards by sex, including marital or parental status, for employment, promotion, salary, recruitment, job classification, or fringe benefits.

Scholarships must be awarded equitably. The regulations require an institution to select students to be awarded financial aid on the basis of criteria other than a student's sex.

Interpretation of Title IX regulations. Some interpretations of Title IX regulations that affect physical education instructional programs are listed here. Interpretations have come from authoritative sources.*

Sex designations associated with class schedules, activities, and budgets are not permitted.

The term *girls' gymnasium* can be used; however, the scheduling of this facility must be nondiscriminatory in respect to each sex.

Policies and procedures in regard to items such as uniforms and attendance must apply to both sexes.

Sex-segregated administrative units, such as departments, do not necessarily have to be merged, although having faculty of men and women in integrated offices in newly combined administrative units is encouraged.

If a significantly greater number of one sex is enrolled in a particular physical education class, the administration, if called on, should be prepared to provide the rationale for such organization.

Supervision of locker rooms may be assigned to teacher

---

*These interpretations come from the following sources:

Arnold, D.E.: Compliance with Title IX in secondary school physical education, Journal of Physical Education and Recreation **48:**19, January, 1977.

New York State Public High School Athletic Association: Spot News, February, 16, 1976.

U.S. Department of Health, Education, and Welfare: Final Title IX regulation implementing education amendments of 1972—prohibiting sex discrimination in education, Washington, D.C., July 25, 1975, Government Printing Office.

U.S. Department of Health, Education, and Welfare Memorandum to chief state school officers, superintendents of local education agencies and college and university presidents, Washington, D.C., September, 1975, Government Printing Office.

aides, paraprofessionals, or teachers in other departments.

Marks or grades given in physical education classes should reflect individual growth and performance and not compare sexes with one another.

Standards of performance that provide an unfair comparison for one sex should not be utilized. In some cases separate standards might be used for each sex; for example, on a physical fitness rating, where boys may be taller and stronger than girls, separate standards may be used.

Coeducational physical education classes. Because the provision for coeducational classes is one of the key implications of Title IX regulations, this topic is further discussed here.

Problems in physical education classes have been cited in the professional literature. Weber* indicates that such problems as the following have developed as a result of Title IX: the teacher is not professionally prepared to teach various activities in a coeducational setting; male and female teachers who traditionally made decisions on their own are finding it difficult to function as a team with the other sex and share the decision-making process; and students are also finding problems such as being unable in some activities to perform satisfactorily in front of members of the opposite sex, and thus lose face, and girls with poor skills are excluded from participation on highly skilled coeducational teams.

Weber also points out how many of these problems can be solved by such means as teachers getting rid of their personal sex biases, using new techniques, seeking a balance between female teachers' and male teachers' instructional methods, and reexamining philosophies regarding the teaching of physical education.

Other problems that have arisen in physical education classes as a result of Title IX include assignment of office space, scheduling a gymnasium for various activities, teaching certain activities such as wrestling, the danger of being accused of making sexual advances against students, supervision of locker rooms, and dressing standards.

---

*Weber, M.: Title IX in action, Journal of Physical Education and Recreation **51:**20, May, 1980.

Fig. 3-16. Judo is sometimes offered in conjunction with self-defense courses. Men and women participate in the judo program in physical education at College of DuPage, Glen Ellyn, Ill.

Administration of physical education and athletic programs

The AAHPERD's book, *Rules for Coeducational Activities and Sports* (1977), contains many examples of coeducational programs in action and suggestions for modifying coeducational college-level team sports for elementary and secondary educational levels.

Mikkelson*conducted a survey of student attitudes about coeducational physical education classes among 263 students. The students included those of "high ability," "medium ability," and "low ability" with regard to their class placement (ability level, previous semester's grade, and sex of their coach). Classes in each group were taught by a woman and by a man. The results are shown in the chart opposite.

Several examples of effective coeducational activities were presented in the May 1976 *Journal of Physical Education and Recreation*. Coeducational sports activities were described for basketball, flag football, fencing, water joust, softball, and several other sports. A brief description of three different sports conducted on a coeducational basis indicate how three institutions provided coeducational sports for students.

Coeducational basketball at Christiansburg High School. To provide intramural basketball on a coeducational basis, only the following modifications or restrictions were required:

1. Teams comprise three boys and three girls.
2. The length of the game is two 10-minute halves.
3. Boys are not allowed to shoot from inside the key (free throw circle).
4. Slow break rules are used (that is, when the ball is controlled by the defensive team, everyone must advance. The ball cannot be moved until everyone is down court).
5. Players must alternate passes between boys and girls when the ball is in the forecourt.
6. One set of passes must be completed before a shot can be attempted.
7. Balls are taken out-of-bounds after a foul, unless it was a deliberate or technical foul.

---

*Mikkelson, M.D.: Coed gym—its a whole new ballgame, Journal of Physical Education and Recreation **50**:63, October, 1979, American Alliance for Health, Physical Education, and Dance, 1900 Association Dr., Reston, Va. 22091

SAMPLING OF FINDINGS

Q—Do you enjoy P.E.?
A—High ability students—98% yes, 2% no
Medium ability students—90% yes, 10% no
Low ability students—87% yes, 13% no

Q—Do you feel that you are good at sports?
A—High ability students—90% yes, 10% no
Medium ability students—74% yes, 26% no
Low ability students—65% yes, 35% no

Q—Do you feel that coed gym is worthwhile?
A—Students whose coach is of the same sex as last year's—56% yes, 44% no
Students whose coach is of the opposite sex as last year's—74% yes, 26% no
All male students—53% yes, 47% no
All female students—80% yes, 20% no

Q—Do you feel comfortable engaging in sports with members of the opposite sex?
A—Students whose coach is of the same sex as last year's—74% yes, 26% no
Students whose coach is of the opposite sex as last year's—85% yes, 15% no
All males students—75% yes, 25% no
All female students—85% yes, 15% no

Q—Compared to last year's class, are the students in your class more or less motivated?
A—Students whose coach is of the same sex as last year's—52% more, 48% less
Students whose coach is of the opposite sex as last year's—62% more, 38% less
All male students—52% more, 48% less
All female students—68% more, 32% less

Coeducational flag football at the University of Texas at Austin. The following modifications were made to equalize competition in flag football:

1. Three men and three women comprise a team.
2. Only women are permitted to run the ball from scrimmage. Men can advance the ball only after catching a pass.
3. Men are limited to passing only to women; women may pass to either sex.

Coeducational softball at the University of Tennessee at Knoxville. The following modifications of rules were instituted:

1. A staggered arrangement by playing position and batting order for men and women is required.
2. Two strikes is an out; three balls is a walk.
3. Men are required to bat using their nondominant stance.

The main consideration in establishing coeducational sports programs is to respond to the interests and ability levels of the participants. Because of their level of skill and other reasons, some males and females will not wish to participate in coeducational sports programs, even on an intramural or recreational level. Opportunities should be provided for these individuals to participate on separate teams. When conducting sports on a coeducational basis, appropriate modifications should be made in the rules and conduct of the activities to equalize competition between the sexes.

Compliance with Title IX. Title IX is being enforced by the Office for Civil Rights of the federal government. The first step seeks to have voluntary compliance. If violations are found, federal financial support may be cut off and other legal measures taken, such as referring the violation to the Department of Justice for appropriate court action.

The Office of Civil Rights is trying to approach Title IX constructively. It wishes to achieve the goals of Title IX, that is, to end discrimination against women, in the shortest time possible. Opportunity for women is the law of the land and must be enforced. The aim will be to use the Department's enforcement machinery by giving priority to systemic forms of discrimination rather than following an approach whereby individual complaints assume priority. This means that the total picture of noncompliance will be assessed, taking into consideration information received from individuals and groups, as a means of determining enforcement priorities and compliance reviews.

Title IX regulations have been evolving for a long time. They should result in increased physical education opportunities for all students.

IMPLICATIONS OF PUBLIC LAW 94-142 FOR INSTRUCTIONAL STRATEGIES*

A milestone in legislative proposals providing for the handicapped was the passage of the Education of All Handicapped Children Act of 1975, which was signed into law by the President of the United States as PL 94-142. This legislation spells out the federal government's commitment to educating handicapped children and provides for annual funding on a sliding scale for this purpose. It provides educational services to handicapped children not receiving a free and appropriate public education and assistance for severely handicapped children receiving inadequate help.

There are specific implications in PL 94-142 for physical education. Special education has been defined within this legislation as ''specially designed instruction, at no cost to parents or guardians, to meet the unique needs of a handicapped child including classroom instruction, instruction in *physical education*, home instruction, and instruction in hospitals and institutions'' (italics added). Other specific provisions of this legislation include the following:

The right of all handicapped children to a free and appropriate public education

Individualized planning of educational programs, with conferences between parents, children, and teachers

Procedural safeguards, including due process for parents and children, so that they may secure their rights under the law

The responsibility of the state educational agency for carrying out the program

The development of a system of personnel training, including pre- and in-service training for teachers

A per pupil expenditure for handicapped children at least as great as that for other children in the state or school district

Proof that free appropriate public education is available to all handicapped children†

All of the regulations apply to physical education as they do to all education.

The term *mainstreaming* has been heard frequently

---

*See also Chapter 4 for a complete discussion of this legislation and physical education for the handicapped.

†Education of All Handicapped Children Act: Implications for physical education and recreation, IRUC Briefings, vol. 1, no. 2, January/February, 1976.

since the passage of PL 94-142, because this law provides for mainstreaming some handicapped children in the public schools and in physical education. Mainstreaming is the movement of handicapped children from a segregated status in special education classes to an integrated status with nonhandicapped children in regular classes. It is a trend in education designed to increase the contact handicapped children have with nonhandicapped children in a normal everyday environment. It can mean an opportunity for children who are handicapped to play with nonhandicapped children.

Each handicapped child does not necessarily have to be mainstreamed. Placement depends on what constitutes the least restrictive environment for the student in relation to his or her handicap.

Physical education must be prepared for having handicapped students in classes with nonhandicapped students. This means understanding children who are handicapped, preparing teachers of physical education to teach these children, and preparing administrators to conform with the law.

Administrative matters related to physical education instructional programs

SCHEDULING

The manner in which physical education is scheduled reflects the physical education leadership and the attitude of the central administration. Physical education is more meaningful for participants when the schedule reflects their interests, rather than administrative convenience.

Scheduling should be done according to a definite plan. Physical education should not be inserted in the overall master scheduling plan whenever there is time left over after all the other subjects have been provided for. This important responsibility cannot be handled on a "hit-or-miss" basis, because that disregards the interests and needs of the students. Instead, physical education should be scheduled first on the master plan, along with subjects such as English and science that are required of all students most of the time they are in school. This allows for progression and for grouping according to the interests and needs

of the individual participants. The three important items to consider in scheduling classes are (1) the number of teachers available, (2) the number of teaching stations available, and (3) the number of students who must be scheduled. This formula should be applied to most subjects in the school offering. Physical education will normally be scheduled correctly, as will other subjects, if this formula is followed.

All students should be scheduled. There should be no exceptions. If the student can go to school or college, he or she should be enrolled in physical education. Special attention should be given, however, to the handicapped or gifted individual to ensure that he or she is placed in a program suited to his or her individual needs. Also, special attention should be given to the weak student who needs extra help developing physical skills.

At the elementary and secondary levels, but especially at the elementary, scheduling should be done on 1-year basis. Special attention should be given to the availability of facilities, equipment, and supplies, and the weather. Planned units of work usually become increasingly longer as the student progresses in grades, because of the student's longer interest span and greater maturity, and the increased complexity of the activities.

Every physical educator should make a point of presenting to the central administration his or her plans for scheduling physical education classes. This need for special consideration should be discussed with the principal and the scheduling committee. Through persistent action, progress will be made. The logic and reasoning behind the formula of scheduling classes according to the number of teachers and teaching stations available and the number of students who must be scheduled cannot be denied. It must be planned this way to ensure progression in instruction.

Flexible scheduling. The introduction of flexible scheduling into school programs has implications for the administration of school physical education programs. Flexible scheduling assumes that the traditional system of having all subjects meet the same number of times each week for the same amount of time each period is passé. Flexible scheduling provides class periods of varying lengths, depending on the type of work being covered by the students, methods of instruction, and other factors pertinent to such a system. Whereas the traditional master plan makes it difficult to have flexible scheduling, the advent of the computer has made such an innovation practical and common.

Flexible scheduling also makes it possible to schedule activities for students of differing abilities differently so that all are not required to have a similar schedule based on a standard format of the school day. Under the traditional system, all students who were the slowest, for example, took as many courses as the brightest. Under flexible scheduling, some students may take as few as four courses and some as many as eight.

Modular scheduling breaks the school day into periods of time called modules. In a high school in Illinois, the school day is composed of 20-minute modules, and classes may vary from one to five modules, depending on the purpose of the course. The school is on a 6-day cycle and operates by day one, two, or three rather than the traditional days of the week. In physical education, each year level meets for three modules per day, 4 days each week. Each year level also has a two-module large group meeting once every cycle. In this meeting students hear guest speakers and lectures concerned with physical education concepts.

In other schools using modular scheduling, students frequently have unscheduled modules that can be used for swimming pool or gymnasium activities. Intramurals, open lab sessions (free time to use facilities), sport clubs, and demonstrations also provide incentives for students to use the skills they have learned.

DRESS

The following are reasons for using special uniforms in physical education classes above the elementary level:

1. It looks better and enhances self-concept if an individual is dressed in clothing that is appropriate to the activity in which he or she is engaging.
2. It provides more comfort and safety and allows freedom of movement.
3. It is more economical, because it saves on street clothes. If uniforms are purchased in lots by the school, there can be a considerable saving to the stu-

dent. Students who cannot afford uniforms should have them provided free of charge.
4. If all students have the same uniform, it aids morale and promotes equality.

Dress does not have to be elaborate. For girls and women, simple, washable shorts and blouses or one-piece suits are suitable. For boys and men, white cotton jerseys and trunks suffice. Of course, appropriate footwear should also be worn. An important consideration is to keep the uniform clean. The instructor should establish a policy on clean uniforms and work diligently to see that hygienic standards are met by all.

TIME ALLOTMENT

Just as scheduling practices vary from school to school, college to college, and state to state, so does the time allotment. In some states there are mandatory laws that require that a certain amount of time each day or week be devoted to physical education, whereas in others permissive legislation exists. For grades one to twelve the requirement varies in different states from none, or very little, to a daily 1-hour program. Some require 20 minutes daily and others 30 mintues daily. Other states specify the time by the week, ranging from 50 minutes to 300 minutes. Colleges and universities do not usually require as much time in physical education as do grades one to twelve. One practice in higher education is to require physical education two times a week for 2 years.

The general consensus among physical education leaders is that for physical education to be of value, it must be given with regularity. For most individuals this means daily periods. There is also agreement among health experts that exercise is essential to everyone throughout life. Smiley and Gould pointed out several years ago the exercise needs of individuals at various ages. These needs still exist today.

Ages 1 through 4. Free play during hours not occupied by sleeping

Ages 5 through 8. Four hours a day of free play (running, jumping, dancing, climbing, teetering, etc.) and of loosely organized group games (tag, nine pins, hoops, beanbags, etc.)

Ages 9 through 11. At least 3 hours a day of outdoor active play (hiking, swimming, gymnastics, group games and relays, soccer, volleyball; broad and high

Fig. 3-17. A player goes for the soccer ball, while a member of the opposing team closes in on him during the soccer competition at the 1980 National Explorer Olympics held at Colorado State University.

Courtesy President's Council on Physical Fitness and Sports.

jump, 25- and 50-yard dashes, folk dancing, etc.)

Ages 12 through 14. At least 2 hours a day of outdoor active play (hiking, swimming, gymnastics, group games, relays, soccer, volleyball, indoor baseball, basketball, baseball, tennis, 60-yard dash, the jumps, shot-put, low hurdles, short relays, folks and gymnastic dancing). Still no endurance contest

Ages 15 through 17. At least 1½ hours a day of outdoor active play (hiking, swimming, apparatus work, group games and relays, soccer, volleyball, indoor baseball, basketball, baseball, tennis, football, golf, ice hockey, 60-yard dash, the jumps, shot-put, low hurdles, short relays, folk and gymnastic dancing). Still no endurance contests

Ages 18 through 30. At least 1 hour a day of active outdoor exercise (all the types listed in the preceding paragraph and, if examined and found phsically fit, in addition, cross-country running, crew, wrestling, boxing, fencing, and polo)

Ages 31 through 50. At least 1 hour a day of moderate outdoor exercise (golf, tennis, riding, swimming, handball, volleyball, etc.)

Ages 51 through 70. At least 1 hour a day of light outdoor exercise (golf, walking, bowling, gardening, fishing, croquet, etc.)*

Some individuals feel that, especially in the elementary schools, a program cannot be adapted to a fixed time schedule. However, as a standard, there seems to be agreement that a daily experience in such

---

*Smiley, D.F., and Gould, A.G.: A college textbook of hygiene, New York, 1940, Macmillan, Inc., pp. 346-347.

a program is needed. Such a recommendation is made and should always be justified on the basis of value and contribution to the student's needs. There should be regular instructional class periods and, in addition, laboratory periods where the skills may be put to use.

On the secondary level especially, it is recommended that sufficient time be allotted for dressing and showering in addition to the time needed for participation in physical education activities. Some leaders in physical education have suggested a double period every other day rather than a single period each day. This might be feasible if the daily class periods are too short. However, the importance of daily periods should be recognized and achieved wherever possible. Administrators should work toward providing adequate staff members and facilities to allow for a daily period.

The amount of time suggested for adults to spend in exercise programs is a minimum of three times a week (not on consecutive days). However, a daily exercise period is considered best.

CLASS SIZE

Some school and college administrators feel that physical education classes can accommodate more students than the so-called academic classes. This is a misconception that has developed over the years and needs to be corrected.

The problem of class size seems to be more pertinent at the secondary level than at other educational levels. At the elementary level, for example, the classroom situation represents a unit for activity, and the number of students in this teaching unit is usually reasonable. However, there are some schools that combine various classrooms for physical education, resulting in large classes that are not desirable.

Classes in physical education should be approximately the same size as classes in other subjects in the school or college offering. This is just as essential for effective teaching, individualized instruction, and progression in physical education as it is in other subjects. Physical education contributes to educational objectives on an equal basis with other subjects in the curriculum. Therefore the size of the class should be comparable so that an effective teaching

job can be accomplished and the objectives of education attained.

After much research, many committees established a standard for an acceptable size of physical education classes. They recommend not more than 35 students as the suitable size for activity classes. Normal classes should never exceed 45 for one instructor. Of course, if there is a lecture or other activity scheduled adaptable to greater numbers, it may be possible to have more persons in the class. For remedial work, the suitable class size is from one-on-one to 20 to 25 and should never exceed 30. With flexible scheduling, the size of classes can be varied to meet the needs of the teacher, facilities, and type of activity being offered.

INSTRUCTIONAL LOADS AND STAFFING

The load of the physical educator should be of prime concern to the administrator. To maintain a top level of enthusiasm and strength, it is important that the load be adjusted so that the physical educator is not overworked.

A few years ago, one state recommended that one full-time physical education teacher should be provided for every 240 elementary pupils and one for every 190 secondary pupils enrolled. If such a requirement is implemented, it would provide adequate staff members in this field and avoid an overload for many of the teachers.

Professional recommendations regarding teaching load at precollege educational levels have been made that would limit class instruction per teacher to 5 hours or the equivalent in class periods per day, or 1500 minutes per week. The maximum would be 6 hours per day or 1800 minutes a week, including afterschool responsibilities. A daily load of 200 students per teacher is recommended and never should exceed 250. Finally, each teacher should have at least one free period daily for consultation and conferences with students.

It is generally agreed that the normal teaching load in colleges and universities should not exceed 15 hours per week.

The work load in a business concern, such as a health spa or industrial physical center is usually a 9 AM to 5 PM workday 5 days each week.

Differentiated staffing. Many innovations, such as differentiated staffing, are directed toward aiding the teacher in the performance of his or her duties. Paraprofessionals, certified undergraduate interns, and student teachers provide a school in Minnesota with valuable staff members.

Differentiated staffing relates to increased responsibilities or differentiation of functions among staff members. For example, in team teaching, higher salaries are given to team leaders or head teachers. Staff members who assume such roles as heads of departments or staff assistants are usually compensated accordingly. Outstanding, competent staff members with expertise in certain areas are assigned to special projects in some systems and compensated accordingly.

The benefits derived from differentiated staffing are obvious from the responsibilities given to various staff members. In schools, for example, the teacher is able to devote more time to help students, and he or she can also be free to work with small groups in different skills. Differentiated staffing allows the teacher to be free to teach and not be directly involved in clerical and physical responsibilities.

Paraprofessionals. Responsibilities include (1) supervised instructional assistance, (2) assisting in swimming pool, (3) clerical duties, (4) student conduct supervision, and (5) preparation of learning materials.

Certified undergraduate interns. Responsibilities include (1) clerical assistance, (2) record keeping, (3) material preparation, (4) conduct supervision in noninstructional areas, (5) individual assistance, and (6) observation.

Student teachers. Responsibilities include (1) observation, (2) supervised clerical teaching experience, (3) assisting supervising teachers, (4) preparation of learning materials, (5) individual assistance, and (6) extracurricular guidance.

TAKING ROLL

There are many methods of taking roll. If a method satisfies the following three criteria, it is usually satisfactory. (1) It is efficient—roll taking should not consume too much time. (2) It is accurate—after the class has been held, it is important to know who was present and who was not and who came late or left early. (3) It should be uncomplicated—any system that is used should be easy to administer.

Some methods for roll taking follow:

1. *Having numbers on the floor*—each member of the class is assigned a number that he or she must stand on at the time the signal for "fall in" is given. The person taking attendance records the numbers not covered.

2. *Reciting numbers orally*—each member of the class is assigned a number that he or she must say out loud at the time the signal for "fall in" is given. The person taking attendance than records the numbers not given.

3. *Tag board*—each member of the class has a number recorded on a cardboard or metal tag that hangs on a peg on a board in a central place. Each member of the class who is present removes his or her tag from the board and places it in a box. The person taking attendance records the absentees from the board.

4. *Delaney stystem*—a special system developed by Delaney involves using a folder with cards that are turned over when a person is absent. It is a cumulative system that records the attendance of pupils over time. Adaptations of this system are used elsewhere.

5. *Squad system*—the class is divided into squads and the squad leader takes the roll for his or her squad and in turn reports to the instructor.

6. *Issuing towels and equipment*—the roll is taken when a towel is issued to each student or when it is turned in, or when a basket with uniform is issued or returned.

7. *Signing a book or register*—students are required to write their names in a book or register at the beginning of the class. Some systems require the writing of a name at the beginning of a period and crossing it out at the end of a period. The person taking attendance records the names not entered.

SELECTING PHYSICAL EDUCATION ACTIVITIES*

Physical education activities represent the heart of the program. They are the means for accomplishing

---

*For more information on the selection of activities, see Chapter 11.

objectives and achieving life's goals. Because activities are so important to the physical education profession, they must be selected with considerable care.

Criteria for selection

1. Activities should be selected in terms of the values they have in achieving the objectives of physical education. This means they should develop not only body awareness, movement fundamentals, and physical fitness, but also the cognitive, affective, and social makeup of the individual.

2. Activities should be interesting and challenging. They should appeal to the participants and present them with problem-solving activities and situations that challenge their skill and ability. For example, golf always presents the challenge of getting a lower score.

3. They should be adaptable to the growth and developmental needs and interests of children, youth, and adults. The needs of individuals vary from age to age. Consequently, movement activities and the pattern of organization must also change to meet these needs. The activity must be suited to the person, not the person to the activity. Wherever possible, participants should be allowed some choice in their activities.

4. Activities should be modifications of fundamental movements such as running, jumping, throwing, walking, and climbing.

5. Activities must be selected in light of the facilities, supplies, equipment, and other resources available in the school, college, or community. One cannot plan an extensive tennis program if only one court is available.

6. Activities should be selected not only with a view to their present value while the child is in school but also with a view to postschool and adult living. Skills learned during school and college days can be used throughout life, thus contributing to enriched living. Patterns for many skills utilized in adult leisure hours are developed while the individual is in the formative years of childhood.

7. Activities must be selected for health and safety values. Such an activity as boxing has been questioned concerning its effect on the health and the safety of individuals.

8. The local education philosophy, policies, and school or college organization must be considered.

9. School activities should provide situations similar to those children experience in natural play situations outside school.

10. Activities should provide the participant with opportunities for creative self-expression.

11. Activities selected should elicit the correct social and moral responses through high-quality leadership.

12. Activities should reflect the democratic way of life.

One survey produced a list of physical education activities offered throughout the country, here classified into various categories. These do not necessarily meet criteria that have been listed. They merely indicate current offerings in physical education programs in the United States:

Team games

Baseball	Soccer
Basketball	Softball
Code ball	Speedball
Field hockey	Touch football
Flag football	Volleyball
Football	

Outdoor winter sports

Ice hockey	Snow games
Roller skating	Snowshoeing
Skating	Tobogganing
Skiing	

Other activities

Camping and outdoor activities	Combatives (judo, karate)
Mountaineering	Correctives
Yoga	Fly-tying
Jogging	Games of low organization
Kayaking	Movement education
Orienteering	Relays
	Self-testing activities

Rhythms and dancing

Folk dancing	Rhythms
Gymnastic dancing	Square dancing
Modern dancing	Social dancing
Movement fundamentals	Tap dancing

Formal activities

Calisthenics	Marching

Water activities

Canoeing	Lifesaving
Surfing	Rowing

Water skiing	Swimming
Scuba diving	Sailing
Diving	Water games
Gymnastics	
Acrobatics	Rope climbing
Apparatus	Stunts
Obstacle course	Trampoline
Pyramid building	Tumbling
Dual and individual sports	
Archery	Handball
Badminton	Horseback riding
Bait and fly casting	Horseshoes
Skeet shooting	Paddle tennis
Trap shooting	Racquetball
Horseback riding	Rifle
Cycling	Rope skipping
Bowling	Shuffleboard
Checkers	Skish
Darts	Table tennis
Deck tennis	Tennis
Fencing	Tether ball
Fishing	Track and field
Golf	Wrestling

GROUPING PARTICIPANTS

Homogeneous grouping in physical education classes is desirable. To render the most valuable contribution to participants, factors influencing performance must be considered when organizing physical education groups. The lack of scientific knowledge and measuring techniques to obtain such information and the administrative problems of scheduling have handicapped the achievement of this goal in many programs.

The reasons for grouping are sound. Placing individuals with similar capacities and characteristics in the same class makes it possible to better meet the needs of each individual. Grouping individuals with similar skill, ability, and other factors aids in equalizing competition. This helps the student realize more satisfaction and benefit from playing. Grouping promotes more effective teaching. Instruction can be better organized and adapted to the level of the student. Grouping facilitates progression and continuity in the program. Furthermore, grouping creates a better learning situation. Being in a group with persons of similar physical characteristics and skills ensures some success, a chance to excel, recognition,

a feeling of belonging, and security. Consequently, this helps the social and personality development of the individual. Finally, homogeneous grouping helps protect the participant physically, emotionally, and socially. It ensures his or her participation with individuals with similar physical characteristics.

The problem of grouping is not so pertinent in the elementary school, especially in the lower grades, as it is in the junior high school and upper levels. At the lower levels the grade classification serves the needs of most children. As children grow older, the complexity of the program increases, social growth becomes more diversified, competition becomes more intense, and consequently, there is a greater need for homogeneous grouping.

At present students are grouped on such bases as grade, health, physical fitness, multiples of age-height-weight, abilities, physical capacity, motor ability, interests, educability speed, skill, and previous experience. Such techniques as health examinations; tests of motor ability, physical capacity, achievement, and social efficiency; conferences with participants; and determination of physiological age are used to obtain such information.

The following suggestions of the American Alliance for Health, Physical Education, Recreation and Dance* are appropriate when considering recommendations for grouping in schools and colleges.

1. The need for grouping students homogeneously for instruction and competition has long been recognized, but the inability to scientifically measure such important factors as ability, maturity, interest, and capacity has deterred physical educators from accomplishing this goal.

2. The most common procedure for grouping today is by grade or class.

3. The ideal grouping organization would consider all factors that affect performance—intelligence, capacity, interest, knowledge, age, height, weight, and so on. To apply all these factors, however, is not administratively feasible at the present time.

4. Some form of grouping is essential to provide a

*American Association for Health, Physical Education, and Recreation: Administrative problems in health education, physical education, and recreation, Washington, D.C., revised 1969, The Association.

Fig. 3-18. Men's volleyball game in action.

Courtesy President's Council on Physical Fitness and Sports.

program that promotes educational objectives and protects the student.

5. On the secondary and college levels, the most feasible procedure is to organize subgroups within the regular physical education class.

6. Classification within the physical education class should be based on age, height, weight statistics, and other factors, such as interest and skill, that are developed after observing the activity.

7. For those individuals who desire greater refinement in respect to grouping, motor capacity, motor ability, attitude, appreciation and sports-skills tests may be used.

To abide by Title IX regulations, physical educators should not group by sex. Some physical education departments have adopted a nongraded curriculum that places students in learning situations according to present levels of skill achievement and physical maturity. A child's chronological age or grade level attainment is not a factor in the nongraded physical education curriculum. This allows for individual student differences and interests.

AREAS OF STUDENT LEADERSHIP AND INVOLVEMENT

In recent years students have been demanding greater involvement in the educational process, and in most cases this increased involvement has been satisfactory to both students and administrators. Some of these areas of involvement are briefly discussed here.

General planning. Students should be involved in planning meetings that discuss schedule changes, curriculum innovations and recent changes in educational method. Students might be invited to attend school board meetings and parent association meetings and could also accompany teachers and administrators to other schools where certain innovations may be directly observed. Some schools and colleges have instituted student advisory boards that meet with staff members to discuss problems, changes, and future planning ideas.

A sports club program at a university in Tennessee is an excellent example of a program for students planned by students. The purposes of this program are the following:

1. To offer activities in sport areas to all interested students.
2. To develop skills in special sports.
3. To provide opportunities for extramural competition.

All students, regardless of the skill in a particular sport, are welcome to join. Instruction is provided for learners in every club. The sports club program is financed through support from the Sport Club Office, dues, games, and contributions. Coaches are usually drawn from faculty or community members, and all coaching is voluntary. These clubs are student organized but under the supervision of the assistant director for sports clubs.

Another interesting example of a student-designed program is an elective physical education program at a high school in Colorado. This course is available to eleventh and twelfth grade students, and its primary objective is to give students a voice in curriculum construction. The course planned by the students includes alpine and Nordic skiing, backpacking, mountaineering, fly fishing, and weekend camping trips. The course has met with active student participation from all school departments. The home economics department has helped keep food costs down, and the shop class has made hunting bows. The community also participates in giving discounts on certain pieces of sports equipment. This student-designed elective course has been successful in expanding the classroom to include the outdoors.

Curriculum planning. Student surveys reveal the extent of curriculum changes desired by the student body. Administrators, teachers, and students should carefully weigh this information in light of the current literature, research studies, and actual curriculum changes in other schools and colleges. Student participation and feedback are esential; however, students do have limited experience in educational matters, and this must also be considered. Frequently the use of experimental programs on a limited basis can test the change before implementing it on a larger scale.

Many schools and colleges have recently instituted independent study programs where students receive credit for individual projects conducted under staff guidance. Some schools, colleges, and universities have eliminated certain requirements for graduation and major field study. In addition, college grades have been replaced in some cases by pass/fail ratings. Many of these innovations were initiated by student groups.

In a high school in Massachusetts, students take an active role in curriculum planning. Students plan what they are going to learn and how they would like to learn the gymnastics unit of the physical education class. Several days are set aside for students to set goals, plan the steps needed to reach a specific goal, and make a commitment to learning and improvement. The students put their goals in writing and then set about to achieve them. Instruction is provided, and grading is a cooperative venture between students and teachers.

Leadership training programs. An innovative student leadership program is the Physical Education Leadership Training Program sponsored by a school in Virginia. As part of an elective course in the physiology of exercise, juniors and seniors can relate their learning experiences to leadership experiences in elementary schools.

The program has as its primary objectives (1) to assist in instruction, particularly when the physical education teacher is absent; (2) to provide in-depth study of health and physical education for students who want to teach as a career; (3) to provide students with leadership opportunities; and (4) to provide individualized instruction. The content and leadership experiences are developed and coordinated by the eleventh and twelfth grade classes. Supervision of the program is provided by the elementary physical education teacher, elementary classroom teacher, senior high school physical education teacher, head of the senior high school physical education department, and supervisor of physical education.

The four phases of the program are (1) in-service training, (2) observation, (3) teaching, and (4) teaching without supervision. This program is valuable to both teachers and students and helps the elementary grade teachers provide individualized help for each student.

Selecting student leaders. Several methods are used by physical educators to select student leaders. Some advocate appointing temporary leaders during the first few sessions of a class until the students become better known to their classmates and instructor. Some selection methods are discussed in the following paragraphs.

Volunteers. Students are asked to volunteer to become a student leader. It may happen that the least qualified persons are the ones who volunteer. If this method is used, it should be with the understanding that the student leader will serve for only a relatively short time. Also, there can be a rotation of student leaders with this method so that all volunteers may have such an experience.

Appointment by the instructor. The physical education instructor may appoint the student leader. One of the limitations of this procedure is that it is not democratic, because it does not involve the students who are going to be exposed to the student leader. However, if the teacher's objective is to let each student in the class have a student leadership experience, this limitation can be overcome.

Election by the class. The students in the class may elect the persons they would like to have as leaders. A limitation of this method is that the persons selected are often the most popular students as a result of participation in sports or student government. Being

the most popular does not mean that they are qualified to be leaders. This is a democratic procedure, however, and if the guidelines for selecting leaders are established and if the proper climate prevails, it can be effective.

Selection based on test results. A battery of tests is sometimes used by physical educators to select student leaders. Tests of physical fitness, motor ability, sports skills, and leadership and personality characteristics yield useful information. They provide tangible evidence that a person has some of the desirable qualifications needed by a student leader in a physical education class. In addition, if the physical educator desires to have the entire class participate in the student leadership program, the test results may also be valuable to the teacher in helping each student identify weaknesses that need to be overcome during the training period.

Selection by Leaders' Club. Physical educators sometimes organize Leaders' Clubs to provide a continuing process for selecting student leaders. The members of the Leaders' Club, under the supervision of a faculty advisor, select new students to participate as leaders-in-training. Then, after a period of training, these students in turn become full-fledged student leaders.

The role of the Leaders' Club in training student leaders. One method of training student leaders is through a Leaders' Club. These clubs commonly have their own constitution, governing body, faculty advisor, and training sessions.

The written constitution of a Leaders' Club usually states the purpose of the club, requirements for membership, qualifications and duties of officers, financial stipulations, procedures for giving awards and honors, and other rules govering the organization.

The governing body of the Leaders' Club may consist of a president, vice-president, treasurer, and secretary, all of whom are elected by the members of the club.

The faculty advisor works closely with the leaders to ensure that the objectives of the Leaders' Club are accomplished. The faculty advisor supervises the affairs of the club and provides inspiration and motivation to the leaders, encouraging creativity and helping the students achieve their goals.

Fig. 3-19. Student Leadership Program at El Camino Real High School in Los Angeles.
Los Angeles Unified School District, Student Auxiliary Services Branch.

Courtesy Gwen R. Waters.

The Leaders' Club usually has regular meetings weekly, biweekly, or monthly.

The students who are interested in becoming student leaders apply for membership in the Leaders' Club. Certain eligibility requirements are usually established for membership in the club. In one school these requirements are listed as follows:

1. Grade of 80% or above in physical education
2. Scholastic average of at least 70% in major subjects
3. Passing grades in all subjects
4. Satisfactory health record
5. Membership in school's general organization
6. Recommendation of the physical education teacher concerning personality, character, and quality of work
7. All-around physical performance
8. Good rating on physical fitness tests

When a student's application for membership in a Leaders' Club is accepted, a period of training for one semester usually follows. During this period students learn the requirements and responsibilities of a student leader, practice demonstrating and leading as an assistant in physical education classes, and become familiar with game rules, officiating techniques, and leadership responsibilities.

After the training period has ended, the qualifications of the trainees are again reviewed by the Leaders' Club. Scholastic average, health and medical record, character, recommendations of physical education teachers, performance on skill tests, scores on written tests of rules, ability to officiate, and skill proficiency are examined. The next step may be the personal interview or a visit before the entire governing body of the Leaders' Club. Here the candidate's record is reviewed, pertinent questions are asked, and action is taken. The faculty advisor, however, usually makes the final decision.

Some physical educators feel that the Leaders'

Fig. 3-20. A student leader instructs disadvantaged youths from Miami and Dade County during the National Summer Youth Sports Program conducted by Miami-Dade Junior College North.

Courtesy President's Council on Physical Fitness and Sports.

Club involvement in selecting and training student leaders is formal and not in the best interests of the goals of the leadership program. These critics especially question the personal interview at the end of the training period and the action taken by a student's peers to determine whether or not a student should become a member of the Leaders' Club. Furthermore, some physical educators object to clubs and societies in general as being contrary to the democratic ideals that should guide any leadership program.

Guiding student leaders. Several effective methods exist for guiding student leaders, either during their training period or while they are actually serving as full-fledged student leaders. They include movies, guest lecturers, leaders' physical education period, and meetings. *Movies* can be shown on strategies involved in sports or how to play a game or sport. *Guest lecturers,* such as visiting physical education teachers, sports personalities, and educational specialists in motor learning and teaching techniques, can be worthwhile. A *leaders' physical education period,* where the student leaders themselves comprise the class and the faculty advisor covers various duties that the student leader must assume, can be helpful. *Meetings* with the faculty advisor to discuss problems are also an excellent medium for guiding student leaders.

Using the student leader. Student leaders may be used in the physical education program in several capacities.

Class leaders. There are many opportunities in the basic physical education instructional class period where student leaders can be effective. These include the following:

1. Acting as squad leader, where the student takes charge of a small number of students for an activity
2. Being a leader for warm-up exercises at the beginning of the class period
3. Demonstrating how skills, games, and strategies are to be performed
4. Taking attendance
5. Supervising the locker room
6. Providing safety measures for class participation, such as acting as a spotter, checking equipment and play areas, and providing supervision
7. Assuming measurement and evaluation responsibilities, such as helping in the testing program, measuring performance in track and field, and timing with a stop watch

Officials, captains, and other positions. Student leaders can gain valuable experience by serving as officials within the class and intramural program, being captains of all-star or other teams, coaching intramural or club teams, and acting as scorers and timekeepers.

Committee members. Many committee assignments should be filled by student leaders so that they gain valuable experience. These include being a member of a *rules committee,* where rules are established and interpreted for games and sports; serving on an *equipment and grounds committee,* where standards are established for the storage, maintenance, and use of these facilities and equipment, and participating on a *committee for planning special events* in the physical education program, such as play, sports, or field days.

Supply and equipment manager. Supplies and special equipment are needed in the physical education program, including basketballs, archery, golf, and hockey equipment, and audiovisual aids. The equipment must be taken from the storage areas, transferred to the place where the activity will be conducted, and then returned to the storage area. The student leader can help immeasurably in this process and profit from such an experience.

Program planner. Various aspects of the physical education program need to be planned, and students should be involved. Student leaders, because of their special qualifications and interest, are logical choices to participate in such planning and curriculum development. Their knowledge and advice can ensure that the program meets the needs and interests of the students who participate in the program.

Record keeper and office manager. Attendance records and inventories must be taken, filing and recording done, bulletin boards kept up to date, visitors met, and other responsibilities attended to. These necessary functions provide worthwhile experiences for the student leader and benefit the program.

Special events coordinator. There are always a multitude of details involved in play days, sports days, demonstrations, and exhibitions. Student leaders should be involved in planning and conducting these events.

Evaluating the program. The student leadership program should be evaluated periodically to determine the degree to which the program is achieving its stated goals. Students should be involved in this evaluation. Such questions as the following might be asked: "Are the experiences provided worthwhile?" "Are the students developing leadership qualities?" "Is the teacher providing the necessary leadership to make the program effective?" "Are any of the assigned tasks incompatible with the objectives sought?" "If a Leaders' Club exists, is it helping to create a better leaders' program?"

Selected administrative problems in instructional programs

The administrator of any physical education program is perennially confronted with such questions

Fig. 3-21. Cheerleaders at College of DuPage, Glen Ellyn, Ill., become involved by registering students for a blood drive to help local residents.

as: Should physical education by required or elective? How much credit should be given? Is it possible to substitute some other activity for physical education? What should be the policy on class attendance? How should one deal with excuses? These and other questions are answered in the following discussion.

SHOULD PHYSICAL EDUCATION BE REQUIRED OR ELECTIVE?

There is general agreement that physical education should be required at the elementary level. However, there are many advocates on both sides of the question of whether it should be required or elective on the secondary and college levels. Both groups are sincere and feel their beliefs represent what is best for the student. Probably most specialists feel the program should be required. Some school administrators feel it should be elective. Following are some of the arguments presented by each.

Required

1. Physical education is a basic need of every student.

2. The student is compelled to take so many required courses that the choice of electives is limited, if not entirely eliminated, in some cases.

3. The student considers required subjects most important and most necessary for success.

4. Various subjects in the curriculum would not be provided unless they were required. This is probably true of physical education. Until state legislatures passed laws requiring physical education, this subject was ignored by many school administrators. If physical education were elective, the course of some administrative action would be obvious. Either the subject would not be offered at all or the administrative philosophy would so dampen its value that it would have to be eliminated because of low enrollment.

5. Even under a required program, physical education is not meeting the physical, social, and cognitive needs of students. If an elective program were instituted, deficiencies and shortages would increase, thus further handicapping the attempt to meet the needs of the student.

Elective

1. Physical education ''carries its own drive.'' If a good basic program is developed in the elementary school, with students acquiring the necessary skills and attitudes, the drive for such activity will carry through in the secondary school and college. There will be no need to require such a course, because students will want to take it voluntarily.

2. Objectives of physical education are focused on developing skills and learning activities that have

carryover value, living a healthful life, and recognizing the importance of developing and maintaining one's body in its best possible condition. These goals cannot be legislated. They must become a part of each individual's attitudes and desires if they are to be realized.

3. Some children and young adults do not like physical education. This is indicated in their manner, attitude, and desire to get excused from the program and to substitute something else for the course. Under such circumstances the values that accrue to these individuals are not great. Therefore it would be best to place physical education on an elective basis where only those students participate who actually desire to do so.

SHOULD SUBSTITUTIONS BE ALLOWED FOR PHYSICAL EDUCATION?

A practice exists in some school and college systems that allows students to substitute some other activity for their physical education requirement. This practice should be scrutinized and resisted aggressively by every administrator.

Some of the activities used as substitutions for physical education are athletic participation, Reserve Officers' Training Corps, and band.

There is no substitute for a sound program of physical education. In addition to healthful physical activity, it is concerned also with developing an individual socially, emotionally, and mentally. The individual develops many skills that can be applied throughout life. These essentials are lost if a student is permitted to take some other activity in place of physical education.

SHOULD CREDIT BE GIVEN FOR PHYSICAL EDUCATION?

Whether or not credit should be given for physical education is another controversial problem with which the profession is continually confronted. Here again can be found advocates on both sides. Some feel the joy of the activity and the values derived from participation are sufficient in themselves without giving credit. On the other hand, some feel that physical education is the same as any other subject in the curriculum and should also be granted credit.

The general consensus among physical education leaders is that if physical education is required for graduation and if it enriches one's education, credit should be given, just as in other subjects.

WHAT POLICY SHOULD BE ESTABLISHED ON CLASS ATTENDANCE?

It is important for every department of physical education to have a definite policy on class attendance that covers absenteeism and tardiness. Because it is felt that students should attend school and college regularly, it follows that they should also attend physical education classes regularly. However, time for independent study should be included in the schedule.

Regular participation in physical education is essential to the value of the program; therefore every physical education department should have a clear-cut policy on attendance regulations. These regulations should be few and clearly stated in writing so that they are recognized, understood, and strictly enforced by teachers and students. They should allow a reasonable number of absences and tardinesses. Perfect attendance at school or college should not be stressed. Many harmful results can develop if students feel obligated to attend classes when they are ill and should be at home. There should probably be some provision for makeup work when important experiences are missed. However, makeup work should be planned and conducted so that the student derives essential values from such participation, rather than enduring it as a disciplinary measure. There should also be provision for the readmission of students who have been ill.

A final point to remember is the importance of keeping accurate, up-to-date attendance records to minimize administrative problems.

WHAT ABOUT EXCUSES?

The principal, nurse, or physical educator frequently receives a note from a parent or family physician asking that a student be excused from physical education. Many abuses develop if all such requests are granted. Many times for minor reasons the student does not want to participate and obtains the parent's or family physician's support.

One survey showed that high schools permitted a

student to be excused on the basis of a parental note, a memorandum from the family physician, or the discretion of the physical education teacher. Although some schools would accept the recommendation of any of these three persons, other schools would accept only an excuse from the school physician. At the college level most programs accept the college physician's excuse or permit the instructor of each class to use his or her own discretion in granting excuses to students.

Those surveyed listed reasons for granting excuses in physical education. Secondary schools grant most of their excuses for participation in athletics and for being in the school band. Some schools permit their athletes to be excused only on the day of the game, whereas others grant a blanket excuse for the entire sports season. Other reasons for excuses on the secondary level included makeup tests, driver training, counseling, a too-heavy extracurricular load, and medical reasons. At the college level, excuses were granted to athletes, veterans, students who could pass physical fitness tests, honor students, older students, for medical reasons, in ''hardship cases,'' and so on.

The survey also reported what was done with the students who were excused. Students in secondary schools were required to attend study halls; to score, officiate, or help around the physical education department; to write reports; to remain on the sidelines; or to report after school. At the college level most colleges did nothing except follow a pattern of failing a student in some cases if he or she exceeded the legal number of excused absences each semester. A few either required the student to observe the class, substitute a health class, or study in the gymnasium; some left it up to the instructor's discretion.

Some school systems have controlled the indiscriminate granting of requests for excuses from physical education. Policies have been established, sometimes through conferences and rulings of the board of education, requiring that all excuses be reviewed and approved by the school physician before they are granted. Furthermore, family physicians have been asked to state specific reasons for requesting excuses from physical education. This procedure has worked satisfactorily in some communities. In other places physical educators have taken particular pains to work closely with physicians. They have established a physical education program in collaboration with the school physician so the needs of each individual are met, regardless of his or her physical condition. They have met with the local medical society in an attempt to clear up misunderstandings about the purpose and conduct of the program. Family physicians have been brought into the planning. As a result of such planning, problems with excuses from physical education have been considerably reduced. It has been found that in those communities where parents, family physicians, and the lay public in general understand physical education, the number of requests for excuses is relatively small. In such communities the values derived from participation in the program are clearly recognized, and because most parents and physicians want children to have worthwhile experiences, they encourage rather than limit such participation.

A few years ago, a conference concerned with close cooperation between physical education and medical doctors drew up this list of statements in respect to the problem under discussion:

1. Orient the student, parent, and physician at an early date in regard to the objectives of the physical education program.

2. Route all requests for excuse through the school physician. In the absence of the physician, the school nurse should have this responsibility. The sympathetic and informed nurse can be a real asset to the physical education program.

3. Discard permanent and blanket excuses. The school physician should share in planning certain areas of the individual physical education program. Instead of being categorically excused, boys and girls can be given an activity in keeping with their special needs.

4. Students involved in the excuse request should have a periodic recheck on the need for excuse (this tends to reduce requests up to 50%).

5. Conferences between the school physicians and the head of the physical education department on the local level need to be emphasized.

6. The problem of excuse from physical education should be tied in with the total guidance program of the school. It helps also if the administrator and classroom teachers are familiar with general physical education aims.

WHO SHOULD CONDUCT THE ELEMENTARY SCHOOL PHYSICAL EDUCATION CLASS?

The question of who should conduct the elementary school physical education class has been continually discussed for many years. Some educators advocate that the classroom teacher handle physical education classes, and many supporters want a specialist to take over this responsibility. The classroom teacher has limited professional education in physical education. Some classroom teachers are not interested in teaching physical education. Furthermore, there is increased interest in physical education today, which implies that qualified and interested persons should handle these classes. There is a trend toward more emphasis on movement education, perceptual motor development, physical fitness, skills, and other aspects of education with which physical education is concerned. There is a need for more research on physical education programs as they relate to the learning and growth of children. There is an increased emphasis on looking to the specialist in physical education for help and advice in planning and conducting the elementary school program. These developments have implications for a sound in-service program to help the classroom teacher do a better job in physical education.

In light of the present status of physical education in the elementary schools of this country, such recommendations as the following should be very carefully considered. Each elementary school should be staffed with a specialist in physical education. The classroom teacher may find his or her best contribution to physical education programs in kindergarten to grade three, but to do the best job he or she needs preparation in this special field and the advice and help of a physical education specialist. Although the classroom teacher can contribute much to the physical education program in grades four to six, factors such as the growth changes and interests taking place in boys and girls and the more specialized program that exists at this level make it imperative to seek the help of a specialist who possesses the ability, experience, and training required to meet the needs of growing boys and girls and to gain their respect and interest. The specialist and the classroom teacher should pool their experience to provide the most desirable learning experience. Each teacher has much to contribute and should be encouraged to do so.

DRESSING AND SHOWERING

Such factors as the age of the participant, time allowed, grade participating, and type of activity should be considered in a discussion of dressing and showering for physical education classes.

The problem of showering and dressing is not so pertinent at the lower elementary level where the age of the participants and type of activities as a general rule do not require special dress and showering. Also the time allotted is too short in many cases. In the upper elementary and at the junior and senior high school and college levels, however, it is a problem.

Physical education embodies activities that require considerable movement, resulting in perspiration. In the interests of comfort and good hygiene practices, provisions should be made for special clothing and showering. The unpleasantness of a student's returning to class after participating in a physical education activity, with clothes malodorous and wet from perspiration, does not establish habits of personal cleanliness and good grooming. Therefore all schools should make special provisions for places to dress in comfortable uniforms and for showering. Such places should be convenient to the physical education areas, be comfortable, and afford privacy. Although boys and girls are increasingly becoming accustomed to using a group shower, many still prefer private showers. In the interests of these individuals, such facilities should be provided. There should also be a towel service. Many schools have facilities for laundering towels that have proved satisfactory.

RECORDS

Records are essential in keeping valuable information regarding the participants' welfare. They also are essential to efficient program planning and administration. They should, however, be kept to a minimum and should be practical and functional. They should not be maintained merely as busy work and for the sake of filling files.

Some of the records should be concerned directly with the welfare of the participant and others with certain administrative factors.

Records that concern the welfare of the participant are the health records, the cumulative physical education form, anecdotal accounts, attendance reports, grades, and accident reports.

Health records are essential. They contain information on the health examination and other appraisal techniques, health counseling, and any other data pertaining to the person's health.

In a school, the cumulative physical education record should start when the student first attends school and contain information about activities engaged in, afterschool play, tests, anecdotal accounts, interests, needs, and other pertinent information about the student's participation in the physical education program.

There should be special records for attendance, grades, and any special occurrences with a bearing on the participant that are not recorded in other records.

If a student is involved in an accident, a full account of the circumstances surrounding the accident should be recorded. Usually special forms are provided for such purposes.

Administrative records provide general information and equipment records, including a list of the year's events: activities; records of teams; play days, sports days, intramurals; events of special interest; techniques that have been helpful; budget information; and any other data that would be helpful in planning for succeeding years. Memory often fails over time, with the result that many good ideas are lost and many activities and techniques of special value are not used because they are forgotten.

There should be records of equipment, facilities, and supplies that show the material needing repair, new materials needed, and the location of various materials, so that they can easily be found.

Records of such items as locker or basket assignments are essential to the efficient running of a physical education program.

PROVIDING FOR THE HEALTH OF THE PARTICIPANT

Physical education staff members must safeguard the health of all individuals in the program. To accomplish this objective, there must be a close working relationship with staff members in the health program.

Every participant should have periodic health examinations with the results of these examinations scrutinized by the physical educator. A physical education program must be adapted to the needs and interests of each person. The physical educator is responsible for health guidance and health supervision in the physical education activities. The physician should be consulted when persons return after periods of illness, when accidents occur, and at any other time that such qualified advice is needed.

Criteria for evaluating physical education instructional programs

Piscopo has developed the checklist at the end of this chapter for evaluating physical education instructional programs.

SELF-ASSESSMENT TESTS

These tests are to assist students in determining if material and competencies presented in this chapter have been mastered:

1. You are a member of a physical education staff in a high school where the instructional program is under attack by the faculty. It has been suggested that the instructional program be abolished. Prepare a brief in defense of the instructional physical education program that describes its nature, scope, and worth in the educational process.

2. You have been invited to speak to the Parent Teachers Association in your community on the topic: "Physical Education from the Preschool through the College Years." Prepare a speech that describes the various instructional physical education programs at each educational level and the purpose and nature of each. Also, discuss some innovative ideas for each educational level. Present your speech to your class.

3. Develop a model for a high school instructional physical education program as a result of Title IX legislation.

4. Compare how traditional physical education instructional programs are conducted with respect to handicapped students and how it is proposed they should be conducted as a result of mainstreaming and the passage of Public Law 94-142.

5. Develop a list of principles for physical education instructional programs that would serve as guides for each of the following: scheduling, time allotment for classes, size of classes, instructional loads, class management, uniforms, taking roll, selecting activities, grouping, and areas of student involvement.

6. Propose a professional solution with supporting evidence for each of the following administrative problems in instructional physical education programs:

Should physical education programs be required or elective?

Should substitutions for physical education be permitted?

Should credit be given for physical education?

How should excuses be handled?

Should a specialist or the classroom teacher teach physical education in the elementary school?

How should a physical education program be evaluated?

SELECTED REFERENCES

American Alliance for Health, Physical Education, and Recreation, education amendments of 1972, update, October, 1975.

American Alliance of Health, Physical Education, and Recreation: Some often-asked questions about Title IX, update, November, 1975.

American Alliance for Health, Physical Education, and Recreation: More often-asked questions about Title IX, update, December, 1975.

American Alliance for Health, Physical Education, and Recreation: Questions about implementation of Title IX, update, January, 1976.

American Alliance for Health, Physical Education, and Recreation: Questions about implementation of Title IX, update, February, 1976.

American Alliance for Health, Physical Education, and Recreation: Management strategies for implementation of Title IX, February, 1977.

American Association for Health, Physical Education, and Recreation: Knowledge and understanding in physical education, Washington, D.C., 1969, The Association.

American Association for Health, Physical Education, and Recreation: Perceptual-motor foundations: a multidisciplinary concern, Washington, D.C., 1969, The Association.

Annand, V.: PELT—physical education leadership training, Journal of Health, Physical Education, and Recreation **44:**50, October, 1973.

Arnheim, D.D., Auxter, D., and Crowe, W.C.: Principles and methods of adapted physical education and recreation, St. Louis, 1977, The C.V. Mosby Co.

Arnheim, D.D., and Sinclair, W.A.: The clumsy child, ed. 2, St. Louis, 1979, The C.V. Mosby Co.

Bucher, C.A.: Physical education for life, New York, 1969, McGraw-Hill Book Co. (A textbook in physical education for high school boys and girls.)

Bucher, C.A.: Foundations of physical education, ed. 9, St. Louis, 1983, The C.V. Mosby Co.

Bucher, C.A., and Koenig, C.: Methods and materials for secondary school physical education, ed. 6, St. Louis, 1983, The C.V. Mosby Co.

Bureau of Health Education, Physical Education, Athletics, and Recreation, California State Department of Education: Evaluation of the effects of flexible scheduling on physical education, Sacramento, Calif., 1972.

Dowell, L.J.: Strategies for teaching physical education, Englewood Cliffs, N.J., 1975, Prentice-Hall, Inc.

Edington, D.W., and Cunningham, L.: Biological awareness, Englewood Cliffs, N.J., 1975, Prentice-Hall, Inc.

Elementary School Physical Education Commission of the American Association for Health, Physical Education, and Recreation, Physical Education Division (1968-69): Essentials of a quality elementary school physical education program, Journal of Health, Physical Education, and Recreation **42:**42, 1971.

Hellison, D.R.: Humanistic physical education; a behavioral perspective, Englewood Cliffs, N.J., 1973, Prentice-Hall, Inc.

Insley, G.S.: Practical guidelines for the teaching of physical education, Reading, Mass., 1973, Addison-Wesley Publishing Co., Inc.

Klappholz, L.A.: There is nothing to fear in the Title IX regulations, Physical Education Newsletter, October 1, 1975.

The National Association for Physical Education for College Women and The National College Physical Education Association for Men: Title IX; moving toward implementation, Briefings 1, 1975, The Association.

Physical Education Division Committee: Guidelines for secondary school physical education, Journal of Health, Physical Education, and Recreation **42:**47, 1971.

Physical Education Division Committee: Guide to excellence for physical education in colleges and universities, Journal of Health, Physical Education, and Recreation **42:**51, 1971.

Schurr, E.L.: Movement experiences for children—a humanistic approach to elementary school physical education, Englewood Cliffs, N.J., 1975, Prentice-Hall, Inc.

U.S. Department of Health, Education, and Welfare, Office of Civils Rights: Elimination of sex discrimination in athletic programs, Washington, D.C., September, 1975, The Department.

U.S. Department of Health, Education, and Welfare, Office of Civil Rights: Prohibiting sex discrimination in education, Washington, D.C., July, 1975. The Department.

U.S. Office of Education, U.S. Department of Health, Education, and Welfare: How teachers make a difference, Washington, D.C., 1971, Superintendent of Documents.

Vannier, M.: Physical activities for the handicapped, Englewood Cliffs, N.J., 1977, Prentice-Hall, Inc.

Wheeler, R.H., and Hooley, A.M.: Physical education for the handicapped, Philadelphia, 1976, Lea & Febiger.

CRITERIA FOR EVALUATING PHYSICAL EDUCATION INSTRUCTIONAL PROGRAMS*

	Poor (1)	Fair (2)	Good (3)	Very good (4)	Excellent (5)
Meeting physical education objectives					
1. Does the class activity contribute to the development of physical fitness?	☐	☐	☐	☐	☐
2. Does the class activity foster the growth of ethical character, desirable emotional and social characteristics?	☐	☐	☐	☐	☐
3. Does the class activity contain recreational value?	☐	☐	☐	☐	☐
4. Does the class activity contain carryover value for later life?	☐	☐	☐	☐	☐
5. Is the class activity accepted as a regular part of the curriculum?	☐	☐	☐	☐	☐
6. Does the class activity meet the needs of *all* participants in the group?	☐	☐	☐	☐	☐
7. Does the class activity encourage the development of leadership?	☐	☐	☐	☐	☐
8. Does the class activity fulfill the safety objective in physical education?	☐	☐	☐	☐	☐
9. Does the class activity and conduct foster a better understanding of democratic living?	☐	☐	☐	☐	☐
10. Does the class activity and conduct cultivate a better understanding and appreciation for exercise and sports?	☐	☐	☐	☐	☐

PERFECT SCORE: 50   ACTUAL SCORE: _____

	Poor (1)	Fair (2)	Good (3)	Very good (4)	Excellent (5)
Leadership (teacher conduct)					
1. Is the teacher appropriately and neatly dressed for the class activity?	☐	☐	☐	☐	☐
2. Does the teacher know the activity thoroughly?	☐	☐	☐	☐	☐
3. Does the teacher possess an audible and pleasing voice?	☐	☐	☐	☐	☐
4. Does the teacher project an enthusiastic and dynamic attitude in class presentation?	☐	☐	☐	☐	☐
5. Does the teacher maintain discipline?	☐	☐	☐	☐	☐
6. Does the teacher identify, analyze, and correct faulty performance in guiding pupils?	☐	☐	☐	☐	☐
7. Does the teacher present a sound, logical method of teaching motor skills, for example, explanation, demonstration, participation, and testing?	☐	☐	☐	☐	☐
8. Does the teacher avoid the use of destructive criticism, sarcasm, and ridicule with students?	☐	☐	☐	☐	☐
9. Does the teacher maintain emotional stability and poise?	☐	☐	☐	☐	☐
10. Does the teacher possess high standards and ideals of work?	☐	☐	☐	☐	☐

PERFECT SCORE: 50   ACTUAL SCORE: _____

*Adapted from Piscopo, J.: Quality instruction: first priority, The Physical Educator **21**:162, 1964.   *Continued.*

CRITERIA FOR EVALUATING PHYSICAL EDUCATION INSTRUCTIONAL PROGRAMS—cont'd

	Poor (1)	Fair (2)	Good (3)	Very good (4)	Excellent (5)
General class procedures, methods, and techniques					
1. Does class conduct yield evidence of preplanning?	☐	☐	☐	☐	☐
2. Does the organization of the class allow for individual differences?	☐	☐	☐	☐	☐
3. Does the class exhibit maximum activity and minimum teacher participation? e.g., overemphasis on explanation and/or demonstration?	☐	☐	☐	☐	☐
4. Are adequate motivational devices such as teaching aids and audiovisual techniques effectively utilized?	☐	☐	☐	☐	☐
5. Are squad leaders effectively employed where appropriate?	☐	☐	☐	☐	☐
6. Does the class start promptly at the scheduled time?	☐	☐	☐	☐	☐
7. Are students with medical excuses from the regular class supervised and channelled into appropriate activities?	☐	☐	☐	☐	☐
8. Is the class roll taken quickly and accurately?	☐	☐	☐	☐	☐
9. Are accurate records of progress and achievements maintained?	☐	☐	☐	☐	☐
10. Are supplies and equipment quickly issued and stored?	☐	☐	☐	☐	☐

PERFECT SCORE: 50 ACTUAL SCORE: _____

	Poor (1)	Fair (2)	Good (3)	Very good (4)	Excellent (5)
Participant conduct					
1. Are the objectives of the activity or sport clearly known to the learner?	☐	☐	☐	☐	☐
2. Are the students interested in the class activities?	☐	☐	☐	☐	☐
3. Do the students really enjoy their physical education class?	☐	☐	☐	☐	☐
4. Are the students thoroughly familiar with routine regulations of class roll, excuses, and dismissals?	☐	☐	☐	☐	☐
5. Are the students appropriately uniformed for the class activity?	☐	☐	☐	☐	☐
6. Does the class exhibit a spirit of friendly rivalry in learning new skills?	☐	☐	☐	☐	☐
7. Do students avoid mischief or "horseplay"?	☐	☐	☐	☐	☐
8. Do students take showers where facilities and nature of activity permit?	☐	☐	☐	☐	☐
9. Do slow learners participate as much as fast learners?	☐	☐	☐	☐	☐
10. Do students show respect for the teacher?	☐	☐	☐	☐	☐

PERFECT SCORE: 50 ACTUAL SCORE: _____

	Poor (1)	Fair (2)	Good (3)	Very good (4)	Excellent (5)
Safe and healthful environment					
1. Is the area large enough for the activity and number of participants in the class?	☐	☐	☐	☐	☐

CRITERIA FOR EVALUATING PHYSICAL EDUCATION INSTRUCTIONAL PROGRAMS—cont'd

	Poor (1)	Fair (2)	Good (3)	Very good (4)	Excellent (5)
Safe and healthful environment —cont'd					
2. Does the class possess adequate equipment and/or supplies?	☐	☐	☐	☐	☐
3. Are adequate shower and locker facilities available and readily accessible?	☐	☐	☐	☐	☐
4. Is the equipment and/or apparatus clean and in good working order?	☐	☐	☐	☐	☐
5. Does the activity area contain good lighting and ventilation?	☐	☐	☐	☐	☐
6. Are all safety hazards eliminated or reduced where possible?	☐	☐	☐	☐	☐
7. Is first aid and safety equipment readily accessible?	☐	☐	☐	☐	☐
8. Is the storage area adequate for supplies and equipment?	☐	☐	☐	☐	☐
9. Does the activity area contain a properly equipped rest room for use in injury, illness, or rest periods?	☐	☐	☐	☐	☐
10. Does the activity area contain adequate toilet facilities?	☐	☐	☐	☐	☐

PERFECT SCORE: *50*   ACTUAL SCORE: _____

Criteria	Perfect score	Actual score
Meeting physical education objectives	50	_____
Leadership (teacher conduct)	50	_____
General class procedures, methods, and techniques	50	_____
Pupil conduct	50	_____
Safe and healthful environment	50	_____
Total points	250	_____

4

The adapted program and physical education for handicapped persons

Instructional objectives and competencies to be achieved

After reading this chapter the student should be able to

■ Discuss what is meant by an adapted program of physical education.

■ Explain the legal and the moral responsibility to provide for the handicapped in physical education programs.

■ Outline the objectives of an adapted physical education program and the guidelines, type of scheduling, and activities essential to achieve these objectives.

■ Describe the various elements that make up an individualized education program (IEP).

■ Define the term *mainstreaming* and set forth the administrative principles that should guide the mainstreaming concept.

■ Describe administrative procedures to follow in order to comply with and implement Public Law 94-142.

■ Discuss various organizational structures and instructional strategies that can be used in providing for handicapped persons.

■ Relate how physical education can contribute to physically handicapped, mentally retarded, emotionally disturbed, culturally disadvantaged, poorly coordinated, physically gifted and creative, and learning disabled students.

Public Law 94-142 has implications for adapted physical education programs. This law, providing for such things as individualized programs for the handicapped and mainstreaming, is bringing about many educational changes. It has particular significance for those handicapped students who can profit from having their physical education with regular students rather than be isolated.

Because of the impact PL 94-142 has had on education and physical education, this chapter is concerned with the adapted program and physical education for the handicapped.

The term *adapted* is used here, although many books and programs use other terms, such as *corrective, individual, modified, therapeutic, remedial, special, restricted,* and *atypical*. In fact, *physical education programs for handicapped persons* is the term being used more frequently. The adapted pro-

gram refers to the phase of physical education that meets the needs of the individual who, because of some physical inadequacy, functional defect capable of being improved through physical activity, or other deficiency, is temporarily or permanently unable to take part in the regular physical education program or in which special provisions are made for handicapped students in regular physical education classes. It also refers to students of a school or college student population who do not fall into the classification "average" or "normal" for their age or grade. These students deviate from their peers in physical, mental, emotional, or social characteristics or in a combination of these traits.

The principle of individual differences is being recognized increasingly by educators. The observance of this principle has resulted in special provisions in the schools for mentally retarded children, as well as

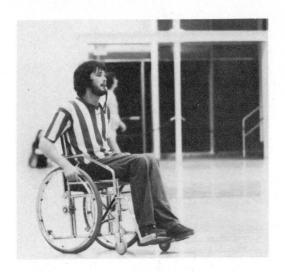

Fig. 4-1.

Courtesy Winona Vannoy, Kent State University, Kent, Ohio.

for gifted children, for those with heart abnormalities, defective sight, physical disabilities, and other deviations from the normal, and for those who are culturally deprived or emotionally disturbed.

The principle of individual differences that applies to education as a whole also applies to physical education. Most administrators believe that as long as a student can attend school or college, he or she should be required to participate in physical education. If this tenet is adhered to, it means that programs must be adapted to individual needs. Many children and young adults who are recuperating from long illnesses or operations or who are suffering from other physical or emotional conditions require special consideration in their programs.

It cannot be assumed that all individuals in physical education classes are not handicapped. Unfortunately, many programs are administered on this basis. One estimate has been made that one out of every eight students in our schools is handicapped to the extent that special provision should be made in the educational program.

Schools and colleges will always have students who, because of many factors such as heredity, environment, disease, accident, or other reason, have

physical or other impairment. Many of these students have difficulty adjusting to the demands society places on them. The responsibility of physical education programs is to help each individual who comes into class. Even though a person may be atypical, this is not cause for neglect. In fact, it should represent an even greater challenge to see that he or she enjoys the benefits of participating in physical activities adapted to his or her needs. Provision for a sound adapted program has been a shortcoming of physical education throughout the nation because of a lack of properly trained teachers, because of the financial cost of remedial instruction, and because many administrators and teachers are not aware of their responsibility and the contribution they can make in this phase of physical education. These obstacles should be overcome as the public becomes aware of the need to educate *all* individuals in *all* phases of the total education program.

The nation's handicapped persons

The nation's estimated 50 million handicapped persons are engaged in an aggressive civil rights movement. Suits have been filed, demonstrations held, and picketing and lobbying have been a common occurrence in recent years. These actions are aimed at obtaining the equal protection promised under the Fourteenth Amendment to the Constitution of the United States.

As a result of the actions on the part of handicapped persons, the nation is finally awakening to their needs. Until recently in the nation's history, handicapped persons were viewed as nonproductive. As a result, it has been common for handicapped persons to be discouraged and not even attempt to accomplish anything in life. Today, however, the picture has changed. The handicapped are demanding and are achieving their rights under the Constitution and are being employed in gainful jobs and taking their rightful place in society.

According to figures provided by agencies such as the National Arts and the Handicapped Information Service, The National Center for Health Statistics, and other sources, the following represent an estimate of the number of persons with various types of handi-

Fig. 4-2. The handicapped are receiving much more attention in physical education programs. Elmer Carey of Cincinnati, a totally blind bowler, is shown here.

Courtesy American Blind Bowling Association.

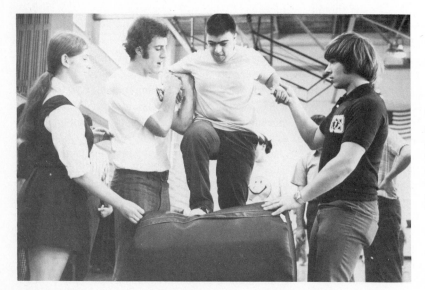

Fig. 4-3. Mentally retarded students can be helped through physical education activities.

Courtesy Arnold College Division, University of Bridgeport, Conn., Parents and Friends Association of Mentally Retarded Children. Photograph by John Tasker.

caps in the United States (some persons fall into more than one category)*:

11.7 million physically disabled persons
12.5 million temporarily injured persons (broken limb, etc.)
2.4 million deaf persons
11 million hearing impaired persons
1.3 million blind persons
8.2 million visually impaired persons
6.8 million mentally disabled persons (retarded, etc.)
1.7 million homebound persons (chronic health disorders, etc.)
2.1 million institutionalized persons

Statistics on the number of handicapped school children vary considerably (from 6 to 9 million). Gearheart and Weishahn† provide the following information:

Visually impaired (includes blind)—55,000
Hearing impaired (includes deaf)—330,000 to 440,000
Speech handicapped—1,925,000 to 2,750,000
Crippled and other health impaired—275,000
Emotionally disturbed—1,100,000 to 1,650,000
Mentally retarded (both educable and trainable)—1,375,000 to 1,650,000
Learning disabled—1,100,000 to 2,200,000
Total—6,160,000 to 9,020,000

The authors also point out that more than half of the handicapped children in the United States do not receive adequate educational services.

Definitions relating to the adapted program and physical education for handicapped persons

HANDICAPPED

Handicapped persons include those who have been identified as being mentally retarded, emotionally disturbed, deaf or hearing impaired, visually impaired, orthopedically impaired, speech impaired, learning disabled, multihandicapped, or otherwise health impaired.

---

*New York Times, p. 8E, Feb. 13, 1977.
†Gearheart, B.R., and Weishahn, M.W.: The handicapped student in the regular classroom, ed. 2, St. Louis, 1980, The C.V. Mosby Co.

PHYSICAL EDUCATION

Physical education as it relates to the handicapped under federal law is the development of (1) physical and motor fitness, (2) fundamental motor skills and patterns, and, (3) skills in aquatics, dance, and individual and group games and sports (including intramural and lifetime sports).

SPECIAL EDUCATION

Under federal law special education means specially designed instruction, at no cost to parents or guardians, to meet the unique needs of a handicapped child, including classroom instruction, physical education instruction, home instruction, and instruction in hospitals and institutions.

IEP (INDIVIDUALIZED EDUCATION PROGRAM)

The individualized education program (IEP) is the program or prescription written for each child in relation to his or her specific disability. It will be discussed in more detail later in this chapter.

LEAST RESTRICTIVE ENVIRONMENT

In essence the least restrictive environment means the handicapped child is placed in a class or setting that is as similar to a normal class as possible and where the child can function safely. This location ranges from a full-time regular physical education class, to a regular physical education class with consultation from specialists in adapted physical education, to part-time regular physical education and part-time adapted physical education, to adapted physical education with regular physical education only for specific activities, to full-time adapted physical education in a regular school, to adapted physical education in a special school.

Types of handicapped individuals

Many terms have been used to classify and define handicapped individuals. These terms vary from publication to publication. Categories of children designated by the United States Congress in relation to legislation for handicapped persons will be the primary classifications used in this text. These categories include the mentally retarded, hard-of-hearing, deaf, speech impaired, visually handicapped, seriously emotionally disturbed, crippled, and other health impaired or learning disabled children who may require educational services out of the ordinary. These handicapping conditions are defined here.*

mentally retarded—Persons characterized by a level of mental development impaired to the extent that the individual is unable to benefit from the standard school program and requires special services. This includes such subcategories as slow learners, educable mentally retarded, and trainable mentally retarded.

hard-of-hearing—Persons in whom the sense of hearing, although defective, is functional with or without a hearing aid. The hearing loss is generally of such a nature and severity as to require one or more special educational services.

deaf—Persons in whom the sense of hearing is nonfunctional for the ordinary purposes of life (inability to hear connected language with or without the use of amplification). This general group is made up of the congenitally deaf and the adventitiously deaf.

speech impaired—Persons experiencing pronounced organic or functional speech disorders that cause interference in oral communication. This includes persons exhibiting language disorders resulting from such specific handicaps as stuttering, cleft palate, speech disorders or voice problems.

visually handicapped—Persons who have such severe visual loss as to require special educational services. This includes subcategories such as blind, legally blind, partially sighted, and visually impaired.

seriously emotionally disturbed—Persons having psychiatric disturbance without clearly defined physical cause of structural damage to the brain, which limits the ability of the individual to govern his or her own behavior. These are of such a nature and severity as to require one or more special services, particularly with reference to education.

crippled—Persons with orthopedic impairments that might restrict normal opportunity for education or self-support. This is generally considered to include individuals having congenital impairments, for example, clubfoot or absence of some body member, impairments caused by some disease, for example, poliomyelitis, bone tuberculosis,

and encephalitis, neurological involvements that may result in conditions such as cerebral palsy, and impairments caused by accidents, for example, fractures or burns that cause contractures.

other health impaired—Persons having health handicaps not covered in other categories, of such a nature and severity as to require one or more special services, particularly with reference to their education. These could include asthma; rheumatic fever; conditions of less than the usual amount of strength, energy, or endurance; conditions resulting from chronic illness or environmental causes; epilepsy; diabetes; or cardiac disease.

learning disabled—Persons with learning dysfunctions that prevent them from learning or functioning in a regular educational program. These individuals exhibit a disorder in one or more of the basic psychological processes involved in understanding or in using spoken or written language. These may be manifested in disorders of listening, thinking, talking, reading, writing, spelling, or arithmetic. They include conditions that have been referred to as perceptual handicaps, brain injury, minimal brain dysfunction, dyslexia, and developmental aphasia. They do not include learning problems that are a consequence primarily of visual, hearing, or motor handicaps; mental retardation; emotional disturbances; or environmental disadvantages.

In addition to these terms just defined, certain other terms used in relation to programs for handicapped persons must also be defined. These terms are *impaired, disabled, handicapped, exceptional person,* and *adapted physical education.*

impaired—This refers to an identifiable organic or functional condition; some part of the body is actually missing, a portion of an anatomical structure is gone, or one or more parts of the body do not function properly or adequately.

disabled—This refers to a limitation or restriction of an individual, because of impairments, in executing some skills, doing specific jobs or tasks, or performing certain activities.

handicapped—Handicapped individuals, because of impairment or disability, are adversely affected psychologically, emotionally, or socially, or in a combination of ways.

exceptional person—The exceptional person, because of some physical, mental, emotional, or behavioral deviation, may require a modification of school practices or

*U.S. Department of Health, Education and Welfare: Better education for handicapped children, annual report, fiscal year 1969, Washington, D.C., 1970, U.S. Government Printing Office.

Fig. 4-4. A physical education instructor working with atypical children.

Courtesy Arnold College Division, University of Bridgeport, Conn., Parents and Friends Association of Mentally Retarded Children. Photograph by John Tasker.

an addition of some special service to develop to his or her maximum potential.

adapted physical education—The Committee on Adapted Physical Education defines adapted physical education as "a diversified program of developmental activities, games, sports, and rhythms suited to the interests, capacities, and limitations of students with disabilities who may not safely or successfully engage in unrestricted participation in the vigorous activities of the general physical education program.*

Functional physical education goals for handicapped persons†

Selected goals that give direction to the physical education program for the handicapped student and that translate into objectives for each participant, as outlined by the AAHPERD, are presented here in the following adapted form:

Informing each student of his of her capacities and limitations

Providing each student within his or her capabilities the opportunity to develop organic vigor, muscular strength, joint function, and endurance

Providing each student with opportunities for social development in recreational sports and games

Providing each student with opportunities to develop skills in recreational sports and games

Helping students meet demands of day-to-day living

Helping students with permanent disabilities in their social development

Developing personal pride in overcoming disabilities or other forms of impairment

Developing an appreciation for individual differences and being able to accept limitations and still be a part of the group

*Stein, J.U.: A clarification of terms, Journal of Health, Physical Education, and Recreation **42**:63, September 1971.
†American Alliance for Health, Physical Education, Recreation: Adapted physical education guidelines—theory and practice for the handicapped, Washington, D.C., 1976, AAHPER.

Public law 94-142*

Many court decisions and laws exist to ensure equality of educational opportunity for handicapped individuals. Because of the specific mention of physical education in the final regulations implementing PL 94-142 (Education of All Handicapped Children Act of 1975), the law is discussed here in some detail.

Overview of the law. The final regulations of PL 94-142 spell out the federal government's commitment to providing all handicapped children with a free and appropriate education. Specifically, full educational services must be provided for (1) handicapped children not currently receiving a free and appropriate education and (2) severely handicapped youngsters receiving inadequate assistance.

Handicapped children, as defined in PL 94-142, are those who require some type of special education and related services. Related services, under the act, are defined as "transportation and developmental, corrective, and other supportive services, including occupational therapy, recreation, and medical and counseling services." Although gifted children might need special education and related services, they are not covered under the law.

Other specific stipulations of PL 94-142 require the following:

1. State and local educational agencies to initiate policies to ensure all handicapped boys and girls the right to a free and appropriate education.
2. Planning of individualized educational programs, with conferences among parents, teachers, representatives of local educational agencies, and, where appropriate, children themselves. These conferences must be held at least once a year.
3. Due process for parents and children, to ensure that their rights are not abrogated.
4. A per pupil expenditure that is at least equal to the amount spent on nonhandicapped children in the state or local school district.
5. The state and local agency shall carry out the man-

dates of the law according to specific timetables provided therein.
6. The development of a comprehensive system of personnel training, including preservice and inservice training for teachers.
7. That handicapped students will be educated in the "least restrictive environment." This means that they will be mainstreamed into the regular class whenever possible.

Aspects of PL 94-142 related to the physical education. Section 121a.307 of the regulations of PL 94-142, which spells out the requirements for physical education, follows.

121a.307 Physical Education

(a) *General.* Physical education services, specially designed if necessary, must be made available to every handicapped child receiving a free appropriate public education.

(b) *Regular physical education.* Each handicapped child must be afforded the opportunity to participate in the regular physical education program available to nonhandicapped children unless:

(1) The child is enrolled full time in a separate facility; or

(2) The child needs specially designed physical education, as prescribed in the child's individualized education program.

(c) *Special physical education.* If specially designed physical education is prescribed in a child's individualized education program, the public agency responsible for the education of that child shall provide the services directly, or make arrangements for it to be provided through other public or private programs.

(d) *Education in separate facilities.* The public agency responsible for the education of a handicapped child who is enrolled in a separate facility shall insure that the child receives appropriate physical education services in compliance with paragraphs (a) and (c) of this section.

The House of Representatives, in a special report, made the following reference to physical education:

The committee expects the Commissioner of Education to take whatever action is necessary to assure that physical education services are available to all handicapped children, and has specifically included physical education within the definition of special education, to make clear that the Committee expects such services, specially designed where necessary, to be provided as an integral part of the educational program of every handicapped child.

*Technical information related to PL 94-142 is taken from the Physical Education Newsletter, Number 87, November, 1977.

Fig. 4-5. The school should do everything within its power to help obtain the necessary medical care for the orthopedically handicapped child. United States Department of Education.

The physical education program for handicapped students must be individualized according to the needs of each handicapped individual. Students should be included in the regular program whenever possible and special adapted programs established as needed. Students should not be mainstreamed into the regular physical education program when their handicap(s) prevents them from receiving an adequate educational experience. Conversely, they should not be placed in a special class and left there. Handicapped youngsters should be scheduled in and out of regular classes, depending on their ability to cope with the specific activity being taught at a particular time. The final consideration is to provide the handicapped child with the ''least restrictive environment'' or one that permits the child to achieve maximum potential.

Other legislation

Other legislative acts relating to handicapped persons and affecting physical education programs are Section 504 of the Rehabilitation Act of 1973 (PL 33-112) and the Education Amendment Act of 1974 (PL 93-380). The provisions of PL 93-380 guarantee the rights of handicapped persons in programs for which schools and other sponsoring groups receive federal funds. PL 93-380 is designed to ensure that handicapped individuals are placed in the least restrictive alternative environment for educational purposes. Part VIB of the law specifically states that

. . . to the maximum extent appropriate, handicapped children should be educated with children who are not handicapped, and that special classes, separate schooling or other means of removal of handicapped children from the regular educational environment, occurs only when the nature or severity of the handicap is such that education in regular classes with the use of supplementary aids and services cannot be achieved satisfactorily.

The adapted program

OBJECTIVES

Physical education can be valuable to the atypical and handicapped individual in many ways. It can help in identifying deviations from the normal and in referring students to proper individuals or agencies, when necessary. It can provide the atypical person with a happy, wholesome play experience. It can help the student achieve, within his or her limitations, physical skill and exercise. It can provide many opportunities for learning skills appropriate for the handicapped person to achieve success. Finally, physical education can contribute to a more productive life for the handicapped individual by developing those physical qualities needed to meet the demands of day-to-day living.

To help students with handicaps achieve effective physical, mental, emotional, and social growth in a program of selected physical education and recreational activities, Crowe and colleagues* have developed objectives for the adapted physical education program, which are given here in the following adapted form:

> To help students correct conditions that are capable of being improved
> To help students protect themselves from injuries and conditions that might occur as a result of participating in physical education activities
> To provide opportunities for students to learn a variety of appropriate recreational activities
> To help students develop optimal organic power and physical condition in light of their physical resources
> To help students understand and appreciate their physical and mental limitations
> To help students develop socially and achieve a worthy self-image

> To help students understand, appreciate, and develop good body mechanics
> To help students understand and appreciate sports at which they will be spectators

An analysis of these objectives indicates that if they are accomplished, the needs of every individual will be provided for, regardless of whether he or she has a temporary or a permanent disability, a need for organic, mental, emotional, or social adjustment, or a need for a broad or limited program. These are excellent goals for physical educators.

SCHEDULING THE ADAPTED PROGRAM

Before scheduling a student in the adapted program, one needs a thorough understanding of the boy's or girl's atypical condition and the type of procedure that will best meet his or her total development.

Because of the shortage of funds, space, and staff, many scheduling difficulties arise concerning the adapted program. Many times equipment has to be improvised, special groups must be scheduled within the regular class period, and staff members have to devote out-of-school time to this important phase of the total physical education program. Unfortunately, some teachers solve the problem by sending the exceptional student to study hall or letting him or her observe from the bleachers, thus failing to provide a modified program.

Some physical education leaders feel that scheduling atypical children and youth in separate groups is not always satisfactory. Many educators who have studied this problem feel the atypical student in many cases should take his or her physical education along with nonhandicapped students and, to provide for the handicapping condition, the program should be modified and special methods of teaching used. In such cases, the administrator should make sure that the modification of the program for the student is physically and psychologically sound. Sometimes mental and emotional defects can be minimized if the teacher acquaints other students with the general problems of the handicapped person and encourages their cooperation in helping the student make the right adjustment and maintain self-esteem and social acceptance.

In larger schools it sometimes has been possible

*Crowe, W.C., Auxter, D., and Pyfer, J.: Principles and methods of adapted physical education and recreation, ed. 4, St. Louis, 1981, The C.V. Mosby Co.

to schedule special classes for students with some types of abnormalities. There also have been special schools established for the severely handicapped. These two procedures have not always proved satisfactory, however, because of the feeling that the handicapped should be scheduled with nonhandicapped students for social and psychological reasons and also because PL 94-142 requires it in many cases.

In some smaller schools and colleges where there is a staff problem, students needing an adapted program have been scheduled in a separate section within the regular physical education class period. In some cases group exercises have been devised together, with the practice of encouraging pupils to assist one another in the alleviation of their difficulties. These methods are not always satisfactory but, according to the schools and colleges concerned, are much better than not doing anything about the problem. In other schools and colleges, atypical pupils have been scheduled during special periods, where individual attention can be given to them.

The procedure any particular school or college follows in scheduling students for the adapted program will depend on PL 94-142, the school's educational philosophy, finances, facilities and staff available, and the needs of the students.

Individualized education programs for handicapped persons

After identification and eligibility have been determined for handicapped students, an individualized education program (IEP) must be developed for each individual. PL 94-142 specifies the requirements for the development of such programs. Section 4(19) provides the following:

The term individualized education program means a written statement for each handicapped child developed in any meeting by a representative of the local educational agency or an intermediate educational unit who shall be qualified to provide, or supervise, the provision of specially designed instruction to meet the unique needs of handicapped children, the teacher, the parents or guardians of such child, and wherever appropriate, such child, which statement shall include:

A. A statement of the present levels of educational performance of such child;
B. A statement of annual goals, including short-term instructional objectives;
C. A statement of the specific educational services to be provided such child, and the extent to which such child will be able to participate in regular educational programs;
D. The projected date for initiation and anticipated duration of such services; and
E. Appropriate objective criteria and evaluation procedures and schedules for determining, on at least an annual basis, whether instructional objectives are being achieved.

The comprehensive IEP should be developed using the team approach. The following persons should be represented on the team: parent; teacher (classroom or physical education teacher, special education teacher); student; and, when appropriate, person responsible for supervising special education, related services such as guidance, and other necessary agencies.

An example of an IEP prepared by the Department of Education of Virginia is shown in Fig. 4-6.

SELECTING ACTIVITIES FOR ADAPTED PHYSICAL EDUCATION

Activities should be selected for the adapted physical education program with the needs of the atypical student in mind after consulting proper medical authorities. The IEP will indicate activities that should be provided. The activities selected should develop worthwhile skills, maintain a proper state of organic fitness, and consider the social and emotional needs of the student. In no case should an activity ever aggravate an existing injury or atypical condition. Of course, all activities should be appropriate to the age level of the student and be ones in which he or she can find success. As far as possible and practical, activities should reflect the regular program of physical education offered at the school or college. The fewer changes made in the original activity, usually, the more the atypical person feels that he or she is being successful and not different from the other students. Activities should contribute to the development of basic movements and skills. There should be as much group activity as possible, because the social-

INDIVIDUALIZED EDUCATIONAL PROGRAM

I. Student name ___John Doe, Jr.___ Date of birth ___1-24-61___ Age ___16___ School divisions ___Stony Point___

Parent/guardian ___Mrs. John Doe___ Date of eligibility ___6-15-77___ Date of IEP implementation ___9-6-77___

Address ___1736 Bay Street___ Categorical identification ___E.M.R.___

II. Present level of performance (summary data)

Academic:

Piat			AAHPER Physical Fitness Test (Refer to charts/age group)	
	Reading recognition	2.3	Items	
	Reading	3.6	Pull-up/flexed arm hang	5
	Spelling	2.0	Sit-ups (flexed legs)	41
	Reading comprehension	4.8	Shuttle run	10.1
	Mathematics	4.2	50 yard dash	6.7
	General knowledge	5.9	600 run-walk	1:55
Key Math			Standing broad jump	6'9"
3.8				
Dolch Sight				
Word Inventory				
263 words mastered				

Behavior:

John is very shy and lacks physical fitness. There is little eye contact with others. He is well mannered. John gets discouraged easily when working in language areas. He performs well in math. His social skills are limited. John is interested in wood-working. Carpentry may provide a setting for advancement and training after he has obtained the necessary prevocational orientation.

III. Long-term goals

1. All items on the *AAHPER Physical Fitness Test* will increase to the 50th percentile (above satisfactory) by the end of the school year.

2. a. To increase sight word vocabulary and survival words.
   b. To increase skills in reading through spelling skills and decoding skills.
   c. To increase math processes skills to include banking and savings.
   d. To demonstrate planning of careers, duties of specific jobs, and survival forms of applications.
   e. To provide instruction in local, state, and national governments.
   f. To increase self-confidence and social adaptability.

Fig. 4-6. An example of an IEP prepared by the Department of Education of Virginia.

IV. Education and/or related services

	Date to begin	Anticipated completion date	Environment	Location	Personnel
E.M.R.	9-6-77	Through high school	4 periods – self-contained	Virginia High School	Mrs. Green
Physical education	9-6-77	Through grade 10	1 period per day regular	Virginia High School	Mr. Dean
Vocational orientation	9-6-77	Through high school	1 period regular	Virginia High School	Vocational Rehabilitation W.I.N. Program

V. Short-term objectives

Objectives	Methods	Special materials and equipment	Dates Begun	Dates Completed	Continuation and/or modification
P.E.	Establish warm-up stations to be used for following activities:				
1. Student's performance levels should show improvement in efforts to reach the 50th percentile	1. To perform sit-ups three times per week	Tape, stop watch, horizontal bar	9/6	5/4	Mastered/ Maintain
	2. To perform pull-ups three times per week		9/6	5/4	Cont./Inc. No. per week
	3. To perform shuttle-run two times per week		9/6	5/4	Cont./Inc. No. per week
	4. To run three 50-yard wind sprints per week		9/6	5/4	Cont./Modif. No.
	5. To jump vertically 1 minute three times per week		9/6	5/4	No. exercise
	6. To run one 600-yard run-walk per week		9/6	5/4	Mastered/ Continue
Academic					
1. To master Dolch sight vocabulary and survival words	Cover and write method	Flash cards, word finds, crossword puzzles	9/15	6/3	Continue/ increase
2. To spell and define 10 words per week			9/15	6/3	Modify
3. To, etc.			9/15	6/3	Continue

Fig. 4-6 cont'd.

VI. Participants

Date	Signature of persons present	Relationship to student
9-1-77	Mrs. Ann Long	Guidance Counselor
9-1-77	Mrs. Louise Green	EMR Teacher
9-1-77	Mr. George Dean	Physical Education Teacher
9-1-77	Mrs. John Doe	Parent
9-1-77	Ms. Matilda Snodgrass	Psychologist
9-1-77	Mr. Oscar Rinklefender	Director of Special Education

I GIVE PERMISSION FOR MY CHILD _John Doe_ to be enrolled in the special program described in the individualized education program plan. I understand that I have the right to review his/her records and to request a change in his/her individualized education program at any time. I understand that I have the right to refuse this permission and to have my child continue in his/her present placement pending further action.

I did participate in the development of the individualized education program. YES _X_ NO ___

I did not participate in the development of the individualized education program, but I do approve of the plan.

YES ___ NO ___

_9/1/77_ _Mrs. John Doe_
Date Signature of parent/guardian

I DO NOT GIVE PERMISSION FOR MY CHILD _____ to be enrolled in the special education program described in the individualized education program. I understand that I have the right to review his/her records and to request another placement. I understand that the action described above will not take place without my permission or until due process procedures have been exhausted. I understand that if my decision is appealed, I will be notified of my due process rights in this procedure.

___ _____
Date Signature of parent/guardian

Fig. 4-6 cont'd.

izing benefits of participation are important in providing students with a feeling of belonging.

The teacher in the adapted program

In the United States today there are several institutions offering specialization in adapted physical education programs. The specialist in adapted physical education usually has a master's degree or a doctorate and has taken courses in special education, psychology, sociology, and other allied areas, as well as in adapted physical education.

It is also important that physical educators and classroom teachers be given the opportunity to take courses in adapted physical education so they will be able to approach their students with greater understanding. Course work in adapted physical education should also be made available to undergraduates.

The teacher of adapted physical education should also understand the student with the atypical condition—the various atypical conditions, their causes, and treatment. The teacher should like to work with students who need special help and be able to establish a good rapport to instill confidence in the work that needs to be done. The teacher should appreciate the various mental and emotional problems confronting an atypical person and the methods and procedures that can be followed to cope with these problems. The teacher must in some ways be a psychologist, creating interest and stimulating motivation toward physical activity for the purpose of hastening improvement. The teacher should be sympathetic to the advice of medical personnel. She or he should be willing to give corrective exercise under the guidance of physicians and to plan the program with their help. It is also necessary to know the implications of medical and other findings for the adapted physical education program, to be familiar with the medical, psychological, or other examinations of each student, and, with the help of the physician, psychologist, social worker, or other specialist, to work out a program that best meets the needs of the student.

Administrative principles

The following statement was prepared for general use in schools and colleges rather than for special schools for handicapped children. It was approved by the Board of Directors, American Alliance for Health, Physical Education, and Recreation, and endorsed in principle by the Joint Committee on Health Problems in Education, American Medical Association, and National Education Association:

It is the responsibility of the school to contribute to the fullest possible development of the potentialities of each individual entrusted to its care. This is a basic tenet of our democratic faith.

1. *There is a need for common understanding regarding the nature of "adapted physical education."*

Adapted physical education is a diversified program of developmental activities, games, and sports suited to the interests, capacities, and limitations of students with disabilities who may not safely or successfully engage in unrestricted participation in the vigorous activities of the general program.

2. *There is a need for "adapted physical education" in schools and colleges.*

The number of children of school age in the United States with physical handicaps is alarmingly high. Of the 33,500,000 in the age groups five to nineteen, approximately 4,000,000 children have physical handicaps which need some kind of special educational consideration. (Of these, 65,000 are blind or partially seeing; 335,000, orthopedic disabilities; and 500,000 each, deaf or hard of hearing, organic heart disease, and delicate or undeveloped.) The major disabling conditions each affecting thousands of children are cerebral palsy, poliomyelitis, tuberculosis, traumatic injuries, and heart disease. Further evidence indicates that, on the college level, there is a significant percentage of students who require special consideration for temporary or permanent disabilities.

3. *"Adapted physical education" has much to offer the individual who faces the combined problem of seeking an education and overcoming a handicap.*

"Adapted physical education" should serve the individual by:

(a) Aiding in discovering deviations from the normal and making appropriate referrals where such conditions are noted.

(b) Guiding students in the avoidance of situations which would aggravate their conditions or subject them to undue risks of injury.

(c) Improving general strength and endurance of individuals who are poorly developed and of those returning to school following illness or injury.

(d) Providing opportunities for needed social and psychological adjustment.

Fig. 4-7. A physical education instructor involved with helping a handicapped student.

Courtesy Arnold College Division, University of Bridgeport, Conn., Parents and Friends Association of Mentally Retarded Children. Photograph by John Tasker.

4. *The direct and related services essential for the proper conduct of adapted physical education should be available in our schools.*

These services should include:

(a) Adequate and periodic health examinations.

(b) Classification for physical education based on the health examination and other pertinent tests and observations.

(c) Guidance of individuals needing special consideration with respect to physical activity, general health practices, recreational pursuits, and vocational planning.

(d) Arrangement of appropriate physical education programs.

(e) Evaluation of progress through observations, appropriate measurements, and consultations.

(f) Integrated relationships with other school personnel, medical and its auxiliary services, and the family to assure continuous guidance and supervisory services.

(g) A cumulative record for each individual, which should be transferred from school to school.

5. *It is essential that adequate medical guidance be available for teachers of adapted physical education.*

Programs of adapted physical education should not be attempted without the diagnosis, written recommendation, and supervision of a physician. Problems of correction may be very profound. Where corrective measures are deemed necessary, they must be predicated upon medical findings and accomplished by competent teachers working with medical supervision and guidance. There should be an effective referral service between physicians, physical education, and parents, aimed at proper safeguards and maximum student benefits.

6. *Teachers of adapted physical education have a great responsibility as well as unusual opportunity.*

Physical educators engaged in teaching adapted physical education should have adequate professional education fitting them for this work. They must be motivated by the highest ideals with respect to the importance of total student development and satisfactory human relationships. They must have the ability to establish rapport with students who may exhibit social maladjustment as a disability. It is essential that they be professionally prepared to implement the recommendations provided by medical personnel for the adapted physical education program.

7. *Adapted physical education is necessary at all school levels.*

The student with a disability faces the dual problem of overcoming a handicap and acquiring an education which will enable him (her) to take his (her) place in society as a respected citizen. Failure to assist a student with his (her) problems may sharply curtail the growth and development process. Offering adapted physical education in the elementary grades, and continuing through the secondary school and college, will assist the individual to improve function and make adequate psychological and social adjustments. It will prevent attitudes of defeat and fears of insecurity. It will be a factor in his (her) attaining maximum growth and development within the limits of the disability. It will help him (her) face the future with confidence.

Mainstreaming

Mainstreaming means that handicapped persons receive their education, including physical education, with persons who are not handicapped, unless the nature of the handicap is such that education in the regular classroom or gymnasium setting cannot be achieved satisfactorily, even with the use of supplementary aids and services. The federal law does not mean that all handicapped children will be a part of the regular class. It does mean that those handicapped students who can profit from having their physical education with regular students should be assigned to regular classes.

Advocates of mainstreaming point out the following advantages:

1. Some psychological testing has been questioned, and tests that have labeled many students as retarded have proved to be unreliable; therefore, many of these students should be in regular classes.

2. Fiscal considerations encourage mainstreaming, because special education with segregated and special classes increases educational costs.

3. Classifying and segregating handicapped students who are retarded result in labeling and cause harm to children.

4. The research does not convincingly show that handicapped children advance scholastically faster when segregated than when grouped with children in the regular classroom.

5. The American way suggests an integration of all types of children into the classroom situation.

6. Many educators are convinced that the nonhandicapped child gains in understanding by exposure to handicapped children.

7. Handicapped children benfit socially and emotionally when they are a part of regular classes.

PRINCIPLES THAT APPLY TO MAINSTREAMING

Some principles that should apply and guide the mainstreaming concept follow:

1. All students should be provided satisfactory learning experiences, whether they are nonhandicapped or handicapped.

2. Class size should be such that all students can receive an adequate educational offering and effective teaching.

3. Facilities should be adapted to meet the needs of all students, including the handicapped (such as providing ramps, if necessary).

4. Mainstreaming should be used only for those students who can benefit from such a practice. In other words, some handicapped students may benefit more from special classes.

5. Periodic evaluation should take place to determine objectively the effectiveness of mainstreaming in terms of students' progress.

6. Adequate supportive personnel, such as a speech therapist or a person trained in physical education for the handicapped, should be provided for handicapped students.

7. The administration should support the program and make it possible for those teachers involved in such a program to have the necessary instructional supplies, space, time, and resources necessary to adequately do the job required.

8. Adequate preservice and inservice teacher preparation should be provided for all teachers who will be involved in working with handicapped students.

LOS ANGELES CITY SCHOOL DISTRICTS
Health Education and Health Services Branch—Auxiliary Services Division
Corrective Physical Education Section

CORRECTIVE PHYSICAL EDUCATION ACTIVITY GUIDE
A Guide for the Teacher and Physician
In Planning a Restricted Program of Physical Education

Pupil _____ Date_____

School_____ Corrective Phys. Ed. Teacher_____

I. TYPES OF MOVEMENTS	OMIT	*MILD	**MODERATE	UNLIMITED	REMARKS
Bending					
Climbing					
Hanging					
Jumping					
Kicking					
Lifting					
Pulling					
Pushing					
Running					
Stretching					
Throwing					
Twisting					

II. TYPES OF EXERCISES	OMIT	*MILD	**MODERATE	UNLIMITED	REMARKS
Abdominal					
Arm					
Breathing					
Foot					
Head					
Knee					
Leg					
Trunk					
Relaxation					

III. TYPES OF POSITIONS	LIMITED	UNLIMITED
Lying supine		
Lying prone		
Sitting		
Standing		

Recommended until_____ 196_

Remarks:

IV. TYPES OF ACTIVITIES	YES	NO
Competitive sports		
Games——Sitting		
Games requiring standing but no running or jumping		
Officiating		
Swimming		
Coeducational activities		
Social dancing		
Square dancing		
Sports and games		

_____
Signature of Physician

*Very little activity.
**Half as much as the unlimited program.

Fig. 4-8. A guide for planning restricted physical education program for students.

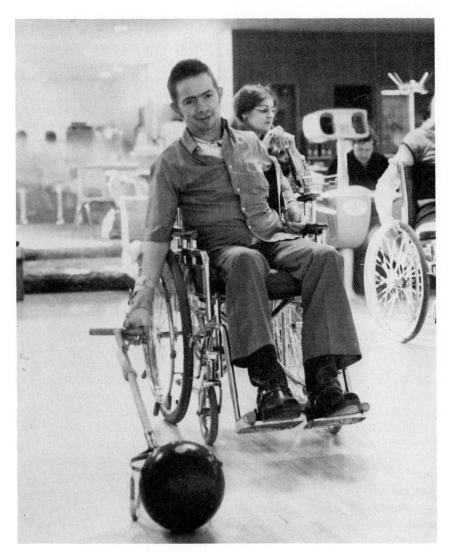

Fig. 4-9. Adapted physical education can enable many handicapped individuals to realize the joy of sports. A patient participating in a bowling program, using bowling device for quadriplegics.

Younker Memorial Rehabilitation Center, Iowa Methodist Hospital, Des Moines, Iowa.

9. To assure full public support, and school should carry on an adequate public information program to ensure that parents, the community, and the general public are aware of the program, its needs, and what it is doing for children.

A NEW CONCEPT OF MAINSTREAMING

The traditional definition of mainstreaming is to take handicapped students from a special class and have them become a part of the regular class with nonhandicapped students. In recent years, this definition has lost favor among some special educators and other teachers who believe that students are frequently placed into the regular class without any support services or modification of regular class instructional procedures. A new concept of mainstreaming being favored by more educators today is that of providing educational services for handicapped students in the "least restrictive environment." In essence, this means that a handicapped child is placed in a special class or a regular class or is moved between the two environments as dictated by his or her abilities and capabilities. Furthermore, the school assumes the responsibility of providing the necessary adjunct services to ensure that handicapped students perform to their optimum capacity, whether integrated into the regular program or left in a special class.

According to many educators, mainstreaming can be successful if certain basic practices are adhered to before and during the process of mainstreaming. The handicapped person should be placed in the educational environment that produces optimal growth and development, that is, the "least restrictive environment." Stein, formerly of the American Alliance for Health, Physical Education, Recreation, and Dance, states "the idea behind mainstreaming is that if an individual can safely, successfully, and with personal satisfaction take part in a regular program or in unrestricted activities, no special program is necessary."* However, this should be viewed as the ideal. It must be realized that some handicapped students must be educated in special self-contained classrooms. Other

handicapped individuals might be able to benefit from some services in a regular class and some activities in the special class.

THE DEVELOPMENTAL CONCEPT—AN AID TO MAINSTREAMING

The use of the developmental approach to programming for handicapped persons will help to promote positive and successful mainstreaming. This approach involves individual planning of educational programs. This developmental concept of education rejects the notion of rigid categories that result in people being stigmatized. Rather, it advances the notion that each individual must progress through a hierarchy of developmental tasks. In other words, each person grows and develops in a sequential pattern in all domains—physically, mentally, emotionally, and socially. By observing behavior manifestations in each of these developmental areas, and on an individual basis, instructional programs can be planned. Crowe, Auxter, and Pyfer* have provided a thorough presentation of the application of the developmental concept.

MAINSTREAMING IN A PHYSICAL EDUCATION PROGRAM FOR HANDICAPPED PERSONS

Physical education is a subject where much can be done for handicapped students if they are mainstreamed, provided the physical educators in charge understand handicapped individuals and the type of program that will best meet their needs. Whether or not the program is successful depends on the teacher and his or her ability to individualize the offering to meet the needs of each student in the class. It is essential to select the program of activities carefully, to begin where the student is at present, and to let the capabilities of the individual determine his or her progress.

The physical educator should use several approaches in teaching various types of handicapped students. A thorough medical examination should be a first step. Personal assistance will be needed from time to time. Modification of the activities will be necessary in many cases. Rapid progress in skill de-

---

*Stein, J.U.: Sense and nonsense about mainstreaming, Journal of Physical Education and Recreation **47**:43, January 1976.

*Crowe, Auxter, and Pyfer, op. cit.

Fig. 4-10. Physical education for the handicapped.

Courtesy South Carolina School for the Deaf and the Blind, Spartanburg, S.C.

velopment should not be expected. Handicapped students should feel they have achieved and are successful in their efforts. Complete records on each student should be kept, with notations concerning the nature of the handicap, recommendations of the physician, and appropriate and inappropriate activities.

Each handicapped student must be made to feel a part of the physical education program. For example, mentally retarded children should gain self-confidence, and physically handicapped students should have fun meeting the challenges that certain activities and exercises provide. In addition, the activities should be challenging and at the same time rewarding for the development of a positive self-concept. Some handicapped students should be taught leisure time activities and ways to play. The need for physical fitness should be stressed. Finally, it is important to stress safety, not to underestimate a student's abilities, and to remember that many handicapped children have a short attention span, tire easily, and are easily distracted.

Suggested administrative procedures for implementing PL 94-142

Cole and Dunn have suggested the following administrative procedures for implementing PL 94-142.*

1. Develop task forces on a local and regional basis and appoint people to leadership positions who know about the law.
2. Appoint someone with responsibility to implement the law and also see that the implementation processes are prescribed in writing.
3. Establish a series of workshops to orient administration and staff personnel to the various components of the law and implementation procedures.
4. Request information about the law and its implementation from organizations concerned with special education.

*Adapted from Cole, R.W., and Dunn, R.: A new lease on life for education of the handicapped: Ohio copes with PL 94-142, Phi Delta Kappan **59**:3, September 1977.

5. Simulate team placement conferences so that administration and staff may become better informed of their responsibilities, the instructional strategies involved, and other administrative details in providing for handicapped students.
6. Prepare a brochure on the program for parents, outlining their rights and the rights of children under the law. Also, explain procedures that may be used and programs under consideration.
7. Organize workshops for administrative and staff personnel to familiarize them with different instructional strategies for individualizing instruction and to acquaint them with the relationships between learning style characteristics and these instructional strategies.
8. Visit schools that are already providing excellent programs under PL 94-142, find out what practices are successful, and get suggestions for implementing the program.
9. Develop a curriculum that meets the needs of various types of handicapped students, including the preparation of such features as learning packages, contract activity packages, multisensory instructional packages, and resource lists for teachers.
10. Involve parents and students in the provision of resources and in helping handicapped students.
11. Decide carefully which students will be mainstreamed and which ones will not be.
12. Encourage all teachers to individualize instruction so that handicapped students will be integrated into their classes as easily as possible.
13. Have all teachers, whether teaching regular or special classes, participate on the reevaluation team.
14. Simplify instructional materials so that they may be easily understood by the students.
15. Participate in regional, state, and national conferences on the implementation of PL 94-142 to discover new techniques and means of instruction that have proved effective in other schools.

Suggested organizational structures for handicapped students

Various organizational structures have been suggested to provide for students with varying degrees of handicapping conditions. Some students may have severe handicaps, and some may have mild handicaps. The organizational structure selected should meet the needs of each student.

Some organizational structures that should be considered include the following:

1. Students placed in special classes
2. Students placed in regular classes, with or without supported services
3. Students placed in special classes for part of the school day
4. Students placed in a special residential school
5. Students provided for at home
6. Students placed in regular classes with supplementary services provided
7. Students placed in special schools that are a part of the public school system
8. Students provided for by utilizing a special diagnostic program

Puthoff* suggests that the following four organizational structures should be considered in physical education:

1. *Integrated or combined class.* Handicapped students are placed in regular classes with modifications made where necessary in respect to goals, activities, and methodology. Individualized instruction is provided and based on a student's needs, interests, goals, and present status. Individual activities, such as track and field and gymnastics, are suggested, because performance in these activities does not affect the success or failure of other students, as is the case with team sports.

2. *Dual class structure.* Handicapped students are placed in an integrated class setting part of the time and in a setting where they can concentrate on their individual needs the rest of the time. Such an arrangement is not to be thought of as remedial instruction. Instead, individual special needs are met when the students are not in an integrated class setting.

3. *Separate class.* Handicapped students are placed in a class separate from the regular physical education class. The reasons for this type of classification could be that students are not yet ready for the regular class or that their handicap is too severe to permit them to participate with nonhandicapped stu-

---

*Puthoff, M.: Instructional strategies for mainstreaming. In Mainstreaming physical education, National Association for Physical Education for College Women and The National College Physical Education Association for Men, Briefing 4, 1976.

dents. Handicapped students who are assigned permanently to separate classes, however, would be in the regular school setting and would have the opportunity to interact with nonhandicapped students during noninstructional hours and experiences. In this way they would not be separated from their nonhandicapped counterparts by being in a separate school.

4. *Flexible model plan.* Handicapped students are placed in regular classes when they can safely and successfully participate in the activities provided and are placed in a separate class when more individualized instruction and experiences are needed because of their handicap.

Suggested instructional strategies for teaching handicapped students

In addition to organizational structures, there is a need to consider what methods will be most effective in teaching handicapped students. Again, as with organizational structures, these methods will vary with the nature of the handicap each child has.

Puthoff* lists four instructional strategies that can be used when teaching physical education to handicapped students, as follows:

1. *Modification of content.* The goal in teaching the handicapped student is to individualize instruction, modifying such elements as goals, behavioral objectives, and activities to meet individual differences. Instructional objectives can be differentiated according to each student's needs, skills, and knowledge. Behavioral objectives can be differentiated in respect to learning outcomes and competencies expected from the handicapped child. Individual selection of activities or modification in these activities can be provided to meet the needs of students.

2. *Modification of learning rate.* The learning rate for the handicapped student can be modified whereby the student sets his or her own pace of learning.

3. *Teaching and learning style options.* The amount of time a teacher spends with each student can be differentiated. This is based on the premise that some students will require more teacher help than others. Furthermore, visual aids and other techniques

will enable some students to move ahead independently in achieving their instructional goals.

4. *Internal class environmental settings.* Within a class the teacher can create different settings to provide for the needs of each handicapped student. For example, there may be opportunities to use methods that involve large and small group instruction, independent study, and an open gymnasium.

Facilities, equipment, and supplies

Appropriate and adequate facilities, equipment, and supplies are important to successful programs of physical education for handicapped persons. However, these items must be emphasized in special or adapted physical education programs because facilities and equipment are designed for students in the regular class. Adaptations are also often necessary when handicapped students are mainstreamed into regular programs.

The passage of recent legislation and the results of various legal decisions have prompted school districts to make available the necessary facilities, equipment, and supplies to ensure a quality education for handicapped students. There is some question, however, about whether handicapped students are being provided with adequate facilities, equipment, and supplies. They are not, according to Stein, a recognized authority on problems of handicapped persons. He believes that "despite federal legislation, mandates in every state, and regulations in some local areas, facilities of all types continue to be built and renovated without consideration of barriers, accessibility, and availability [to the handicapped person]." Stein states that the major problem and cause of these situations and conditions are "attitudinal barriers."*

The types of facilities and equipment needed for adapted physical education will vary according to the nature of the program (adapted sports, remedial or corrective exercises, or rest and relaxation), the type of student (mentally retarded, physically handi-

---

*Puthoff, op. cit.

*American Alliance for Health, Physical Education, and Recreation: Making physical education and recreation facilities accessible to all: planning, designing, adapting, Washington, D.C., 1977, The Alliance, p. i.

capped, or some other), and the school level at which the program is conducted. For example, the elementary school program in adapted physical education may be taught in the regular gymnasium, or in less desirable circumstances, in the classroom. In secondary schools and colleges, however, a special room for adapted physical education should be provided.

The Virginia State Department of Education, in its instructional booklet of *Physical Education for Handicapped Students,* outlines some of the factors that should be taken into consideration for handicapped students. A few of these factors are as follows:

Within building
Doors easy to open
Ramps with handrails on both sides
Elevators or chair lifts when necessary
Floors with nonslip surfaces
Toilet seats of proper height with rails provided

Outside building
Loading and parking areas close to entrances
Convenient parking places
Ramps suitable for wheelchairs
Doorways wide enough for wheelchairs
Emergency exits for wheelchairs

Adaptive physical education equipment (for bowling)
Providing a wheelchair student with a bowling ball ramp
Providing a blind student with a bowling rail
Providing a student with limited strength with lightweight, plastic bowling balls and pins

Contribution of physical education to various types of atypical conditions*

No one way exists to group students in the adapted program. As has been indicated, many different types of boys and girls are in the program. It would be wise for the physical educator to sit down with the school physician, school psychologist, and nurse and include in their planning the various types of atypical students they have in their institution. The discussion in this section includes the following atypical conditions: (1) physically handicapped, (2) mentally retarded, (3)

emotionally disturbed, (4) learning disabled, (5) multihandicapped, (6) culturally disadvantaged, (7) poorly coordinated, and (8) physically gifted and creative students.

PHYSICALLY HANDICAPPED STUDENTS

Whatever the physical disability, a physical education program must be provided. Some handicapped students will be able to participate in a regular program of physical education with certain minor modifications. A separate adapted program must be provided for those students who cannot participate in the basic instructional program of the school. The physically handicapped student cannot be allowed to sit on the sidelines and become only a spectator. The handicapped student needs to have the opportunity to develop and maintain adequate skill abilities and fitness levels.

Physical handicaps, which may stem from congenital or hereditary causes or may develop later in life through environmental factors, such as malnutrition, disease, or accident, sometimes cause negative psychological and social traits to develop because of the limitations imposed on the individual. Physically handicapped students are occasionally ignored or rebuffed by classmates who do not understand the nature of the disability or who ostracize them because the disability prevents them from participating fully in the activities of the school. These attitudes toward the handicapped force them to withdraw to avoid becoming hurt and result in their becoming further isolated from the remainder of the students.

Some experts have noted that the limitations of the handicap often seem more severe to the observer than they are in fact to the handicapped individual. When this misconception occurs, the handicapped student must prove his or her abilities to gain acceptance and a chance to participate and compete equally with nonhandicapped classmates.

The blind or deaf student or the student with a severe speech impairment has a different set of problems from the orthopedically handicapped student. The partially sighted, the blind, the deaf, and the speech-impaired student cannot communicate easily. The orthopedically handicapped student is limited in the physical education class but not necessarily

*Parts of this section have been adapted from Bucher, C.A., and Thaxton, N.: Physical education and sport, change and challenge, St. Louis, 1981, The C.V. Mosby Co.

in the academic classroom. The student with vision, hearing, or speech problems may be limited in both physical education and the academic classroom.

Very often there is a tendency toward overprotection of handicapped children. Recent programs, however, have specifically included the visually handicapped child in the regular physical education program. Injuries and accidents among these children were proved to be negligible. The purposes of having these children participate in regular physical education programs are to provide activities with their peers and to aid them in developing skills in lifetime sport areas so they can enjoy these sports outside school and in later life.

Some handicapped students will be able to participate in almost all the activities that nonhandicapped students enjoy. Blind students have successfully engaged in team sports where they can receive oral cues from their sighted teammates. Some athletic equipment manufacturers have placed bells inside game balls; the blind student is then able to rely on this sound, as well as on supplementary oral cues. Ropes or covered wires acting as hand guides also enable the blind student to participate in track and field events. Still other activities such as swimming, dance, calisthenics, and tumbling require little adaptation or none at all, except regarding heightened safety precautions.

In general, deaf students will not be restricted in any way from participating in a full physical education program. Some deaf students experience difficulty in activities requiring precise balance, such as balance beam walking, and may require some remedial work in this area. The physical educator should be prepared to offer any extra help needed.

Other physically handicapped students will have a variety of limitations and a variety of skill abilities. Appropriate program adaptations and modifications must be made to meet this range of individual needs. The physician is the individual most knowledgeable about the history and limitations of a student's handicap.

The student's abilities and levels of fitness should be tested in those areas where medical permission for participation has been granted. This will not only help to ensure a proper program for the individual but will also help in placing the student in the proper class or section of a class. Careful records should be kept showing the student's test scores, activity recommendations, activities, and progress through the program.

Organized competition for the handicapped has been successful and meaningful for its participants. An innovative competitive program in the form of an "activity day" was introduced at Cypress Orthopedic School in California. This activity day served as a climax to the learning of physical skills developed as a part of the vigorous physical education program. Such activities as a wheelchair beanbag race, balloon bounce, and crutch walking race demonstrated some of the activities these children can and do participate in.

Physically handicapped students need the challenge of a progressive program. They welcome the opportunity to test their abilities, and they should experience the fun of a challenge and the success of meeting it. The handicapped should be given an opportunity to seek extra help and extra practice after school hours. During this time they can benefit from more individualized instruction than is possible during the class period. The fitness level of each student, his or her ability, recreational needs, sex, age, and interests will help to determine the activities the student will engage in pleasurably. Safe facilities and safe equipment are essential. Intramural and club programs should be provided, but they should be such that physically handicapped students can enjoy them in a safe and controlled atmosphere that precludes the danger of injury.

Some suggestions for physical education programming

The nature and extent of physical handicaps differ widely, resulting in many functional levels and capacities. Therefore physical activities should be modified according to the person's functional ability, for example, persons who have prosthetic devices or persons who use canes or crutches.

The basic instructional and program strategies for any sound physical education program should be observed when teaching handicapped students. However, certain other guidelines may be helpful when teaching students with physical handicaps.*†

1. Obtain medical approval for the planned program.

2. If the person with the physical handicap is receiving physical therapy, the program of physical education should be planned to complement the therapeutic exercises.

3. Plan an individualized program of exercises and activities to meet the special needs of each student.

4. Be aware of the dangers of twisting, bending, falling, and lifting motions for those persons with spinal cord impairments such as spina bifida (a congenital abnormality characterized by a developmental defect in one or more vertebral arches through which the contents of the spinal canal may protrude.‡ Because of a lack of motor dexterity and the increased possibilities for further injury, including paralysis, the teacher should be extremely careful of the types of physical activities included in a physical education program for persons with spina bifida.

5. In activities in which there is an impairment or disability of the lower extremities, substitute sitting or lying positions for standing positions. When the person is fitted with a prosthetic device, wears braces, or is able to ambulate with a cane or crutches, physical activities may be modified whereby the handicapped person can participate while standing.

6. Provide frequent periods of rest and less vigorous games and activities for those with limited endurance.

7. Use the maximum number of sensory modalities appropriate for a specific physical impairment or disability. For example, visual communication would not be used for students with visual handicaps, but kinesthetic stimuli (guiding the body parts through the desired movement), tactile stimuli (use of touch to relate to the person which body part is to be used), and verbal stimuli (oral instructions) would be emphasized.

8. Teach the person with an orthopedic handicap to fall

correctly from crutches, wheelchairs, or unsupported positions.

9. Have the nonhandicapped students simulate the handicap to gain a better insight into the problems and difficulties handicapped students face in performing physical activities. For example, require students to use only one hand for some activities in classes in which there are some students with only one hand.

10. Promote self-acceptance and help to instill confidence in handicapped students by providing opportunities whereby they can achieve success.

11. Help the students develop skills and talents that compensate for a physical disability or impairment. The person who has paralysis of the lower limbs and is confined to a wheelchair, for instance, might be taught and encouraged to develop the upper body through weight training. Such a person might also be taught track and field skills that require only the use of the upper body, such as the discus and javeline throw.

12. Help alleviate a student's fears about dressing and showering with others if that student has an obvious deformity or loss of limb. This objective might be accomplished by having a talk with the student about the handicap and helping him or her find a solution that is satisfying and realistic. The student should be encouraged to meet the challenges of his or her handicap with humor rather than with fear of ridicule or embarrassment.

13. Provide body awareness activities to compensate for the loss of limb or lack of mobility. Specific activities for body awareness might include the teacher pointing to different parts of the body and asking the students to do the same, the teacher asking students to draw pictures of themselves, the teacher requiring the students to play games such as "Do This, Do That" and "Simon Says," in which they have to point to and move different parts of their bodies on command.

14. Provide exercise programs that increase range of motion, alleviate contractures, and improve postural maintenance, balance, muscular power, endurance, and coordination. For example, exercises such as the gorilla walk (flexibility and coordination), frog stand (balance and arm strength), and wheelbarrow (arm, shoulder, and abdominal strength) might be used.*

15. Pay special attention to the concept of progression

---

*Adapted from Geddes, D.: Physical activities for individuals with handicapping conditions, ed. 2, St. Louis, 1978, The C.V. Mosby Co., pp. 105-106.

†Most books on adapted physical education contain information specifically related to the organization of programs and teaching strategies for physically handicapped students. For example, see Geddes; Crowe, Auxter, and Pyfer; and Fait.

‡Adams, R.: Program implications for children with orthopedic and related impairments. In AAHPER: Physical education and recreation for impaired, disabled, and handicapped individuals: past, present, and future, Washington, D.C., 1975, The Alliance, p. 125.

*These are three of the suggested exercises for the primary grades for developing physical fitness. These and other exercises suggested for primary through intermediate grades were recommended by the President's Council on Physical Fitness and Sports. See Bucher and Thaxton for a description of these exercises.

Fig. 4-11. Boy being helped in adapted physical education program at the University of Bridgeport.

Courtesy Arnold College Division, University of Bridgeport, Conn., Parents and Friends Association of Mentally Retarded Children. Photograph by John Tasker.

for students who have been inactive for a long time. Often these students need a period of relearning; therefore, start with basic movement skills and body mechanics, stressing large muscle activity. Gradually include modified or adapted activities requiring specific fine motor activities.

16. Modify ambulatory or locomotor activities for those students with lower extremity impairments. For example, students in a relay race might be required to hop instead of run when there are students in the class with only one leg.

MENTALLY RETARDED STUDENTS

Mental retardation can be a result of hereditary abnormalities, birth injury, or an accident or illness that leads to impairment of brain function. Degrees of mental retardation range from the severely mentally retarded, who require custodial care, to the educable mentally retarded, who function with only a moderate degree of impairment.

Many agencies are conducting research in mental retardation to try to discover the causes and nature of mental retardation and the methods through which retardation may be prevented. Some agencies are operating innovative training schools for the mentally retarded. The Joseph P. Kennedy, Jr., Foundation is spearheading much of the research concerned with mental retardation and is also a leader in providing camping and recreational programs for the mentally retarded. The Kennedy Foundation has also sponsored training programs for teachers of the mentally retarded. The United States government is sponsoring experimental physical education programs for mentally retarded persons staffed by special education teachers, specially trained physical educators, vocational rehabilitation technicians, and architectural engineers. Special programs and special equipment have been designed especially for the mentally retarded. Climbing devices, obstacle courses, and unique running areas, as well as a swimming pool, are part of the special facilities. The objectives of this program include social and personal adjustment and development of physical fitness, sports skills, and general motor ability.

Mentally retarded students show a wide range of intellectual and physical abilities. Experts seem to agree that a mentally retarded person is usually closer to the norm for chronological age in physical development than in mental development. Some mentally

Fig. 4-12. Special fitness awards for the mentally retarded, AAHPERD—Kennedy Foundation.

retarded students are capable of participating in a regular physical education class, whereas others have been able to develop only minimal amounts of motor ability. In general, most mentally retarded students are 2 to 4 years behind their normal peers in motor development alone.

Despite a slower development of motor ability, mentally retarded students seem to reach physical maturity faster than do nonretarded students of the same chronological age. The mentally retarded tend to be overweight and to lack physical strength and endurance. Their posture is generally poor, and they lack adequate levels of physical fitness and motor coordination. Some of these physical problems develop because the mentally retarded have had little of the play and physical activity experiences of normal children. The problems of some mentally retarded youngsters are further multiplied by attendant physical handicaps and personality disturbances.

The mentally retarded require a physical educator with special training, special skills, and a special brand of patience because they lack confidence and pride and need a physical educator who will help them change their negative self-image. The physical educator must be able to provide a program designed to give each student a chance for success and be ready to praise and reinforce each minor success. He or she must be capable of demonstrating each skill, given simple and concise directions, and be willing to participate in physical education activities with the students. Discipline must be enforced and standards adhered to, but the disciplinary approach must be kind and gentle.

The physical educator must be especially mindful of the individual characteristics of each mentally retarded student. Students who need remedial work should be afforded this opportunity, whereas students who can succeed in a regular physical education program should be placed in such a class or section.

Most mentally retarded students need to be taught how to play. They are frequently unfamiliar with even the simplest of childhood games, and they lack facility in the natural movements of childhood, such as skipping, hopping, and leaping. The mentally retarded are often seriously deficient in physical fitness and need work in postural improvement. Further, the mentally retarded find it difficult to understand and remember game strategy, such as the importance of staying in the right position, and cannot relate well to the rules of sports and games.

The majority of mentally retarded students need a specially tailored physical education experience. For students who can participate in a regular physical education class, care must be taken so that they are not placed in a situation where they will meet failure. Physical fitness and posture improvement, along with self-testing activities and games organized and designed according to the ability and interests of the group, will make up a vital part of the program. Activities can be easily modified and new experiences introduced before interest wanes. Research has indicated that specially tailored physical education classes can help mentally retarded students progress rapidly in their physical skill development. Movement education is especially suited to the mentally retarded. These students have often not engaged in the natural play activities of childhood and need to develop their gross motor skill abilities to find success in some of the more sophisticated motor skills.

There are many new and exciting innovations in physical education programs for mentally retarded youngsters. The AAHPERD-Kennedy Foundation Special Fitness Awards program encourages retarded children and youths to engage in vigorous physical activities to compete in the Olympics for the retarded. To qualify for these Olympics, the child must first earn the ''champ'' award. The three awards given are silver, gold, and champ. Standards of performance are based on a national sample of educable retarded children. To achieve awards in this program, the child must meet the standards of seven test items and spend 30 hours in active sports participation within a 3-month period.

In July, 1968, the first International Special Olympics for mentally retarded boys and girls was held at Chicago's Soldier Field. More than 1,000 boys and girls participated. The Olympics are currently held regularly.

Olympics programs for children with all types of handicaps including retardation have also been held. The first Special Olympics was held in southwest Cook County, Illinois, and involved the entire community in the program. Children were divided into nonphysically handicapped and physically handicapped groups and then into chronological age, ability, and sex groupings.

Some suggestions for physical education programming

The scope of the program for mentally retarded persons should include such activities as swimming, basic movement skills, self-testing, gymnastics and tumbling, trampolining, rhythms and dance, and some of the simple individual and dual games. Team games and others that require extensive rules and strategy should not be included because of the limited intellectual development and low frustration level of the retarded persons.

Because of the great diversity among mentally retarded persons, specific guidelines would not be meaningful or very helpful. However, there are some general suggestions that might prove beneficial to teachers or leaders of programs for mentally retarded persons.*

1. Base the selection of activities on the present level of functioning of the mentally retarded person. Classifications of retarded persons should be used only as a guide for describing the needs, abilities, and characteristics of individuals and the remediation required.

2. Be aware of the extremely slow process of learning and achievement in mentally retarded persons. Constant repetition, drill, and review of skills are needed more often than with nonretarded persons.

3. Consider the principle of progression—from the known to the unknown and from the simple to the complex. When teaching young educable mentally retarded persons, for example, start with a program of activities that stresses basic movement skills, such as running, climbing on stall bars, tumbling, and bouncing on a small trampoline. Once these children learn to control their bodies through basic movement activities, they might be taught simple activities (hopscotch, croquet, ring toss, and the like) that require the use of these basic movement skills.

4. Provide for vigorous physical acitvity on a daily basis. Because research has shown that the mentally retarded as a group are less developed physically then nonretarded persons, the provision of regular, vigorous physical activity in the physical education program is an important objective.

5. Provide opportunities for group interaction to foster social development and coping skills. Including simple group games and lead-up games to team sports in the program and teaching recreational games that can be played and enjoyed by the family (bowling, bicycling, fishing, sledding, and so on) are ways of fostering the development of social interaction and acceptable social traits. Having retarded youngsters work on group assignments such as setting-up and removing equipment, marking off

*Adapted from AAHPERD: Recreation and physical activity for the mentally retarded, Washington, D.C., 1966, The Alliance.

fields, and planning a short story or physical activity for class is another means of developing desirable social behavior.

6. Introduce new or complex activities at the start of the class when students are fresh and alert. For example, do not introduce tumbling and gymnastic skills to the class during the last 15 minutes, after group games have been taught for the first 15 minutes of class.

7. Be firm in the exercise of discipline but also be fair and consistent.

8. Do not remain with one activity too long because of the short attention span of the children; provide for many and varied activities.

9. Make instructions short and simple. Demonstrate often.

10. Remove a disruptive person temporarily from the class situation and deal with him or her in a small group or individually.

11. If discipline is a constant problem during a particular activity, consider the appropriateness of the skill or activity being taught. The activity possibly requires too much skill, has too many rules, or entails too many verbal instructions.

12. Correlate physical activities with basic classroom activities to reinforce academic concepts, for example, use games such as hopscotch and the bean bag toss to teach word recognition and number concepts. Specifically, arrange the letters of the alphabet in the blocks of a hopscotch drawing. Have the children hop from one box to another, and require them to say the letter on which they hop, spell out words, and so on. When numbers are placed in the blocks, mathematics concepts can be taught. Students may also use bean bags to toss in the boxes that contain either letters or numbers to reinforce alphabet or word recognition and number concepts.

13. Do not expect much transfer of skill to be made by retarded youngsters from one activity to another. Be prepared to assist them in making generalizations by emphasizing the common principles of the skills. In teaching the high jump in track and field and the jump for a rebound in basketball, for instance, emphasize the lowering of the body by bending at the knees and the upward thrust of the arms for added momentum.

14. Provide a wide range of stimuli in teaching skills:
   a. Tactile stimuli—Use touch to relate more effectively the body part to be used in a skill. Touching the triceps muscle when asking the person to perform a push-up is one example of the use of tactile stimulation.
   b. Kinesthetic stimuli—Manually guide the body parts through the desired movement to give the person the feeling of the movement pattern. An example of this principle is manually turning a child's head in the water when teaching rhythmic breathing.
   c. Visual stimuli—Use visual aids such as diagrams, wall posters, demonstrations, and films. Using film strips in teaching tennis strokes is an example of visual stimuli.
   d. Verbal stimuli—Use oral instructions in teaching. Keep verbal instructions to a minimum when teaching mentally retarded persons, especially severely retarded persons.

15. Extend free and lavish praise for good performances.

16. For severely and profoundly retarded persons, alternate short periods of activity, work, and rest. Anticipate when these individuals are tired and make changes accordingly.

17. Structure and administer the program whereby all children will experience some success.

EMOTIONALLY DISTURBED STUDENTS

Emotionally disturbed students present special problems for the physical educator, who must be concerned not only with teaching but also with the safety of the students in the class.

A single emotionally disturbed student can have a disastrous effect on a class and can affect the behavior of the rest of the students in that class. Effective teaching cannot take place when discipline deteriorates.

Emotionally unstable students have difficulty maintaining good relationships with their classmates and teachers. Some of their abnormal behavior patterns stem from a need and craving for attention. Sometimes the disruptive student exhibits gross patterns of aggressiveness and destructiveness. Other emotionally unstable students may be so withdrawn from the group that they refuse to participate in the activities of the class, even to the extent of refusing to report for class. In the case of physical education, the emotionally disturbed student may refuse to dress for the activity when he or she does report. Such behavior draws both student and teacher reaction and focuses attention on the nonconforming student.

Emotionally unstable students are often restless and unable to pay attention. In a physical education class they may poke and prod other students, refuse to line up with the rest of the class, or insist on bouncing a game ball while a lesson is in progress. These are also ploys to gain attention. The student may behave similarly in the academic classroom for the same reason.

Some emotionally disturbed students may have physical or mental handicaps that contribute to their behavior. Others may be concerned about what they consider to be poor personal appearance such as extremes of height or weight or physical maturity not in keeping with their chronological age. Still other emotionally disturbed students may simply be in the process of growing up and are finding it difficult to handle their adolescence.

If negative student behavior stems from some aspect of a student's personality, then the physical educator must take positive steps to resolve the problem so that teaching can take place. The physical educator must deal with each behavior problem individually and seek help from school personnel who are best equipped to give aid. The school psychologist and the student's guidance couselor will have information that will help the physical educator. A conference with these individuals may reveal methods that have proved effective with the student in the past. Further, the observations made by the physical educator will be valuable to the continuing study of the student.

The physical educator will find that not all emotionally disturbed students are continual and serious behavior problems. The physical educator should have a private conference with the student whose behavior suddenly becomes negative and try to understand why the student has reacted in a way unusual for him or her. Such a conference may lead to mutual understanding and often help allay future problems with the same student.

Much of the physical educator's task is student guidance. In individual cases of disruptive behavior, the physical educator should exhaust all personal resources to alleviate the problem before enlisting aid from other sources. Any case of disruptive behavior demands immediate action on the part of the physical educator to prevent minor problems from becoming major ones.

The majority of school pupils enjoy physical activity and physical education. They look forward to the physical education class as one part of the school day in which they can express themselves and gain a release of tension. For this reason, the student who is disruptive in the classroom is often one of the best citizens in the physical education class.

Physical education is uniquely suited to help the emotionally disturbed student. Most students profit from the activities of physical education, and through their actions in this phase of the school curriculum, teachers can gain many insights into student behavior. Individual knowledge of each student is of utmost importance in physical education and in understanding individual behavior patterns. Recognizing a student's needs and problems early in the school year will help offset future behavior problems.

Whereas physical education classes are conducted less formally than are classroom subjects, this does not mean that lower standards of behavior are acceptable. Students should know what the standards are on the first day of class and should be expected to adhere to these standards in all future classes.

Respect for the individual student is a necessity. No student likes to be criticized or embarrassed in front of his or her peers. When a student is singled out from a group and used as a disciplinary example, the atmosphere in the class will deteriorate. Respect for the student means maintenance of respect for the teacher. If disciplinary matters are handled on a one-to-one basis, rapport is enhanced. If the disruptive student knows that the physical educator expects him or her to behave in a bizarre manner, he or she will react in just this way. Good behavior should be expected until the student acts otherwise. Constant failure only abets disruptive behavior. If a student is known to be hostile and disruptive, an attempt should be made to avoid placing that student in situations where he or she feels inadequate and shows this in his or her behavior. If, for example, a disruptive student does not run well, he or she may still make a superior goalie in soccer, a position that does not require running. If the emotionally disturbed student has a special skill, he or she might be asked to demonstrate for the class. This will help to give the recognition and attention needed. Praise should be given for a skill well performed.

No student is going to participate in extra class activities unless he or she really wants to. Therefore, behavioral standards should be set for each activity, and it should be available to all students in the school who meet the standards. Acceptance into a club or participation on an intramural team may help the disruptive student gain self-respect and peer recognition and approval.

Some suggestions for physical education programming

1. Become acquainted with the characteristics of emotionally disturbed persons and keep a record of all pertinent data of children in your classes. Note such behavior as constantly talking during verbal instructions to the class, daydreaming, a student poking a classmate, or students who are completely withdrawn from class activities. Refer students with emotional problems that impair learning or disrupt classroom management to the proper school authorities (psychologist or nurse).

2. Be firm with students who display disruptive behavior. Make them responsible for such behavior. For example, prohibit a student from playing in a team game if he or she constantly disrupts such games with arguing, hitting, or the like.

3. Develop a system for "selectively ignoring" students who act out in class; failing to call attention to a minor disruptive act of a student is one means of accomplishing this objective. Whereas the teacher may ignore the student during the class, the teacher should talk to the student in private after class about his or her disruptive behavior. Students often exhibit disruptive behavior to gain attention. If attention is not gained by such behavior, sometimes that is enough to cause the student to discontinue the behavior. Teachers should be very careful in using this strategy. They should not ignore a student who is asking for help. Sound judgment is needed to know when to ignore and when to offer help.

4. Praise those students who demonstrate improvement in their behavior patterns, in both small group and large group situations.

5. Teach students how to relax by providing relaxing activities such as aquatics and rhythms and dance. There are also specific methods of teaching relaxation. For example, have children assume a comfortable position, preferably on mats, lying on their backs, and have them think about breathing and breathe slowly and deeply. Next, have students try to make their bodies as "tight" and "hard" as possible, and then have them make their bodies "soft" and

"light as a feather." Practice in slow, deep breathing should be alternated with the tightening and relaxing of the muscles.

6. Increase the attention span of students by removing distracting objects. For example, keep all equipment out of sight that is not being used.

7. Plan several games and activities for each class to allow for the short attention span of students.

8. Provide for aquatics in the program. The warm water is relaxing and provides a sedative effect for hyperactive students.

9. Stress program material that aids in the development of social and personal development. Such activities as rhythms and dance, team games such as field hockey and softball, and self-testing activities are recommended.

10. Modify the rules when appropriate for students to achieve success.

11. Organize classes according to a routine or set procedure; however, discourage stereotyped play activities that develop rigid behavioral patterns, such as constantly playing with a ball, jumping rope, and playing hopscotch alone.

12. Establish rapport with students by being firm and consistent in dealing with them, yet letting them know that you care about them as people and want to help them succeed both in school and in life.

13. Plan for behavior control by using the following intervention techniques:
   a. Allow free-play periods and other activities at times when control is not necessary.
   b. Plan activities that allow for success by all. Acting out behavior is sometimes engaged in because of a feeling of frustration and failure.
   c. When necessary, physically restrain students.
   d. Provide both positive and negative reinforcement.
   e. Use humor in the classroom or gynmasium.

14. Use emotionally disturbed students as teacher's aids when possible.

15. Use direct, eye-to-eye contact when dealing with students.

16. Establish a feeling of mutual respect among the children.

17. Protect students from embarrassment and ridicule while behavior is unstable.

LEARNING DISABLED STUDENTS

Individuals with learning problems that affect the development of processes associated with speech, language, reading, writing, and arithmetic are said to have a "specific learning disability" if the problems are caused by one or more of the following conditions: perceptual handicaps, brain injury, minimal brain dysfunction, dyslexia, and developmental aphasia. Specific learning disabilities do not include learning problems that are caused primarily by visual, hearing, or motor handicaps, mental retardation, emotional disturbance, or environmental disadvantage. In essence, an individual with a discrepancy of 50% or more from expected achievement based on his or her intellectual ability is considered to have a specific learning disability.

Some research (Ismail and Gruber* and Dillon, Heath, and Biggs†) has suggested that programs of motor development and movement stimulation can help to ameliorate, and in some cases prevent, learning problems.

Learning disabled children exhibit many of the same traits as children with other handicaps. However, some characteristics are unique to people with learning disabilities. Gearheart indicates that all learning disabled children have only three characteristics in common: (1) they must have average or above average intelligence, (2) they must have adequate sensory acuity, and (3) they must be achieving considerably less than the composite of their IQ, age, and educational opportunity (health, availability of schooling, and cultural opportunity) would predict.‡

Many children with learning disabilities also exhibit one or more of the following characteristics: hyperactivity, hypoactivity (not found in many cases), lack of motivation, clumsiness and awkwardness, inattention, belligerence, and unwillingness to relate to peers. Physical educators should be very careful to note any of these characteristics in children while they are in the gymnasium. If the physical educator cannot cope with the condition, he or she should contact the appropriate person in the school.

The literature dealing with the causes of learning problems is voluminous. These causes are often said to include factors such as perceptual problems, cerebral dysfunctions, or behavioral disturbances. Bateman further defined the cerebral dysfunctions and other physiological factors as: (1) damage to or dysfunction of certain localized areas of the brain such as angular gyrus, second frontal gyrus, connection between the cortical speech mechanism and the brain stem cetrencephalic system, and the parietal and parietal-occipital areas, (2) hereditary or developmental lag factors such as inherited underdevelopment of directional function, hereditary delayed development of parietal lobes, slow tempo of the neuromuscular maturation, and (3) other factors such as lack of cerebral dominance, minimal brain injury, endocrine disturbance and chemical imbalance, and primary emotional factors.*

The consequences of learning disabilities are poor achievement in school, inadequate social development, and poor motor development. These conditions may often cause a child to give up and become a delinquent. In too many cases, children who have learning problems are diagnosed and labeled as mentally retarded and are placed in environments with other mentally handicapped children. To prevent this, special education teachers, physical education teachers of students with learning problems, and others dealing with such children must be careful to make accurate diagnoses and referrals.

Some suggestions for physical education programming

Proper diagnosis is necessary to ascertain the specific learning problem a person has. (The listing of characteristics indicated there is a wide range of individual differences in students with learning problems.) Once children are diagnosed, the teacher should be careful to plan the physical education program to meet the needs of those with specific learning problems. (It might be necessary to seek the services of a specialist such as an audiologist, optome-

---

*Ismail, A.H., and Gruber, J.J.: Motor aptitude and intellectual performance, Columbus, Ohio, 1967, Charles E. Merrill Publishing Co.

†Dillon, E.J., Heath, E.J., and Biggs, C.W.: Comprehensive programming for success in learning, Columbus, Ohio, 1970, Charles E. Merrill Publishing Co.

‡Gearheart, B.R.: Learning disabilities: educational strategies, ed. 3, St. Louis, 1981, The C.V. Mosby Co.

---

*Bateman, B.: Learning disabilities—yesterday, today, and tomorrow. In Frierson, E.C., and Barbe, W.B., editors: Educating children with learning disabilities, New York, 1976, Appleton-Century-Crofts, pp. 13-14.

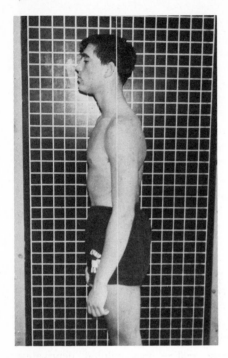

Fig. 4-13. Project ACTIVE posture screening program, Township of Ocean School District, N.J.

Courtesy Project ACTIVE.

trist, or psychologist to make diagnoses.) For example, if a group of children is diagnosed as having perceptual-motor problems, specific difficulties such as poor eye-hand or eye-foot coordination, laterality, or directionality must be identified and provided for.

The following suggestions are offered to help teachers improve programs in which there are students with learning disabilities.*

1. Provide the maximum stimuli in teaching motor skills; for example, the teacher would not use verbal stimulation with persons with aphasia because they do not understand spoken words because of cerebral dysfunction.

2. Plan a wide variety of activities that includes basic movement, rhythms, movement exploration, perceptual-motor activities, games, self-testing activities, and aquatics.

3. Keep hyperactive students together in groups and allow them to calm down. Keep them busy with activ-

*Adapted from Geddes and Harvat (Chapter 1).

ity; for example, have the children play quiet games such as checkers, old maid, or cribbage. They may also be given self-testing exercises to perform, or they may be assigned to keep score or act as student managers during the class.

4. Keep an uncluttered environment, free from outside noises and distractions.

5. Correlate physical activities with academic work; for example, when working on directionality, have the students identify their body parts as they make certain movements.

6. Create an atmosphere of trust and confidence by being fair but firm and by structuring activities whereby children can succeed.

7. Emphasize an "action" atmosphere by having children act out the activity and describe what is taking place at the same time. Including story plays and drama and games such as charades in which the students are required to act out the story or activity is one means of providing an "action" atmosphere. Another technique is to have students describe to the class an activity or stunt before they perform it, then perform the activity, and finally have the class perform it.

8. Prepare many activities that will relate to language because many children with learning problems have difficulty in this area. Having children write their own descriptions of games, requiring them to explain the rules of a game to the class, and requiring students to write and give an oral report on a current sports event are ways this can be implemented.

9. Prepare children for assuming responsibility before giving them wide options for action; it might be necessary to start with command teaching, for example, and then work toward movement exploration. Students with learning problems need more help in finding solutions to problems than other children because of the problems they have with language, speech, and other cognitive areas. Therefore, they would probably be overwhelmed by too much freedom in making choices. The teacher can assist in their learning by demonstrating a certain stunt, for example, and then asking students to perform the stunt. If students are able to perform the stunt with relative ease, the teacher might then ask students if they can perform the stunt in any other manner. By gradually giving the students more options to assume responsibility, they will feel more confident and will be less likely to become frustrated.

10. Imitation works well with young children; use it freely. For instance, the teacher might create a certain posture or shape and ask the class to repeat the movement.

11. Have children repeat instructions before they perform the activity to reinforce auditory clues.

12. Prepare a conducive learning atmosphere, paying special attention to room light that avoids shadows and other visual illusions.

13. Seek additional help if children do not respond to the program being conducted. It might be necessary for rediagnosis of those children or a change in some aspects of the program.

MULTIHANDICAPPED STUDENTS

A person with a physical handicap may become so withdrawn that he or she becomes emotionally disturbed. Likewise, an emotionally handicapped person may develop certain learning problems that will adversely affect academic performance. Other situations exist in which one handicap will cause decreased functioning in other developmental areas.

Teachers working with handicapped individuals should realize that some people may have two or more major handicaps simultaneously. For instance, a person might be both blind and deaf, or a person might be mentally retarded and have an orthopedic handicap.

Working with handicapped individuals is a tedious, demanding, and sometimes frustrating job. Obviously, dealing with people who have multiple handicaps is even more difficult. However, the enjoyment and satisfaction gained from helping the handicapped individual make progress, whether there is a single or multiple handicap, should more than outweigh the difficulties.

In dealing with persons with multiple handicaps, the teacher should become as familiar as possible with the handicaps and attempt to help those persons make the best adjustment possible. Emphasis in program planning should be on those aspects of a person's personality and physical self that can be fully developed. The program should be modified to meet the needs of the handicapped person. Ideally, the program of physical education will enable the person with multiple handicaps to develop the necessary physical fitness, motor skill, and general body mechanics to enjoy life to the fullest, in spite of the handicaps.

Guidelines for program planning and instruction will not be presented for multiple handicapped persons as they were for persons with only one handicap.

Such guidelines would be so hypothetical (because of the possible combinations of handicaps) that they would be virtually useless. Teachers of multiple handicapped persons would need to teach those individuals according to their specific handicap. For example, the teacher would need to use different instructional strategies when teaching physically and emotionally handicapped persons than when teaching a person who is visually handicapped and learning disabled. The guidelines for program planning indicated for specific handicaps, along with the other information presented in this section, are intended to aid in developing programs to meet the needs of persons with more than one handicap.

CULTURALLY DISADVANTAGED STUDENTS

Recently, culturally disadvantaged students have become a real concern to various communities and to the schools serving these communities. It is a common error for the public to associate only the black child with cultural deprivation. Professional educators especially must realize that cultural deprivation crosses all color lines. The culture of poverty is especially apparent in the large urban centers. Culturally disadvantaged persons may be found in Appalachia, suburbia, and isolated small towns and rural villages all across the United States.

The culturally disadvantaged student feels isolated from the mainstream of life. Home and neighborhood environments serve as negative influences, destroying confidence, robbing him or her of a chance for success, and defeating any aspirations he or she may have. A culturally disadvantaged student does not achieve success in school, because the cultural standards of the school and the home environment are usually inconsistent. Even schools in the inner city are staffed by teachers who represent the middle-class segment of society. Continual failure in the classroom negatively affects the school behavior of the culturally disadvantaged student. Short attention spans, emotional instability, excitability, and restlessness often contribute to disruptive behavior patterns.

In physical education the culturally disadvantaged student can be given an opportunity to meet success. Physical activity has a strong appeal for these youngsters, whether they are students in a school in their neighborhood or community or part of the student body in a school in an affluent area.

The physical educator is the most important single factor in a school physical education program for the disadvantaged. The physical educator should have a sincere interest in these students and must be willing to assume the responsibility for physically educating them. He or she should have an adequate background and special training in general education and physical education courses concerned with teaching the disadvantaged. These courses will help in attaining a fuller understanding of the culturally disadvantaged student and the educational problems he or she faces. The physical educator should have the ability to develop rapport with the culturally disadvantaged so that he or she can better respect, understand, and help these students. The physical educator should be able to provide an enriched program that will help motivate the culturally disadvantaged student to make the best use of his or her physical, intellectual, and creative abilities.

Through physical education activities, many general educational knowledges, skills, and abilities can be enhanced. Through folk dances, for example, it is possible to acquaint the student with the dress and customs of various cultures. This knowledge will help a class in history to become more interesting to the student and develop pride in his or her own culture. Through a sport such as baseball, mathematics can be brought to life. The students will be able to see the relationship between mathematics and its uses in determining baseball batting averages, computing team won-lost percentages, and the importance of understanding angles as applied to laying out a baseball diamond.

The school physical education program frequently is the only supervised physical activity program for the culturally disadvantaged student. These students usually do not have a neighborhood recreational facility available and must conduct their sports and games on unsupervised streets or in dangerously littered lots. The school physical education experience must be designed to afford this student the physical education and recreational activities that are denied elsewhere.

Lack of structured programs outside the school denies culturally disadvantaged students the opportunity to participate in a regular program of physical activity. This often prevents these students from maintaining even minimal fitness levels. Competitive sports and games must be a part of the class program, but time must also be allotted for the individual to compete with himself or herself to raise a physical fitness test score or to improve in a skill performance.

Some suggestions for physical education programming

1. Provide a wide choice of physical education activities so students can select not only those experiences they find pleasurable but also those in which they can find success.

2. Include activities that will help students to increase their physical fitness and optimal skill levels.

3. Include in the program such lifetime sports as swimming, dancing, and tennis, as well as other recreational activities such as bowling.

4. Records, a phonograph, and a variety of rhythm instruments should be available. Students enjoy rhythmic activities and find that they are successful in such activities as dance, gymnastics, and tumbling, where they can demonstrate their creativity and express their individuality. Many warm-up activities, as well as many games, can be done to a musical accompaniment.

5. Culturally disadvantaged students are especially conscious of their individuality, and the program should allow ample opportunity for self-expression and creativity.

6. Teacher recognition and praise for the most minor accomplishments are essential to the continued success of these students.

7. If possible, culturally disadvantaged students should not be in a large class, because little teaching may take place and the individual student may become lost in the mass.

POORLY COORDINATED STUDENTS

The student with low motor ability is often ignored by the physical educator. This person may be unpopular with classmates and considered a detriment in a team sport. He or she may be undesirable as a partner in a dual sport and may wind up paired with an equally uncoordinated and awkward partner. Students with low motor ability need special attention so they can improve physical skill performances, derive pleasure from success in physical activity, and gain a background in lifetime sports.

Poorly coordinated students are frequently placed in regular physical education classes when they have no mental or physical handicaps. The only concession made to their problem is through ability groupings in schools where facilities and personnel are adequate. Even then, ability grouping sometimes is used only to separate the "duds" from the "stars," thus increasing the poorly coordinated student's feelings of inadequacy. The poorly coordinated student may be held up to ridicule by fellow students, as well as by physical education teachers who use him or her as an example of how not to perform a physical skill.

The poorly coordinated student will resist learning new activities because the challenge this presents offers little chance for success. The challenge of a new skill or activity to be learned may create such tension within the student that he or she becomes physically ill. In other instances this tension may result in negative behavior.

Poor coordination may be the result of several factors. The student may not be physically fit, or may have poor reflexes, or may not have the ability to use mental imagery. For some reason such as a lengthy childhood illness, the poorly coordinated student may not have been normally physically active. Other poorly coordinated students may enter the secondary school physical education program from an elementary school that lacked a trained physical educator, had no facilities for physical education, or had a poor program.

In working with poorly coordinated students the physical educator must exercise the utmost patience. He or she must know why the student is poorly coordinated and be able to devise an individual program for each student that will help the student to move and perform more effectively. The physical educator must be sure that the student understands the need for special help and try to motivate him or her to succeed. When a skill is performed with even a modicum of improvement, the effort must be praised and the achievement reinforced.

With a large class and only one instructor, there can be relatively little time spent with each individual. Buddy systems—that is, pairing a poorly coordinated student with a well-coordinated partner—often enables both students to progress faster. The physical educator must be careful not to push the student beyond his or her limits. A too difficult challenge coupled with the fatigue that results from trying too hard may result in deterioration rather than acceleration of improvement. Any goal set for the poorly coordinated student must be reasonable.

The objectives of the program for poorly coordinated students will not differ from the objectives of any physical education program.

Some suggestions for physical education programming

1. Before a program is devised, the status of the students should be known to identify their individual abilities and needs.

2. Physical fitness and motor ability testing should be ongoing phases of the program. Through the physical education program poorly coordinated students should come to realize that their special needs are being met because in the eyes of the physical educator they are as important as the well-skilled students.

3. Separating students into ability groups may cause poorly coordinated students to feel they are being pushed out of the way. If ability grouping is used, poorly coordinated students must receive adequate instruction, a meaningful program, and equal access to good equipment and facilities.

4. If a student has poor eye-hand or eye-foot coordination, he or she will not succeed in such activities as tennis or soccer. Activities should be chosen that suit the abilities of the students and at the same time help them develop the needed coordinations.

5. Work on improving fitness and self-testing activities should form only a part of the program. Appropriate games, rhythmics, dance, and such activities as swimming and archery will help stimulate and maintain interest. Physical fitness clubs, swimming clubs, and other clubs open to all students will also benefit poorly coordinated students.

6. With carefully arranged teams and schedules in an intramural program, poorly coordinated students can be given a chance to compete with other students at their own level of ability. Preparation for intramural competition should be a part of the class program.

7. Dancing is appropriate for coeducational instruction. When coeducational instruction is offered, poorly coordinated students have an opportunity to develop social skills. Different groupings for different activities will stimulate interest and provide students with a variety of partners.

8. The student's progress should be evaluated periodically.

ANNUAL PHYSICAL ACTIVITY FORM

Junior and Senior High School

Sponsored by Bureau of School Health Service, Division of Pupil Personnel Services,
New York State Department of Education and New York State Heart Assembly, Inc.

Date _____

To Dr. _____

From Dr. _____ School Physician
_____ School

Address
Re: _____   _____
    Name of pupil   Grade in school

     All pupils registered in the schools of New York State are required by the
education law to attend courses of instruction in physical education   These courses
are required to be adapted to meet individual needs. This means that a pupil who is
unable to participate in the entire program should have his activities modified to
meet and/or improve his condition. The physical education classes are approximately
_____ minutes in length and are held __ times a week.
     The final responsibility for the determination of a student participation rests
with the school physician. Your recommendation will assist him in making a decision.
If further clarification is needed, the school physician will arrange a conference with
you.
     This child may participate in all physical education class activities and in
competitive sports, intramural and interscholastic.   Yes_____ No_____

DIAGNOSIS: _____

If activity is limited, please check what he may do, in the following list:

PHYSICAL EDUCATION CLASS ACTIVITIES

( ) Basketball   ( ) Trampoline   ( ) Square dancing
( ) Baseball   ( ) Tumbling   ( ) Social dancing
( ) Football   ( ) Volleyball   ( ) Apparatus
( ) Soccer   ( ) Wrestling   ( ) Archery
( ) Softball   ( ) Track   ( ) Field hockey
                                           ( ) Swimming

INTRAMURAL AND INTERSCHOLASTIC SPORTS

( ) Basketball   ( ) Wrestling   ( ) Golf
( ) Baseball   ( ) Track and field ( ) Swimming
( ) Football   ( ) Cross country   ( ) Cheerleading
( ) Soccer   ( ) Bowling

1. Does this child require a rest period during school hours?   Yes_____ No_____
2. Duration of restrictions: weeks_____ months_____ school year_____
3. Do you wish the patient to return to you for reevaluation?   Yes_____ No ___Date___

_____ _____ M. D. _____
Date   Address
Prepared and pretested by: Nassau TB, Heart and Public Health Association, Inc.

Fig. 4-14. Adapted physical education record.

Bureau of School Health Service,
Division of Pupil Personnel Services,
New York State Department of Education
and New York State Heart Assembly, Inc.

PHYSICALLY GIFTED AND CREATIVE STUDENTS

Physically gifted and creative students in physical education also need a specially tailored physical education experience.

The physically gifted student has superior motor skill abilities in many activities and maintains a high level of physical fitness. This student may be a star athlete, but in general is simply a good all-around performer. In a game situation, the student always seems to be in the right place at the right time. The physically gifted student learns quickly and requires a minimum of individual instruction. He or she is usually enthusiastic about physical activity and practices skills without being told to do so. Any individual instruction required is in the form of coaching rather than remedial correction. The physically gifted student has a strong sense of kinesthetic awareness and understands the principles of human movement. The student may not be able to articulate these last two qualities, but observation by the physical educator will reveal that the student has discovered how to exploit his or her body as a tool for movement.

The creative student with a well-developed sense of kinesthetic awareness knows how to use his or her body properly. This student is the girl or boy who dances with ease and grace, who is highly skilled in free exercise, or who is a lithe tumbler or gynmast. These students develop their own sophisticated routines in dance, tumbling, gymnastics, apparatus, and synchronized swimming. They may or may not be extraordinarily adept in other physical education activities, but they are as highly teachable as are the physically gifted.

The beginning physical educator may find it especially difficult to teach a student who possesses many more physical abilities than the teacher. However, no students in school know everything about an activity. Many experiences will still be new to them.

Physically gifted and creative students may not have attempted a wide range of activities, but they may have experienced all the activities offered in the school physical education program. The physically gifted students, the creative student and the average student, will be stimulated and challenged by the introduction of new activities. The creative student in dance may be introduced to a new kind of music, or

the boy skilled on apparatus may enjoy adding new moves to his routines. The athlete may be a good performer, but perhaps needs to become a better team player. Or he or she may rely on superior skills rather than on a complete knowledge of the rules and strategies of sports and games.

A well-planned physical education program will be adaptable to the needs of all the students it serves. But before the program can be definitively developed, the specific needs, limitations, and abilities of the students in the program must be defined. The activities offered must be adapted to the needs of the students, for the students cannot be adapted to the program.

Some suggestions for physical education programming

1. The exceptional student needs a structured program of physical activity, because this is a vital part of his or her mental, social, emotional, and physical development. Some schools have made it a policy to excuse athletes from the activity program when their varsity sport is in season. This is a disservice to the student, especially when the varsity sport and the unit being taught in class are different. A student benefits from physical activity in a regular program. The physical educator can keep the interest of the exceptional student high by adopting some tested methods.

2. A leaders' program has proved valuable in many schools. Leaders can assist the physical educator in innumerable ways, and they develop a sense of responsibility for the program because they are directly involved. Members of Leaders' Clubs have served as gymnastics and tumbling spotters in classes other than their own and can assist as officials in both the class program and during intramural contests. Members of Leaders' Clubs thus still participate in the activities of their own class, but at the same time receive the benefit of extra exposure to activities.

3. Movies, film strips, loop films, and slides interest and benefit all students. The exceptional student can compare his or her performance with those of experts and can gain new insights into skills.

4. Textbooks in physical education are not in wide use in secondary school physical education programs. Students can benefit from the use of a textbook, special outside readings, assignments, and research problems, and these provide additional challenges for the exceptional student.

5. Many highly skilled or creative students will be able to assist those students who have low motor skill abilities. By working on a one-to-one basis, the amount of individu-

alized instruction will be increased. The student with low motor ability will receive the special assistance he or she needs, and the gifted student will learn that not all students possess high ability levels.

6. The exceptional student can assist in the intramural program by acting as a coach on a day when his or her team is not playing. Coaching a team will help the student become more cognizant of the importance of team play, sportsmanship, and the need for rules.

7. The gifted student can especially profit from independent study programs where he or she can choose a desired area of study and proceed at his or her own rate. Resource centers, field trips, and library research are all important parts of independent study programs.

8. The gifted or creative student may also want to contribute to the physical education programs by suggesting and demonstrating innovative methods of learning an activity or by creating new activities. These students should be encouraged, and physical education should be discussed as a possibility for a future career.

SELF-ASSESSMENT TESTS

These tests are to assist students in determining if material and competencies presented in this chapter have been mastered:

1. What is meant by an adapted physical education program?

2. A parent of a gifted varsity basketball player has questioned why you have decided to provide a physical education program for handicapped students. State your answer, giving the legal and moral bases for providing such a program.

3. You are a director of a school physical education program and have been asked by the superintendent of schools to plan an adapted program of physical education for the entire school system—elementary school through high school. Prepare the plan you will submit to the superintendent, including the objectives you will strive to achieve, the guidelines you will follow, how you plan to schedule the students, and the activities you will offer.

4. Without consulting your text, define the term *mainstreaming* and discuss its advantages.

5. You are a member of a school physical education staff and have been selected by your college to see that PL 94-142 is fully implemented in your program. Prepare a plan that will ensure your school physical education program has fully complied with this law.

6. There are many different organizational structures and instructional strategies that may be used with handicapped students. List each and discuss the conditions under which each one would be utilized.

7. Prepare and complete the chart according to the format shown on the following page.

SELECTED REFERENCES

Adams, R., et al.: Games, sports and exercises for the physically handicapped, Philadelphia, 1975, Lea & Febiger.

American Alliance for Health, Physical Education, and Recreation: Foundations and practices in perceptual motor learning—a quest for understanding, Washington, D.C., 1971, The Alliance.

American Alliance for Health, Physical Education, and Recreation: Guidelines for professional preparation programs for personnel involved in physical education and recreation for the handicapped, Washington, D.C., 1973, The Alliance.

American Alliance for Health, Physical Education, and Recreation: Annotated bibliography in physical education, recreation and psychomotor function of mentally retarded persons, Washington, D.C., 1975, The Alliance.

American Alliance for Health, Physical Education, and Recreation: Update, March, 1977, Law to provide education for handicapped has far-reaching implications for physical education.

American Alliance for Health, Physical Education, Recreation and Dance: Adapted physical education guidelines: theory and practices for 70's and 80's, Reston, Va., 1976, The Alliance.

American Alliance for Health, Physical Education, Recreation and Dance: Making physical education and recreation facilities accessible to all: planning, designing, adapting, Washington, D.C., 1977, The Alliance.

American Alliance for Health, Physical Education, Recreation and Dance: Physical education and recreation for individuals with multiple handicapping conditions, Washington, D.C., 1978, The Alliance.

Arnheim, D., and Sinclair, W.A.: The clumsy child, ed. 2, St. Louis, 1979, The C. V. Mosby Co.

Auxter, D.: Integration of the mentally retarded with normals in physical and motor fitness training programs, Journal of Health, Physical Education, and Recreation 41:61, 1970.

Bucher, C.A., and Thaxton, N.A.: Physical education and sport: change and challenge, St. Louis, 1981, The C. V. Mosby Co.

Bucher, C.A., and Thaxton, N.A.: Physical education for children: movement foundations and experiences, New York, 1979, Macmillan, Inc.

Carlson, R.E.: A diagnosis and remediation plan for physical education for the handicapped, Journal of Health, Physical Education, and Recreation 43:73, 1972.

A clarification of terms, Journal Health, Physical Education, and Recreation 42:63, 1971.

Crowe, W.C., Auxter, D., and Pyfer, J.: Principles and methods of adapted physical education and recreation, ed. 4, St. Louis, 1981, The C.V. Mosby Co.

Drowatzky, J.: Physical education for the mentally retarded, Philadelphia, 1971, Lea & Febiger.

Ersing, W.F.: Current direction of professional preparation in

Type of handicapped or exceptional student	Characteristics	Needs	Type of physical education program needed
Physically handicapped Mentally retarded Emotionally disturbed Culturally disadvantaged Poorly coordinated Physically gifted or creative Learning disabled			

adapted physical education, Journal of Health, Physical Education, and Recreation **43:**78, 1972.

Fait, H.F.: Special physical education; adaptive, corrective, developmental, Philadelphia, 1978, W.B. Saunders Co.

Gearheart, B.R., and Weishahn, M.W.: The handicapped student in the regular classroom, ed. 2, St. Louis, 1980, The C.V. Mosby Co.

Geddes, D.: Physical activities for individuals with handicapping conditions, ed. 2, St. Louis, 1978, The C.V. Mosby Co.

Kalakian, L.H., and Motan, J.M.: Physical education and recreation for the mentally retarded and emotionally disturbed, Minneapolis, 1973, Burgess Publishing Co.

Kolstoe, O.P.: Teaching educable mentally retarded children, New York, 1976, Holt, Rinehart and Winston, Inc.

Logan, G.A.: Adapted physical education, Dubuque, Iowa, 1972, William C. Brown Co.

Milofsky, D., Schooling the kids no one wants, New York Times Magazine, January 2, 1977.

Moran, J.M., and Kalakian, L.H.: Movement experiences for the mentally retarded or emotionally disturbed child, Minneapolis, 1977, Burgess Publishing Co.

National College Physical Education Association for Men and National Association of Physical Education for College Women: Mainstreaming physical education, Briefings 4, 1976, The Associations.

Nyquist, E.B.: Mainstreaming; idea and actuality, New York, 1975, New York State Department of Education.

Parish, T.S., et al.: Stereotypes concerning normal and handicapped children, Journal of Psychology **102:**63, May 1979.

Riessman, F.: The culturally deprived child, New York, 1962, Harper & Row, Publishers.

Soane, M.: Handbook of adapted physical education equipment and its use, Springfield, Ill., 1973, Charles C Thomas, Publisher.

Telford, C.W., and Sawrey, J.M.: The exceptional child, Englewood Cliffs, N.J., 1977, Prentice-Hall, Inc.

Tillman, K.: Recreational activities reinforce learning experiences for the disadvantaged student, Journal of Health, Physical Education, and Recreation **43:**32, 1972.

Vannier, M.: Physical activities for the handicapped, Englewood Cliffs, N.J., 1977, Prentice-Hall, Inc.

Vedola, T.: Individualized physical education program for the handicapped child, Englewood Cliffs, N.J., 1972, Prentice-Hall, Inc.

Wheeler, R.H., and Hooley, A.M.: Physical education for the handicapped, Philadelphia, 1976, Lea & Febiger.

Winnick, J.: Issues and trends in training adapted physical education personnel, Journal of Health, Physical Education, and Recreation **43:**75, 1972.

5

Intramural, extramural, and club programs

Instructional objectives and competencies to be achieved

After reading this chapter the student should be able to

■ Define what is meant by *intramural, extramural,* and *club programs* and the objectives each is designed to achieve.

■ Prepare a list of policies that, if followed, will enable a person to organize and administer intramural, extramural, and club physical education programs.

■ Understand the roles played by various administrative personnel in conducting intramural, extramural, and club programs.

■ Describe how each of the following tasks is involved in intramural and extramural programs: selecting activities, scheduling, establishing awards and point systems, maintaining records, determining player eligibility, planning health examinations, financing, and coordinating publicity and promotion.

■ Discuss how intramural, extramural, and club programs are administered in elementary schools, secondary schools, colleges, universities, and other organizations.

■ Organize various types of competition for intramural and extramural activities.

■ Show the importance of and the procedures for administering sport clubs, corecreation, and programs for handicapped students and faculty members.

Intramurals and extramurals comprise that phase of a physical education program in a school, college, industry, or other organization geared to the abilities and skills of the entire student body or the members of the organization. It consists of voluntary participation in games, sports, and other activities. This phase offers intramural activities within a single school or other institution and such extramural activities as "play" and "sports" days that bring together participants from several institutions.

A club program is usually devoted to one activity such as tennis, skiing, or mountain climbing, and it encourages students and other individuals to participate at all levels of skill. It may be managed by members of an organization, such as students in schools and colleges, or by the central administration of an organization. Members, advisors, or community volunteers provide instruction. Clubs are popular in schools and colleges, as well as in other organizations.

Intramurals were started many years ago as a result of student motivation in schools and colleges. Initial-

ly, they received little administrative support and were poorly organized. However, as student interest grew there was increased demand for departmental control. In 1913 intramural sports came under faculty control at the University of Michigan and Ohio State University. Since that time intramurals, extramurals, and club programs have continued to grow and in most cases today are under the administration and direction of full-time faculty personnel. The National Intramural Sports Council was organized in Washington, D.C., May 27-28, 1965, and held its first meeting in 1966.

Intramural and extramural programs
OBJECTIVES

The worthy objectives of intramural and extramural programs are one indication of why there has been a great expansion of such programs throughout the country.

The objectives of intramural and extramural activities are compatible with the overall objectives of

Fig. 5-1. Intramurals at Colgate University, Hamilton, N.Y.

physical education and also with those of education in general. The objectives as listed by one university are as follows:

1. To provide the students at the institution with opportunities for fun, enjoyment, and fellowship through participation in sports
2. To provide the students at the institution with opportunities that will be conducive to their health and physical fitness
3. To provide the students at the institution with opportunities for release from tensions and aggressions and to provide a feeling of achievement through sports participation, all of which are conducive to mental and emotional health

The objectives of the intramural and extramural programs may be classified under four headings: (1) health, (2) skill, (3) social development, and (4) recreation.

Health. Intramural and extramural activities contribute to the physical, social, and emotional health of the individual. They contribute to physical health through participation in activities affording healthful exercise. Such characteristics as strength, agility, speed, and body control are developed. They contribute to social health through group participation and working toward achieving group goals. They contribute to emotional health by helping one achieve self-confidence and improve one's self-concept.

Skill. Intramural and extramural activities offer the opportunity for every individual to display and develop his or her skill in various physical education activities. Through specialization and voluntary par-

Fig. 5-2. Girls' intramurals at Panama Central School, Panama, N.Y.

Fig. 5-3. Intramural basketball at Iowa State University, Ames, Iowa.

ticipation they offer people the opportunity to excel and to experience the thrill of competition. It is generally agreed that an individual enjoys activities in which he or she has developed skill. Participation in athletics offers the opportunity to develop proficiency in group activities where each person is equated according to skill, thus providing for equality of competition, which helps guarantee greater success and enjoyment. Intramurals also enable many persons to spend leisure moments profitably and happily.

Social development. Opportunities for social development are numerous in intramural and extramural activities. Through many social contacts, coeducational experiences, playing on teams, and other situations, desirable qualities are developed. Individuals learn to subordinate their desires to the will of the group, develop sportsmanship, fair play, courage, group loyalty, social poise, and other desirable traits. Voluntary participation exists in such a program, and persons who desire to play under such conditions will live by group codes of conduct. These experiences offer training for citizenship, adult living, and human relations.

Recreation. Intramural and extramural programs help develop an interest in many sports and physical education activities, which carries over into adult living and provides the basis for many happy leisure hours. These programs also provide for excellent recreational activities during school days, when idle moments have the potential to foster antisocial behavior, as well as constructive social behavior.

Relation to basic instructional and highly organized athletic programs

Intramural and extramural activities and interscholastic and intercollegiate athletics are integral phases of the total physical education program in a school or college, which consists of the instructional program, the adapted program, the intramural and extramural program, and the varsity athletic program. Each has an important contribution to make to the achievement of physical education objectives. It is important to maintain a proper balance so each phase enhances and does not restrict the other phases of the total program.

The basic instructional program in physical education is looked on by most physical education leaders as the foundation on which the adapted, intramural and extramural, and highly organized athletic programs rest. The instructional program includes teaching such things as concepts, skills, and strategies. Intramural, extramural, and club programs provide opportunities for students and others to use these concepts, skills, and strategies in games and contests that are usually competitive. This part of the total physical education program is often referred to as the laboratory where the individual has an opportunity to experiment and test what has been learned in the instructional program.

Whereas intramurals and extramurals are for everyone, varsity athletics are usually for those individuals skilled in various physical activities. Intramurals and extramurals are conducted primarily on an intrainstitutional basis, whereas varsity athletics are conducted on in interinstitutional basis.

No conflict exists between these two phases of the program if the facilities, time, personnel, money, and other factors are apportioned according to the degree to which each phase achieves the outcomes desired, rather than the degree of public appeal and interest stimulated. One should not be designed as a training ground for the other. It should be possible for a person to move from one to the other, but this should be incidental rather than planned.

If conducted properly, each phase of the program can contribute to the other, and through an overall, well-balanced program the entire student body or members of an organization will come to respect sports and the great potentials they have for improving physical, mental, social, and emotional growth. When a physical education program is initially developed, it seems logical first to provide an intramural program for the majority of persons, with the varsity athletic program becoming an outgrowth of it. The first concern should be for the majority. This is characteristic of the democratic way of life. Although the intramural and extramural athletic programs in a school or college are designed for every student, in practice they generally attract poorly skilled and moderately skilled individuals. The skilled person finds a niche in the varsity interschool athletic program. This has its benefits in that it is an equalizer for competition.

The philosophical model depicted in Fig. 5-5, *A*, illustrates one basis for the placement of intramurals in physical education programs. This triangular model displays an interdependency and a building of skills from the instructional level to the intramural level and finally to the athletic attainment level. This model conveys the philosophy that instruction is basic to the other programs and that intramural skills are essential to producing the athletic skills found in varsity play.

The model in Fig. 5-5, *B,* is presented because of its implications for viewing the phases of the physical education program as both interdependent and equal. It establishes each phase as independent of the others. Intramurals and athletics are placed in their close position because each is related to the other more closely than are recreation and instruction. Recreation has been added to the model because of its contribution to intramural activities and because both have as a primary objective the satisfaction derived from participation.

Administrative personnel

Many administrative personnel are needed if an intramural and extramural program is to be a success. Some key persons involved are the director, student leaders, student directors and unit managers, intramural and extramural council members, and officials.

The director

Many schools, colleges, businesses, and other organizations have established the position of director of intramurals and extramurals. In some cases other titles are used. The director is responsible for establishing programs, getting adequate funding, involving the community, and evaluating the success of the program. Some of the more specific duties of the director include the following:

1. Providing an organizational structure that will best serve the program
2. Planning programs
3. Organizing tournaments and other forms of competition
4. Supervising the maintenance of facilities, equipment, and supplies

5. Supervising personnel
6. Attending and planning intramural council meetings
7. Interpreting the program to the membership, the administration, and the public in general
8. Coordinating the program with allied areas such as the physical education instructional program, the program for the handicapped, and varsity athletics
9. Attending professional meetings
10. Surveying student or member opinion about program needs
11. Supervising the program in action
12. Preparing budgets
13. Evaluating the worth of the program

Place in administrative structure. The director of intramurals in a school is usually responsible to the director of physical education. In a college or university the intramural director is also usually responsible to the director of the department of health, physical education, and recreation and athletics. In some cases, not all of these various components are under the same department. However, intramural programs are usually a responsibility of the director of the physical education department. Several colleges appoint one person to administer the entire campus recreation program of which intramurals, extramurals, and club activities are a part.

Intramural and extramural activities should be based in the physical education program. However, they should be separate divisions of the overall program, receiving equal consideration with the other athletic divisions concerning staff members, finances, facilities, equipment, supplies, and other essentials. One staff member who is well trained in physical education and whose chief interest is intramural and extramural activities should be directly responsible for the program. Working with the director should be assistant directors, supervisors, student managers, and other staff members as needed, depending on the size of the organization. There should also be adequate numbers of officials.

Student leaders

Student involvement in all phases of education has been steadily increasing. Involvement in the administration of intramurals and extramurals is happening in high schools and on college campuses. Roles of stu-

Fig. 5-4. Intramural track and field at Iowa State University, Ames, Iowa.

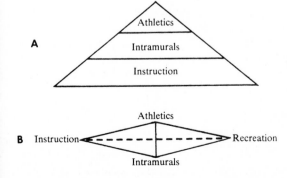

Fig. 5-5. A, The traditional triangular conception of physical education and intramurals. **B,** A modern conceptualization of physical education and intramurals.

From Jones, T.R.: Needed; a new philosophical model for intramurals, Journal of Health, Physical Education, and Recreation **42:**34, 1971.

dent leaders may range from serving as officials to being managers and office assistants. For example, many colleges have "drop-in" centers where student supervisors are available to establish programs, reserve equipment, and arrange for the gymnasium or swimming pool to be open for additional hours. Some colleges have student managers who supervise intramural activity.

Student directors and unit managers

In some school programs the director of intramurals and extramurals appoints an upperclass student who has been involved with the program as student director. This student director may have such responsibilities as contacting officials, working with managers, issuing supplies, and scheduling.

Student unit managers have an important responsibility because they are in charge of a particular sport or activity. They usually work closely with the team captains and manage supplies and equipment, team rosters, and entry sheets, notifying teams of the time and date of contests, and clarifying eligibility rules.

Intramural and extramural council members

An important feature of the overall administration of an intramural or extramural program is an intramural and extramural council. This is usually an elected council with representatives from the participants, central administration, intramural staff, health department, and staff. The council is influential in establishing policy and practices for a broad athletic program.

The council assists and advises the director and the staff members. In some cases it plays an important role in the decision-making process. Councils usually have representatives from the various participating units who communicate information to the participating teams. The council also helps make decisions about program operation and serves as a sounding board for ways in which the program may be improved.

Officials

Excellent officials are necessary for a sound intramural program. They should have special qualifications, including a knowledge of the activity, the participants, the goals of the program, and the organiza-

tion's philosophy of competition. Some of the responsibilities of the administrators of the intramural program are to find sources for good officials and then to select and train them so they enhance the program. Some of the duties performed by officials are to have game equipment ready before the contest, see that accurate score sheets are prepared, check for any hazards to safety, prepare accident reports if needed, and officiate the game or activity objectively and impartially. Some institutions put officials through a training program, supervise them during the playing season, and evaluate their performance after the season is over. Studies have shown that most colleges pay their intramural officials, although some colleges and many schools use volunteer officials.

Policies for organization and administration

A list of policies governing the various features of the program should be written down and well publicized, perhaps as a handbook.

Policies for intramurals and extramurals should be developed in at least each of the following areas:

- A policy supporting the thesis that, if properly conducted, intramurals and extramurals complement and supplement the total physical education program, as well as the welfare of the entire school or organization
- A policy for participant and student involvement in the organization and administration of these programs
- A policy for the health and welfare of all participants, including medical examinations and safe facilities
- A policy for a variety of activities that meet the interests and needs of the participants
- A policy for equalizing competition so all participants experience success
- A policy for qualified officiating to promote better play and maintain safety
- A policy for properly handling protests
- A policy for eligibility standards and the publicizing of these standards
- A policy for properly financing the program, including clarifying fees, if they are to be charged
- Policies also covering such items as postponements, point systems, and awards
- A policy for coeducational recreation

Organizational considerations

The organization of an intramural or extramural program involves selecting activities, scheduling, determining eligibility, establishing awards and point systems, maintaining records, planning health examinations, financing, and directing publicity and promotion.

Activities. The activities constituting the intramural and extramural program determine the amount of resulting participation. It is therefore important to select the right activities. Some administrative guidelines that will help in selecting activities follow:

1. Activities should be selected in accordance with the season of the year and local conditions and influences.
2. Activities should reflect the needs and interests of the students or the members of the organization.
3. Coeducational recreational activities should be provided.
4. The activities included in the physical education school instructional program should be coordinated with the activities included in the intramural and extramural program. The latter should act as a laboratory for the former.
5. Many desirable activities require little special equipment and do not require long periods of training to get the participant in appropriate physical condition.
6. Consideration should be given to such recreational activities as field trips, dramatics, hiking, and handicraft.
7. Activities should be selected with special attention to the ability and safety of the participant.

The following are some activities that have been used with success in various intramural and extramural programs throughout the nation:

Selected individual activities

Archery	Racquetball
Badminton	Rope climbing
Billiards	Scuba diving
Bowling	Shooting
Curling	Shuffleboard
Cycling	Skiing
Deck tennis	Swimming
Golf	Table tennis
Gymnastics	Tennis
Handball	Track and field
Horseshoes	Tumbling
Paddle tennis	Weight lifting
Physical fitness	Wrestling

Selected recreational activities

Camping and cookouts	Hosteling
Canoeing	Ice skating
Cycling	Rifle
Dance	Roller skating
Figure skating	Rowing
Fishing	Sailing
Hiking	Tumbling
Horseback riding	

Selected team sports*

Baseball	Softball
Basketball	Speedball
Field hockey	Swimming
Football	Touch (or flag) football
Gymnastics	Track and field
Ice hockey	Volleyball
Lacrosse	Water games
Soccer	

Scheduling. The time when intramural and extramural activities are scheduled will depend on the facilities, season of year, community, faculty availability, student needs, and budget requirements.

One of the most popular and convenient times for schools is late afternoon. This has proved best for elementary schools, junior high schools, and senior high schools. In the spring and fall it has also been popular in college. It is an economical time, does not require lights, and has the outdoors available. It also ensures faculty supervision to a greater degree.

Evenings have been used quite extensively at colleges during the winter. This is not recommended for elementary schools, junior high schools, or senior high schools.

Some schools use hours during the school day. The physical education class is primarily an instructional period, however, and to use this period for intramurals or extramurals does not seem to be in conformance with the standards set by the profession. However, some schools have satisfactorily used free periods, activity periods, and club periods for the program when facilities are available.

The noon hour has been popular in some schools, especially in elementary schools and secondary schools, and particularly in rural schools where students do not go home for lunch. Because students will be active anyway, such a period offers possibili-

*See intramural programs for various educational levels for more activities.

Fig. 5-6. The judo mat can be an accident-prone setting unless the activity is carefully supervised.

Courtesy Florissant Valley Community College in St. Louis. Photograph by LeMoyne Coates.

Fig. 5-7. Women's track.
Courtesy Barbara Ann Chiles,
Aledo, Ill.

ties in selected situations, if strenuous activities are not offered.

Recess periods in elementary schools are a good time for many communities to conduct some of their intramural activities.

Saturdays have also been used in some situations. Although the weekend is a problem in some localities because many individuals have to work or have planned this time to be with their families, it has worked successfully in many communities.

The time before school in the morning has also been satisfactory in a few schools.

Special days are set aside in some schools for "field days" when all the students participate in a day or a half-day devoted entirely to the program's activities.

In recent years, the computer has been used with greater frequency in scheduling intramural events. Most schools, especially colleges, have a computer for registration or financial procedures, and this computer may also be used for scheduling.

Intramural activities in industry, youth-serving agencies, and other organizations are scheduled at various times to meet the convenience of the mem-

bers. Activities might be scheduled at any time during the day and the night.

Eligibility. A need exists for a few simple eligibility rules. These should be kept to a minimum, because the intramural and extramural programs should offer something for the vast majority of students.

It is generally agreed that in schools and colleges there should be no scholarship rules. There should be rules that forbid players from participating in activities when they are on the varsity team or squad. Professionals should be barred from those activities in which they are professional. A student should be allowed to participate on only one team in a given activity during the season. Students, of course, should be regularly enrolled in the school and carrying what the institution rules is a normal load. Unsportsmanlike conduct should be dealt with in a manner that is in the best interests of the individual concerned, the program, and the established goals. Certain activities by their very nature should not be engaged in by individuals with certain health problems. Therefore, such individuals should be cleared by the health department of the school before participation is allowed in such activities.

Following are the eligibility rules established by one college that have implications for high schools and colleges.

1. All students of the college (school) in good standing shall be eligible to compete in any activity promoted by the Intramural Department, except as provided later in these articles.
2. A varsity team member is one who is retained by the coach after the final cut has been made.
3. The varsity and freshman coaches are requested to pass on the list of their respective squads. Participation on these squads will automatically make an individual ineligible for intramural athletics in that particular sport.
4. An individual may represent one team in a given sport in a given season.
5. A team shall forfeit any contest in which an ineligible player was used. The director shall eliminate any points made by an ineligible person in meets. These infractions of the rules must be discovered within 48 hours after the contest.
6. Members of the freshman or varsity squads who become scholastically ineligible in any particular sport shall be ineligible to participate in any allied intramural activity.
7. The director may declare an individual ineligible to participate in intramural athletics for unsportsmanlike conduct toward officials or opponents.
8. An individual receiving a varsity award is ineligible to participate in that particular intramural sport until one season has passed since earning his or her letter.

Awards. There are arguments pro and con concerning granting awards for intramural and extramural competition. Some argue that awards stimulate interest, are an incentive for participation, and recognize achievement. Some argue that awards make the program more expensive, that a few individuals win most of the awards, and that they are unnecessary, because individuals would participate even if no awards were given. Leaders who oppose awards also stress that there should be no expectation of awards for voluntary, leisure-time participation; it is difficult to make awards on the basis of all factors that should be considered; the incentive is artificial; and the joy and satisfaction received are reward enough.

One study indicates that approximately four out of five intramural directors give awards. Letters, numerals, and similar awards are used most frequently at junior high schools. Medals and trophies are given more extensively at junior colleges, colleges, and in other organizations.

Awards, if given, should be inexpensive, such as medals, ribbons, certificates, plaques, cups, or letters.

Point systems. Most intramural programs have a cumulative point system figured on an all-year basis, maintaining interest and enthusiasm over the course of the school year and encouraging greater participation.

A system of keeping points should be developed that stimulates wholesome competition, maintains continued interest, and is in conformance with the objectives of the total program. The system should be readily understood by all and easy to administer. Under such conditions, points should be awarded on the basis of contests won, championships gained, standing in a league or order of finishing, participation, sportsmanship, and contribution to the objectives of the program.

A point system used by one school system is based on the following items:

Each entry: 10 points
Each win: 2 points
Each loss: 1 point
Forfeits: 0 points
Each team championship: 10 points
Second-place team championship: 6 points
Third-place team championship: 3 points
Each individual championship: 6 points
Second-place individual championship: 4 points
Third-place individual championship: 3 points
Each game an official works: 3 points
Being homeroom representative: 10 points
Each meeting attended by homeroom representative: 2 points

Records. Efficient administration of the program will necessitate keeping records. These should not be extensive but should contain the information needed to determine the worth of the program and the progress being made.

Such records allow for comparison with other similar organizations. They show the degree to which the program is providing for the needs of the entire membership and the extent of participation. They show the

Fig. 5-8. Trophies awarded by Youth Services Section, Los Angeles City Schools.

activities that are popular and the ones that are not so popular. They focus attention on the best units of competition, needs of the program, effective administrative procedures, and leadership strengths and weaknesses. Record keeping is an important phase of the program that should not be overlooked.

Health examinations. Health examinations should be required of all participants as a safeguard to their health. Sometimes this is taken care of through an annual health examination and at other times through special examinations given before a seasonal activity starts.

Finances. The finances involved in intramural and extramural programs are raised in various ways. Because these programs have as many contributions to make to educational objectives as other parts of the educational program, or more, they should be financed out of board of education and central administration funds, just as other phases of the program are financed. They should be included in the regular physical education budget and supported through regularly budgeted school or college income.

Another method of financing the programs that has proved satisfactory in some high schools and colleges incorporates the cost of running the programs in the regular activity fee that includes such student activities as dramatics, the interscholastic athletic program, musicals, and band concerts. This provides funds in proportion to the student enrollment and can be anticipated in advance. Also, this method eliminates any additional charges to the student.

Other methods of financing used by some organizations include using money taken from athletic gate receipts, equipment rental, requiring participant entry fee, and such special fund-raising projects as athletic nights, carnivals, and presenting talented athletic and other groups. Some argue that such practices create an overemphasis on gate receipts, that they discourage spectators from attending and persons from participating, and that they require special projects to raise money, which should not be necessary for such a valuable phase of the program.

Publicity and promotion. Members of an organization and the public in general must understand the

Fig. 5-9. Intramural competition at the elementary school level.

Courtesy President's Council on Physical Fitness and Sports.

intramural and extramural programs, the individuals they service, the activities offered, and their objectives. Such information can be disseminated to the right individuals only through a well-planned publicity and promotion program.

Newspapers should be encouraged to give appropriate space to these activities. Brochures, bulletin boards, posters, and the school or organization's newspaper can help focus attention on the program. Notices can be prepared and sent home to parents in elementary and secondary schools. A handbook can be prepared that explains all the various aspects of the total program and can be given to all who are interested. Record boards can be constructed and placed in conspicuous settings. Clinics can be held on the various sports. Orientation talks and discussions can be held in school and college assemblies and at other gatherings. Special days can be held with considerable publicity, and such catch slogans as ''It Pays to Play'' can be adopted. A good job of publicity and promotion will result in greater student participation and better public understanding.

At Downers Grove (Illinois) North High School, where they offer 40 activities a year, people responsible feel they have the ingredients to publicize the program. These ingredients include a *Weekly Trojans Intramural Report,* T-shirts for champions, team uniforms paid for by local merchants, pictures of winners on the Intramural Bulletin Board, community-oriented events such as the Trojan mile for runners, and an annual Intramural Champions Pizza Party.

Patterns of organization

INTRAMURAL AND EXTRAMURAL PROGRAMS IN THE ELEMENTARY SCHOOL

The intramural and extramural programs in the elementary school should be outgrowths of the instructional program. They should consist of a broad variety of activities including stunts, rhythmic activities, relays, and tumbling. They should be suited to the age and interests of children at this level and should be carefully supervised. The younger children in the primary grades probably will benefit most from free

SUGGESTED PROGRAM OF ACTIVITIES FOR ELEMENTARY SCHOOLS*

Fall and spring

Beat the runner	Prisoner out
Bicycle distance race	Punchball
Cosom hockey	Relays
Dodge ball	Rope jumping
Endball	Soccer
Fitness day	Soccer kick
Flag football	Softball
Foursquare	Speedball
Hopscotch	Stealing sticks
Kickball	Tetherball
Longball	Track and field
Playdays	Wiffleball

Winter

Badminton	Newcomb
Basket shooting	Relays
Basketball	Rhythms
Battleball	Rope climbing
Bowling	Shuffleboard
Cageball	Trampolining
Cosom bowling	Tug-of-war
Cosom hockey	Tumbling
Dodge ball	Volleyball
Gym scooters	Wiffleball
Gymnastics	Wrestling
Ice skating	

*Hyatt, R.W.: Intramural sports: organization and administration, St. Louis, 1977, The C.V. Mosby Co.

play. In the upper elementary grades, recess periods and afterschool activities can take place on both intragrade and intergrade bases. The programs should be broad, varied, and progressive, with participants similar in maturity and ability.

Guidelines for intramural and extramural programs at the elementary school follow:

A basic instructional offering geared to the needs, interests, and growth and developmental levels of elementary school children should be prerequisite to and foundational for intramural and extramural programs.
Qualified leadership should be provided, including com-

petencies involving understanding the physical, mental, emotional, and social needs of elementary school children.
Competition should only involve children compatible in maturity, size, and ability.
Intramurals and extramurals should be limited to grades four through six in the elementary school. In grades kindergarten through three the regular basic instructional physical education program provides sufficient competition.
Desirable social, emotional, physical, and health outcomes for students should be the aim of intramural and extramural programs.
Activities such as tackle football and boxing should not be permitted.
The planning of the program should involve students, parents, and community.

INTRAMURAL AND EXTRAMURAL PROGRAMS IN THE MIDDLE SCHOOL AND JUNIOR HIGH SCHOOL

The main concentration in athletics should be on intramurals in the middle school and intramurals and extramurals in the junior high school. At these educational levels students are taking a special interest in sports, but at the same time their immaturity makes it unwise to allow them to engage in a highly organized interscholastic program. The program should involve both boys and girls, appeal to the entire student body, have good supervision by a trained physical educator, and be adapted to the needs and interests of the pupils.

Many authoritative and professional groups favor broad intramural and extramural programs and oppose a varsity interscholastic, competitive program in junior high school. They feel this is in the best interests of youths at this age.

The junior high school provides a setting for giving students fundamental skills in many sports and activities. It is a time of limitless energy when physiological changes and rapid growth are taking place. Youths in junior high schools should have proper outlets to develop themselves healthfully.

INTRAMURAL AND EXTRAMURAL PROGRAMS IN THE SENIOR HIGH SCHOOL, COLLEGE, AND UNIVERSITY

At senior high schools, colleges, and universities the intramural and extramural programs should re-

SUGGESTED ACTIVITIES FOR JUNIOR HIGH AND MIDDLE SCHOOLS*

F = fall
W = winter
S = spring
A = all seasons (popular sport)

Team sports

A	Basketball	W	Ice hockey	A	Speedball
S	Baseball (boys)	FS	Kickball	F	Touch (or flag) football
A	Dodge ball	W	Newcomb ball	S	Track and field
S	Fieldball	A	Soccer	F	Tug-of-war
FS	Field hockey	S	Softball	W	Volleyball
W	Gymnastics				

Individual and dual sports

FS	Archery	FS	Horseshoes	A	Table tennis
A	Badminton	FS	Paddle tennis	FS	Tennis
A	Basketball goal shooting	A	Paddleball	A	Tetherball
A	Bounce ball	FS	Paddle tetherball	FS	Track and field
A	Bowling	A	Quoits	AW	Tumbling
W	Deck tennis	A	Rope climbing	W	Wrestling (boys)
A	Handball (1-wall)	A	Shuffleboard		

Corecreational activities

A	Badminton	FS	Golf	W	Skiing
A	Bicycling	FS	Horseshoes	A	Table tennis
A	Bowling	W	Ice skating	FS	Tennis
FS	Canoeing	FS	Roller skating	FS	Track and field
A	Dance (social and folk)	A	Shuffleboard	AW	Volleyball
W	Deck tennis				

Club activities

A	Bicycling	FS	Fishing	S	Outings
S	Canoeing	A	Hiking	FS	Roller skating
A	Dance (social, folk, square, modern)	W	Ice skating	A	Tumbling

Special events

FS	Track-and-field meet	FS	Field day	WS	Relay carnival
WA	Basketball-skills contest	S	Baseball and softball field meet		

*Hyatt, R.W.: Intramural sports: organization and administration, St. Louis, 1977, The C.V. Mosby Co.

Fig. 5-10. Intramural competition at the junior high school level.

Courtesy Jafro Corporation, Waterford, Conn.

SUGGESTED PROGRAM OF ACTIVITIES FOR SENIOR HIGH SCHOOLS*

Aerial darts	Gymnastics	Social, square, and folk dancing
Archery	Handball	Softball
Badminton	Hiking	Speedball
Basketball	Horseshoes	Swimming
Basket shooting	Ice skating	Table tennis
Bicycle distance race	Jogging	Tennis
Bowling	Kickball	Touch, or flag, football
Chess and/or checkers	Paddleball	Track and field
Cross-country	Physical fitness	Trampolining
Deck tennis	Roller skating	Tug-of-war
Field hockey	Rope climbing	Tumbling
Fitness day	Shuffleboard	Volleyball
Golf	Skating	Water polo
GRA	Soccer	Wrestling

*Hyatt, R.W.: Intramural sports: organization and administration, St. Louis, 1977, The C.V. Mosby Co.

Fig. 5-11. High school boys engaging in intramural team handball competition.

Courtesy North Castle Department of Parks and Recreation, Wilmington, Del.

ceive a major emphasis. At this time the interests and needs of students require such a program. These students want and need to experience the joy and satisfaction that are a part of playing on a team, excelling in an activity with one's own peers, and developing skill. Every high school, college, and university should see to it that a broad and varied program is part of the total physical education plan.

The intramural and extramural programs should receive more emphasis than they are now getting at senior high schools and colleges. They are basic to sound education. They are settings where the skills learned and developed in the instructional program can be put to use in a practical situation, with all the fun that comes from such competition. They should form a basis for applying skills that will be used during leisure time, both in the present and in the future.

There should be adequate personnel for such programs. Good leadership is needed if the programs are to prosper. Each school should be concerned with developing a plan where proper supervision and

leadership are available for afterschool hours. Qualified officials are also a necessity to ensure equal and sound competition. Facilities, equipment, and supplies should be apportioned equitably for the entire physical education program. No part of any group or any program should monopolize facilities and equipment.

The college and university level offers an ideal setting for play and sports days for both men and women.

Sports clubs should be encouraged in those activities having special appeal to groups of students. Through such clubs, greater skill is developed in the activity, and the social experiences are worthwhile.

Coeducational recreational activities should play a prominent part in the program, and Title IX ensures that this will take place. Girls and boys need to participate together. Many of the activities in the high school and college programs adapt well to both sexes. Such activities include volleyball, softball, tennis, badminton, table tennis, folk and square dancing, bowling, swimming, and skating. In some cases the

MIAMI-DADE COMMUNITY COLLEGE* Miami, Florida	
Men's events	Women's events
Fall	
Water polo	Speed and novelty
Swimming	swimming
Bowling	Golf
Flag football	Volleyball
Archery	Bowling
Volleyball	Scavenger hunt
Billiards	Kickball
Tug-of-war	Sit-down
Turkey run	volleyball
Wrestling	Turkey run
	Badminton
Winter	
Novelty swim	Games night
Basketball	Basketball and free throw
Falcon 50 (bicycle race)	contest
Track and field	Filly 440
Table tennis	Track and field
Racquetball	Frisbee
Golf	Archery
Softball	Deck tennis
Badminton	Softball
Gym hockey	Speed and novelty swim
Tennis	Easter egg throw

*Hyatt, R.W.: Intramural sports: organization and administration, St. Louis, 1977, The C.V. Mosby Co.

rules of the games will need to be modified. The play and sports days also offer a setting where both sexes can participate and enjoy worthwhile competition together.

INTRAMURAL AND EXTRAMURAL PROGRAMS IN OTHER ORGANIZATIONS

Intramural and extramural programs play a major role in many organizations outside the educational domain. For example, in industry there are many intramural leagues for employees in a variety of sports and other physical activities. In many instances, baseball diamonds, basketball courts, jogging areas, plat-

form and lawn tennis courts, swimming pools, and even golf courses are provided. Employees usually take an active role in these programs, which contribute much to their morale and well-being.

What is true in business is also true in YMCAS, Boys Clubs, and other youth- and adult-serving agencies. Intramurals represent an important part of their curricular offering.

The same types of tournaments and forms of competition employed in schools and colleges are used in these nonschool organizations.

Units and types of competition

The careful selection of appropriate units and types of competition will help enhance the values that accrue from intramural and extramural activities.

Units of competition. Many ways exist for organizing competition for the intramural and extramural programs. The units of competition should lend interest, create enthusiasm, and allow for identity with some group where an esprit de corps can be developed and where a healthy attitude is added to the competition.

At the elementary school level, the classroom provides a basis for such activity. It may be desirable in some cases to organize on some other basis, but the basic structure of the homeroom lends itself readily to this purpose.

At middle, junior high, and senior high schools, several units of organization are possible. Organization may be by grades or classes, homerooms, age, height, weight, clubs, societies, residential districts, physical education classes, study groups, or the arbitrary establishment of groups by staff members. The type of unit organization will vary from school to school and from community to community. The staff member in charge of the program should try to determine the method of organization best suited to the local situation.

At a college or university or in an industry or other organization several units for organization are also possible. Organization may be on the basis of fraternities or sororities, classes, colleges within a university, departments, clubs, societies, physical education classes, boarding clubs, churches, residential

UNIVERSITY OF TENNESSEE*

Men	Women	Faculty/staff	Corecreation
Fall			
Team:	Team:		
Football	Football	Football	Paddleball
Bowling	Tug-of-war	Golf	Racquetball
Handball	Volleyball	Handball	Tennis
Tug-of-war	Badminton	Paddleball	Badminton
Volleyball		Racquetball	
Golf		Squash	
		Tennis	
Individual and dual:	Individual and dual:	Badminton	
Handball	Paddleball	Turkey trot	
Paddleball	Racquetball		
Racquetball	Squash		
Squash	Tennis		
Tennis	Golf (par 3)		
Golf (par 3)	Pass, punt, and kick		
Pass, punt, and kick	Turkey trot		
Turkey trot			
Winter			
Team:	Team:		
Basketball	Basketball	Three-player basketball	Paddleball
Racquetball	Inner tube water polo	Handball	Racquetball
Inner tube water polo	Swimming and diving	Paddleball	Badminton
Swimming and diving	Bowling	Racquetball	Table tennis
Track relays		Squash	
Individual and dual:	Individual and dual:		
Handball	Paddleball		
Paddleball	Racquetball		
Racquetball	Squash		
Squash	Badminton		
Badminton	Basketball free throw		
Basketball free throw			
Wrestling			

*Hyatt, R.W.: Intramural sports: organization and administration, St. Louis, 1977, The C.V. Mosby Co.

Fig. 5-12. Women's intramural touch football at Colgate University, Hamilton, N.Y.

districts, geographic units or zones of the campus, dormitories, marital status, social organization, assignment by lot, honorary societies, or groups set up arbitrarily. Again, the best type of organization will vary from situation to situation.

Types of competition. Several different ways of organizing competition are possible. Three of the most common are leagues, tournaments, and meets. These methods of organization take many forms, with league play popular in the major sports, elimination tournaments utilized to great extent after league play has terminated, and meets held to culminate a season or year of sports activity.

Individual and group competition may be provided. Individual competition is adaptable to such team activities as basketball, softball, and field hockey.

Various types of tournament competition have been widely written up in books specializing in intramurals and other aspects of sports. For this reason only a brief discussion of these items will be included here.

The round robin tournament is probably one of the most widely used and one of the best types of compe-

tition, because it allows for maximum play. It is frequently used in leagues, where it works best when there are not more than eight teams. Each team plays every other team at least once during the tournament. Each team continues to play to the completion of the tournament, and the winner is the one who has the highest percentage, based on wins and losses, at the end of scheduled play.

The elimination tournament does not allow for maximum play; the winners continue to play, while the losers drop out. A team or individual is automatically out when it or he or she loses. However, this is the most economical form of organization from the standpoint of time in determining the winning player or team.

The single or straight elimination tournament is set up so that one defeat eliminates a player or team. Usually there is a drawing for positions, with provisions for seeding the better players or teams on the basis of past experience. Such seeding provides more intense competition as the tournament moves toward the finals. Under such an organization, byes are awarded in the first round of play whenever there is not an

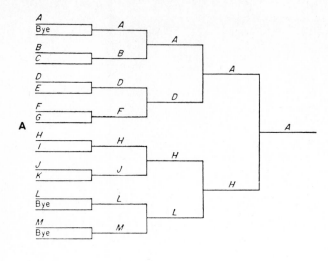

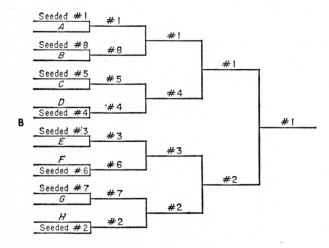

Fig. 5-13. A, Single elimination tournament. **B,** single elimination tournament with seedings.

even number of entrants. Although such a tournament is a timesaver, it is weak because it does not adequately select the second- and third-place winners. The actual winner may achieve the championship because another player who is better has a bad day. Another weakness is that the majority of participants play only once or twice in the tournament.

The double elimination tournament does not have some of the weaknesses of the single elimination, because it is necessary for a team or individual to have two defeats before being eliminated. This is also characteristic of various types of consolation elimina-

tion tournaments that permit the player or team to play more than once.

In some consolation tournaments all the players who lose in the first round and those who, because they received a bye, did not lose until the second round get to play again to determine a consolation winner. In other similar tournaments they permit any player or team who loses once, irrespective of the round in which the loss occurs, to play again. There are also other tournaments, such as the Bagnall-Wild Elimination Tournament, that place emphasis on second and third places.

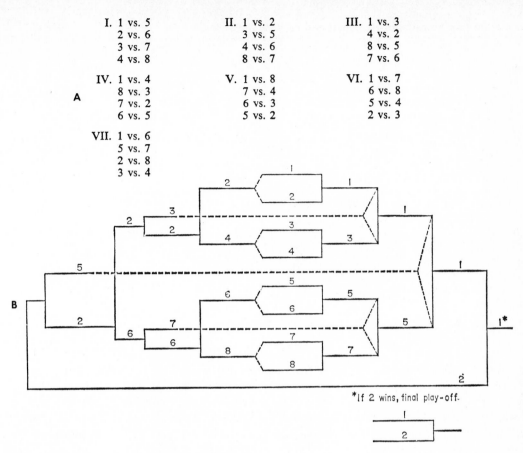

A

I. 1 vs. 5	II. 1 vs. 2	III. 1 vs. 3
2 vs. 6	3 vs. 5	4 vs. 2
3 vs. 7	4 vs. 6	8 vs. 5
4 vs. 8	8 vs. 7	7 vs. 6

IV. 1 vs. 4	V. 1 vs. 8	VI. 1 vs. 7
8 vs. 3	7 vs. 4	6 vs. 8
7 vs. 2	6 vs. 3	5 vs. 4
6 vs. 5	5 vs. 2	2 vs. 3

VII. 1 vs. 6
5 vs. 7
2 vs. 8
3 vs. 4

B

*If 2 wins, final play-off.

Fig. 5-14. A, Round robin rotation for an eight-team league. **B,** Double elimination tournament. **C,** Consolation tournament—teams. **D,** Ladder tournament.

From Intramurals for senior high schools, The Athletic Institute, Chicago.

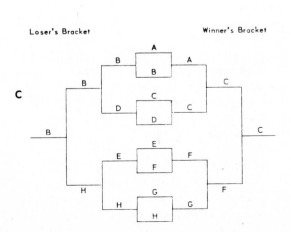

C

Loser's Bracket

Winner's Bracket

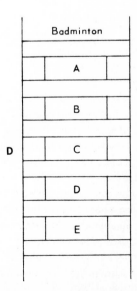

D

Badminton

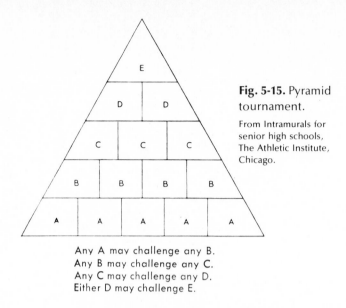

Fig. 5-15. Pyramid tournament.

From Intramurals for senior high schools, The Athletic Institute, Chicago.

Any A may challenge any B.
Any B may challenge any C.
Any C may challenge any D.
Either D may challenge E.

The ladder tournament adapts well to individual competition. Here the contestants are arranged in ladder, or vertical, formation with rankings established arbitrarily or on the basis of previous performance. Each contestant may challenge the one directly above or in some cases two above, and if he or she wins, the names change places on the ladder. This is a continuous type of tournament that does not eliminate any participants. However, it is weak because it may drag and interest may wane.

The pyramid tournament is similar to the ladder variety. Here, instead of having one name on a rung or step, there are several names on the lower steps, gradually pyramiding to the top-ranking individual. A player may challenge anyone in the same horizontal row, and then the winner may challenge anyone in the row above him or her.

The spider web tournament takes its name from the bracket design, which is the shape of a spider's web. The championship position is at the center of the web. The bracket consists of five (or any other selected number) lines drawn radially from the center, and the participant's names are placed on concentric lines crossing these radial lines. Challenges may be made by persons on any concentric line to any person on the next line closer to the center. This tournament provides more opportunity for activity.

The type of tournament organization adopted should be the one best for the group, activity, and local interests. The goal should be to have as much participation as possible for the facilities and time available. Tournaments encourage participant interest and enthusiasm and are an important part of intramural and extramural athletic programs.

Extramurals

Extramurals are a part of the total physical education program that represent an increase in the intensity of competition above that of intramurals. Whereas intramurals are conducted within a school, college, or other organization, extramurals represent informal competition with other schools, colleges, and organizations. Extramurals usually involve participants regardless of their skills and abilities. Also, they are less highly organized than varsity athletic programs. Furthermore, the emphasis is more on the social outcomes than on the winning. Three types of extramurals are discussed here: sports days, play days, and invitation days.

SPORTS DAYS, PLAY DAYS, AND INVITATION DAYS

Sports days, play days, and invitation days are rapidly growing in popularity and deserve a prominent place in the extramural athletic program of any

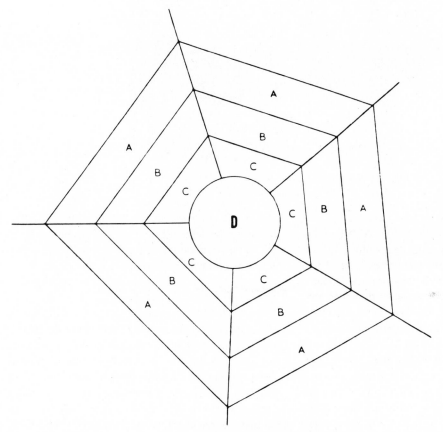

Fig. 5-16. Spider web tournament.

From Intramurals for senior high schools, The Athletic Institute, Chicago.

Note: Any A may challenge any B.
Any B may challenge any C.
Any C may challenge D.

Fig. 5-17. Sports day conducted by the Youth Services Section, Los Angeles City Schools.

school, college, or other organization. Although they have been used mainly by girls' and women's physical education programs, they are equally important for boys and men. They have received the endorsement of AAHPERD, the National Association for Girls and Women in Sport, and many other prominent associations concerned with physical education.

Sports days refer to a program when one or several schools, colleges, or other organizations participate in physical education activities. They may enter several teams in various sports. When thus organized, each team is identified with the institution it represents. Sports days may also be used to culminate a season of activity for participants within, for example, the same school or college. When several schools or colleges participate in a sports day, the number of activities may range from one to eight, although it is generally agreed that having too many activities is sometimes a disadvantage. No significant awards are granted for the various events, and the publicity does not encourage fierce competition.

Play days usually refer to a day or part of a day set aside for participation in physical education activities. It may be for participants from the same school, col-

lege, or other organization from several institutions in the same community, or from many schools and colleges in various communities and organizations . In the play day each team is composed of individuals from different organizations. Here the organization loses its identity, whereas it is maintained in the sports day. The teams are usually labeled by distinctively colored uniforms, arm bands, numbers, or some other device. The activities can be individual or team and competitive or noncompetitive. It would be noncompetitive, for example, if several students desired to engage in horseback riding, not for the purpose of competing against one another but simply for the sociability of the occasion.

Invitation days refer to a time when two schools, colleges, or other organizations usually meet for competition in an activity. This practice has worked out successfully at the end of a seasonal activity, when the winning intramural team or representatives from several teams compete against a similar group from another school, college, or other organization. The emphasis, however, is not on placing selected, highly skilled players on one team to enhance the chances of winning but on the social benefits and fun that can be gained from the occasion.

The advantages of sports days, play days, and invitation days are evident. They offer opportunities for all members of a school or an organization to participate in wholesome competition regardless of skill. They offer the individual an opportunity to participate in many varied activities in a spirit of friendly rivalry. They stress both social and physical values. They eliminate the pressures and undesirable practices associated with highly competitive athletics. They are available to all. They are especially adaptable for immature youngsters who should not be exposed to the practices and pressures of high-level competition. They add interest to student participation and offer innumerable opportunities for leadership.

Sports clubs

The concept of a sports club originated in Europe where many community sports clubs exist. A sports club specializes in a particular activity. Club teams are often established, and equipment and other expenses are usually paid for by the club members. The administration of the club is composed of voluntary or paid coaches, managers, and officers.

Some advantages of sports clubs include the following: they provide opportunities for students and others to engage in activities in which they have an interest but that are not provided in other parts of the physical education program; they provide opportunities for self-administration, self-financing, and self-planning; and they provide opportunities for students and faculty members to participate together.

According to Hyatt* a definite plan is needed whereby sports clubs can be readily organized and also disbanded if sufficient interest is not in evidence. He suggests the following steps:

1. Appoint a central coordinator
2. Determine which sports clubs the students might be interested in forming
3. Organize the club
4. Hold the first meeting
5. Write the constitution

6. Meet regularly
7. Find funds
8. Establish rules and regulations
9. Schedule practices
10. Secure equipment
11. Establish a sports club council
12. Evaluate the club
13. Phase out unneeded clubs
14. Provide for safety

Sports clubs provide interested participants an opportunity for social group experiences and the enjoyment of a particular sports activity. Clubs have many different interests, including water ballet, table tennis, boating, and ice skating. Most sports clubs in schools and colleges provide for student administration and financing. Financing may be derived from students through student fees, dances, and exhibition games. The club should provide for some relationship to the athletic administration of the institution. Procedures and policies clarifying this relationship should be a part of the club's bylaws. Such a relationship is necessary in matters of equipment and facility use, eligibility insurance, travel, injuries, and program assistance.

Sports clubs in operation today include those concerned with such activities as the following: skiing, soccer, karate, trap and skeet shooting, weightlifting, archery, bowling, boxing, canoeing, cricket, racquetball, judo, lacrosse, dance, mountaineering, parachuting, hang gliding, rifle and pistol target practice, rodeo, rugby, sailing, scuba, fencing, and flying.

Sports clubs are the responsibility of the intramural administrator in many organizations. As such, the administrator sees that constitution and bylaws, membership qualifications, fees, advisors, officers, coaches, scheduling, and financing are provided for.

In some cases clubs are financially self-sufficient as a result of fees and assessments of the members of the organization. In other instances, the school, college, business, or other organization underwrites the cost of operating the club. In other cases, finances are provided by the members themselves.

Equipment and facilities for clubs may be provided by the organization or may be rented. Travel and transportation may be provided by the organization or paid for by the participants.

---

*Hyatt, op. cit.

Fig. 5-18. Intramural racquetball, part of the industrial fitness program at the Forbes Magazine Fitness Center, New York.

The responsibility for insurance usually rests with the club member. Some organizations obtain reduced group insurance rates for their members.

Coeducational recreation

In light of Title IX and in view of the desire and interest on the part of the girls and women to engage in sports, physical education, and recreation activities, coeducational recreation (corecreation) is growing very rapidly, not only in schools and colleges, but also in community recreation and other organizational programs.

According to Hyatt* the objectives of corecreational sports in adapted form are as follows: (1) to provide opportunities for both sexes to engage in wholesome play experiences; (2) to provide opportunities for cooperative efforts of both sexes; (3) to provide new programs and activities for couples; (4) to enable participants to enjoy themselves, have fun, and develop friendships; (5) to provide opportunities for both sexes to experience new activities and develop skills; and (6) to provide the skills and information needed for spending leisure hours constructively in physical pursuits.

The corecreational program should offer opportunities for participation in many types of activities, including individual sports, team sports, noncompetitive activities, social activities, and both indoor and outdoor activities. Such activities as golf, tennis, swimming, archery, raquetball, dance, and skating are especially suited to corecreational programs. Competition, when offered, should meet the needs, abilities, and interests of both sexes. In certain cases it may be necessary to modify the rules of some sports.

One southern educational institution offers the following corecreational activities:

Fall quarter —tennis, shuffleboard, horseshoes, turkey trot
Winter quarter —paddleball, racquetball, badminton, table tennis
Spring quarter —basketball, softball, volleyball, paddleball, racquetball
Summer quarter —softball, volleyball, paddleball, racquetball, tennis

The corecreational program will enhance intramural, extramural, and club activities. It is greatly needed and should represent an important part of these programs in the future.

*Hyatt, op. cit.

CHECKLIST FOR SCHOOL CLUB AND ACTIVITY PROGRAMS

	Yes	*No*
1. Are club activity programs a normal outgrowth of the regular school program?	_____	_____
2. Are there clearly stated objectives for the club or activity program?	_____	_____
3. Does the club program supplement the formal curriculum by increasing knowledge and skills?	_____	_____
4. Are clubs organized in terms of educational value rather than administrative convenience?	_____	_____
5. Does the administration set adequate policies to guide the program?	_____	_____
6. Have the aims and objectives of the club or activity program been determined?	_____	_____
7. Can any student join a club?	_____	_____
8. Is a student limited to the number of clubs he or she may join?	_____	_____
9. Does each club have a simple constitution and bylaws that can guide students in the conduct of the organization?	_____	_____
10. Do the clubs prepare the student for democratic living?	_____	_____
11. Do the activities help to develop school spirit?	_____	_____
12. Does the school schedule club activities so that they do not conflict with regularly scheduled school activities?	_____	_____
13. Does the school administrator ensure the program of adequate space and funds to carry on a worthwhile program?	_____	_____
14. Can a student discover and develop special aptitudes and abilities through the club and activity program?	_____	_____
15. Does the club and activity program offer opportunities for vocational exploration?	_____	_____
16. Is the individual student able to develop socially acceptable attitudes and ideals through the club program?	_____	_____
17. Does the club experience provide situations that will contribute to the formation of improved behavior patterns in the student?	_____	_____
18. Do all club members actively participate in program planning?	_____	_____
19. Are the projects and activities of the club initiated primarily by the students?	_____	_____
20. Do the activities performed pertain to the club purposes?	_____	_____
21. Are students allowed to select clubs and activities according to interests?	_____	_____
22. Are students issued a calendar of events?	_____	_____
23. Does the school library make available books and periodicals needed by club and activity groups?	_____	_____
24. Does the club faculty advisor enlist the confidence of boys and girls?	_____	_____
25. Is the club faculty advisor willing to give time and thought to making the club or activity program a success?	_____	_____
26. Is the club faculty advisor able to find his or her chief satisfaction in pupil growth and not in appreciation of personal efforts?	_____	_____
27. Does the administration of the school evaluate the club periodically?	_____	_____
28. Does the club allow time for the evaluation of activities?	_____	_____

Faculty, staff, and family programs

Faculty members, staff members, and families of members of educational institutions need to have opportunities to engage in recreational activities. In some institutions programs that include such activities as volleyball, softball, basketball, tennis, golf, handball, racquetball, badminton, swimming, jogging, and bowling have been very popular. Sometimes teams and leagues are organized to add variety to the competition. Faculty sports clubs and fitness programs have been exceptionally well received. Faculty-family recreation nights or Saturday or Sunday afternoons are favorites. In such cases, children are usually not admitted unless accompanied by their parents. Faculty-student activities and sports nights are also scheduled in some schools and colleges.

In institutions where the faculty members, staff members, and families have been provided for in the recreational program, dividends have accrued for these programs in the form of support and financial help. Participants greatly appreciate it if dressing and locker room facilities can also be furnished.

Intramurals for the handicapped

In the same way that instructional physical education programs are provided for the handicapped so should intramural, extramural, and club programs be provided for them. The University of New Mexico has shown how this objective can be accomplished.* After assessing the needs of the handicapped at this institution it was determined that a variety of recreational activities should be available for the handicapped population on campus. It was felt that the involvement of the handicapped in sports and related activities would be of great value to these students if they were provided with this means of relaxation, the constructive use of leisure, and the means for maintaining good health. Next, facilities were sought that met the specialized needs of the disabled person. Then, when needed, rule modifications were made in the activities to be offered. For example, wheelchair tennis was played as doubles in the singles court,

and the ball was allowed to bounce twice before returning it over the net.

Sports activities at the University of New Mexico include such activities as swimming, tennis, archery, table tennis, badminton, bowling, and chess. These activities are scheduled at the same time as the rest of the intramural program. In this way handicapped students feel a part of the regular program and social environment and at the same time the other students become aware of the needs and interests of the handicapped students.

An important effort is put forth by the intramural staff members to contact personally all of the handicapped students on campus and urge them to participate in this program.

Funding for such programs comes from student fees, because such fees are appropriated for all students regardless of abilities and skills.

Evaluation

One of the most important functions of the intramurals administrator is the continual evaluation of the program to see if its goals are being met. It must also be evaluated in terms of budget and numbers of persons participating in programs. If a program has few participants and a relatively high cost of operation, it may have to be phased out.

Evaluation techniques will differ, but it can be generally stated that the process should include: (1) definition of program objectives; (2) data collection and evaluation including participation count, team numbers, and games played and forfeited; (3) appraisal forms, including player ratings, scores, and team surveys; (4) study groups and consultant advice; and (5) participant opinion about specific activities.

Recent forms of evaluation have used consultants on a voluntary, advisory basis. Consultants are usually objective and can provide information without prejudice. Evaluation score cards, such as Ridgeway's Scorecard for Evaluation of Men's Intramural Sports Programs in Colleges and Universities, have also been found to be functional. In addition, many schools have used computers in evaluating intramural programs. In some cases the cost of computers for evaluations is not practical.

*Perez, F.V., and Gutierrez, T.: Participation for the handicapped, Journal of Physical Education and Recreation, **50**:81, October 1979.

AN INTRAMURAL PROGRAM EVALUATION CHECKLIST*

A program can be evaluated in terms of the stated principles and objectives or according to prevalent acceptable standards.

How does the intramural program measure up to the acceptable minimum standards? By taking a few minutes to check off the items listed below, a quick evaluation can be made of the present status of the excellence of the program.

	Yes	No
Philosophy and objectives		
1. Is a written philosophy or a set of objectives available to the participants?	_____	_____
Organization and administration		
1. Is the director professionally qualified to administer the program?	_____	_____
2. Does the director devote sufficient time per week to administering his or her program?	_____	_____
3. Are participants included in the management of the program?	_____	_____
4. Is there an advisory committee?	_____	_____
Units of competition		
1. Are participants classified according to ability, age, height, or weight within the competitive unit?	_____	_____
2. Within the basic unit, are participants permitted to choose the members of their teams?	_____	_____
Program of activities		
1. Does the director consult with the participants to make sure that their interests are of prime consideration in the choice of activities in the program?	_____	_____
2. Are there both strenuous and nonstrenuous sports in the program?	_____	_____
3. Are there both team and individual sports in the program?	_____	_____
4. Are there at least five different sports making up the program?	_____	_____
5. Do corecreational activities make up part of the program?	_____	_____
Time periods		
1. Do the hours that participants are free receive top priority for scheduling?	_____	_____
2. Is the noon hour used for intramurals?	_____	_____
Methods of organizing competition		
1. Is the round robin tournament used whenever possible in preference to others?	_____	_____
Point system of awards		
1. Is recognition of any kind given to the participants for their achievements?	_____	_____
2. Is the award primarily for achievement instead of incentive for participants?	_____	_____
Rules and regulations		
1. Are the rules defining such things as eligibility, health, safety, forfeits, postponements, and team membership distributed to all participants?	_____	_____
2. Is the lack of good sportsmanship regarded as a rule violated?	_____	_____
3. Is equipment provided for all the activities offered?	_____	_____

*From Matthews, D.O.: Intramural administration principles, The Athletic Journal **46**:82, 1966. Reproduced courtesy The Athletic Journal. Adapted and updated, 1979.

Continued.

AN INTRAMURAL PROGRAM EVALUATION CHECKLIST—cont'd

Publicity

1. Is there a special bulletin board for intramural information?   _____ _____

Finances

1. Does the organization provide funds for the operation of the program?   _____ _____

Rating scale

A "yes" answer must be given in each category if a program is to be considered *good* or *excellent*.

Excellent	15 to 22
Good	13 to 14
Fair	10 to 12
Poor	9 or below

SELF-ASSESSMENT TESTS

These tests are to assist students in determining if material and competencies presented in this chapter have been mastered:

1. Justify the place of intramural, extramural, and club programs in the total physical education plan of a school, college, or other organization, in terms of their objectives and activities.

2. Imagine you are the director of physical education in a high school, college, or other organization. You have been requested by your superior to develop a list of policies for a newly organized intramural and extramural program in your organization. Prepare the policies and submit them to your class for their critical evaluation.

3. Conduct a job analysis of the roles played by various administrative personnel involved with the intramural and extramural program of the college you are attending. Compare it to the personnel discussed in this chapter.

4. Develop a set of policies that could be used as guides to accomplish the following tasks for intramural and extramural programs: selecting activities, scheduling, establishing awards and point systems, maintaining records, determining player eligibility, planning health examination, financing, and coordinating publicity and promotion.

5. Develop what you consider to be a model intramural and extramural program for an elementary school, high school, college, and large corporation.

6. Identify the following: round robin tournament, straight elimination tournament, ladder tournament, pyramid tournament, and double elimination tournament. Using

one of these tournaments, prepare a hypothetical competitive program for 16 teams in basketball.

7. Describe the procedure you would use for organizing a scuba diving club in your school.

SELECTED REFERENCES

Adkins, R.M.: Almost anything goes at ECU, Journal of Physical Education and Recreation **49**:44, 1978.

Alsager, D.: Intramural programming in Ohio high schools, Oxford, Ohio, Miami University, unpublished material, 1977.

Baren, D.E.: Improving response and participation in intramural programs, Journal of Physical Education and Recreation **51**:50, 1980.

Bucher, C.A.: Foundations of physical education, ed. 9, St. Louis, 1983, The C.V. Mosby Co.

Bucher, C.A., and Cohane, T.: Little league baseball can hurt your boy, Look, p. 74, August 11, 1963.

Bucher, C.A., and Dupee, R.K., Jr.: Athletics in schools and colleges, New York, 1965, The Center for Applied Research in Education, Inc. (The Library of Education.)

Calder, J., and McGregor, I.: How to succeed in intramurals without really trying, Journal of Physical Education and Recreation **51**:48, 1980.

Carey, D.M.: Activity hours: the commuter solution, Journal of Physical Education and Recreation **51**:67, 1980.

Clark, E.: Intramural officiating—the sport club concept, Journal of Physical Education and Recreation **51**:71, February 1980.

Colgate, J.A.: Administration of intramural and recreational activities; everyone can participate, New York, 1978, John Wiley & Sons, Inc.

Cooney, L.: Sports clubs: their place within the total intramural-recreational sports program, Journal of Physical Education and Recreation **50**:40, 1979.

Educational Policies Commission: School athletics—problems and policies, Washington, D.C., 1954, National Education Association.

Edwards, R.W.: Effective intramural publicity, Journal of Physical Education and Recreation **49:**46, 1978.

Fabian, L., and Evans, K.: Intramurals in Pennsylvania high schools, Proceedings of the National Intramural Recreation Sports Association, 1977.

Felton, H.F.: Sports clubs at commuter colleges, Journal of Physical Education and Recreation **49:**48, 1978.

Gehrke, D.: Guys and gals intramurals, Journal of Health, Physical Education, and Recreation **43:**75, 1972.

Hyatt, R.W.: Intramural sports: organization and administration, St. Louis, 1977, The C.V. Mosby Co.

Jandris, T.P.: Possibilities and potentials—high school intramurals, Journal of Physical Education and Recreation **51:**49, 1980.

Jandris, T.P.: Responding to today's diversity, Journal of Physical Education and Recreation **49:**48, 1978.

Jeter, J.M.: Extramural sports clubs and varsity athletics, Journal of Physical Education and Recreation **50:**42, 1979.

Jones, T.R.: Needed: a new philosophical model for intramurals, Journal of Health, Physical Education, and Recreation **42:**34, 1971.

Kidd, B., and Pandau, M.: Extension of the elementary physical education class through an intramural program, Journal of Physical Education and Recreation **51:**46, 1980.

Lohmiller, V.: National intramural sports council, Journal of Physical Education and Recreation **50:**50, 1979.

Maas, G.M.: Promoting high school intramurals, Journal of Physical Education and Recreation **49:**40, 1978.

Maas, G.M.: The sports club council—a vital administrative tool, Journal of Physical Education and Recreation **50:**45, 1979.

Maas, G.M.: Survey of intramural sports programs in Iowa high schools, Proceedings of the National Intramural Recreational Sports Association, 1977.

McCase, R., and Hardin, P.: Intramurals at six, Journal of Physical Education and Recreation **52:**64, 1981.

Mueller, P.: Intramurals, programming and administration, New York, 1971, The Ronald Press Co.

Mueller, P., and Rexnik, J.W.: Intramural-recreational sports: programming and administration, New York, 1979, John Wiley & Sons.

Nave, J.L.: Community junior college intramurals: guidelines for success, Journal of Physical Education and Recreation **51:**70, 1980.

Pankau, M.A.: New twists to old routines, Journal of Physical Education and Recreation **49:**45, 1978.

Perez, F.F., and Gutierrez, T.: Participation by the handicapped, Journal of Physical Education and Recreation **50:**81, 1979.

Peter, J.A., editor: Intramural administration—theory and practice, Englewood Cliffs, N.J., 1976, Prentice-Hall, Inc.

Rule books for all boys' sports. Available from the National Federation of State High School Athletic Associations, 7 South Dearborn Street, Chicago, Ill. 60603

Rule books for all girls' sports. Available from the Division for Girls' and Women's Sports, American Alliance for Health, Physical Education, Recreation, and Dance, 1201 16th Street, N.W., Washington, D.C. 20036.

Shields, E.W.: Intramurals: an avenue for developing leisure values, Journal of Physical Education and Recreation **50:**75, 1979.

Summerlin, S.K.: Initiating public school intramurals, Journal of Physical Education and Recreation **49:**43, 1978.

Turner, M.: Scheduling student officials, Journal of Physical Education and Recreation **49:**42, 1978.

Wasmer, L.: Visibility—the key to building a successful intramural program, Journal of Physical Education and Recreation **51:**54, 1980.

6

Interscholastic, intercollegiate, and other highly organized athletic programs

Instructional objectives and competencies to be achieved

After reading this chapter the student should be able to

■ Discuss the purpose of and the values derived from participating in highly organized athletic programs.

■ Specify the duties performed by such key administrative personnel in athletic programs as the athletic director, coach, athletic trainer, and members of the athletic council.

■ Explain some of the administrative considerations involved in athletic programs relating to scheduling, providing for the health of participants, contracts, officials, transportation, game management, crowd control, protests and forfeitures, awards, and records.

■ Understand some of the central issues involved in such administrative problems concerned with athletics as recruitment, eligibility, scholarships, proselyting, scouting, finances, and extra pay for coaching.

■ Describe the nature and scope of athletic programs in elementary, junior high, and senior high schools, colleges and universities, and in other organizations.

■ Identify some of the key athletic associations and the role they play in influencing highly organized athletic competition in schools, colleges, and other organizations.

Varsity interscholastic, intercollegiate, and other highly organized athletic programs represent an integral part of the total physical education program. In most cases they should evolve from the intramural and extramural athletic programs.

Athletics, with the appeal they have to youths and adults alike, should be the heart of physical education and should help achieve goals that will enrich living for all who participate.

The varsity interschool athletic program is designed for individuals most highly skilled in sports. It is one of the most interesting and receives more publicity than the other phases of physical education. The reason for this is not that it is more important or renders a greater contribution; instead, it is largely the result of popular appeal. That sportswriters and others discuss

it in glowing terms and that it involves competition pitting one school or college against another school or college also increases its public appeal. A spirit of rivalry develops, which seems to be characteristic of American culture.

Varsity interscholastic and intercollegiate athletics programs have probably had more difficulties attached to them than any other phases of the physical education program. The desire to win and to increase gate receipts has resulted in some unfortunate practices, such as unethical recruitment procedures, changing transcripts to make players eligible, admitting students who may be academically unqualified, and extensive public relations programs. Large stadiums and sports palaces have been constructed that require huge financial outlays for their upkeep.

Fig. 6-1. Intercollegiate wrestling at the State University College, Potsdam, N.Y.

The challenge of providing sound educational programs in varsity interscholastic and intercollegiate athletics is one that all physical education personnel recognize. The challenge can be met and resolved if physical educators aggressively bring to the attention of administrators and the general public the true purposes of athletics in a physical education program. It is important to stress that there is a need for having an athletic program that meets the needs of all; that such a program is organized and administered with the welfare of the individual in mind; that it is conducted in light of educational objectives that are not compromised when exposed to pressures from sportswriters, alumni, and community members; and that it has leaders trained in physical education.

What sport does for people

Wilkerson and Dodder* have conducted research to determine what sport does for people. They found that sport has the following seven functions in society:

Emotional release —sport releases emotions, acts as a safety valve, and relieves aggressive tendencies.
Affirmation of identity —sport offers opportunities to be recognized and to express one's individual qualities.
Social control —in a society where deviance is prevalent, sport provides a means of control over people.

*Wilkerson, M., and Dodder, R.A.: What does sport do for people? Journal of Physical Education and Recreation **50**:50, February, 1979. American Alliance for Health, Physical Education, Recreation, and Dance, 1900 Association Dr., Reston, Va. 22901.

Socialization —sport serves as a means of socializing those individuals who identify with it.

Change agent —sport results in social change, introduces new behavior patterns, and changes the course of history (for example, it allows for interaction of all kinds of people and for upward mobility based on ability).

Collective conscience —sport creates a communal spirit that brings people together in search of common goals.

Success —sport provides a feeling of success both for the participant and for the spectator when a player or team with whom one identifies achieves. To win in sport is also to win in life.

Values claimed for highly competitive athletics

The values of athletics are discussed under the headings of physical fitness, skill, individual development, and social development.

PHYSICAL FITNESS

Athletics contributes to physical fitness by developing organic vigor, neuromuscular skill, and desirable attitudes toward play and exercise. To develop and maintain a high degree of physical fitness, the individual must voluntarily submit to a vigorous program of exercise. Perhaps the strongest force capable of motivating a person to engage in strenuous conditioning programs is the desire to excel in competitive athletics. Athletic skills are a source of social esteem, and therefore persons will try to excel in athletic competition to enhance their peer status. The contribution to a high degree of physical fitness is an obvious concomitant.

SKILL

To achieve success in athletics, an individual must develop neuromuscular skills that will enable him or her to respond instantly and effectively in a game situation. The resulting skill development will enable the individual to respond to situations requiring strength, endurance, speed, or coordination.

Acquiring skill through athletics also leads to a high level of proficiency and a desire to engage in physical activity. Some research shows that persons who engage in sports when they are young are more likely to lead physically active lives when they are older.

The development of physical skill has many other benefits for the individual, such as feelings of accomplishment, recognition, and belonging, a more positive self-image, and less expenditure of energy.

INDIVIDUAL DEVELOPMENT

Self-realization, self-sufficiency, self-control, and self-discipline are individual qualities frequently developed through athletics. An individual's self-image is gained through comparing one's self with others; athletics provides many such opportunities for comparison.

Self-sufficiency and self-reliance are developed because athletics provides opportunities for a person to make decisions and to profit from mistakes, thereby also gaining self-direction.

Self-control may be developed; the ability to withstand or to adjust to emotional stress is believed to be a result of the stress adaptation mechanism conditioned by exercise. The increased adrenal activity that follows exercise increases the reserve of steroids available to counter stress. Furthermore, the highly charged atmosphere inherent in athletic contests provides opportunities for participants to test and develop their ability to exercise self-control.

Athletic competition develops self-discipline. Participation and success in athletics require a great deal of self-sacrifice. The individual is called on to subordinate personal wishes and desires to those of the group and to submit to strenuous conditioning programs and rigid training rules. Such sacrifices can lead to the development of both mental and physical discipline.

SOCIAL DEVELOPMENT

Athletics provides opportunities for competition and cooperation. Although competition is a part of our way of life, at the same time our way of life demands cooperation, self-sacrifice, and respect for other persons. Competition and cooperation must therefore be interdependent. Athletics provides a natural opportunity to achieve this dual objective, because individuals must be both competitive and cooperative.

Athletics also stresses fairness, adherence to the rules, ability to accept defeat, and respect for other players.

Fig. 6-2. Varsity basketball at the University of Nevada, Las Vegas.

Fig. 6-3. Wrestling contributes to physical fitness.

Courtesy Cramer Products, Inc., Gardner, Kan.

Current problems associated with athletics

Some current problems associated with athletics include a stress on false values, such as when the game becomes more important to the player than do other aspects of education; harmful pressures the community and parents place on players to win; stirred-up emotions leading to aggression and violence; and inequitable use of facilities and money to support varsity athletics for the few at the expense of athletics for all.

Problems particularly abound at the college level. In a recent article on the student athlete, Underwood* made a series of charges against several colleges and their athletic programs. For example, players at several

*Underwood, J.: The writing is on the wall, Sports Illustrated, May 19, 1980.

colleges were declared ineligible because they received credit for courses they never attended and coaches were suspended because they doctored academic transcripts. Underwood recommended several changes to help correct such abuses: abolish freshman eligibility to give an athlete a year to adjust to college; make it mandatory for an athlete to attend classes; institute a formula restricting scholarships when a university does not graduate a certain number of its student athletes; remove all matters of eligibility from the jurisdiction of coaches; and make it possible for the student athlete who leaves school for professional athletics to come back to college to finish acadmic studies at the college's or professional organization's expense. Underwood summed up his report by pointing out that the real solution to the problem is caring for young people, wanting to see them get an education, and helping them make a contribution to society.

The changing role of girls' and women's athletic competition

There is considerable emphasis on girls' and women's athletic competition today in schools, colleges, and other organizations. Traditionally, girls and women have suffered in some school, college, and other organizational athletic programs. In some cases they have had limited access to many athletic activities and have at times been subjected to poor equipment and facilities and other hardships. The arguments that traditionally have been used by a few physical educators and administrators to justify their actions and decisions often centered on a woman's delicacy, health, and femininity. Studies, however, indicate that girls and women can benefit from sports participation, just as their male counterparts.

The women's movement, proponents of equality in girls' and women's sports, and Title IX have altered the concept of women's sports in recent years. Women are becoming more and more accepted as athletes, with a full right to experience all kinds of sports activities. Many persons wrongly interpret this kind of statement to mean that women want to compete with men in all sports activities. Although women may compete with men in certain coeducational activities, such as bowling, tennis, and volleyball, they also want sepa-

Fig. 6-4. Women's gymnastics at Smith College, Northampton, Mass.

rate but equal athletic programs, including equal funding, equipment, and facility use.

Procedures and practices concerning interscholastic and intercollegiate athletic competition for girls vary from state to state. Some schools and colleges have broad programs of interscholastic athletics, others have few, and some have modified programs. Most states do not set up specific requirements for girls' athletics but feel that their established regulations apply to both girls and boys. A few states have athletic associations for girls that are similar to those for boys.

The National Association for Girls and Women in Sport (NAGWS) of the AAHPERD believes that teams should be provided for all girls and women desiring competitive athletic participation. Adequate funds, facilities, and staff should be provided for these programs.

Key administrative personnel involved in athletic programs

Key administrative personnel involved in athletic programs include the director of athletics, the coach, the athletic trainer, and members of the athletic council.

Many other personnel are involved in athletic programs, particularly at the college level, such as assistant or associate athletic directors, sports information director, athletic business manager, facility director, travel coordinator, administrative assistant, fund raiser, equipment manager, game manager, ticket manager, and coordinator of special events. Only the four major administrative positions will be discussed here.

THE DIRECTOR OF ATHLETICS

The director of athletics implements the athletic policies as established by the council, board, or committee. Responsibilities of the athletic director include preparing the budget for the sports program, purchasing equipment and supplies, scheduling athletic contests, arranging for officials, supervising eligibility requirements, making arrangements for transportation, seeing that medical examinations of athletes and proper insurance coverage are adequate, and generally supervising the program.

The athletic director should be prepared in physical education and athletics. The best qualifications include a major in physical education, as well as experience as a player and as an athletic coach.

In a large school, college, or other organization with a large athletic program, the athletic director might work closely with a faculty manager or business manager of athletics. This manager might handle officials, hire ticket sellers and ticket takers, develop programs, keep financial records, pay guarantees, and be in charge of security.

The director of athletics in some large programs might also have an assistant to help with such responsibilities as scheduling, staff supervision, eligibility, budgets, purchasing, travel, and insurance.

There might also be a director of sports information who handles media releases, develops brochures, and handles such things as athletic statistics and photography. Furthermore, there may be a coordinator of

Fig. 6-5. Girl gymnastic champion on the balance beam. Championships conducted by the Youth Services Section, Los Angeles City Schools.

athletic alumni relations with whom the athletic director will need to work in recruiting athletes and in fund raising.

A question continually asked concerns whether athletic directors should also be coaches. Very often athletic directors at small community or junior colleges are asked to coach along with their other responsibilities. In an attempt to answer this question, Poorman, athletic director of Lakeland Community College, Mentor, Ohio, surveyed 206 athletic directors and coaches in junior and community colleges with enrollments ranging from 3000 to 5000 students.

The coaches and athletic directors were asked the following question: "Should athletic directors at 2-year junior or community colleges be involved in coaching an intercollegiate sport?" In general, most athletic directors felt they should not coach, but because of budgetary problems, coaching became necessary. The coaches, many of whom expected to eventually enter administration, felt they would like to continue coaching after becoming administrators and thought athletic directors should coach. Some athletic

administrators indicated that if athletic directors coached, they would not have adequate time to complete administrative functions.

Bryson* has compiled a complete list of duties performed by athletic directors. Although these are listed for secondary school athletic directors, most of the duties would also apply equally to college and university athletic directors. This list of duties, adapted as follows, provides a complete picture of an athletic director's functions.

GENERAL ADMINISTRATIVE TASKS

In the general area of administrative tasks, Bryson says the major responsibilities of athletic directors are to

- Keep office hours
- Perform office routines including correspondence and clerical duties
- Prepare notices and announcements
- Help in preparing bulletin and catalog statements

---

*Bryson, L.A.: Duties performed by secondary school athletic directors. The athletic educator's report, Old Saybrook, Conn., April 1981, Physical Education Publications.

Fig. 6-6. Varsity basketball at the University of Nevada, Las Vegas.

- Assist in selecting noncoaching personnel
- Orient noncoaching personnel
- Help in preparing daily work schedules for noncoaching personnel
- Develop an evaluation program for noncoaching personnel
- Serve on athletic department committees
- Serve on school committees outside the athletic department
- Participate and take a leadership role in developing athletic department aims and objectives

- Attend staff meetings
- Develop and maintain an accident report system
- Provide detailed reports to superiors—principal, superintendent, board of education
- Obtain information and reports from staff members
- Maintain complete records for each sport each year
- Develop a comprehensive crowd control program with procedures to be employed in specific situations
- Coordinate the department's program with those of other departments in the school district

PUBLIC RELATIONS AND COMMUNITY SERVICE

In the area of public relations and community service, Bryson says athletic directors are generally expected to:

- Plan public relations programs
- Conduct public relations programs personally
- Provide publicity for the press and broadcast media
- See that coaches perform public relations functions
- Be aware of public relations procedures
- Collaborate with the sports information director or other responsible personnel in planning publicity campaigns for the athletic department
- Join appropriate community service organizations
- Be speakers for community service groups
- Speak to school-related organizations
- Be advisors to public and private agencies
- Promote joint school-community activities
- Entertain or meet casually with students and athletes
- Sponsor club activities
- Assist in planning and supervising faculty recreation activities
- Cooperate and work with athletic booster clubs
- Arrange for community use of facilities
- Arrange special receptions and dinners at appropriate times and for appropriate purposes
- Evaluate coverage given the athletic program by the news media
- Plan and conduct clinics and workshops
- Plan ways of teaching spectator sportsmanship, proper behavior, and rules of various sports

PROFESSIONAL ACTIVITIES

Bryson says athletic directors should be active in professional organizations. They should, as part of their professional activity:

- Serve on professional committees on the national, state, and local levels
- Participate in professional meetings and conferences
- Represent the school or district at meetings in some capacity other than that of athletic directors
- Write for professional journals, magazines, and bulletins
- Contribute to professional knowledge and research by completing checklists and questionnaires
- Take graduate courses for professional advancement
- Visit other schools and cities to observe outstanding programs
- Read in own and allied fields for professional improvement
- Teach classes in health, physical education, and recreation

- Observe sports events at other schools, as time permits, to obtain ideas to improve their own programs
- Substitute for coaches who are absent
- Help plan workshops and clinics
- Encourage professional growth of coaches
- Keep a log or diary of professional activities

EQUIPMENT AND FACILITIES

With respect to equipment and facilities, Bryson says athletic directors should:

- Assist in developing and planning an inventory
- Take an inventory annually or at periodic intervals
- Assist in the care and repair of supplies, equipment, and facilities
- Assist in selecting equipment to be used in various sports
- Assist in planning new facilities
- Work with architects, engineers, and others involved in constructing new facilities
- Supervise maintenance and custodial personnel working in or assigned to the athletic department
- Inspect and evaluate equipment for safety
- Develop an equipment evaluation safety form
- Devise a plan for issuing and returning equipment
- Develop a plan for inspecting and repairing facilities
- Provide an overall facilities master plan to meet the present and future athletic needs of the school or district
- Interview persons selling athletic equipment
- Be current in knowledge of equipment and facilities
- Advise departmental personnel with respect to installing equipment

BUDGET AND FINANCE

Secondary school athletic directors have many responsibilities in budget and finance. Among those cited by Bryson are:

- Request and review annual budgets with coaches in each sport
- Discuss final budgets with coaches
- Approve general office spending
- Discuss proposed and final budgets with the budget director
- Keep records and inform coaches of monthly expenditures
- Approve travel receipts
- Arrange for purchasing all athletic equipment and supplies for the school or district
- Assume legal responsibility for department equipment
- Plan and conduct fund-raising activities and seek donations from various groups to supplement school board appropriations for athletics

- Approve all requisitions for purchases of athletic supplies and equipment
- Meet with appropriate administrators to set prices for tickets to games and meets
- Check all bills pertaining to the athletic department
- Purchase or see to it that insurance is purchased to protect the department from damages (liability, accident, equipment, facilities)
- Arrange payment for all personnel including game officials
- Evaluate the financial structure of the athletic department to eliminate extravagance and to make sure actual needs are met
- Make arrangements for concessions at athletic contests
- Acknowledge all contributions and donations made to the Athletic Department

SPECIALIZED SPORTS TASKS

In the all-encompassing category of specialized sports tasks, Bryson says athletic directors should:

- Interpret school rules and regulations with and for coaches
- Represent the school or district at sports meetings
- Interpret conference and state rules and regulations for coaches
- Establish job descriptions for various head and assistant coaching positions
- Prepare and sign game contracts
- Determine, with the help and cooperation of the administrators and the school board, the sports in which the school will participate
- Supervise athletic contests
- Accompany teams on trips
- Prepare a system for keeping records of all athletic contests
- Meet with individual coaches to discuss maters pertaining to their teams and athletes
- Prepare guidelines for all sports
- Arrange for transportation for teams
- Make reservations for meals and lodging when needed
- Issue passes for appropriate individuals attending athletic contests
- Assist coaches in performing routine duties
- Work with coaches in selecting and contacting officials and in preparing contracts for officials
- Make arrangements for scouting athletic contests (both scouting other schools and for scouts attending games at their school)
- Coach, as necessary, but never at the expense of the overall administration of the athletic program
- See that athletic facilities are ready and in good condition for contests

- Help in acquiring nonofficiating personnel for athletic contests
- See that all participants in the athletic program have appropriate medical examinations
- Provide medical and dental services for all athletes who need them as a result of participation in the athletic program
- Counsel athletes on academic matters
- Counsel athletes on personal matters
- Establish procedures for reviewing the academic progress of athletes
- Prepare disciplinary policies governing the athletic program
- Establish recruiting policies and procedures to be used by representatives of colleges and universities visiting their school or district to provide the best possible service to student athletes
- Determine suitable standards for awards
- Plan awards dinners in cooperation with coaches and booster clubs
- Discipline athletes for violation of school rules
- Develop eligibility rules as necessary
- Arrange suitable excuses from class so that athletes can participate in away games and meets
- Prepare schedules for athletic teams in conjunction with coaches of individual sports
- Serve on the athletic committee
- Coordinate and direct special championship events held on the school grounds or in the school's facilities
- Present appropriate awards at athletic contests or assemblies
- Interview prospective staff members
- Orient new department staff members, including head and assistant coaches

USING THE LIST FOR EVALUATION

With a little imagination and a slight revision in format, school administrators can use Bryson's list as an instrument for evaluating athletic directors. A school district might list all the items—or appropriate items—in each category and rate the athletic director on the performance of each item on a scale of zero to ten. Zero would indicate a failure to perform, five would be an average performance, and ten would be superior. A predetermined minimum standard should be established that the athletic director must attain.

Because five is suggested as an average performance level, the administration might establish a 6 to 6.5 required level of performance in each category. Many options are available, but the main concern is to see that the athletic director knows what he or she is expected to do, and that his or her performance is evaluated.

THE COACH

One of the most popular phases of physical education professional work is coaching. Many students who show exceptional skill in an interscholastic sport feel they would like to become members of the profession so that they may coach. They feel that because they have proved themselves outstanding athletes in high school, they will be successful in coaching. This, however, is not necessarily true. There is insufficient evidence to show that exceptional skill in any activity necessarily guarantees success in teaching that activity. Many other factors such as personality, interest in youths, knowledge of human growth and development, psychology, intelligence, integrity, leadership, character, and a sympathetic attitude are essential to coaching success.

Coaching should be recognized as teaching. Because of the nature of the position, a coach may be in a better position to teach concepts that affect daily living than any other member of a school faculty. Youths, with their inherent drive for activity and action and their quest for the excitement and competition found in sports, look up to the coach and in many cases feel that the coach is a person to emulate. Therefore, the coach should recognize his or her influence and see the value of such attributes as character, personality, and integrity. Although a coach must know thoroughly the game he or she is coaching, these other characteristics are equally important.

Coaching is characterized in some organizations by insecurity of position. Whether a coach feels secure depends to great extent on the administration. Coaching offers an interesting and profitable career to many individuals. However, the coach should recognize the possibility of finding himself or herself in a situation where the pressure to produce winning teams may be so great as to cause unhappiness, insecurity, and even the loss of a job.

Four qualifications are found in the outstanding coach. First, the coach is able to teach the fundamentals and strategies of the sport; he or she *must* be a good teacher. Second, the coach needs to understand the player: how a person functions at a particular level of development—with a full appreciation of skeletal growth, muscular development, and physical and emotional limitations. Third, the coach understands the game coached; thorough knowledge of techniques, rules, and similar information is basic. Fourth, the coach has a desirable personality and character. Patience, understanding, kindness, honesty, sportsmanship, sense of right and wrong, courage, cheerfulness, affection, humor, energy, and enthusiasm are imperative.

The only qualification some coaches have is that they have played the game or sport in high school, college, or professionally. It is generally recognized that the best preparation a coach can have is training in physical education. In light of this, several states are attempting to see that coaches, particularly at the precollege level, have at least some training in physical education.

Sabock* indicates the following adapted list as the qualities of a good coach:

Transparent realism—Allow personal and human qualities to show and not pretend to be someone else.
Reasoning—plans involved in coaching should be thought through rationally.
Interest in individuals—Know individually each member of the squad.
Respect—This quality must be earned.
Ability to motivate—Get players to want and to strive to be better athletes.
Dedication—This is the desire and will to try to do the best job possible.
Ability to discipline—A firm sense of discipline is essential.
Identification of goals—Goals must be established for oneself and for the program.
Ability to recognize talent—The ability to be able to recognize prospective athletes is essential.
Ability to use available talent—The ability to do well with the talent available at any particular time is important.
Enthusiasm—When the coach is enthusiastic, the players will also be enthusiastic.
Intense desire to win—Just as enthusiasm is important, so is the desire to win.
Willingness to work—Long hours of work are necessary to achieve success.
Knowledge of the sport—A critical quality for the master coach.

---

*Modified from Sabock, R.J.: The coach, Philadelphia, 1979, W.B. Saunders Co.

Fig. 6-7. The coach must be a good teacher. A pole vaulter is coached in the Youth Services Section, Los Angeles City Schools.

Dislike of mediocrity—Whatever is done must be done correctly.

Understanding boys and girls—It is important to know the participant, as well as the game.

Know what factors make the difference between winning and losing—Such factors as personnel, conditioning, and mental attitude are important.

Ability to develop pride—Pride is contagious.

Ability to organize—This is an essential quality to get the best results.

Language—A coach is also an English teacher.

Moral standards—Coaches are role models for boys and girls.

Dignity—Keeping oneself under control at all times is essential.

Courage of convictions—A coach should believe in something.

Ethical standards—Living by the rules is important.

Good judgment—This quality, if put to use, helps to solve many of the coach's problems.

Consistency—Consistency in discipline and other factors is important.

Fairness—All members of the squad should be treated alike.

Imagination—Being creative will help to bring success.

Sense of humor—People like to hear humorous things.

Behavioral guidelines specifically for coaches

The following behavioral guidelines specifically for coaches who work with children and youths are based on research conducted by Smoll and Smith.*

1. Provide immediate rewards for good performance. Reward children for good effort, as well as for positive results of performance. A positive statement such as "Good catch" or "Good try" and a pat on the back represent adequate rewards. Expensive, tangible rewards are not necessary.

2. Give encouragement to players immediately after mistakes. Provide corrective instruction when needed to minimize occurrence of the particular mistake in the future. Use positive instructional techniques. ("You will have a better chance to catch the ball if you use two hands instead of one hand.")

3. Do not give corrective instruction in a hostile or threatening manner. Be positive and use an encouraging tone of voice when correcting an athlete who has made a mistake.

4. Do not punish to correct mistakes. For example, do not require a player to run the bases ten times because he or she failed to touch a base after a hit.

5. Maintain order by clearly outlining expectations of all personnel associated with the team. Involve players in the formulation of rules and regulations.

6. Provide instruction as a central focus of coaching. Use demonstrations as a teaching strategy when possible, provided you possess the necessary skill. For example, show the players the correct method of dribbling a soccer ball instead of simply telling them how to dribble.

7. Give instruction in a positive manner. Avoid using sarcasm and ridicule when instructing youngsters.

8. Set a good example for team unity and behavior. Treat all players fairly and do not yell or use abusive language when communicating with officials.

9. Teach all players the necessary skills of the sport. Do not spend more time with highly skilled players.

10. Never stop striving to communicate effectively with your players.

11. Communicate with players at the most opportune time. Wait until the youngster is receptive to your communication. Remember that different individuals are receptive to communication from the coach at different times. For instance, some players respond to immediate corrections while others profit more if the feedback is delayed.

12. Communicate to parents the need to let children have fun while participating in sports. Encourage parents not to place too much emphasis on winning and, most of all, implore parents not to berate their children when they make mistakes in sports. Urge them instead to give positive support and encouragement.

Certification of coaches

Standards for coaching certification were identified by the AAHPERD through their Task Force on Certification of High School Coaches. The essential areas identified by the Task Force were (1) medical aspects of athletic coaching, (2) sociological and psychological aspects of coaching, (3) theory and techniques of coaching, (4) kinesiological foundations of coaching, and (5) physiological foundations of coaching.

Coaches should be encouraged to seek training even if certification standards have not yet been required by their particular state. The trend toward certification is growing, but more important, the thorough training of all coaches is essential to the health and performance of athletes.

Nobel and Sigle* surveyed the 50 states and Washington, D.C., regarding the certification of coaches. The responses provide the following information:

In 34 states nonteachers are allowed to coach either regularly or in an emergency.

In 20 states there are no minimum requirements other than age.

In 8 states a teaching certificate is required.

In 1 state a Red Cross First Aid course is required.

In 1 state attendance at a rules clinic in the particular sport coached is required.

In 1 state a knowledge of developmental skills of the sport coached is required.

In 5 states (Iowa, Minnesota, Pennsylvania, South Dakota, and Wyoming) paraprofessionals are required to complete a coaching preparation program

In 15 states limitations are placed on nonteaching

---

*Smoll, F.B., and Smith, R.E.: Behavioral guidelines for youth sport coaches, Journal of Physical Education and Recreation **49**:46, March 1978.

*Noble, L., and Sigle, G.: Minimum requirements for interscholastic coaches, Journal of Physical Education and Recreation **51**:32, November/December 1980.

Fig. 6-8. Athletics is a source of great public interest.

Courtesy Cramer Products, Inc., Gardner, Kan.

coaches, such as not allowing them to be head coaches or that a teacher must be present on road trips.

In 8 states (Arkansas, Iowa, Minnesota, New York, Oklahoma, Oregon, South Dakota, and Wyoming) additional requirements are necessary, such as taking certain courses, having work in physical education, being versed in first aid, having coaching experience, and being certified in physical education.

Evaluation of coaches

As an example of the evaluation of coaches, the Beaverton (Oregon) School District's* form for evaluating their coaches is depicted in Fig. 6-9.

THE ATHLETIC TRAINER

The profession of athletic training has taken on greater significance in recent years with the increase in sports programs and the recognition that the health of the athlete is an important consideration.

Today's athletic trainers need special preparation to carry on their duties, which include prevention of injuries, first aid and postinjury treatment, and rehabilitation work. Such preparation, if possible, should include a major in physical education, certification by the National Athletic Trainers Association or being a registered physical therapist. Furthermore, such personal qualifications are needed as emotional stability under stress, ability to act rationally when injuries occur, and a standard of ethics that places the welfare of the participant uppermost. For further information see Chapter 15.

In many schools and colleges the financial situation does not permit hiring a full-time athletic trainer. Some schools and colleges therefore find that if a full-time athletic trainer is not a possibility, it may be feasible to provide such a service by hiring a person who is a part-time teacher and a part-time trainer; is a secretary or nurse and is also a trainer; is a trainer–assistant athletic director; is a trainer–health service person; is a trainer who can also teach in the adapted physical education program; or is a teacher on the faculty who instructs in an athletic training degree program and who also is an athletic trainer.

---

*Pflug, J.: Evaluating high school coaches, Journal of Physical Education and Recreation, **51**:76, April 1980. Courtesy of the American Alliance for Health, Physical Education, Recreation, and Dance, 1900 Association Dr., Reston, Va.

Special qualifications for athletic trainers

Athletic trainers should complete a 4-year college curriculum that emphasizes the biological and physical sciences, psychology, coaching techniques, first aid and safety, nutrition, and other courses in physical education. The athletic trainer should be competent in accident prevention, emergency treatment, and rehabilitation of injured athletes. The athletic trainer should be able to work closely with administrators, coaches, physicians, the school nurse, students, and parents in a cooperative effort to provide the best possible health care for all athletes under his or her jurisdiction. He or she is also responsible in many college programs for development and supervision of a student athletic training staff.

Klafs and Arnheim* list the following as the personal qualifications needed by athletic trainers: good health, sense of fair play, maturity and emotional stability, good appearance, leadership, compassion, intellectual capacity, sense of humor, kindness and understanding, competence and responsibility, and a sound philosophy of life.

The courses required in professional preparation programs for athletic trainers also indicate some of the competencies needed. These courses include: anatomy, physiology, physiology of exercise, applied anatomy and kinesiology, psychology, first aid and safety, nutrition, remedial exercise, health, techniques of athletic training, and laboratory practice in the techniques of athletic training.

More women need to become involved in athletic training. In many undergraduate physical education programs, women have not received adequate preparation in athletic training courses. Most athletic training in women's competitive sports is performed by men who often cannot handle the physical and emotional trauma suffered by female athletes. In addition, a female athlete may be reluctant to seek the services of a male athletic trainer. Women are more likely to be open about personal problems with other women. Athletic training is important in all sports, male and female. Injuries and other related problems occur regularly in women's sports, and women should be adequately trained to meet these situations.

---

*Klafs, C.E., and Arnheim, D.D.: Modern principles of athletic training, ed. 5, St. Louis, 1977, The C.V. Mosby Co.

DEPARTMENT OF ATHLETICS

Name_____   SCHOOL DISTRICT NO. 48   Evaluator _____

Beaverton, Oregon

Assignment _____   Date _____

COACH'S EVALUATION

COACH'S SELF-EVALUATION (To be completed prior to the start of coaching assignment.)

1. Statement of personal goals and/or program goals as they relate to your coaching
    assignment.

    _____

    _____

    _____

2. Statement of self-evaluation on applicable criteria relative to completion of goals
    statement. (To be completed at the conclusion of your coaching assignment.)

    _____

    _____

    _____

3. ATHLETIC COORDINATORS EVALUATION (To be completed subsequent to the coaching assign-
    ment then reviewed with the coach.)
    CODE: Scale of 1 to 5, with 5 highest competency. If blank, not applicable.

    A. Administration   Circle one
        1. Care of equipment (issue, inventory, cleaning, etc.) 1 2 3 4 5
        2. Organization of staff   1 2 3 4 5
        3. Organization of practices   1 2 3 4 5
        4. Communication with coaches   1 2 3 4 5
        5. Adherence to district and school philosophy and policies
            (eligibility reports, inventories, budgets, rosters,
            insurance forms, and follow-up, scores reported)
        6. Public relations   1 2 3 4 5
        7. Supervision   1 2 3 4 5
    B. Skills
        1. Knowledge of fundamentals   1 2 3 4 5
        2. Presentation of fundamentals   1 2 3 4 5
        3. Conditioning   1 2 3 4 5
        4. Game preparation   1 2 3 4 5
        5. Prevention and care of injuries (follow-up with parents) 1 2 3 4 5
    C. Relationships
        1. Enthusiasm   1 2 3 4 5
            a. For working with students   1 2 3 4 5
            b. For working with staff (support of other programs) 1 2 3 4 5
            c. For working with academic staff   1 2 3 4 5
            d. For the sport itself   1 2 3 4 5
        2. Discipline   1 2 3 4 5
            a. Firm but fair   1 2 3 4 5
            b. Consistent   1 2 3 4 5
        3. Communication with players
            a. Individual   1 2 3 4 5
            b. As a team   1 2 3 4 5
    D. Performance
        1. Appearance of team on the field or floor   1 2 3 4 5
        2. Execution of the team on the field or floor   1 2 3 4 5
        3. Attitude of the team   1 2 3 4 5
        4. Conduct of coach during game   1 2 3 4 5
    E. Self-improvement
        1. Attends in-district meetings and clinics   1 2 3 4 5
        2. Attends out-of-district clinics   1 2 3 4 5
        3. Keeps updated by reading current literature   1 2 3 4 5
4. Review by Building Athletic Coordinator with Coach
    (District Athletic Coordinator will review all evaluations before
    forwarding to principal.)

    _____

    _____

    _____

    _____

5. To be placed in working papers of principal and forwarded to the personnel office
    with yearly teaching evaluation.

Original-Building Principal
  Canary-District Athletic Coordinator   Signed by Coach
    Pink-Building Athletic Coordinator
    Gold-Coach
                                               Signed by Evaluator

Fig. 6-9. An example of a form for evaluating coaches.

Courtesy of the American Alliance for Health, Physical Education, Recreation,
and Dance, 1900 Association Dr., Reston, Va.

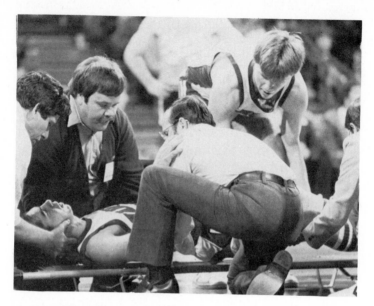

Fig. 6-10. Athletic trainer at work.

Courtesy Cramer Products, Inc., Gardner, Kan.

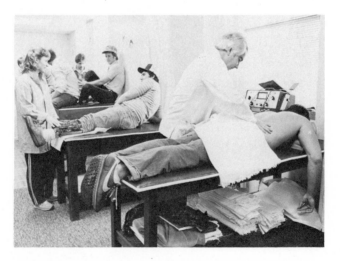

Fig. 6-11. Athletic trainer at work.

Courtesy Cramer Products, Inc., Gardner, Kan.

THE ATHLETIC COUNCIL

Most colleges and many schools have some type of athletic council, board, or committee, that establishes athletic policies for the institution. It may involve only faculty members, or it may also involve students. Such councils, boards, or committees are responsible for giving the athletic program proper direction in the educational program.

The composition of such committees or councils varies widely from school to school and college to college. In a school, the principal may serve as chairperson, or this position may be held by the director of physical education or other faculty member. The committee may include coaches, members of the board of education, faculty members, students, or members of the community at large. In a college or university, the composition of the committee may consist of administrators, faculty members, students, athletic directors, coaches, and others.

Some of the functions of athletic councils at the high school and college levels include making policy, approving awards, advising athletic department on problems, endorsing and approving schedules and budgets, evaluating the athletic program, investigating complaints, interviewing and recommending coaches to athletic directors, developing eligibility guidelines, considering postseason play, approving codes of ethics, reviewing scholarship programs, and deciding if sports should be added or dropped.

Administrative functions in athletic programs

Many administrative functions are pertinent to conducting highly organized athletic programs, including schedules and practice periods, contracts, health of the players, officials, transportation, game management, crowd control, protests and forfeitures, awards, and records.

SCHEDULES AND PRACTICE PERIODS

Scheduling involves maintaining a proper balance between home and away contests, seeking contests with organizations and institutions of approximately the same size and caliber of play, and trying to restrict the scope of the geographical area where contests are held to keep transportation costs to a minimum.

Where leagues and conferences are involved, schedules are usually made many months or years in advance and involve representatives from each of the institutions involved.

Athletic directors frequently involve the coaches or in many instances permit the coaches to schedule their own sports and limit their activity to negotiating the contracts involved.

There should be defined limits for the length of seasons. These should have the approval of school, college, or other organizational authorities. The length of seasons should be arranged so they interfere as little as possible with other school and college work. There should be adequate practice before the first game so the players are in good physical condition. Depending on the sport, there should be limits on the total number of games and also on the number of games played in any one week. Postseason games are not considered advisable by many educators.

Some factors that may affect scheduling include climatic conditions, maximizing gate receipts, number of participants, state playoffs and invitational tournaments, transportation, school facilities available, different sports that appeal to the same students, and maximum number of games or contests permitted.

Practice periods should be scheduled equitably and according to Title IX regulations. All coaches and other personnel involved in using the facilities should be involved in decision making.

CONTRACTS

Written contracts are usually essential in the administration of interscholastic and intercollegiate athletics. On the college level, in particular, games are scheduled many months or years in advance. Memories and facts tend to fade and become obscure with time. To avoid misunderstanding and confusion, it is best to have in writing a contract between the schools or colleges concerned.

Contracts should be properly executed and signed by official representatives of both schools or colleges. Many athletic associations provide specially prepared forms for use of member schools or colleges. Such forms usually contain the names of the schools, dates, and circumstances and conditions

ATHLETIC EVENTS AGREEMENT
Department of Intercollegiate Athletics
University of Nevada, Las Vegas

ATHLETIC ACTIVITY _____

_____ VS UNIVERSITY OF NEVADA, LAS VEGAS

I. THE PARTIES HERETO HEREBY AGREE AS FOLLOWS:

(1) _____
         (Location)   (Date)   (Time)

(2) _____
         (Location)   (Date)   (Time)

(3) _____
         (Location)   (Date)   (Time)

(4) _____
         (Location)   (Date)   (Time)

II. THE FINANCIAL AGREEMENT SHALL BE SPECIFIED SUBSEQUENTLY:

(1) _____
   (Financial Sum)

(2) _____
   (Complimentary Tickets)

(3) _____
   (Other)

FOR: UNIVERSITY OF NEVADA, LAS VEGAS   FOR: VISITING TEAM

Signature: _____   Signature: _____

Title: _____   Title: _____

Date: _____   Date: _____

DISTRIBUTION:

   WHITE: University of Nevada, Las Vegas

   PINK: Visiting Team

Fig. 6-12. Athletic events agreement.

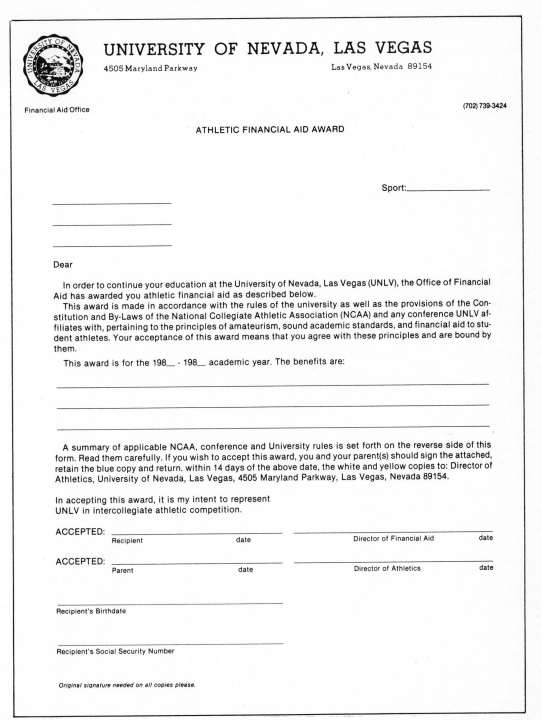

UNIVERSITY OF NEVADA, LAS VEGAS

4505 Maryland Parkway   Las Vegas, Nevada 89154

Financial Aid Office   (702) 739-3424

ATHLETIC FINANCIAL AID AWARD

Sport:_____

_____

_____

_____

Dear

    In order to continue your education at the University of Nevada, Las Vegas (UNLV), the Office of Financial Aid has awarded you athletic financial aid as described below.

    This award is made in accordance with the rules of the university as well as the provisions of the Constitution and By-Laws of the National Collegiate Athletic Association (NCAA) and any conference UNLV affiliates with, pertaining to the principles of amateurism, sound academic standards, and financial aid to student athletes. Your acceptance of this award means that you agree with these principles and are bound by them.

    This award is for the 198__ - 198__ academic year. The benefits are:

_____

_____

_____

    A summary of applicable NCAA, conference and University rules is set forth on the reverse side of this form. Read them carefully. If you wish to accept this award, you and your parent(s) should sign the attached, retain the blue copy and return. within 14 days of the above date, the white and yellow copies to: Director of Athletics, University of Nevada, Las Vegas, 4505 Maryland Parkway, Las Vegas, Nevada 89154.

In accepting this award, it is my intent to represent
UNLV in intercollegiate athletic competition.

ACCEPTED: _____   _____
                Recipient   date   Director of Financial Aid   date

ACCEPTED: _____   _____
                Parent   date   Director of Athletics   date

_____
Recipient's Birthdate

_____
Recipient's Social Security Number

Original signature needed on all copies please.

Fig. 6-13. Athletic financial aid award.

under which the contests will be held. Furthermore, they usually provide for penalties if contracts are not fulfilled by either party.

HEALTH OF THE PLAYERS*

Athletics should contribute to the health of the players. Through wholesome physical activity the participant should become more physically, mentally, emotionally, and socially fit.

Medical examination. One of the first requirements for every participant in an athletic program should be a medical examination to determine physical fitness and capacity to engage in such a program. The strenuous nature of athletics and the demands placed on the participant make it imperative that a thorough medical examination should be required.

Safety. Everything possible should be done to ensure the safety of the participant. A coach should always conduct the program with the health of the players in mind. He or she will have a knowledge of first aid and will continually be alert to stop players from further participation if they are unduly fatigued; have received head, spine, or neck injuries; or are dazed. He or she will not allow a player who has been unconscious as a result of injury to resume play until a thorough check and approval have been given by a qualified physician. The coach will also work closely with the team or school physician, trying to make every effort possible to guard the health of the players.

Proper conditioning and training should take place before any player is subjected to competition. Such conditioning and training should be progressive and gradual. There should always be enough players on the squad to allow for substitutions in the event a person is not physically or otherwise fit for play.

Proper facilities and equipment should be available to guard the safety and health of the players. This means that facilities are constructed according to recommended standards concerning size, surfacing, and various safety features. Protective equipment should be provided as needed in the various sports. If desirable facilities and equipment are not available, such competition should not be provided.

Games should be scheduled that result in equal and safe competition. The desire of small schools to defeat larger schools, where the competition is not equal, often brings disastrous results to the health and welfare of the players. Under such circumstances, one often hears the remark, "They really took a beating." Competition should be as equitable as possible.

Prompt attention should be given to all injuries. Injured players should be examined by a physician and given proper treatment. There should be complete medical supervision of the athletic program. The trainer is not a substitute. A physician should be present at all games and practices involving the most strenuous contact sports. The physician should determine the extent of injury. A player after being ill or hurt should not be permitted to participate again until the coach receives an approved statement from the family, school, or college physician.

Proper sanitary measures should be taken. Individual towels and drinking cups should be provided. The day of the team towel and the team drinking cup has passed. Equipment and uniforms should be cleaned as often as necessary. Locker, dressing, shower, toilet, and other rooms used by players should be kept clean and sanitary. Playing areas should be kept clean and safe. Gymnasiums should be properly heated, and every measure taken to ensure as nearly ideal conditions as possible.

Injuries and insurance.* The state athletic association in many states sponsors an athletic insurance plan. Such plans pay various medical, x-ray, dental, hospitalization, and other expenses according to the terms of the plan. Some private insurance companies also have such plans. Their purposes are to provide enrolled athletes with benefits that will help meet the cost of medical, dental, and hospital care in the event of accidental injury resulting from participation in physical education or athletics sponsored by a participating school. The amount of any payment for an injury is only the amount of the actual expenses incurred but not in excess of the amounts listed in the schedule of allowance for such injury. To collect benefits, plan requirements must be met.

The insurance provided by various state and independent plans usually includes benefits for accidental death or dismemberment, hospital expenses, x-ray

*See also Chapter 15.

*See also Chapter 16.

UNIVERSITY OF NEVADA, LAS VEGAS

Controller's Office
Accounts Payable Department
CLAIM FOR GROUP TRAVEL EXPENSES

Note: Do not use this form for submitting Travel expenses for individual faculty/staff of UNLV.

Department to Travel: _____

Destination: _____

Dates of Travel: _____

Number of Students and Staff Members: _____

SUMMARY OF EXPENDITURES

Transportation:

    Method: _____

    Cost (Do not enter cost of any agency vehicle.) _____

Meals, lodging, and miscellaneous:

Dates						Total
Breakfasts						
Lunches						
Dinners						
Lodging						
Other						
Student Allowance						

Total Meals, Lodging, and Miscellaneous: ....

Total All Expenditures and/or Student Allowances.......................
(Must be substantiated by receipts)

Advance Received: ....

Balance Due or to be reimbursed.....................................
(If balance is to be reimbursed to the traveler submit a request
for check in the amount of reimbursement.)

Account to be Charged: _____

Signed by: _____

Approved by: _____
                          Department Head

(1) Controller's Office
(2) Controller's Office
(3) Department

UNLV AP 270 4-76

Fig. 6-14. Claim for group travel expenses.

TEAM TRAVEL

Name of Sport_____

Date Leaving_____

Date Return_____

Destination _____

Method of Travel_____

Travel Agency_____

Flight No. and Time_____

Name of Airline_____

Price of Airline Ticket_____

Place Where the Team will be Staying_____

Telephone Where the Team will be Staying_____

Entry Fee Amount_____

Room and Meal Money_____

Name of Athletes and Staff_____

Fig. 6-15. Team travel.

fees, physicians' fees, and surgical and dental expenses. Dental benefits may or may not be included in the schedule of surgical benefits. In some plans, catastrophe benefits are also available for injuries requiring extensive medical care and long-term hospitalization. Coverage is normally provided on a deductible basis, with the insurance company paying 75% to 80% of the total cost over the deductible amount up to a maximum amount.

State high school athletic associations in a few states operate successful benefit plans, primarily by adopting many of the benefits used by the insurance industry, namely, nonallocated benefits, catastrophic coverage, and nonduplication of benefits.

Every school, college, and other organization should have a written policy concerning financial and other responsibilities associated with injuries. The administrator, parents, and players should be thoroughly familiar with the responsibilities of each regarding injuries.

Drug abuse. Drug abuse among high school and college students is a reality—one that must be recognized and treated. The athlete is no exception to the growing use of drugs among students. Many coaches and physical educators assume the rigid training and health requirements of athletes somehow protect them from drug abuse. However, athletes are a part of the whole school social environment, and intense peer group pressures are exerted on them just as they are on other students.

It is important that programs be developed to come face-to-face with the drug problem. Some suggestions in formulating an anti–drug abuse program follow:

1. A major effort for coordinating and exchanging information concerning drug abuse by universities and professional organizations is vitally important.
2. Teacher training programs for physical educators and coaches should include courses in adolescent psychology and human development.
3. Athletic administrators should demonstrate to their communities that athletic activities contribute to an effective anti–drug abuse program.
4. Support must be elicited from community members and public service groups in the fight against drug abuse.
5. It is important to involve a student's family in activities to aid in cementing family relationships. Athletic activities may be enjoyed by all family members and help bridge the communication gaps that may exist.
6. Ergogenic aids are not recommended. Also, the use of dimethyl sulfoxide (DMSO) is frowned on by most athletic trainers.

OFFICIALS

Officials greatly influence the athletic program and determine whether it is conducted for the benefit of the players. Officials should be well qualified. They should know the rules and be able to interpret them accurately; recognize their responsibility to the players; be good sportsmen; and be courteous, honest, friendly, cooperative, impartial, and able to control the game at all times.

To ensure that only the best officials are used, procedures should be established to register and determine those who are qualified. Officials should be required to pass examinations on rules and to demonstrate their competency. Rating scales have been developed to help make such estimates. Most athletic associations have some method of registering and certifying acceptable officials. The National Association for Girls and Women in Sport of the AAHPERD has a rating committee that certifies officials. In some states the officials who are used, in turn, rate the schools or colleges as to facilities, environment, and circumstances surrounding the game.

Subject to contract differences, officials are frequently chosen by the home team with approval of opponents. The practice of the home team selecting officials without any consideration of the wishes of other organizations or regard for impartial officiating has resulted in relations that have not been in the best interests of players or of athletics in general. A growing practice of having the conference or association select officials has many points in its favor.

Officials should be duly notified of the date and time of the contests to which they have been assigned. Officials' fees vary from school to school, although some associations have set up standard rates. It is usually considered best to pay a flat fee that includes salary and expenses, rather than to list both separately.

Fig. 6-16. Officials play a very important role in athletic contests.

Courtesy Iowa State University, Ames, Iowa.

TRANSPORTATION

Transporting athletes to games and contests presents many administrative problems, such as: Who should be transported? In what kinds of vehicles should athletes be transported? Are athletics part of a regular program? Should private vehicles or school- and college-owned vehicles be used? What are the legal implications involved in transporting athletes to school-sponsored and college-sponsored events?

The present trend is to view athletics as an integral part of the educational program so that public funds may be used for transportation. At the same time, however, statutes vary from state to state, and persons administering athletic programs should examine carefully the statutes in their own state.

The energy crisis created a transportation problem. Because of the increased expense of fuel, many interscholastic and intercollegiate programs are being curtailed or dropped from the calendar. Schools should try to conduct athletic activities on school days and use public transportation and carpools wherever possible.

Many administrators feel that athletes and representatives of the school or college concerned, such as band members and cheerleaders, should travel only in transportation provided by the school. Where private cars belonging to coaches, students, or other persons are used, the administrator should be sure to determine whether the procedures are in conformity with the state statutes regarding liability. Under no circum-

Fig. 6-17. Umpires play a major role in baseball competition.

Courtesy Cramer Products, Inc., Gardner, Kan.

stances should students or other representatives be permitted to drive unless they are licensed drivers. Under most circumstances students should not be used as drivers.

The business administrator is usually responsible for the transportation program. He or she will, therefore, make a provision in the transportation program for buses to carry athletic teams to sport contests so they will arrive safely on time. The director of athletics must be informed of the mode of transportation that will be available so he or she can plan accordingly. This involves a direct relationship between the director of athletics and the transportation supervisor. All requests for special athletic trips should be in writing and acknowledged by the secondary school principal or college administrator where he or she is involved. This is necessary because the principal or

college administrator will be aware of any conflicts with other parts of his or her program. The business administrator finds it difficult to schedule special athletic trips on a moment's notice, although this situation can arise when games are canceled because of the weather or other unforeseen events. The director of athletics should submit a monthly calendar of athletic events, listing the date, time and place of departure, event, destination, number of participants, time of pickup, and remarks.

As the boxed material on page 208 shows, the events scheduled on April 8 are routine, and the transportation supervisor can request a bus accordingly. The events on April 9 are more complex, and the director of the athletics can state a preference for a station wagon. It is more economical for a school district or college to furnish a station wagon rather

---

MONTH OF APRIL

April 8

Depart: 3:00 PM
From: Senior High School
Team: Junior Varsity Baseball
To: Jones High School
Students: 35
Pickup: 5:30 PM
Remarks:

April 9

Depart: 3:00 PM
From: Junior High School
Team: Varsity Tennis
To: Albany High School
Students: 5
Pickup: 5:00 PM
Remarks: Station wagon requested; Coach Lewis will
  drive.

April 10

Depart: 3:00 PM
From: Senior High School
Team: Varsity Baseball and Varsity Tennis
To: Baseball to Jones High School
  Tennis to Albany High School
Students: 40
Pickup: Baseball—5:00 PM
  Tennis—5:30 PM
Remarks: One bus for both teams—drop off baseball
  first.

than a 60-passenger bus to transport five students. The events on April 10 are more complex, and the remarks indicate that one bus can be used for both teams. It is necessary to list the number of participants so the proper size bus, or buses, can be assigned. This calendar should be submitted in triplicate (carbons) to the business administrator. After the transportation department has scheduled the trips, the business administrator initials all three copies and returns two copies to the athletic director. The director keeps one copy, and the other copy is sent to the principal or college administrator. The procedure for submitting transportation requests could vary in different schools. The administrator might receive the schedule for approval before the business office.

GAME MANAGEMENT

Because so many details are connected with game management, it is possible to include only a brief statement of the more important items. To have an efficiently conducted contest, it is important to have good organization. Someone must be responsible. There must be planning. Many details must be attended to, including (1) before-game responsibilities, (2) game responsibilities, (3) after-game responsibilities, and (4) preparation for out-of-town games. Before a home game such details as contracts, eligibility records, equipment, facilities, tickets, public relations, medical supervision, officials, and physical examinations must be thoroughly checked. Game responsibilities at home games include checking such items as supplies and equipment, entertainment, tickets and ushers, scoreboards, public-address system, presence of physician, and quarters for visiting teams. The responsibilities after a home game consist of checking such items as payments to officials and visiting school, records of officials, and participation records. When preparing for an out-of-town game, such important details as parents' permissions, transportation, funding, contracts, personnel, and records must be attended to.

CROWD CONTROL

Crowd control at athletic contests is becoming increasingly important in light of dissent, riots, violence, and disturbances both on high school and college campuses and in public gathering places. The elimination of night athletic activities has been on the increase, particularly in large cities. School districts and college authorities are taking increased precautions to avoid any disturbances. More police are being brought in to help supervise the crowds at athletic contests, sportsmanship assemblies are being held, townspeople are being informed, administrators are discussing the matter, and careful plans are being developed.

The California Interscholastic Federation—Southern Section published crowd management guidelines

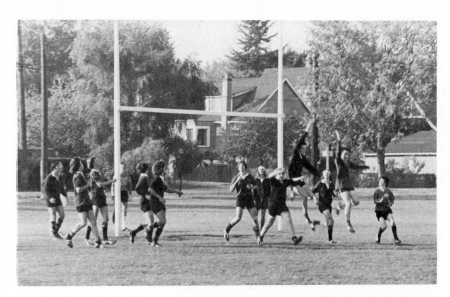

Fig. 6-18. Practice periods are important but should not intrude on students' time excessively. High school rugby at Balaclava Park in Vancouver.

Courtesy Board of Parks and Public Recreation, Vancouver, B.C.

Fig. 6-19. Guidelines exist to help control crowds at sporting events. Students at a pep assembly at Prairie Senior High School, Cedar Rapids, Iowa.

after several years of research into crowd control problems in southern California. The suggested guidelines were general and not specifically applicable to all communities. In substance, these guidelines urged civic leaders to meet first with local school administrators to determine precisely in what activities during athletic events civic group assistance would be most helpful. The guidelines would then be expanded or revised to suit the situation.

The Sixth National Conference of City and County Directors of the AAHPERD spent considerable time on the subject of crowd control at athletic contests. A summary of their discussions is listed on pp. 211-213.

Fig. 6-20. Everything possible should be done to guard the safety of players. NCAA championship competition in lacrosse on the Astro Turf of Hofstra Stadium, New York.
Courtesy NCAA.

PROTESTS AND FORFEITURES

There should be a set procedure for handling protests and forfeitures in connection with athletic contests. Of course, there should be careful preventive action beforehand to avoid a situation when such protests and forfeitures occur. Proper interpretation of the rules, good officiating, elimination of undue pressures, and proper education of coaches on the objectives of athletics will help prevent such action.

However, the essential procedure for filing protest and forfeitures of contests should be established. This procedure should be clearly stated in writing and contain all the details, such as the person to whom the protest should be sent, time limits involved, person or group responsible for action, and any other necessary information. A frequent reason for a protest is the use of ineligible players. Most associations require the forfeiture of any game in which ineligible players participate.

AWARDS

The basis for awards in interscholastic and intercollegiate athletics is the same as that for intramural and extramural athletics. There are arguments for and against giving awards. Some individuals feel that the values derived from playing a sport—joy and satisfaction, physical, social, and other values—are sufficient and that no awards should be given. Others argue that awards are traditional and symbolic of achievement and should be given.

The awards policy should be determined locally. A definite policy should be established that cuts across all the affairs of the school or college. The practice of giving awards in the form of letters, insignia, or some other symbol is almost universal. When awards are given they should be simple and inexpensive. Some state athletic associations, for example, have stated that the award should not cost more than $1.00. Furthermore, it seems wise not to distinguish between so-called major and minor sports when giving awards. They should be treated equally.

APPROACHES TO CROWD CONTROL
Summary of reports: small group discussions

The nature and seriousness of the problems in crowd control have recently become more drastic and bizarre as they have occurred with increasing frequency. They take on the collective character of a deliberate attempt either to ignore or confront the system. This social problem may be impossible to eliminate completely, but an attempt must be made to cope with the immediate symptoms. Our only hope is for imaginative and coordinated efforts by the school administration, the majority of students, and community authorities to promote standards of conduct conducive to continuing spectator sports in comparative tranquility. The alternatives are to allow a disruptive element to completely negate the nature of school athletics, to play with no spectators, or to abandon the activity.

The following will present some causes of crowd control problems and some approaches to solutions.

Some causes of problems

Lack of anticipation of, and preventive planning for, possible trouble

Lack of proper facilities

Poor communication resulting in lack of information

Lack of involvement of one or more of the following: school administration, faculty, student body, parents, community, press, and law enforcement agencies

Lack of respect for authority and property

Attendance at games of youth under the influence of narcotics

Increased attitude of permissiveness

School dropouts, recent graduates, and outsiders

Some approaches to solutions

Develop written policy statements, guidelines, and regulations for crowd control

1. Consult the following before writing policy statements or promulgating regulations: a school administration, athletic director, coaches, faculty members involved in the school sports program, school youth organizations, local police departments

2. Properly and efficiently administer regulations and provide for good communications

3. Constantly evaluate regulations and guidelines for their relevance and effectiveness

4. Make guidelines and regulations so effective that the director of athletics who follows them is secure in knowing he or she has planned with the staff for any eventuality and has sufficient help to cope with any situation that may arise

Provide adequate facilities

1. Plan and design stadiums, fieldhouses, and gymnasiums for effective crowd control

2. Provide for adequate rest room facilities

3. Establish a smoking area when indoor contests are held

4. Complete preparation of facilities before game time

Teach good sportsmanship throughout the school and the community

1. Begin education in good sportsmanship in the earliest grades and continue it throughout the school life

2. Make frequent approving references to constructive and commendable behavior

3. Arrange for program appearances by faculty members and students jointly to discuss the true values of athletic competition including good sportsmanship

4. Make use of all news media through frequent and effective television, radio, and press presentations and interviews, commentaries, and frequent announcement of good sportsmanship slogans

5. Distribute a printed Code of Ethics for Good Sportsmanship

6. Include the good sportsmanship slogan in all printed programs at sports events

7. Urge the use of athletic events as an example in elementary school citizenship classes, stressing positive values of good conduct at games, during the raising of the flag, and singing of the national anthem; courtesy toward visitors

Continued.

APPROACHES TO CROWD CONTROL
Summary of reports: small group discussions—cont'd

8. Involve teachers in school athletic associations, provide them with passes to all sports events, and stress the positive values of their setting an example of good sportsmanship

Intensify communications before scheduled games

1. Arrange for an exchange of speakers at school assembly programs; the principals, coaches, or team captains could visit the opposing school
2. Discuss with appropriate personnel of the competing school the procedures for the game, including method and location of team entry and departure
3. Provide superintendent or principal, athletic director, and coach with a copy of written policy statement, guidelines and regulations
4. Meet all game officials and request them to stress good sportsmanship on the field
5. Meet with coaches and instruct them not to question officials during a contest; stress the importance of good sportsmanship and that their conduct sets the tone for spectator reaction to game incidents
6. Instruct students what to expect and what is expected of them
7. Schedule preventive planning conferences with local police to be assured of their full cooperation and effectiveness in spectator control

Inform the community

1. Request coaches and athletic directors to talk to service groups and other community groups
2. Stress the need for exemplary conduct of coaches at all times
3. Invite community leaders (nonschool people) to attend athletic events
4. Post on all available notice boards around town, in factories and other public places, posters showing the Sportsmanship Code of Ethics and Guidelines in brief
5. Release constructive information and positive statements to news media and request publication of brief guidelines on sports pages
6. Provide news media with pertinent information as to ways in which the community may directly

and indirectly render assistance in the crowd control problem

Involve law enforcement personnel

1. Police and other security personnel should be strategically located so as to afford the best possible control
2. Law enforcement professionals should handle *all* enforcement and disciplining of spectators
3. Strength in force may be shown by appearance of several policemen, motorcycles, police cruise cars, et cetera, at and near the site of the game
4. Women police may be stationed in women's rest rooms
5. Civil Defense organizations could patrol parking areas
6. A faculty member from the visiting school may be used as a liaison with police and local faculty in identifying visiting students
7. Attendents, police, county sheriffs, deputies should be in uniform. Uniformed authority figures command greater respect

Use supervisory personnel other than police

1. Select carefully teacher supervisors who are attentive and alert to signs of possible trouble
2. Identify faculty members by arm bands or other means
3. Provide for communication by means of walkie-talkie systems
4. Assign some faculty members to sit behind the visiting fans; this reduces verbal harassment of visitors
5. Employ paid ticket takers and paid chaperones to mingle strategically among the crowd and to remain on duty throughout the game, including half-time
6. Issue passes to junior high physical education teachers to provide more adult supervision

Plan for ticket sales and concession stands

1. Arrange for advance sale of student tickets to avoid congestion at the gate
2. Sell tickets in advance only to students in their own schools, and avoid sale of tickets to outsiders and nonstudents

APPROACHES TO CROWD CONTROL
Summary of reports: small group discussions—cont'd

3. Provide for a close check at the gate or entrance
4. Arrange for concession stands to be open before the game, during half-time, and after the game, but closed during actual play
5. Channel the flow of traffic to and from concession stands by means of ropes, or other means; keep traffic moving

Prepare spectators and contestants

1. Encourage as many students as possible to be in the uniforms of the athletic club, pep club, booster clubs, band, majorettes, cheerleaders
2. Bus participants to and from the site of the game
3. Have participants dressed to play before leaving for a game or contest
4. Adhere to established seating capacity of stadiums and gymnasiums
5. Request home team fans to remain in their own stands until visiting team fans have left
6. Try to arrange for a statewide athletic association regulation prohibiting all noise makers including musical instruments except for the school band or orchestra under professional supervision
7. Request the assistance of visiting clubs
8. Educate cheerleaders, student leaders, band captains, pep squads, and faculty supervisors by means of a one day conference program
9. Keep spectators buffered from the playing area as much as practical
10. Request that elementary school children be accompanied by an adult

Miscellaneous

1. Inform and involve school superintendents fully when problems arise in connection with sports events
2. Impose severe penalties on faculty and student leaders guilty of poor conduct

3. Publish the identity of offenders at games and notify parents, if possible; any penalties inflicted should also be noted (Note: If the offense leads to Juvenile Court action, care should be taken not to contravene laws about publishing names of juvenile offenders)
4. Consistently enforce rules and regulations; this is a necessity
5. Work toward the assumption of responsibility for strong regulation and enforcement of team behavior on the part of the state athletic associations
6. Attempt to work with the courts toward greater cooperation
7. Avoid overstressing the winning of games
8. Discontinue double headers and triple headers
9. After-game incidents away from the proximity of the stadium or gymnasium are out of the control of school officials, but cause bad public reaction

Summary

Sound safety controls and crowd controls at school athletic functions are a must! Greater concentration on treating the causes of the problem is essential. Preliminary groundwork is the key to good crowd control. Coordination and cooperation of school and law enforcement agencies is the key to success.

Youths should be taught to know what to expect and what is expected of them. Consistent enforcement of rules and regulations in a necessity if youth is to respect authority. Adult behavior should be such that it may be advantageously and admirably emulated by youth whose actions hopefully may result in deserving praise instead of negative criticism and disapproval.

The athletic program is a constructive and valuable school activity. It should be permitted to function in a favorable, healthful, and friendly environment.

RECORDS

The wise administrator and coach will keep accurate records of all the details concerned with the administration of athletics. There should be records of participation for eligibility purposes and to show the extent of the program; records of the conduct of various sports from year to year so they can be compared over time and also compared with other organization; statistical summaries of player and game performance that will help the coach determine weaknesses in game strategy or identify players' performances and other items essential to well-organized play; records of equipment and supplies; officials' records; financial records, and other items in connection with conducting the total program. Sound business and administration demand record keeping.

Administrative problems concerned with highly competitive athletics

The director of athletics or other administrator responsible for interscholastic, intercollegiate, or other highly organized athletic programs is bound to encounter many problems, including recruitment, eligibility, scholarships, proselyting, scouting, finances, and extra pay for coaching. In addition, certain problems arise in school situations in working with the business administrator.

RECRUITMENT

Recruiting athletes is a controversial issue. Some educational institutions indicate it is not condoned if it is for the primary purpose of developing winning teams. They feel the procedure for admittance should be the same for all students, regardless of whether they are athletes, chemistry students, music students, or others. No special consideration should be shown to any particular group. The same standards, academic and otherwise, should prevail.

Some educational institutions, however, actively recruit athletes for their varsity teams. The main consideration here is to live up to rules of the league, the conference, the NCAA, or other rules under which the organization participates. To do otherwise is not condoned.

Each organization will need to establish its own code of ethics and philosophy regarding recruitment.

In schools and colleges, however, athletic teams should be composed of matriculated students attracted to the school or college because of its educational advantages.

The NCAA cites the following definitions regarding recruiting rules and regulations in their *1982-83 NCAA Guide for the College-Bound Student-Athlete*. NOTE: This material is subject to annual review by the NCAA membership and may change annually.

1. An individual, who is not enrolled in the member institution and has not exhausted eligibility for intercollegiate athletics under NCAA regulations, becomes a "prospective" student-athlete if a member institution's athletic staff member or other representative of its athletic interests:
   (a) provides transportation for the individual to visit the campus;
   (b) entertains the individual in any way on the campus, except that the institution may make available to the prospect a complimentary admission to an athletic contest;
   (c) initiates or arranges telephone contact with the individual or a member of the individual's family (or guardian) for the purpose of recruiting;
   (d) visits the individual or a member of the individual's family (or guardian) for the purpose of recruiting, or;
   (e) entertains members of the family (or guardian) of the individual on its campus.
2. An individual becomes a "representative of an institution's athletic interests" when an institutional staff member requests the individual to recruit a particular prospect or has knowledge that the individual is recruiting a prospect. Further, an institution's responsibility for the conduct of its intercollegiate athletic program includes responsibility for the acts of an individual when the institution's executive or athletic administration has knowledge that such an individual is promoting the institution's intercollegiate athletic program. Once a person is identified as a representative, it is presumed the person retains that identity.

ELIGIBILITY

Standards regarding the eligibility of contestants are essential. These should be in writing, disseminated widely, and clearly understood by all concerned. They should be established well ahead of a season's or year's play so players, coaches, and others will not become emotional when they suddenly real-

Fig. 6-21. Varsity crew in rowing tank with mirrors.

Courtesy Trinity College, Hartford, Conn.

Fig. 6-22. Angell Field, Stanford University, with an intercollegiate dual meet in progress. The rim of Stanford Stadium is visible in the center background.

ize they will lose their chance to win a championship because they cannot use a star player who is ineligible.

Standards of eligibility in interscholastic circles usually include an age limit of not more than 19 or 20 years of age; a requirement that an athlete be a bona fide student; rules on transfer students that frequently require their being residents in the community served by the school; satisfactory grades; a limit of three or four on number of seasons of competition allowed (playing in one game usually constitutes a season); regular attendance at school; permission to play on only one team during a season; and a requirement that the participant have a medical examination, amateur status, and parent's consent. These regulations vary from school to school and state to state.

The National Federation of State High School Athletic Associations considers a student ineligible for amateur standing if the student (1) has accepted money or compensation for playing in an athletic contest, (2) has played under an assumed name, (3) has competed with a team whose players were paid, or (4) has signed a contract to play with a professional team.

Eligibility requirements at the college and university level include rules about residence, undergraduate status, academic average, amateur status, limits of participation, and transfer. In some cases players must have been in residence for at least 1 year, whereas in others they can play as freshmen. Furthermore, they must be fully matriculated students carrying a full program of studies, have a satisfactory grade-point average, and have had only so many years of competition. Also, a student cannot participate after the expiration of four consecutive 12-month periods following the date of initial enrollment in an institution of higher learning. Amateur status is also a requirement.

The NCAA lists the following general principles of eligibility in their *1982-83 NCAA Guide for the College-Bound Student-Athlete*. NOTE: This material is subject to annual review by the NCAA membership and may change annually.

A prospective student-athlete SHALL BE SUBJECT TO LOSS OF ELIGIBILITY if the prospect:

1. Following completion of high school eligibility in the sport and prior to enrollment in college, participates in an all-star football or basketball contest that is not specifically approved either by the appropriate state high school athletic association or, if interstate, by the NCAA All-Star High School Games Committee, or participates in more than two approved all-star football contests or more than two approved all-star basketball contests.

2. Violates NCAA legislation related to the receipt of financial assistance.

3. Is guilty of fraudulence in connection with an entrance or placement examination.

4. Exhibits dishonesty in evading or violating NCAA regulations.

5. Enrolls in a member institution which violated NCAA regulations in recruiting the individual. [NOTE: This loss of eligibility to be for NCAA championships or postseason football games only.]

SCHOLARSHIPS

Should athletes receive scholarships or special financial assistance in schools and colleges? This subject is argued pro and con and is mainly a problem at the college level. Those in favor of scholarships and financial assistance claim that a student who excels in sports should receive aid just as much as one who excels in music or any other subject. They claim that such inducements are justified in the educational picture. Those opposed point out that scholarships should be awarded on the basis of the need and general academic qualifications of a student, rather than skill in some sport. Another controversy concerns the right of women to also receive athletic scholarships, although Title IX provides that women be able to receive scholarships the same as men.

One solution is to list criteria for making such grants and have them handled by an all-school or all-college committee. This plan is based on the premise that scholarships and student aid should not be granted to the athletic or to any other department. Instead, they should be handled on an all-school or all-college basis and given to students who need them most and are best qualified. In this way, those students who are in need of assistance, regardless of the area in which they specialize, will be the ones who will receive aid.

The NCAA provides the following information on

Fig. 6-23. High school cross country meet.

Courtesy Regis High School, New York

financial aid for athletes in their *1982-83 NCAA Guide for the College-Bound Student-Athlete.* NOTE: This material is subject to annual review by the NCAA membership and may change annually.

A student MAY:

1. Receive unearned athletically related financial aid administered by the institution for any regular term the student is in attendance, provided it does not exceed that amount equal to tuition and fees, room and board, and required course-related books, and provided the student is not under contract to or currently receiving compensation from a professional sports organization.

2. Receive unearned athletically related financial aid awarded only by an institution's regular financial aid committee for a maximum period of one year, it being understood that such aid may be renewed for additional, maximum one-year periods by the institution while the recipient is an undergraduate or a graduate student with remaining eligibility.

3. Receive income from employment during term time or nonathletic grants for educational purposes in combination with unearned athletically related financial aid, provided the total from all sources does not exceed the actual cost of room and board, tuition and fees, and required course-related books. Income from employment during official institutional vacation periods need not be considered in this limit.

A student SHALL NOT:

1. Receive athletically related financial aid from an NCAA member institution to attend its summer term prior to the student's initial enrollment as a regular student during the regular academic year at the institution. This prohibition does not apply to a summer orientation program for which participation (by both athletes and nonathletes) is required and financial aid is administered on the same basis for all participants in the program.

2. Receive financial aid other than that administered by the institution if the aid has any relationship whatsoever to athletic ability. This prohibition shall not apply to earnings from a professional organization in a sport other than the student's collegiate sport.

3. Accept a scholarship or grant-in-aid from an organization, individual or agency outside of the student's institution for which selection is based primarily on athletic ability or participation.

4. Receive an extra benefit not available to members of the student body in general.

*NOTE: Division III member institutions generally may not award financial aid to student-athletes except on a showing of financial need by the recipient.

PROSELYTING

Proselyting is a term applied to a high school or college that has so strongly overemphasized athletics that it has stooped to unethical behavior to secure outstanding talent for winning teams. High schools are not troubled with this problem as much as colleges, but sometimes they also have difficulties. There have been incidents where a father was provided employment so he would move his family to a particular section of a city or a particular community so his child would be eligible to play with the local team. However, thanks to vigilant state athletic associations, such incidents have been kept to a minimum. The following represent some of the rules in force in many states to eliminate special inducements to attract athletes. These rules have been established by many state high school athletic associations:

1. Only acceptable forms of recognition should be presented to athletes. These usually include letters, monograms, or school insignias.
2. The educational institution or athletic association should be the only source of awards to athletes.
3. No student should be the recipient of special treatment from any outside organization.
4. Complimentary dinners (from local organizations) may be accepted by athletic teams if approved by the superintendent of schools.

SCOUTING

Scouting has become an accepted practice at high school and college levels. By watching another team perform, one will learn the formations and plays used and discover certain weaknesses. One coach said his scouting consisted of watching players to determine little mannerisms they had that would give away the play going to be used.

Many schools and colleges are spending considerable money on scouting. Some scout a rival team every game during the season, using three or four persons on the same scouting assignment and taking moving pictures at length so the opponent's play can be studied in great detail. Such money, it is felt by some physical educators, could be spent more wisely if used to enhance the value of the game for the participants, rather than to further any all-important effort to win.

Many unethical practices have entered into scouting. Coaches have been known to have scouts observe secret practice sessions. Scouting is considered unethical under any circumstances except by means of observing regularly scheduled games. If scouting does occur, the head coach at the institution has direct responsibility for the action.

Many coaches say the only reason they scout is that they themselves are being scouted. Therefore, they feel it will work to their disadvantage unless they follow the same procedure. If something could be done to eliminate or restrict scouting, considerable time and money could be put to much more advantageous use.

FINANCES

Throughout the country, interscholastic and intercollegiate athletic programs are financed through many different sources. These include gate receipts, board of education and central university funds, donations, special projects, students' fees, physical education department funds, magazine subscriptions, and concessions. In high schools a "general organization" frequently handles the funds for athletics. Some colleges finance part of the program through endowment funds.

It has long been argued by leaders in physical education that athletic programs have great educational potential. They are curricular in nature rather than extracurricular. This means they contribute to the welfare of students, like any other subject in the curriculum. On this basis, therefore, the finances necessary to support such a program should come from board of education or central university funds. Athletic programs should not be self-supporting or used as a means to support part or all of the other so-called extracurricular activities of a school or college. They represent an integral part of the educational program and as such deserve to be treated the same as other aspects of the program. This procedure is followed in some schools and colleges with benefits to all concerned and should be an ideal toward which all should strive.

Gate receipts are the source of many unfortunate practices in athletics. Too often they become the point of emphasis rather than the valuable educational out-

Fig. 6-24. Varsity volleyball for girls at Northland College, Ashland, Wis.

comes that can accrue to the participant. When this occurs, athletics cannot justify their existence in the educational program. Furthermore, the emphasis on gate receipts results in a vicious cycle—the money increases the desire for winning teams so there will be greater financial return, which in turn results in greater financial outlays to secure and develop even better teams. This goes on and on, resulting in a false set of standards forming the basis for the program.

One survey indicates that one out of every five U.S. schools has cut back athletic programs or may soon do so, as a result of budgetary difficulties. Declining athletic support has also resulted in lessened support for other nonacademic activities.

EXTRA PAY FOR COACHING

A frequent topic of discussion at school meetings is: Should teachers receive extra pay for extra ser-

vices? Parents, taxpayers, and school boards have been trying to decide whether or not athletic coaches, band leaders, dramatics supervisors, publication consultants, and others who do work in addition to their teaching load should receive additional compensation for such services.

A sensible solution to this problem is essential to the good morale of a school staff. Because school systems are demanding more and more services, a policy must be formulated to cover the extra duties being heaped on the shoulders of teachers.

The many-faceted problem of extra pay and extra services concerns a large number of educators, administrators, and laymen. Following are ideas that represent the thinking of many teachers and administrators throughout the country.

The educational program in all school systems should rest on a sound financial base. Coaches' salaries should be sufficient to provide a comfortable living. They should not have to seek extra work in school or elsewhere to make ends meet.

If possible, there should be enough staff members in every school to make it unnecessary for anyone to take on an extra load.

Extra work means loss of efficiency. A teacher or coach can perform at his or her best for only a certain number of hours a day; then the law of diminishing returns sets in.

All teachers and coaches work beyond the school day. They prepare teaching assignments, grade papers, keep records, and take on other professional responsibilities. It is difficult, therefore, to determine what is "extra work."

Extra work in education is not comparable to extra work in business or industry. Professional ethics dictate that positions in public service cannot be categorized in the same way as many other types of work.

Coaching loads should be equalized as far as possible. If inequalities exist that cannot be corrected through extra staff, extra pay is justified.

Where extra pay is provided, it should be distributed equitably for all who work beyond a normal school day. Teachers and coaches should perform extra work only in areas where they are qualified.

The most acceptable form of compensation for additional duties is extra pay. The practice of released time does not seem to meet the wishes of most coaches.

The problem of extra pay for extra service is not easy to resolve. Convincing arguments can be given for both sides. Because local needs differ, a nationwide solution cannot be prescribed. However, any community wrestling with this problem may well be guided by the foregoing points.

PROBLEMS BUSINESS ADMINISTRATORS ENCOUNTER

Some of the pitfalls and problems encountered by business administrators in working with athletic directors and coaches, as seen through the eyes of business administrators, follow:

1. Overestimation of budget requests with the ideal of expecting a reduction in the request
2. Not being able to justify budget requests as they relate to the total educational program
3. Deadlines not met in submitting requests for transportation, supplies, and other needs
4. Lack of awareness of the school district or college philosophy regarding the place of the athletic program in the curriculum; hence, budget complications
5. Lack of cooperative planning regarding the transportation equipment available and scheduling special athletic events away from school or college necessitating the use of buses
6. Late notification to the business administrator's office when a special athletic event is cancelled that requires cancellation of a prearranged bus
7. Negligence in filing accident reports on students injured in sports or classes, no matter how insignificant an accident may seem at the time
8. Incomplete records on students participating in sports—especially regarding the requirement that all students receive a physical examination *before* trying out for the sport
9. Lack of concern for accident victims
10. Lack of knowledge of an injured student's rights and privileges under the student accident policy
11. Failure to realize that the educational goals represented in the philosophy of the school or college take priority over selfish, petty, and political interests
12. Lack of respect for the chain of command—a physical education teacher or coach should not bypass the director of the department when communicating with the business office
13. Lack of interest in the facilities at his or her disposal, causing breakdowns and extra added expense

Highly competitive athletic programs

Highly competitive athletic programs exist in schools, colleges, universities, and other organizations.

INTERSCHOLASTIC ATHLETIC PROGRAMS IN ELEMENTARY AND JUNIOR HIGH SCHOOLS

Since athletics was first introduced into the educational picture, there has been a continual pushing downward of these competitive experiences into the lower education levels. Educational athletics started at the college level with a crew race between Harvard and Yale in 1852. Then other sports were introduced to campuses throughout the United States. As higher education athletic programs expanded and gained

Fig. 6-25. An Olympic swim meet in the elementary school of the Cumberland Valley School District, Mechanicsburg, Pa.

recognition and popularity, the high schools felt sports should also be a part of their educational offerings. As a result, most high schools in America today have some form of interscholastic athletics. In recent years, junior high schools have also felt the impact of interscholastic athletic programs. A survey made by the National Association of Secondary School Principals that included 2296 junior high schools showed 85.2% had some program of interscholastic athletics, whereas 14.8% did not.

There should not be any interscholastic athletics at the elementary school level. In kindergarten to grade six, physical activities should be geared to the developmental level of the child. Starting with grade four it may be possible to initiate an informal intramural program. However, there should not be undue emphasis on developing skill in a few sports or requiring children to conform to adult standards of competition.

The special nature of grades seven through nine, representing a transition period between the elementary school and the senior high school and between childhood and adolescence, has raised a question in the minds of many educators about whether an interscholastic athletic program is in the best interests of the students concerned.

Many of the guidelines of the American Academy

of Pediatrics listed below apply to the junior high school level, as well as to the elementary school level, and to the type of athletic competition that should be offered:

1. All children should have opportunities to develop skill in a variety of activities.
2. All such activities should take into account the age and developmental level of child.
3. a. Athletic activities of elementary school children should be part of an over-all school program. Competent medical supervision of each child should be ensured.
   b. Health observation by teachers and others should be encouraged and help given by the physician.
4. Athletic activities outside the school program should be on an entirely voluntary basis without undue emphasis on any special program or sport, and without undue emphasis on winning. These programs should also include competent medical supervision.
5. Competitive programs organized on school, neighborhood, and community levels will meet the needs of children 12 years of age and under. State, regional, and national tournaments and bowl, charity, and exhibition games are not recommended for this age group. Commercial exploitation in any form is unequivocally condemned.
6. Body-contact sports, particularly tackle football and

boxing, are considered to have no place in programs for children of this age.

7. Competition is an inherent characteristic of growing, developing children. Properly guided, it is beneficial and not harmful to their development.

8. Schools and communities as a whole must be made aware of the needs for personnel, facilities, equipment, and supplies, which will assure an adequate program for children in this age group.

9. All competitive athletic programs should be organized with the cooperation of interested medical groups, who will ensure adequate medical care before and during such programs. This should include thorough physical examinations at specified intervals, teaching health observation to teachers and coaches, as well as attention to factors such as: (a) injury, (b) response to fatigue, (c) individual emotional needs, and (d) the risks of undue emotional strains.

10. Muscle testing is not, per se, a valid estimate of physcial fitness, or of good health.

11. Participation in group activities is expected of every child. When there is a failure to do so or lack of interest, underlying physical or emotional causes should be sought.

12. Leadership for young children should be such that highly organized, highly competitive programs are avoided. The primary consideration should be a diversity of wholesome childhood experiences that will aid in the proper physical and emotion development of the child into a secure and well-integrated adult.

The research regarding a highly organized athletics program at the junior high school level indicates the following points of substantial agreement:

1. The junior high school educational program should be adapted to the needs of boys and girls in grades seven, eight, and nine. This is a period of transition from elementary school to senior high school and from childhood to adolescence. It is a time when students are trying to understand their bodies, gain independence, achieve adult social status, acquire self-confidence, and establish a system of values. It is a time when a program of education unique to this age group is needed to meet the abilities and broadening interests of students.

2. The best educational program at the junior high school level provides program enrichment to meet the needs of students in grades seven through nine, rather than using the senior high school or other educational level as a blueprint to follow.

3. There is need for a distinct and separate educational climate for these grades to ensure the program will not be influenced unduly by either the elementary or the senior high school.

4. There is a need for coaches whose full responsibilities involve working with grades seven, eight, and nine and whose training has included an understanding of the needs of these students and of the educational program required to meet those needs.

5. The junior high school should provide for exploratory experiences with specialization delayed until senior high school and college.

6. The junior high school should provide for the mental, physical, social, and emotional development of students.

7. Out-of-class, as well as in-class, experiences should be provided.

8. There should be concern for the development of a sound standard of values in each student.

9. The principal and other members of the administration have the responsibility for providing sound educational leadership in all school matters. The type of physical education and athletic programs offered will reflect the type of leadership provided.

10. The physical education program at the junior high school level should consist of a class program, an adapted program, and intramural and extramural programs. (The interscholastic athletics program is controversial.)

11. The interscholastic athletics program, if offered, should be provided only after the prerequisites of excellent physical education class, adapted, and intramural and extramural programs have been developed, and only as special controls regarding health, facilities, game adaptations, classification of players, leadership, and officials have been provided.

12. The physical education program should be adapted to the needs of the student. There is a need for a wide variety of activities, based on physical and neuromuscular maturation, that will contribute to the development of body control, enable each student to experience success, provide for recognition of

energy output and fatigue, and take into consideration the "growth spurt" of early adolescence.

13. The physical education program should represent a favorable social and emotional climate for the student. There should be freedom from anxiety and fear, absence of tensions and strains, a feeling of belonging for each student, a social awareness that contributes to the development of such important traits as respect for the rights of others, and an atmosphere conducive to growing into social and emotional maturity.

14. Personal health instruction should be closely integrated into the physical education program.

15. Coeducational activities should be provided.

16. All physical activities should be carefully supervised medically and conducted under optimal health and safety conditions.

17. Students who are not physiologically mature should not engage in activities that are highly competitive or require body contact, a high degree of skill, or great amounts of endurance.

18. Physiological maturity is the best criterion for determining whether a student is physiologically ready for participation in most interscholastic athletic activities.

19. Competition itself is not the factor that makes athletics dangerous to the physiologically mature student. Instead, such items as the manner in which the program is conducted, type of activity, facilities, leadership, and physical condition of students are the determining factors.

20. Physiological fitness can be developed without exposure to an interscholastic athletic program.

21. Competitive athletics, if properly conducted, have the potential for satisfying such basic psychological needs as recognition, belonging, self-respect, the feeling of achievement, as well as providing a wholesome outlet for the physical activity drive. However, if conducted in light of adult interests, community pressures, and other questionable influences, they can prove psychologically harmful.

22. Interscholastic athletics, when conducted in accordance with desirable standards of leadership, educational philosophy, activities, and other pertinent factors, have the potential for realizing beneficial social effects for the student; but when not conducted in accordance with desirable standards, they can be socially detrimental to the student.

23. Tackle football, ice hockey, and boxing have questionable value for junior high school students.

INTERSCHOLASTIC (HIGH SCHOOL) AND INTERCOLLEGIATE ATHLETIC PROGRAMS

Selected recommended standards for high school and college athletic programs follow:

1. Organization
   a. The wholesome conduct of the athletic programs should be the ultimate responsibility of the school administration.
   b. Athletic policy should be adapted, evaluated, and supervised by a faculty committee.
   c. Athletic policy should be implemented by the director of physical education and the director of athletics.
   d. Athletics should be organized as an integral part of the department of physical education.

2. Staff
   a. All members of the coaching staff should be members of the faculty.
   b. All coaches should be hired on their qualifications to assume educational responsibilities, and not on their ability to produce winning teams.
   c. All coaches should enjoy the same privileges of tenure, rank, and salary accorded other similarly qualified faculty members.
   d. All public school coaches should be certified in physical education.

3. Finances
   a. The financing of interscholastic and intercollegiate athletics should be governed by the same policies that control the financing of all other educational activities within an institution.
   b. Gate receipts should be considered an incidental source of revenue.

4. Health and safety
   a. An annual physical examination should be required of all participants; a physical examination on a seasonal basis would be preferable.
   b. Each school should have a written policy for the implementation of an injury-care program.
   c. Each school should have a written policy concerning the responsibility for athletic injuries and should provide or make available athletic accident insurance.
   d. All coaches should be well qualified in the care and prevention of athletic injuries.

e. A physician should be present at all contests at which injury is possible.

f. Only that equipment offering the best protection should be purchased.

g. Proper fitting of all protective equipment should be ensured.

h. Competition should be scheduled only between teams of comparable ability.

i. Games should not be played until players have had a minimum of 3 weeks of physical conditioning and drill.

j. Playing fields should meet standards for size and safety.

5. Eligibility

a. All schools should honor and respect the eligibility rules and regulations of respective local, state, and national athletic associations.

b. A student who is not making normal progress toward a degree or diploma should not be allowed to participate.

6. Recruiting

a. The athletic teams of each school should be composed of bona fide students who live in the school district or who were attracted to the institution by its educational program.

b. All candidates for admission to a school should be evaluated according to the same high standards.

c. All financial aid should be administered with regard to need and according to the same standards for all students. The recipient of financial aid should be given a statement of the amount, duration, and conditions of the award.

7. Awards

a. The value of athletic awards should be limited.

b. There should be no discrimination between awards for different varsity sports.

c. The presentation of all-star and most valuable player awards should be discouraged.

The checklist on p. 226 provides an evaluation aid in determining the relationship of the high school athletic program to the total educational program.

HIGHLY COMPETITIVE ATHLETIC PROGRAMS IN OTHER ORGANIZATIONS

Other organizations also have highly competitive athletic programs. These are frequently found in such organizations as corporations and businesses, YMCAs, commercial clubs that specialize in one or more sports, and Police Athletic Leagues.

The main consideration in such athletic programs is to gear them to the age and needs of the participants. Youth-serving agencies, for example, should observe the established standards for interscholastic programs, whereas adults might follow the standards applicable at the college and university level.

Many advantages accrue from belonging to leagues and conferences rather than playing independently. Leagues and conferences result in several people getting together and establishing procedures, rules, and regulations that are more likely to benefit the participant than if a team were organized independently.

Usually athletics sponsored by educational institutions take special pains to provide for the health of the participants. They frequently have insurance, athletic trainers, physicians in attendance, and other provisions that help guarantee safer participation for the players. Sometimes in highly competitive athletic programs in other organizations, there is not the same concern and, as a result, sometimes players participate at their own risk.

It would be helpful if organizations think through and apply many of the procedures and standards set forth in this chapter for educational institutions.

Athletics for handicapped persons

Persons with handicaps can receive the same benefits from a program of competitive sports as nonhandicapped persons. The following reasons for including adapted sports activities in the physical education program are listed by Crowe, Auxter, and Pyfer:*

1. There are many students assigned to an adapted physical education class who are unable to correct an existing condition, but who also are unable to participate in regular physical education. A program of adapted sports would be ideal for such students [because it would give them some form of physical activity].

2. Students in the adapted physical education program need activities that have carry-over value. They may continue exercise programs in the future, but they also need training in carry-over types of sports and games that will be useful to them in later life.

---

*Crowe, W.C., Auxter, D., and Pyfer, J.: Principles and methods of adapted physical education, ed. 4, St. Louis, 1981, The C.V. Mosby Co.

3. Adapted sports activities may have a therapeutic value if they are carefully structured for the student.

4. Adapted sports and games should help the handicapped individual learn to handle his or'her body under a variety of circumstances.

5. There are recreational values in games and sports activities for the student who is facing the dual problem of overcoming some type of handicap; some of his or her special needs can best be met through recreational kinds of activities.

6. A certain amount of emotional release takes place in play activities and this is important to the student with a disability.

7. The adapted sports program, whether it is given every other day or several weeks out of the semester, tends to relieve the boredom of a straight exercise program. No matter how carefully a special exercise program is planned and organized, it is difficult to maintain a high level of interest if students participate in this kind of activity on a daily basis for one or more semesters.

Federal legislation, specifically PL 94-142 and Section 504 of PL 93-112, has undoubtedly played a great part in improving the educational opportunities of the handicapped. However, the Joseph P. Kennedy Jr. Foundation probably has focused more attention on sports for handicapped persons than any other single organization or legislation. The Kennedy Foundation can also be credited with promoting and causing others to provide significant services to handicapped persons through its many programs and activities.

The most visible activity promoted by the Kennedy Foundation is the Special Olympics, which was organized in 1968. It was designed to provide mentally retarded youths, 8 years of age and over, with opportunities to participate in a variety of sports and games on local, state, regional, national, and international levels.

The basic objectives of the Special Olympics are to

1. Encourage development of comprehensive physical education and recreation programs for the mentally retarded in schools, day care centers, and residential facilities in every community.
2. Prepare the retarded for sports competition—particularly where no opportunities and programs now exist.
3. Supplement existing activities and programs in schools, communities, day care centers, and residential facilities.
4. Provide training for volunteer coaches to enable them to work with youngsters in physical fitness, recreation, and sports activities.*

Thousands of people volunteer to coach mentally retarded youngsters in Special Olympic events such as track and field, swimming, gymnastics, floor hockey, and volleyball. The volunteers include professional athletes in many sports.

A Special Winter Olympics was started in 1975 for mentally retarded children and young adults. These Games are sponsored by New York Special Olympics, Inc., which is affiliated with the International Special Olympics.

Nearly 300 retarded and handicapped children and young adults gathered at a Catskill Mountain ski resort in Woodridge, New Jersey to participate in the Fourth Annual Winter Games. Events included tobogganing, snowshoeing, downhill and cross-country skiing, and figure and speed skating.

Wheelchair sports are another specialized series of athletic events designed for handicapped individuals. Wheelchair sports were initiated in Veterans' Administration Hospitals all over the United States as part of the medical treatment for disabled veterans returning home after World War II. The stated purpose of wheelchair sports is to "permit those with permanent physical disabilities to compete vigorously and safely under rules that are kept as close to normal rules as possible."

Wheelchair basketball was the first sport in the Wheelchair Games. Presently, track and field events, archery, dartchery, lawn bowling, table tennis, snooker, weightlifting, and swimming are also included in the Wheelchair Games.

The first National Wheelchair Games in the United States were held at Adelphi College in 1957. A total of 371 athletes competed at the twenty-third National Wheelchair Games at St. John's University, Queens, New York, in 1979.

Competitors are grouped at the Wheelchair Games according to various disability classes: quadriplegic,

---

*Stein, J.U., and Klappholz, L.A.: Special Olympics instructional manual, Washington, D.C., 1977, AAHPER and the Kennedy Foundation, pp. 1-2.

Evaluation of a high school athletic program   Yes   No

1. Athletic program an integral part of total curriculum
   a. The sports are an outgrowth of the physical education program
   b. A variety of sports are available for all students
   c. The educational values of sport are foremost in the philosophy
   d. All students have an opportunity to participate in a sport
   e. Athletics are used appropriately as a school's unifying force
   f. Athletes are not excused from courses, including physical educaion, because of athletic participation
2. Coaches as faculty members
   a. Coaches have an adequate opportunity to exercise the same rights and privileges as other faculty members in determining school and curricular matters
   b. Coaches attend, and they are scheduled so they may attend, faculty meetings
   c. Coaches are not expected to assume more duties of a general nature than are other faculty members
   d. Teaching tenure and other faculty privileges are available to athletic personnel
   e. Assignments for extra duties are made for coaches on the same basis as for other teachers
3. Participants encouraged by activities to perform adequately in academic areas
   a. Athletes are held accountable scholastically at the same level as other students
   b. Practices are of such length and intensity that they do not deter students' academic pursuits
   c. Game trips do not cause the students to miss an excessive number of classes
   d. Counseling services emphasize the importance of academic records in regard to career education
   e. Athletes are required to attend classes on days of contests
4. Meeting philosophy of school board
   a. New coaches are made aware of the board policies and informed that they will be expected to follow them in spirit as well as letter
   b. All coaches are regularly informed by the principal and athletic director that they must practice within the framework of board policy
   c. A procedure is available for the athletic director and coaches to make recommendations regarding policy change
   d. Noncoaching faculty members are made aware of board policy regarding athletics so they may discuss it from a base of fact
   e. The philosophy of the board is written and made available to all personnel
5. Awards
   a. Only those intrinsic awards authorized by local conferences and state athletic associations are given
   b. Diligence is exercised to ensure that outside groups do not cause violations of the award regulations
   c. Care is taken to assure that athletes are not granted privileges not available to the general student body
6. Projected program outcomes
   a. It is emphasized that participation in athletics is a privilege
   b. Development of critical thinking as well as athletic performance is planned into the program

*National Council of Secondary School Athletic Directors: Evaluating the high school athletic program, Washington, D.C., 1973, American Association for Health, Physical Education, and Recreation.

		Yes	*No*
c.	Development of self-direction and individual motivation is a real part of the athletic experience	_____	_____
d.	The athletes are allowed to develop at their own cognitive, psychomotor, and effective readiness level	_____	_____
e.	The accepted social values are used as standards of behavior both on and off the playing area	_____	_____

7. Guarding against student exploitation

		Yes	*No*
a.	The student is not used in athletic performance to provide an activity that has as its main purpose entertainment of the community	_____	_____
b.	The student's academic program is in no way altered to allow him to maintain eligibility with less than normal effort on his part	_____	_____
c.	The student is not given a false impression of his athletic ability through the device of suggesting the possibility of a college scholarship	_____	_____
d.	The athletes are not given a false image of the value of their athletic prowess to the material and cultural success within the school and community*	_____	_____

Fig. 6-26. Interscholastic gymnastics at Thornwood High School, South Holland, Ill.

Fig. 6-27. Second-year college students practicing their golf at Florissant Valley Community College in St. Louis.

Photograph by LeMoyne Coates.

Fig. 6-28. Intercollegiate basketball.

Courtesy Cramer Products, Inc., Gardner, Kan.

paraplegic, and amputee. The various classes are also broken down into levels, based on degree of disability. For example, Class IA includes incomplete quadriplegics who have involvement of both hands, weakness of triceps, weakness throughout the trunk and lower extremities, and loss of voluntary control. The most severely disabled compete in this class. The next classification (IB) includes those incomplete quadriplegics who have some upper extremity involvement, but less than IA, with other disabilities similar to those of IA. There are three additional classifications.

Sports opportunities are also available for handicapped persons in the special schools for the handicapped, as well as the regular schools where handicapped students are mainstreamed. In some cases, handicapped students in special schools are permitted to compete against athletes in regular schools. For instance, the Texas University Interscholastic League (UIL) has rules that allow mentally retarded students to participate in all levels of interscholastic athletic competition. Provided they meet certain requirements, special students are allowed to compete in athletic contests when they participate in Texas Education Agency–approved secondary school programs.*

Selected athletic associations

An individual school or college, by itself, finds it difficult to develop standards and control athletics in a sound educational manner. However, uniting with other schools and colleges makes such a project possible. This has been done on local, state, and national levels in the interest of better athletics for high schools and colleges. Establishing rules and procedures well in advance of playing seasons provides educators and coaches the necessary control for conducting a sound athletic program. It helps them resist pressures of alumni, students, spectators, townspeople, and others who do not always have the best interests of the program in mind.

There are various types of athletic associations. The ones most prevalent in high schools and colleges are student athletic associations, local conferences or leagues, state high school athletic associations, National Federation of State High School Athletic Associations, National Collegiate Athletic Association, and various college conferences that exist throughout the nation.

The student athletic association is an organization within a school designed to promote and participate in the conduct of the athletic program of that school. It is usually open to all students in attendance. Through the payment of fees, it often helps support the athletics program. Such associations are found in many high schools throughout the country. They can be helpful in the development of a sound athletic program.

Various associations, conferences, or leagues bind together athletically several high schools within a particular geographical area. These are designed to regulate and promote wholesome competition among the member schools. They usually draw up schedules, approve officials, handle disputes, and have general supervision over the athletic programs.

The state high school athletic association that now exists in almost every state is a major influence in high school athletics. It is open to all professionally accredited high schools within the state. It has a constitution, administrative officers to conduct the business, and a board of control. The number of members on the board of control varies usually from six to nine. Fees are usually paid to the association on a flat basis or according to the size of the school. In some states there are no fees, because the necessary revenue is derived from the gate receipts of tournament competition. State associations are interested in a sound program of athletic competition within the confines of the state. They concern themselves with the usual problems that have to do with athletics, such as rules of eligibility, officials, disputes, and similar items. They are interested in promoting sound high school athletics, equalizing athletic competition, protecting participants, and guarding the health of players. They are an influence for good and have won the respect of educators.

*American Association for Health, Physical Education and Recreation: The best of challenge, vol. II, Washington, D.C. 1974, The Association, p. 21.

THE NATIONAL COUNCIL OF SECONDARY SCHOOL ATHLETIC DIRECTORS

The American Alliance for Health, Physical Education, and Recreation established the National Council of Secondary School Athletic Directors. The increased emphasis on sports and the important position of athletic directors in the nation's secondary schools warranted an association where increased services could be rendered to enhance the services given to the nation's youth. The membership in the National Council is open to members of the AAHPERD who have primary responsibility in directing, administering, or coordinating interscholastic athletic programs. The purposes of the Council follow:

To improve the educational aspects of interscholastic athletics and their articulation in the total educational program

To foster high standards of professional proficiency and ethics

To improve understanding of athletics throughout the nation

To establish closer working relationships with related professional groups

To promote greater unity, good will, and fellowship among all members

To provide for an exchange of ideas

To assist and cooperate with existing state athletic directors' organizations

To make available to members special resource materials through publications, conferences, and consultant services

THE NATIONAL FEDERATION OF STATE HIGH SCHOOL ATHLETIC ASSOCIATIONS

The National Federation of State High School Athletic Associations was established in 1920 with five states participating. At present nearly all states are members. The National Federation is particularly concerned with the control of interstate athletics. Its constitution states this purpose:

The object of this Federation shall be to protect and supervise the interstate athletic interests of the high schools belonging to the state associations, to assist in those activities of state associations, which can best be operated on a nationwide scale, to sponsor meetings, publications and activities which will permit each state association to profit by the experience of all other member associations, and to coordinate the work so that waste effort and unnecessary duplication will be avoided.

The National Federation has been responsible for many improvements in athletics on a national basis, such as eliminating national tournaments and working toward a uniformity of standards.

THE NATIONAL COLLEGIATE ATHLETIC ASSOCIATION

The National Collegiate Athletic Association was formed in the early 1900s. The alarming number of football injuries and the fact that there was no national control of the game of football led to a conference of representatives of universities and colleges, primarily from the eastern United States, on December 12, 1905. Preliminary plans were made for a national agency to assist in the formulation of sound requirements for intercollegiate athletics, particularly football, and the name Intercollegiate Athletic Association was suggested. At a meeting March 31, 1906, a constitution and bylaws were adopted and issued. On December 29, 1910, the name of the association was changed to National Collegiate Athletic Association. The purposes of the NCAA are to uphold the principle of institutional control of all collegiate sports; to maintain a uniform code of amateurism in conjunction with sound eligibility rules, scholarship requirements, and good sportsmanship; to promote and assist in the expansion of intercollegiate and intramural sports; to formulate, copyright, and publish the official rules of play; to sponsor and supervise regional and national meets and tournaments for member institutions; to preserve athletic records; and to serve as headquarters for national collegiate athletic matters.

Membership in the NCAA requires that an institution be accredited and compete in a minimum of four sports each year on an intercollegiate level. At least one sport must be competed in during the normal three major sport seasons.

The services provided by the NCAA are as extensive as its stated purposes for existence. These services include publication of official guides in various sports, provision of a film library, establishment of

Fig. 6-29. Intercollegiate baseball at the University of Nevada, Las Vegas.

an eligibility code for athletes and provisions for the enforcement of this code, provisions for national meets and tournaments in 12 sports with appropriate eligibility rules for competition, provision of financial and other assistance to groups interested in the promotion and encouragement of intercollegiate and intramural athletics, and provision of administrative services for universities and colleges of the United States on matters of international athletics. The NCAA now offers women's, as well as men's, championships in various sports.

NATIONAL ASSOCIATION OF INTERCOLLEGIATE ATHLETICS

Also on the college and university levels is the National Association of Intercollegiate Athletics, which has a large membership, especially among the smaller colleges. This organization has become affiliated with the American Alliance for Health, Physical Education, Recreation, and Dance.

THE NATIONAL JUNIOR COLLEGE ATHLETIC ASSOCIATION

The National Junior College Athletic Association is an organization of junior colleges that sponsor athletic programs. It has nineteen regional offices with an elected regional director for each. Regional business matters are carried on within the framework of the constitution and bylaws of the parent organization. The regional directors hold an annual legislative assembly in Hutchinson, Kansas, are run by an executive committee, and determine the policies, programs, and procedures for the organization. The *Juco Review* is the official publication of the organization. Standing and special committees are appointed each year to cover special items and problems that develop. Membership entitles each member to the services provided by the NJCAA.

National championships are conducted in such sports as basketball, cross country, football, wrestling, baseball, track and field, golf, and tennis.

National invitation events are also conducted in such activities as soccer, swimming, and gymnastics.

The NJCAA is affiliated with the National Federation of State High School Athletic Associations and the National Association of Intercollegiate Athletics. It is also a member of the United States Track and Field Federation, Basketball Federation, the United States Collegiate Sports Council, United States Olympic Committee, United States Gymnastics Federation, National Basketball Committee, and American Alliance for Health, Physical Education, Recreation, and Dance.

Some of the services offered by the NJCAA to its members include an insurance plan for athletics, recognition in official records, publications, film library, and participation in events sponsored by the association.

AMATEUR ATHLETIC UNION (AAU) OF THE UNITED STATES

Founded in 1888, the Amateur Athletic Union of the United States is probably the oldest, as well as the largest single, organization designed to regulate and promote the conduct of amateur athletics. Certainly it is the most influential organization governing amateur sports in the world. The AAU is a federation of athletic clubs, national and district associations, educational institutions, and amateur athletic organizations.

Many persons associate the AAU only with track and field events. However, it is concerned with many more sports and activities, including basketball, baton twirling, bobsledding, boxing, diving, gymnastics, handball, judo, karate, luge, power lifting, swimming, synchronized swimming, water polo, weightlifting, and wrestling. In addition to governing the multiplicity of sports and activities, the AAU is vitally concerned with ensuring that the amateur status of athletes is maintained at all times when participating in amateur sports. To this end, the leaders of the AAU have developed and promulgated a precise set of guidelines describing amateurism.

Some of the other activities of the AAU include registering athletes to identify and control the amateur status of participants in sports events, sponsoring national championships in many sports, raising funds for American athletes in international competition and the Olympic Games, conducting tryouts for the selection of Olympic competitors, and sponsoring Junior Olympic competition. The AAU has established a number of committees for the various sports and activities (e.g., Age Group Diving, Track and Field, Youth Activities, Swimming) to help with the monumental task of performing the myraid duties associated with governing such a large number of sports and activities. An executive director directs and coordinates all activities of the AAU.

The address of the AAU is 3400 West 86th Street, Indianapolis, Indiana 46268 (Telephone: 317-297-2900). Ollan C. Cassell is the executive director.

OTHER ORGANIZATIONS

In higher education are also many leagues, conferences, and associations formed by a limited number of schools for athletic competition. Examples are the Ivy League and the Big Ten Conferences. These associations regulate athletic competition among their members and settle problems that may arise in connection with such competition.

Conclusion

The standards for athletics at school and college levels have been clearly stated. There should be no doubt in any individual's mind about the types of interscholastic and intercollegiate programs that are sound educationally and in the best interests of students who will participate in them. It is the responsibility of administrators and others concerned with such programs to implement the various standards that have been established. *In every case, it is not a question of deemphasis but a question of reemphasis along educational lines. Good leadership will make the interscholastic and intercollegiate programs forces for good education that have no equal.*

Athletics are a part of a total physical education program. The objectives stated earlier in this text for physical education also apply to interschool and intercollegiate athletics. The administrator can evaluate his or her program in terms of the extent to which the listed objectives are being achieved. There should be no question about where a school or college stands.

SELF-ASSESSMENT TESTS

These tests are to assist students in determining if material and competencies presented in this chapter have been mastered:

1. Imagine you are at a school budget hearing where a taxpayer attacks the varsity athletic program as costing too much money for the values derived from such a program. As a member of the physical education staff you are asked to react to the taxpayer's statement. What values can you cite to support the need for a varsity athletic program?

2. Write a profile of what you consider to be an ideal athletic director, coach, and athletic trainer.

3. List some essential points to keep in mind concerning each of the following: contracts, officials, protests and forfeitures, game management, awards schedules, records, and medical examinations for athletes.

.**4.** As a director of athletics, what administrative policy would you recommend regarding the following: gate receipts, tournaments and championships, eligibility, scholarships, recruiting, proselyting, and scouting?

5. Develop a set of standards that could be used to appraise an athletic program in an elementary school, high school, college, or other organization.

6. What is the role of the athletic association in the conduct of athletics? Identify three athletics associations and the role each plays.

SELECTED REFERENCES

Ambron, S.R.: Child development, San Francisco, 1975, Rhinehart Press.

American Alliance for Health, Physical Education, and Recreation: Equality in sports for women, Washington, D.C., 1977, The Alliance.

American Alliance for Health, Physical Education, and Recreation: HPER omnibus, Washington, D.C., 1976, The Alliance.

American Association for Health, Physical Education, and Recreation: Professional preparation in physical education and coaching, Washington, D.C., 1974, The Association.

American Alliance for Health, Physical Education, and Recreation: Programs that work—Title IX, Washington, D.C., 1978, The Alliance.

American Alliance for Health, Physical Education, and Recreation: Ulrich, C., To seek and find, Washington, D.C., 1976, The Alliance.

American Association for Health, Physical Education, and Recreation: Women's athletics: coping with controversy, Washington, D.C., 1974, The Association.

Banks, O.: How black coaches view entering the job market at major colleges, Journal of Physical Education and Recreation **50:**62, 1979.

Broyles, J.F., and Hay, R.D.: Administration of athletic programs—a managerial approach, Englewood Cliffs, N.J., 1979, Prentice-Hall, Inc.

Bucher, C.A.: After the game is over, The Physical Educator **30:**171, 1973.

Bucher, C.A.: Athletic competition and the developmental growth pattern, The Physical Educator, **28:**3, March 1971.

Bucher, C.A.: Foundations of physical education, St. Louis, 1983, The C.V. Mosby Co.

Bucher, C.A., and Dupee, R.K., Jr.: Athletics in schools and colleges, New York 1965, The Center for Applied Research in Education, Inc. (The Library of Education).

Bucher, C.A., and Koenig, C.: Methods and materials for secondary school physical education, St. Louis, 1983, The C.V. Mosby Co.

Bucher, C.A., and Thaxton, N.: Physical education and sport: change and challenge, St. Louis, 1981, The C.V. Mosby Co.

Burke E., and Kleiber, D.: Psychological and physical implications of highly competitive sports for children, The Physical Educator **33:**63, May 1976.

Colgate, J.A.: Administration of intramural and recreational activities: everyone can participate, New York, 1978, John Wiley & Sons, Inc.

Collison, R.: Master coach certification proposed. The Prep Coach, February, 1972, Publication of Minnesota High School Coaches Association.

Competitive sports for the handicapped, Journal of Health, Physical Education, and Recreation **41:**91, November-December 1970.

Crowe, W.C., Auxter, D., and Pyfer, J.: Principles and methods of adapted physical education and recreation, ed. 4, St. Louis, 1981, The C.V. Mosby Co.

Deatherage, D., and Reid, C.P.: Administration of women's competitive sports, Dubuque, Iowa, 1977, William C. Brown Co., Publishers.

Division for Girls' and Women's Sports: 1973 guidelines for intercollegiate athletic programs for women, Washington, D.C., 1973, American Association for Health, Physical Education, and Recreation.

Division for Girls' and Women's Sports: 1973 guidelines for interscholastic athletic programs for junior high school and high school girls, Washington, D.C., 1973, American Association for Health, Physical Education, and Recreation.

Durso, J.: The sports factory: an investigation into college sports, New York, 1975, Quadrangle/The New York Times Book Co.

Educational Policies Commission: School athletics—problems and policies, Washington, D.C., 1954, National Education Association.

Eitzen, D.S.: Athletics in the status system of male adolescents: a replication of Coleman's *The Adolescent Society.* Adolescence **10:**266, Summer 1975.

Eitzen, D.S.: Sport in contemporary society, New York, 1979, St. Martin's Press.

Encyclopedia of associations, Booktower, Detroit, Mich., 1979, Gale Research Co.

Fuoss, D.E., and Truppmann, R.J.: Creative management techniques in interscholastic athletics, New York, 1977, John Wiley & Sons, Inc.

Gerson, R.: Redesigning athletic competition for children, Motor Skills: Theory into Practice **2**:3, Fall 1977.

Gilbert, B., and Williamson, N.: Programmed to be losers, Sports Illustrated **38**:60, 1973.

Gould, D., and Martens, R.: Attitudes of volunteer coaches toward significant youth sport issues, Research Quarterly **50**:369, October 1979.

Hardy, R.: Checklist for better crowd control, Journal of Physical Education and Recreation **52**:70, May 1981.

Hotchkiss, S.: Parents and kids' sports, Human Behavior **7**:35, March 1978.

Howe, H., II: On sports, Educational Record **58**:218, Spring 1977.

Hult, J.: Equal programs or carbon copies, Journal of Physical Education and Recreation **47**:24, May 1976.

Lopiano, D.A.: A fact-finding model for conducting a Title IX self-evaluation study in athletic programs, Jounrnal of Physical Education and Recreation **47**:26, May 1976.

Lugo, J.O., and Hershey, G.L.: Human development, New York, 1974, Macmillan Inc.

Lumpkin, A.: Let's set the record straight, Journal of Physical Education and Recreation **48**:40, March 1977.

Magill, R., Ash, M., and Smoll, F.: Children in sport: a contemporary anthology, Champaign, Ill., 1978, Human Kinetics Publishers.

Martens, R.: Joy and sadness in children's sports, Champaign, Ill., 1978, Human Kinetics Publishers.

The National Association for Physical Education of College Women and The National College Physical Education Association for Men: Perspectives for sport, Quest Monograph 29, Winter Issue, 1973 (entire issue devoted to sport).

The National Association for Physical Education of College Women and The National College Physical Education Association for Men: Sport in America, Quest Monograph 27, Winter Issue, 1977 (entire issue devoted to sport).

Netcher, J.R.: A management model for competency-based HPER programs, St. Louis, 1977, The C.V. Mosby Co.

Noble, L., and Sigle, G.: Minimum requirements for interscholastic coaches, Journal of Physical Education and Recreation **51**:32, November/December 1980.

Orr, R.E.: Sport, myth, and the handicapped athlete, Journal of Physical Education and Recreation **50**:33, March 1979.

Parkhouse, B.L., and Lapin, J.: The woman in athletic administration, Santa Monica, Calif., 1980, Goodyear Publishing Co.

Penman, K.A.: Planning physical education and athletic facilities in schools, New York, 1977, John Willey & Sons, Inc.

Pflug, Jerry: Evaluating high school coaches, Journal of Physical Education and Recreation, **51**:76, April 1980.

Policies on women athletes change: Journal of Health, Physical Education, and Recreation **44**:51, 1973.

Poorman, D.: Should A. D.'s coach? Juco Review **25**:10, 1973.

Rarick, G.L., editor: Physical activity; human growth and development, New York, 1977, Academic Press, Inc.

Reed, J.D.: A miracle! or it is a mirage? Sports Illustrated, April 20, 1981.

Resick, M.C., and Erickson, C.E.: Intercollegiate and interscholastic athletics for men and women, Reading, Mass., 1975, Addison-Wesley Publishing Co., Inc.

Richardson, H.D.: Athletics in higher education: some comparisons, Journal of Physical Education and Recreation **50**:56, June 1979.

Rule books for all boys' sports. Available from the National Federation of State High School Athletic Associations, 7 South Dearborn St., Chicago, Ill.

Rule books for all girls' sports. Available from the Division for Girls' and Women's Sports, American Alliance for Health, Physical Education, and Recreation, 1900 Association Dr., Reston, Va.

Sabock, R.J.: The coach, Philadelphia, 1979, W.B. Saunders Co.

School athletics face austerity budgets, Sportscope, September-October 1973.

Seefeldt, V., coordinator: Youth sports, Journal of Physical Education and Recreation **49**:38, March 1978.

Shaffer, T.E.: Athletics for elementary-school youth: a medical viewpoint, Motor Skills: Theory into Practice **3**:97, June 1964.

Shults, F.D.: Toward athletic reform, Journal of Physical Education and recreation **50**:18, January 1979.

Smoll, F.B., and Smith, R.E.: Behavioral guidelines for youth sport coaches, Journal of Physical Education and Recreation **49**:46, March 1978.

Smoll, F.B., and Smith, R.E., editors: Psychological perspectives in youth sports, Washington, D.C., 1978, Hemisphere Publishing Corp.

Stevenson, C.L.: Socialization effects of participation in sport: a critical review of the research, Research Quarterly **46**:287, October 1975.

Talamini, J.T., and Page, C.H.: Sport and society—an anthology, Boston, 1973, Little, Brown and Co.

Tutko, T., and Burns, W.: Winning is everything and other American myths, New York, 1976, Macmillan Inc.

Underwood, J.: The writing is on the wall, Sports Illustrated May 19, 1980.

Wilkerson, M., and Dodder, R.A.: What does sport do for people? Journal of Physical Education and Recreation **50**:50, February 1979.

Zeigler, E.F., and Spaeth, M.J.: Administrative theory and practice in physical education and athletics, Englewood Cliffs, N.J., 1975, Prentice-Hall, Inc.

7

The administration of girls' and women's athletic programs*

Instructional objectives and competencies to be achieved

After reading this chapter the student should be able to

- Trace the history of girls' and women's athletic programs.
- Discuss some of the reasons why girls' and women's athletic programs were not stressed before the feminist movement.
- Indicate the role of the Division of Girls' and Women's Sports in the development of athletic programs.
- Outline the various provisions of Title IX.
- Describe the present status of girls' and women's athletics.
- Give the reasons why a man or a woman should be a director of athletics, coach, athletic trainer, or official for girls' and women's athletic contests.

The growth of girls' and women's sports has been so rapid in recent years that a separate chapter is needed to discuss the many administrative ramifications of this growth. Popular magazines devote much space to the liberation of American women. Best-selling books, television talk shows, and nationwide lecturers stress the new female freedom and woman power. The Harris poll, having realized the growing influence of women, sampled their views. Women are playing a more important role in American life. For instance, more than 300 women now sit on corporate boards. In a 1977 report the executive search firm of Heidrick and Struggles found 325 women officers in a sampling of 1000 companies; by 1979 the number had grown to 485, and today it is nearly 600. This change is taking place not only in business, government, and politics, but also in sports. But it has not always been that way.

When the first Olympic Games were held in 776 BC in ancient Greece, women were not even permitted to be spectators on Mount Olympus. Those who had the audacity to peek and then were caught were thrown to their death from the highest peak of a giant rock. Years later, when the modern Olympics were started in 1896 by Pierre de Coubertin, women were not permitted to compete in any event.

Discrimination against girls and women has been a part of the history of this country. Reasons for this included the stress on activity for boys and men and the concepts of femininity and masculinity. Masculinity meant being aggressive, hard, and tough, whereas femininity meant being submissive, soft, and non-assertive. Girls could be cheerleaders but not combative participants. Too often the public and parents associated physical education and sports with boys and never thought of girls as athletes or watched them participate in sports.

I conducted a survey some years ago and found that parents did not feel sports and girls are compatible. The reasons: "Parents want girls to be fancy," "It's not feminine for a girl to get hot and sweaty," "Girls are discouraged from participating because it isn't ladylike," and, "Girls can get all the exercise they need cooking and cleaning house."

*Parts of this chapter were adapted from Bucher, C.A., and Dupree, R.K., Jr.: Athletics in schools and colleges, New York, 1965, The Center for Applied Research in Education, Inc., and Bucher, C.A., and Thaxton, N., Physical education and sport: change and challenge, St. Louis, 1981, The C.V. Mosby Co.

Fig. 7-1. Girls' athletics in Aledo, Ill.

Courtesy Barbara Ann Chiles.

Some of the arguments against girls' and women's athletics, especially of a highly competitive nature, frequently heard before the present feminist movement, may be summarized as follows:

1. Athletics for girls should stress those activities offered in a broad intramural program. Any interschool athletics should stress the social aspects of athletic competition rather than the development of varsity teams and highly skilled players.

2. Interschool athletics for girls should be limited to extramurals and informal competition, such as play days, sports days, and invitational meets. There should be an emphasis on having fun rather than on winning a school championship or staging a show for spectators.

3. The athletically gifted girl should not be a major concern of physical education leaders. Too many poorly skilled girls and women need attention first. The challenge facing physical educators today is to provide a sound sports program for all girls and women.

4. The social status of girls and women in the American culture is an important consideration. The Olympic champion who puts the shot or throws the discus is not looked on as reflecting the best image of the American woman. There is no place in highly competitive sports for women who want to reflect the qualities of femininity according to the American standards.

5. The athletic program for girls and women should not duplicate that designed for boys and men. Girls and women have their own special needs and occupy a different role in our society. Therefore, their athletic program should reflect these needs and roles. Furthermore, many of the undesirable practices that have become a part of interscholastic athletics for boys and men must never be permitted to invade the domain of the physical education program for girls and women.

6. There are at present too many pressures on girls' and women's physical education programs without adding those that would be involved in such things as conditioning and training girls and women for highly organized athletics.

7. Equipment and facilities in schools and colleges are already limited; therefore it is neither practical nor wise to promote an interschool or intercollegiate athletic program for girls and women. Furthermore, the physical education teacher is already overloaded with classes, intramurals, and other girls' activities. Why add new responsibilities when there is not enough time now to do those already assigned?

8. High school girls are not sufficiently mature—physically, mentally, or emotionally—to withstand the strains and tensions of highly organized athletic competition.

There were also advocates of highly organized sports competition for girls and women. Some of the arguments they presented in favor of girls' and women's athletics may be summarized as follows:

1. Sports competition for girls and women, as for boys and men, can develop physical fitness, skills,

Fig. 7-2. Girls' competitions at the National Finals of the Hershey's National Track and Field Youth Program.

Courtesy President's Council on Physical Fitness and Sports.

and desirable social qualities. As long as sports activities are adapted to the girls and their needs, an athletic program will have great value.

2. The highly skilled girl should have the opportunity to compete against other girls of comparable skill. To deny her such a privilege is not educationally sound. Girls and women should have the same opportunities as boys and men to achieve a high standard of achievement of physical efficiency, skill, and emotional control.

3. Girls and women engage in all sorts of interscholastic and intercollegiate competition such as music festivals, debates, dances, science fairs, and other educational activities. It is also important for them to have the opportunity to compete in a highly organized competitive sports program.

4. If girls and women are denied the right to participate and utilize their superior skill in a school or college sports program, they may seek to use this skill in other situations that may be highly undesirable. For example, they may be induced to play with

teams that gamble on the outcome of the game, with organizations that do not supply adequate protective equipment, or with individuals of questionable character. The school and college have the responsibility to provide a program for gifted girls and women so they will not have to look elsewhere.

5. If a highly organized program of athletics for skilled girls and women is administered and conducted by women leaders of physical education, it can have many values for the participants. The competition itself is not harmful; the type of leadership provided will determine whether or not the activity has value.

6. A desirable program of varsity sports for girls and women can be provided if the coaches and officials are women; if the competition is in selected sports such as tennis, badminton, golf, archery, and bowling; and if the standards of play are established by women.

7. Athletics will provide girls and women with an incentive to achieve a high degree of skill and emo-

tional control; a high level of performance, poise, health, and appearance; and a greater interest in the overall physical education program.

8. This is a highly competitive world, and women, as well as men, have to compete. Athletics provides a good training ground for such competition.

9. Although girls or women may not, because of certain biological factors, ever achieve some of the physical feats of boys or men, there appears to be little biological damage in athletic competition, except where it might interfere with menstruation and the reproductive functions. Furthermore, this appears to be an individual matter: girls and women react to exercise in different ways. The Educational Policies Commission in their report, *School Athletics* (published several years ago), cited the fact that medical opinion has recommended that girls and women engage only in mild exercise during the first 2 days of their menstrual flow to avoid physiological damage. It has also been recommended that girls and women should avoid activities involving holding the breath, hard vertical landings, or heavy lifting, because such activities increase abdominal pressures on the floor of the pelvis, which may lead to undesirable effects on the reproductive organs and on the menstrual flow.

Division of Girls' and Women's Sports

The most influential organization, particularly in the early years of athletics for girls and women, was the Division for Girls' and Women's Sports (DGWS) of the American Association for Health, Physical Education, and Recreation (AAHPER). The DGWS was responsible for establishing the standards by which most athletic programs were conducted in schools and colleges throughout the nation. The DGWS was composed of leaders in physical education and recreation who served in such organizations as schools, colleges, clubs, recreational agencies, military establishments, and industrial plants. The purpose of the DGWS included the following:

1. Promoting desirable sports programs for girls and women
2. Providing leadership for sports programs

3. Developing guiding principles and standards for use by people responsible for sports programs, including administrators, leaders, officials, and players
4. Being on call at all times whenever they can be of help to the profession
5. Continually evaluating the role of girls and women in sports programs
6. Furnishing materials and information concerned with such items as rules, teaching techniques, and other material for the benefit of players, officials, and sports leaders and teachers

HISTORY

The history of the DGWS goes back about 80 years, when organized sports attracted the interest of many girls and women in sports clubs, recreational agentices, the YWCA, and schools and colleges. (It is interesting to note that a game of basketball was held in 1899 at Smith College.) During these early years there was little attempt to organize and control athletic activities nationally. Then, in 1907, *The Women's Basketball Guide* was published. Also, a committee of women was appointed to establish rules for the game. Other attempts to supervise sports occurred in rapid succession following this initial action. In 1916, the American Physical Education Association—now the AAHPERD—appointed the Women's Athletic Committee to give some direction to women's sports. This group later became known as the National Section for Women's Athletics and continued to provide leadership for girls and women by preparing guides for various sports, establishing policy, writing rules, and providing consulting and other services. Still later there developed a larger organization, the National Section for Girls and Women's Sports of the AAHPER. Then, in 1957, the AAHPER invited this group to become the Division for Girls' and Women's Sports. This milestone was an indication of the outstanding growth and value of this organization to the profession. It is now known as the National Association for Girls and Women in Sport (NAGWS), one of the seven associations in the American Alliance for Health, Physical Education, Recreation, and Dance.

Another organization that contributed much to the establishment of standards was the Women's Division of the National Amateur Athletic Federation, organized as a private agency in 1923. Other groups, such as the National Joint Committee on Extramural Sports for College Women, did much to establish standards and procedures for conducting tournaments for college women, as well as providing outstanding leadership in many other areas of education.

The DGWS—through its publications, consulting services, speakers, and conferences—spelled out policies and procedures and desirable practices, rules, techniques, and regulations for governing the athletic programs for girls and women in schools and colleges. It also established standards for the construction of the program, the conduct of the program, the leadership that should be provided, and the responsibilities of the participant.

STANDARDS

Some of the standards in sports for girls and women that represent guiding principles in the organization and administration of such programs established by the DGWS were as follows.*

The program. The sports program for girls and women should be developed on the basis of such factors as individual characteristics and needs, individual differences, and the environment surrounding the activity in question.

The leaders of the program should exemplify outstanding physical, mental, social, and emotional traits; possess excellent teaching techniques; be well-informed as to the needs and interests of girls and women; realize that the results of her teaching are enhancing the physical powers and social adjustment of her students.

The participant in the program should assume responsibility for her own health and behavior. The conduct of the sports program should aim to help each player lead and follow according to her merit, skill, willingness, and ability to adapt to the individuals and purposes concerned.

The sports activities should be selected on the basis of the best scientific evidence available and on the contribution such activities can make to the health and welfare of girls and women. Health safeguards should be taken into consideration; the health status of the participant should be evaluated and measures provided to adapt the individual's activity and extent of participation to it. The extent to which a girl or woman can participate in athletic activity

during the menstrual period should be recognized as an individual matter and proper provisions made.

Competition should be designed to function constructively in the sports program. All players should have the opportunity to participate and compete at their own level of ability. Furthermore, each participant should understand and appreciate the fundamental values that can be gained from participation in a sports program.

Officials should fulfill the qualifications for outstanding leadership—including a consistent and expert knowledge of the girl and the activity.

The rules established by the DGWS are the official rules and should be used.

The administrator. The administrator in charge of the sports program for girls and women is responsible for accomplishing the objectives for which the program is established. She has the responsibility for providing a safe, healthful, and desirable physical environment for the conduct of sports activities, and for seeing that the publicity in regard to the sports program is in accordance with the purpose for which the program has been established.

The administrator should hire only properly qualified teachers to conduct the sports program. Teachers should be expert in their task of leading others and understand and utilize the best techniques for teaching and conducting sports. They should reflect all those physical, mental, emotional, and social qualities that they seek to develop in others.

The participant. The participant should develop the desire for participation in accordance with her own individual needs. She should be interested in her own health, in having it periodically appraised by qualified persons, and in engaging in those hygienic practices which reflect such interest.

She should also be interested in developing skills which will yield satisfaction both in the present and in the future, and should utilize her role in the competitive sports situation wisely and in a manner that yields enjoyment.

Finally, the participant should recognize her responsibility as a cooperative member of the group and her potential as a leader.

The change in attitude toward girls' and women's athletics

There has been a gradual change in the attitude of the public in general, as well as professionals in physical education, regarding participation by girls and women in sports.

When college men began to organize athletic com-

---

*The Division of Girls' and Women's Sports, Standards in Sports for Girls and Women, Washington, D.C., 1958, American Association for Health, Physical Education, and Recreation.

Fig. 7-3. Women's field hockey.

Courtesy Cramer Products, Inc., Gardner, Kan.

petition in the 1800s, participation by girls and women was frowned on. At this time, however, girls and women were allowed to be spectators, and some were even encouraged to be cheerleaders. The dictates of society still forbade participation by females in competitive sports, however.

By the beginning of the twentieth century, women began to participate in sports at some colleges. In the eastern colleges this participation was limited mainly to play days and sports days, with an occasional invitational meet with several schools participating. The situation was different in other parts of the United States. For example, a survey in 1909 revealed that nearly half the colleges in the Midwest and West engaged in intercollegiate competition.*

The attitude of leaders in women's physical education toward sports for girls and women paralleled the

attitude of the general society. The platform statement issued in 1923 by the Women's Division of the National Amateur Athletic Federation indicated the thinking at that time. The stress was on informal participation and not on high-level competition. The group endorsed participation in athletics by girls and women that:

Promotes competition that stresses enjoyment of sport and development of good sportsmanship and character rather than those types that emphasize the making and breaking of records and the winning of championships for the enjoyment of spectators or for the athletic reputation or commercial advantage of institutions and organizations.*

The emphasis was clearly on intramural and informal extramural sports activities for girls and women in 1923. The attitude of leading women physical

---

*Dudley, G., and Kellor, F.A.: Athletic games in the education of women, New York, 1909, Henry Holt and Co. Cited in Van Dalen, D.B., and Bennett, B.: A world history of physical education, Englewood Cliffs, N.J., 1971, Prentice-Hall, Inc., p. 451.

*Sefton, A.A.: The Women's Division—National Amateur Athletic Federation, Stanford, 1941, Stanford University Press. Quoted in Lumpkin, A.: Let's set the record straight, Journal of Physical Education and Recreation **48:**40, March 1977.

educators remained that way until the 1960s. Probably the first tangible sign of a change in philosophy by women leaders of physical education toward the participation by girls and women in varsity athletics was in 1967 with the organization of the Commission on Intercollegiate Athletics for Women (CIAW) by the DGWS. The women acted on their changed attitude in 1969 by sponsoring national championships in both gymnastics and track and field. Athletics for girls on the precollegiate level usually followed the lead of the institutions of higher learning.

In some cases girls and women participated in highly competitive athletics before it was approved by leaders of women's physical education organizations. In Michigan, for instance, the girls' high school team of Marshall won the state basketball championship in 1905 and was greeted by ''bonfires, 10,000 Roman candles, crowds, noise, Superintendent Garwood, ex-major Porter, and all red-corpuscled Marshall.''*

Females in a few black colleges in the South also participated in highly competitive sports during the early 1900s, especially basketball. It was noteworthy, however, that a highly competitive track and field program for girls and women (known as the Tuskegee Relays) was started in 1929 by Tuskegee Institute in Tuskegee, Alabama. Several of the schools and colleges in the local area participated in these relays.†

Today women are freely participating in almost all phases of American society on an increased basis, including participation in sports and athletics.

Some benefits of physical education and sport

''I like it because it makes me look and feel better.'' ''It helps me to use up extra energy, work off excess calories, and develop a nice body.'' These were the replies given by two eleventh grade girls to the question, ''Do you feel physical education and sport are important?''

*Van Dalen and Bennett, op. cit.
†Thaxton, N.A.: A documentary analysis of competitive track and field for women at Tuskegee Institute and Tennessee State University, unpublished doctoral dissertation, Springfield College, 1970, Springfield, Massachusetts, pp. 77-79.

To determine how students feel about physical education and sport, I surveyed more than 200 high school girls. The comments made by the girls, students in grades nine through twelve, reflect personal reactions to their own physical education and sport programs. Their feelings, of course, may be different from those of girls in programs in other communities.

The answers given by high school girls who feel physical education and sport are important may be grouped into the following four categories:

Personal health—body development. Physical education and sport make a valuable contribution to their personal health and well-being, according to many girls. Some typical student comments: ''Just as the mind needs knowledge, the body needs exercise.'' ''It's great for one's health.'' ''It builds energy, improves coordination, strength and endurance, and makes you feel good.'' ''Everyone needs exercise, and physical education and sport are important for a healthy life, especially in a society that is automated like ours.''

Mental and physical both important. High school girls also recognize the need to stress both the mental and the physical in their school programs. As one freshman commented, ''I think a sound body and sound mind are both important.'' A senior expressed her thoughts this way: ''While your academic classes provide a chance to develop your mental ability, physical education and sport represent the only opportunity during school to develop your body and physical ability.''

Several girls felt the change of pace that physical activity provides is very worthwhile. ''It gives a chance for relief from the pressures of academic courses,'' one student commented. Another said, ''It is nice to run and let off some steam after tension has been built up during the school day.''

Personality. Girls are very much interested in experiences that contribute to their personality development, and physical education and sport, many students feel, contribute to this objective. One girl's feelings: ''It contributes to a personality that is more outgoing.'' Another girl felt it tested her will: ''It challenges my perseverance and self-discipline.''

Develops interest in sports. High school girls also feel physical education is important because it de-

Fig. 7-4. Women's intercollegiate athletics at the University of Kansas, Lawrence, Kan.

Courtesy Cramer Products, Inc., Gardner, Kan.

velops an interest in participating in sports. The reasons for wanting to become involved in sports range from that cited by one coed—''Boys like girls who are active''—to the desire to engage in competitive experiences, as expressed by a high school basketball star, ''I like to test my skill against girls who play on teams from other schools.''

From a more scientific point of view, Klafs and Lyon* list some of the physiological capabilities of girls and women, as follows:

1. A woman is competent to participate in strenuous activity under all conditions in which a man can participate.
2. She has not in any way reached her potential in terms of performance and is thoroughly capable of attaining much greater heights.
3. Physiologically, she compares favorably to the male in most parameters. However, in the area of power or strength she will always function at a 20% to 30%

handicap because of her size and structure.
4. Obstetrical and gynecological data obtained to date refute the idea that severe exercise is damaging and the cause of undesirable effects.
5. Endurance performance is no more damaging or overtaxing to the female than to her male counterpart. She is capable of great endurance.
6. The female's emotional reactions under stress are no different from those of the male; so-called ''emotional'' reactions are more likely to be the result of social and cultural mores than psychophysiological factors.
7. Such differences as do exist between the sexes must be kept in mind when selecting physical activities and sports for the female. Activities should be designed or modified when necessary to take advantage of both her body structure and functions.
8. Age is not, nor should it be permitted to be, a barrier to sports activity and competition. The values of such participation are pointed up not only by the beneficial aspects that can accrue but by the fact that participating mothers are most insistent that their daughters should be activity conscious.

*Klafs, C.E., and Lyon, M.J.: The female athlete, St.Louis, 1978, The C.V. Mosby Co.

Fig. 7-5. Intercollegiate basketball for women at the University of Nevada, Las Vegas.

Furthermore, these authors stress that through a training and conditioning program it is possible to achieve such results as increased muscular strength, increased oxygen consumption, higher maximum volume of blood per heart beat, lowered pulse rate, more economical lung ventilation, ability to perform more work aerobically, quicker recovery after exercise, and more efficient heat dissipation.

Title IX*

"No person in the United States shall on the basis of sex be excluded from participation in, be denied the benefits of, or be subjected to discrimination under any education program or activity receiving Federal financial assistance." This, in essence, is the theme of the legislation that Congress passed in June 1972, and that affects nearly all educational institutions in the United States. The law was initiated in 1971 as an amendment to the Civil Rights Act of 1964. After some changes the bill emerged as what is known as Title IX of the Education Amendments of 1972. This legislation is having wide-reaching effects on physical education and athletic programs in the United States.

One of the major reasons Title IX came into being was to ensure that girls and women received the same rights as boys and men. Testimony before congressional committees before the enactment of this legislation indicated that girls and women were being discriminated against in many education programs, including physical education and athletics. A survey conducted by the National Education Asso-

---

*Parts of this section have been taken directly from government documents relating to Title IX, particularly the following documents:

U.S. Department of Health, Education, and Welfare, Office for Civil Rights: Final Title IX regulation implementing education amendments of 1972—prohibiting sex discrimination in education, Washington, D.C., July 21, 1975, Government Printing Office.

U.S Department of Health, Education, and Welfare, Office for Civil Rights: Memorandum to chief state school officers, superintendents of local educational agencies and college and university presidents. Subject: Elimination of sex discrimination in athletic programs, Washington, D.C., September 1975, Government Printing Office.

ciation showed that although women constituted 67% of all public school teachers nationally, at the time the survey was conducted, they held only 15% of the principalships in the schools and 0.6% of the superintendencies. Another survey conducted by the National Center for Educational Statistics showed that salaries for women faculty members in colleges and universities were considerably lower than for their male counterparts. Furthermore, it was well established that for many years girls and women were discriminated against in many educational institutions regarding physical education and athletics facilities, budgets, salaries, and scholarships.

While the proposed legislation was under consideration in the Congress, voluminous amounts of mail and public comments showed that there was great public concern in six areas:

Sex discrimination in sports and athletic programs

Coeducational physical education classes

Sex stereotyping of textbooks

Impact of the law on fraternities and sororities

Scholarships

Employment

Although Title IX applies to all types of educational programs, probably the most dramatically affected have been sport and physical education programs. Girls' and women's athletic programs, in particular, have grown rapidly in only a few years. In the early 1970s there were comparatively few varsity interscholastic and intercollegiate teams for girls and women. Today, however, as a result of the federal regulation banning sex discrimination, it is a different story. Girls' and women's sport teams have come into their own and are in evidence throughout the nation.

PROVISIONS OF TITLE IX AFFECTING ATHLETIC PROGRAMS

Some of the provisions of Title IX affecting physical education and athletic programs include the following:

GENERAL PROVISIONS

Military and religious schools are exempted from the law where the provisions of the legislation are inconsistent with the basic religious tenets of the institution.

Fig. 7-6. Women's field hockey at Smith College, Northampton, Mass.

Membership requirements for social fraternities and sororities at the postsecondary level who receive federal funds, including the Boy Scouts, Camp Fire Girls, YWCA, and YMCA, are exempted from the regulation with the provision that where their educational programs are conducted for nonmembers, these programs must not discriminate on the basis of sex.

Scholarships may be restricted in nature if created by means such as a will, trust, or similar legal instrument or act of a foreign government.

Discrimination in housing is forbidden, with the exception that single-sex housing is permissible.

Comparable facilities for each sex are mandated, including locker rooms, shower facilities, and toilets.

Enrollment in course offerings and extracurricular activities should be open and not involve discrimination except that classes in health education may hold separate sessions in elementary and secondary schools when the subject matter concerns human sexuality exclusively.

PROVISION FOR PHYSICAL EDUCATION CLASSES

Physical education classes must be organized on a coeducational basis.

Classes may be separated by sex for contact sports such as wrestling, boxing, basketball, and football. Also, within classes students may be grouped on ability or other basis, except that of sex, even though such grouping results in single-sex or predominantly single-sex grouping.

PROVISION FOR ATHLETICS

Separate teams for boys and girls, or a coeducational team, must be provided in schools and colleges. For example, if there is only one team in a particular school, such as swimming, then students of both sexes must be permitted to try out for this team.

Equal opportunities must be provided for both sexes in educational institutions in equipment and supplies, use of facilities for practice and games, medical and training services, coaching and academic tutoring, travel allowances, housing and dining facilities, compensation of coaches, and publicity.

Equal aggregate expenditures are not required; however, equal opportunity for men and women is mandated.

Where men are given the opportunity for athletic scholarships, women must also be given the same opportunity.

Contact sports such as football, basketball, boxing, wrestling, rugby, and ice hockey may be offered either separately or on a unitary basis.

The emphasis of Title IX is that of providing equal opportunity for both sexes. In determining whether equal opportunity is provided, it is important to know whether the interests and abilities of students of both sexes have been met and whether such things as adequate facilities and equipment are available to both sexes in each sport.

In a fact sheet dated December 4, 1979, the Department of Health, Education and Welfare sought to clarify the proposed policy "Title IX and Intercollegiate Athletics," which was issued in 1978.* The policy interpretation of Title IX of the Education Amendments of 1972 was published in the Federal Register on December 11, 1979. The policy is designed to clarify what the regulation requires and proposes to determine whether a school's athletic program is in compliance with Title IX by assessing three factors of the athletic program:

1. *Financial assistance*—scholarships and grants-in-aid provided on the basis of athletic ability.
—The Title IX regulation requires that:
Colleges and universities provide reasonable opportuni-

ties for male and female students to receive scholarships and grants-in-aid in proportion to the number of male and female participating athletes.
—The policy explains that:
Schools must distribute all athletic assistance on a substantially proportional basis to the number of participating male and female athletes. (Example: Total scholarship fund = $100,000 in a school with seventy male and thirty female athletes. Male athletes are entitled to $70,000. Female athletes are entitled to $30,000.) Unequal spending for either the men's or the women's program may be justified by sex-neutral factors, such as a higher number of male athletes recruited from out-of-state.

2. *Athletic benefits and opportunities*—equipment and supplies, travel, compensation of coaches, facilities, housing, publicity, and other aspects of a program.
—The Title IX regulation specifies the factors that HEW should assess in determining whether a school is providing equal athletic opportunity. This "equal opportunity" regulation applies to all aspects of athletic programs, such as equipment and supplies, scheduling of games and practices, compensation of coaches, housing and dining services, publicity, travel and per diem costs, opportunities for coaching, locker rooms and other facilities, medical and training services, and other relevant factors.
—The policy explains that schools must provide "equivalent" treatment, services, and benefits in those areas. HEW will assess each of those factors by comparing:
  • Availability
  • Kind of benefits
  • Quality
  • Kind of opportunities

3. *Accommodation of student interests and abilities*—the third section of the policy sets out how schools can meet the requirement of the regulation to "effectively accommodate the interests and abilities of both sexes."
—The Title IX regulation requires that schools effectively:
Accommodate the interests and abilities of students of both sexes in the selection of sports and levels of competition.
—The policy explains how to accommodate interests and abilities through:
  • Selection of sports
    1. When there is a team for only one sex, and the excluded sex is interested in the sport, the university may be required to:
       —Permit the excluded sex to try out for the team if it is not a contact sport; or

---

*HEW Fact Sheet: Title IX and Intercollegiate Athletes Policy, Washington, D.C., December 4, 1979, U.S. Department of Health, Education and Welfare, p. 1.

—Sponsor a separate team for the previously excluded sex if there is a reasonable expectation of intercollegiate competition for that team.

2. Teams do not have to be integrated.
3. The same sports do not have to be offered to men and to women.

• Levels of competition
Equal competitive opportunity means:

1. The number of men and women participating in intercollegiate athletics is in proportion to their overall enrollment, or
2. The school has taken steps to ensure that the sex underrepresented in athletic programs is offered new opportunities consistent with the interests and abilities of that sex; or
3. The present program accommodates the interests and abilities of the underrepresented sex.
4. Men and women athletes, in proportion to their participation in athletic programs, compete at the same levels; or
5. The school has a history and practice of upgrading the levels at which teams of the underrepresented sex compete.
   —Schools are not required to develop or upgrade an intercollegiate team if there is no reasonable expectation that competition will be available for that team.

• Measuring of interests and abilities
The recipient must:

1. Take into account the increasing levels of women's interests and abilities;
2. Use methods of determining interests and ability that do not disadvantage the underrepresented sex;
3. Use methods of determining ability that take into account team performance records; and
4. Use methods that are responsive to the expressed interests of students capable of intercollegiate competition who belong to the underrepresented sex.

These Title IX guidelines provided that expenditures on men's and women's athletics be proportional to the number of men and women participating in athletics. This standard of substantially equal per capita expenditures must be met unless the institution can demonstrate that the differences are based on nondiscriminatory factors, such as the costs of a particular sport (for example, the equipment required) or the scope of the competition (national rather than regional or local). This proportional standard applies to athletic scholarships, recruitment, and other readily measurable financial benefits such as equipment, supplies, travel, and publicity.

According to the Department of Health and Human Services, the policy is designed to eliminate, over a reasonable period of time, the discriminatory effects, particularly at the college level, of the historic emphasis on men's sports and to facilitate the continued growth of women's athletics. It requires colleges and universities to take specific active steps to provide additional athletic opportunities for women—opportunities that will fully accommodate the rising interests of women in participating in athletics.

The staff attorney of the Department of Health and Human Services indicated that guidelines have three basic parts. First, there must be equal expenditure of money per person involved in intercollegiate athletics. Second, there must be comparable standards set where there are elements that are not easily measurable. Third, colleges must have policies and procedures for upgrading women's athletics such as showing how they will upgrade a women's club team to a varsity team.

The staff attorney explained that if a college gives out 95 full athletic scholarships to men for football, the guidelines do not mean that college must also give out 95 full athletic scholarships to women. It does mean, however, that if a college has 200 male varsity athletes and spends $200,000 on scholarships for an average of $1000 per scholarship per male athlete, that college must spend an average of $1000 per athletic scholarship for women. Thus, if that college has 50 women in varsity sports, it must spend $50,000 on women's athletic scholarships. Also, if a college spends $300 for each football helmet, that does not mean it must spend a similar amount for a piece of equipment for women. But it does mean that if tennis racquets cost $40 each, a college with women tennis players must spend the money to make the racquets as available to these women as the helmets are to the football players. Another example given by the attorney was that if a college sends its football team by first-class charter flight to a game,

Fig. 7-7. Women's racquetball at Smith College, Northampton, Mass.

Fig. 7-8. Girl's track in Aledo, Ill.

Courtesy Barbara Ann Chiles.

it must spend a proportionately similar amount on some aspect, not necessarily travel, for its women's teams. It might spend the proportionately similar amount on living quarters or something else.

INTERPRETATIONS OF REGULATIONS CONCERNING TITLE IX

Although the Title IX regulations have been effective since July 21, 1975, there are few fixed guidelines emanating from the Department of Health and Human Services to assist in implementing this legislation. In fact, persons who have written to the department for interpretations have found that it takes several months to get a reply. Therefore it is helpful to know that the interpretation of certain provisions of Title IX that affect physical education and athletic programs have caused confusion among physical educators throughout the nation. The following interpretations have been made only after careful study or communication with officers of the Office of Civil Rights of the Department of Health and Human Services. These interpretations are provided in the following question-and-answer format.

QUESTIONS AND ANSWERS ON ATHLETICS UNDER TITLE IX PROVISION*

Question: If a school operates a baseball team for boys and a softball team for girls in the spring, must the school permit a girl to try out for the baseball team?

Answer: No, assuming that the interests and abilities of most of the female students are satisfied by the softball team and other teams offered for them.

Question: If a school has a boys' soccer team and a girls' field hockey team in the fall, must it permit girls to try out for the soccer team?

Answer: No.

Question: If a school has a team for girls in a noncontact sport such as badminton, but not for boys, must it permit boys to try out for the team?

Answer: No, unless—and this would be rare—boys' athletic opportunities at the school have been limited.

Question: A school has sponsored separate teams for boys and girls in golf, tennis, track and field, swimming, and diving. For some reason the school terminates the dual

program and starts single programs in these sports. All but a few girls are eliminated from these programs. Assuming that the rest of the boys' and girls' sports programs are equal, has the school violated any provision of Title IX?

Answer: Assuming there are still a sufficient number of girls to field teams in these sports and the interests and abilities are not accommodated by the remaining sports, it would appear that the school has violated Title IX.

Question: If there are sufficient women interested in basketball to form a viable women's basketball team, is an institution that fields a men's basketball team required to provide such a team for women?

Answer: One of the factors to be considered in determining whether equal opportunities are provided is whether the selection of sports and levels of competition effectively accommodate the interests and abilities of members of both sexes. Therefore, if a school provides basketball for men and the only way in which the school can accommodate the interests and abilities of women is to offer a separate basketball team for women, such a team must be provided.

Question: If there are insufficient women interested in participating on a women's track team, must the institution allow an interested woman to compete for a position on a men's track team?

Answer: If athletic opportunities have previously been limited for women at that school, it must allow women to compete for the men's team if the sport is of the noncontact variety such as track. The school may preclude women from participating on a men's team in a contact sport. A school may preclude men or women from participating on teams for the other sex if athletic opportunities have not been limited in the past for them, regardless of whether the sport is contact or noncontact.

Question: Can a school be exempt from Title IX if its athletic conference forbids men and women on the same noncontact team?

Answer: No. Title IX preempts all state or local laws or other requirements that conflict with Title IX.

MORE TITLE IX INQUIRIES*

The NCAA posed a total of 45 questions to the Department of Education regarding the implementation of the Title IX regulation. The department answered the following questions.

---

*Schnee, Ronald G.: Frying pan to fire: school advocacy of Title IX, Phi Delta Kappan **58**:423, January 1977.

*National Collegiate Athletic Association, NCAA **17**:1, November 30, 1980.

The answers indicated the position of the Department of Education as to what Title IX requires. Because that department had responsibility for implementing and enforcing the Title IX regulation, its interpretations of the regulation are important.

However, the validity of these interpretations and of the Title IX regulation itself ultimately will be determined by the courts.

Question: The policy interpretation indicates that Title IX compliance will be assessed by examining, among other factors, the equivalence for men and women of the "time of day competitive events are scheduled." In making scheduling decisions, may an institution take into account differences in the level of spectator interest in men's and women's sports programs? Will equivalency of scheduling be assessed on a sport-by-sport basis?

Answer: No program component, including equivalency of scheduling, will be assessed on a sport-by-sport basis. An institution may take into account differences in the level of spectator interest in various sports when making scheduling decisions. However, an institution may not justify all scheduling decisions based on spectator interest since the time of day competitive events are scheduled may have a significant impact on whether a sport ever develops a spectator following.

Question: If the student-athletes, coaches and administrators of a women's basketball program choose to schedule games within the institution's home state and contiguous states despite the fact that the men's program is conducted on a national level, is the institution in violation of Title IX?

Answer: Evaluation of compliance will not be based on a sport-by-sport comparison. An institution which chooses to conduct a nationally competitive program in men's basketball may develop some sport other than basketball for women. If an institution asserts program comparability of men's teams which compete nationwide and women's teams which compete locally, it must show that sufficient competition at the appropriate level is available to the women's teams within the institution's home state and contiguous states.

Question: An institution provides a training table for members of the football team because, due to the extended practice session for the sport, regular student dining facilities are closed by the conclusion of football practice. To be in compliance with Title IX, is the institution required to make a training table available to other male student-athletes and/or to a proportionally equal number of female student-athletes?

Answer: Provision of a training table for football players will not mandate similar provisions for other male athletes. Since dining services constitute direct benefits to students, they will be considered in evaluating overall program comparability. If a training table is provided for football players due to extended practice sessions and if women's teams have practice sessions which conflict with student cafeteria hours, it would be appropriate to make similar arrangements for women's team members.

Question: An institution has special locker-room facilities for its football team. Assuming that the locker-room facilities for male and female student-athletes in sports other than football are equivalent, is the institution in compliance with Title IX?

Answer: If locker rooms used by female athletes are significantly poorer in quality and availability than those provided for male athletes, including football players, the institution may not be providing equivalent benefits and opportunities to female athletes in this program area. As with all program components, if these deficiencies are substantial enough in and of themselves to deny equality of athletic opportunity, the institution will be found in noncompliance. It shall not be a defense to say that locker facilities for women are equivalent to those provided for all nonfootball male athletes.

Question: Will financial aid awarded on the basis of need ever be considered to be an athletic scholarship or grant-in-aid? Specifically, an institution recruits a student because of his or her athletic ability. However, no preference regarding athletic ability is shown in admission and the student simply is referred to the financial aid office, where financial aid is determined on the basis of the applicant's financial need and he or she receives no special treatment. Is financial assistance awarded to the student subject to the proportionality requirement merely because the student was recruited as an athlete?

Answer: No. Aid which is demonstrably unrelated to athletic ability will not be included in the calculation of athletic financial assistance.

Question: If an institution gives a student a preference in admission because of his or her athletic ability but extends financial aid to that student solely on the basis of need, is that aid subject to the proportionality requirement?

Answer: No, so long as the financial aid is demonstrably unrelated to athletic ability.

Question: An institution gives a student an advantage in the admissions process because of athletic ability and awards financial aid to that student solely on the basis of need. If the institution's financial aid package for the student-athlete contains a greater-than-standard proportion of scholarship assistance (as compared to loan assistance) because of the student's athletic ability, is the aid received by that student subject to the proportionality requirement?

Answer: Funds based solely on need (i.e., demonstrably unrelated to athletic ability) are not subject to the proportionality requirement. The packaging of need-based aid will be reviewed to determine that equivalent benefits based on athletic ability are proportionately available to athletes of both sexes. It may be permissible, for example, for an institution to award a greater-than-standard proportion of scholarship assistance (as compared to loan assistance) to athletes so long as a greater-than-standard proportion is given to athletes of each sex.

Question: An institution sets aside sufficient financial assistance funds to aid all athletes who demonstrate financial need. The aggregate amounts awarded by sex are not proportionate because of different distributions of need levels among male and female participants. Would the funds awarded be considered athletic grants-in-aid (or scholarships)? Would the disproportionality violate Title IX, or would the difference in need distributions constitute a nondiscriminatory factor justifying the lack of proportionality?

Answer: So long as the determination of need is based on sex-neutral, nondiscriminatory formulas or procedures, the proportionality requirement will not apply. However, distribution of the need-based aid will be examined to determine whether equivalent benefits are proportionately available to male and female athletes. Examples of "equivalent benefits" include proportions of grants and waivers (as compared with loans) awarded, favorable job assignments and pay rates under a work-study program and assistance in obtaining employment during the academic year.

Question: In what circumstances, if any, is it permissible for an NCAA Division III member institution (which does not award athletic financial assistance to men) to award athletic financial assistance to women who participate in intercollegiate athletics under AIAW regulations at any divisional level?

Answer: An institution may choose not to make any awards of financial assistance based on athletic ability. If an institution awards athletic financial assistance to students of either sex, it must do so for students of both sexes. One exception to this rule is that an institution may provide athletic financial assistance to members of one sex to overcome the effects of conditions that have limited opportunities of that sex to participate in the athletic program. This exception is based on the Title IX regulatory section on voluntary affirmative action, 34, C.F.R. 106.3(b).

PROCEDURES FOR ASSURING COMPLIANCE WITH TITLE IX

To make sure the provisions of Title IX have been complied with by an educational institution, certain procedures are followed. Each educational institution usually has some member of the faculty or staff coordinate a self-evaluation and assure compliance.

The steps that have been followed in some physical education and athletic programs involve first developing a statement of physical education philosophy that provides a guide for equality of opportunity for both sexes. Then, student interest is determined regarding the activities they desire in the physical education and athletic program. Furthermore, all written materials concerned with items such as curriculum, employment, administration, and course content are reviewed to see that needed changes are made to ensure that physical education activities are being taught coeducationally. Also, such things as practice times for all teams, provision for supplies and equipment, travel expenses, number of coaches assigned to teams, and salaries of coaches are examined to see if there are any discrepancies between the sexes. The membership requirements for clubs and other student organizations associated with physical education and athletics are reviewed. The amount of publicity and information services provided for physical education and athletic programs are checked. Eligibility requirements for scholarships and financial aid, medical and accident policies, award systems, and employment procedures are examined. Teaching loads, coaching assignments, and facility assignments are also included in such an appraisal.

The procedure followed by the Oklahoma City Public Schools illustrates what one school system has done in implementing the regulations advocated by Title IX. The school system followed this procedure:

Fig. 7-9. Women's field hockey.
Courtesy President's Council on Physical Fitness and Sports.

It appointed an assistant superintendent as Title IX co-cordinator.

It committed itself to the implementation of Title IX according to the letter and intent of the law.

Tasks involved in implementing Title IX were assigned to the following committees: athletics, curriculum and physical education, employment/affirmative action, extracurricular activities, and guidance. These committees were composed of teachers, students, principals, and concerned patrons.

It obtained inservice training assistance from the University of Oklahoma.

It clearly defined the information needed regarding possible discrimination in each of the committee areas.

It enlisted more than 200 people in collecting and assessing data following the inservice training program provided by the University of Oklahoma.

It prepared a report recommending remedial actions and began implementing changes.

The Oklahoma City Schools, in implementing this plan, stressed the need to recognize that affirmative actions are necessary, remedial actions are necessary, and clear affirmative policies are needed. When in doubt, decisions should be made in favor of equalized opportunity, and every effort should be made to follow the full intent of the law.

According to the AAHPERD,* many questions can

be asked to determine if equality exists between men and women. For example, under *employment conditions* the question might be asked, "Are men and women paid the same salaries for essentially the same work for both teaching and coaching?" Under *physical education classes* the question might be asked, "Are physical education requirements for graduation the same for boys and girls, men and women?" Under *recreational opportunities,* "Are intramural programs provided for both sexes?" Under *athletics,* "Does the total budget reflect comparable support to both the men's and women's programs?" Many other questions are listed in their publication to determine if equality exists.

In some cases where equality does not exist between men and women, litigation is initiated. For example, in one case a high school girl wanted to participate on the boys' golf team. There was no golf team for girls, and the court ruled in favor of the girl and allowed her to participate. Another case involved girls who wanted to play on the high school football team, thus challenging a state athletic association rule excluding girls. The court ruled in favor of the girls and said the association rule discriminated on the basis of sex.

The publication *In the Running* * a project of the

*AAHPERD: Equality in sports for women, Reston, Va., 1977, The Alliance.

*Rosensweig, M.: Want to file a Title IX complaint? In the Running **1:**1, Fall 1978.

Women's Equity Action League Educational and Legal Defense Fund, has indicated the following pros and cons of bringing a legal suit:

Some *pros of filing a complaint* are: It is possible to win. You may convince other women to take legal action for other complaints. You may change discriminatory practices at your school or college. Many girls and women may benefit from your action. Your action may result in the Title IX compliance plan at your school becoming the subject of scrutiny. Schools that have been cited for complaints are more likely to be closer to compliance with the law.

Some *cons of filing a complaint are:* You can lose. You may lose your position or scholarship. You may become frustrated in dealing with the many organizations involved. The procedure sometimes takes years to resolve. You may be labeled a trouble-maker.

Organizations that will be of help in case you find that inequality exists are: Department of Health and Human Services; Office for Civil Rights; Equal Employment Opportunity Commission; Office of Federal Contract Compliance; and the U.S. Department of Labor—Wage and Hour Division of the Employment Standards Administration.

The NCAA indicates that new Title IX athletics complaints have been filed against several institutions, bringing the total number of colleges and universities with such complaints pending against them to approximately 100. The new complaints were filed with regional Office of Civil Rights (OCR) offices and have been referred to the national OCR headquarters office in Washington, D.C. OCR intends eventually to conduct comprehensive intercollegiate athletics compliance reviews of all institutions against which complaints have been filed.

COEDUCATIONAL SPORTS AND TITLE IX

Coeducational sports should be provided for students in schools and institutions of higher education because of the benefits (mainly sociological and cultural) that can accrue from such participation. However, coeducational sports, in some cases, should be limited to the intramural and recreational levels.

In instances when one or two highly skilled females would not otherwise have the opportunity to participate in a particular sport, they must be allowed to participate with males.

The main reason for not advocating coeducational sports participation on interscholastic and intercollegiate levels in many sports is the physiological differences between males and females. The ratio of strength to weight is greater in males than in females. Females would thus be at a decided disadvantage in those sports requiring speed and strength, including all contact sports and some noncontact sports such as track and field and volleyball.

There are other reasons for advocating separate teams for males and females. For instance, if coeducational varsity teams were encouraged, males would comprise most of the teams. Because of the "speed, size, and strength" factors, girls would not be able to make varsity teams in any great numbers. Consequently, there would be mostly male-dominated teams.

The attempt by Ann Myers (a former women's all-American basketball player from UCLA) to make the roster of an NBA basketball team demonstrates the athletic differences between top-level male and female athletes. Myers failed to make the NBA team. The coach said her weight and overall strength militated against her making the team. He said she possessed excellent basketball skills. The skills of most of the other basketball hopefuls at that level of play were probably also very high. Thus size and strength became critical factors. This would not be the case on the intramural and recreational levels. Some females might possess more skill than their male counterparts and thereby make up for the differences in strength and size.

A 1977 Gallup Youth Survey poll revealed that the most popular coeducational sports among teen-aged boys and girls were tennis, swimming, track, basketball, and baseball.

PROBLEMS CREATED BY THE RAPID GROWTH OF GIRLS' AND WOMEN'S SPORTS AND TITLE IX

The number of girls and women participating in sports has grown by leaps and bounds but so have their problems, most of which are the result of this growth.

One problem relates to the need to achieve and maintain high-quality athletic programs. The budget crunch and distressed economy have not provided for needed additional facilities such as locker rooms, gymnasia, athletic fields, and equipment. Although girls and women are entitled to an equitable share of these necessities, these items exist in insufficient number to accommodate the expanded girls' and women's sport programs.

Girls' and women's athletic programs are beginning to be faced with the same concerns that boys' and men's programs have faced over the years: emphasis on winning, recruiting, unethical means of obtaining star players, and the demand for scholarships. Some women physical educators, as a result, are being exposed to the same temptations to produce winning teams.

Present practices indicate that women leaders in physical education and athletics are encountering the same problems that beset the men when they were deciding whether to go "big time" in athletics. In an effort to gain parity with athletic programs for men, some practices that have been adopted by men are now being endorsed by women. In 1978, for instance, the AIAW recommended that women coaches be paid to scout high school and junior college athletic prospects.

Girls' and women's programs are also finding it difficult in some instances to be prepared adequately for coaching responsibilities. Title IX has brought about so many changes in such a short period that many women are assigned to coaching responsibilities, and they are finding that coaching is different from teaching. During many years of teaching and little varsity team coaching they have developed philosophies that at times are in conflict with the demands on them to coach highly skilled varsity teams who are supposed to win games.

Girls' and women's programs are also being engulfed in publicity and promotion of a magnitude they never experienced before the present emphasis on highly organized competition for women. Girls' and women's sports are featured in the newspaper headlines, television coverage, and radio news. They have become "big time." As a result of such exposure, girls and women are having difficulty keeping their sports programs in proper perspective and observing sound ethical practices.

Present status of girls and women in sports

During the year before the birth of Title IX, 3,366,000 boys and 294,000 girls competed in interscholastic sports in the United States. Seven years later the figures showed 4,109,000 boys and 1,645,000 girls in the same activities. The participation by girls in interscholastic sports increased 460% during the interim. Furthermore, the participation of girls increased from 7% of the total number of students involved to 29%. In addition, approximately 500 colleges offer athletic scholarships to women athletes. The Association for Intercollegiate Athletics for Women (AIAW), now defunct, had more than 1000 member schools a few years ago and was the largest collegiate athletic association in the United States. Since that time, however, the NCAA has taken over control of women's athletics in many colleges and universities. The AIAW is no longer active in governing womens' intercollegiate athletics.

A 1979 survey by the College and University Administrators Council* indicated that the average institution employed more coaches for athletic activities for men than coaches for women for all three divisional levels of the NCAA and AIAW. The greatest disparity was in the Division I institutions (those with the largest enrollments); there were 1320 coaches for men's athletic activities and only 575 coaches for women's athletic activities. There was an average of 13 coaches of sports for men and 6 coaches of sports for women in each institution in Division I. The average number of sports offered for men and women in each institution did not differ greatly—seven sports per institution for men and five for women. In Division II institutions, the average number of sports offered for men and women was six and five, respectively.

Another revealing conclusion drawn from the survey was that more coaches for women's sports are tenured regular faculty appointments or have split academic and athletic assignments than are coaches of

---

*Richardson, H.D.: Athletics in higher education: some comparisons, Journal of Physical Education and Recreation **50**:56, June 1979.

sports for men. However, future trends indicate that new coaches, both men and women, are being hired without regular faculty status. Also, coaches retaining regular academic appointments will be replaced with nonacademic appointees.

The data for this survey were based on the responses of 65% of 344 institutions of higher education. A random sample was used to select the 344 institutions, all within the geographical divisional structure of the National Collegiate Athletic Association. The NCAA's *Blue Book of College Athletics 1977-1978* was used as a resource in selecting the institutions.

The situation on the secondary school level is about the same as it is on the college level; males are participating in organized athletic programs in greater numbers than females. Although girls on the secondary school level have made tremendous gains insofar as the total number of participants in interscholastic athletics, they still represent only half the total number of boys who participate in interscholastic athletics.

Figures in a recent survey by the National Federation of State High School Associations indicate there are more than 1.85 million female participants in athletics on the high school level.* The total number of girls participating in high school athletics represents a drop from over 2 million who participated during the 1977-1978 school year. This decrease in participants resulted from dropping from the figures all Canadian high school participation and all United States junior high school participation previously included in the surveys. However, when compared with only 294,000 female participants in 1970-1971, the 1.85 million female participants for the 1978-1979 figure is impressive.

Girls participated in a total of 29 high school sports. The three most popular sports, in terms of both schools sponsoring teams and number of participants, were basketball, track and field, and volleyball. Over 15,000 schools sponsored basketball teams for girls with almost 500,000 participants. Field hockey was the tenth most popular sport, with 1959

*National Federation of State High School Associations: 1979 sports participation survey, Kansas City, Mo., 1979, NFSHSA.

schools sponsoring teams in the sport.

A 1973-1974 survey by the editors of *Women Sports* revealed that budgets for boys' sport activities at the interscholastic level were on the average five times larger than the budgets for girls' sport activities. On the college level, the men received 30 times that received by women, and in some universities, they received 100 times what the women received. At Ohio State, for example, the men's sports program was funded at $2.8 million, while the women's program received only $50,000. Although sports programs for men and women are still not equal in terms of funding, legislation such as Title IX has had a positive impact. Sports programs for males and females on all levels are much more equal in the 1980s.

Prospects for the future

Title IX is now the law of the land. All institutions, including most schools and colleges, who receive federal financial assistance must comply. Furthermore, because it is difficult for the federal government to supervise and make decisions for the 16,000 schools and 2700 postsecondary educational institutions, a major share of the responsibility rests with each individual institution. Each school district and each college or university or other institution is unique and as a result must develop its own plan for compliance. Noncompliance can present many problems and difficulties. The government will no longer tolerate and this nation can no longer justify inequities in the manner in which both sexes are treated.

Each institution and each educational program will face many problems in complying with Title IX. This is true particularly in light of the budget crises that many schools and colleges face at present. For example, it will be difficult for many institutions to increase items such as the course offerings, budgets, and facilities for an expanded athletic program for girls without curtailing some other parts of the educational program at the same time, possibly that of the boys. It will be difficult to bear the increased costs of adding faculty, facilities, supplies and equipment, and scholarships to provide girls and women with a physical education and athletics program comparable with what boys and men now possess. There will be many problems concerned with implementing coeducational class activities.

All of these problems can be solved, however, as they are being solved in thousands of educational institutions from coast to coast. For example, in many schools and colleges athletic and physical education activities are being modified so students may engage in them on a coeducational basis. Basketball is being played with modifications such as three women and two men on a team, with field goals scored by women counting four points and those by men two points, and with men not being permitted to enter the freethrow lane at any time at either end of the court. Volleyball is being played with four men and four women; men are not permitted to spike and must serve underhand. Furthermore, at least one woman must touch the ball before it is volleyed back over the net by her team. Adaptations and modifications can be developed in most activities to make them suitable for coeducational use.

Instructors of physical education classes and coaches of athletic teams, when assigned to teams of the opposite sex or on a coeducational basis, have proved successful. Budgets have been increased for girls' and women's programs in many cases without harming the overall physical education and athletic program. Schedules have been revised so that both males and females have equitable access to facilities. Many other changes have also taken place to comply with Title IX.

Compliance may be achieved according to the letter and the spirit of the federal mandate providing there is a willingness to comply and a desire to cooperate with other members of an educational institution. The first and foremost way to achieve desirable results is to work through the system in one's local situation. It should be recognized that resistance in some cases will be encountered, because change seldom comes easily. However, the law demands equity for both sexes, and as a result such changes will eventually take place. The Office for Civil Rights is willing to assist school officials in meeting their Title IX responsibilities. Regional offices exist in ten different locations throughout the nation where help may be secured.

Physical education and athletics occupy a very important place in the American culture. The turmoil and reorganization implicit in the federal requirement for equity offer an opportunity to let this field of endeavor contribute to the health and welfare of all human beings rather than to only a few.

Selected administrative personnel involved in girls' and women's athletic programs

Many of the administrative functions discussed in Chapter 6 are equally applicable to girls' and women's sports. However, some pertinent questions regarding the administration of girls' and women's sports are discussed here.

THE ATHLETIC ADMINISTRATOR— MAN OR WOMAN?

Some questions continually raised concerning the sex of the athletic director include: Should there be an athletic director for the women's and also for the men's program? Is the plan whereby the woman is an associate or assistant athletic director responsible to the male athletic director satisfactory? Should there be one department of athletics with a man and a woman given equal stature and responsibility? Should the director of the physical education department be in charge of all athletic programs?

No one kind of organization exists in all schools and colleges. It appears the conditions that exist in each specific situation dictate what plan is to be followed. However, in an attempt to clarify the problem, some recommendations by selected leaders in the field are given here.

Sisley* argues that Title IX and the equal opportunity movement have opened up many opportunities for women who desire to become athletic directors. She implies that women should be the persons to administer girls' and women's athletic programs. However, she is concerned that women's athletics may be following the same road men's athletics have. She stresses the need for quality leadership among

---

*Sisley, B.L.: Women in administration—a quest for leadership, Journal of Physical Education and Recreation **52**:77, April 1981.

Fig. 7-10. Girls and women are increasingly involved in intramural activities. These girls are participating in intramurals as part of The Youth Services Section of the Physical Education Program in the Los Angeles City Schools.

women that fosters ethical behavior. She lists the following activities that today's administrators must perform if they are to achieve these goals:

- Keep in close contact with student athletes and focus the program on what is good for them
- Hire quality personnel to direct and manage the program
- Keep informed of AIAW rulings and NCAA and AAIA developments
- Set priorities based on a sound philosophy
- Develop excellent channels of communication among staff members, students, and administration

- Recognize that the participants are the main ingredient in the program
- Meet the demands of change

Deatherage and Reid* state that for intercollegiate sports the program should definitely be under the jurisdiction of women physical education teachers. For interscholastic sports they also stress that responsibility should be delegated to women physical edu-

---

*Deatherage, D., and Reid, C.P.: Administration of women's competitive sports, Dubuque, Iowa, 1977, Wm. C. Brown Co.

cators by the central administration, recognizing that the ultimate authority rests with the central administration.

Parkhouse and Lapin* point out that although some women administrators have some managerial deficiencies, at the same time, women with an athletic background have other skills that will enable them to be better managers than nonathletic women. Some of the managerial weaknesses they cite include women do not accept criticism well, they wait to be told what to do instead of acting on their own, they seldom master their emotions, they are not innovative, they accept what they are told without questioning, they focus on the present instead of planning for the future, they try too hard to please, and they are not willing to take risks.

At the same time, these authors point out that women can overcome these deficiencies and, in addition, women have the ingredients for success as managers. They have a strong self-image, they are articulate, they have an intuitive sense, they are more quick-witted than men, they pay attention to detail, they are less easily flustered, and they retain self-possession for a longer time.

THE COACH—MAN OR WOMAN?

Should the coach of girl's and women's sports teams be a man or a woman? Parkhouse and Lapin† point out that federal law indicates the most qualified person should be hired as coach, whether man or woman. However, a study by Parkhouse showed that in 320 AIAW institutions 40% of the female athletic directors indicated a different kind of preparation was needed to coach girls' and women's sports than for coaching boys' and men's sports. She also notes that the current trend is for women athletic directors to hire a female coach if she is qualified. However, men are not excluded and are hired in most cases if their qualifications are superior to those of the women candidates. Indeed, 42% of those surveyed had no preference for gender of the coach.

Two considerations in hiring a coach for girl's and women's teams are that the coach should have a good relationship with and the ability to communicate with girls and women, and that the coach's character should be beyond reproach.

THE ATHLETIC TRAINER—MAN OR WOMAN?

The question of whether an athletic trainer should be a man or a woman also seems to suggest the most qualified person should be hired regardless of sex. Parkhouse and Lapin list several reasons why a coeducational training room works well, providing both sexes derive the same benefits: all persons should receive equal treatment; a coed training room works best with a full-time trainer who supports the women's program; two part-time trainers, one male and one female, should be present; and at least one woman should be on the athletic training staff because some girls and women feel uncomfortable when treated by men, and a woman will take a special interest in injuries to female athletes.

THE OFFICIALS—MEN OR WOMEN?

Deatherage and Reid* state that in intercollegiate sports officials should be rated by the National Association for Girls and Women in Sports. In interscholastic sports they state that qualified women should be used as officials whenever possible. Also, it is important for officials to have a NAGWS rating. In reality this is not always possible because such qualified women are not always available.

Officials may obtain their training or their rating through such means as clinics sponsored by local officiating boards, state associations, sports federations, NAGWS, officiating classes, and courses offered by colleges and recreation associations.

Parkhouse and Lapin† indicate the general quality of officiating for girls and women's sports leaves much to be desired. In a survey they conducted, female athletic directors rated men and women officials about the same:

	Men (%)	Women (%)
Excellent	31	28
Fair	61	61
Poor	8	11

---

*Parkhouse, B.L., and Lapin, J.: The woman in athletic administration, Santa Monica, Calif., 1980, Goodyear Publishing Co.

†Parkhouse and Lapin, op. cit.

*Deatherage and Reid, op. cit.

†Parkhouse and Lapin, op. cit.

Administrative guidelines

Some guidelines to help school personnel who are faced with the task of starting a program of athletics for girls and women or for providing coeducation sports are listed below. The guidelines should be consistent with the latest, current information related to medical, psychological, sociological, and educational aspects of sports for girls and women. They reflect a philosophy of athletics as an educational experience for the highly skilled, as well as for the less skilled, student.

1. Conduct athletic programs in accordance with regulations promulgated by athletic governing bodies; that is, the National Federation of State High School Associations, National Association for Girls and Women in Sport, and the National Collegiate Athletic Association. However, seek to change those regulations and resolutions that are contrary to the best interests of student-athletes.
2. As a general rule, when size, strength, or other special conditions place girls and women at a disadvantage in some sports (football and wrestling, for example), provide separate teams for males and females. In special cases when a highly skilled girl or woman wishes to participate in a sport offered for males only, allow her to try out for that sport.
3. Maintain an educational emphasis in the athletic program. Keep schedules to a point that students will not be away from school and classes for long periods.
4. When coeducational teams are provided, modify the rules to equalize competition.
5. Provide qualified coaches for all girls' and women's sports. Allow qualified men to coach sports for girls and women, with the ultimate aim toward having the best qualified person coaching athletic teams.
6. Base the athletic program on the needs, interests, and capacities of the participants.
7. Encourage and facilitate research on the effects of athletics on girls and women.
8. Although wide differences of opinion exist concerning athletics for girls and women, there is agreement that in any type of athletics program for girls and women—intramural, extramural, or varisty—special consideration must be made for the participants. The program cannot be a duplication of boys and men's athletics. Strong support also exists for the idea of having women responsible for the administration, coaching, officiating, and conduct of the athletics program.

Selected athletic associations for girls and women*

NATIONAL ASSOCIATION FOR GIRLS AND WOMEN IN SPORTS (NAGWS)

The National Association for Girls and Women in Sport is one of the seven associations of the American Alliance for Health, Physical Education, Recreation, and Dance and is concerned with the governance of sports for girls and women.

The specific functions of the National Association for Girls and Women in Sport are the following:

1. To formulate and publicize guiding principles and standards for the administrator, leader, official, and player.
2. To publish and interpret rules governing sports for girls and women.
3. To provide the means for training, evaluating, and rating officials.
4. To disseminate information on the conduct of girls' and women's sports.
5. To stimulate, evaluate, and disseminate research in the field of girls' and women's sports.
6. To cooperate with allied groups interested in girls' and women's sports in order to formulate policies and rules that affect the conduct of women's sports.
7. To provide opportunities for the development of leadership among girls and women for the conduct of their sports programs.

For more information, contact the national office of the American Alliance for Health, Physical Education, Recreation, and Dance, located at 1900 Association Drive, Reston, Va. 22091 (Telephone: 703-476-3400).

ASSOCIATION FOR INTERCOLLEGIATE ATHLETICS FOR WOMEN (AIAW)

The Association for Intercollegiate Athletics for Women (now defunct) established in 1971 as a structure of the National Association for Girls and Women in Sport, was an autonomous organization with its own charter and bylaws. It established its own legal identity on June 1, 1979. The purpose for establishing the organization was to provide governance and

---

*Other athletic associations, such as the NCAA, are discussed in Chapter 6.

leadership for women's intercollegiate athletics. There was a total of 1007 member schools in the AIAW for the 1978-1979 academic year.*

The functions and activities of the AIAW were many and varied. For example, the organization sponsored national championships in many sports; fostered programs that encouraged excellence in performance of participants in women's intercollegiate athletics; sponsored conferences, institutes, and meetings designed to meet the needs of individuals in member schools; stimulated the continual evaluation of standards and policies for participants and programs; and cooperated with other professional groups of similar interests for the ultimate development of sports programs and opportunities for women. The expressed purpose of all the activities and work of the AIAW was ''to foster broad programs of women's intercollegiate athletics which were consistent with the educational aims and objectives of the member schools and in accordance with the philosophy and standards of the NAGWS.''*

Membership was open to any institution if:

The institution is an accredited college or university of higher education in the United States or its territories;
The institution provides an intercollegiate athletic program for women in one or more sports;
The institution is willing to abide by the policies and regulations of the organization;
The institution is a member of the appropriate regional organization.
Additionally, associate, affiliate, junior/community college allied or subscription memberships are available.*

Since the National Collegiate Athletic Association is also sponsoring sports for women there is some doubt as to the future of the AIAW.

SELF-ASSESSMENT TESTS

These tests are to assist students in determining if material and competencies presented in this chapter have been mastered:

1. Write an essay of 250 words on the topic ''The History of Girls' and Women's Sports.''

2. Prepare a report that provides pertinent facts regarding the impact of Title IX on girls' and women's sports. Identify the various aspects of Title IX legislation.

3. Discuss the role the Division of Girls' and Women's Sports, now the National Association for Girls and Women in Sport, has had on the growth of sports programs.

4. List some of the problems that have evolved as a result of the growth of girls' and women's sports.

5. You are the athletic director in a high school. The principal has asked for your recommendations for hiring a coach for the women's basketball team. Prepare a set of recommendations.

6. What role has the AIAW played in sports for women at the college level?

SELECTED REFERENCES

AAHPERD: Rules for coeducational activities and sports, Reston, Va., 1977, The Alliance.

American Alliance for Health, Physical Education, and Recreation: Equality in sports for women, Washington, D.C., 1977, The Alliance.

American Alliance for Health, Physical Education, and Recreation: Professional preparation in physical education and coaching, Washington, D.C., 1974, The Association.

American Alliance for Health, Physical Education, and Recreation: Programs that work—Title IX, Washington, D.C., 1978, The Alliance.

American Association for Health, Physical Education, and Recreation: Women's athletics: coping with controversy, Washington, D.C., 1974, The Association.

Broyles, J.F., and Hay, R.D.: Administration of athletic programs—a managerial approach, Englewood Cliffs, N.J., 1979, Prentice-Hall, Inc.

Bucher, C.A.: After the game is over, The Physical Educator **30:** 171, December 1973.

Bucher, C.A.: Athletic competition and the developmental growth pattern, The Physical Educator, **28:**3, March 1971.

Bucher, C.A.: Foundations of physical education, ed. 8, St. Louis, 1983, The C.V. Mosby Co.

Bucher, C.A., and Dupree, R.: Athletics in schools and colleges, New York, 1965, The Center for Applied Research in Education, Inc.

Bucher, C.A., and Thaxton, N.: Physical education and sport: change and challenge, St. Louis, 1981, The C.V. Mosby Co.

Burke, E., and Kleiber, D.: Psychological and physical implications of highly competitive sports for children, The Physical Educator **33:**63, May 1976.

Cobb, R.A., and Lepley, P.M., editors: Contemporary philosophies of physical education and athletics, Columbus, Ohio, 1973, Charles E. Merrill Publishing Co.

Deatherage, D., and Reid, C.P.: Administration of women's competitive sports, Dubuque, Iowa, 1977, Wm. C. Brown Co.

Durso, J.: The sports factory: an investigation into college sports,

---

*Association for Intercollegiate Athletics for Women: AIAW handbook, 1979-1980, Washington, D.C., 1979, American Alliance for Health, Physical Education, Recreation, and Dance, p. 11.

New York, 1975, Quadrangle/The New York Times Book Co.

Eitzen, D.S.: Athletics in the status system of male adolescents: a replication of Coleman's *The Adolescent Society,* Adolescence **10:**266, Summer 1975.

Eitzen, D.S.: Sport in contemporary society, New York, 1979, St. Martin's Press.

Encyclopedia of associations, Booktower, Detroit, Mich., 1979, Gale Research Co.

Fuoss, D.E., and Troppmann, R.J.: Creative management techniques in interscholastic athletics, New York, 1977, John Wiley & Sons.

Gerson, R.: Redesigning athletic competition for children, Motor Skills: Theory into Practice **2:**3, Fall 1977.

Gould, D., and Martens, R.: Attitudes of volunteer coaches toward significant youth sport issues, Research Quarterly **50:** 369, October 1979.

Hoepner, B.J., editor: Women's athletics—coping with controversy, Reston, Va, 1974, AAHPERD.

Hotchkiss, S.: Parents and kids' sports, Human Behavior **7:**35, March 1978.

Howe, H.H.: On sports, Educational Record **58:**218, Spring 1977.

Journal of Sport and Social Issues **4:**entire issue, Fall/Winter 1979.

Klafs, C.E., and Lyon, M.J.: The female athlete, St. Louis, 1978, The C.V. Mosby Co.

Lopiano, D.A.: A fact-finding model for conducting a Title IX self-evaluation study in athletic programs, Journal of Physical Education and Recreation **47:**26, May 1976.

Lumpkin, A.: Let's set the record straight, Journal of Physical Education and Recreation **48:**40, March 1977.

Magill, R., Ash, M., and Smoll, F.: Children in sport: a contemporary anthology, Champaign, Ill., 1978, Human Kinetics Publishers.

Martens, R.: Joy and sadness in children's sports, Champaign, Ill., 1978, Human Kinetics Publishers.

The National Association for Physical Education of College Women and The National College Physical Education Association for Men: Perspectives for sport, Quest Monograph 29, Winter Issue, 1973 (entire issue devoted to sport).

The National Association for Physical Education of College Women and The National College Physical Education Association for Men: Sport in America, Quest Monograph 27, Winter Issue, 1977 (entire issue devoted to sport).

Noble, L., and Siglo, G.: Minimum requirements for interscholas-

tic coaches, Journal of Physical Education and Recreation **51:**32, November/December 1980.

Orr, R.E.: Sport, myth, and the handicapped athlete, Journal of Physical Education and Recreation **50:**33, March 1979.

Parkhouse, B.L., and Lapin, J.: The woman in athletic administration, Santa Monica, Calif., 1980, Goodyear Publishing Co.

Rarick, G.L., editor: Physical activity; human growth and development, New York, 1977, Academic Press, Inc.

Richardson, H.D.: Athletics in higher education: some comparisons, Journal of Physical Education and Recreation **50:**56, June 1979.

Seefeldt, V., coordinator: Youth sports, Journal of Physical Education and Recreation **49:**38, March 1978.

Shults, F.D.: Toward athletic reform, Journal of Physical Education and Recreation **50:**18, January 1979.

Sisley, B.L.: Women in administration—a quest for leadership, Journal of Physical Education and Recreation **52:**77, April 1981.

Smoll, F.B., and Smith, R.E.: Behavioral guidelines for youth sport coaches, Journal of Physical Education and Recreation **49:** 46, March 1978.

Smoll, F.B., and Smith, R.E., editors: Psychological perspectives in youth sports, Washington, D.C., 1978, Hemisphere Publishing Corp.

Steitz, E.S., editor: Administration of athletics in colleges and universities, Washington, D.C., 1971, National Association of College Directors of Athletics and Division of Men's Athletics, AAHPER.

Stevenson, C.L.: Socialization effects of participation in sport: a critical review of the research, Research Quarterly **46:**287, October 1975.

Thaxton, N.A.: A documentary analysis of competitive track and field for women at Tuskegee Institute and Tennessee State university, unpublished doctoral dissertation, Springfield College, Springfield, Massachusetts, 1970.

Tutko, T., and Burns, W.: Winning is everything and other American myths, New York, 1976, Macmillan Inc.

Vanderzwaag, H.J., and Sheehan, T.J.: Introduction to sport studies, Dubuque, Iowa, 1978, Wm. C. Brown Co.

Weber, M.: Title IX in action, Journal of Physical Education and Recreation **51:**20, May 1980.

Wilkerson, M., and Dodder, R.A.: What does sport do for people? Journal of Physical Education and Recreation **50:**50, February 1979.

Administration of physical education and athletic–related school and community programs

8

School and college health education

Instructional objectives and competencies to be achieved

After reading this chapter the student should be able to

■ Explain why health education is important, describe the three dimensions of a health education program, and identify the people who compose the health team.

■ Compare health education with physical education as professions and describe the role physical educators can and do play in health programs throughout the nation.

■ Outline the topics covered in health science instruction at preschool, elementary school, secondary school, and college levels.

■ Determine how health classes may be organized and the teaching methods that may be used.

Health education programs should be discussed in an administration text for several reasons. Many administrators whose primary area of expertise is physical education are responsible for health education programs in addition to their physical education, athletic, and other responsibilities. These administrators will be better able to carry out their functions, particularly concerning health education, if they have an understanding of what school and college health programs are about. Many physical educators teach health science courses, even though this may not be the most desirable practice; therefore they need some orientation to health education. Many physical educators serve on health councils in schools and colleges and participate in the decision-making process in these groups. Being informed about health matters will assist them in making informed decisions.

Physical educators should work closely with health educators so both areas of specialization can grow and prosper. This chapter is designed to urge physical educators to have an excellent working relationship with health educators. It is further designed to impress on physical educators, athletic administrators, coaches, and others the importance of health education and health programs, the need for well-trained teachers and other personnel, and the contribution

physical educators can make to these programs. Although this chapter covers school and college health education programs briefly, ideally it will encourage the reader to investigate further the nature and scope of this dynamic field. If one is to make the greatest contribution, further study is necessary.

The nature and scope of health education

Communities, schools, colleges, and individual families have a responsibility to educate young people and adults in health-related matters. Society needs to be made aware of new health developments and how they affect us.

Throughout the history of education, the schools and colleges have indicated an interest in health. In 1918 the report of a commission on education of the National Education Association listed health as its first objective. The Educational Policies Commission, an important policy-making group in education, pointed out that an educated person understands basic facts concerning health and disease, protects his or her own health and that of his or her dependents, and strives to improve the health of the community. The American Council on Education, another policy-

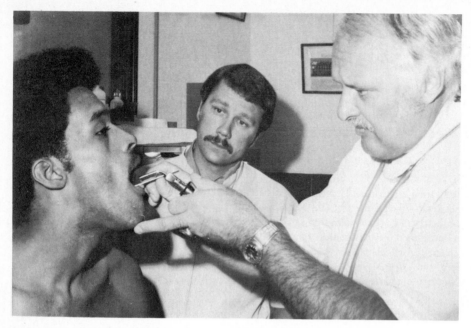

Fig. 8-1. Inspection of teeth and mouth should be done periodically.

Courtesy Cramer Products, Inc., Gardner, Kan.

making group, encouraged schools and colleges to help pupils improve and maintain their health. White House Conferences on Education have stressed physical and mental health as important educational objectives.

There are well-supported reasons for these statements emphasizing the importance of health in education. Research has shown that the healthy person has a better chance to be a success in school and college, to be more effective scholastically and academically, and to be more productive. The school also acts in loco parentis and, as such, has a legal and moral responsibility to concern itself with the health of the student. Other reasons why a health education program is needed follow:

- Healthful living should be inculcated at an early age so persons may live their lives in the best possible manner.
- Health should be a primary objective of education, and health-directed behavior should be established early in life.
- In our ever-shrinking world, the possibility of con-

tracting disease increases, and health education can help us anticipate and solve this problem.
- Health problems encompass our daily lives, and we should be educated in such areas as drug, alcohol, and tobacco abuse; obesity; heart disease; nutrition; environmental problems; and accidents.
- Mental health problems increase each year. An important emphasis of health instruction includes mental and emotional well-being.
- Understanding human sexuality, marriage, problems of divorce, and family life education is essential to the well-being of a person growing up to today's society.

THE THREE DIMENSIONS OF HEALTH WITHIN EDUCATION

Health within the educational structure includes health instruction, health services, and healthful school and college living.

Health instruction. In health science instruction, which is treated at length in this chapter, scientific knowledge is imparted and experiences are provided so that students may better understand the importance

Fig. 8-2. Health education teacher in Greenbelt, Md., takes her class on a food shopping trip as part of a nutrition unit.

Courtesy Eileen Cleinman Forman.

of developing desirable attitudes and health practices. Information concerning such subjects as nutrition, communicable disease, health quackery, rest, exercise, sanitation, drugs, alcohol, tobacco, environmental pollution, human sexuality, first aid, and safety is presented.

On the elementary school level the responsibility for such health education rests primarily with the classroom teacher, although in some school systems trained specialists are provided as resource persons. On the secondary school and college levels, individuals who have had special training in health education should be responsible for concentrated health instruction.

A concentrated course in health education should be required of all students for at least 1 and preferably 2 years at the secondary school level. At the college level there should be at least a one-semester health course for all students. Health educators should teach such courses, and these subjects should be given the same credit and time allotments as other important courses.

Nearly two thirds of the states now certify teachers of health education; about one third of these states offer dual certification in health and physical education. The remaining states do not have any specific requirements for teachers of health education. Most

require only a general teaching certificate. Physical educators teach health in many of these states.

Health services. The health services phase of school and college health programs includes health appraisal, health counseling, correction of defects, provision of the exceptional student, prevention and control of communicable disease, and emergency care of injuries. This area of the educational program is discussed at greater length in Chapter 15.

In this phase of the health program, it is important to recognize concern for mental, emotional, social, and physical health. In providing health services that include all these phases of health, several persons in addition to the health educator play prominent roles.

The classroom teacher has an important responsibility in health services. He or she can detect deviations from the normal, provide first aid when necessary, administer certain screening tests, and oversee the general welfare of the child.

The nurse plays a prominent role in the administration of the health program through counseling, acting as a resource person for other staff members, developing close relationships with parents, helping physicians, and other responsibilities peculiar to the profession.

The physician has the potential for playing an

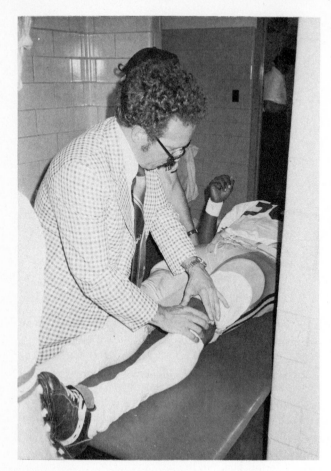

Fig. 8-3. The physician plays an important role in athletic programs.

Courtesy Cramer Products, Inc., Gardner, Kan.

important part in school and college programs. Through medical examinations, health guidance, protection of students from communicable diseases, development of health policies, and consultations with parents, the physician can be a positive influence on the health of students and parents. The physician often does not realize the educational implications of his or her role in the health program. As a result, the physician does not take advantage of teachable moments that occur whenever a student is being given a medical examination or when conferences are held with parents.

Dentists and dental hygienists play an important role whenever they appraise the dental needs of students. This is an unlimited opportunity to educate the student and the parent on the importance of proper oral hygiene.

Psychologists, psychiatrists, social workers, guidance counselors, speech therapists, and others are increasingly being brought into school and college health services programs. All have an important contribution to make to the total health of young people.

Healthful school and college living. Healthful school and college living is also an important part of the total health program. Both a healthful physical environment and a wholesome emotional environment are important to the health of the student. This phase of the educational program is examined more fully in Chapter 15.

The physical environment should provide an attractive, safe, and wholesome place for students to congregate, with adequate lighting, ventilation, heating, location, sanitary facilities, play space, and equipment in the buildings and areas used for educational purposes. It also means there is proper maintenance by the custodial staff and includes any other factors that influence the physical arrangements of the school or college.

The emotional environment is as important to the student's health as the physical environment. To ensure a wholesome emotional environment, proper rapport must exist between the teacher and pupils and among the pupils themselves; educational practices regarding grades, promotions, assignments, schedules, play periods, attendance, class conduct, and discipline must be sound; and the teachers themselves must be emotionally well adjusted.

RELATIONSHIP OF HEALTH EDUCATION AND PHYSICAL EDUCATION

Health education and physical education as professions are closely allied; in many schools and colleges, both come under one administrative head. They are concerned with the accomplishment of similar objectives. In many small communities both health education and physical education are taught by the same person, although this is not always desirable. Professional preparation institutions usually incorporate both in the same schools or departments. Individuals working in these specialized areas share facilities, personnel, funds, and other items essential to their programs.

These are only a few of the reasons why a close administrative relationship should and must exist between these specialized fields. Although professionals realize the place of each and the need for specialists in each area, at the same time they also recognize the importance of maintaining a close and effective working relationship. The administrator is a key person in seeing that such a relationship is maintained. In some quarters there has been disunity and strained relations between these areas because the administrator did not assume his or her role of appeaser and unifier.

In recent years the place of health education and physical education in school and college programs has become more apparent. Each is closely related to the other, but at the same time each is distinct. Each area has its own specialized subject matter content, its specialists, and media through which it is striving to better the living standards of human beings. In the larger professional preparation institutions, each has its own separate training program. There is continual demand for separate certification of its leaders in the various states. Some sections of the country have recognized this need and have established state certification standards.

A close relationship among teachers in these areas is evidently necessary because, to a great degree, they work on committees together and have professional books and magazines that cover the literature of both fields. Both are concerned with the total health of the individual. Both recognize the importance of activity in developing and maintaining good personal health. Both are concerned with the physical, as well as the social, mental, emotional, and spiritual aspects of good health. Both are interested in promoting the total health of the public at large as a means to enriched living, accomplishment of worthy goals, and increased happiness.

The trend at present recognizes the close relationship that exists between health education and physical education and at the same time provides for greater autonomy and visibility on the part of each. An example of this is the American Alliance for Health, Physical Education, Recreation, and Dance, which has changed to a federation status to accomplish this goal.

THE HEALTH TEAM

The school health team includes the following persons.

Health teacher. The health teacher is a key person in an effective health science program. This person needs an understanding of what constitutes a well-rounded health program and the teacher's part in it. Preparation should include a basic understanding of the various physical, biological, and behavioral sci-

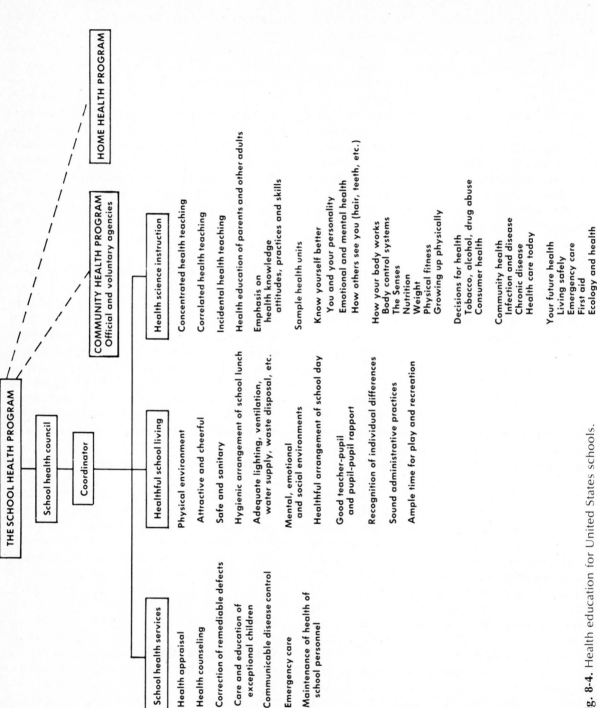

Fig. 8-4. Health education for United States schools.

ences that help explain the importance of health to the optimal functioning of the individual, including understanding of such areas as structure and growth of the human body, nutrition, and mental health. The teacher should possess personal characteristics that exemplify good health, and have the skill to make health education meaningful and interesting. The teacher should be able to organize health teaching units in terms of the health needs and interests of students, motivate them to be well and happy, and perceive the individual differences of the pupils. The teacher should also be able and willing to interpret the school health program to the community and enlist its support in solving health problems.

Health coordinator. The health coordinator has special qualifications that enable him or her to serve as a coordinator, supervisor, teacher, or consultant for health education. He or she is concerned with developing effective working relationships with school, college, and community health programs and coordinating the total school or college health program with the general educational program, integrating health instruction with many subject matter areas. A health coordinator can see that a well-rounded health program exists and that health instruction is carefully planned. Resource materials can be provided for the health teachers. School, college, and community relationships can be developed. The total health program can be guided to function as an integrated whole. Each administrator should recognize the importance of the position of health coordinator and designate a person qualified for such a responsibility. The Nebraska State Departments of Health and Education outline the responsibilities for the health coordinator in the box on p. 272.

School or college administrator. The school or college administrator makes important decisions regarding health programs, such as the personnel appointed to teach health course, the methods of instruction, the topics to be covered, and the budget needed for the necessary equipment and supplies.

School or college physician. The school or college physician can be an effective member of the health team by discussing results of medical examinations with teachers, drawing implications from the medical examinations for health science instruction, stressing to administrators and the community at large the need for health instruction, visiting classes, and periodically being a visiting lecturer in the health classes.

Nurse. The nurse works closely with medical personnel on one hand and with students, teachers, and parents on the other. As the person who administers health tests, assists in medical examinations, screens for hearing and vision, holds parent conferences, keeps health records, teaches health classes, helps control communicable disease, and coordinates school, college, and community health efforts, the nurse can play an effective and important role in giving support and direction to the health instruction program. The school nurse can help identify the topics that need to be covered, emphasizing the health needs of the students, and interpreting to administrators the importance of health in the school or college program.

Physical educator. Although the physical educator may not be qualified to teach health courses, he or she can contribute much to the health program. Training in such areas as first aid and the foundational sciences and the role of directing the physical education program place the physical educator in a position to impress on students the importance of learning about health, developing sound health attitudes, and forming desirable health practices. Physical education offers frequent opportunities for correlated health teaching using situations closely related to the health and fitness of students.

Dentist. The dentist employed to work with school children is frequently involved in conducting dental examinations, giving or supervising oral prophylaxis, and advising on curriculum material in dental hygiene. The health teacher can be helped by the dentist in the selection of curriculum material for classroom teaching, by discovering dental problems of students, and by participating in the classroom as a resource person.

Dental hygienist. The dental hygienist usually assists the dentist and does oral prophylaxis. The health teacher can therefore benefit from a close working relationship with this specialist in much the same way as she or he works with the dentist.

Custodian. All aspects of the school or college health program must be carefully coordinated—the

Fig. 8-5. In health studies class at Kaiser High School in Honolulu, Hawaii, students of Japanese, Hawaiian, and American backgrounds analyze the effects of smoking.
Courtesy Ed Arrigoni.

The school health coordinator should:*

Coordinate the health activities of all school personnel.

Provide leadership in the development of a health curriculum based upon the progression of health knowledge, concepts, and activities from kindergarten through high school.

Serve as a liaison person between school, public, and voluntary health agencies to establish desirable working relationships and coordination of school and community health efforts.

Be a resource person for teachers needing help with health education materials, references, teaching aids, and methods.

Establish good relationships with the community's professional medical and dental resources so that the school's program is properly understood.

Promote inservice training for the teaching of health through faculty meetings, small group meetings, workshop sessions with nurses and other school health personnel, and individual interviews with teachers.

With the assistance of the school health council, study needs and present activities of the school health program; from the findings make recommendations that will develop an improved program.

*From Health policies and procedures for Nebraska schools, Lincoln, Nebraska Department of Health and the Nebraska Department of Education.

health instruction program, health services, and healthful living. Therefore, the cleanliness of the building and a healthful physical environment are contributions to the health program. The custodian can be invited to help plan pertinent aspects of the health curriculum that specifically relate to his or her area of responsibility, to have the school or college be a model of cleanliness, and to adhere to lighting, ventilation, and heating standards that promote good health.

Nutritionist. The nutritionist can supplement the health science curriculum by contributing nutritional information, speaking about food and nutrition, and discussing nutritional problems of students.

Guidance counselor. The guidance counselor is too frequently overlooked as an effective member of the school health team. Because many academic problems are health related and because the guidance counselor is interested in helping each student have a successful school experience, the counselor must be concerned with areas of health. He or she can make suggestions for health topics to be discussed in classes and can be an effective guest speaker in health classes to discuss the relationship of health to scholastic and vocational success.

The health council. Every school and every school system should have health councils or committees to help ensure a desirable and adequate health program. This means that optimally there should be a health council for each school and one central health council for all the schools in a particular school system. The number of members composing such councils may vary from 3 or 4 persons in a small school to 15 or 16 in a larger school. Potential members of such councils are the school principal, health coordinator, nurse, psychologist, guidance counselor, custodian, dental hygienist, speech therapist, physician, dentist, physical education teacher, science teacher, home economics teacher, classroom teacher, teacher of handicapped persons, nutritionist, students, parents, public health officer, mayor, clergymen, and any other individual who is particularly interested in the health of the school or community and has something to contribute.

Health councils are responsible for coordinating the entire health program of the school, including deter-

mining curriculum, resources to use, and experiences to provide; securing a healthful environment for the school; arranging inservice training in health-related areas; encouraging closer school-parent relationships concerning such important health procedures as medical examinations, promoting sanitary conditions, providing for the safety of children, and distributing health literature.

Representatives from various community and school groups who are interested in health can accomplish much when discussing their problems at a conference table. A spirit of cooperation and oneness will aid in developing procedures and taking action that will promote better health for all.

Organization and curriculum of health education

The administration of health science instruction varies with each educational system.

ADMINISTRATIVE STRUCTURE AND HEALTH SCIENCE INSTRUCTION

In some schools and colleges health science instruction is placed in such departments as physical education, science, and home economics. In other schools and colleges it is a separate area by itself. Most often health is administratively located in the health and physical education department. In the larger schools especially, and in colleges and universities, there may be a separate health education department with full-time personnel who have been trained in health education. Such an administrative arrangement is conducive to good interrelationships between the school and college and public health agencies, to the development of a health council, and to a well-coordinated and well-integrated health program. In smaller and medium-sized schools and colleges, there should also be full-time health educators charged with this important responsibility.

The physical education person many times is assigned such responsibilities as coaching, intramurals, and special events, in addition to physical education classes. If the responsibility for health education is given to a teacher of physical education, in addition to these numerous other duties, some responsibility is going to suffer. In many cases, with pressure for winning teams and successful intramural programs, the class instruction program is neglected. School and college administrators should recognize that health education is an important part of the curriculum. It should be assigned only to qualified persons and should receive ample time and facilities to make it effective.

Every school and college, regardless of size, should have someone on its staff assigned to coordinate the various aspects of the health program. In larger schools and colleges this might be a full-time position. In smaller ones it could be the principal, chairperson of the health department, or some qualified and interested staff member.

The administration of the health education program should also include a health council or committee. Such a group of individuals, regardless of type or size of school, can play an important part in planning and carrying out the health education program.

ADMINISTRATIVE GUIDELINES FOR DEVELOPING A HEALTH EDUCATION CURRICULUM

The Curriculum Commission of the School Health Division of AAHPERD has proposed a guide for developing a health curriculum that will meet the needs of individuals associated with schools. The guide was developed by curriculum directors and others responsible for health curriculum development.

The guide proposes the following steps to be taken in developing a curriculum.

Preplanning. For a program to succeed, it must have community support and support from the administration and staff. A written policy should include reference to funds, time allocations, class space, and instructional material.

Two committees should be formed. The first would be an in-school steering committee, consisting of representatives from the students, teachers, administrators, parents, school nurses, and special interest or ethnic groups. A second or advisory committee would be out-of-school and consist of community personnel (counselors, lawyers, physicians, health specialists,

and others), and representatives from the PTA and other organizations.

The basic considerations necessary in the development of any curriculum include: (1) meeting all state and local requirements; (2) identifying behavioral objectives; (3) meeting the needs of community members, students, and specific community requirements; (4) developing a health education philosophy; (5) considering controversial areas; (6) developing a work schedule; and (7) exploring fully all sources of funding.

Review of existing school health education program. The status of the present health education program should be evaluated in terms of pupil knowledge and behavioral objective standards, as well as in terms of staff, policies, budget, and facilities. The conclusions and recommendations should be thoroughly discussed and evaluated.

Broad content areas. Content areas should be based on student needs and opinions of the steering and advisory committees. Student health records and absences might also be evaluated.

Format. The format of the curriculum guide should include the specific content area, behavioral or instructional objectives, concepts, student learning experiences, student and teacher resources, and evaluation techniques for students and teachers.

Field testing. Field testing should be conducted at a variety of levels. Both novice and experienced teachers should be used, as well as all types of students: rural, urban, and disadvantaged. Changes should be made where indicated.

Implementation. The plan for implementation should be specific in terms of target date and schedule. Administration approval should be included.

Reevaluation. All programs should be reevaluated every 3 to 5 years. Students' needs change over the years, and the curriculum must also change to meet these needs.

ADMINISTRATIVE GUIDELINES FOR DETERMINING CONTENT AREAS FOR THE HEALTH SCIENCE INSTRUCTION PROGRAM

Considerable knowledge and information may be taught in health education. With all the literature available in such forms as textbooks, resource books,

Table 8-1. A schematic health science spiral curriculum for kindergarten to grade twelve*†

Major health instruction areas	Primary grades				Intermediate grades			Junior high grades			Senior high grades		
	K	1	2	3	4	5	6	7	8	9	10	11	12
1. Human ecology and health, disease, longevity	X	X	X	X	X		X		X				X
2. Human growth, development, maturation, aging	X	X	X	X	X		X		X				X
3. Healthful living and physical fitness	X	X	X	X	X		X		X				X
4. Nutrition and personal fitness	X	X	X	X	X		X		X				X
5. Alcohol, tobacco, and narcotics	X	X	X	X	X		X		X				X
6. Prevention and control of disease	X	X	X	X		X		X				X	
7. Community and environmental health	X	X	X	X		X		X				X	
8. Consumer health education	X	X	X	X		X		X				X	
9. Rise of modern scientific medicine	X	X	X	X		X			X			X	
10. Safety education	X	X	X	X	X		X	X		X			X
11. First aid and home nursing	X	X	X	X		X			X		X		X
12. Personality development and mental health	X	X	X	X		X		X			X		X
13. Family life and sex education	X	X	X	X		X		X			X		X
14. Current health events and problems	X	X	X	X	X	X	X	X	X	X	X	X	X

*From Hoyman, H.S.: An ecologic view of health and health education, The Journal of School Health **25**:118, 1965.
†In kindergarten to grade three the X's denote topics, in grades four to twelve, units, or major parts of combined units.
Note: Separate health courses may be scheduled at the junior and senior high school levels as a part of the health science spiral curriculum where this method of scheduling is preferred.

pamphlets, and promotional material, it is important that content be selected with care.

Some basic principles for selecting curriculum experiences in the health science instruction program follow:

1. The content of health science instruction should be based on the needs and interests of the students. Developmental characteristics of children and youths and psychological needs of students, such as security, approval, success in athletics, appearance, and peer group approval, are considerations in relating teaching to the interests of students.

2. The problems and topics covered must be appropriate to the maturity level of the students.

3. The materials used should be current and scientifically accurate. The course should not be a textbook course. Many materials and experiences should be provided.

4. Pupils should be able to identify with the health problems discussed. As such, the problems should be geared to or related to the daily living experiences of the student body.

5. Health should be recognized as a multidisciplinary subject, and, as such, subject matter, projects, and methods of teaching should take cognizance of the new developments in the related sciences.

6. Health science instruction should be taught in light of a rapidly changing society and knowledge of new ways of affecting the behavior of human beings.

7. Health teaching should take place in a healthful psychological and physical environment.

8. To be most effective, the health teacher must exemplify good health and be well informed, happy, and successful.

9. The basic concepts in health should be identified and taught.

10. New technological methods and aids should be used to improve visual presentations of health material to students.

11. Students' previous health experiences should be considered.

12. Planning for health science instruction should be a total school or college endeavor, with students, teachers, specialists, and consultants participating.

Furthermore, health instruction should permeate the entire school or college curriculum.

13. Objectives of the school or college health program, including knowledge, attitudes, practices, and skills, need to be reviewed and the program planned intelligently and meaningfully in light of these goals.

14. The community should be involved in health science instruction, including personnel from the public health department, voluntary health associations, medical and dental professions, and other health associations and agencies.

15. School health science instruction should be closely integrated with home conditions.

16. New methods of organizing for teaching, including the nongraded school, team teaching, individualized instruction, and programmed instruction, should be considered.

17. Constant research and evaluation of the program should take place.

18. Health instruction in general should share the same prestige and respect in the eyes of school or college administrators, teachers, and students as other respected school or college offerings, with time allotments and other considerations receiving equal attention.

Sex education, drugs, and other critical content areas in health science instruction. The question often arises as to whether such critical subjects as sex, drug abuse, and alcohol education should be included in the health science instruction program. That some of these problems are more pronounced in certain communities, and possibly restricted to some population groups, and that such education might tend to stimulate curiosity are reasons put forth for not including them in courses of study.

On the other hand, instruction concerning the ill effects of drug and alcohol abuse is required by law in many states. Furthermore, it is felt that if children and youths are provided with the facts, intelligent instruction in these subjects will act as a preventive measure. In sex education, it is believed the term *sex education* creates opposition among many parents and church groups and consequently should not be used. If it is introduced in the natural process of instruction without undue emphasis, much good, it is felt by many educators, can be done.

The nature of the instruction will depend on the local situation. Where a drug abuse or alcohol problem exists, there should be provision in the school curriculum for the presentation of sociological, physiological, and psychological facts, as well as the legal aspects of such a problem. Students should understand these facts and be guided intelligently in making the right decisions and establishing a sound standard of values.

Health education is not the only area in which discussions of sex, drug abuse, and alcohol should take place. Social studies, biology, general science, physical education, and other classes also have a responsibility. Many phases of these subjects logically fit into certain aspects of these courses. Teachers should appreciate the importance of such instruction and the need for treating these subjects objectively on the basis of the facts. It is not necessary for the teacher to take a definite stand on the subject. Instead, if students obtain the necessary facts through research or some other method and then interpret them intelligently, the right answers will be clear. The students make their own decisions not on the basis of the teacher's position, but on the basis of the facts they have collected.

Regarding sex education, the emphasis should be on the psychological and sociological aspects rather than only on the biological aspects. The goal is to have students recognize what is desirable behavior and what constitutes a healthy sexuality rather than only to gain knowledge of reproductive organs. Sex education should not be a separate course in elementary and secondary schools but should be included and discussed in every course where its various aspects arise during regular discussions. Parents and representative community groups should be consulted and participate in discussions relative to the planning for sex education. It is important to have qualified teachers handling such instruction. If the right leadership is provided, the result can be beneficial, but if poor leadership exists, results can be harmful.

HEALTH SCIENCE INSTRUCTION AT THE PRESCHOOL AND ELEMENTARY SCHOOL LEVELS

The committee on Health Education for Pre-School Children of the American School Health Associa-

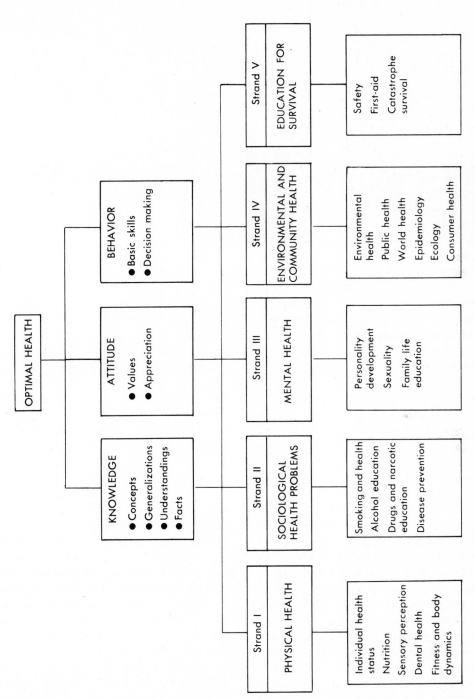

Fig. 8-6. Content and basic aims of New York Health Education Program.

Fig. 8-7. Nutrition instruction as part of the health education program.

tion has listed the following as a topical outline of content for preschool children:

Cleanliness and grooming
Dental health
Eyes, ears, nose
Rest and sleep
Nutrition
Growth and development
Family living
Understanding ourselves and getting along
Prevention and control of disease
Safety

For each of these topics the committee has identified key concepts, suggested learning experiences, and means of evaluation.

Health education at the elementary school level is aimed primarily at having the child develop good health habits and health attitudes, and at helping him or her live happily, healthfully, and safely. This is achieved in great measure by adapting good health practices to the regular routine of school and home living, rather than by dispensing irrelevant facts concerning health. The responsibility for the guidance, planning, and stimulation of good health practices and

attitudes falls on the classroom teacher. He or she is the guiding influence, and his or her understanding of good health will determine to a great degree the effectiveness of such a program.

The type of health program offered should be adapted to the child's level of understanding and planned in accordance with his or her interests and needs. Health education is a continuous process and cannot be compartmentalized within a definite subject area or within a class period. It embraces all activities and subjects that are part of the child's life.

At the primary or intermediate grade levels the emphasis should be more on the child and his or her daily routine as it is affected by certain health practices and attitudes. The child's various routines and associations at school and at home form the basis for the health emphasis. The importance of a healthful classroom environment is stressed. Such items as cleanliness, eating, use of lavatories, safety, and good mental hygiene are brought out as the child plays, eats, and shares experiences common to all youngsters.

The committee on Health Education for Elementary School Children of the American School Health Association has listed the following as a topical outline of content for this age group:

Fig. 8-8. As shown here, elementary school youngsters enjoy using apparatus as a means of developing physical fitness.

GRADES 1, 2, AND 3

Cleanliness and grooming
Rest and exercise
Growth
Posture
Role of physician and dentist
Individual responsibility for one's health
Responsibility for the health of others
Dental health
Vision and hearing
Babies
Nutrition
Making new friends
Being alone sometimes
Family time
Protection from infection
Food protection
Safety

GRADES 4, 5, AND 6

Health care
Cleanliness and grooming
Vision and care of eyes
Hearing and care of ears
Heart
Teeth
Exercise, rest, and sleep
Nutrition
Growth and development
Family living
Understanding ourselves
Getting along with others
Making decisions
Environmental health
Prevention and control of diseases
Safety and first aid

For each of these topics the committee has identified key concepts, suggested learning experiences, and means of evaluation.

In the upper elementary school years a planned progression in instruction is developed. Although there is still stress on the actual practices and attitudes concerned with the daily routines and associations, more factual information is incorporated to form the basis for such habits. Furthermore, more and more responsibility is placed on the child for his or her own self-control.

Trips and textbooks that point up the value of healthful living and include interesting and inspiring stories, visual aids, class discussions, and projects will leave their impression on the child's thinking.

Because health experiences should be based on the needs and interests of the child, the wise teacher will use various means to obtain accurate information about these needs and interests. Such techniques as talks with parents and pupils, observations of children under various situations, a perusal of health records, a study of the home environment and community, together with scientific measuring devices that have been developed to determine health knowledge and attitudes will be used.

The Joint Committee on Health Problems in Education of the National Education Association and the American Medical Association has listed the following health instruction activities in which pupils in intermediate and elementary grades can engage:

1. Conducting animal feeding experiments and experiments to test for food nutrients
2. Taking field trips to local dairies, markets, restaurants, bakeries, water supply and sewage treatment plants, and housing projects
3. Visiting museums
4. Preparing charts and graphs for visualizing class statistics, such as absence due to colds or school accidents
5. Making pin maps of sources of mosquitoes, rubbish depositories, and slum areas
6. Making health posters
7. Setting up room and corridor health exhibits
8. Preparing health bulletin boards and displays
9. Making murals and dioramas
10. Maintaining class temperature charts
11. Arranging a library corner of health materials on the subject being studied
12. Using sources of printed material—reference books, texts, bulletins, newspapers, and magazines—for the study of a particular topic
13. Giving reports in various ways—chalkboard talks, dramatizations, role-playing, panels
14. Serving on the safety patrol
15. Joining the bicycle safety club
16. Participating in a home or school cleanup campaign
17. Planning menus
18. Preparing meals for class mothers or other guests
19. Sharing health programs with primary grades
20. Securing a health examination
21. Having all dental corrections made

22. Taking inoculations
23. Keeping records of growth through charts or graphs
24. Keeping diaries of health practices
25. Studying text or references to find answers to problems
26. Thinking through solutions to problems
27. Applying in daily practices health principles learned

Health suggestions for the classroom teacher.
The classroom teacher is the key school person involved in the health of the elementary school child. The organization of the school with the self-contained classroom enables him or her to continually observe the pupils and to note deviations from normal. Continuous contact with the same children over a long period of time also makes it possible to know a great deal about their physical, social, emotional, and mental health. The teacher can help them develop the right knowledge, attitudes, and practices. Some of the responsibilities of the classroom teacher in regard to the health of the pupils are to

1. Possess an understanding of what constitutes a well-rounded school health program and the teacher's part in it.
2. Meet with the school physician, nurse, and others to determine how he or she can best contribute to the total health program.
3. Become acquainted with parents and homes of students and establish parent-school cooperation.
4. Discover the health needs and interests of the pupils.
5. Organize health teaching units that are meaningful in terms of the health needs and interests of his or her students.
6. See that children needing special care are referred to proper places for help.
7. Know first aid procedures.
8. Participate in the work of the school health council. If none exists, interpret the need for one.
9. Provide an environment for children while at school that is conducive to healthful living.
10. Continually be on the alert for children with deviations from normal behavior and signs of communicable diseases.
11. Provide experiences at school for healthful living.
12. Help pupils assume an increasing responsibility for their own health, as well as for the health of others.
13. Set an example of healthful living for the child.
14. Motivate the child to be well and happy.
15. Be present at health examinations of pupils and contribute in any way helpful to the physician in charge.
16. Follow through in cooperation with the nurse to see that remediable health defects are corrected.
17. Interpret the school health program to the community and enlist its support in solving health problems.
18. Provide a well-rounded class physical education program.
19. Help supervise various activities that directly affect health—school lunch, rest periods.
20. Become familiar with teaching aids and school and community resources for enhancing the health program.
21. Be aware of the individual differences of pupils.

HEALTH SCIENCE INSTRUCTION AT THE SECONDARY SCHOOL LEVEL

The structural organization of the secondary school level differs from that of the elementary school level. At the elementary school level, the classroom teacher frequently takes overall charge of a group of children. He or she teaches them in various subjects, stays with them throughout the entire day, and supervises their activities. At the secondary school level, the student has many different teachers who specialize in subject matter to a greater degree than they specialize in pupils. Departmentalization into such subject areas as mathematics, social studies, and English affects health education.

First, this structural organization points up the need for concentrated courses in health education, such as those found in the other subject areas.

Second, it emphasizes the need for a specialist in teaching health education. Just as specialists are needed in English and the other subjects offered at the secondary school level, so are they needed in the field of health education. The body of scientific knowledge, the training needed, and the importance of the subject make such a specialist a necessity.

Third, this structural organization stresses the need for coordination and cooperation. Health cuts across many subject areas, as well as the total school life of the student. That it may be properly treated in the various subject areas such as science, physical education, home economics, and social studies, that the physical environment and the emotional environment may be properly provided for, that health services may be most effectively administered, and that close cooperation and coordination between the school and the rest of the community may be obtained, there is an essential need for some type of coordinating machinery, such as a school health council.

The junior high school. Junior high school students need knowledge and attitudes that will result in desirable health practices. That students may not be interested in such information represents a challenge for the junior high school educational program. The consumption of many sweets as a substitute for essential foods, omission of breakfast, an interest in personal grooming, a need to understand one's bodily makeup, the maturing sexual drive, and other factors make it imperative to get across health information at this time.

Health content should be adapted to the needs and interests of the students in this age group. Stress should be on the personal health problems of the students themselves, how hereditary factors affect their health, how good or poor health is manifested, and how health practices affect the attainment of life ambitions and goals. Such topics as food, rest, exercise, first aid, safety, alcohol and drug abuse, mental health, communicable disease, growth and functions of the human body, death and dying, personality development, family life, and community health should be included.

The health teaching in the junior high school should consider the developmental tasks that characterize the early adolescent. These include the desire for independence from adults, self-respect, and peer identification, as well as accepting one's physical makeup, adjusting to the opposite sex, and establishing values.

The committee on Health Education for Junior High School of the American School Health Association had listed the following as a topical outline of content for this age group:

Health status
Cleanliness and grooming
Rest, sleep, and relaxation
Exercise
Posture
Recreation and leisure time activities
Sensory perception
Nutrition
Growth and development
Understanding ourselves
Personality
Getting along with others
Family living
Alcohol
Drugs
Smoking and tobacco
Environment
Air and water pollutions
Consumer health
Disease

For each of these topics the committee has identified key concepts, suggested learning experiences, and means of evaluation.

The senior high school. During grades ten, eleven, and twelve, the stress continues to be on many subject areas that were emphasized for the health content in the junior high school years. However, the material and experiences presented should be more advanced and adapted to the age group found in the later high school years. Such topics as the structure and function of the human body could stress more scientific concepts as found through research, evaluation of individual health needs in the light of proper balance in one's daily routine, and the means of attaining proper emotional maturity and mental health.

The committee on Health Education for Senior High School of the American School Health Association has listed the following as a topical outline of content for this age group:

Health status
Fatigue and sleep
Exercise
Recreational activities
Sensory perception
Nutrition
Growth and development toward maturity
Family living
Alcohol

Fig. 8-9. Athletes need to observe sound health practices.

Courtesy Cramer Products, Inc., Gardner, Kan.

Drugs
Smoking and tobacco
Health protection
Noise pollution
Health agencies
Health careers
World health
Safety and accidents

For each of these topics the committee has listed key concepts, suggested learning experiences, and means of evaluation.

Although personal health receives considerable attention during the high school years, a major part of the teaching is concerned with problems of adult and family living and community health. Such health areas as marriage and family life, communicable and noncommunicable disease control, evaluation of professional health services, environmental health, death and dying, industrial health, consumer health education, accident prevention, emergency care, protection from environmental hazards such as radiation, health agencies at the local, state, national, and international levels, and the various health careers open to high school students are included.

Some students will not be going to college. This means that the senior high school years offer the last opportunity to impress boys and girls with their health

responsibilities—to themselves, their loved ones, and the members of their community.

Health education at the secondary school level can have a lasting effect for the betterment of human lives. The leadership provided, the methods used, and the stress placed on such an important aspect of living will determine in great measure the extent to which each school fulfills its responsibility.

HEALTH SCIENCE INSTRUCTION AT THE COLLEGE AND UNIVERSITY LEVEL

Years ago the college and university health education offerings consisted mainly of lectures on various aspects of the anatomy and physiology of the human body. These were usually given by medical personnel and were often a collection of uninteresting facts unrelated to the student's interests and health problems. In more recent years this kind of presentation has changed. The emphasis has shifted from the factual medical knowledge to health problems students themselves encounter in day-to-day living and also to those subjects in which students are especially interested. Consequently, discussions are now held on subjects concerned with family living, sex education, personal and community health, mental health, drugs, environmental health, nutrition, prevention of disease, and related subjects.

Fig. 8-10. First aid and emergency care are included in the health science instruction program. Students from College of DuPage, Glen Ellyn, Ill., participating in local emergency rescue unit and hospital emergency procedures.

A President's Commission on Higher Education stressed the importance of health instruction for college students. It particularly stressed instruction based directly on the practical problems of personal and community health.

The American College Health Association recommended that every college and university have a requirement in health education for all students who fall below acceptable standards on a college-level health knowledge test.

The junior college is a particularly strategic position to offer health instruction. The 2-year college reaches a significant segment of the population that does not go on to the 4-year colleges and universities. Furthermore, research has shown that junior college students have demonstrated as much as 25% more interest in health problems than high school students. Junior college students are more mature, and this may be an explanation of their increased interest in health problems. Topics such as sex instruction, marriage, mental health, emotional health, alcohol, tobacco, drug abuse, and death and dying are of particular interest to this segment of the college population.

One survey concerning the status of required health education courses in colleges and universities revealed a trend toward eliminating the requirement for health courses in many such institutions. Furthermore, the course content trend seemed to be emphasizing discussion of such topics as alcohol, drugs, narcotics, mental health, personal adjustment, marriage preparation, and parenthood and child care.

It is generally felt that a health education department should be established to coordinate the instruction in health, that student needs should help determine subject content, that only qualified faculty members should be permitted to teach health education classes, and that classes should be limited to a maximum of 35 students. Testing of new students is also recommended, after which those students who fall below desirable standards should be required to take the required health education course.

Presently, health education courses offered in colleges and universities are listed in college catalogues under such names as Personal Hygiene, Health Education, Personal and Community Health, Health Science, Hygiene, Healthful Living, Health and Safety,

Health Essentials, and Problems of Healthful Living. Courses are taught in such departments as health, physical education, and recreation; health education; biology; education; health and safety; basic studies; psychology; and biological sciences. Students required to take such courses vary from only those students in schools of education or in departments of health, physical education, and recreation, or elementary education major students, to liberal arts students. In some institutions courses are required for women but not for men.

There is a need for a uniform requirement for all college students to demonstrate that they know basic facts in the field of health.

HEALTH EDUCATION FOR ADULTS

Adults are the guiding force in any community. Their prestige, their positions, and their interests determine the extent to which any project or enterprise will be a success. Therefore, if schools are to have an adequate health education program, if the knowledge disseminated, the attitudes developed, and the practices encouraged are to become a permanent part of the child's being and routine, the adult must be considered. Unless this is done, the schools' efforts will be useless.

There is a great need for parental education and for education regarding the many health problems that confront any community. Adults are interested not only in children's health problems but also in the causes of sickness and death in the population and ways in which they can live a healthier life. Adult education is increasing in this country. It is important that health education be included in any such program.

Schools and colleges should play a key part in adult education programs because of the facilities, staff, and other resources at their disposal. They should cooperate fully with the many official and voluntary health agencies and other interested community groups in the furtherance of health objectives. Adult health education programs should be designed to discover community health problems, understand the health needs of children, and understand school health programs. Such discovery and understanding should lead to active participation in meeting health

ACCIDENT AND/OR ILLNESS REPORT*

Date _____

Time _____

1. Name of injured/sick person: _____
                                   (last)   (first)   (m.i.)

2. Age: _____ Sex: _____ Date of birth: _____ Social Security ____/____/____

3. Address: _____ City: _____ State: _____

4. Telephone number: _____ 5. Date of injury: _____ Time: _____

6. Status at time of accident: Student _____ Faculty _____ Staff _____ Visitor _____

7. Specific location of accident/illness: _____
    _____

8. Describe accident/illness fully using back of paper if necessary: _____
    _____
    _____
    _____
    _____
    _____

9. Names and addresses of witnesses:

    a. _____

    b. _____

10. Treatment and disposition: _____
    _____
    _____
    _____

    _____
    Signature of Gym Supervisor

    _____
    Signature of Investigating Officer

*To be filled out by the Gym Supervisor on duty when an accident or illness occurs in
the Gym Complex.

Fig. 8-11. Accident and/or illness report.

needs and in solving health problems. Such a program would also improve the health knowledge, attitudes, and practices of adults.

Methods of teaching health

Lecture, recitation, and assignments in textbooks represent a limited array of approved techniques for the modern health class. Although good textbooks are important, many other methods can motivate students and create interest in health topics.

The methods used should be adapted to the group of students being taught, be in accordance with the objectives sought, be capable of use by the instructor, stimulate interest among the students, and be adaptable to the time, space, and equipment in the school program. Some of the more popular methods for teaching health are discussed in the following paragraphs.

Problem solving is one of the most effective and best methods for teaching health. Health topics can be stated in the form of problems, and then the students can use a systematic approach to obtain an answer. For example, the problem can be stated: "What are the effects of narcotics on health?" A systematic approach to this problem might include (1) stating the nature and scope of the problem; (2) defining the various possible solutions to the problem; (3) collecting scientific information to support each of the various aspects of the problem; (4) analyzing the information gathered as to its source, authoritativeness, date of origin, and other pertinent factors; and (5) drawing conclusions to solve the problem.

Textbook assignments may be given, followed by class discussions based on the readings.

Field trips can include planned visits to an agency or place where health matters are important, such as a hospital, local health department, water purification plant, health clinic, or fire department.

Class discussions on health topics of interest can be encouraged among members of the class.

Demonstrations are an excellent method to show how something functions or is constructed, such as good and poor forms of posture or first aid procedures.

Experiments, such as observing the growth of animals when certain types of diet are administered, are informative.

Independent study in which the students are assigned health topics to investigate is helpful.

Resource people, such as physicians, dentists, firemen, or other specialists, can be brought in to speak to health classes.

Audiovisual aids, such as films, network educational television and cable television, filmstrips, slides, radio, and recordings, help make health material interesting and clear.

Graphic materials such as posters, graphs, charts, bulletin boards, and exhibits are valuable for motivating students regarding health matters, arousing interests, attracting attention, and visualizing ideas.

Interviews can be arranged in which students get views and recommendations of such persons as officers of the local health department, representatives of safety councils, members of voluntary health agencies, and heads of medical and dental societies.

Panels can be made up of students for an informal exchange of ideas or viewpoints regarding pertinent health matters.

Buzz sessions in which a class is organized into small groups of students for the purpose of discussing health topics, permitting each student more opportunity for discussion, is an excellent method.

Class committees can be formed by dividing a class and assigning topics for exploration.

Dramatizations, such as a play or a skit, can be put on by a class to bring to the pupils' attention a health matter such as the importance of safety on the playground.

Surveys of health problems in the school, college, or community that need investigating and solving can be suggested. Survey forms can be constructed by pupils themselves or standard forms may be available.

Games and quizzes patterned after popular shows on radio or television can provide interesting methods and challenge the thinking of students.

Health aids can be provided in which community health agencies may offer opportunities for students to obtain experience by keeping records or engaging in various activities where the jobs do not require

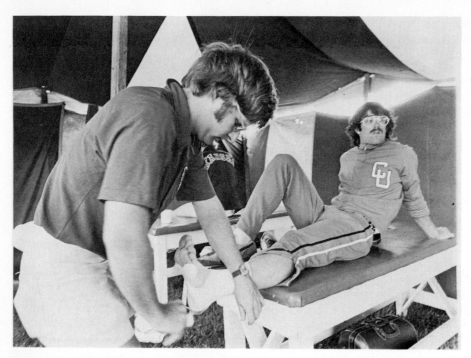

Fig. 8-12. Athletic trainer wrapping athlete's ankle.

Courtesy Cramer Products, Inc., Gardner, Kan.

experience and special training. Working on a Red Cross blood program is an example.

Concentrated, correlated, integrated, and incidental health teaching

Four ways of including health education in the school offering are through concentrated, correlated, integrated, and incidental teaching.

CONCENTRATED HEALTH TEACHING

Concentrated health education refers to the provision in the school offering for regularly scheduled courses confined solely to a consideration of health, rather than a combination with some other subject area. It implies a scheduled time for class meetings and a planned course of study. Such courses should be given on the secondary school level. Furthermore, such courses should be held for a daily class period at least one semester during the ninth or tenth grade and also during eleventh or twelfth grade.

Concentrated health education courses required of all students result in many educational benefits. There is a specialized body of knowledge to impart that can best be given to students in a concentrated manner, rather than by depending on some other subject to provide this information. It allows for better planning, teaching progression, and evaluation. It further allows for giving credit, such as is given for any other course. It is more likely to result in health instruction by teachers who have specialized in this particular area and who are qualified and interested in participating in such a course. It offers greater opportunities for discussing personal health problems, for guidance and counseling in regard to these problems, and for using teaching methods appropriate to such a course.

CORRELATED HEALTH TEACHING

Correlated health education refers to the practice of including health concepts in the various subject areas. For example, in History the relationship of

Table 8-2. Health education correlation*

Subject	Schools	Subject	Schools
Science	244	Conservation	1
Physical education	217	Driver education	1
Home economics	183	Educational guidance	1
Biology	165	Elective living	1
General science	34	Home arts	1
Family living	29	Home living	1
Sociology	11	Household mechanics	1
Social studies	10	Life adjustment	1
Psychology	6	Modern problems	1
Orientation	4	Nursing	1
Civic	3	Personal biology	1
Guidance	3	Personal living	1
Reading	3	Physics	1
Art	2	Political science	1
Chemistry	2	Sex education	1
Life science	2	Social living	1
Natural science	2	Teen living	1
Physiology	2		

*From State Department of Education: Patterns and features of school health education in Michigan public schools, East Lansing, 1969, Michigan State Department of Education, p. 4.

the rise and fall of various groups of people could be related to their health and the prevalence of disease, as could the increased speed of transportation and the transfer of disease from one country to the other. In English, a study of the works of literature could be selected with a view to pointing up the health problems of individuals during various periods of history. The relationship of music and of art to mental health could be brought out. Mathematics could be used as a tool to figure the costs of various health projects. Science could bring out the health aspects in relation to the structure and functions of the human body. Home Economics provides an excellent setting for teaching such topics as nutrition and personal cleanliness. There is hardly a subject that cannot be correlated with health education. (See Table 8-2.)

INTEGRATED HEALTH TEACHING

In integrated health teaching, health learnings are integrated into other aspects of the classroom program. Learning experiences are organized around a central objective. Whereas in correlated teaching, health is brought into various subject areas, such as

physical education and mathematics, in integrated health teaching various parts of a unit of study are related to a central theme. Two such themes might be that of living in a city or planning a visit to a foreign country. Health is one consideration involved in the planning, discussion, and assignments concerning this central theme. Health factors, for example, can be an important consideration in living in a large metropolitan city or in going to a foreign country. There are problems concerned with water supply, sewage treatment, fire prevention, disease control, immunizations, and medical examinations. Integrated health teaching finds its best setting in the elementary school.

INCIDENTAL HEALTH TEACHING

Incidental health education refers to the education that takes place during normal teaching situations, where attention is focused on problems concerned with health. Such occasions may arise as the result of a question asked by a student; a problem that is raised in class; a personal problem that confronts a member of the class, a family, or the community; or a sudden illness, accident, or special

Fig. 8-13. Incidental health education can take place when an athlete is injured. Other students can learn how such injuries affect health.

Courtesy Cramer Products, Inc., Gardner, Kan.

project. It represents an opportunity for the teacher, physician, dentist, or nurse to provide educational information. When a student has his or her eyes examined or chest x-rayed, for example, many questions arise and opportunities are afforded to give the student beneficial information. In many cases this will benefit the health of the child more than information given in more formalized, planned class situations. Teachers and others should constantly keep in mind the necessity for continually being alert to these "teachable moments." When a child is curious and wants information, this establishes a time for dynamic health education. Incidental health education can be planned for in advance. Situations and incidents should be anticipated and utilized to their fullest in the interests of good health.

Organization of health classes

A problem frequently arising in connection with the organization of health science classes is whether boys and girls should meet together or separately. Where health science instruction is a combined pro-

gram with physical education, and where the boys and girls are in separate classes, it would probably be best to conduct the health class separately. However, in most situations classes will be coeducational because of Title IX; therefore it would probably be best to have integrated health education classes.

If health science and physical education are not combined, they should be handled in the same manner as any other subject. This means that there would be mixed groups. That the subject matter is health science should not mean separation of sexes. Some leaders in the field maintain this concept is wrong and advocate keeping the sexes separate as a means of obtaining better organization.

If boys and girls meet as a mixed group for health science they should continue as a mixed group throughout the entire course. It is not wise to have them meet separately when certain topics are considered. To do so tends to place undue emphasis on certain aspects of health science. It is best to treat all subjects in a natural and educational manner.

CHECKLIST FOR EVALUATING THE HEALTH SCIENCE INSTRUCTION PROGRAM*

General   *Yes*   *No*

1. The school has a clear statement of the philosophy and principles upon which an effective school health instruction program is based.

2. Teachers on the staff appreciate the importance of health instruction and understand the contributions it makes to the total education program.

3. The school administration has assigned a qualified person from the staff to coordinate the entire school health program and provides him or her time to carry out duties and responsibilities.

4. The school has an active health committee that helps in planning and coordinating the school health program.

5. The school provides a physical environment and an emotional atmosphere that help to make possible the achievement of the goals of the health instruction program.

6. Teachers and other school staff members set a good example, in terms of good physical and mental health habits and attitudes, as part of the health instruction program.

7. The health instruction program is based upon the health needs, problems, interests, and abilities of the pupils.

8. The school has developed a teaching guide outlining a progressive plan of health instruction from grades 1 through 12.

9. The school has established definite goals of achievement in relation to habits, understanding, attitudes, and skills for each.

10. The school administration promotes the integration of health and safety instruction with all curricular areas and extracurricular activities of the school.

11. The school includes in its in-service education program opportunities for its staff to become better qualified for conducting the health instruction program.

12. The school administration provides adequate materials, such as books, charts, filmstrips, and pamphlets needed for the program.

13. Textbooks used in health classes are authoritative, up-to-date, written in an interesting manner, and suitable for the grade level in which they are used.

14. The school evaluates its health instruction periodically to determine its effectiveness in achieving established goals.

Elementary school program

15. In grades 1 to 3 sufficient time is provided during the school day for incidental and integrated teaching of health.

16. In grades 4 to 6 a minimum of three periods a week is allotted for direct health instruction.

17. The planned health instruction is supplemented in the upper grades by incidental teaching, correlation, and integration.

18. Classroom teachers meet the state's minimum standards relative to college preparation in health education.

19. The health instruction program centers around the daily living of the child instead of rote learning of health facts and rules.

*From State of Ohio Department of Education: A guide for improving school health instruction programs, Columbus, Ohio, State of Ohio Department of Education, Division of Elementary and Secondary Education.

Continued.

CHECKLIST FOR EVALUATING THE HEALTH SCIENCE INSTRUCTION PROGRAM—cont'd

Elementary school program—cont'd   Yes   No

20. The program provides many interesting and worthwhile activities that are helpful   _____   _____
    to the child in solving his or her health problems related to growth, develop-
    ment, and adjustment.

21. If the school attempts to integrate health instruction with large teaching units, the   _____   _____
    services of a health educator are utilized in planning those phases of unit dealing
    with health.

22. The health instruction program includes the major health areas and problems.   _____   _____

Junior and senior high schools

23. The time required for direct health instruction at the junior high school level is   _____   _____
    equivalent to one full semester of daily classes.

24. The time provided for direct health instruction in the senior high school is equiv-   _____   _____
    alent to one full semester of daily classes.

25. In addition to specific health courses, health instruction is correlated with other   _____   _____
    subject areas and programs.

26. Teachers of health classes in the school have at least a minor in health education   _____   _____
    or a major in health and physical education.

27. The health teacher is keenly interested in the health instruction program and at-   _____   _____
    tempts to achieve the potentialities inherent in the program.

28. The number of pupils assigned to health classes is no greater than that assigned   _____   _____
    to other classes in the school.

29. The school provides suitable classrooms and adequate facilities for health   _____   _____
    classes.

30. The teacher utilizes the films, materials, and other resources available from local   _____   _____
    and state health agencies.

31. The content of the program is interesting and meaningful to the pupils and helps   _____   _____
    them meet their health problems.

32. The school has established definite policies relative to the teaching of controver-   _____   _____
    sial areas in health education.

33. The health instruction program in the junior high school includes the health areas   _____   _____
    recommended by leaders in the field.

34. The health instruction program in the senior high school includes the health areas   _____   _____
    recommended by leaders in the field.

SELF-ASSESSMENT TESTS

These tests are to assist students in determining if material and competencies presented in this chapter have been mastered:

1. Construct a diagram delineating the three main divisions of a school health education program: health instruction, health services, and healthful school living. Identify the key elements under each. Also, include in the diagram the outcomes expected from each of the three main divisions.

2. If a physical education person is teaching health education, what should be his or her qualifications to do an acceptable job?

3. What are eight content areas in health education? Which do you feel are most important and why, at each educational level? Describe the controversial content areas and indicate why they are controversial.

4. As a physical educator teaching health at the high school level, prepare a plan to submit to your superior outlining how you would organize your classes and the methods you would use in the instructional process.

SELECTED REFERENCES

American School Health Association: School health in America—a survey of state school health programs, Kent, Ohio, 1976, The Association.

Anderson, C.L., and Creswell, W.: School health practice, ed. 7, St. Louis, 1980, The C.V. Mosby Co.

Bucher, C.A.: Health, Morristown, N.J., 1981, Silver Burdette Co.

Bucher, C.A., Olsen, E., and Willgoose, C.: The foundations of health, Englewood Cliffs, N.J., 1976, Prentice-Hall, Inc.

Cornacchia, H., and Staton, W.M.: Health in elementary schools, ed. 5, St. Louis, 1979, The C.V. Mosby Co.

Essentials of life and health, New York, 1977, Random House, Inc.

Grawunder, R., and Steinmann, M.: Life and health, New York, 1980, Random House, Inc.

Jones, K.L., et al.: Principles of health science, New York, 1975, Harper & Row, Publishers.

O'Connor, R.: Choosing for health, New York, 1980, Saunders College.

Read, D.A., and Greene, W.: Creative teaching in health, New York, 1980, Macmillan, Inc.

Report of the Study Committee on Health Education in the Elementary and Secondary Schools of the American School Health Association: Health instruction suggestions for teachers, The Journal of School Health **34:**entire issue, 1964.

Schiffres, J., and Synovitz, R.: Healthier living, New York, 1980, John Wiley & Sons, Inc.

Schiller, P.: Creative approach to sex education and counseling, New York, 1973, Association Press.

Sinacore, J.S., and Sinacore, A.C.: Introductory health—a vital issue, New York, 1975, Macmillan, Inc.

Willgoose, C.: Health education for secondary schools, Philadelphia, 1977, W.B. Saunders Co.

Willgoose, C.: Health education in the elementary school, Philadelphia, 1974, W.B. Saunders Co.

Your health and safety for better living, New York, 1977, Harcourt Brace Jovanovich, Inc.

9

Administration of physical education–related community-based programs

Instructional objectives and competencies to be achieved

After reading this chapter the student should be able to

- Identify the relationship between physical education and related community-based programs.
- Discuss the influence the community has on physical education programs.
- Describe physical education programs in industry, health clubs, and centers for the aged.
- Discuss the various types of recreation programs, the goals they are designed to achieve, and how they are administered.
- Prepare a list of guiding administrative principles that could be used in planning recreational programs.
- Explain the role of the school and the community in recreation, environmental education, and camping programs.
- Describe the role of physical education in various community service organization programs.

Physical education programs are not limited to schools, colleges, and other educational institutions. Many are located within the community at large. Furthermore, many programs in the community are closely related to physical education regarding such factors as their goals, activities, and personnel. Such programs include those concerned with physical education and fitness, community and school recreation, school and community camping and outdoor environmental education, and physical education in community service organizations.

The relationship between physical education and these community-based programs takes many forms. Community-based programs in many cases are coordinated and interwoven with school programs to prevent repetition and overlapping in offered activities. Physical educators in schools and colleges in many cases provide leadership for community-based organizations. Prospective physical educators in pro-

fessional educational programs are often enrolled in curricula that will prepare them for employment in community-based organizations. Frequently, school and college physical education and community-based programs share facilities and personnel. School programs, college programs, and community-based programs are attempting to achieve many similar goals: physical fitness, recreation, health, and, in general, an improvement in the quality of life of their clientele. Indeed, some predict that sometime in the future all school and community physical education and recreation programs will be administratively under the direction of one person and staff to carry out an effective and coordinated program for community residents for their entire lives.

A discussion of the community, the setting for community-based physical education–related programs will precede a discussion of these programs.

Fig. 9-1. Skiing as a recreational activity at Colgate University, Hamilton, N.Y.

The community and physical education–related programs

When developing physical education programs for a particular population, one should remember that the community is the real focus of decision making. The program must be planned around its needs and interests. The physical education program must be related to the individual, the family, and the community.

Economic conditions. One of the problems facing every community today is how to obtain enough money to close the gap between the amount and quality of needed physical education and the available financial support. For example, concerning physical education–related community-based programs, factors determining the cost include the problem of securing adequate staff members at salaries high enough to attract and hold them, the need for adequate facilities and equipment, and the need to raise poverty-stricken areas to respectable levels.

The community able and willing to meet these needs has sound programs, well-planned physical plants, and sufficient qualified personnel to adminis-

ter an excellent, safe, and varied program. In the community not able to afford what it needs are lower salaries, larger classes, less equipment and supplies, fewer personnel, and limited programs.

Fiscal problems have no easy solution, and their implications for physical education are monumental. The economy of a community may have particular impact on physical education programs. In an economically weak situation, equipment may be worn out or inadequate and new equipment difficult to obtain. When students are employed after school, it may be difficult to operate a recreation program. Lack of staff members may dictate that physical education personnel assume a variety of duties. In a community where physical education programs enjoy strong economic support, the reverse will ideally be true.

Religious groups. Fifty to 100 years ago, religious groups had a great and direct influence on the administration of a community's affairs. In recent years the stress on the separation of church and state has been great, and the influence of religious groups is frequently less than before.

A few religious groups frown on certain activities,

Fig. 9-2. Students enjoying a golf game during their leisure hours at Colgate University, Hamilton, N.Y.

including social dancing, Saturday or Sunday athletic contests, and family life courses. A particular church with considerable influence could completely break down some parts of the program, even though the program may be needed and wanted by youths in the community.

To meet these problems, physical educators must base programs on sound principles and should be certain the community is supporting the program. If a question arises, they should be prepared to explain the program with supportive evidence to representatives of the community's churches and to listen carefully to valid criticisms and suggestions for improvement.

Politics. In communities where recreation boards and other community boards are appointed, merit and qualifications for the job may be taken into consideration. In other instances, however, appointments may be made on the basis of political patronage. When board members are elected, the entire voting community has a voice; however, this system may also have drawbacks. Interested candidates who will do a good job run and often win election. However, aspiring politicians often run for the board and then use their position as a stepping-stone for their careers.

Recreation and fitness are frequently only of minor consideration for such politically motivated individuals. Further, in a community that favors one political party over another, the candidates of that party, rather than the best person for the job, may be elected.

Not only the recreation board and other community boards, but also politicians, may have a voice in running the programs of a community. The local press and radio and television stations reflect local political views through editorial comments. The board, however, has great influence in hiring staff members, approving budgets, and deciding on new construction. A staff member is ultimately responsible to the board, which is in turn responsible to the community.

Strong community support of a board is reflected in the program. Qualified staff members are hired, they teach in a healthful environment, and, if satisfactory, they are retained for further service. Budget requests and appropriations are most likely to be honored when the board receives community support and, in turn, supports its staff members and their programs. When the board is ineffective and inefficient because it is politically maneuvered, the program suffers.

Fig. 9-3. Bicycling is an excellent form of recreation.

Courtesy Department of Recreation, Intramural and Club Sports
at Colgate University, Hamilton, N.Y.

Climate. The climate and the geographical location of the community are other community conditions physical educators must consider. Planning must take the following into consideration:

1. Amount of time it will be possible to be outdoors. It would be unreasonable and detrimental to outdoor facilities to spend large amounts of money equipping and maintaining an oversized gymnasium in southern California or Florida where the amount of time spent outdoors will be much greater than time spent indoors. Conversely, in the northern states more time will be spent inside because of the weather.

2. Activities of interest to local residents. The inclusion of and emphasis on skiing and ice skating in a program in northern states would certainly be understandable, whereas more emphasis on tennis would be reasonable in Arizona and Texas. This does not exclude ice skating from the program in the South or the Southwest, although facilities would have to be available. The emphasis on winter sports in the South, however, would not approximate that in the North.

It is necessary to determine the activities and interests of the community as they relate to the climate and make efficient use of funds in light of it.

Sociological and cultural backgrounds. The composition of the community has a bearing on physical education and related programs. The races, nationalities, wealth, poverty, educational backgrounds, and ages of the residents are just a few of the sociological and cultural factors that should be considered when planning a program.

The program in a low socioeconomic area should include many opportunities for active participation as an outlet for aggressive tendencies that may be apparent in this area. In requiring proper gymnasium attire it is important to recognize that some participants may not have the money to purchase sneakers or gym suits.

If a youngster resides in the inner city, play space is usually limited to the streets and neighborhood playgrounds. If the parents of a child work and are poverty stricken, they will have little money for recreational activities. If different ethnic groups live in the community, new sports and activities might be included in the program to enhance the participants' pride and respect for their heritage. This is in keeping with making activities relevant to a per-

Fig. 9-4. Corporate physical education program in action.
Courtesy The Forbes Magazine Fitness Center, New York.

sons's background. It makes much more sense, for example, than trying to teach deck tennis to inner-city youths.

The community residents may be college graduates and financially stable. Physical education programs should make use of the educational interests of these fathers and mothers to encourage support for programs, facilities, special equipment, volunteer help, and supplies. The program may include individual activities such as golf, tennis, and archery, because the students will probably have the opportunity to use these skills.

The great problem of meeting the needs of participants from varied backgrounds presents a challenge to the physical educator in working not only with youths but also in working with parents. It is therefore important to know the parents in the community. Such knowledge could partially come from analyzing the following items concerning parents: (1) participation in various organizations important in the community (e.g., the League of Women Voters, garden clubs, and Junior League may indicate a higher educational background and socioeconomic status), (2) participation in hobbies and leisure activities (golf and tennis clubs and riding stables may indicate a higher socioeconomic area), (3) interest in sports

activities, and (4) desire to conform (a danger lies in the possibility of conforming to mediocrity).

Differences in taste, attitude, race, or nationality are minimized in the gymnasium and on the athletic field. Breaking down false beliefs, recognizing ability, and instilling a feeling of belonging can often be accomplished in sports. Physical educators can help combat harmful social and cultural variances within a community through a good physical education program.

Attitudes toward physical education and related programs. Is the community willing and able to support physical education and related programs? How have the residents voted in recent referendums relating to expenditures for recreation, health, and fitness programs? Do they regularly cut the budget? If they do, is it possible that the community is either unable or unwilling to meet desirable expenses?

A beginning physical educator should be conscious of the handicap of working where the equipment and supplies are old or in short supply, classes are overcrowded, or facilities are inadequate. The amount of expected relief largely depends on the attitude of community members.

The degree of community acceptance of trends approved and used in other communities or sections

Fig. 9-5. Intramural, club and recreational activities at Colgate University, Hamilton, N.Y.

of the country is also important. For instance, are antiquated strength tests, an excessive amount of formal work such as calisthenics, or heavy apparatus being used? Are jogging and aerobic dancing considered a waste of time? The answers to these questions indicate attitudes of the community that may affect the eventual success of physical education and related programs.

The physical educator must give consideration to parents' ideas for their youngsters' education when designing a program. All social groups have goals for their offspring, and these determine what programs the community will support. Clear lines of communication between curriculum planners and the community are necessary.

Pressure groups. A pressure group can be defined as an organization or group of people working to achieve a common goal. Groups or organizations in every community attempt to pressure the community to elect a certain candidate, repair a street, reduce a tax, or perhaps change the physical education or related programs. Examples of pressure groups are a dads' club desiring to sponsor a football league, a church group wanting to eliminate social dancing, and a citizens' group trying to rally support for a referendum.

Not all pressure groups try to tear down a program. In fact, the opposite is often true. One of the strongest possible allies for combating the goals of one pressure group may be another group. Many organizations believe they are helping physical education programs by their actions when in reality they are doing them a great disservice. For example, a fraternal organization that gives expensive prizes or awards or sponsors a football league for young children usually does so out of a desire to be of service to the community. It is only by fostering an understanding of the possible harm that can be caused by such a program that the physical educator can combat these influences effectively.

When physical educators are members of the community, they often have opportunities to discuss ideas informally. Such discussions are excellent opportunities to encourage, dissuade, or rechannel the desires of a group of interested community members. Speaking at meetings, interpreting a good program,

and sending home happy, understanding young people are probably the best ways to combat undesirable group pressures.

Community physical education and fitness programs

Selected community physical education and fitness programs include those found in industry, health clubs, and centers for the aged.

INDUSTRIAL PHYSICAL FITNESS PROGRAMS

The hidden costs to American industry of the physical degeneration of its employees are staggering. For example, loss of production in the United States as a result of premature death caused by chronic cardiovascular disease alone, according to Dr. Roy J. Shephard of the University of Toronto's Department of Physiological Hygiene, is $19.4 billion per year. There are also other losses: in terms of illness, $5 billion; disruption of home life, $5 billion; hospital and other services, $3 billion. Heart attacks alone cost industry about 132 million workdays yearly, or approximately 4% of the gross national product. Backaches, which many doctors feel are caused by physical degeneration, cost American industry $1 billion each year in lost goods and services and another $225 million in workmen's compensation according to the National Safety Council. Such statistics do not consider other important factors, such as shortened workdays caused by workers' fatigue and minor aches and pains, or absenteeism for several days from illness caused by lowered physical resistance to disease.

The values, on the other hand, that accrue to American industry by instituting fitness programs in its establishments pay huge dividends, and not only for the nation but also for industry itself. Research studies have shown that companies with fit employees have higher performance, greater production, improved morale among their workers, reduced absenteeism, more creative ideas, and better cooperation between labor and management.

W.W. Keeler, Chairman of the Board of Phillips Petroleum Company, who earned a certificate for jogging 400 miles in 1 year, was thinking of many psychological as well as physical benefits of fitness pro-

Fig. 9-6. Recreational activities for children.

Courtesy Cosom, Minneapolis, Minn.

Fig. 9-7. Industrial physical fitness program.
Courtesy The Forbes Magazine Fitness Center,
New York.

Fig. 9-8. Industrial physical fitness program
Courtesy The Forbes Magazine Fitness Center, New York.

grams when he pointed out, ''For most of us, the benefits of a physical conditioning program go beyond our personal well-being. They accrue to the business with which we are associated. When our employees are gaining physical fitness through regular exercise they become more productive and happier individuals.''

Executives, in particular, should recognize the value of being physically fit, because it may provide them with a larger salary check. A survey conducted among 50,000 executives by the Robert Half Personnel Agencies and reported in *The Wall Street Journal* found that fitness and company position were related. About one out of three of those persons in the $10,000 to $20,000 salary bracket was overweight by more than 10 pounds, whereas in the $25,000 to $50,000 bracket only one out of ten was overweight by the same amount.

That fitness is good business and pays dividends was shown in a study conducted by the National Aeronautics and Space Administration in cooperation with the U.S. Public Health Service. The study included 259 executives, ranging in age from 35 to 55 years, who volunteered to exercise regularly as part of their daily routine. After 1 year, the results showed that: 93% of the persons who participated in the study reported feeling better, more than 60% lost weight, 89% had greater stamina, 15% of those who smoked cut down, and one out of two became more diet conscious and involved in more physical activity beyond the required program. The subjects in the study also improved their work performance and had a more positive attitude toward their jobs; their enthusiasm caused others outside the study with whom they associated to become interested and involved in fitness activities.

I surveyed 10 corporations and found that each had some kind of fitness or sports program, providing a source for much needed exercise; some were for executives only, and some served all the employees.

Whereas 10 to 15 years ago when occasional participation in recreational sports was the base of any fitness program within a corporation, the trend today is to provide in addition to recreational sports, cardiovascular fitness programs with new and separate fitness facilities and a specialized staff for testing, diagnosis, and individual program planning. One reason for the stress on cardiovascular fitness today is the awareness of the sedentary life-styles of many corporate employees. Therefore programs are geared to individual needs based on testing and then are scientifically planned with a definite progression to obtain the goal of maximum fitness.

The majority of corporations surveyed that had a fitness program had one only for top executives and administrative staff personnel. One reason for this seemed to be the lack of space and the financial cost of providing such a program for all employees. Another reason is the prevailing philosophy that fitness is most important for top executives because they carry the load of responsibility and therefore live under more stressful conditions. Also, behind the movement toward physical conditioning of executives is mounting statistical evidence that administrators who regularly undergo controlled strenuous exercise stay healthier, perform better, and hold down the cost of health insurance programs.

Many corporations today have in-house physical fitness directors who supervise programs to keep their people in optimum physical condition. Pepsico, Xerox, and Exxon are three examples of the corporations studied. Physical educators are also in charge of recreational activities in corporate physical education programs.

Fitness is becoming a key word in the vocabulary of business, and many corporations are contributing, through fitness and recreational programs, to counteract the destructive nature of a sedentary, stress-laden life-style so prevalent in much of society today. As one executive stated, ''I feel certain that, since the program started, we have prevented a number of fatal heart attacks, and for those who have had heart attacks, I think exercise has provided the basis for their full recovery. Even more important, those who take advantage of this opportunity for self-improvement are finding it to be a pleasant and rewarding experience.'' The Vice President of Pepsico, after jogging his noontime mile, described the general consensus regarding corporate fitness programs: ''This is a great recharge. It clears away the cobwebs. Keeping fit is the best way I know to maintain peak performance.''

A large life insurance company in the South has a

Fig. 9-9. Industrial physical fitness program.

Courtesy The Forbes Magazine Fitness Center, New York.

physical fitness program that has the strong and enthusiastic endorsement of the president and other corporate officers. This program, including the fitness testing and diagnostic program, is open to all 13,000 employees. About 40% of the employees are involved. Of this number, the majority are male, because the sports teams are not coeducational, and the fitness program is not yet open to women. The recreational program was started when the gymnasium was built around the turn of the century at the request of employees. It was one of the first corporate facilities built within the city limits. The fitness testing and counseling program began in 1970 because of the concern over the high incidence of heart attacks occurring in men between 20 and 40 years of age.

The Director of Employee Activities is in charge of coordinating activities for the total employee population, including physical fitness and recreational sports. He also has a full-time salaried staff working with him to coordinate the various activities.

The fitness program is emphasized for all employees, including stress testing, counseling, prescriptive exercises, periodic checkups, and various instructional classes in many physical education activities. Recreational sports include basketball, weight training, handball, gymnastics, volleyball, exercise sessions, and tennis. Intramurals are played among the various teams in basketball and among employees in handball. Basketball and tennis leagues exist where teams representing the corporation play against other corporate clubs.

The indoor facilities include a full-size basketball court complete with markings for other sports, such as handball. Practice sessions for basketball are held every Monday, Tuesday, and Thursday after 5 PM, and other activities are held on Wednesday and Friday after 3 PM. There are also separate fitness testing areas, four-wall handball courts, a room with gymnastic mats and a horse, and an area for weight lifting and weight training. There are no outdoor facilities.

Another corporation, located in the Midwest, has a fitness program for both executives and other employees not involved in management. About 50% of the 12,000 employees participate in the program, which originated a few years ago as a result of the concern for executive fitness. Recently, the fitness and recreational programs were opened to all employees because of their interest and their requests.

Fig. 9-10. Industrial physical fitness program.
Courtesy The Forbes Magazine Fitness Center, New York.

The fitness director is in charge of the fitness program and the recreational program. There are two complete testing and exercise programs, one for executives and one for the rest of the employees.

Recreational sports include softball and basketball, played in newly constructed outdoor facilities and available to all employees.

There are two fitness gymnasiums, one for executives and one for the rest of the employees. Both are fully equipped with various types of exercise equipment. There is no indoor gymnasium for any type of sports program.

The North American Rockwell Corporation program

North American Rockwell Corporation has one of the best industrial fitness programs in the country, at El Segundo, California. Begun in 1960, it has as its goal to have each employee and family member participate daily in the many physical activities provided. E.A. Emmick, manager of Employee Services, and Ken White, personnel representative, spent 7 years selling the values of the program within the company and the community.

The North American Rockwell program requires each participant to first have a medical examination and then be tested for such components of fitness as cardiovascular efficiency and lung capacity. The test results determine the person's level of fitness and accordingly he or she is placed in one of five color squads: *green* (novice), *red* (average), *blue* (better), *gold* (good), and *purple* (outstanding). Employees are encouraged to try to progress from one squad to another one representing a higher level of fitness. A typical session, of which there are three to five per week for each squad, includes warmup exercises for 10 to 20 minutes, then vigorous exercising for 5 to 30 minutes, and finally tapering-off exercises for 5 to 15 minutes. Charts are posted on the walls where the performance of each participant is recorded for all to see. The activities are tailored to the needs of each individual, and competition is avoided because of the danger that some persons may overextend themselves and harm themselves physically.

Special awards may be earned in several activities by persons who reach the blue or higher division; *Running*—by jogging 1200 miles in 1 year or 75 miles in 1 week; *swimming*—by swimming 500 miles in 1 year or 26 miles in 2 weeks; *bicycling*—by pedaling 5000 miles in 1 year or 200 miles in 2 days, and *hiking*—by covering 50 miles in 2 days.

Executives, as well as workers, participate at El Segundo. As North American Rockwell's Vice President for Marketing Services, Jim Daniell, says, "When the workers see their bosses out there huffing and puffing, and sweat streaming down their faces, they say to themselves, 'There's got to be something to this physical fitness, or these fellows wouldn't be working so hard at it.' "

The Metropolitan Life Insurance Company program

The Metropolitan Life Insurance Company has developed an effective physical fitness program in their home office in New York City for men aged 20 to 40. Dr. William Cunnick, Medical Director, who believes he is working with people at a vulnerable age because it is a time when men increase their caloric input and cut down on their physical activity, developed a program that includes a physical fitness test involving jogging, rowing, bicycling, and sit-ups. The test determines how the subject's pulse rate responds to exercise. The yardstick is the length of time it takes the pulse to return to normal after exercise— the longer it takes, the poorer physical condition the person is in. After the testing is over, subjects are informed of their physical status, provided with literature on the importance of keeping fit, and encouraged to exercise regularly. A special motivating device is a leaflet each participant is given, *Measure Up To Par,* which gives the distance from various locations throughout New York City to the Metropolitan office and provides a scoring system for covering distances in a certain amount of time.

The Xerox Corporation program

The Xerox Corporation has invested large sums of money in its fitness program at Webster, New York, where its superb facilities include an executive fitness laboratory, putting green, skating rink, and jogging paths. The company also has an executive fitness program in downtown Rochester. Clubs are organized for the employees in sailing, skiing, scuba diving, horseback riding, judo, and square dancing. Men's

and women's physical fitness classes are also offered at various times of the day throughout the year. Part of the program's success is because it has become a matter of prestige to participate—there is always a waiting list, and only as participants drop out can new persons be added. To remain on the list, an employee must participate at least five times every 2 weeks and no fewer than two times in any 1 week. This regulation reaffirms a basic belief that the fitness level begins to deteriorate rapidly if training is interrupted.

Guidelines for industrial physical fitness programs

Although any company desiring to develop a physical fitness program for its employees does not necessarily have to spend large amounts of money on facilities, it should strive to meet the following six administrative criteria developed by the President's Council on Physical Fitness and Sports:

1. The program should be an adjunct of the company's health program.
2. It should include a medically oriented screening test as a criterion for participation.
3. A person skilled in prescribing exercise should direct it.
4. Exercise should be tailored to the individual participant, and should be progressively more strenuous, in order for him or her to benefit from it.
5. Activities should be noncompetitive; that is, individuals should compete only against other participants in the program.
6. A system of periodic evaluation should be included to measure progress and to aid in program design.

Some administrative guidelines have also been established for physical fitness programs in business and industry. These guidelines were prepared by the President's Council on Physical Fitness and Sports and the American Medical Association's Committee on Exercise and Physical Fitness:

1. A written set of operational procedures and objectives should be developed for all physical fitness programs.
2. Specific hours of operation of the facility should be established.
3. Participants should be required to make a commitment to an established set of goals before entering

Fig. 9-11. Fitness participants jogging at Xerox Corporation fitness and recreation center, Leesburg, Va.

Fig. 9-12. Courtesy Fitness and Recreation Center, Xerox Corporation, Leesburg, Va.

the program. These goals should be expressed in terms of length of time in the program; number of days to be spent per week in the program; and physiologic accomplishments such as weight loss, cardiovascular improvement, and strength development.

4. Participants should receive a specific training program to follow.
5. Evaluation of the participant's progress should be noted by the fitness director before each training session and related to the participant in terms of increased or decreased work output or change of conditioning routine.
6. Motivational devices in the form of awards of progress and/or completion should be developed.
7. Strict safety rules should be developed in regard to use of equipment and adherence to conditioning routines.
8. Dress codes should be established commensurate with the degree of program sophistication.
9. Research and evaluation studies should be conducted to determine the effect of the program in meeting stated objectives.

HEALTH CLUBS

The health club business has increased significantly in the last decade. The European Health Spas alone have more than 144 locations in 80 cities and 28 states They employ nearly 3000 people, and in 1 year their gross sales totaled about $65 million. The membership consists of both men and women, and a typical facility costs between $250,000 and $750,000. Their facilities consist of exercise rooms, resistive-type exercise equipment of the Universal Gymnasium or Nautilus design, treadmills, stationary bicycles, swimming pools, whirlpools, saunas, steam rooms, cold plunges, oil baths, and locker and shower areas. Their programs include jogging, weight training, yoga, ballet, and athletic competition. Their instructors include physical educators, business executives, and high school graduates.

Some estimates of the total number of health clubs (spas) in this country range from 2000 to 5000.

Glen Swengros, former vice-president of Health Industries, Inc., points out that the health spa idea will expand in the years ahead for such reasons as the following:

1. The high cost of other types of recreation
2. The accessibility of health spas to the general population.

3. The gasoline problem—the public will use leisure time close to home
4. The high divorce rate with the desire for improved body cosmetics by those who are newly divorced or separated
5. Great amount of leisure time of American public
6. Heavily populated areas with few natural outlets for physical activity
7. National advertising programs relating to the values of physical fitness

Descriptions of three health clubs follow, together with a candid evaluation of each club by a professional physical educator. These descriptions are based on interviews and visits to selected establishments. The names of the health clubs are omitted, because the purpose of these descriptions is to provide the reader with a better understanding of what health clubs are and what they purport to do.

Health club no. 1

This health club has been operating for several years. When a person applies for membership, he or she has a personal interview with the manager where they discuss the client's goals. Sometimes, depending on the apparent physical condition of the customer, a complete physical exam is recommended before a program is started. Body measurements are taken, and depending on an individual's height, weight, bone structure, and daily activity schedule, a program of exercises and diet suited for attaining the person's goals is prescribed.

Three types of programs are offered to all customers: gaining weight, losing weight, and conditioning. For men, the instruction is personalized and is conducted by three rotating floor directors. These instructors, as well as all other members of the staff, must possess either a degree in physical education or have a minimum of 3 years' experience in the field. All activity is under constant supervision. For women, whose exercises are primarily concerned with stretching and toning the body, there are voluntary group classes to supplement individualized programs. There is an hourly class in calisthenics that consists of two parts. One half is devoted to military-like drills commonly performed in traditional physical education settings. The other half is composed of dance, rhythms, and movements accompanied by ''music of

Fig. 9-13. Staff members playing racketball at Xerox Corporation fitness and recreation center, Leesburg, Va.

Fig. 9-14. Industrial fitness program at Forbes Magazine Fitness Center, New York.

distinction.'' Additional classes offered to women are yoga, which meets five times per week, and belly dancing, which meets twice weekly. The instructors of these special classes are qualified personnel, possessing appropriate degrees or other credits.

Some of the facilities at the health club include a whirlpool, a mirrored fitness room and gymnasium, sauna baths, customized outdoor jogging track, year-round tropical swimming pool, solarium and roof garden, ultraviolet suntan room, eucalyptus inhalation room, reducing equipment, steam baths, women's figure salon, a food bar and lounge, and private showers and dressing booths. All of these facilities are open to all members at all times for no additional cost. Also, there is a professional salon where one can get a massage from a registered masseur or masseuse. There is an extra charge for this service.

This health spa advertises in newspapers, on the radio, on billboards, and by circulating flyers to local residents. It also attracts customers through constant discount membership promotions, such as joining before a specific date and two-for-one sales.

The club's basic philosophy is to bring people back to health, This, they feel, can be achieved by getting them in shape, motivating them to stay fit, and improving their self-concept. Because the safety of the public is another of its prime concerns, this club has imposed a ceiling on its membership to limit overcrowding and to provide adequate supervision.

Evaluation. This club is a ''top-notch'' operation. The facilities and equipment are the finest. The staff is qualified, and the programs offered are reasonably individualized. Group classes, however, if open to women, should be available to men as well. The supervision is adequate. One major criticism of the spa is the way it promotes its product. The gymnasium and fitness rooms are highlighted by tinted mirrors, which improve the appearance of the clientele. Although motivating the customers should be a prime consideration, accomplishing this objective deceitfully is wrong. People want to see results, but not from artificial methods. There should be enough of an inherent drive to look and feel better so that ploys of this type can be avoided.

The manager's statement that there is a ceiling on membership might be questioned. This does not appear to be financially feasible, nor is it congruous with the club's philosophy of bringing everybody back to health.

Health club no. 2

This health club has been serving the public for several years. The organization is one of the largest women's health clubs in America. The salon's goal is to better one's physical health through a scientific plan of exercise. The customer discusses her objectives with the manager, who then suggests a series of exercises. If a person is not willing to embark on the entire program outlined for her, she will not be admitted. There is no claim for spot reducing. The salon believes that its product is total fitness, and this cannot be achieved by working on only one part of the body. If one is granted membership, the first three visits consist of individualized instruction and becoming acquainted with the operations and uses of the equipment. The woman is then on her own to carry out her program of reducing, gaining, or maintaining body tone.

Each member receives her own program card, which identifies the prescribed activities she is to follow. Body measurements are also recorded on this sheet along with the woman's weight. The card is reviewed on every visit so that appropriate changes in exercise routines can be made when needed. In addition, if a customer is on a reducing program and is *gaining* weight, the salon will not hesitate to question the individual about why the desired results are not being attained. If it is discovered that the recommended procedures are not being adhered to, the management indicates they will terminate the membership and refund the unused portion of money. The underlying reason for this is that the organization is highly concerned with its image, and thus feels that unfit women are detrimental to its reputation.

The staff does not prescribe any diets, but does provide food sheets for each member. On these sheets the women record what they eat, so that they will become more aware of what they're consuming. The sheets are due every third visit.

The facilities are limited. There is one large exercise room, containing belts and rollers for stimulating circulation and various forms of reducing equipment. The members are told that the belts and rollers will not eliminate or redistribute fatty tissues, that this equipment will only improve circulation. The salon believes that little machinery is required to bring about fitness and that vigorous exercise with heavy equipment will not ensure a healthier body. Group classes are conducted in yoga, dance, and calisthenics on request from the public.

The basic requirements of the staff women are that they must be personable and hard-working. They are trained by the manager. There is constant supervision of the patrons by these floor directors to avoid any unsafe practices. For every seven people in the gymnasium at one time, there is one supervisory staff member.

This organization advertises in the newspapers and on television. The price of membership (which is very low) is included in each advertisement. However, the salon attracts 75% of its customers through the "buddy" system, that is, customers bringing in their friends. The salon believes that its low-key philosophy of attaining a better figure through a planned series of simple, daily exercises is its best selling point.

Evaluation. How can a scientific plan of exercise for each member be achieved when the staff members may have no background at all in physical education? In addition, the space and equipment are so limited that accommodating 40 or 50 women at one time seems impossible. Also, because group classes and individual programs are carried out in the same room, distractions are maximized, and safety hazards result.

It is hard to believe that members are threatened with expulsion if they are not reducing. First of all, no two people lose weight at the same pace, and one should not be punished if her body is not reacting to the exercises as quickly as one might expect. Second, and more important, if a spa must be that concerned with the upkeep of its image to the detriment of its patrons, it cannot be a first-class operation. It is easy to see why this club has a negligible renewal rate and must profit through a high level of turnover. The fee is small because they simply have nothing to offer.

Health club no. 3

This health club for men is privately owned and has been in existence for several years. It takes a serious approach to physical fitness by offering complete programs in weight training and body building, conducted in a large and complete gymnasium.

A person entering the spa for the first time is assumed to be in poor physical condition. He is given a complete body workout beginning with the large muscle groups, paying particular attention to building up the heart and lungs. No specialization takes place until the whole body has passed through the initial stages of conditioning. The client is then ready to begin an exercise program developed by the owner of the club, based on the individual's objectives.

Each club member is given a thorough orientation with each piece of equipment and machinery before he is allowed to use it. Individualized instruction is given as much as possible, but the ratio of customers in the gymnasium to members of the staff at any one time necessitates that a person be able to follow through on his own. Good form in exercising is stressed to achieve optimum results. Every individual has his own program card for recording progress. It is reviewed every 3 weeks. The customers are encouraged to visit the spa at least three times per week to improve and maintain fitness. The club offers no group classes and does not prescribe or suggest any diets. The club feels that every person should care enough about his body to know what foods he should be eating.

This club offers a complete program in aerobic training. Three times a year, a 10-week clinic in aerobics is given to all interested members. Aerobic training, the club maintains, serves many vital functions, such as strengthening the muscles of respiration and facilitating the rapid flow of air; improving the strength and pumping efficiency of the heart; toning muscles throughout the body, thus improving blood pressure; increasing the total amount of blood circulating through the body; and increasing the number of red blood cells and the hemoglobin content.

The facilities include a gymnasium stocked with the latest and finest equipment available. There is also a whirlpool, sauna, steam room, television lounge, sun room, and health juice bar. One can also receive a rubdown from a licensed professional masseur.

There are three rotating instructors in the gymnasium. At least one is always present to supervise, and all three are available during peak hours. Each has significant knowledge of exercise, body building, and weight training. They must also be personable, easy to communicate with, and someone with whom the patrons can identify. Once hired, staff members are further trained by the management.

This club attempts to attract the ''city crowd'' by advertising in newspapers and periodicals. It also depends largely on the buddy system. The spa claims to have a high renewal rate, uncommon to some clubs, because it is a high-level physical fitness facility. It does not take members long to realize that it is concerned with fitness first and business second. That attitude of personal interest in everyone's health is the chief reason why customers return season after season. The health club believes that all areas of human existence should be in balance, beginning with physical fitness.

Evaluation. This health spa for men is serious about physical fitness, and this is reflected in its members' attitudes. They do not come to the club to socialize; they are there to work. Group classes do not exist because they are not wanted and not needed. The customers know what they want and are able to get it, with the help of excellent equipment and instruction by a knowledgable floor instructor who is readily available. The facilities are more than adequate. The owner cites that he would like to add more to his spa, but there is simply no room. This organization has an outstanding public relations plan: the patrons can identify with the people who work there; the employees are friendly, helpful, and know what they are talking about. I was totally impressed by everything at the spa, particularly the candor of the owner. If pure physical fitness is one's goal, then this health spa for men has much to offer.

Code of ethical practices for health clubs

The Association of Physical Fitness Centers, which was formed to upgrade establishments engaged in promoting physical fitness, has set forth a Code of Ethical Practices for health clubs to follow. A knowledge of these practices will be helpful to the physical educator who is interested in and desires to improve this field. The following have been selected as representative of the Code and the administrative practices that should be followed by health clubs:

1. Members at all times should administer their organizations at the highest professional level.
2. Members should continually seek to increase their professional knowledge in the field of physical fitness.
3. Members will make proper provision for the physical fitness requirements of each consumer of their services.
4. Employees of these establishments should be trained in the use of exercise facilities, in designing exercise programs, and in the proper use of equipment. Qualified staff should be maintained at all exercise facilities in sufficient numbers to meet consumer needs.
5. Members will stress the importance of physical activity and proper nutrition and keep their facilities in a clean and healthful condition.
6. Members of the Association will not discriminate in employment or sales of memberships on the basis of race, creed, sex, religion, or national origin.
7. Members will maintain a high standard of ethics in advertising and sales promotion.
8. Members of the Association will not describe the price or cost of a membership program in any misleading or deceptive manner.
9. Special provisions will be set forth for releasing consumers from contractual obligations. Such provisions will be reasonable.
10. Members of the Association will publish their membership policies and rules and regulations for their consumers.

CENTERS FOR THE AGED

A national adult physical fitness survey conducted for the President's Council on Physical Ftiness and Sports by the Opinion Research Corporation of Princeton, New Jersey, indicates that the physical fitness of adults is inadequate. Furthermore, it shows that the aged of America, in particular, need physical education programs as much as or more than any other age group. Such programs can delay the aging process, deter the onset of degenerative diseases, and enhance the quality of life for the elderly.

The Congress of the United States, as well as many private organizations, have encouraged the development of more physical education programs for the aged. For example, the National Association for Human Development in cooperation with the President's Council on Physical Fitness and Sports, under a grant from the Administration on Aging, has conducted a

Fig. 9-15. Activity for the elderly at Westwood Home, Clinton, Mo.

national campaign aimed at encouraging older persons to become more physically active. The program included regional workshops to stimulate a series of state and local workshops through which a fitness program for the elderly can be fully implemented.

Many of the centers have not developed physical education programs that the profession would consider excellent; however, these programs are being initiated, and professional leadership is greatly needed so they may be upgraded and receive the approval of physical educators. A sampling of four programs selected at random are described in the following.

Center for the aged no. 1

The program in this center consists of folk dancing and square dancing twice a week, Monday afternoons from 2:00 to 4:00 and Thursday nights from 7:30 to 9:30. The program is held in a gymnasium, and the instructor is a slender man of 60, who is graceful, enthusiastic, and friendly. The music is supplied by a sound system set up in the gymnasium.

The first dance performed at the center during the visit was called ''Sweet Sir Galahad'' and reportedly was arranged by the instructor. It is a dance similar

to ''The Bus Stop,'' which was popular in discotheques. The dance consisted of walking steps to music. The 20 participants seemed to have little trouble in learning this dance and performed with great enthusiasm.

The next dance was called ''Tango Pacquito.'' The participants made a circle, held hands, and danced various steps. The dance was easy to learn and proved excellent for coordination, balance, and general physical conditioning.

Next was a dance involving sets of two couples and involved an interchange of partners. This dance required a considerable amount of timing, balance, and coordination, which most of the participants seemed to possess. The final dance was ''Alley Cat.''

The atmosphere in which the dancing was conducted was relaxing, and the participants had an excellent sense of timing, rhythm, and coordination. They danced for 2 hours with only short breaks between dances. They were enthusiastic about the program and seemed to want longer than a 2-hour period. All participated in all the dances.

One lady said she did not know how to dance until she came to the program 1 year earlier and now she

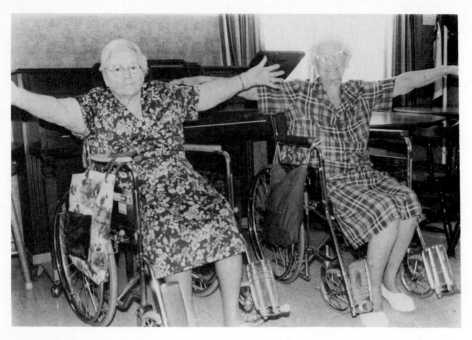

Fig. 9-16. Part of square dance call, "Take your arms out to the side, like you can hold the ocean tide."

Courtesy Westwood Home, Clinton, Mo.

loves the activity. Another woman said she could not play football or basketball, but she loved dancing, and it provided her with healthful physical exercise.

The instructor's philosophy concerning the program was that he thought it was excellent for socialization purposes and, in addition, the dancing provided a full range of movements for coordination and balance. The program also enhanced the self-concepts of the participants and gave the elderly a better, more confident image of themselves.

Center for the aged no. 2

The program at this center offers folk and social dancing three times a week for ½ hour at a time. Music is piped into a large recreational room in the basement of the building. An instructor, however, is present for dancing only once or twice a month. As a result, participants dance only if they desire. However, because there is little motivation, there are few dancers. Most of the senior citizens seem to be content to sit, talk, and play cards. The center also has two table tennis tables, neither of which were used

during the visit, and a shuffleboard court and a pool table, which were in use.

This program, in addition to the dance, has a daily exercise class from 11:15 to noon. It is conducted by a man of 60, who is not a physical educator. The exercises included various stretching exercises, abdominal exercises, modified push-ups, breathing exercises, and marching in place followed by running in place for ½ minute. The exercises lasted about 20 minutes.

The participants in this program were not enthusiastic. Furthermore, the exercises, card playing and conversations all took place in the same room at the same time. The card players and the persons talking outnumbered the physically active senior citizens about 10 to 1.

Center for the aged no. 3

This center conducts bowling for the aged every Thursday from 3:00 to 4:00, a yoga class on Mondays from 11:30 to noon, and a dance class from 1:00 to 2:00 on Tuesdays and Thursdays. The setting for the dance classes is a large ballroom with a sound system. The activity consists of a combination of ballroom, folk, and social dances. The dances during the visit included a social dance to "Volare," a Slavic folk dance, a waltz, and a Greek dance.

The instructor is well liked and motivates the people to want to dance. One woman said that when the program first started there were only six participants but now there are 40.

This program is varied and appears to meet the needs and interests of the elderly who participate.

Center for the aged no. 4

This center schedules bowling and square and social dancing once a week. In addition, it offers an exercise class from 10:30 to 11:45 each morning. The instructor is a slim young woman who has a background in dancing. She is friendly and has good rapport with the people who visit the center. The exercises are done to music, and the benefits that accrue from each are explained by the instructor. The exercises include stretching, shoulder, upper trunk, abdominal, and leg exercises given progressively to cover the entire body. The instructor places the emphasis on relaxing while performing the exercises. In addition, she explains how to do each exercise. To wind up the exercise session, the instructor introduces total body activity, including jogging and jumping jacks to stimulate the cardiorespiratory system.

The instructor stated that her philosophy is to try to get everyone to relax and let every person work at his or her own level. She is particularly interested in getting everyone motivated to perform the exercises.

Administrative guidelines for physical education programs for the aged

Some important guidelines to observe in administering programs for the aged include the following:

1. All participants should have medical clearance before engaging in any strenuous exercise program.
2. Comfortable clothing should be worn while exercising.
3. There should be a warmup period before the exercise program.
4. The exercises should be tailored to the individual participants.
5. The exercises should be administered progressively; that is, the tempo and the number of repetitions should begin slowly and increase gradually. This will minimize stiffness and soreness.
6. Exercises with music add to the enjoyment of participation.
7. Exercises performed with family and friends provide added incentive and interest for participants.
8. There should be a cooling down period after exercising.
9. It is helpful to keep a record of exercises performed and number of repetitions and to set performance goals for accomplishment.
10. A cheerful, healthful environment should be chosen for the physical activity sessions.

Recreation programs

It has been estimated that the American worker has an average of 675 hours of free time annually. This does not include vacation time. When this is added, the net gain of free time is close to 800 hours annually or roughly 1 month out of every 12.* With this much free time, it is essential that recreation programs be developed to help people enjoy their leisure hours fully and constructively.

Recreation involves socially acceptable and worthwhile activities in which a person voluntarily participates during leisure hours and through which he or she has opportunities to develop physically, mentally, emotionally, and socially.

Five key concepts of any form of recreation are advocated here. First, the activity must be conducted in hours other than work. It is a *leisure time activity*. The activity must not be associated with productive labor aimed at profit. Second, recreation is an *enjoyable activity* from which one gains satisfaction, serenity, and happiness. Third, recreation is *constructive*—it is wholesome. Recreation should contribute to the individual's physical, mental, emotional, or social welfare. Fourth, recreation is *nonsurvival in nature*. Therefore, sleep cannot be labeled a form of recreation in the sense discussed in this chapter. Finally, recreation is *voluntary*. The person engages in the activity because he or she has freely chosen to

---

*Hodgson, J. D.: Leisure and the American worker, Journal of Health, Physical Education, and Recreation **43**:38, 1972.

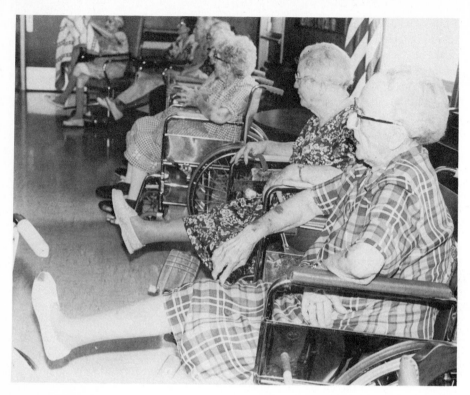

Fig. 9-17. Warm up with leg and foot exercises at Westwood Home, Clinton, Mo.

participate. These five criteria must be satisfied for an activity to be considered recreation.

Types of recreation

Some of the better-known kinds of recreation are community, industrial, therapeutic, school, family, and commercial. The kinds of recreation considered primarily in this chapter are community and school recreation.

Community recreation. Community recreation is sponsored by villages, towns and cities for their inhabitants. It is controlled, financed, and administered by the community.

Industrial recreation. Industrial recreation is sponsored by an industrial concern or other business establishment for its own employees.

Therapeutic recreation. Therapeutic recreation is set up in hospitals, nursing homes, and other establishments for the benefit of ill and disabled patients. The therapeutic values of recreation are increasingly being recognized.

School recreation. School recreation is provided by a board of education for the persons who attend a particular school system.

Family recreation. Family recreation involves the activities a family chooses to engage in during leisure hours.

Commercial recreation. Commercial recreation is found in such places as amusement parks and is conducted for profit.

Goals of recreation

Community recreation enriches lives. Many goals have been listed for the field of recreation that reflect this contribution: physical, cognitive, emotional, and social health; happiness; satisfaction; balanced growth; creativity; competition; learning; citizenship; socialization; and the development of one's talents.

Following are six goals for American recreation put forth by The Commission on Goals for American Recreation. They represent one of the best professional statements on recreational goals.

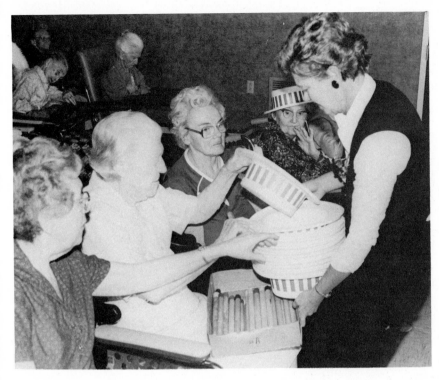

Fig. 9-18. Westwood Home, Clinton, Mo., has found that props add extra motivation.

Personal fulfillment. The democratic ideal is based on the concept that the individual is the most important consideration in society. To achieve one's place in our culture, each person needs self-fulfillment. Each person wants to belong and to feel important. Each person should strive to become all he or she is capable of becoming. Therefore, recreation should help each person achieve full integration of total personality; contribute to mental, physical, social, and emotional development; and help fill in the gaps that work does not provide.

Democratic human relations. Democratic society functions best through associated effort directed toward accomplishing goals in the best interests of the majority. The recreation profession recognizes that its goals exist on the level of the individual, as well as on the level of the democratic society. Recreation, therefore, constantly keeps in mind such important tenets as (1) each individual has worth and each personality must be respected, (2) the citizen in a democracy cooperates for the common good, (3) the

citizen abides by the laws—rules that have been established to guard each individual's rights, and (4) the citizen living in a democracy guides his or her behavior by acceptable moral and ethical values.

Leisure skills and interests. Recreation is concerned with meeting the interests of those people who voluntarily participate in its programs, developing skills that provide the incentive, motivation, and medium for spending free time constructively. As such, recreation must be concerned with a breadth and variety of interests, ranging from physical activities, social activities, and artistic activities to community service programs and learning activities.

Health and fitness. Many individuals are sedentary and thus have poor health and fitness. Recreation emphasizes the importance of a vigorous and active life and seeks to meet the challenge of a society in which mental illness, stress, and inactivity are prevalent.

Creative expression and esthetic appreciation. Each individual needs to give vent to personal expres-

Fig. 9-19. Jogging on the Bronx River Parkway during "Bicycle Sunday" sponsored by the Westchester County, N.Y., Department of Parks, Recreation, and Conservation.

Fig. 9-20. Senior citizens enjoying their learn-to-swim program.

Courtesy Westchester County, N.Y., Department of Parks, Recreation, and Conservation.

sion, to creativity, and to the appreciation of the most beautiful and cultured activities in the various cultures of the world. Recreation seeks to contribute to each individual's desire for creative expression and esthetic appreciation by providing the environment, leadership, materials, and motivation for such experiences, recognizing that creativity can flourish only in a climate that has been properly prepared for its development and growth.

Environment for living in a leisure society. The environment is important in determining the quality and extent of the recreative experience. Therefore, recreation is particularly interested in preserving our natural resources; in constructing parks, playgrounds, hobby centers, and other recreation centers; in seeing that recreation programs are considered in city planning; and in awakening the populace to the need for an appreciation of esthetic and cultural values.

Guides for planning recreation programs

Recreation programs should not be developed on a hit-or-miss basis. Instead, leaders in recreation have thoroughly and carefully studied the types of programs that best serve the needs of people and have developed guides for planning programs, such as the following, set forth by Brightbill*:

1. Individual interests, characteristics, needs, and capabilities should be considered when planning recreation programs.
2. The recreational interests and skills of individuals may be determined to some degree by the cultural, economic, religious, and social phenomena that characterize them.
3. Recreation should be planned cooperatively, with the recreator consulting interested individuals, departments, agencies, and organizations.
4. Program planning requires that national standards be modified to local conditions.
5. Program planning should consider individual differences in skills and the progressive planning of skill experiences.
6. Creativity and self-expression are considerations in program planning.

7. Opportunities should be available for individuals to serve others and gain personal satisfaction.
8. Recreation programs should provide a wide spectrum of activities.
9. Leadership, financial means, and facilities are essential considerations in program planning.
10. Physical and human resources in the community should be mobilized for the recreation program.
11. The recreation program should provide equal opportunity for participation for all persons in the community.
12. Flexibility to change activities as people's interests change should be possible within a recreation program.
13. The health and safety of participants should always be considered in planning recreation programs.
14. The recreation program should seek to help each person exemplify acceptable standards of human behavior.
15. The participant in the recreation program should never be exploited for such means as raising money or personal glory.
16. Recreation should be continually evaluated to determine how the goals are being achieved in light of the investment being made.

Recreation activities

The range of recreation activities is infinite. Any activity that meets the criteria listed earlier in the chapter can be a recreational activity. This means that drama, music, art, crafts, games, sports, camping, literature, fairs, nature study, dance, and community work are possible avenues for millions of people to obtain the benefits recreation can offer.

A list of a few of the possible activities for recreation purposes follows:

Arts and crafts	**Outdoor activities**
Ceramics	Campfires
Graphic arts	Camping
Leathercraft	Canoeing
Metalcraft	Conservation
Photography	Fishing
Plastics	Orienteering
Sewing	Outdoor cooking
Stenciling and block printing	Woodcraft

Sports and games	**Dramatics**
Archery	Clubs
Badminton	Festivals
Bowling	Plays

*Adapted from Langton, C.V., Duncan, R.O., and Brightbill, C.K.: Principles of health, physical education, and recreation, New York, 1962, The Ronald Press Co., pp. 251-261.

Fencing
Golf
Hopscotch

Music

Barber shop quartets
Choral groups
Community sings
Instrumental
Orchestral

Dancing

Folk
Modern
Social
Square

Miscellaneous

Cards
Flowers
Forums
Hobby clubs

Recreation agencies

The three major types of recreation agencies in the United States are: (1) public recreation agencies, (2) private or voluntary agencies, and (3) commercial agencies. Some examples of each type are listed, as follows:

1. Public recreation agencies
   a. Municipal public agencies—the park department, recreation department, youth commission, education department, and other city or community departments that operate recreation programs

Fig. 9-21. Bicycling is excellent exercise for old and young alike.

b. State public agencies—state park departments, state conservation departments, and state education departments
c. Federal public agencies—national parks, Forestry Service, Children's Bureau, Fish and Wild Life Service, and Tennessee Valley Authority
2. Private or voluntary agencies
   a. Youth-serving organizations—Boys' Clubs of America, YMCAs, YWCAs, Campfire Girls, Boy Scouts, and church centers
   b. Organizations serving an entire population—museums, libraries, athletic clubs, outdoor clubs, and granges
   c. Private voluntary agencies organized around special interests of certain groups—music specialties, photographic specialties, and sports specialties
3. Commercial agencies (operated for profit—theaters, bowling alleys, art galleries, night clubs, and concert halls

National Recreation and Park Association. A major development in recreation was the unification of five of the national organizations serving lay people and professional recreation. The American Institute of Park Executives, the American Recreation Society, the American Zoological Association, the National Council of State Parks, and the National Recreation Association were merged into a unified national organization known as the *National Recreation and Park Association.* Lawrence S. Rockefeller was elected as the first president. The merger was designed to bring together a single organization supported by private citizens and professional groups and dedicated to helping all Americans devote their free time to constructive and satisfying activities.

Recreation program administration

The following are five major methods of administering community recreation programs in this country.

The recreation board. A recreation board can be set up in any community where enabling legislation exists and permits such action. The board usually consists of five to nine members: representatives of the city government, the school district, the recreation or park department, and the community at large. Terms of office usually run for varying periods of time depending on the community, and the members usually serve without compensation. Members of the board are either elected or appointed to their positions.

The school board. In many communities the board of education, under a broad interpretation of its powers or under the provisions of state extension education law or enabling acts, conducts recreation programs. In some communities this responsibility is interpreted as providing a program only for its children and youth, whereas other programs are designed for persons of all ages.

The park board. In such cities as Detroit and Seattle, the department of parks administers the recreation program. Because the community parks are used so extensively for recreation purposes, and to avoid duplication of facilities, budgeting, and planning, some citizens feel the park board is the logical form of administration for community recreation programs. Those opposed to this arrangement, however, point out that recreation does not get priority under such an administrative setup.

The recreation board and the school board. In some communities the recreation board and school board cooperatively work in administering the recreation program. The school board, for example, may provide the facilities and sometimes the funds, whereas the recreation board provides the personnel, equipment, and supplies. Regardless of how the responsibilities are shared, a close working relationship is developed between the two groups.

The recreation association, nonprofit agency, and corporation. In villages and other communities where the park, recreation, or school board has not assumed the administration of the recreation program, sometimes recreation associations, clubs, and other organizations provide a program. The Boys' Clubs of America, YMCAs, and Recreation Promotion and Service Corporations are examples of this type of administrative organization.

School recreation

Schools should play a vital role in recreation. At present they are contributing staff members and facilities. The program of studies also has implications for recreation. The school, with wide and varied educational offerings in such fields as science, art, music, physical education, and industrial arts, has infinite opportunities to develop many resources for leisure.

Fig. 9-22. Biking on the Bronx River Parkway during "Bicycle Sunday" sponsored by the Westchester County, N.Y., Department of Parks, Recreation, and Conservation.

The school's responsibility does not end when the final bell rings. Its influence extends into the student's life throughout the school day and is also reflected in those activities in which he or she engages after regular school hours. How the student spends free time after school and on weekends and holidays influences his or her health and success. During the school years the student may want to find out more about photography, choral singing, dramatics, or sports. The out-of-class program, such as intramurals and clubs, as well as course offerings, provides opportunities to pursue there interests.

The recommendations of the Second National Conference on School Recreation included the following adapted series of principles regarding school-centered recreation and municipal school recreation.

SCHOOL-CENTERED RECREATION

1. Schools should accept, as a major responsibility, education for leisure.
2. Schools and colleges should provide their students with opportunities for participation in wholesome, creative activities.
3. The facilities and resources of a school should be made available for recreation.
4. Where community recreation programs are missing or inadequate, the school should take the initiative and provide recreation programs for both young and old.
5. The school should cooperate with community organizations and agencies interested in or sponsoring recreation programs.
6. The school should appoint a person to act as a community school director; he or she would be responsible for the recreation education program in the school.
7. Recreation and education are not identical; each has its own distinctive features.
8. The community school director should provide in-service recreation education for his or her staff members.
9. The federal government has a responsibility to stimulate recreation programs.
10. Recreation depends on public understanding and support for its existence.
11. Recreation should be concerned with exploiting the interests of people.
12. The recreation program should consist of many varied activities.
13. Recreation should be concerned with contributing to the mental health of the individual.

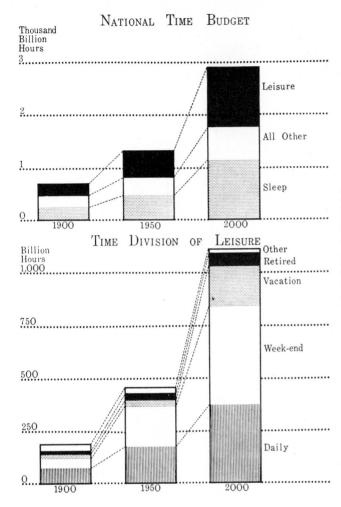

Fig. 9-23. National time budget and time division of leisure — 1900, 1950, and 2000.

From The American Academy of Political and Social Science: Leisure in America; blessing or curse? Philadelphia, 1964, The Academy.

MUNICIPAL SCHOOL RECREATION

1. The school should teach people to use leisure time productively, contribute to recreation in the instructional program, mobilize community resources, and cooperatively plan facilities for recreation. The college and university should promote research in recreation and provide professional preparation programs in this specialized area.
2. There should be joint planning of municipal school recreation based on stated principles and brought about by state departments of education and local boards of education.
3. School facilities should be available for recreational use.

The recreation leader

The recreation leader should have most of the qualifications of the physical education specialist and some that are pertinent to his or her field of work.

Qualifications. The recreation leader, who works with people much of the time, needs integrity, friendliness, enthusiasm, initiative, and organizing ability. Recreation leaders should possess a broad cultural background, with an understanding of the needs and problems facing society. This entails a fundamental knowledge of history, sociology, and anthropology. In addition, they should have the skills necessary to

Fig. 9-24. Track meet conducted at the Westchester County Center, N.Y.

Courtesy Westchester County, N.Y., Department of Parks, Recreation, and Conservation.

Fig. 9-25. Inner-city youths in Los Angeles enjoy and benefit from recreational experiences.

Courtesy Youth Services Section, Los Angeles City Schools.

Fig. 9-26. Physical education programs are needed for inner-city youths. A baseball game offered by the Youth Services Section of the Los Angeles City Schools.

Fig. 9-27. There is insufficient stress on family recreation today.

Fig. 9-28. Chess as a recreational activity in Milwaukee.

Courtesy Division of Municipal Recreation and Adult Education
Milwaukee Public Schools.

cope with such needs and problems, which include the communicative arts, knowledge of psychology, and other allied areas.

The recreation leader must have respect for the human personality; a broad social viewpoint; the desire to inculcate a high standard of moral and spiritual values; a recognition of the needs, interests, and desires of individuals; an appreciation of the part that recreation can play in meeting these needs and interests; and a desire to serve humanity.

A special need exists to understand and appreciate community structure and the place of recreation at the grass roots level of this structure. The ability to use scientific survey techniques and other methods of social research is also an essential qualification.

Recreation skills are necessary; however, they should not be limited to games and sports but should branch out into such areas as arts and crafts, dramatics, camping and outdoor education, music, social recreation, and other important aspects of the total offering.

The philosophy of recreation, with the importance of constructive leisure time activities to human beings, should be understood. In addition, special knowledge, attitudes, and skills concerned with methods and materials, safety, first aid, principles of group work, health, juvenile delinquency, and crime prevention are necessary.

Recreation positions and areas of recreation service. Recreation positions for which the aspiring student can prepare and areas where recreation service may be rendered include the following:

Recreation positions

Superintendent of recreation
Assistant superintendent
Recreation director
Consultant
Field representative
Executive director
Hospital recreation supervisor
Campus recreation coordinator
Extension specialist

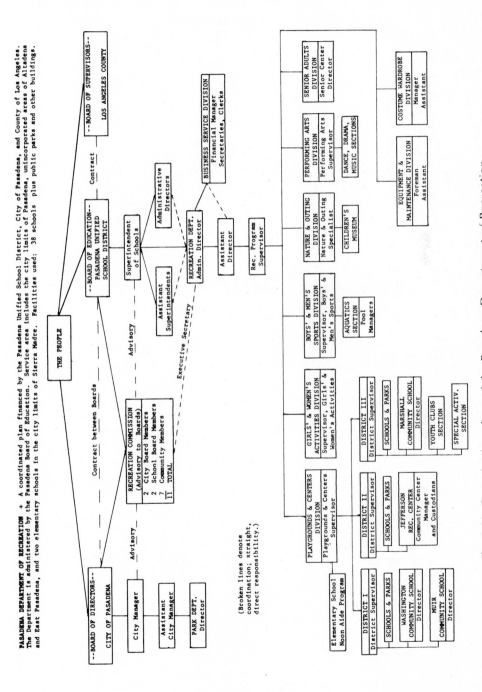

Fig. 9-29. Organization chart of the Pasadena Department of Recreation, Pasadena, Calif.

Service club director
Girls' worker—boys' worker
District recreation supervisor
Recreation leader
Supervisor of special activities
Recreation therapist
Recreation educator

Areas of recreation service

Community recreation departments
Park departments
Schools
Service clubs for the armed forces
Churches and religious organizations
Hospitals
Institutions—public and private
Voluntary youth-serving agencies
Rural
Colleges and universities
Industry
State and federal agencies

Community and school outdoor environmental education and camping programs

A commitment to outdoor education has steadily increased in recent years. A variety of methods have been used to stimulate better use of the immediate school environment for educational purposes.

In Michigan, a junior high school was developed for environmental education. The school site includes a courtyard with plantings and a waterfall. A greenhouse opens into the science classrooms.

In California, a school has created a nature trail and a playground area with observation towers.

In an inner city area of Washington, D.C., the students of an elementary school and local residents developed an abandoned lot and converted it into an outdoor environmental laboratory.

These are only a few of the projects that concerned

TEN GUIDELINES FOR THE ADMINISTRATION OF SCHOOL RECREATION*

1. The acceptance and commitment of the administration regarding the role of recreation in education.
2. The establishment of a representative ad hoc committee by the Board of Education to survey recreational needs and interests in the school district. Appropriate funds should be provided for the routine services for such a committee, including secretarial and consultant services.
3. The appointment of a qualified professional staff member, preferably the school district director of health, physical education, and recreation, to serve as coordinator of the study and liaison to the ad hoc committee.
4. The conduct of the study by the committee to determine the status of organized recreation in the school district. This should include: a review of the understanding and philosophy of people in the school district regarding recreation; existing recreational services available.
5. Arranging for technical, professional, consultant services in recreation through recognized agencies for the purpose of appraising the findings of the survey in terms of quality recreation for the school district.
6. Develop, in cooperation with the professional consultant, a proposed plan of recreation for the school district. Such a plan should include a statement of philosophy, principles, policies, procedures, and a financial plan.
7. A review of the ad hoc committee plan by the Board of Education and administration.
8. The acceptance or modification of the plan by the Board of Education.
9. The ratification of the plan and the adjustment of general school district administrative policies to appropriately provide for recreation.
10. The administrative implementation of recreation as officially adopted by the Board of Education, with emphasis on clear communication.

*New York State Department of Education, Albany, N.Y.

Fig. 9-30. Play and recreation are important aspects of a healthy regimen for students. Students at Florissant Valley Community College in St. Louis have opportunities for recreation at the pool table.

Photograph by LeMoyne Coates.

citizens, teachers, and students have helped develop. Both the urban and rural school offer numerous opportunities for outdoor education experiences.

The outdoors is nature's laboratory, a setting that offers excellent opportunities to gain knowledge and skills and to develop wholesome attitudes. Experiments and research have shown that students who use nature's classroom will be more interested and learn more readily those things that directly relate to the outdoors.

Outdoor education and school camping are not synonymous. Outdoor education includes school camping. The camp provides a laboratory in which many facets of the outdoors can be studied firsthand. And the camp experience helps develop qualities that prepare young people for the future.

SETTINGS FOR OUTDOOR ENVIRONMENTAL EDUCATION

The American Alliance for Health, Physical Education, and Recreation lists the following significant settings for outdoor environmental education activities.*

1. *School sites and adjacent areas.* The trees, shrubs, streams, ponds, and outdoors in general offer many opportunities to develop outdoor laboratories that can be used for experiences related to such areas as science, social studies, arts and crafts, and physical education.

*American Association for Health, Physical Education, and Recreation: Leisure and the schools, Washington, D.C., 1961, The Association, p. 108.

2. *Parks, forests, and farms.* Most communities have parks, farms, or other available outdoor areas nearby that can be used for outdoor education.

3. *School farms.* School farms are being developed in some communities and are providing agricultural experiences and a variety of learning situations that revolve around rural living. Such farms offer opportunities for studying birds, animals, conservation, gardening, milk production, home management, care of farm machinery, and community life.

4. *School forests.* School forests or nearby municipal, county, state or national forests provide excellent outdoor education settings. School experiences relating to art, music, conservation, forestry, zoology, shop, archery, shelter construction, fire protection, camp crafts, and hiking can be provided.

5. *School and community gardens.* The opportunity to till the soil and see plants grow can be provided in school and community gardens.

6. *Museums and zoos.* An opportunity to study animals, collections of historic materials, works of art, and other important aspects of our culture is provided by museums and zoos.

7. *School camps.* Camps, either day or extended, offer opportunities for group living, work experience, development of outdoor skills, and many other experiences important to a well-rounded education.

VALUES OF OUTDOOR ENVIRONMENTAL EDUCATION AND SCHOOL CAMPING

The values of outdoor environmental education and school camping are evident as a result of the many experiments that have been conducted throughout the United States. The values of such experiences are threefold: (1) they meet the social needs of the child, (2) they meet the intellectual needs of the child, and (3) they meet the health needs of the child.

A camping experience is an essential part of every child's school experience because it helps the child develop socially. In a camp setting, children learn to live democratically. They mix with children of other creeds, national origin, color, economic status, and ability. They help plan the program that will be followed during their camp stay; they assume part of the responsibility for the upkeep of the camp, such as making their own beds, helping in the kitchen, sweeping their cabins, and fixing the tennis courts; and they experience cooperative living. The children get away

from home and from their parents. They lose their feeling of dependency on others and learn to do things for themselves. They learn to rely on their own resources. The camp also provides an enjoyable experience. Children are naturally active and seek adventure. Camping provides the opportunity to release some of this spirit of adventure and to satisfy the wanderlust urge.

A camping experience is an essential part of every child's school experience because it helps the child develop intellectually. While living in a camp, young people learn about soil, forests, water, and animal and bird life. They learn about the value of the nation's natural resources and how they should be conserved. They learn of ecology, the science concerned with the interrelationship between living organisms and their environment and between organisms themselves. They learn by doing rather than through textbooks. Instead of looking at the picture of a bird in a book, they actually see the bird chirping on the branch of a tree. Instead of reading about soil erosion in a textbook, they see how it actually occurs. Instead of being told about the four basic groups of food, they live on a diet that meets the right standards. Instead of reading about the value of democratic living, they actually experience it. They engage in many new activities they cannot possibly do at home or within the four walls of a school building. Camping is especially valuable to children who do not learn easily from books. In many cases the knowledge accumulated through actual experience is more enlightening and beneficial.

Camping is an essential part of every child's school experience because it helps meet the health needs of the child. Camps are located away from the turmoil, confusion, noise, and rush of urban life. Children have their meals at a regular time, get enough sleep, and participate in wholesome activity outdoors. They wear clothing that does not restrict movement, that shields from the sun, and that they are not afraid to get dirty. The food is good. They do things that are natural for them to do. It is an outlet for their dynamic personalities. It is more healthful, both physically and mentally, than living in a push-button existence, with its lack of recreation, relaxation, and opportunity for enjoyable experiences. It is like living in another world, and children come away refreshed.

Fig. 9-31. The annual regatta sponsored by the Youth Services Section, Los Angeles City Schools.

Fig. 9-32. Babysitting as a recreational study activity—a 3-week series of sessions on caring for infants and young children sponsored by the North Castle County Department of Parks and Recreation, Wilmington, Del.

Fig. 9-33. Feeding the animals is one of the outdoor education experiences provided young children at Oak Ridge Farm.

Courtesy Milwaukee Public Schools, Division of Municipal Recreation and Community Education.

Fig. 9-34. Outdoor environmental education experiences meet many needs of the child. Children in outdoor education program at Brea Canyon Camp sponsored by the Youth Services Section of the Los Angeles City Schools.

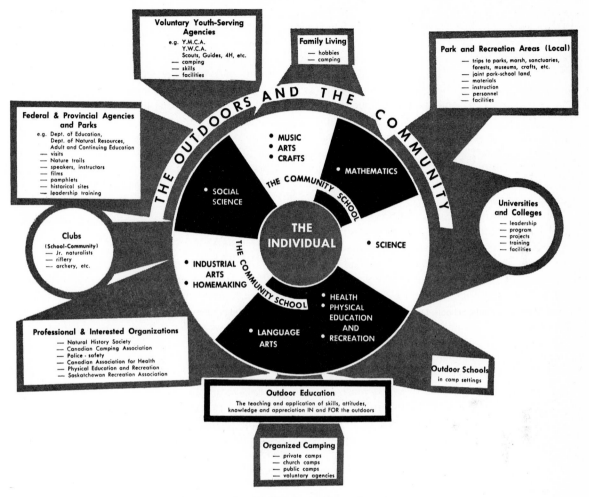

Fig. 9-35. The world of outdoor education.

From MacKenzie, J.: Saskatchewan Community
14:4, 1963-1964.

THE FUTURE OF OUTDOOR ENVIRONMENTAL EDUCATION

Outdoor education holds great promise for the future. In the future it will become available to more people. Communities will become more involved in outdoor education, and government funding for special projects will be increased.

Schools in the near future will also look to their staff members to develop outdoor education programs. Teachers will take inservice courses that will help them develop excellent outdoor education programs.

Outdoor education has numerous advantages; one of the most significant is providing a greater understanding of the environment and its problems. In this time when pollution, ecological disruption, and the energy crisis are important national and world considerations, understanding contributed by outdoor education programs is invaluable.

CAMPS

Camping has grown in popularity until today there are numerous camps located in nearly every section of the country, and over 20,000 camps throughout the nation. These are operated by cities, counties, and states; by social agencies such as churches, schools, and settlements; by youth-serving agencies such as the YMCA, YWCA, YMHA, YWHA, Boy Scouts, Girl Scouts, Campfire Girls, 4-H Clubs, and Boys' Clubs of America; by employer and labor organizations; and by private individuals and corporations. Some camps are operated for profit, whereas others work on a nonprofit basis. Some are open only during the summer months, others during the spring, summer, and fall, and others all year. Some are for children, others for adults, and still others for adults and children. Some are day camps, whereas others operate seasonally. Some are for just one sex, and others are corecreational. Tennis, football, basketball, baseball, horseback riding, and other activity camps have been opened to provide a place for the young person interested in developing further skill in a particular sports activity.

The program in most camps consists of such sports activities as swimming, boating, fishing, horseback riding, tennis, badminton, hiking, horseshoes, basketball, and softball; such social activities as campfires, frankfurter and marshmallow roasts, dancing mixers, and cookouts; and opportunities to develop skills and an appreciation in arts and crafts, photography, Indian lore, drama, music, and nature study.

The educational aspects can include a variety of experiences. Some of these are campfires, outdoor cooking, woodcraft, campsites, canoeing, conservation, astronomy, birds, animals, indoor and outdoor gardening, fishing, hiking, hunting, and orienteering.

Some states have passed legislation making tax money available to the schools for camping programs. This trend in state provisions for camping in the public schools means that more and more opportunities are going to be made available for children to have this worthwhile experience. For example, in Michigan a bill was passed several years ago providing that boards of education, with the exception of those in primary school districts, could operate camps independently or jointly with other boards of education or governing bodies for recreation and instruc-

tion. Provision was made for charging fees, if necessary, to cover expenses incurred in maintaining the camp. However, these camps are to be run on a nonprofit basis. Provisions were also made for boards of education to employ personnel to operate these camps, to maintain essential facilities, and to locate camps on property other than that owned by the board of education, provided the consent of the owner of the property had been secured. Finally, a provision was made stipulating that the cost of operating a school camp should not be included in the determination of per capita costs of the regular school program.

Community service organization programs

Many service organizations such as the YMCA, American Red Cross, settlement houses, Boy Scouts, Girl Scouts, Boys' Clubs of America, and American Youth Hostels, Inc., have programs that involve physical education activities, and these organizations frequently employ physical educators.

These service organizations serve the people of various communities where they have been established, both the young and the adults. Religious training, physical training, and other goals are objectives of these organizations. Physical activities are an important part of most of their programs. Classes in various physical activities; athletic leagues and contests for industries, churches, young people's groups, and boys' and girls' groups; and camping programs are a few of the activities organized and administered by these voluntary agencies. The cost of financing such organizations is usually met through membership dues, community chest drives, and contributions of private individuals.

These organizations are designed to improve society members physically, morally, mentally, and spiritually through their programs of physical activity. Usually these agencies have directors for the physical activities who have received specialized training in their field. Many organizations have complete staffs of trained physical education personnel who aid in organizing and administering the programs.

Fig. 9-36. Outdoor education is fun and healthful.

OUTDOOR EDUCATION

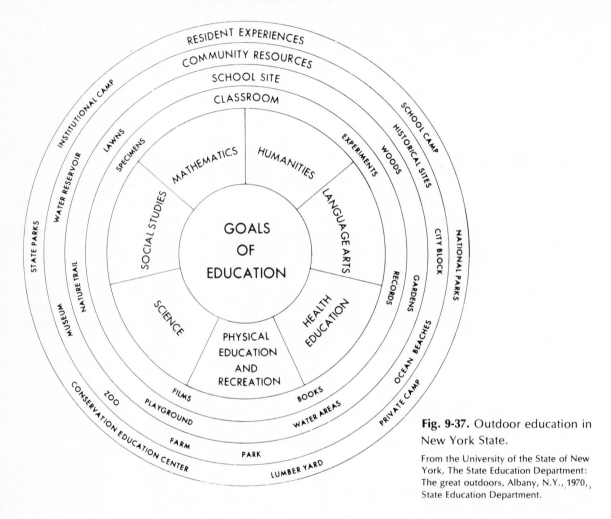

Fig. 9-37. Outdoor education in New York State.

From the University of the State of New York, The State Education Department: The great outdoors, Albany, N.Y., 1970, State Education Department.

SELF-ASSESSMENT TESTS

These tests are to assist students in determining if material and competencies presented in this chapter have been mastered:

1. What economic, political, social, and religious factors in a community can have an impact on physical education and related programs? Discuss how these factors influence these programs.

2. Prepare sets of guidelines you would follow if you were asked to administer an industrial fitness program, a health club, and a center for the aged.

3. Define the term *recreation*. What kinds of recreation programs are there? How are they administered? Why should physical educators be interested in recreation programs?

4. Prepare a set of administrative guidelines for conducting a community recreation program.

5. In what way can outdoor environmental education contribute to ecology?

6. To what extent is camping a popular activity in communities throughout the United States?

7. List 10 community service organizations and indicate the role physical education activities play in each.

SELECTED REFERENCES

Bannon, J.J.: Leisure resources—its comprehensive planning, Englewood Cliffs, N.J., 1976, Prentice-Hall, Inc.

Britton, J.H., and Britton, J.O.: Personality changes in aging; a longitudinal study of community residents, New York, 1972, Springer Publishing Co., Inc.

Bucher, C.A.: Foundations of physical education, ed. 9 St. Louis, 1983, The C.V. Mosby Co.

Bucher, C.A., and Bucher, R.: Recreation for today's society, Englewood Cliffs, N.J., 1974, Prentice-Hall, Inc.

Bucher, C.A., and Engelbardt, S.: Exercise: it's plain good business, Reader's Digest, February 1976.

Bucher, C.A., and Thaxton, N.: Physical education and sport: change and challenge, St. Louis, 1981, The C.V. Mosby Co.

Bucher, C.A., et al.: The foundations of health, Englewood Cliffs, N.J., 1976, Prentice-Hall, Inc.

Commission on Goals for American Recreation: Goals for American recreation, Washington, D.C., 1964, American Association for Health, Physical Education, and Recreation.

Cooper, K.H.: The new aerobics, New York, 1970, M. Evans & Co., Inc.

Donaldson, G.W., and Donaldson, A.: Outdoor education: its promising future, Journal of Health, Physical Education, and Recreation 43:23, 1972.

Donnely, K.: Current trends in commercial recreation, Journal of Health, Physical Education, and Recreation 44:33, 1973.

Dustin, D.L., and Rentschler, G.J.: Magical outcomes of organized camping, Journal of Physical Education and Recreation, **51**:46, 1980.

Getchell, B.: Physical fitness: a way of life, New York, 1976, John Wiley & Sons, Inc.

Goldstein, J.: Environmental education for teachers, Journal of Healthy, Physical Education, and Recreation **44**:38, 1973.

Ibrahim, H., and M.F.: Leisure: an introduction, Los Alamitos, Calif., 1977, Hwong Publishing Co.

Johnson, W.R., and Buskirk, E.R., editors: Science and medicine of exercise and sport, New York, 1974, Harper & Row, Publishers.

Kraus, R.G.: Recreation today—program planning and leadership, Santa Monica, Calif., 1977, Goodyear Publishing Co., Inc.

Kraus, R.G., and Bates, B.J.: Recreation leadership and supervision; guidelines for professional development, Philadelphia, 1975, W.B. Saunders Co.

Larson, L.A., editor: Fitness, health, and work capacity, New York, 1974, Macmillan, Inc.

Linck, D.B.: Outdoors at grassroots, Journal of Physical Education and Recreation 52:48, 1981.

President's Council on Physical Fitness and Sports, Washington, D.C. 20201. (Many different publications are available on such topics as industrial fitness and fitness for aging.)

Report of the Second National Conference on School Recreation: Twentieth century recreation, re-engagement of school and community, Washington, D.C., 1963, American Association for Health, Physical Education, and Recreation.

Sinacore, J., and Sinacore, A.: Introductory health: a vital issue, New York, 1975, Macmillan, Inc.

Smith, N.W.: Community involvement through a curriculum study project, Journal of Physical Education and Recreation **52**:16, 1981.

Stark, S.L., and Parker, B.E.: A viable partnership: community education and parks and recreation, Journal of Physical Education and Recreation 52:17, 1981.

Weiskopf, D.C.: A guide to recreation and leisure, Boston, 1975, Allyn & Bacon, Inc.

Wilson, G.T.: Evaluating the results of community recreation, Journal of Physical Education and Recreation 51:53, 1980.

PART FOUR

Administrative functions

10

Personnel administration and supervision

Instructional objectives and competencies to be achieved

After reading this chapter the student should be able to

- Understand the need for personnel policies.
- State the basic principles underlying effective personnel administration.
- Summarize the qualifications needed by physical educators who work in such settings as educational institutions, health clubs, industrial fitness programs, centers for the aged, and youth-serving agencies.
- Trace the process for recruitment, selection, orientation, and in-service training of new staff members.
- Discuss the subject of supervision, including the qualities needed by supervisory personnel, the role of group dynamics in the supervisory process, and the basic principles that should guide effective supervisory working relationships with staff members.
- Describe various methods of evaluating physical educators and other personnel in physical education programs.

Personnel administration originally was mainly concerned with selecting, placing, and retaining people who were staff members of an organization. Today, however, personnel administration has taken on a more mature connotation. It does not involve manipulating people to get them to produce as much as possible. Instead it involves the entire organization and the procedures by which the organization can best achieve its goals. Recruitment, selection, morale, and other considerations become the responsibility not only of the administration but of all staff members. As a result, it depends on various individuals and groups understanding and accepting each other and working closely together to achieve the organization's goals.

The nature of personnel administration and supervision is changing. Students, faculty, and employees are participating more in administrating and supervising. Administrators and supervisors are consulting with staff members before making final decisions on curriculum, scheduling, evaluations, and working conditions. Administrators are also being required to negotiate with unions in collective bargaining sessions. Administration and supervision are no longer unilateral prerogatives but increasingly cooperative endeavors involving students, faculty, and staff.

For all these reasons personnel administration and supervision are perhaps the most challenging responsibilities of an effective leader. A leader who does not have the cooperation of his or her personnel will have great difficulty in implementing any decision or policy.

Personnel policies

The administration with the help of staff members should see that a detailed list of personnel policies is developed. These policies should be sound, up to date, and consistent with the best thinking on personnel management. Furthermore, these policies,

Fig. 10-1. Students and faculty are participating more in administering and supervising in today's physical education and athletic programs.

Courtesy Smith College, Northampton, Mass.

after careful thought and deliberation, should also be put into writing and be made available to all staff members and administrators to whom they apply. Selected areas that should be covered by personnel policies include assignments, promotions, separations, evaluation, hours of work, compensation, fringe benefits, absences, leaves, travel, in-service training, and conduct on the job.

Principles of personnel and supervisory administration

Productive personnel administration and supervision do not just happen. They occur only as a result of adhering to a prescribed set of basic principles.

COOPERATION

To achieve cooperation the specialties and unique abilities of individuals must be noted and used when their services will be most effective. The permanence of cooperation will depend on the degree to which the purposes of the organization are achieved and individual motives are satisfied. The function of administration and supervision is to see that these essentials are accomplished.

THE INDIVIDUAL AS A MEMBER OF AN ORGANIZATION

Administration and supervision should seek to imbue the organization with the idea that every individual has a stake in the enterprise. The undertakings can be successful only if all persons contribute to the maximum of their potential and with success bringing satisfaction to all. Submergence of self is necessary for the achievement of the organization's goals.

THE FALLACY OF FINAL AUTHORITY

The existing authority belongs to the job and not to the person. The administrator and supervisor should never feel powerful and all-important. Authority does not reside in one human being but in the best thinking, judgment, and imagination the organization can command. Each individual has the authority that goes with his or her position and only that much. In turn, this authority is conditioned by other members whose work is closely allied to achieving the objectives for which the organization exists. Authority comes from those who perform the more technical aspects of the organization's work, as well as from those who, because of their positions, are responsible for ultimate decisions. Department heads and staff consultants issue reports interpreting the facts. Their judgments, conclusions, and recommendations contribute to the formulation of the final decisions, which are the responsibility of the administrator. If these interpretations, judgments, conclusions, and recommendations are not accepted, the organization may fail. Its best thinking has been ignored. Furthermore, individuals cannot be induced to contribute their efforts in an organization that has little respect for their thinking. Authority permeates the entire organization from top to bottom.

STAFF MORALE

The administration should continually strive to create conditions that contribute to staff morale. The degree to which high staff morale exists will be in direct proportion to the degree to which such conditions are satisfied.

Leadership. The quality of the leader will determine staff morale to a great degree. From the top down, there should be careful selection of all leaders. Other things being equal, individuals will contribute better service, produce more, have an overall better morale, and have more respect for individuals who are leaders in the true sense of the word.

Physical and social environment. A healthful physical and social environment is essential to good staff morale. The physical health of the worker must be provided for. There must also be provisions for mental health that include proper supervision, opportunity for advancement, emergency plans, and avenues for intellectual improvement.

The social environment is also an important consideration. The individuals with whom one works and the activities in which one engages can strengthen or dampen the human spirit. An individual is the product of his or her interactions with others. Therefore, to improve oneself, it is important to associate with those who can contribute to this improvement. Because the working day represents, to a great degree, the majority of an individual's social relationships, it is important that these relationships be wholesome and conducive to individual improvement.

Advancement. Human beings like to feel that they are getting ahead in the world. To develop and continue high staff morale, each member of an organization must know what is essential for progress and promotion. Opportunities should be provided for learning new skills, gaining new knowledge, and having new experiences. Encouragement should be given those who are anxious to improve and are willing to devote extra time and effort to this end.

Recognition of meritorious service. All human beings need to be recognized. Those who make outstanding contributions to the organization should be so honored. This is important to further greater achievements.

Individual differences. An important principle of personnel management is recognizing individual differences and different types of work. Individuals differ in many ways—abilities, skills, training, and physical, mental, and social qualities. There are also various types of work that require different skills, abilities, and training. These differences must be recognized by the administrator, who must make sure that the right person is in the right niche. An individual who is a round peg in a square hole does not contribute to his or her own or the organization's welfare. To be placed in a position that should be held by a person with lesser qualifications or vice versa is unjust and devastating.

It is important for the administrator and supervisor to recognize formally individual differences existing in the organization. To develop efficient communication, a sense of responsibility, and the basis for personnel improvement and advancement within the organization, such status systems must be readily understood, authoritative, and authentic. The status granted any one person should be in line with the capacities and importance of the function he or she performs. Many disruptive features can develop in status systems if there is no recognition of individual abilities, if the system is allowed to become an end rather than a means to an end, and if proper incentives are not provided at each level.

Differentiated staffing. Administration must recognize staff members' interests, talents, and general suitability for each position. Teachers should be assigned activities where they demonstrate particular skills. Schools are also employing staff members to perform specialized tasks, such as paraprofessionals, activity specialists, interns, teachers, teacher aides, clerks, custodians, and equipment and facility managers.

Personnel recruitment and selection

Personnel recruitment and selection are important functions of administration and management. They include a consideration of the general qualifications of physical educators and the special qualifications for teaching and working in health clubs, industrial fitness centers, and other agencies. Orientation and in-service training are also responsibilities that go with staff recruitment and selection.

GENERAL QUALIFICATIONS FOR PHYSICAL EDUCATORS*

The most important consideration in administration is personnel. The members of an organization determine whether it will succeed or fail. Therefore the administration must recognize the following qualifications of physical educators.

The physical educator should be a graduate of an approved training institution that prepares persons for physical education. The college or university should be selected with care.

Because physical education is based on the foundation sciences of anatomy, physiology, biology, kinesiology and biomechanics, sociology, psychology, and research, the physical education leader should be well versed in these disciplines.

The general education of physical educators is under continuous scrutiny and criticism. Speech, knowledge of world affairs, mastery of the arts, and other educational considerations are important in the preparation of the physical educator. Because the position requires frequent appearances in public, communication skills are essential.

Physical education work is strenuous and therefore demands that members of the profession be in buoyant, robust health to carry out their duties with ef-

ficiency and regularity. Physical educators are supposed to build healthy bodies. Therefore they should be good testimonials for their teachings.

Many moral and spiritual values are developed through participation in games and other physical education activities. It is essential, therefore, that the physical educator stress fair play, good sportsmanship, and sound values. His or her leadership should develop a recognition of the importance of high moral and spiritual values.

The physical educator should have a sincere interest in physical education: one must enjoy teaching, participating in the activities, helping others realize the thrill of participation and becoming physically fit, and encouraging citizenship traits conducive to democratic living. Unless the individual has a firm belief in the value of his or her work and a desire to help extend the benefits of such an endeavor to others, he or she will not be an asset to the profession.

The physical educator should possess an acceptable standard of motor ability. To be able to teach various games and activities to others, it is necessary to have skill in many of them. The physical educator must enjoy working with people, for there is continuous informal association when teaching physical education activities. The values of such a program will be greatly increased if the physical educator elicits happiness, cooperation, and a spirit of friendship.

The qualifications for teachers of physical education to be certified in New Jersey are listed in the box on p. 346.

SPECIAL QUALIFICATIONS FOR TEACHING

Several persons were interviewed concerning the qualities and characteristics they thought existed in the best teachers to whom they were exposed. A list of those qualities mentioned most frequently follows:

1. Teacher knew the subject matter well.
2. Teacher took a personal interest in each student.
3. Teacher was well respected and respected the students.
4. Teacher stimulated the students to think.
5. Teacher was interesting and made the subject matter come to life.

---

*Qualifications for physical education administrators, athletic directors, and coaches can be found in Chapters 3, 5, and 6.

6. Teacher was an original thinker and creative in his or her methods.
7. Teacher was a fine speaker, presented a neat, well-groomed appearance.
8. Teacher had a good sense of humor.
9. Teacher was fair and honest in dealings with students.
10. Teacher was understanding and kind.

Beginning teachers need considerable encouragement and help. The administration should be aware of these needs and work to ensure that they are met. A survey of 50 teachers indicated the following problems of beginning teachers:

1. Difficulties arising from a lack of facilities
2. Large size of classes, making it difficult to teach effectively

3. Teaching assignments in addition to the primary responsibility of teaching health education or physical education
4. Discipline problems with students
5. Conflicting methods between what the beginning teacher was taught in professional preparing institution and established patterns of experienced teachers
6. Clerical work—difficulty in keeping records up to date
7. Problems encountered in obtaining books and supplies
8. Problems encountered in obtaining cooperative attitude from other teachers
9. Lack of departmental meetings to discuss common problems
10. Failure to find time for personal recreation

Fig. 10-2.

Paraprofessional in physical education program at Regina High School, Minn., takes attendance and keeps all records for program.

Photograph by Rollie Baird, Dellarson Studios.

PHYSICAL EDUCATION

Authorization

This certification is required for teaching physical education in elementary and secondary schools. (Health education shall be included in this authorization if the curriculum contains at least eighteen semester-hour credits in this field.)

Requirements

I. A bachelor's degree based upon a four-year curriculum in an accredited college
II. Successful completion of *one* of the following:
   A. A college curriculum approved by the New Jersey State Department of Education as the basis for issuing this certificate

Or

   B. A program of college studies including:

General background

1. A minimum of thirty semester-hour credits in *general background* courses distributed in at least three of the following fields: English, social studies, science, fine arts, mathematics, and foreign languages. Six semester-hour credits in English and six in social studies are required.

Professional education

2. A minimum of eighteen semester-hour credits in *professional education* courses distributed over four or more of the following groups, including at least one course in each starred area. A maximum of three semester-hour credits will be accepted in health education. These eighteen credits do not include student teaching.

   *Methods of teaching physical education in elementary and secondary schools.

   *Educational psychology. This group includes such courses as psychology of learning, human growth and development, adolescent psychology, educational measurements, and mental hygiene.

   *Health education. A maximum of three semester-hour credits will be accepted in this area. This group includes such courses as personal health problems, school health problems, nutrition, health administration, and biology.

   Curriculum. This group includes such courses as principles of curriculum construction, the high school curriculum, a study of the curriculum in the field of specialization, and extracurricular activities.

   Foundations of education. This group includes such courses as history of education, principles of education, philosophy of education, comparative education, and educational sociology.

   Guidance. This group includes such courses as principles of guidance, counseling, vocational guidance, educational guidance, research in guidance, and student personnel problems.

Student teaching

3. One hundred and fifty clock hours of *approved student teaching*. At least ninety clock hours must be devoted to responsible classroom teaching; sixty clock hours may be employed in observation and participation. This requirement is in addition to the eighteen credits in professional education.

Specialized field

4. A minimum of forty semester-hour credits in the *field of specialization*, distributed among the following areas and covering both the elementary and secondary fields:

   Anatomy, physiology, kinesiology

   Coaching, development of personal skills, nature and function of play

   History, principles, and organization and administration of physical education

   Materials and methods in physical education for the elementary grades and materials and methods in physical education for the high school

   Health education including personal and community hygiene, first aid, and safety

Fig. 10-3. Future coaches at the Tuskegee Institute, Ala.

SPECIAL QUALIFICATIONS FOR PHYSICAL EDUCATORS IN OTHER SETTINGS

The physical educator who seeks employment in settings other than schools and colleges needs to possess the general qualifications listed and, in addition, the special training and qualifications needed for work in the agency or area where he or she seeks employment. For example, a physical educator who seeks employment in an industrial executive fitness program should have as much preparation as possible in exercise physiology, because many of the duties will involve helping assess the physical status of executives and planning and supervising programs to develop and maintain an optimum state of physical fitness in employees. It would also be helpful to be familiar with the various types of exercise equipment that are used in these programs. If the physical educator plans to seek a position in the employee recreation program in industry, he or she should have a wide variety of skills in activities that will interest adults. Furthermore, special qualifications will be needed in program planning, scheduling, facility maintenance, public relations and promotion, conducting various types of tournaments, and physical fitness evaluation.

To be successful in such settings as health clubs, nursing homes, centers for the aged, and youth-serving agencies, it is important to know the characteristics and needs of the special population being served.

For example, a physical educator working with the elderly must understand senior citizens—their lifestyles, interests, needs, physical fitness status, and the activities and programs that will contribute to their well-being.

In a health club one must be able to assess, as far as a physical educator is qualified, the physical fitness of the patrons, analyze this assessment, advise patrons of their remedial physical needs, and then supervise their fitness programs.

GUIDELINES FOR STAFF RECRUITMENT

Several guidelines regarding the recruitment of qualified personnel follow:

1. A job description should be prepared for the position that includes the various duties and qualifications the position requires. These items should be spelled out in detail, including such things as the title of the position, a list of specific duties involved, salary, and educational and experience requirements. In addition, it is a practice to declare that the organization is an Equal Opportunity Employer.
2. Notices of the position vacancy should be widely distributed, within the organization itself and to professional programs and placement offices in colleges and universities, respected leaders and colleagues in the field, and professional organizations such as the AAHPERD. Some organizations also advertise such positions in newspapers and professional journals.

Fig. 10-4. Play leaders receiving leadership training in Milwaukee.

Division of Municipal Recreation and Adult Education, Milwaukee Public Schools.

3. Members of the administration can also obtain excellent recommendations through personal contacts with professional colleagues in other institutions and agencies and through people who know of persons who have outstanding qualifications for such positions. Furthermore, confidential information that cannot be obtained in writing can be secured through a phone conversation.
4. Candidates for the position should be asked to send their credentials, including college transcripts, confidential references (or persons who can be contacted by the employing organization), and a record of work and professional experiences.
5. A file should be prepared on each candidate being considered.

GUIDELINES FOR SELECTION

Guidelines for the selection of personnel follow:

1. Many organizations have a search or personnel committee that recruits and interviews candidates for vacancies and makes recommendations to the administration.
2. The search, personnel, or other committee or individual should review the files of all candidates, select the three to five best prospects for the position, and then invite them for a personal interview.
3. Persons within the organization who apply for the position should be evaluated according to the same criteria applied to candidates from outside the organization.

4. The personal interview offers an opportunity to see the candidate firsthand and to discuss the position with him or her. During a personal interview it is important to assess the candidate's personality, character, education, experience, and qualifications. Questions asked might revolve around his or her interest in the position, qualifications, understanding of the employing organization, involvement in professional activities, and background experience and preparation.
5. Based on personal interviews and a further examination of credentials, a recommendation should be made to the administration that includes either one name or more than one name, giving the administration the prerogative to select the best-qualified person.

ORIENTATION OF THE NEW STAFF MEMBER

The staff member who has been employed needs considerable orientation and help in adjusting satisfactorily to the new position. Therefore the administration should provide guidance and assistance during the first days on the job. Help should be provided, if needed, with housing, transportation, and getting settled. An orientation to the organization through a tour of the facilities and meeting with key personnel is necessary. A social hour might be held for a person and his or her family to become better acquainted with the people in the organization. The first staff

Fig. 10-5. These future leaders of physical education will attempt to realize the values that can be achieved from highly competitive athletics.

Courtesy Tuskegee Institute, Ala.

meeting also offers an opportunity to introduce the new staff member to the group.

The administration will want to discuss and clarify the new staff member's duties and responsibilities. Furthermore, the new member should know the person to whom he or she is responsible, as well as the lines of communication within the organization and any protocol that should be observed. The new person will have many questions; these should be expected and taken care of. Salary and fringe benefits should be further clarified. Proper orientation will result in a happier and more productive member of the organization.

IN-SERVICE TRAINING

Staff members need periodic in-service training to keep abreast of their profession. Changes are taking place continually. New methods of teaching, programming, and evaluating have implications for physical education. Physical educators should weigh these innovations carefully and incorporate them into their programs. The public expects physicians, lawyers, architects, and other professionals to incorporate the latest techniques and knowledge into their practice, and physical educators should do the same.

Some suggestions for in-service training include the following:

- Conducting workshops for staff members in which new trends and developments in physical education are examined
- Urging consultants and professional colleagues who are specialists in facilities, curriculum development, methods, activity skills, and visual aids to meet with staff members to discuss these new developments
- Encouraging staff members to take graduate courses in their fields of specialization
- Developing a professional library with the latest books and periodicals in physical education and making them readily accessible to staff members
- Devoting some staff meetings to discussions of new developments in physical education
- Encouraging staff members to attend professional meetings and, if possible, subsidizing some of the costs
- Using staff members with special talents to upgrade the knowledge and competence of other staff members
- Providing preschool or summer orientation sessions for staff members
- Conducting research and experimentation within one's own program in such areas as facilities and methods

Supervision

Supervisory leadership, among other requirements, must recognize each individual staff member and the contribution he or she makes to the organization, see that staff members are assigned to tasks in line with their abilities, be willing to delegate responsibility, establish high, attainable standards, provide a complete analysis of each position in the organization, establish accountability for each staff member, and help each member to feel a sense of accomplishment.

Supervision will be effective if sound leadership is provided for the organization.

QUALITIES OF THE SUPERVISOR WHO IS A LEADER

In the last 30 years research has indicated that some beliefs or certain qualities indicate who leaders are, that leaders are born and not made, and that some people will lead and others will follow. These statements are not exactly true. Instead, personal characteristics must be related to the characteristics of the followers because of the interaction of the two. The identification of qualities of certain individuals as leaders without relating these qualities to the persons they are going to try to lead has little meaning.

Stogdill* studied the relationship of personality factors to leadership and found that the leader of a group exceeds the average of the group regarding such characteristics as intelligence, scholarship, acceptance of responsibility, participation, and socioeconomic status.

Berelson and Steiner† surveyed the scientific findings in the behavioral sciences and formulated the following propositions and hypotheses relating to leadership:

1. The closer an individual conforms to the accepted norms of the group, the better liked he will be; the better liked he is, the closer he conforms; the less he conforms, the more disliked he will be.
2. The higher the rank of the member within the group,

the more central he will be in the group's interaction and the more influential he will be.
3. In general, the "style" of the leader is determined more by the expectations of the membership and the requirements of the situation than by the personal traits of the leader himself.
4. The leadership of the group tends to be vested in the member who most closely conforms to the standards of the group regarding the matter in question or who has the most information and skill related to the activities of the group.
5. When groups have established norms, it is extremely difficult for a new leader, however capable, to shift the group's activities.
6. The longer the life of the leadership, the less open and free the communication within the group and probably the less efficient the group in the solution of new problems.
7. The leader will be followed more faithfully the more he (she) makes it possible for the members to achieve their private goals along with the group goals.
8. Active leadership is characteristic of groups that determine their own activities, passive leadership of groups whose activities are externally imposed.
9. In a small group, authoritarian leadership is less effective than democratic leadership in holding the group together and getting its work done.

Other studies that provide pertinent information on leadership include those of Myers,* Hemphill,† Homans,‡ and Halpin.§

The physical educator who desires to exercise a leadership and supervisory role in an organization should study the administrative theory reflected in the research studies available on supervision. This will help assure success as a leader in any particular situation.

The physical educator should also recognize that

---

*Stogdill, R.M.: Personal factors associated with leadership, a survey of the literature, Journal of Psychology **25:**63, 1948.

†Berelson, B., and Steiner, G.A.: Human behavior; an inventory of scientific findings, New York, 1964, Harcourt Brace Jovanovich, Inc., pp. 341-344.

*Myers, R.B.: The development and implications of a conception for leadership education, unpublished doctoral dissertation, University of Florida, 1954.

†Hemphill, J.K.: Administration as problem solving. In Halpin, A.W., editor: Administrative theory in education, Chicago, 1958, Midwest Administration Center, University of Chicago.

‡Homans, G.C.: The human group, New York, 1950, Harcourt Brace Jovanovich, Inc.

§Halpin, A.W.: A paradigm for the study of administrative research in education. In Campbell, N.R., and Gregg, R.T., editors: Administrative behavior in education, New York, 1957, Harper & Row, Publishers.

various personal qualities are essential for providing supervisory leadership. These personal qualities include a sense of humor, empathy, sensitivity, feeling of adequacy, ability to win confidence and respect, enthusiasm, originality, sincerity, and resourcefulness. Supervision requires the ability to assist staff members to see their own strengths and weaknesses, provide assistance in helping them to solve problems, resolve its personnel conflicts, improve morale, and judge objectively personal performance and make recommendations for promotions and other rewards. To accomplish these tasks the supervisor must be able to promote staff development, create effective channels of communication, establish accountability, set goals, and provide adequate rewards.

GROUP DYNAMICS

Group dynamics are important in supervision. They are concerned with understanding the nature and role of groups in modern living. As used in this text, they are considered in light of the supervisory role in physical education programs. Research has revolved around the structure of groups, how groups operate, the relationships of members within a group and between groups, the factors that affect group attitudes and productivity, and what types of leadership are most effective in varying group relationships.

Physical educators can benefit from a study of group dynamics because they work with various groups of people in their programs, and they are interested in getting groups to enter and participate in their activities and support their programs. Teamwork is essential when working with other professional groups, and administrators and supervisors must work closely with various groups both inside and outside the organization.

Shaw* has noted the following research approaches to the study of groups:

Formal models research: theoretical models of the structure and behavior of groups are developed.
Field theory: the behavior of groups and individuals within a group results from many interrelated and interdependent phenomena.

Sociometric research: the choices of the group on an interpersonal basis among members of the group play a major role.
Systems approach: the group is viewed as a structure of interlocking elements, and group inputs and outputs are analyzed.
Psychoanalytic approach: the factors that groups and individuals use for motivation and defensive actions form the basis for investigation.
Empirical approach: groups are observed with observations recorded and statistical procedures used to develop basic concepts and guidelines regarding group decisions.

According to Hemphill and Westie,* research has shown that supervisors must understand certain factors concerning groups in order to work effectively with them. These factors include an understanding of the group's *autonomy* in working with other groups, the *control* the group has over its own members, the *flexibility* of the group's activities (whether they are informal or highly structured), and the *hedonic tone* or satisfaction derived by members of the group as a result of such group association. Other factors include *homogeneity*, the characteristic similarities of members of the group; *intimacy*, whether or not members of the group have a close relationship with each other; *participation*, the degree to which members actively participate in group activities; *permeability*, the ease of access to membership to the group; *polarization*, group orientation to one goal subscribed to by all members; *potency*, significance of the group to its members; *stability*, durability and stability of the group; and *stratification*, the structure of the group as it affects the status of its members.

Shaw† suggests the following five reasons why groups are effective:

1. Group performance provides increased motivation over individual performance.
2. Judgments of group are superior to individual ones that involve random error.
3. Groups usually produce better solutions to problems than do persons working alone.

*Shaw, M.E.: Group dynamics; the psychology of small group behavior, New York, 1971, McGraw-Hill Book Co.

*Hemphill, J.K., and Westie, C.: In Hilton, B.L., and Reitz, H.J., editors: Groups and organization, Belmont, Calif., 1971, Wadsworth Publishing Co., Inc.
†Shaw, op. cit.

Fig. 10-6. The poorly coordinated child getting considerable personal attention from the teacher in physical education class at the Hudson Falls Central School, Hudson Falls, N.Y.

4. Groups are able to learn faster than individuals by themselves.

5. More new and different ideas are generated by both individuals and groups where there is an absence of critical evaluation.

An understanding of group dynamics can enhance the physical educator's role in the supervisory process. It is an evolving area that has great potential for increasing the productivity and interpersonal relationships of any organization.

SUPERVISORY WORKING RELATIONSHIPS WITH STAFF

Effective working relationships between supervisors and staff members may be discussed under the headings of (1) responsibilities of supervisors, (2) responsibilities of staff members, (3) common points of conflict, and (4) checklist for effective working relationships.

Responsibilities of supervisors

1. *Supervisors should possess a sound understanding of human nature to work effectively with people.* Physical educators should not look on supervising as impersonal but should always keep in mind human

dimensions and give human problems high priority.

2. *Supervisors should understand their own behavior.* They should see conflicts where they exist and not fabricate them where they do not exist. They should give an accurate account of group expectations although they may not be in agreement with them. They should recognize the differences and rationale between their own views and those of other people.

3. *Supervisors should exercise wisely the authority vested in their positions.* The authority goes with the office and not with the person. Supervisors should recognize that the position exists to further the goals of the organization. It should never be used for personal reasons.

4. *Supervisors should establish effective means of communication among members of the organization.* Opportunities should be readily available to discuss personal and professional problems, new ideas, and ways to improve the effective functioning of the organization.

5. *Supervisors should provide maximum opportunity for personal self-fulfillment.* Each person has a basic psychological need to be recognized, to have self-respect, and to belong. Within organization require-

ments, supervisors should make this possible for every member of the organization.

6. *Supervisors should provide leadership.* Supervising requires leadership qualities that bring out the best individual effort of each staff member and a total coordinated effect working toward common goals.

7. *Supervisors should provide clear-cut procedures.* Sound procedures are essential to the efficient functioning of an organization; therefore they should be carefully developed, thoroughly discussed with those concerned, written in clear, concise language, and then followed.

8. *Supervisors should plan meaningful meetings.* Staff meetings should be carefully planned and efficiently conducted. Meetings should not be called on impulse or dominated by the supervisor. Plans and procedures agreed on should be carried out.

9. *Supervisors should recommend promotions only on the basis of merit, without politics or favoritism.* Recommendations for promotions, when requested, should be arrived at through careful evaluation of each person's qualifications and objective criteria.

10. *Supervisors should protect and enhance the mental and physical health of staff members.* In carrying out this responsibility, the supervisor should attempt to eliminate petty annoyances and worries that can weigh heavily on staff members, increase the satisfactions each person derives from the organization, promote friendly relationships, develop an esprit de corps, improve respect for the social status of staff members, and establish a climate of understanding that promotes good will.

Responsibilities of staff members

1. *Physical educators should support the total program.* Each staff member must see his or her responsibility to the program. This means serving on committees, attending meetings, contributing ideas, and giving support to worthy new developments regardless of the phase of the program to which he or she belongs. Also, staff members should view their own fields of specialization in proper perspective with the total endeavor.

2. *Physical educators should take an interest in supervision* by participating in policy making and decision making, role playing the problems and pres-

sures faced by the supervisor, and contributing ideas that will help cut down on red tape and thus streamline the process.

3. *Physical educators should carry out their individual responsibilities with dispatch.* If each job is performed effectively, the total organization will function more efficiently.

4. *Physical educators should get their reports in on time.* Purchase requisitions, attendance, excuse and accident reports, and the multitude of other forms and reports that have to be completed and then collated in the supervisor's office must be done on time. Punctuality makes supervising easier.

5. *Physical educators should be loyal.* Each staff member has the responsibility to be loyal to his or her organization. There can be disagreement about the supervision, but loyalty to the leaders and the organization is essential.

6. *Physical educators should observe proper protocol.* Administrators and supervisors do not appreciate a staff member going over their heads to a higher authority without their knowing about it. There are lines of authority that must be recognized and followed in every organization.

7. *Physical educators should be professional.* In relationships with colleagues, supervisors, or the general public, a staff member should recognize that there is a professional way of behaving. Confidences are not betrayed, professional problems are ironed out with the people concerned, and personality conflicts are discussed with discretion.

COMMON POINTS OF CONFLICT BETWEEN SUPERVISORS AND STAFF MEMBERS

Areas where poor working relationships occur include the following:

- The failure of supervisors to recognize physical education as a vital subject
- The existence of authoritarian and undemocratic supervision
- The failure to clarify goals and responsibilities for the organization and for each member of the organization
- The failure of supervisors to provide dynamic leadership
- The failure of supervisors to provide clearly defined procedures

Fig. 10-7. Supervisory personnel should provide maximum opportunity for personal self-fulfillment. A supervisor working with students and teachers at Tuskegee nstitute, Ala.

- The practice of supervisors encroaching on classes and schedules without good reason or adequate previous announcement
- The assignment of unreasonable work loads and assignments
- The failure of staff members to read bulletins that contain important announcements
- The failure of supervisors to assume conscientiously the duties and responsibilities associated with supervision
- The existence of unsatisfactory working conditions
- The lack of adequate materials, supplies, and equipment

Personnel problems requiring special attention

Selected personnel problems needing special attention are teacher burnout, unionism, affirmative action, and use of certified and noncertified personnel.

TEACHER BURNOUT

Teacher burnout has been defined by one person as ''a physical, emotional, and attitudinal exhaustion.'' More stable school and college faculties, shrinking employment opportunities, austere budgets, back-to-

basics movements, public criticism, lack of community support, heavier teaching loads, accountability, discipline problems, and inadequate salaries are a few of the conditions resulting in teacher burnout.

Some teachers are tired of their work and the many educational problems they face. As a result, in many cases the students are being shortchanged and the teachers are complacent, dissatisfied, restless, and suffering emotionally and sometimes physically.

What can be done to cope with teacher burnout? How can teachers who are suffering from it be helped? What procedures will result in self-renewal for teachers? More important, how can teacher burnout be prevented?

Many suggestions have been made for eliminating and avoiding teacher burnout. They are listed here so beginning teachers and those on the job will be familiar with ways to avoid it or, if already afflicted, can find a cure for it.

Langlois* has found that fitness is the answer. She has initiated faculty fitness classes at her college that have paid dividends in eliminating and avoiding teacher burnout.

---

*Langlois, S.: Faculty fitness: a program to combat teacher burnout, Update, March 1981.

Crase* suggests the following activities as antidotes to teacher burnout and complacency: reassess teaching technologies, reevaluate curricular offerings, participate in visitations and exchange programs, participate in structured learning experiences, become involved in professional organizations, reassess reading habits, contribute to professional publications, develop quest for new knowledge, get involved in local service functions, and explore additional development opportunities.

Wendt† implies that change may help in avoiding teacher burnout.

Austin‡ lists several possible solutions: use holidays and vacations for personal and professional revitalization, change the way material is taught, transfer to another school, play a new role within the educational structure, find a job outside education, or participate in in-service education.

UNIONISM

Unionism is widespread and administrators, teachers, and other staff members should understand and be able to work effectively with unions.

The emphasis in physical education over the years has been for professionals to know their professional organizations. The student and administrator are well oriented to these organizations. But how much orientation is there to unionism? It would seem very little, yet teacher, labor, and other unions are calling on physical educators to strike, to agree to binding arbitration agreements, and to give allegiance to union leaders who may or may not act in the best interests of physical education and sports.

There is a need, particularly for administrators, to understand unionism and to be able to work with unions. Some recommendations for administrators to follow if involved with professional negotiations with unions are given by Wood et al.,§ as follows:

---

*Crase, D.: Development activities: a hedge against complacency, Journal of Physical Education and Recreation, **51**:53-54, November/December 1980.

†Wendt, J.: Resistance to change, Journal of Physical Education and Recreation **51**:56, November/December 1980.

‡Austin, D.A.: Renewal, Journal of Physical Education and Recreation **51**:57-59, 1980.

§Adapted from C.L. Wood, E.W. Nicholson, and D.G. Findley, The secondary school principal, manager and supervisor, Copyright © 1979 by Allyn and Bacon, Inc. Used with permission.

1. Recognize that negotiations can be a positive force in the relationship of administrators and staff. Since negotiation is necessary, it should be looked upon as a time to attempt to improve relationships rather than harm such relationships.
2. Perceptive administrators can adjust to negotiations and make the best of their working relationship.
3. A positive result of professional negotiations can be the involvement of greater human resources to advance the organization and to improve its democratic atmosphere.
4. Administrators should insist on being a part of the negotiation process.
5. Administrators should protect their right to be the professional leader of their organizations.
6. Administrators should at all times strive to promote mutual respect, cooperation, and shared decision making in the negotiation process.
7. Administrators should know what their responsibilities are in professional negotiations and these should be spelled out in a written job description. If administrators perform within the responsibilities as stated, they then should receive solid backing from their superiors.

AFFIRMATIVE ACTION

Administrators need to understand and conform to affirmative action guidelines. Among other things, these guidelines indicate that no discrimination can exist on the basis of sex, race, ethnic background, or creed. All individuals must be afforded equal opportunities to achieve their destinies. In hiring personnel, for instance, attention must be given to adequate publicity of vacancies, consideration of all applications, and selection based on each individual's qualifications. There can be no discrimination against minority groups in employment, salary, or promotion. Also, organizations should strive for balance and a representative number of staff members who are, for example, male and female, nonwhite and white, handicapped and nonhandicapped.

Many organizations have individuals whose responsibility it is to promote and oversee the process of equal opportunity within their department, school, or division. Administrators should consult with these individuals periodically to see that affirmative action guidelines are being met. If no such individual exists in an organization, then the administrator should see that proper conditions exist.

Fig. 10-8. The physical educator should have a sincere interest in teaching physical activities. An instructor at Morehouse College in Atlanta works with some youngsters in track.

Courtesy President's Council on Physical Fitness and Sports.

Fig. 10-9. Each individual should be made to feel that he or she belongs to the group and has something to contribute, as shown here in Thornwood High School, South Holland, Ill.

CHECKLIST FOR EFFECTIVE WORKING RELATIONSHIPS AMONG ADMINISTRATORS, SUPERVISORS, AND PHYSICAL EDUCATORS

	Yes	*No*
1. Job descriptions of all personnel are formulated, written, and disseminated to each individual involved.	_____	_____
2. Policies are cooperatively formulated.	_____	_____
3. Staff members are encouraged to participate in the determination of policies. Administration utilizes committees of faculty to develop policies.	_____	_____
4. Policies cover priorities in the use of physical education facilities.	_____	_____
5. Policies have been developed and are in writing for the major areas of the enterprise, as well as specifically for physical education.	_____	_____
6. Departmental policies and procedures are up to date and complete.	_____	_____
7. Board of education establishes and approves policies and programs.	_____	_____
8. Physical educators know the policies for their organization and work within this framework.	_____	_____
9. Open channels of communication are maintained between administrator, supervisor, and staff.	_____	_____
10. In-service education is provided.	_____	_____
11. Staff members are encouraged to participate in the activities of professional organizations.	_____	_____
12. Supervisors act in an advisory and not an administrative capacity.	_____	_____
13. The teaching load of all teachers is equitable in that the following factors are considered: work hours per week, number of students per week, and number after-school activities scheduled.	_____	_____
14. Athletics are open to all students and conducted according to sound educational principles.	_____	_____
15. Policies are in writing and disseminated and cover the organization and administration of interscholastic athletics.	_____	_____
16. Coaches are certified in physical education.	_____	_____
17. The group process is effectively used in staff and committee meetings.	_____	_____
18. There is a strong belief in and a willingness to have a democratic administration.	_____	_____
19. Staff meetings are well organized.	_____	_____
20. New staff members are oriented in respect to responsibilities, policies, and other items essential to their effective functioning in the organization.	_____	_____
21. Departmental budgets and other reports are submitted on time and in proper form.	_____	_____
22. Staff members attend meetings regularly.	_____	_____
23. Staff members participate in curriculum studies.	_____	_____
24. Class interruptions are kept to an absolute minimum.	_____	_____
25. Proper administrative channels are followed.	_____	_____
26. Relationships with colleagues are based on mutual integrity, understanding, and respect.	_____	_____
27. The administration is interested in the human problems of the organization.	_____	_____
28. Maximum opportunity is provided for personal self-fulfillment consistent with organization requirements.	_____	_____
29. Department heads are selected on the basis of qualifications rather than seniority.	_____	_____
30. Staff members are enthusiastic about their work.	_____	_____
31. All personnel are provided opportunities to contribute to the improved functioning of the organization.	_____	_____

Continued.

CHECKLIST FOR EFFECTIVE WORKING RELATIONSHIPS AMONG ADMINISTRATORS, SUPERVISORS, AND PHYSICAL EDUCATORS—cont'd

	Yes	No
32. The school board's executive officer executes policy.		
33. Faculty and staff assignments are educationally sound.		
34. The administration works continually to improve the working conditions of personnel.		
35. Out-of-class responsibilities are equitably distributed.		
36. The administration provides recreational and social outlets for the staff.		
37. The administration recognizes and records quality work.		
38. Physical educators seek to improve themselves professionally.		
39. Physical educators view with proper perspective their special fields in the total enterprise.		
40. Physical educators organize and plan their programs to best meet the needs and interests of the participants.		
41. Health and physical educators continually evaluate themselves and the professional job they are doing in the organization.		
42. Budgetary allocations are equitably made among departments.		
43. The administration is sensitive to the specific abilities and interests of staff.		
44. Physical educators take an active role in planning.		
45. Physical education objectives are consistent with general education objectives.		
46. The administration recognizes and gives respect and prestige to each area of specialization in the organization.		
47. Physical educators are consulted when new facilities are planned in their areas of specialization.		
48. Funds are available for professional libraries, professional travel, and other essentials for a good in-service program.		
49. Physical educators carefully consider constructive criticism when given by the administration.		
50. The administration is skilled in organization and administration.		

Fig. 10-10. The staff member needs considerable orientation and help in adjusting satisfactorily to a new position. Dance class receives the attention of a well-qualified instructor at Tuskegee Institute, Ala.

Fig. 10-11. Staff members need in-service training to keep abreast of their profession, including new techniques for handling underwater equipment.

Courtesy Tuskegee Institute, Ala.

USE OF CERTIFIED AND NONCERTIFIED PERSONNEL

A trend in recent years has been to use noncertified personnel in physical education to teach activities when permanent certified personnel do not have the proper expertise or when work loads have become too heavy for the full-time faculty. The National Association for Sport and Physical Education (NASPE)* has studied this problem and recommends the following

1. The profession recognizes the need to offer new activities into the curriculum in which students and other consumers are interested in participating.
2. The profession should attempt to have regular full time faculty members become qualified to teach new activities. Furthermore, in hiring new faculty attention should be given to applicants who have the qualifications to teach these new activities.
3. During the interim period when no faculty member is available to teach the new activity, non-certified personnel can be hired under such conditions as the following:
   a. The non-certified person has expertise in the activity to be taught.

---

*National Association for Sport and Physical Education: The use of certified and non-certified instructors in the basic physical education instruction program in higher education, Journal of Physical Education and Recreation, **50**:19-22, November/December 1979. Courtesy American Alliance for Health, Physical Education, Recreation, and Dance, 1900 Association Dr., Reston, Va.

   b. Proper supervision is provided for the non-certified person.
   c. An understanding exists that the non-certified person will be replaced when regular full time faculty become qualified to teach the new activities.
   d. The compensation for the non-certified person should be less than that of a regular full time faculty member.

EVALUATION

Administrators and supervisors need to establish methods to measure staff effectiveness to make sound decisions for retention, salary adjustments, and promotion, as well as to help staff members improve.

The administration should encourage a program of evaluation. Staff members need to be helped to improve their own effectiveness. Records should be kept to determine progress.

Some guidelines for evaluating staff members follow:

1. *Appraisal should involve staff members themselves.* Evaluation is a cooperative venture, and staff members should be involved in developing the criteria for evaluation, because they need to understand the process.

2. *Evaluation should be centered on performance.* The job to be accomplished should be the point of focus with extraneous factors omitted.

3. *Evaluation should be concerned with helping staff members grow on the job.* The purpose of evaluation is to help the person evaluate himself or herself and maintain strengths and reduce weaknesses.

4. *Evaluation should look to the future.* It should be concerned with developing a better physical education program and a better organization.

5. *Evaluation of staff members should be well organized and administered.* The step-by-step approach should be clearly outlined.

TEACHER EVALUATION

Fawcett* suggests the following list, which includes some of the broad areas in which a teacher might be evaluated, as a means of initiating an evaluation program.

INTERPERSONAL RELATIONS

Teacher-teacher
Teacher-students
Teacher-parents
Teacher-community
Teacher-administrators

CLASSROOM MANAGEMENT

Setting of classroom goals and individual learning goals for each student
Assignment and acceptance of individual responsibility by each student in the class
Confirmation of desired behavior of students and redirection of undesirable behavior
Exercise of authority to secure necessary decisions in the classroom
Research behavior of the teacher to keep goals and activities of the classroom consistent with the culture
Record-keeping behavior of the teacher essential to the conduct of the classroom
Coordination of the instruction in the classroom not only with other instructional activities of the school but with out-of-school learning experiences of the students
Inclusion of each student in the learning activities of the class
Communication in the classroom not only to make the teacher understand, but to make it possible for each person to share in classroom activities

---

*Fawcett, C.W.: School personnel administration, New York, 1964, Macmillan, Inc. pp. 58-59.

Judgment in the allocation of time and resources to different activities in the classroom

TEACHER-LEARNING

1. Analysis of students:
   Skills
   Attitudes
   Knowledge
2. Presentation of subject matter through:
   Lectures
   Group discussions
   Student research
   Programmed learning
3. Utilization of instructional material and resources:
   Libraries
   Books
   Machines
   Television
   Radio
   Films
   Supplementary materials, organizations, and people of the community
4. Creation of an efficient learning environment through organization of the physical surroundings in the classroom

Some methods of evaluating teachers follow.

1. *Observation of teachers in the classroom or in the gymnasium.* The National Education Association Research Division, in studying this method, reported that the median length of time for the most recent observation was 22 minutes, about 25% of the teachers were notified 1 day in advance that the observation would take place, and about 50% of the teachers reported that a conference followed up the observation with the teacher's performance being discussed and evaluated. Nearly 50% of the teachers reported that the observation was helpful to them.

2. *Student progress.* With this method standardized tests are used to determine what progress the student has made as a result of exposure to the teacher.

3. *Ratings.* Ratings vary and may consist of an overall estimate of a teacher's effectiveness or consist of separate evaluations of specific teacher behaviors and traits. Self-ratings may also be used. Ratings may be conducted by the teacher's peers, by students, or by administrative personnel and may include judgments based on observation of student progress. To be effective, rating scales must be based on such cri-

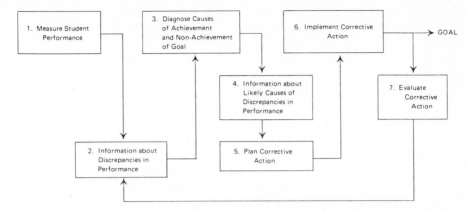

Fig. 10-12. Accountability is a term familiar to all physical educators today. The model of the accountability system.

From McDonald, F.J., and Forehand, G.A.: A design for accountability in education, New York University Education Quarterly **4:**7, 1973.

teria as objectivity, reliability, sensitivity, validity, and utility.

At colleges and universities the evaluation of teacher performance is sometimes more difficult than at other schools because of the unwillingness of the faculty to permit administrators or others to observe them. Various methods have been devised to rate faculty members, including statements from department heads, ratings by colleagues, ratings by students, and ratings by deans and other administrators.

What constitutes effective evaluation as it relates to a teacher in a particular school or college? Several studies have been conducted with some interesting findings. For example, there is only a slight correlation between intelligence and the rated success of an instructor. Therefore, the degree of intelligence a teacher has, within reasonable limits, seems to have little value as a criterion. The relation of knowledge of subject matter to effectiveness appears to depend on the particular teaching situation. A teacher's demonstration of good scholarship while in college appears to have little positive relationship to good teaching. There is some evidence to show that teachers who have demonstrated high levels of professional knowledge on National Teachers Examinations are more effective teachers. However, the evidence here is rather sparse. The relationship of experience to effectiveness also seems to have questionable value.

Experience during the first 5 years of teaching seems to enhance teacher effectiveness but then levels off. There is little, if any, relationship between effectiveness and cultural background, socioeconomic status, sex, and marital status. Finally there is little evidence to show that any specified aptitude for teaching exists. More research needs to be done to establish what constitutes teacher effectiveness on the job.

Innovations in teacher evaluation

With schools plagued by austerity budgets, an excess of teachers, community relations problems, and rural and minority group controversies, teacher accountability has come of age. The community wants to know what the teachers are doing and how well they are doing it. Administrators, students, and parents are demanding standards for teacher performance.

Accountability. Accountability may be simply defined as a means of holding the teacher (and other school or college staff members) responsible for what the students learn. Articles are frequently appearing in newspapers that cite high school students reading at grade levels far below their present grade. Many persons feel that the teachers and administrators should be held accountable for such situations.

"The emphasis behind accountability must be

learning on the part of the students rather than teaching on the part of the teachers."* When the subject matter or method of teaching has become useless, relevant learning cannot take place. For accountability to be valid, curriculum revision must take place to allow for the best possible student progress. Once this has been accomplished (continuous program evaluation is essential), the teacher can direct his or her time and energy toward learning motivation. When an atmosphere of enjoyment is created, learning comes more naturally.

How can accountability be assessed? The first obstacle that must be overcome to have a valid accountability program is the acceptance by educators that certain student objectives must be met. This can usually be accomplished by developing performance objectives. Such tests as the AAHPERD Cooperative Physical Education Tests for major students, distributed by the Educational Testing Service in Princeton, for example, are helpful. Once objectives have been developed, both the student and teacher know what is expected of them. Accountability can be based on how well the students satisfy the stated performance objectives for each unit. Some have suggested that student performance should be a basis for teacher bonuses. This method of accountability has many pros and cons.

Student evaluations. The student is the one most exposed to the teacher and his or her method. Therefore, the student should have some say about whether the teacher is doing a satisfactory job of teaching. Harristhal's study,† devoted exclusively to women physical educators in colleges, was designed to obtain information concerning the desirable characteristics of teachers in a given subject. The following factors were found to be related to teacher effectiveness based on student responses in this study:

1. Subject familiarity
2. Interest in individuals
3. Fairness

4. Patience
5. Leadership that was amicable but firm
6. Enthusiasm
7. Skill in activities

Many teachers are using a student questionnaire for teacher evaluation. The student is asked to respond to multiple choice questions that indicate such items as (1) interest level in activity, (2) skills learned, (3) time spent outside of class on activity, (4) knowledge gained, and (5) rating of instructor regarding understandability of his or her instructions, organization of presentation, enthusiasm, knowledge, skill, and interest in students. There is often a space left for the student to express himself or herself in paragraph form concerning changes in curriculum or teaching methods.

Self-evaluation. An area of evaluation often overlooked is self-evaluation, which is often the key to self-improvement. One should ask himself or herself some of the following questions:

1. Have I been innovative?
2. Do I alter my teaching to meet the different ability levels I encounter?
3. Are my classes planned well in advance to be sure of teaching space, equipment, and facility use?
4. Do I involve all my students in activities?
5. Do I stress cognitive, social, and behavioral objectives?
6. Do I change my activities from year to year and try new concepts such as contact grading, performance objectives, self-directed learning, and resource centers?
7. Do I continually evaluate my activity programs?
8. Do I try to improve myself by continuing my education?

Such questions as these can help the teacher begin to evaluate himself or herself. Self-evaluation is not easy, but can be valuable in improving one's teaching.

Independent evaluators. In recent years there has been a trend toward using independent evaluators, because they may be more objective in assessing a teacher's abilities. Independent evaluators should be thoroughly trained and familiar with the subject they are evaluating and should have a teaching and administrative background. Often evaluators are drawn

---

*Field, D.: Accountability for the physical educator, Journal of Health, Physical Education, and Recreation **44**:37, 1973.

†Harristhal, J.: A student reaction inventory for rating teachers in the college women's physical education service program, Eugene, Ore., 1962, unpublished doctoral dissertation.

Fig. 10-13.

Accountability aims at making sure students learn from their educational experiences. A teacher instructing jazz dancing at El Camino Real High School in Los Angeles Unified School District, Student Auxiliary Services Branch.

Courtesy Gwen R. Waters.

from education consultant groups, education specialists in civil service positions, or university or college professors.

Evaluating the prospective teacher. The competence of the prospective teacher is an important facet of the total educational evaluation system. Traditionally the undergraduate education major was evaluated in terms of grade-point average, completion of required course work, and a minimum grade level in major subjects. Obviously, such evaluation techniques are not sufficient to produce quality teachers. New criteria of assessment must be established to include such factors as (1) comprehensive testing to ascertain mastery of both general and specific knowledge, as well as teacher education objectives; (2) performance testing based on teaching task analysis; and (3) an internship to develop teaching skills.

The prospective teacher should be field oriented, with much of his or her 4 years spent in school or doing school-related tasks. During undergraduate years, the individual should have experience in grading papers, keeping records, individual tutoring, and actual classroom teaching. The teacher who has graduated from such a program and has satisfied the

assessment criteria will be a better teacher and will also have an easier and more enjoyable adjustment to the first few years of teaching.

Performance-based teacher education

The trend today, as has been pointed out earlier in this text, is toward performance-based teacher education. Under this plan the prospective teacher is evaluated, not in terms of courses taken, but in terms of certain competencies (skills, knowledge, abilities) that have been determined essential to satisfactory teaching. The prospective teacher is evaluated by scientific assessment techniques, and the stress is on his or her performance. A major consideration is whether this prospective teacher can change student behavior through his or her teaching.

EVALUATION OF PHYSICAL EDUCATORS IN OTHER SETTINGS

Much of what has been said about the evaluation of teachers of physical education is also true about the evaluation of physical educators who work in other capacities. They are held accountable for the effective performance of assigned duties. This accountability is determined by observing physical educators on the job, by eliciting opinions from persons who have been served by them, and by their productivity. One form of productivity in a commercial establishment, such as a health club, unfortunately, is how many customers are attracted to the organization and the bottom line profit or loss figure for the business.

The main concern of all physical educators wherever they are employed is to do the best job possible, and then evaluation will take care of itself. In other words, one should be enthusiastic, develop as much expertise as possible concerning the position and responsibilities one has, and provide the best service possible to the persons being served. One should also develop good human relations with everyone concerned. If these suggestions are adhered to, the physical educator should not have to worry about the evaluation process; professional advancement will result.

SELF-ASSESSMENT TESTS

These tests are to assist students in determining if material and competencies presented in this chapter have been mastered:

1. Define what is meant by *personnel administration* and *supervision* and the principles you would follow if you were a supervisor of a physical education staff.

2. If you were the employing officer hiring a physical educator in a school, college, health club, or corporation, what qualifications would you look for in the person you desire to employ?

3. Prepare a step-by-step procedure for the recruitment, selection, orientation, and inservice training of a new member of a physical education staff.

4. You are scheduled to be interviewed by a superintendent of schools who is looking for a person to supervise the work of those physical educators who teach at the elementary school level in her school system, During the interview she asks you to state your qualifications for such a position, how you will use group dynamics in the position, and how you plan to work most harmoniously and productively with staff members. Tell your class what you told the superintendent of schools. Then, have the class decide whether or not you were hired for the position.

5. Develop a rating sheet you would use to evaluate the work of a physical educator teaching at the high school level, and a health club or industrial physical fitness employee.

SELECTED REFERENCES

American Association of School Administrators: Profiles on the administrative team, Washington, D.C., 1971, The Association.

Austin, D.A.: Renewal, Journal of Physical Education and Recreation **51**:57-59, November/December 1980.

Bucher, C.A.: Foundations of physical education, ed. 9, St. Louis, 1983, The C.V. Mosby Co.

Bucher, C.A., and Koenig, C.: Methods and materials for secondary school physical education, ed. 6, St. Louis, 1983, The C.V. Mosby Co.

Bucher, C.A. and Thaxton, N.: Physical education and sport: change and challenge, St. Louis, 1981, The C.V. Mosby Co.

Carter, G.F.: Part-time staffing: a management dilemma, Journal of Physical Education and Recreation **50**:49, January 1979.

Castetter, W.B.: The personnel function in educational administration, New York, 1971, Macmillan, Inc.

Center for the Advanced Study of Educational Administration: Perspectives on educational administration and the behavioral sciences, Eugene, Ore., 1965, The Center.

Clayton, R.D., and Clayton, J.A.: Concepts and careers in physical education, Minneapolis, 1977, Burgess Publishing Co.

Committee on Organizational Pattern: Organizational patterns for instruction in physical education, Washington, D.C., 1971, American Association for Health, Physical Education, and Recreation.

Crase, D.: Development activities: a hedge against complacency, Journal of Physical Education and Recreation **51**:53-54, November/December 1980.

Frith, G.H., and Roswal, G.M.: Teacher aides: a discussion of roles, Journal of Physical Education and Recreation **52**:37, 70, June 1981.

McIntyre, M.: Organization development: a cast study in blockages, Journal of Physical Education and Recreation **52**:71-74, March 1981.

The National Association for Physical Education for College Women and The National College Physical Education Association for Men: Sports in America, Quest, Monograph 27, entire issue, Winter 1977.

National Association for Sport and Physical Education: The use of certified and non-certified instructors in the basic physical education instruction program in higher education, Journal of Physical Education and Recreation **50**:19-22, November/December 1979.

Seker, J.: Are we preparing teachers for the reality of unionism? Journal of Physical Education and Recreation **51**:16, April 1980.

Simon, H.A.: Administrative behavior, New York, 1957, The Free Press.

Sparks, D., and Hammond, J.: Managing teacher stress and burnout, Reston, Va., 1981, American Alliance for Health, Physical Education, Recreation, and Dance.

Wood, C.L., et al.: The secondary school principal—manager and supervisor, Boston, 1979, Allyn & Bacon, Inc.

11

Program development

Instructional objectives and competencies to be achieved

After reading this chapter the student should be able to

- Explain why program development is an important part of the administrative process, and what the program of physical education should accomplish.
- Identify the factors that influence program development.
- Outline a step-by-step process for program development, including the people or groups who will be involved.
- Describe a systems and competency-based approach to program development.
- Discuss significant trends in program development.
- Develop a procedure for evaluating a program.

The term *program development* as used in this text refers to the total learning experiences provided to consumers to achieve the objectives of physical education. It is concerned with all of the component parts of the physical education program, as well as with the resources involved in implementing these learning experiences, such as personnel, facilities, and money. The physical educator is involved with programs in schools, colleges, industry, and other organizations. Today the trend is to provide programs planned in light of such considerations as: (1) the needs and abilities of the consumer, (2) the needs of society, (3) the practical usefulness of various knowledge and skills, and (4) the psychology of learning.

What should the physical education program accomplish?

In brief, the main goals the physical education program should accomplish pertain to four areas. The physical education curriculum should (1) develop physical powers, (2) develop skill in activities, (3) develop an understanding of physical activity, and (4) provide a meaningful social experience.

DEVELOP PHYSICAL POWERS

The physical education program should develop such physical characteristics as adequate cardiovas-cular function, proper body composition, strength, flexibility, body awareness, endurance, muscular power, coordination, speed, balance, accuracy, and proper posture.

DEVELOP SKILL IN ACTIVITIES

The physical education program should develop skill in activities such as movement fundamentals, fundamental activities (running, jumping, skipping), individual sports, team sports, gymnastics, aquatics, and rhythmic activities such as dance.

DEVELOP AN UNDERSTANDING OF PHYSICAL ACTIVITY

The physical education program should develop an understanding of such things as the contribution of physical activity to physical health (weight control, absence of fatigue, etc.), to biomechanical principles (role of gravity, force, etc.), and to mental health (relief of nervous tension, body image, etc.).

PROVIDE A MEANINGFUL SOCIAL EXPERIENCE

The physical education program should provide for such social goals as the human desire for affiliation with other people, success in play activities, a feeling of belonging, recognition of ability, and respect for leadership and followership.

Fig. 11-1. Developing physical powers is an objective of physical education and athletics.

Courtesy President's Council on Physical Fitness and Sports.

Importance of program development and the role of administration

Program development determines what needs to be learned and achieved and provides the means for seeing that these are accomplished. Because no two persons are exactly alike, there is need for flexibility and for a wide range of experiences that meet the requirements of all individuals.

The administration plays an important part in program planning. The goal of all administrative effort is to provide better teaching, better learning situations, and better experiences and activities to achieve the established objectives. Because new problems constantly arise and unmet needs continue to exist or go unrecognized, there is an urgent need for continuous planning. The administrator provides the required leadership.

Program construction requires the selection, guidance, and evaluation of experiences and activities to achieve both long-term and more immediate goals. It provides for an orderly periodic evaluation of the entire program to make changes whenever necessary. It considers such factors as participants, the community, the organization, existing facilities, personnel, time allotments, national trends, and state rules and regulations. It sets up a framework for orderly progression. It offers a guide to physical education personnel so they are better able to achieve educational goals.

Although program development is in many cases a staff and faculty responsibility, the administration plays a very important role in effecting program reform. The administration assesses the organization's needs and sees that the wheels are set in motion to develop a program meeting the organization's objectives.

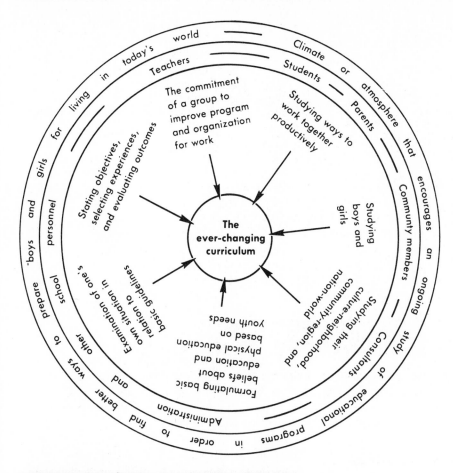

The commitment of a group to improve program and organization for work

Stating objectives, selecting experiences, and evaluating outcomes

Studying ways to work together productively

The ever-changing curriculum

Studying boys and girls

Examination of one's own situation in relation to basic guidelines

Formulating basic beliefs about education and physical education based on youth needs

Studying their culture-neighborhood, community-region, and nation-world

Teachers *Students* *Parents* *Community members* *Consultants* *Study of educational programs* *Administration* *and better ways to find order in to school prepare "boys and girls for living in today's world* *Climate or atmosphere that encourages an ongoing*

Fig. 11-2. The curriculum merry-go-round.

From Cassicy, R.: Curriculum development in physical education, New York, 1954, Harper & Row, Publishers.

People involved in program development

Program planning should be characterized by broad participation of many people. The considerations of administrators, staff members, state groups, consumers, parents and community leaders, and other individuals are important.

ADMINISTRATORS

Administrators are key personnel in program planning. They serve as the catalytic forces that set curriculum studies into motion; the leadership that encourages and stimulates interest in providing better learning experiences; the obstacle clearers who provide the time, place, and materials to do an effective job; and the implementors who help carry out appropriate recommendations of such studies.

STAFF

At the grass-roots level of the program, staff members actually know what is feasible. The staff member can contribute his or her experiences and knowledge and present data to support recommendations of desired changes. Committees are an effective way to use staff members. They can be established to study philosophy, specific instructional areas, pertinent case studies, immediate and specific objectives, needs of participants, means of implementing changes, and the program of evaluation.

STATE GROUPS

Throughout most states are many people and agencies who can help in physical education planning. These include the state department of public instruction or education, the state department of health, colleges and universities, industrial groups, and voluntary health agencies. These groups may provide program guides, courses of study, advice, teaching aids, other materials, and help that will prove invaluable in program planning.

THE CONSUMER

Consumers can play a part in program development. Their thinking in regard to what constitutes desirable activities and methods of instruction, for example, is worthwhile.

PARENTS AND COMMUNITY LEADERS

Discussions with parents and other interested citizens can sometimes help communicate to the public what the school is trying to achieve and how it can best be accomplished. Parents and other community-minded people can make significant contributions in evaluating participant behavior in terms of desired outcomes.

OTHER INDIVIDUALS FROM SPECIALIZED AREAS

Program development should use the services of interested individuals, such as physicians, nurses, recreation leaders, and industrial leaders, who can make a worthwhile contribution by looking at the program from all sides and all angles.

Cooperative planning by people involved in program development

The most effective activities to be considered in cooperative planning of the physical education program include the following:

1. Finding a group of individuals committed to work cooperatively in the study and organization of program-related materials
2. Formulating a philosophy of physical education related to consumer needs and goals
3. Understanding thoroughly the objectives of physical education
4. Analyzing the consumer and the organization in reference to their needs, attitudes, values, and objectives in terms of programs and facilities
5. Designing objectives consistent with consumer needs and general principles of the formulating group

6. Selecting activity units that satisfy the statement of objectives
7. Developing teaching aids and resource materials
8. Developing evaluation techniques and provisions for continuous program assessment

Factors that influence program development

Several factors that directly and indirectly influence program development in physical education include (1) the community; (2) federal and state legislation; (3) research; (4) professional organizations; (5) attitudes of administrators, faculty, students, and consumers; (6) facilities and equipment; (7) scheduling classes; (8) class size; (9) physical education staff members; (10) climate and geographical considerations; and (11) social forces.

THE COMMUNITY

The community has considerable influence on physical education program development. In public schools and other institutions, in particular, where the community provides the funds for the program, there are implications for program development. The community wants to be involved.

Smith[*] indicates the extent of community involvement in Darien, Connecticut public schools. She notes how various groups within this community were involved in a curriculum study project. A task force on physical education was appointed by the board of education consisting of thirteen members who were active in the community and business life. The task force established the objectives they wished to accomplish and the strategy they would use to achieve these goals. The strategy provided for a survey of 600 students in the school system, coaches and staff members, 1000 Darien residents selected from tax rolls, and 40 organizations with a direct or indirect interest in athletics and recreation. Furthermore, the task force established evaluation criteria for program assessment.

The result of this community involvement project

[*]Smith, N.W.: Community involvement through a curriculum study project, Journal of Physical Education and Recreation, **52:**16-17, June 1981.

Fig. 11-3. Dance is an important activity in a physical education program.
Courtesy State University College at Potsdam, N.Y.

Fig. 11-4. A dance class at the State University College at Potsdam, N.Y.

was rewriting curriculum guides for each level of instruction kindergarden to grade six, grades seven through nine, and grades ten through twelve, setting up student advisory boards and student intramural councils, creating a physical education inventory system, appointing faculty manager positions in the secondary school, instituting a full-day in-service workshop for physical education teachers, holding regular meetings with community agencies, and developing a coaches' handbook.

FEDERAL LEGISLATION

Although the governmental authority primarily responsible for education is the state, the federal government is active in shaping educational programs. The Department of Health and Human Services is responsible for recommending many legislative changes in various fields, including education.

Title IX has had a profound effect on educational programs by prohibiting sex discrimination in educational programs. As a result, many school districts have had to revise their curricula to meet the mandate. For example, those schools with separate classes for boys and girls must now have coeducational classes.*

PL 94-142 has also had an effect on school programs in physical education by requiring schools to provide educational services for handicapped students.†

STATE LEGISLATION

The state is the governmental authority primarily responsible for education. Local boards of education are responsible to the state for operating schools in their respective local school districts. They must adhere to the rules and regulations established by state departments of education.

State departments of education set policies concerning credits to be earned for graduation, courses to be included in the curriculum, and the number of days and the amount of time to be spent in class.

In most cases the regulations adopted by state departments of education set minimum standards. Ideal-ly, school administrators will go beyond these minimum standards.

RESEARCH

Although some school districts rely on research to aid them in developing and revising their physical education curricula, too many schools fail to be guided by the latest research in developing their curricula.

Important research studies are being conducted by people in a variety of disciplines that affect curriculum offerings in physical education. An example of the results of research that have influenced physical education curricula are studies relating to the fitness of American children and youths. The results have shown that American children and youths are lacking in many fitness components, and curricula have been revised accordingly to upgrade their physical fitness status.

Relevant research in the social, psychological, and physical sciences, as well as in physical education, should guide physical education program planning. Researchers are investigating motor learning, learning theory, and movement education, and their research has implications for curriculum development in elementary school physical education.

PROFESSIONAL ORGANIZATIONS

National, state, and local professional organizations are constantly engaged in activities that influence physical education programs. Through such activities as workshops, conferences, research, and publications, these organizations provide much-needed information of value in developing curricula.

The AAHPERD, for example, sponsors many national conferences of vital importance to physical education. Research studies, panels, and a general exchange of ideas are presented at these conferences. Also, the AAHPERD on request will suggest knowledgable consultants to work with school personnel in curriculum development and revision.

State and local professional organizations also provide valuable professional information. Individuals responsible for program development and revision should keep abreast of the latest activities of their state and local professional organizations.

---

*For further information on Title IX see Chapters 3, 6, and 7.
†For further information on PL 94-142 see Chapter 4.

Fig. 11-5. Research is an important part of meaningful physical education and athletic programs.

Courtesy Smith College, Northampton, Mass.

ATTITUDES OF ADMINISTRATORS, FACULTY, STUDENTS, AND CONSUMERS

The scope and content of physical education programs are influenced by school administrators and teachers. If physical education is viewed as an integral part of the school program, attempts will be made to provide the necessary support, financial and otherwise, for a quality program. If, on the other hand, it is viewed as extraneous, attempts to create and administer sound programs may be thwarted. The attitudes of teachers and students toward physical education can also affect the kind of program offered.

Physical educators have the responsibility for interpreting the program to students, faculty, the chief school administrator of the district, and the community. A written statement of philosophy and policies should be provided and included in the curriculum guide.

Students' and consumers' attitudes should not be overlooked by program planners. The way students and consumers feel about physical education will influence their participation in the program. A questionnaire written in language that students and consumers can understand is one means of assessing attitudes toward physical education.

FACILITIES AND EQUIPMENT

The provision of adequate facilities and equipment influences the physical education program. Both indoor and outdoor facilities help in providing a quality

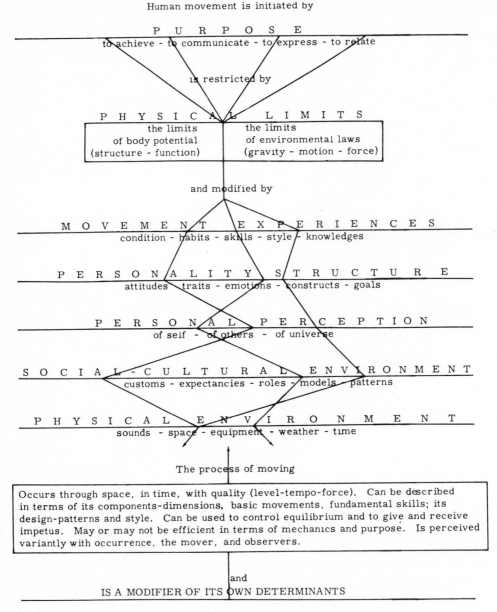

Human movement is initiated by

P U R P O S E
to achieve - to communicate - to express - to relate

is restricted by

P H Y S I C A L   L I M I T S

| the limits of body potential (structure - function) | the limits of environmental laws (gravity - motion - force) |

and modified by

M O V E M E N T   E X P E R I E N C E S
condition - habits - skills - style - knowledges

P E R S O N A L I T Y   S T R U C T U R E
attitudes - traits - emotions - constructs - goals

P E R S O N A L   P E R C E P T I O N
of self - of others - of universe

S O C I A L - C U L T U R A L   E N V I R O N M E N T
customs - expectancies - roles - models - patterns

P H Y S I C A L   E N V I R O N M E N T
sounds - space - equipment - weather - time

The process of moving

Occurs through space, in time, with quality (level-tempo-force). Can be described in terms of its components-dimensions, basic movements, fundamental skills; its design-patterns and style. Can be used to control equilibrium and to give and receive impetus. May or may not be efficient in terms of mechanics and purpose. Is perceived variantly with occurrence, the mover, and observers.

and
IS A MODIFIER OF ITS OWN DETERMINANTS

Fig. 11-6. Movement education, an approach to the study of observable movement, is an objective of many elementary school physical education programs.

From Abernathy, R., and Waltz, M.: Toward a discipline; first steps first, Quest, monograph II, p. 3, April, 1964.

program. The extent and nature of the facilities depend on such factors as the number of students and the geographical location of the school.

CLASS SCHEDULES

The number of periods of physical education provided each week and the length of these periods affect the program. The minimum time for all subjects is set by state departments of education. However, local school administrators can increase the amount of time spent in physical education classes, as in other subjects.

CLASS SIZE

The type of activity being taught and the number of instructors will determine the class size. It is recommended that under normal circumstances the number of children in a physical education class not exceed 30. Classes in adapted physical education should be limited to 20 or less. In school districts where physical education is accepted as an integral part of the school curriculum, class size is kept at a level to promote optimum learning.

PHYSICAL EDUCATION STAFF MEMBERS

The number and qualifications of physical education staff members influence the program. Are there qualified teachers of physical education? Is there a supervisor of physical education to coordinate physical education in the school district? These are important questions because a sound physical education program will depend on the quality of its teaching staff. The faculty of every school should include personnel who have expertise in physical education.

The physical education specialist responsible for physical education should have completed a sequence of courses relating to his or her specialty. Too often physical education specialists with only two or three courses in physical education are assigned to teach or coach in the school program.

CLIMATE AND GEOGRAPHICAL CONSIDERATIONS

The content of the program in physical education is also influenced by weather conditions and the geographical location of the school. Program designers should emphasize the environmental aspects of school locations. For example, many outdoor activities can be scheduled in areas where the weather is normally warm for most of the year, and schools in areas with an abundance of water can stress aquatic activities.

SOCIAL FORCES

Such social forces as the civil rights movement, the feminist movement, automation, mass communication, student activism, and sports promotion have implications for program development. Times change, customs change, habits change, and the role of institutions and their responsibilities to society also change.

Principles to consider in program development

Although program development varies from organization to organization, the following general principles are applicable to all situations:

1. Learning experiences and activities should be selected and developed to achieve desired outcomes.
2. The value of program development is determined by improved instruction and results.
3. Program development is a continuous effort rather than one accomplished at periodic intervals.
4. The leadership in program development rests primarily with administrators and supervisors.
5. The administration should consult (wherever possible and practicable) teachers, laymen, students, participants, state consultants, and other persons who can contribute to the development of the best program possible. The work should not, however place an unreasonable demand on any person's time and effort.
6. Program development depends on a thorough knowledge of the needs and characteristics, developmental levels, capacities, and maturity levels of participants, as well as an understanding of their environments and life-styles.
7. Program development should permit staff members to exploit sound principles of learning when selecting and developing experiences.
8. Physical education should be viewed in its broadest scope and include all programs provided by the physical education department.

Fig. 11-7. Students engaged in dance exercise at the Dow Health and Physical Education Center, Hope College, Holland, Mich.

9. Physical education should be integrated with other subject areas in the organization.
10. Physical education activities should be selected using valid criteria.
11. Program development should be continuous.

Steps in program development

The major steps involved in program development include (1) determining the objectives, (2) analyzing the objectives in terms of the program, (3) analyzing the objectives in terms of activities, (4) providing program guides and teaching aids, and (5) assessing the program.

DETERMINING THE OBJECTIVES

Determining the objectives involves studying such factors as the nature of society, developmental program trends, the learning process, and the needs of the consumer so that objectives may be clearly formulated.

ANALYZING OBJECTIVES IN TERMS OF THE PROGRAM

Having determined the objectives and knowing the characteristics of the consumer, those developing a program can outline and analyze broad categories of experiences and activities and assign relative emphases to the various phases of the process. The specialized fields of physical education and athletics should be viewed as part of the total organizational program. Consequently, their specific objectives should relate to the overall objectives of the organization.

ANALYZING OBJECTIVES IN TERMS OF ACTIVITIES

The next step is to focus attention on the activities needed to achieve the set objectives. Obviously, for example, the physiological needs of the consumer necessitate providing a wide range of physical activities. Growth and developmental characteristics of children and physical capacities and abilities need to be studied in the school.

PROVIDING PROGRAM GUIDES AND TEACHING AIDS

Curriculum and program guides and teaching aids such as books and visual aids offer opportunities to use educationally sound materials to achieve objectives.

ASSESSING THE PROGRAM

Evaluation represents the culmination of the program development process—what actually takes place in the classroom, gymnasium, fitness center, or swimming pool. The learning that takes place, the physical fitness achieved, the aids, methods, and materials used, and the outcomes accomplished determine the success or the failure of program development.

Selected approaches to organizing curriculum experiences

Three approaches that have been used to organize curriculum experiences are the systems, conceptual, and competency-based approaches.

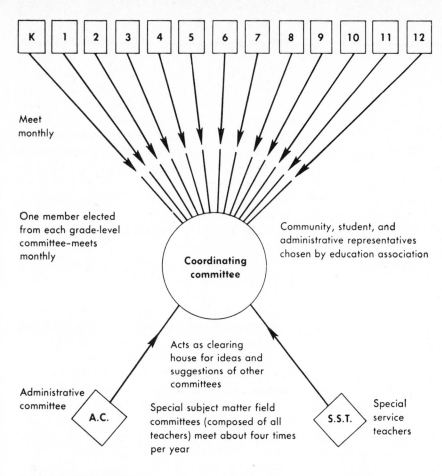

| K | 1 | 2 | 3 | 4 | 5 | 6 | 7 | 8 | 9 | 10 | 11 | 12 |

Meet
monthly

One member elected
from each grade-level
committee–meets
monthly

**Coordinating
committee**

Community, student, and
administrative representatives
chosen by education association

Acts as clearing
house for ideas and
suggestions of other
committees

Administrative
committee

A.C.

Special subject matter field
committees (composed of all
teachers) meet about four times
per year

S.S.T.

Special
service
teachers

Fig. 11-8. Grade-level committees. Purpose of program is to ascertain the needs of children and to devise means of meeting those needs.

From Oliver, A.I.: Curriculum improvement—a guide to problems, principles, and procedures, New York, 1965, Dodd, Mead & Co.

SYSTEMS APPROACH

In recent years many physical educators have tried to develop a more logical means of determining the activities to include in a program. In some cases formulas have been created; in other cases, step-by-step procedures have been developed to match activities to goals. Such methods of program development are encouraging because they represent an attempt to make program development in physical education a more scientific procedure.

A systems approach for developing a physical education program may be helpful to the physical educator because it provides a scientific, logical method for preparing a program of physical education that meets the needs of children and adults. This systems approach to program development comprises the following seven steps:

1. *Identify the developmental objectives* to be achieved in physical education (for example, organic development, skill development, cognitive development, and social-affective development).

2. *Divide each of the developmental objectives listed in the first step into subobjectives.* Identifying the subobjectives brings into sharper focus what needs to be accomplished and makes more manageable the achievement of the developmental objective. The following are examples of subobjectives of each of the developmental objectives:

ORGANIC DEVELOPMENTAL OBJECTIVE

Subobjectives
    Cardiorespiratory endurance
    Muscular strength and endurance
    Coordination
    Balance
    Posture
    Flexibility
    Speed
    Agility
    Accuracy

SKILL DEVELOPMENTAL OBJECTIVE

Subobjectives
    Locomotor and nonlocomotor skills

Movement fundamentals
General motor ability
Specific motor ability in game and sport skills

COGNITIVE DEVELOPMENTAL OBJECTIVE

Subobjectives
Understanding of principles of movement (role of gravity, force)
Knowledge of rules and strategies of games and sports
Knowledge of contribution of physical activity to health
Awareness of contribution of physical activity to academic achievement
Problem-solving ability

SOCIAL-AFFECTIVE DEVELOPMENTAL OBJECTIVE

Subobjectives
Sportsmanship
Clarifying values
Cooperation in group work
Positive attitude toward physical education
Respect for other students and leadership

3. *Identify the characteristics of the participants in terms of each subobjective identified in step 2.* A cardiorespiratory endurance characteristic, for example, of students in grades seven to nine under the developmental objective of organic development is that they tire easily because of their rapid, uneven growth, whereas in grades ten to twelve, students have or nearly have reached physiological maturity and therefore are better equipped to engage in extended vigorous activity.

The characteristics of students at each educational level must be determined in terms of each of the subobjectives identified in step 2. Where pertinent, characteristics of boys and girls should be differentiated. It is now possible to see the relationship between the goals and the specific characteristics of the students.

4. *Determine students' needs in relation to the characteristics outlined in step 3.* For each subobjective, the needs of the students concerned must be identified. For example, a cardiorespiratory endurance characteristic of students in grades seven to nine indicates that they tire easily because of their rapid, uneven growth. Therefore there is a need for physical education experiences that overcome fatiguing factors associated with time, distance, and game pressures. On the other hand, because a characteristic of students in grades ten to twelve is greater physio-

logical maturity, more vigorous activities are required. Students also need guidance related to such items as amounts of activity, food habits, rest, and sleep.

5. *Identify appropriate activities.* For example, the activities scheduled for students in grades seven to nine that meet their needs should include such sports as soccer or field hockey, depending on the school's facilities, using modified rules, including shortened periods of play, smaller playing areas, frequent time-outs, and unlimited substitutions.

6. *List specific performance objectives for the participants in relation to their objectives, characteristics, and needs and the activities appropriate to their age, physical condition, and ability.* For each of the subobjectives, specific performance objectives will be listed. For example, a performance objective for the cardiorespiratory endurance subobjective for seventh to ninth grade students could be: "Given an exercise that measures cardiorespiratory endurance (example, running a quarter mile), the student is able to perform without undue fatigue and with a quick heart rate recovery." A performance objective for tenth to twelfth grade students might be: "The student runs one-half mile and is able to perform without undue fatigue and with a quick recovery of pulse and heart rate." Of course, all performance objectives should consider the characteristics and needs of the specific students in question. Performance objectives provide specific levels of accomplishment that indicate whether the desired goals have been accomplished.

7. *Identify the teaching methods and procedures that will most effectively achieve the desired goals.* These methods provide variety and apply sound motor learning theories (mass versus distributed practice, for example). They reinforce concepts related to accomplishing the objectives (for example, follow-through helps guarantee accuracy, a concept in skill development).

Methods that can be used to develop the subobjective of cardiorespiratory endurance for seventh to ninth graders include a laboratory experiment with conditioned and nonconditioned animals, an explanation of the role and worth of cardiorespiratory endurance in organic development and physical fitness, a discussion of research that outlines the physical fitness status of their age group, and actual participation in activities that develop this endurance, together with an explanation of performance objectives and practice to accomplish them.

The seven-step systems approach to curriculum development provides a logical, scientific, step-by-step method for determining the activities that will achieve the objectives, meet the characteristics and needs of participants, and provide the performance objectives to assess whether or not students have met each objective. A systems approach may provide a meaningful physical education program aimed at helping participants become truly physically educated and making physical education a viable, well-planned offering that achieves specific developmental goals.

CONCEPTUAL APPROACH

During the past two decades many disciplines have instituted major curriculum reforms that emphasize the concept approach to curriculum development. New curriculum models based on the conceptual approach have been designed for mathematics, science, biology, social studies, and health education. Examples are the national School Health Education Study,* and the social studies curriculum developed for the Wisconsin Public Schools.†

In addition to studying national curriculum models, physical education curriculum planners and other educators interested in the conceptual approach to curriculum development should also become acquainted with the theoretical aspects of concept development.

To better understand the conceptual approach to curriculum development a definition of a concept is presented. Woodruff defines a concept as follows:

. . . some amount of meaning more or less organized in an individual's mind as a result of sensory perception of external objects or events and the cognitive interpretation of the perceived data.‡

---

*School Health Education Study: Health education: a conceptual approach to curriculum design, Washington, D.C., 1967, The 3M Press.
†State Department of Public Instruction, Madison, Wisconsin: A conceptual framework for the social studies, Madison, 1964, State Department of Public Instruction.
‡Woodruff, A.D.: The use of concepts in teaching and learning, Journal of Teacher Education **20**:84, March 1964.

According to Woodruff several kinds of concepts can be identified. He indicates that a concept might be a mental construct, an abstraction, a symbolic response, or some other connotation.* It should be added that although a concept might be a high-level abstraction, many concepts might also be presented as concrete, easy-to-understand ideas. For example, Edington and Cunningham† presented and illustrated several concepts related to applied exercise physiology. One specific concept indicated was related to the cardiac response to exercise: the heart rate increases during exercise. It can be illustrated by having students take their resting pulse rate, engage in exercise, and then take their pulse rate again to note the increase as a result of exercise. Another concept was related to energy metabolism whereby the body must provide energy compounds needed for the function of any active tissue. This concept is somewhat more abstract than the first. These and other concepts have been tested and found useful for students at the upper elementary school level.‡ Edington and Cunningham developed several minilessons, each lesson being based on a single concept.

The following example of the concept approach is based on movement activities. It is broken down into the key concept, the concept, and subconcepts. Some conceptual statements are then given.

> *Key concept:* Individual development can be enhanced through movement activities.
> *Concept:* The development of locomotor skills is necessary for effective and efficient movement. These skills are also necessary for later development of competency in specialized sports and other activities.
> *Subconcept:* Sprints and distance running are two specialized forms of one locomotor movement—running.

CONCEPTUAL STATEMENTS

1. Proper techniques and skill in starting are necessary for mastery of sprint running.
2. The ability to understand and carry out the concept of pacing (the idea of running at a gradually increased speed to have enough energy left to sprint the last part of the race) is necessary for distance running.

---

*Ibid, p. 83.
†Edington, D.W., and Cunningham, L.: Applied physiology of exercise: a biological awareness concept, Journal of Health, Physical Education, and Recreation **44**:30-31, October 1973.
‡Edington and Cunningham, op. cit.

3. Proper leg strength is important in sprint running.
4. Proper leg strength, endurance, and cardiovascular-respiratory endurance are important in distance running.
5. A knowledge of the cognitive aspects of concepts related to both sprint and distance running and a proper attitude toward and feeling about running are necessary to the development of these running skills.

COMPETENCY-BASED APPROACH

Competency-based learning has evolved because of a public and professional concern for accountability. Students are taught by means of defined performance objectives based on psychomotor, cognitive, and affective tasks. Students are not in competition with each other but with themselves. The teacher becomes an aid to learning rather than a demonstrator, and each student proceeds at his or her own rate. In addition, resource materials are made available to students to help further their behavioral and cognitive skills.

How competency-based instruction or learning actually takes place can better be understood by reviewing the competency-based instruction at a university in Texas. This program is used in the physical education department with prospective teachers.

In this approach the professor explicitly outlines all factors essential for success in the program. Objectives are thoroughly defined and understood by students entering the program. This helps to focus professor-student effort toward a specific training result rather than toward nonproductive work. Students are tested before entering a particular program to assess those competencies the student already has. Learning units are individualized to suit the needs of each student. Instruction is divided into psychomotor, cognitive, and affective tasks, and students must attain competencies in each. Resource material is available to aid students in attaining competency. At the completion of a unit students are tested for psychomotor, cognitive, and affective performance.

Competency-based learning is also used as a grading method. For example, in a high school in Illinois the performance objectives were written by a group of physical educators and were based on general organic, neuromuscular, emotional, social, and cognitive goals. A competency-based learning unit for fresh-

man gymnastics, for example, was divided into a 10-day introductory unit and a 3-week advanced unit. A lecture and demonstration of the 40 selected gymnastic stunts were presented to the students, followed by an introductory unit in instruction and practice. The grading system for the introductory unit was as follows, based on satisfactory performance as predetermined by the instructor:

16 to 28 stunts = A
10 to 15 stunts = B
6 to 9 stunts = C
3 to 5 stunts = D
0 to 2 stunts = F

The advanced unit required a 3-week, instruction–demonstration period with the students, continuing from the introductory unit. A student who satisfactorily completed 20 to 40 stunts received an A, 16 to 27 stunts a B, and 10 to 15 stunts a C. A performance objective unit was also prepared for sophomores required to take a 3-week unit in soccer.

The committee wrote performance objectives for all activities in the 4-year high school curriculum. The freshmen and sophomores started in the program with teachers who desired to work with the performance objective concept. The initial evaluation was positive for both students and teachers.

Other competency-based programs in physical education have been developed in such places as North Haven, Connecticut (Cripton Project), Florida, Michigan, and Oregon. The Cripton Project curriculum, entitled "Continuous Progress, K-12," consists of a comprehensive set of competencies and provides for student levels of achievement to be assessed periodically and a student profile card that tracks each student's progress throughout his or her school experience. The competencies are grouped into 10 clusters consisting of 44 competency packages.

Selected trends in program development

Some selected trends that administrators should be familiar with in program development are Basic Stuff Series I and II, health-related physical fitness, the wellness movement, mastery learning, movement education, Title IX and PL 94-142, humanistic education, Olympic curriculum, New Games, lifetime sports, high adventure leisure activities, nongraded schools, and accountability.

BASIC STUFF SERIES I AND II*

The National Association of Physical Education and Sport of the AAHPERD has created Basic Stuff Series I and II. The purpose behind this project has been to identify the basic knowledge that applies to physical education programs and organize it in a manner that can be used by physical educators. It is applicable to elementary and secondary school children and youth, a time when the foundations are being laid down for future adult years. It stresses basic concepts presented in simple, concise language, involved with the six areas of exercise physiology, kinesiology, motor learning, psychosocial aspects of physical education (movement), humanities (art, history, and philosophy), and motor development. A pamphlet has been prepared covering the basic concepts in each of the six areas and designed for preservice and in-service teachers. Series I represents the body of knowledge that supports the worth of physical education. The chapters in each pamphlet in the series share a similar organizational format relating to questions asked by students, such as (1) What do you have to help me? (2) How do I get it? (3) Why does it happen this way? Concepts are presented and then the student is shown how it can be best accomplished. It also explains why the concept is valid and works.

In Series II, which has been designed for teachers in the field, examples of instructional activities are provided for early childhood (ages 3 to 8), childhood (ages 9 to 12), and adolescence (ages 13 to 18). The scientific knowledge in the six areas in Series I is related directly to the physical education class and enables the physical education practitioner to have at his or her disposal the basic information and learning activities that will make it possible to educate the students. Such general concepts as how to learn a new skill, how to better one's performance, and the beneficial effects of exercise are identified and then it is

shown how they may be included in activity programs and presented to students by showing them why these concepts are important. This is accomplished by relating the concepts to the motives most children and young people desire for themselves. These motives are health (they want to feel good), appearance (they want to look good), achievement (they want to achieve), social (they want to get along with other people), esthetic (they want to develop esthetic and affective qualities), and coping with the environment (they want to survive). Furthermore, the Basic Stuff Series makes it possible for teachers to tell and show students what concepts are important in physical education and how and why they are important.

Basic Stuff Series I and II have been developed by scholars and teachers who are experts in their particular disciplines. Heitmann* has presented a plan for integrating Basic Stuff Series I and II into curriculum models.

HEALTH-RELATED PHYSICAL FITNESS
(see also pp. 57, 613)

The AAHPERD through its Task Force on Youth Fitness has advocated for the general population the need for health-related physical fitness consisting of an emphasis on cardiovascular function, body composition, strength, and flexibility. These components also represent the ingredients for performance-related fitness. Curriculum designers will want to keep health-related and performance-related fitness in mind in developing programs for various segments of the population. Pate and Corbin† have indicated some implications for curriculum development in physical education of health-related physical fitness.

THE WELLNESS MOVEMENT

The emphasis today on the wellness movement has implications for curriculum development in physical education. The trend today is toward an emphasis on seeing how humans can stay well and fit. Self-help

---

*Basic Stuff Series I and II may be ordered through AAHPERD Publications, P.O. Box 870, Lanham, MD 20801.

*Heitmann, H.M.: Integrating concepts into curricular models, Journal of Physical Education and Recreation **52**:42-45, February 1981.

†Pate, R., and Corbin, C.: Implications for curriculum, Journal of Physical Education and Recreation **52**:36-38, January, 1981.

Fig. 11-9. Students walking on stilts in the Oakview Elementary School physical education program at Fairfax, Va.

medicine is the answer. People need to follow a personal health regimen and adopt a life-style that stresses fitness. Physical activity, physical fitness, and physical education programs thus have an increased value and importance for all segments of the population. Curriculum designers in physical education should therefore take the wellness movement into consideration in developing their programs.

MASTERY LEARNING

Mastery learning is based on the assumption that nearly all students and other people can master material if they are given sufficient time and the material is presented in an understandable way. The procedure followed in places where it has proved successful is that material is presented to an entire group of persons. Then an evaluation is conducted and those persons or students who have not mastered the material are given a second chance. The material is presented again but in a different way and in a more understandable manner. Mastery learning operates under the assumption that there are few failures—everyone succeeds. Curriculum designers should take this new development into consideration in developing physical education programs.

MOVEMENT EDUCATION
(see also pp. 59, 60, 62-65, 322)

Movement education has been of value in elementary school physical education programs. Therefore it should be seriously considered by physical educators developing curricula for elementary school children. A discussion of movement education is presented in Chapter 3.

TITLE IX AND PL 94-142

Chapters 4 and 7 discuss at length Title IX and PL 94-142 and the manner in which they affect curriculum development in physical education. Because these are federally mandated laws, physical educators must abide by them.

HUMANISTIC EDUCATION

Change is needed in our society to humanize our schools and other organizations so students and other persons feel a sense of identity and belonging and are actively involved in the decision-making processes that affect them. Physical education curriculum designers need to be concerned with humanization and involvement processes.

Fig. 11-10. Title IX provides that women cannot be discriminated against in various sports and physical education activities. Women's varsity athletics has a large following at College of DuPage, Glen Ellyn, Ill., which offers women opportunities in volleyball, football, swimming, tennis, softball, basketball, and gymnastics.

OLYMPIC CURRICULUM*

The education committee of the United States Olympic Committee has prepared booklets designed to incorporate the ideals associated with the Olympic Games into the curriculum of several subjects in elementary, junior high, and senior high schools. One of the subjects in which these Olympic concepts can be taught is physical education. Curriculum designers will want to review these booklets and determine if this material should be a part of their program.

NEW GAMES

New Games represents an innovative approach being used by some physical educators. It is based on such concepts as ''any game can be a new game,'' ''anyone can play,'' ''creating a new game is part of the fun,'' ''we play for the fun of it,'' ''it is the process of finding a game that we will want to play,'' and ''we learn about play by playing.'' The New Games organization holds training sessions for individuals interested in learning more about this movement.

LIFETIME SPORTS

There is considerable emphasis today on the importance of including lifetime sports in a physical education curriculum. The term *lifetime sports* refers to sports that can be engaged in throughout a person's life, such as tennis, golf, and swimming. A significant part of the physical education curriculum should be devoted to these activities.

HIGH ADVENTURE LEISURE ACTIVITIES

More people today are engaging in such high adventure leisure activities as skydiving, hang-gliding, and rock climbing. The risks involved in participating in such activities appeal to some individuals who want to be challenged, desire a thrill, and are looking for excitement. It is questionable whether such activities should be a part of any school physical education curriculum. If they are a part of the curriculum in an adult organization other than schools, there should be considerable stress on participants knowing the funda-

mentals of the activity and on their being fit to cope successfully with these activities.

NONGRADED CURRICULA

Nongraded schools are based on the premise that individual differences exist among students. Therefore grade levels are abolished in some subjects, and children with similar abilities study together regardless of their chronological age. For example, a science class might have students ranging in age from 5 to 8 years. A student progresses as rapidly as desired, based on individual potential. The desirability of nongrading in physical education is controversial.

ACCOUNTABILITY

Accountability generally denotes various ways of making persons answerable for their performance. Performance or productivity may be measured by prespecified goals, the outcomes of which must meet certain standards. Accountability in education may include students as well as teachers and administrators.

New curriculum developments for the 1980s

A survey of physical educators indicates what they feel will be curriculum developments in the 1980s. These include the following:

More electives
Individualized learner goals
Interdisciplinary emphasis
Elimination of repetitious content
Relevant course choices for students
Needs of consumer better met
Curriculum reinforced with behavioral objectives
A more relevant curriculum
Curriculum interesting and enjoyable for all students
Recognition of individual abilities
Flexible program
Recreation-oriented program
Greater use of community resources
Stress on individualized curriculum
More coeducational activities
Increased voluntary participation
Greater use of audiovisual aids
Teacher-student-community planning
Emphasis on behavioral change in participants

---

*United States Olympic Committee: The Olympics: an educational opportunity, enrichment units K-6 and enrichment units 7-9, Colorado Springs, Colo., 1981, U.S. Olympic Committee.

The administration and program change

Because so many factors continually influence programs, the physical educator must assess the recommended changes to make informed and wise decisions. Four questions that administrators might ask themselves in evaluating suggested changes follow:

1. *What are the functions of the organization?* How does the suggested change conform to the philosophy and purpose of the organization?

2. *Am I sufficiently well informed so I can make an intelligent decision?* Administrators need to be knowledgeable about the learning process, the patterns of human growth and development, current program needs, and the needs and interests of the people in the local community.

3. *How does the change relate to staff, plant, budget, and other important administrative considerations?* The change must be practical to implement and make the best use of staff and plant.

4. *What do the experts say?* What is the thinking of professionals who have done research, studied the problem intensively, and tested the proposal widely? Expert opinion may be helpful in making a wise program decision.

CONSIDERATIONS IN PROGRAM CHANGE

Program revision cannot occur without considering the following:

1. *Participants.* The number of participants, their characteristics and needs, and their socioeconomic backgrounds and interests need to be considered before initiating any pertinent program change.

2. *Staff members.* Staff members play a key role in program revision. For example, the attitude of the faculty in a school toward change, present teaching loads, comprehension of goals of the school, attitudes toward in-class and out-of-class programs, competencies in curriculum revision, and past training and experience are a few important considerations. Change in curriculum might mean new members being added to the faculty or a different type of competency being represented on the staff.

3. *Physical plant.* The adequacy of the physical plant for present and future programs must be con-

sidered. Information should be available on capabilities and limitations of the present plant. There may be new demands placed on facilities through a program revision that brings about changes in class size.

4. *Budget.* The budget is another important consideration. What will the new program cost? What are the sources of support? Before staff members expend time and effort to study program change, they need reasonable assurance that proposed changes are economically feasible. In systems using PPBS, budgets are formulated considering the objectives of the program; PPBS also provides for evaluation techniques that require curriculum change if goals are not being met.

5. *Program.* Because any new proposal is likely to reflect present practices to some degree, it seems logical that the present program needs careful scrutiny to determine what has happened over the years, the degree to which staff members have brought about change, and the general direction in which the institution is moving.

6. *Administration.* Staff members must take a hard look at the administrative leadership. The philosophy of the administration and its views toward change should be carefully weighed. Administrators will need to approve budgetary allocations and necessary expenditures, as well as pass on the proposed changes.

RESEARCH IN PHYSICAL EDUCATION AND PROGRAM CHANGE

There is an urgent need to advance the frontiers of knowledge in physical education and athletics. There have been too many unsupported claims for the value of physical education. There is a need to determine its worth through valid research findings—basic research that will advance knowledge and applied research that will determine the best ways to use this knowledge.

Many questions are still unanswered, such as: What is the best way to develop physical fitness? What activities are most effective for weight control? How much can retarded children learn? What activities can the employee on the job perform to promote his or her physical fitness? What are the most important biomechanics of human movement? What areas of exercise physiology need the greatest attention and

Fig. 11-11. Men are very much a part of college dance companies, as evidenced here in the University of Mississippi Dance Company.

Photograph by Nelson Neal.

research? What activities are best conducted co-educationally? What is the relationship of personality development to motor performance? What is the relationship of scholastic achievement to physical fitness? What is the therapeutic value of physical activity? What instructional strategies are most effective in mainstreaming?

Evaluation

Once a program has been developed, evaluation is essential to determine the extent to which the experiences provided have produced desirable outcomes for participants. Unless the outcomes are acceptable, the program cannot be considered successful. Essential characteristics of an evaluation program follow:

1. The relationship between program planning and evaluation is recognized and understood by all individuals involved in the program.

2. Changes are based on evaluation techniques and results.
3. All learning experiences are evaluated.
4. Evaluation is primarily concerned with: (a) meeting consumer needs, (b) meeting the objectives of the program, and (c) considering the requirements of parents, staff members, and organization members.

Goodlad* indicates that program evaluation to date has used the following four means to determine the worth of a new program: (1) observing individuals who have been exposed to the new program and the progress they have made, (2) systematic questioning of persons involved in the program, (3) testing participants periodically to determine their progress, and (4) comparative testing of participants under the new and under the old programs to determine progress under each.

*Goodlad, J.I.: School curriculum in the United States.

SUGGESTED OUTLINE OF A SCHOOL CURRICULUM EVALUATION CHECKLIST

The following evaluation checklist for physical education programs suggests methods of assessing curriculum development in this area.

	Yes	No
1. Does the physical education curriculum meet the established objectives?	———	———
2. Does the physical education curriculum provide for the keeping of records to show student progress?	———	———
3. Is evaluation used to help each student in the physical education program find out where he or she is in relation to the program objectives?	———	———
4. Are objective as well as subjective measures used to determine the progress of students in attaining program objectives?	———	———
5. Are the students protected by periodical medical examinations to see if they have health deficiencies?	———	———
6. Does the physical education curriculum provide for the administration of physical fitness tests to evaluate the fitness of each student?	———	———
7. Does the physical education program provide for the testing of skills and use specific ability tests?	———	———
8. Does the physical education curriculum provide for cognitive testing of students?	———	———
9. Does the physical education curriculum provide for the testing of the social adjustment of each student?	———	———
10. Are the attitudes and interests of the students evaluated?	———	———
11. If scientific methods of testing are not feasible, does the physical education curriculum provide for teacher-made tests?	———	———
12. Does the physical education program use test results in planning and assessing units of activity?	———	———
13. Does the physical education curriculum provide for mobility of students based on evaluation results?	———	———
14. Does the physical education curriculum provide for student evaluation as well as teacher evaluation?	———	———
15. Does the physical education program provide for the recognition of curriculum problems and then try to bring about change?	———	———
16. Once change in the curriculum is recognized, is it easy to bring about change?	———	———
17. Is the physical education staff receptive to change?	———	———
18. Is there a provision for ongoing evaluation of programs in reference to satisfying objectives according to an established schedule?	———	———

SELF-ASSESSMENT TESTS

These tests are to assist students in determining if material and competencies presented in this chapter have been mastered.

1. Explain to the class what is meant by program development, the role of the administration in this process, and the ways in which program change occurs.

2. If you were an administrator in a junior high school, what factors would influence the various activities included in your program?

3. You have been assigned to chair a committee to develop a physical education program for a particular school or organization. What people would you select to serve on the committee with you?

4. List and discuss several principles you would observe in developing the curriculum to which you have been assigned in number 3.

5. Trace program development using the systems approach for a high school.

6. You have been hired as a consultant to evaluate a physical education program. Develop a method you will follow in conducting this evaluation.

SELECTED REFERENCES

American Alliance for Health, Physical Education, Recreation, and Dance: Guidelines for secondary school physical education, Reston, Va., 1979, The Alliance.

Annarino, A.A., Cowell, C.C., and Hazelton, H.W.: Curriculum theory and design in physical education, ed. 2, St. Louis, 1980, The C.V. Mosby Co.

Bain, L.L.: Basic Stuff Series, Journal of Physical Education and Recreation **52:**33-34, February 1981.

Bain, L.L.: Socialization into the role of participant: physical education's ultimate goal, Journal of Physical Education and Recreation **51:**48-50, September 1980.

Bonanno, D., Dougherty, N., and Feigley, D.: Competency by contract: an alternative to traditional competency testing techniques, Journal of Physical Education and Recreation **49:**49-51, November/December 1978.

Bucher, C.A., and Thaxton, N.: Physical education and sport: change and challenge, St. Louis, 1981, The C.V. Mosby Co.

Council on Physical Education for Children: Essentials of a quality elementary school physical education program, Reston, Va., 1981, American Alliance for Health, Physical Education, Recreation, and Dance.

Evaul, T.: Organizing centers for the 1980s, Journal of Physical Education and Sport **51:**51-54, September 1980.

Harrington, W., and Enberg, M.L.: Developing competencies: questions and consequences, Journal of Physical Education and Recreation **49:**52-54, November/December 1978.

Heitmann, H.M.: Integrating concepts into curricular models, Journal of Physical Education and Recreation **52:**42-45, February 1981.

Jewett, A.E., and Mullan, M.R.: Curriculum design: purposes and processes in physical education teaching–learning, Reston, Va., 1977, American Alliance for Health, Physical Education, Recreation, and Dance.

Marsh, D.B.: Competency based curriculum: an answer for accountability in physical education, Journal of Physical Education and Recreation **49:**45-48, November/December 1978.

Melograno, V.: Designing curriculum and learning: a physical coeducation approach, Dubuque, Iowa, 1979, Kendall/Hunt Publishing Co.

Melograno, V.: Physical education curriculum for the 1980s, Journal of Physical Education and Recreation **51:**39, September 1980.

Meredith, M.: Expand your program step off campus, Journal of Physical Education and Recreation **50:**21-22, January 1979.

Pate, R., and Corbin, C.: Implications for curriculum, Journal of Physical Education and Recreation **52:**36-38, January 1981.

Robinson, S.M.: Anticipating the 1980s: living and being in physical education, Journal of Physical Education and Recreation **51:**46-47, September 1980.

Rothstein, A.: Basic Stuff Series I, Journal of Physical Education and Recreation **52:**35-37, 46, February 1981.

Sanborn, M.A., and Meyer, C.L.: Curricular constructs and parameters for today's elementary physical education, Journal of Physical Education and Recreation **51:**42-43, September 1980.

Siedentop, D.: Physical education curriculum: an analysis of the past, Journal of Physical Education and Recreation **51:**40-41, 50, September 1980.

Smith, N.W.: Community involvement through a curriculum study project, Journal of Physical Education and Recreation **52:**16-17, June 1981.

Taylor, J.L.: Styles of secondary school physical education curriculum **51:**44-45, September 1980.

Trimble, R.T., and Mullan, M.: Basic Stuff Series II, Journal of Physical Education and Recreation **52:**38-39, 46, February 1981.

Ward, D.S., and Werner, P.: Two curricular approaches: an analysis, Journal of Physical Education and Recreation **52:**60-63, April 1981.

12

Facility management

Instructional objectives and competencies to be achieved

After reading this chapter the student should be able to

- Prepare a list of 10 principles that could be used by an administrator in planning, constructing, and using facilities for physical education and athletic programs.
- List the procedure involved in working with an architect.
- Describe the indoor facilities (type, size, location) needed in physical education and athletic programs, and prepare guidelines for administrators to follow in planning such facilities.
- Describe the outdoor facilities (type, size, location) needed in physical education and athletic programs, and prepare guidelines for administrators to follow in planning such facilities.
- Compute the number of teaching stations needed, given the total number of participants, size of classes, and periods per week.
- Discuss new features and developments in the construction of physical education and athletic facilities.
- Show how to provide facilities that will be conducive to a healthful and safe environment for conducting physical education and athletic programs.

Facility management is a very important administrative responsibility. Physical education and athletics have more facilities than most other educational programs. The planning, scheduling, and maintenance of these facilities is a major function for an administrator, particularly during these current critical times.

Some recent developments have implications for facility management. Moratoriums have been placed on new capital construction in many organizations. The cost of materials and labor is rising as a result of inflation. High interest rates make it difficult to get bond issues passed for facility construction. Title IX requires that facilities must be available to girls, women, and minorities. PL 94-142 and other legislation for the handicapped mandates certain facility changes for the disabled. Energy conservation and costs must be taken into consideration. Community involvement must be given priority in many facility projects.

That little or no money is available in some situations has resulted in alternative methods for seeing that physical education and athletic programs have the necessary facilities to conduct excellent programs. Such methods as renovating existing structures and instituting multiple use of present facilities are being adopted. Where funds are limited, cost-cutting involves following construction plans that are most economical in cost and in the use of energy.

Physical plants require careful planning, and specialists in architectural planning must be consulted. Administrators, physical educators, and other personnel should participate in planning new facilities and be knowledgeable about their structure and functions. Trends and innovative structural concepts should be thoroughly examined to provide a healthful and efficient physical plant.

The physical plant is a major consideration in most physical education, athletic, and recreational programs. New architectural ideas are being introduced and new concepts developed to have a more economi-

Fig. 12-1. Houston's Astrodome.

Courtesy Houston Sports Association, Inc., Houston, Tex.

cal and functional plant. Some building concepts include *convertibility,* for example, rearranging interiors by using movable walls and partitions and using the gymnasium and ampitheater for a variety of activities such as basketball, ice skating, and baseball. Such versatility is needed to accommodate a number of different activities so small and large group instruction and independent study spaces may be provided. This flexibility also ensures such important functions as team teaching and proper installation and use of electronic aids.

Many excellent books are devoted exclusively to facilities for physical education and athletics. Some of these are listed in the references at the end of this chapter. They should be consulted by physical educators who desire a more thorough treatment of this subject.

Planning the facility

At the outset two principles should be prominent in the minds of physical educators in relation to facility management: (1) facilities emanate as a result of program needs, and (2) cooperative planning is essential to avoid common mistakes. The objectives, activities, teaching methods and materials, administrative policies, and equipment and supplies represent program considerations regarding facilities. The educational and recreational needs of both the school and community, the thinking of both administrators and physical educators, and the advice of both architects and lay persons are other considerations if facilities are to be planned wisely.

Penman* has set forth the following 17 general principles for planning facilities:

1. Establish a priority for use of facilities.
2. Design facilities that are compatible with the unique characteristics of the community.
3. Specify the age group for which the facility is planned.
4. Project the population growth rate in early stages of planning.
5. If it is a new school, it should be designed for 50 years of use.

6. Design facilities for efficient supervision.
7. Eliminate duplication of school and park facilities in the same neighborhood.
8. Park and school officials should have close working relationships in regard to facilities.
9. The physical educator will have to persuade key officials to incorporate new concepts in facilities.
10. Physical educators should have adequate knowledge of facility planning.
11. The physically handicapped must be considered in the planning.
12. The maintenance of facilities after construction must be considered.
13. Facilities should not be copied from other facilities, because of the unique needs that characterize each situation.
14. Facilities should be planned primarily for participants.
15. A model of the proposed facility should be built.
16. Physical educators should attempt to obtain the best possible facility, recognizing at the same time that compromise may be necessary.
17. Planning for schools should recognize the different types of activities in the programs at each educational level.

A second set of principles has been developed by Bookwalter.* These may be used as guides for planning, constructing, and using facilities for school physical education programs:

1. *Validity.* Standards for space, structure, and fixtures must be compatible with the rules essential for the effective conduct of the program.
2. *Utility.* Facilities should be adaptable for different activities and programs without affecting such items as safety and effective instruction.
3. *Accessibility.* Facilities should be readily and directly accessible for the individuals who will be using them.
4. *Isolation.* Facilities should be planned to reduce to a minimum distractions, offensive odors, noise, and undesirable activities and groups.
5. *Departmentalization.* Functionally related services and activity areas should be continuous or adjacent for greatest economy and efficiency.
6. *Safety, hygiene, and sanitation.* The maintenance of

---

*Penman, K.A.: Planning physical education and athletic facilities in schools, New York, 1977, John Wiley & Sons, Inc.

*Bookwalter, K.W.: Physical education in the secondary schools, Washington, D.C., 1964, The Center for Applied Research in Education, Inc. (The Library of Education), pp. 84-86.

proper health standards should be a major consideration in all facility planning.

7. *Supervision.* Facilities should take into consideration the need for proper teacher supervision of activities under his or her jurisdiction. Therefore, visibility and accessibility are essential considerations.

8. *Durability and maintenance.* Facilities should be durable, and easy and economical to maintain.

9. *Beauty.* Facilities should be attractive and esthetically pleasing with the utilization of good color dynamics and design.

10. *Flexibility and expansibility.* Changes in program and other considerations for future expansion should be considered. Modern thinking has stressed the principle of flexibility in regard to physical education facilities. Flexibility should provide for immediate change through folding partitions, such as doors that separate gymnasiums, for overnight change with very little effort in cases in which partitions cannot be removed immediately, and for greater change that can be made within a period of 1 or 2 months, such as during the summer vacation.

11. *Economy.* The best use of funds, space, time, energy, and other essential factors should be considered as they relate to facility planning.

A summary of some of the important guidelines and principles for facility planning includes the following:

1. All planning should be based on goals that recognize that the total physical and nonphysical environments must be safe, attractive, comfortable, clean, practical, and adapted to the needs of the individual.

2. The planning should include a consideration of the total school or college health and physical education facilities and the recreational facilities of the community. The programs and facilities of these areas are essential to any community. Because they are closely allied, they should be planned coordinately and based on the needs of the community. Each should be a part of the overall community pattern.

3. Facilities should be geared to health standards, which are important in protecting the health of individuals and in determining the outcomes.

4. Facilities play a part in disease control. The extent to which organizations provide play areas ample space, sanitary considerations, proper ventila-

tion, heating, and cleanliness will to some extent determine how effectively disease is controlled.

5. Administrators must make plans for facilities long before an architect is consulted. Technical information can be procured in the forms of standards and guides from various sources, such as state departments of education, professional literature, building score cards, and various manuals. Information may also be secured from such important groups as the American Association of School Administrators and the American Institute of Architects.

6. Standards used as guides and as a starting point will prove helpful. However, it is important to keep in mind that standards cannot always be used entirely as developed. They usually have to be modified in light of local needs, conditions, and resources.

7. Building and sanitary codes administered by the local and state departments of public health and the technical advice and consultation services available through these sources should be known and used by administrators during the planning and construction of facilities. Information concerned with acceptable building materials, specifications, minimum standards of sanitation, and other details may be procured from these informed sources.

8. Physical education and recreation personnel should play important roles in planning and operating facilities. The specialized knowledge that such individuals have is important. Provisions should be made so their expert opinion will be used to promote a healthful and proper environment.

9. Facilities should be planned with an eye to the future. Too often, facilities are constructed and outgrown within a very short time. Units should be large enough to accommodate peak-load participation in the various activities. The peak-load estimates should be made with future growth in mind.

10. Planning should provide adequate allotment of space to the activity and program areas, which should receive priority in space allotment. The administrative offices and service units, although important, should not be planned and developed in a spacious and luxurious manner that goes beyond efficiency and necessity.

11. Geographical and climatic conditions should be considered when planning facilities. By doing this,

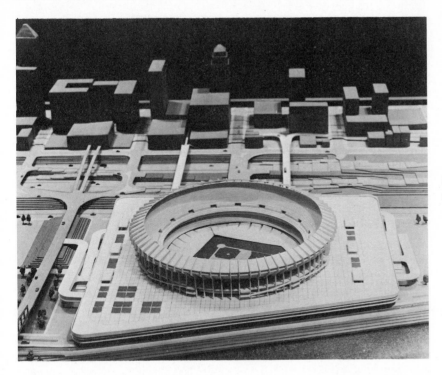

Fig. 12-2. Home of the Cincinnati Reds.

the full potential for conducting activities outdoors, as well as indoors, can be realized.

12. Architects do not always pay as much attention as they should to the educational and health features when planning buildings and facilities. Therefore, it is important that they be briefed on certain requirements that physical educators feel are essential so the health and welfare of children, youth, and adults may be provided for. Such a procedure is usually welcomed by the architect and will aid him or her in rendering a greater service to the community.

13. Facilities should include all the necessary safety features essential in physical education programs. Health service substations near the gymnasium and other play areas, proper surfacing of activity areas, adequate space, and proper lighting are a few of these considerations.

14. The construction of school or college physical education facilities often tends to set a pattern that will influence parents, civic leaders, and others. This in turn promotes a healthful and safe environment for the entire community.

Selected health considerations in facility planning

A healthful environment must consider the participant. He or she must be given a safe, healthful, pleasant, and emotionally secure environment. The environment also includes the outdoors, where everything possible should be done to control land, water, and air pollution. The total environment must also be healthful and pleasant for staff members, faculty members, and employees.

Another set of principles basic to facility planning relates particularly to the optimal promotion of a healthful environment for students. Included in this set of principles is the provision for facilities that consider the physiological needs of the student, including proper temperature control, lighting, water supply, and noise level. A second principle is to provide safe facilities. The facilities should be planned so the danger of fire, the possibility of mechanical accidents, and the hazards involved in traffic would be eliminated or kept to a minimum. A third principle

Fig. 12-3. Louisiana's Superdome, New Orleans, showing Superdome superscreens. Louisiana's Superdome features a closed-circuit, full-color television system (six screens, each 56 feet wide and 36 feet high), attached to a gondola suspended from the stadium ceiling. The TV system, which is adjustable for height, provides close-up showings of in-stadium events (sports, entertainment, conventions) as they happen, as well as instant replay from your seat in the stadium. The giant screens have a multiplicity of uses, including commercial advertising, attractiveness to conventions and trade shows, and closed-circuit showings of out-of-stadium events such as prize fights and collegiate football.

is concerned with protection against disease. This means attention to such items as proper sewage disposal, sanitation procedures, and water supply. Finally, a fourth principle is the need to provide a healthful psychological environment. This has implications for space, location of activities, color schemes, and elimination of distractions through such means as soundproof construction.

The general health features of the physical environment include site, building, lighting, heating and ventilation, plant sanitation, and acoustics.

Site. There are many aspects to consider in selecting a suitable site. These considerations will differ, depending on the community. Whether it is a rural or an urban community will have a bearing on the location of the site. In an urban community it is desirable to have a school situated near transportation facilities, but at the same time located away from industrial concerns, railroads, noise, heavy traffic, fumes, and smoke. Consideration should be given to the trends in population movements and future development of the area in which the buildings are planned. Adequate space for play and recreation should be provided. Some standards concerning schools recommend 5 acres of land for elementary schools, 10 to 12 acres for junior high schools, and 20 acres for senior high schools. The play area should consist of a minimum of 100 square feet for every child.

Attention should be given to the esthetic features of a site because of its effect on the physical and emotional well-being of participants and staff members. The surroundings should be well landscaped, attractive, and free from disturbing noises or odors.

Building. The trend in schools is toward one-story construction at the precollege level, where possible, with stress on planning from a functional rather than an ornamental point of view. The building should be constructed for *use*. The materials used should make the building attractive and safe. Every precaution should be taken to protect against accidents from fire, slippery floors, and other dangers. The walls should be painted with light colors and treated acoustically. Doors should open outward. Space for clothing should be provided. Provisions for handicapped persons are major considerations, including ramps and toilet facilities.

It is important that an architect plan such facilities with special regard to the needs of those who use them.

Lighting. Proper lighting is important to conserve vision, prevent fatigue, and improve morale. There should be proper lighting in both quality and quantity. In the past it had been recommended that natural light should come into the room from the left and that artificial light should be provided as needed. There is a trend now toward allowing natural light from more than one direction. Artificial light, moreover, should come from many sources rather than one to prevent too much concentration of light in one place. Switches for artificial light should be located in many parts of the room.

In gymnasiums and swimming pools light intensity should range from 10 to 80 footcandles, depending on the activity being conducted.

Glare is undesirable and should be eliminated. Fluorescent lights should be properly installed and adjusted for best results. Strong contrasts of color such as light walls and dark floors should be avoided.

Heating and ventilation. Efficiency in the classroom, gymnasium, special activities rooms, and other places is determined to some extent by thermal comfort, which is mainly determined by heating and ventilation.

The purposes of heating and ventilation are to remove excess heat, unpleasant odors, and, in some cases, gases, vapors, fumes, and dust from the room; to prevent rapid temperature fluctuations; to diffuse the heat within a room; and to supply heat to counter-

act loss from the human body through radiation and otherwise.

Heating standards vary according to the activities engaged in, the clothing worn by the participants, and the section of the country.

Concerning ventilation, the range of recommendations is from 8 to 21 cubic feet of fresh air per minute per occupant. Adequate ventilating systems are especially needed in dressing, shower, and locker rooms, toilet rooms, gymnasiums, and swimming pools. The recommended humidity ranges from 35% to 60%. The type and amount of ventilation will vary with the specific needs of the particular area.

Plant sanitation. Plant sanitation should not be overlooked. Sanitation facilities should be well planned and well maintained. The water supply should be safe and adequate. If any question exists, the local or state health department should be consulted. Concerning water supply, one authority suggests that at least 20 gallons per individual per day is needed for all purposes.

Drinking fountains of various heights should be recessed in corridor walls and should be of material that is easily cleaned. A stream of water should flow from the fountain so it is not necessary for the mouth of the drinker to get too near the drain bowl.

Water closets, urinals, lavatories, and washroom equipment such as soap dispensers, toilet paper holders, waste containers, mirrors, bookshelves, and hand-drying facilities should be provided as needed, also keeping the handicapped person in mind.

Waste disposal should be adequately cared for. There should be provision for cleanup and removal of paper and other materials that make the grounds and buildings a health and safety hazard, as well as unsightly. Proper sewage disposal and prompt garbage disposal should also be provided.

Acoustics. Noise distracts, causes nervous strain, and results in the loss of many of the activity's benefits. Therefore noise should be eliminated as effectively as possible. This can be achieved by acoustical treatment of such important places as corridors, gymnasiums, and swimming pools.

Acoustical materials include plasters, fibers, boards, tiles, and various fabrics. Some areas should be given special attention. Floor covering that reduces noise can be used in corridors, and acoustical mate-

Fig. 12-4. The Kingdome, Seattle, Wash.

Fig. 12-5. Gymnasium at Fitness and Recreation Center, Xerox Corporation, Leesburg, Va.

Fig. 12-6. The University of Notre Dame's Athletic and Convocation Center provides a healthful environment for part of its athletic program.

Courtesy University of Notre Dame.

rial can be used in walls. Swimming pools and gymnasiums need special treatment to control the various noises associated with enthusiastic play participation. Ceiling and wall acoustical treatment help control noises in the gymnasium, whereas using mineral acoustical material, which will not be affected by high humidity, is helpful in the swimming pool.

Determining number of teaching stations needed

The teaching station concept should be considered when scheduling physical education classes. A teaching station is the space or setting where one teacher or staff member can carry on physical education activities for one group of students. The number and size of teaching stations available together with the number of teachers on the staff, the size of the group, the number of times the group meets, the number of periods in the school or college day, and the program of activities are important items to consider in planning.

According to the participants in the National Facilities Conference,* the following formulas help determine the number of teaching stations needed.

*Participants in National Facilities Conference: Planning areas and facilities for health, physical education, and recreation, rev. ed., Washington, D.C., 1965, American Association for Health, Physical Education, and Recreation, pp. 29, 31.

ELEMENTARY SCHOOLS

The formula for computing the number of teaching stations needed for physical education in the elementary schools is

$$\text{Minimum number of teaching stations} = \frac{\text{Number of classrooms of students}}{} \times$$

$$\frac{\text{Number of physical education periods per week per class}}{\text{Total periods in school week}}$$

For example, in an elementary school with six grades, with three classes at each level (approximately 450 to 540 students), ten 30-minute physical education periods per day, and physical education conducted on a daily basis, the teaching station needs are calculated as follows:

$$\text{Minimum number of teaching stations} = 18 \text{ classroom units} \times$$

$$\frac{5 \text{ periods per week}}{50 \text{ periods per week}} = \frac{90}{50} = 1.8$$

SECONDARY SCHOOLS AND COLLEGES

The formula for computing the number of teaching stations needed for physical education in colleges and secondary schools is as follows:

$$\text{Minimum number of teaching stations} = \frac{\text{Number of students}}{\text{Average number of students per instructor}} \times$$

$$\frac{\text{Number of periods class meets each week}}{\text{Total number of class periods in school week}}$$

For example, if a school system projects its enrollment to 700 students and plans six class periods a day with an average class size of 30 students, and physical education is required daily, the formula is as follows:

$$\text{Minimum number of teaching stations} = \frac{700 \text{ students}}{30 \text{ per class}} \times$$

$$\frac{5 \text{ periods per week}}{30 \text{ periods per week}} = \frac{3,500}{900} = 3.9$$

Colleges should substitute pertinent facts into the same formula to determine the number of teaching stations they would need.

Role of administration in facility management

Kraus and Curtis* have indicated the role of administrators in facility management. They are presented here in the following adapted form:

1. The administration should familiarize itself with background information pertinent to the facility plan and should be actively involved in all planning sessions.
2. The administration should meet and discuss the facility project with all leaders and important people who have a stake in the project. The administration should be familiar with the views of such people and consider their suggestions carefully.
3. The administration should insist on being involved in selecting the architect or engineer who is going to do the plan. The administration should press strongly for selecting competent and qualified people to do the job rather than the lowest bidder or firm with political connections.
4. The administration should be at all planning conferences to present the department's point of view and programs to be considered.
5. The administration should visit the site regularly after construction begins. All problems should be noted and a follow-up of recognized errors made.
6. The administration should insist that all details and standards incorporated in the project plan be carried out exactly as specified. The administration should not approve any facility or authorize payment unless this has been done.

The team approach to facility planning

Facility planning requires a team approach that includes the architect, consultants, and physical education and athletic professionals. Flynn* has indicated the steps that should be followed in achieving the best results from the team approach. *First,* form a planning team that will identify needs and prepare a project proposal. Included on this team would be the project coordinator for the organization for whom the facility is being planned, the architect, and a specialist from physical education. Team members should understand the role each plays in the planning process. *Second,* hire a consultant during the early stages of the project because the other team members usually do not have expertise in all aspects of programming and design. The consultant can help in closing the gap between architectural theory and physical education and athletic practice. *Third,* stress faculty and staff member involvement to provide information about special areas and facilities for which they are responsible. For example, a biomechanist, exercise physiologist, adapted physical education teacher, or dance instructor could provide information about his or her projected laboratory or other facility. *Fourth,* visit other facilities in other locations to obtain ideas that may contribute to a better facility. The planning team should also be alert when making recommendations for controlling maintenance and operational costs as much as possible after the facility has been built. When construction is underway, not only the architect and consultant but also the physical education and athletic specialist should monitor the work going on. In this way many errors can be avoided or corrected.

WORKING WITH THE ARCHITECT

The architect is the specialist in facility planning and the leader in designing physical education facilities. The architect, through his or her training and experience, is a specialist who is competent to give advisory service in all aspects of facility management.

---

*Kraus, R.G., and Curtis, J.E.: Creative administration in recreation and parks, ed. 3, St. Louis, 1982, The C.V. Mosby Co.

*Flynn, R.B.: The team approach to facility planning, Athletic Purchasing and Facilities **5:**12-18, 20-22, 24, June 1981.

The architect's qualifications should include the following:

1. The architect should be legally qualified to practice in the state and should be in good standing in the profession. He or she must have unquestioned professional character and integrity and must possess high ethical standards.
2. The architect should have had previous successful experience in designing buildings that demonstrate competence in architectural work. The buildings previously designed by the architect should also reflect a careful study of the peculiar needs of each client.
3. The architect should possess the vision and imagination to translate the educational aims and program specified by the educator into functional buildings. The architect should not possess set, preconceived ideas that are hard to change. He or she must be able and willing to mold design to fit needs and avoid stereotypes.
4. The architect must have a record of working cooperatively and harmoniously with clients, educational advisors, and contractors.
5. The architect must have an adequate staff of trained personnel to carry out the building program without undue delay. The architect should either have qualified engineering services available in his or her own organization or should specify qualified engineering specialists who will work with him or her.
6. The architect should keep abreast of recent research and study concerning materials and mechanical equipment used in school buildings.
7. The architect should show such economy in the use of space and materials as is consistent with educational needs.
8. The architect should be competent in site planning and in using space for education and recreation.
9. The architect must give adequate supervision to his or her buildings.
10. The architect should be informed concerning state and municipal building regulations and codes and must show care in complying with them.
11. The architect must demonstrate sound business judgment, proper business procedures, and good record keeping on the job.*

Physical educators should carefully think through their own ideas and plans for their special facilities

*Adapted from Leu, D.J.: Planning education facilities, New York, 1965, The Center for Applied Research in Education, Inc. (The Library of Education), p. 50.

and submit them in writing to the architect during the early stages of planning. There should also be several conferences in which the architect and physical education specialist exchange views and consider architectural possibilities.

Many architects know little about physical education programs and therefore welcome the advice of specialists. The architect might be furnished with such information as the names of plants where excellent facilities exist, kinds of activities that will constitute the program, space requirements for various activities, storage and equipment areas needed, temperature requirements, relation of dressing, showering, and toilet facilities to program, teaching stations needed, best construction materials for activities, and lighting requirements. The physical educator may not have all this information readily available, including some of the latest trends and standards recommended for his or her field. However, such information can be obtained through professional organizations, other schools and organizations where excellent facilities have been developed, and facility books developed by experts in the area.

Mr. William Haroldson, former Director of Health and Physical Education for the Seattle, Washington, public schools, developed a procedural outline in cooperation with three architectural firms, which lists some essential considerations for physical educators in their relationships and cooperative planning with architects. Some of the main points from this outline are discussed here.

Educational specifications. Adequate educational specifications provide the basis for good planning by the architect:

1. General description of the program, such as the number of teaching stations necessary to service the physical education program for a total student body of approximately _____ boys and _____ girls
2. Basic criteria that pertain to the gymnasium: the number of teaching periods per day, capacities, number, and size of courts, lockers, and projected total uses contemplated for the facility
   a. Availability to the community
   b. Proximity to parks
   c. Parking
   d. Size of groups that will use gymnasium after school hours

e. Whether locker rooms will or will not be made available to public use

3. Specific description of aspects of the physical education program that affect the architects
   a. Class size and scheduling, both present and possible future; number of instructors, present and future
   b. Preferred method of handling students, for example, flow of traffic in classrooms, locker rooms, shower rooms, and going to outside play area (This item has a direct bearing on the design of this area.)
   c. Storage requirements and preferred method of handling all permanent equipment and supplies (Here, unless a standard has been established, requirements should be specific—for example, request should state number and size of each item rather than "ample storage.")
   d. Team and other extracurricular use of facilities (It helps the architect if the educational specifications can describe a typical week's use of the proposed facility, which would include a broad daily program, afterschool use, and potential community use.)

Meeting with the architect. At this point, it is advisable to meet with the architect to discuss specifications to ensure complete understanding and to allow the architect to point out certain restrictions or limitations that may be anticipated even before the first preliminary plan is made.

Design. The factors to be considered in the design of the facility and discussed with the architect should include the following:

1. *Budget*. An adequate budget should be allowed. Gymnasiums are subject to extremely hard use, and durability should not be sacrificed for economy.
2. *Acoustics*. Use the service of acoustical consultants.
3. *Public address system*. How is it to be used—for instruction, athletic events, general communication?
4. *Color and design*. Harmonize with surrounding neighborhood.
5. *Fenestration* (window treatment). Consider light control, potential window breakage, vision panel; gymnasium areas should have safety glass (preferred) or wire protectors.
6. *Ventilation*. The area should be zoned for flexibility of use. This means greater ventilation when a larger number of spectators are present, or a reduction for single class groups, or isolated areas, such as locker rooms. Special attention must be given to proper ventilation of uniform drying rooms; gymnasium

storage areas, locker and shower areas. (Current and off-season uniform storage areas require constant ventilation when plant is shut down.) Ventilation equipment should have a low noise level.
7. *Supplementary equipment in the gymnasium*. Such equipment should be held to a minimum. Supplementary equipment, such as fire boxes, should be recessed.
8. *Compactness and integration*. Keep volume compact—large, barnlike spaces are unpleasant and are costly to heat and maintain. Integrate as far as budget permits.
9. *Mechanical or electrical features*. Special attention should be given to location of panel boards, chalk boards, fire alarm, and folding doors.

Further critique with the architect. The architect begins to develop plans from an understanding of the initial requirements he or she has considered in relation to the design factors listed.

When the basic plan is set, the architect will usually call in consulting engineers to discuss the structural and mechanical systems before approval of the plan. These systems will have been outlined by the architect but cannot be discussed with the consultants other than in generalities before the plan is in approximate final form.

More meetings are then held regarding approval of preliminary plans and proposed structural and mechanical systems and the use of materials after the incorporation in the preliminary plans.

If supplementary financing by governmental agencies is involved, the drawing or set of drawings will have been submitted to those agencies with a project outline or specifications as soon as the plan has been sufficiently developed to establish the area. If the agency approves the application as submitted by the architect, the final preliminary working drawings are started.

Final processing. It is advisable to settle all matters that can be settled during preliminary planning to save time. If this method is used, greater clarity is assured and less changing or misunderstanding results. Preliminary plans are drawn with the intent of illustrating the plan; working drawings are technical and often difficult to interpret. However, if personnel wish to check the working drawings before their completion, they should be welcome to do so.

Common errors made by physical educators in facility management

Some common mistakes made by physical educators and athletic directors in facility planning and management include the following:

1. Failure to adequately project enrollments and program needs into the future (Facilities are difficult to expand or change, so this is a significant error.)
2. Failure to provide for multiple use of facilities
3. Failure to provide for adequate accessibility for students in physical education classes and also for community groups for recreation
4. Failure to observe basic health factors in planning facilities regarding lighting, safety, and ventilation
5. Failure to provide adequate space for the conduct of a comprehensive program of physical education activities
6. Failure to provide appropriate accommodations for spectators
7. Failure to soundproof areas of the building where noise will interfere with educational functions
8. Failure to meet with the architect to present views on program needs
9. Failure to provide adequate staff offices
10. Failure to provide adequate storage space
11. Failure to provide adequate space and privacy for medical examinations
12. Failure to provide entrances large enough to transport equipment
13. Failure to observe desirable current professional standards
14. Failure to provide for adequate study of cost in terms of durability, time, money, and effective instruction
15. Failure to properly locate teaching stations with service facilities

Indoor facilities

Several special areas and facilities are needed by physical education and athletic programs.

ADMINISTRATIVE AND STAFF OFFICES

It is important, as far as practical and possible, for physical educators and athletic directors to have a section of a building set aside for administrative and staff offices. As a minimum there should be a large central office with a waiting room. The central office provides a place where the secretarial and clerical work can be performed, space for keeping records and files, and storage closets for office supplies. The waiting room can serve as a reception point where persons can wait until staff members are ready to see them.

Separate offices for the staff members should be provided, if possible. This provides a place where conferences can be held in private and without interruption. This is an important consideration for health counseling and for discussing scholastic, family, recreational, and other problems. If separate offices are not practical, a desk should be provided for each staff member. There should then be a private room available to staff members for conferences.

Other facilities that make the administrative and staff setup more efficient and enjoyable are staff dressing rooms, departmental library, conference room, and toilet and lavatory facilities.

LOCKER, SHOWER, AND DRYING ROOMS

Physical education and athletic activities require facilities for storage of clothes, showering, and drying. These are essential to good health and a well-organized program.

Locker and shower rooms should be readily accessible to activity areas. Locker rooms should not be congested places that persons want to get out of as soon as possible. Instead, they should provide ample room, both storage and dressing lockers, stationary benches, mirrors, recessed lighting fixtures, and drinking fountains.

An average of 14 square feet per individual at peak load, exclusive of the locker space, is generally required to provide proper space.

Storage lockers should be provided for each individual. An additional 10% should be installed for expanded enrollments or membership. These are lockers for the permanent use of each individual and can be used to hold essential clothing and other supplies. They can be smaller than the dressing lockers; some recommended sizes are 7½ by 12 by 24 inches, 6 by 12 by 36 inches, and 7½ by 12 by 18 inches. Basket lockers are not favored by many experts because of hygiene problems, because an attendant is

Fig. 12-7. The University of Idaho has a portable football field. The Tartan Turf is 200 by 370 feet and can be rolled up and stored on a 210-foot long steel drum.

Courtesy Scholastic Coach.

required for good administration of this system, and because of the necessity of carting the baskets from place to place.

Dressing lockers are used by participants only when actually engaging in activity. They are large, usually 12 by 12 by 54 inches or 12 by 12 by 48 inches in elementary schools, and 12 by 12 by 72 inches for secondary schools and colleges and for community recreation programs.

Shower rooms should be provided that have both group and cubicle showers. Some facility planners recommend that girls and women have a number of shower heads equal to 40% of the enrollment at peak load, and boys and men, 30% of the enrollment at peak load. Another recommendation is one shower head for four boys or men and one for three girls or women at peak load. These should be 4 feet apart. If showers are installed where a graded change of water temperature is provided and where the individual progresses through such a gradation, the num-

ber of shower heads can be reduced. The shower rooms should also be equipped with liquid soap dispensers, good ventilation and heating, nonslip floors, and recessed plumbing. The ceiling should be dome-shaped so it will more readily shed water.

The drying room adjacent to the shower room is an essential. This should be equipped with proper drainage, good ventilation, towel bar, and a ledge that can be used to place a foot on while drying.

A report of a conference sponsored by the Athletic Institute and the AAHPERD on the planning of facilities for health, physical education, and recreation lists the following common errors in service facilities:

Failure to provide adequate locker and dressing space
Failure to plan dressing and shower area so as to reduce foot traffic to a minimum and establish clean, dry aisles for bare feet
Failure to provide a nonskid surface on dressing, shower, and toweling room floors
Failure to properly relate teaching stations with service facilities

Fig. 12-8. Gymnasium, McPherson High School, McPherson, Kan.

Courtesy Shaver & Co., Salina, Kan.

Fig. 12-9. Locker rooms at Sinclair Community College, Dayton, Ohio.

Inadequate provision for drinking fountains

Failure to provide acoustical treatment where needed

Failure to provide and properly locate toilet facilities to serve all participants and spectators

Failure to provide doorways, hallways, or ramps so that equipment may be moved easily

Failure to design equipment rooms for convenient and quick check-in and check-out

Failure to provide mirrors and shelving for boys' and girls' dressing facilities

Failure to plan locker and dressing rooms with correct traffic pattern to swimming pool

Failure to construct shower, toilet, and dressing rooms with sufficient floor slope and properly located drains

Failure to place shower heads low enough and in such a position that the spray is kept within the shower room

Failure to provide shelves in the toilet room

Fig. 12-10. Suggested indoor surface materials.

ROOMS	\ FLOORS \ Asphalt, Rubber, Linoleum Tile	Cement, Abrasive and Non-absorbent	Maple, hard	Terrazzo Abrasive	Tile, ceramic	Brick	Brick, glazed	Cinder Block	\ LOWER WALLS \ Concrete	Plaster	Tile, ceramic	Wood Panel	Moisture-proof	Brick	Brick, glazed	Cinder Block	\ UPPER WALLS \ Plaster	Acoustic	Moisture-resistant	Concrete or Structure Tile	Structure Tile	\ CEILINGS \ Plaster	Tile, acoustic	Moisture-resistant
Apparatus Storage Room	1	2			1				C															
Classrooms	2	1	1							2							2			C	1	1		
Clubroom	2	1		2						2							2			C	1	1		
Corrective Room			2		1				1		2		2	2	1	2					1	1		
Custodial Supply Room	1		2										2								1			
Dance Studio	2	1																		C	1	1		
Drying Room (equip.)		1	2	1	2	1	1		1	1	2		1	1	1	2	1				1	1		
Gymnasium	1		2		1				1		2						2		*	C	1	1		
Health-Service Unit	1	1	2		1				1		2						2			C	1	1		
Laundry Room	2		2	1	2		2	2	1		C							*			1	1	*	
Locker Rooms	3		2	1	2		2	3				*			1	2		*			1	1	*	
Natatorium			2	1	2	1	3	2	1		1	*	1	2	1		1		*	G	1		*	
Offices	2	1	2				2		1				2		2	1		*			1	1		
Recreation Room	2	1	2				2		1		1		2		2	1	*				1	1	*	
Shower Rooms	3	1		2		1		2	1		1	*	2	1	1	2		*			1	1	*	
Special-activity Room	2	1	2		1				1		1	*	1	1	1	1				C	1	1	*	
Team Room	3		2	1	2	2			2		2	*	1	2	1	2		*		C	1	1		
Toilet Rooms	3		2	1	2	2			2		1	*	1	2	1	2					1	1	*	
Toweling-Drying Room (bath)	3		2	1	2	2			2		1	*	2	1	1	2		*			1	1		*

Note: The numbers in the Table indicate first, second, and third choices. "C" indicates the material as being contrary to good practice. An "*" indicates desirable quality.

From Participants in National Facilities Conference: Planning areas and facilities for health, physical education, and recreation, revised, Chicago, 1965, The Athletic Institute.

Fig. 12-11. Locker room at the University of Notre Dame accents a healthy environment for athletes.

Special attention should be paid to the health aspects of shower facilities. The shower room should be kept clean, and soap and warm water should be available. Proper heating and ventilation should be provided; a nonslip floor surface should be installed; and ceilings should be constructed to prevent condensation. The drying area should be washed daily to prevent athlete's foot and other contaminations. A towel service should be initiated if it does not already exist.

Locker rooms should provide dressing and storage lockers for all participants. Adequate space should be provided so dressing is not done in cramped quarters.

GYMNASIUMS

The type and number of gymnasiums that should be part of a school or organizational plant depend on the number of individuals who will be participating and the variety of activities that will be conducted in this area.

General construction features include smooth walls, hardwood floors (maple preferred—laid lengthwise),

recessed lights, recessed radiators, adequate and well-screened windows, and storage space for the apparatus and other equipment. It is also generally agreed that in schools it is best to have the gymnasium located in a separate wing of the building to isolate the noise and also as a convenient location for community groups that will be anxious to use such facilities.

The AAHPERD has listed the following important factors to keep in mind when planning the gymnasium:

1. Hard maple flooring that is resilient and nonslippery.
2. Smooth interior walls to a height of 10 or 12 feet.
3. Upper walls need not be smooth.
4. The ceiling should reflect light and absorb sound, and there should be at least 22 to 24 feet from the floor to exposed beams.
5. Windows should be 10 to 12 feet above floor and placed on long side of room.
6. Heating should be thermostatically controlled, radiators recessed with protecting grill or grate if placed at floor level.

7. Subflooring should be moisture- and termite-resistant and well ventilated.
8. Suspension of apparatus from the ceiling and the erection of wall-type apparatus must be well planned.
9. Mechanical ventilation may be necessary.
10. Proper illumination meeting approved standards and selectively controlled for various activities must be designed.
11. Floor plates for standards and apparatus must be planned, as well as such items as blackboards, electric clocks and scoreboards, public address system, and provisions for press and radio.
12. Floor markings for various games should be placed after prime coat of seal has been applied and before application of the finishing coats.

Many gymnasiums have folding doors that divide them into halves, thirds, or fourths and allow activities to be conducted simultaneously on each side. This has proved satisfactory where separate gymnasiums could not be provided.

In elementary schools that need only one teaching station, a minimum floor space of 36 by 52 feet is suggested. Where two teaching stations are desired, floor space of 54 by 90 feet may be divided by a folding partition.

In junior and senior high schools where only one teaching station is desired, a minimum floor space of 48 by 66 feet is necessary. An area 66 by 96 feet of floor space, exclusive of bleachers, will provide two teaching stations of minimum size. The folding partition that provides the two teaching stations should be motor driven. Where seating capacity is desired, additional space will be needed. If more than two teaching stations are desired, the gymnasium area may be extended to provide an additional station or activity rooms may be added. Of course, the addition of a swimming pool also provides an additional teaching station.

Other considerations for gymnasiums should include provisions for basketball backboards, mount-

Fig. 12-12. Main gymnasium at Plymouth Canton High School, Plymouth Community School District, Plymouth, Mich. This gymnasium is approximately 110 by 170 feet and features three teaching stations and room for badminton, tennis, volleyball, and basketball and also a 14 lap-per-mile track.

ings for various apparatus that will be used, recessed drinking fountains, places for hanging mats, outlets for various electric appliances and cleaning devices, proper line markings for activities, bulletin boards, and other essentials to a well-rounded program.

Just as safe and properly constructed equipment should be a part of outdoor facilities, so should they be a part of indoor physical education facilities. Adequate space should be provided for all the activity phases of the program, whether they are in the gymnasium, swimming pool, or auxiliary areas. Mats should be used as a protective measure on walls and other areas where participants may be injured. Drinking fountains should be recessed and doors should open away from the playing floor. Proper flooring should be used—tile-cement floors are sometimes undesirable where activity takes place. Space should be provided for the handicapped where persons in wheelchairs and on crutches can be accommodated.

Clothing and equipment used in physical education activities should meet health standards. If not, odors and germs will thrive, causing an unpleasant environment that may help spread disease. Gymnasium mats, for example, should be kept clean. Regular physical education clothing, not street clothes, should be worn, except in social dancing or similar activities. Clean clothing, including all types of athletic costumes, should be required. Footwear should be fitted properly. Socks should be clean.

Guidelines in gymnasium planning. The following guidelines are valid for administrators, architects, board members, and other persons involved in gymnasium planning. Many of these guidelines are overlooked by those responsible for gymnasium construction.

The roof. If the roof is not properly designed before construction, costly changes in equipment installation may occur later. Ceiling support beams are also essential for the physical educator to make maximal use of the facility. The design of the roof should allow for support beams strong enough to absorb the stress placed on them in various activities. Support beams should be placed to allow maximal flexibility in the location of apparatus. The design should also consider the placement of gymnastic apparatus so students are saved from obstructions in the event of falls.

The floor. The floor is a vital part of the gymnasium and should be constructed from hardwood, not tile. Although expensive, hardwood is safer, does not become slick, and is better for athletic performance. Plates for floor apparatus such as the high bar should be designed with safety and flexibility in mind.

The walls. Electrical outlets should be provided throughout the gymnasium so audiovisual areas can be used at each activity station. Walls behind baskets should be recessed and padded. This is safer than hanging pads near glazed tile walls. It is a good idea to provide a wall for participants to practice their tennis skills. A line should be painted along the wall to indicate the height of the tennis net. The wall can also be used for hardball and other ball skills.

Lighting. Adequate durable lighting with recessed fixtures is essential. This helps prevent bulb breakage from ball activities.

Acoustics. Noise control should be a primary consideration in any gymnasium construction. Acoustic treatment of ceilings and walls can help reduce or eliminate noise.

Special activity areas. Although gymnasiums take up considerable space, there should still be additional areas for activities essential to physical education and athletic programs.

Wherever possible, additional activity areas should be provided for remedial or adapted activities, apparatus, handball, squash, weight lifting, dancing, rhythms, fencing, and dramatics and for various recreational activities, such as arts and crafts, lounging and resting, and bowling. The activities to be provided will depend on interests of participants and type of program. The recommended size of such auxiliary gymnasiums is 30 by 50 by 24 feet, or 40 by 60 by 24 feet. A 75 by 90 foot auxiliary gymnasium is ideal.

In reference to special activity areas, it should also be pointed out that regulation classrooms and other space can be converted into these special rooms. This may be feasible where the actual construction of such costly facilities may not be practical.

The remedial or adapted activities room should be equipped with items such as horizontal ladders, mirrors, mats, climbing ropes, stall bars and benches, pulley weights, dumbbells, Indian clubs, shoulder

Fig. 12-13. A, Main doors to the Branch Rickey Gymnasium at Ohio Wesleyan University, Delaware, Ohio.

wheels, and other such equipment suited for the particular needs of the individuals participating. (See also p. 414-418.)

Auxiliary rooms. The main auxiliary rooms are supply, check-out, custodial, and laundry rooms.

Supply rooms should be easily accessible from the gymnasium and other activity areas. In these rooms are stored balls, nets, standards, and other equipment needed for the programs. The size of these rooms varies according to the number of activities offered and the number of participants.

Check-out rooms should be provided seasonally. They house the equipment and supplies used in various seasonal activities.

Custodial rooms provide a place for storing equipment and supplies used to maintain these specialized facilities.

Laundries should be large enough to accommodate the laundering of such essential items as towels, uniforms, and swimming suits.

INDOOR SWIMMING POOLS

Major design decisions must be made if an organization decides to construct a pool. These include such items as the nature of the program to be conducted in a pool, type of overflow system, dimensions and shape of pool, depth of the water, type of finish, type of filters and water treatment system, construction material, amount of deck area, climate control, illumination, and number of spectators to be accommodated.

Some mistakes that should be avoided in the construction of a pool include entrances to the pool from the locker rooms opening onto the deep rather than the shallow end of the pool, pool base finished with slippery material such as glazed tile, insufficient depth of water for diving, improper placement of ladders, insufficient rate of recirculation of water to accommodate peak bathing loads, inadequate storage space, failure to use acoustic material on ceiling and walls, insufficient illumination, slippery tile on decks, and an inadequate overflow system at the ends of the pool.

Some trends and innovations in pool design and operation include: the Rim-Flow Overflow System, inflatable roof structure, the skydome design, pool tent cover, floating swimming pool complex, prefabrication of pool tanks, automation of pool recirculating and filter systems, regenerative cycle filter system, adjustable height diving platform, variable depth bottoms, fluorescent underwater lights, automatic cleaning systems, and wave-making machines.

Present types of swimming pools have two main

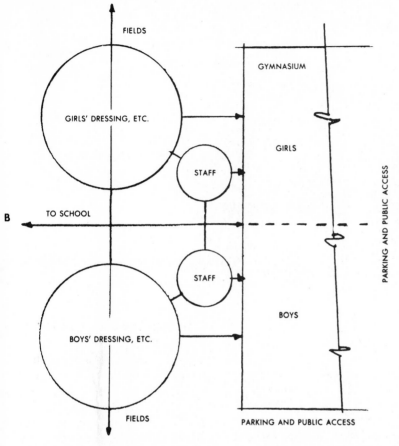

FIELDS

GYMNASIUM

GIRLS' DRESSING, ETC.

GIRLS

STAFF

PARKING AND PUBLIC ACCESS

B TO SCHOOL

STAFF

BOYS

BOYS' DRESSING, ETC.

FIELDS

PARKING AND PUBLIC ACCESS

Fig. 12-13, cont'd. B, Orientation of gymnasium to related areas.

B, from Participants in National Facilities Conference, op. cit.

objectives: to provide instructional and competitive programs and to provide recreation.

The swimming pool should be located on or above the ground level, have a southern exposure, be isolated from other units in the building, and be easily accessible from the central dressing and locker rooms. Materials that have been found most adaptive to swimming pools are smooth, glazed, light-colored tile or brick.

The standard indoor pool is 75 feet long. The width should be a multiple of 7 feet, with a minimum of 35 feet. Depths vary from 2 feet 6 inches at the shallow end to 4 feet 6 inches at the outer limits of the shallow area. The shallow or instructional area should comprise about two thirds of the pool. The deeper areas taper to 9 to 12 feet deep. An added but important factor is a movable bulkhead that can be used to divide the pool into various instructional areas.

The deck space around the pool should be constructed of a nonslip material and provide ample space for land drills and demonstrations. The area above the water should be unobstructed. The ceiling should be at least 25 feet above the water if a 3-meter diving board will be used. The walls and the ceiling of the pool area should be acoustically treated.

The swimming pool should be constructed to receive as much natural light as possible, with the windows located on the sides rather than on the ends. Artificial lighting should be recessed in the ceilings. Good lighting is especially important near the diving boards. Underwater lighting is beautiful but not essential.

There should be an efficient system for adequately heating and circulating the water. The temperature of the water should range from 75° to 80° F.

If spectators are to be provided for, a gallery sepa-

Fig. 12-14. Swimming pool complex, Brigham Young University, Provo, Utah.

Fig. 12-15. Swimming pool at University of Montevallo, Montevallo, Alabama.

rate from the pool room proper should be erected along the length of the pool.

An office adjacent to the pool where records and first aid supplies can be kept is advisable. Such an office should be equipped with windows that overlook the entire length of the pool. Also, there should be lavatory and toilet facilities available.

The swimming pool is a costly operation. Therefore, it is essential that it be planned with the help of the best advice obtainable. Specialists who are well acquainted with such facilities and who conduct swimming activities should be brought into conferences with the architect, a representative from the public health department, and experts in such essentials as lighting, heating, construction, and acoustics.

Different designs in swimming pool complexes are a current trend. The Art Linkletter Natatorium at Springfield College, Springfield, Massachusetts, measures 44 by 169 feet. One wall can be positioned anywhere along the length of the pool, thus forming two areas of any chosen size. Beneath the water level in the pool are picture windows that look into classrooms where swimming techniques can be studied.

Another design in swimming pools is the aquatic center at Princeton University. This complex was designed to meet the needs of swimming as a spectator sport. Seating is provided for 3500 persons, and the 50-meter pool features a submersible deck that can be lowered to divide the pool into varsity and teaching areas. The diving decks are hydraulically operated for height adjustments, and sidewall windows have been eliminated because of the possible danger of mistaking window glare for the pool surface.

Health considerations for swimming pools

Swimming pools need special attention whether indoor or outdoor. First, the pool should be properly constructed to provide for adequate filtration, circulation, and chlorination. A daily diary should be kept of such things as water temperature, hydrogen ion concentration, residual chlorine, and other important matters. Regulations for pool use should be established and students acquainted with them. Pool regulations advocated by the National Education Association and the American Medical Association follow:

1. Everyone using the pool should have a bath in the nude, with soap and water, washing carefully the armpits, the genital and rectal areas, and the feet.
2. Before taking a shower, the bladder should be emptied. Pupils needing to urinate during the swimming period should be excused to go to the toilet.
3. Anyone leaving the pool to go to the toilet must take another cleansing bath with soap and water before returning.
4. Pupils should expectorate only in the overflow trough.
5. Boys and men should swim in the nude or wear sanitized trunks. Girls and women should wear sanitized tank suits.
6. Girls and boys with long hair should wear rubber bathing caps. Caps keep hair, dandruff, and hair oil from contaminating the water. They also keep hair out of the eyes.
7. Each pupil should be inspected by the instructor or the pool guard before entering the pool. Pupils with evidence of skin infection, eye infection, respiratory disease, open cuts or sores, or bandages should be excluded.
8. There must be no rough or boisterous play and no running or playing tag in or around the pool area.
9. Pupils should wear ear plugs or nose clips if these have been recommended by their physicians. Some pupils, on medical recommendation, may need to be excused, at least temporarily, from participation in the aquatic program.
10. A qualified person, either the instructor or other person qualified as a lifeguard, should be on duty whenever the pool is in use. No pupil should enter the pool unless a guard is present. All doors leading to the pool should be locked when the pool is not in use and a guard on duty.
11. Since dirt from shoes may be tracked into the pool and contaminate the water, spectators should be prohibited from entering the pool deck.*

ATHLETIC TRAINING AND HEALTH SERVICE FACILITIES

Athletic training and health services are an important part of the program and require adequate facilities. They are discussed in Chapter 15.

---

*Joint Committee on Health Problems in Education of the National Education Association and the American Medical Association: Healthful School Environment, Washington, D.C., 1969, The Associations, pp. 234-235.

Outdoor facilities

The outdoor facilities discussed in this section are play areas, game areas, outdoor swimming pools, and camps.

PLAY AREAS

Many factors must be considered when planning outdoor facilities for schools and colleges. Before a site is selected, it is important to appraise the location, topography, soil drainage, water supply, size, shape, and natural features. The outdoor facilities should be as near the gymnasium and locker rooms as possible and yet far enough from the classrooms so the noise will not be disturbing.

The play areas should serve the needs and interests of the students for the entire school year and at the same time should provide a setting for activities during vacation periods. The needs and interests of the citizens of the community must also be considered, for the play areas can be used for part of the community recreation program. This is especially important in some communities where such facilities can be planned as education and recreation centers. Because the community uses the areas after the school day is over, the plan is feasible.

The size of the playground area should be determined on the basis of activities offered in the program and the number of individuals who will be using the facilities at peak load. Possibilities for expansion should also be kept in mind. Playing fields and playgrounds should have good turf and be clear of rocks, holes, and uneven surfaces. A dirty, dusty surface, for example, can aggravate such conditions as emphysema, chronic bronchitis, and allergies. Artificial turf is now being used more and more. However, it needs several improvements to reduce injuries and other problems associated with it. Safety precautions should also be provided in terms of well-lined areas, regularly inspected equipment, and fenced-in playfields and playgrounds, particularly where there is heavy traffic adjoining these facilities. Rubber asphalt, synthetic materials, and other substances that require little maintenance and help to free an area from cinders, gravel, stones, and dust are being used more and more on outdoor surfaces. In some sections of the country limited shelters are also being used to provide protection from the rain, wind, and sun. All outdoor areas should have sanitary drinking fountains and toilet facilities as needed.

Elementary school. The activities program in the elementary school suggests what facilities should be available. Children of the primary grades engage in big muscle activity involving adaptations of climbing, jumping, skipping, kicking, throwing, leaping, and catching. The children in the intermediate and upper elementary grades perform these activities and others in games of low organization, team games, and fundamental skills used in playing these games.

The playground area for an elementary school should be located near the building and should be easily accessible from the elementary classrooms. The kindergarten children should have a section of the playground for their exclusive use. This should be at least 5000 square feet and separated from the rest of the playground. It should consist of a surfaced area, a grass area, and a place for sand and digging. The sand area should be enclosed to prevent the sand from being scattered. It is also wise to have a shaded area where storytelling and similar activities may be conducted. Some essential equipment includes swings, slides, seesaws, climbing structures, tables, and seats.

The children older than kindergarten age in the elementary school should have play space that includes turf, apparatus, shaded, multiple-use paved, and recreation areas.

The turf area provides space for many field and team games. Provisions for speedball, soccer, field hockey, softball, and field ball could be included.

The apparatus area should provide such equipment as climbing bars in the form of a jungle gym, horizontal bars, and Giant Strides. There should be ample space to provide for the safety of the participants.

The shaded area may provide space for such activities as marbles, hopscotch, ring toss, and storytelling.

The multiple-use paved area may serve a variety of purposes and activities year-round by both school and community. It can house basketball, tennis, and handball courts, games of minimum organization, and other activities. This area should be paved with material that provides resiliency, safety, and durability.

Fig. 12-16. Swimming pool, Sinclair Community College, Dayton, Ohio.

Fig. 12-17. Outdoor gymnasium, University of Tampa, Tampa, Fla.

Rapid and efficient drainage is essential. Lines may be painted on the area for various games. Schools should allow additional space adjacent to this area for possible future expansion.

Other recreation areas that have important implications for the community are a landscaped, parklike area, a place for quiet activities such as dramatics and informal gatherings, a wading pool, a place for older adults to congregate, and a place for children to have gardening opportunities.

Junior high school. The junior high school play and recreation area, planned and developed for the children who attend the school and also for the adults in the community, should be located on a larger site than that for the elementary school. It should be from 10 to 25 or more acres. Local conditions will determine the amount of area available.

Many of the facilities of the elementary school will be a part of the junior high school. In many cases, however, the various areas should be increased in size. The necessary facilities should provide for those activities that will be part of the regular physical education class and of the intramural program.

A landscaped, parklike area should be provided for various recreational activities for the community, such as walking, picnicking, skating, and fly casting.

Senior high school. The senior high school physical education program is characterized to a more pronounced degree by a team game program in various activities. This emphasis, together with the fact that facilities are needed for the recreational use of the community, requires an even larger area than those for the two previous educational levels. Estimates range from 10 to 40 acres for such a site.

Most of the areas that have been listed in discussing the elementary and junior high schools should be included at the senior high school.

Considerably more space for physical education class instruction in the various field games is necessary to provide fullsized official fields for softball, field hockey, soccer, speedball, lacrosse, football, and baseball. The intramural and the interscholastic programs, as well as the community recreation program, could use these facilities.

Football and track can be provided for in an area of approximately 4 acres, with the football field placed within the track oval. A baseball field is questionable in such an area, because track and baseball are both spring sports. Baseball needs an area about 350 feet square. This allows a minimum of 50 feet from home plate to the backstop and also allows adequate space outside the first and third base lines.

GAME AREAS

The recommended dimensions for game areas for school physical education programs have been outlined by a group of experts as shown in Table 12-1. One acre will accommodate four tennis courts, four handball courts, three badminton courts, and two volleyball courts.

The game area should permit basic physical education instructional classes to be held and also provide fields for softball, field hockey, soccer, speedball, lacrosse, and court areas that include basketball, softball, and other activities. There should be proper space for track if desired, an oval one-fourth mile around or at least a straightaway of 380 feet and 15 to 20 feet wide. Of course, an interschool athletic area, which usually includes football, track, baseball, and soccer, is also needed.

The winter activities should not be forgotten. With such activities gaining increased popularity, provision should be made for skiing, sledding, skating, and other winter activities.

One state recommends the outdoor facilities for the basic needs of a physical education and recreation program, from kindergarten to grade twelve, should consist of a minimum of 12 acres. This area should be divided into an elementary area of 3 acres; courts area of 1 acre; high school girls' and boys' intramural area of 5 acres, and an interschool athletic area of 3 acres. With the trend toward coeducational activities, the boys' and girls' areas are combined.

A concept in play areas is the multipurpose sports court. This small, self-contained, fenced-in court provides for a variety of activities in a small area. The average sports court is 12 by 24 by 10½ feet and is completely enclosed (including top) with a weatherproofed steel tube and link fence that rests like a box on the floor of the court. Low-cost lighting and canvas covering can be used for evening and colder weather activities. The floor is frequently a raised wooden

Table 12-1. Recommended dimensions for game areas*†

	Elementary	Upper grades	High school (adults)	Area size (sq. ft.)
Basketball	40' × 60'	42' × 74'	50' × 84'	5000
Volleyball	69' × 50'	25' × 50'	30" × 60'	2800
Badminton			20' × 44'	1800
Paddle tennis			20' × 44'	1800
Deck tennis			18' × 40'	1800
Tennis		36' × 78'	36' × 78'	7200
Ice hockey			85' × 200'	17,000
Field hockey			180' × 300'	54,000
Horseshoes		10' × 40'	10' × 50'	1000
Shuffleboard			6' × 52'	648
Lawn bowling			14' × 110'	7800
Tetherball	10' circle	12' circle	12' circle	144
Croquet	38' × 60'	38' × 60'	38' × 60'	2275
Handball	18' × 26'	18' × 26'	20' × 34'	1280
Baseball			350' × 350'	122,500
Archery		50' × 150'	50' × 300'	20,000
Softball (12" ball)‡	150' × 150'	200' × 200'	250' × 250'	62,500
Football—with 440-yard track—220-yard straightaway			300' × 600'	180,000
Touch football		120' × 300'	160' × 360'	68,400
6-man football			120' × 300'	49,500
Soccer			165' × 300'	57,600

*From Participants in National Facilities Conference, op. cit., p. 26.
†Table covers a single unit; many of above can be combined.
‡Dimensions vary with size of ball used.

deck that allows for quick drainage and a weather-resistant playing surface. However, pads of other playing surfaces can be laid over the wooden deck. The court can be used for basketball, volleyball, paddle tennis, handball, and other activities. This type of court is excellent for crowded urban areas, industrial recreation programs, schools, apartments, and individual homes.

OUTDOOR SWIMMING POOLS

The outdoor swimming pool is a popular and important facility in many communities. To a great degree climatic conditions determine the advisability of such a facility.

Outdoor pools are built in various shapes, including oval, circular, T-shaped, and rectangular. Rectangular pools are most popular because of easier construction and because they lend themselves better to competitive swimming events.

The size of pools varies, depending on the number

of persons they are to serve. One recommendation has been made that 12 square feet of water space per swimmer be allotted for swimming purposes, or, if the deck is taken into consideration, 20 square feet of space for swimming and walking area per swimmer.

The decks for outdoor pools should be larger than those for indoor pools. This larger space will accommodate more people and also provide space for sunbathing.

Shower facilities should be provided to ensure that every swimmer takes a soapy shower in the nude before entering the water. A basket system for storing clothes has been found practical. Where the pool is located adjacent to a school, it is sometimes practical to use the locker and shower facilities of the school. However, it is strongly advised that wherever possible separate shower and basket facilities be provided. Toilets should also be provided.

Because swimming is popular at night, as well as in

Fig. 12-18. Swimming pool, Wallace Rider Farrington High School, Honolulu, Hawaii.

the daytime, lights should be provided so a great percentage of the population may participate in this healthful and enjoyable activity.

Diving boards generally are of wood or metal, but in recent years fiber glass and plastic ones have proved popular. The standard heights of boards are 1 and 3 meters. The 1-meter board should be over water 9 to 10 feet deep and the 3-meter board over 10 to 12 feet deep. The board or any diving takeoff area should have a nonskid covering. The boards should be securely fastened to the ground or foundation.

The rules and regulations concerning diving equipment should be clearly posted near the diving areas. Roping off and patrolling the area are safety precautions.

The checklist at the end of the chapter provides further information on swimming pool standards.*

CAMPS†

Because camping is becoming an increasingly popular activity in both school and recreational programs, it should receive consideration.

Camps should be located within easy reach of the school and community. They should be in locations

desirable from the standpoints of scenic beauty, safety, accessibility, water, and natural resources pertinent to the program offered. Activities usually offered include fishing, hiking, swimming, campcraft, boating, nature study, and appropriate winter sports. The natural terrain and other resources can contribute much toward such a program.

There should be adequate housing, eating, sanitary, waterfront, and other facilities essential to camp life. These do not have to be as elaborate as those in the home or school Adequate protection against the elements is essential, however. Facilities should also meet acceptable standards of health and sanitation. In general, camp structures should be adapted to the climatic conditions of the particular area in which the camp is located. It is wise to consult public health authorities when selecting a campsite. Sometimes existing facilities can be converted to camp use. The campsite should be purchased outright or a long-term lease acquired.

Facilities for the handicapped

Since the passage of PL 94-142 more consideration has been given to the facility needs of the handicapped. These facilities in particular are concerned with the student's program of developmental exercises, perceptual-motor activities, modified sports,

*For more information on swimming pools, see pp. 406-409.
†See Chapter 12.

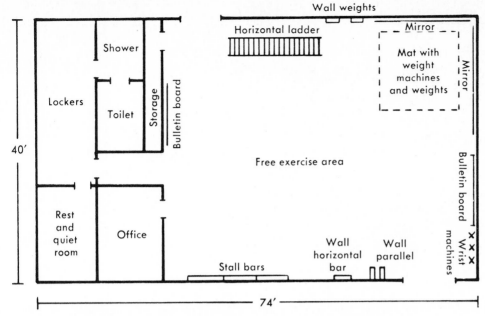

Fig. 12-19. Self-contained adapted physical education room.

From Crowe, W.C., Auxter, D., and Pyfer, J.: Principles and methods of adapted physical education and recreation, ed. 4, St. Louis, 1981, The C.V. Mosby Co.

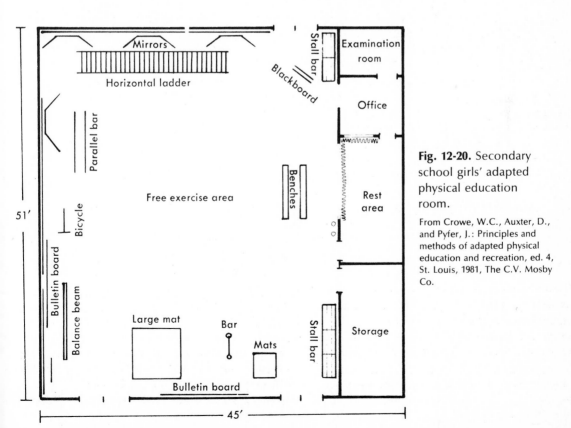

Fig. 12-20. Secondary school girls' adapted physical education room.

From Crowe, W.C., Auxter, D., and Pyfer, J.: Principles and methods of adapted physical education and recreation, ed. 4, St. Louis, 1981, The C.V. Mosby Co.

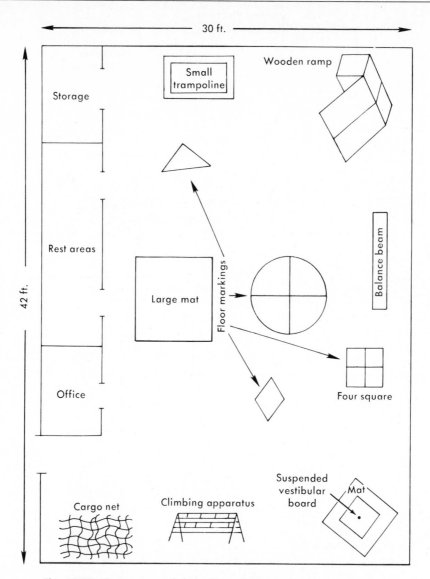

Fig. 12-21. Elementary school adapted physical education room.

From Crowe, W.C., Auxter, D., and Pyfer, J.: Principles and methods of adapted physical education and recreation, ed. 4, St. Louis, 1981, The C.V. Mosby Co.

and rest and relaxation. These facilities usually vary from school to school and according to the type of handicapped persons served.

Facilities in elementary schools for the adapted program vary from a classroom to a gymnasium, swimming pool, or outside play area. Some schools take their students to special centers for the handicapped, or to another school within the district. The minimum facility for the elementary school would be ample space to enable a program of adapted physical education involving such things as performing special exercises, playing with balls and hoops, and participating on various pieces of climbing apparatus.

Facilities in secondary schools should include an adapted physical education room large enough to accommodate such things as specialized equipment

Fig. 12-22. A, Use of the open space area in an adapted physical education room to conduct formal group exercises. **B,** Elementary school class uses a college facility. Each student performs an individual exercise on a piece of equipment.

From Crowe, W.C., et al.: Principles and methods of adapted physical education and recreation, ed. 4, St. Louis, 1981, The C.V. Mosby Co.

(horizontal ladder, pulleys), exercises, and play activities. The minimum size for a junior or senior high school room would be 40 by 60 feet. There should also be an adapted sports area located adjacent to the adapted physical education room. On this sports area would be conducted such activities as volleyball, paddle tennis, badminton, table tennis, shuffleboard, and croquet. A swimming pool at any educational level would be especially desirable because most handicapped persons enjoy and profit from swimming activities. As in the case with elementary school students, secondary schools and colleges sometimes use locations in the community, private facilities, or recreation centers to carry on their program.

Other special facilities

Other facilities needing special attention include those in dance, gymnastics, weight training, wrestling and martial arts, racquetball, and other sports and research and teaching areas.

DANCE FACILITIES

Because dance is becoming very popular as an activity, special facilities should be provided. It is recommended that a minimum of 100 square feet per student be provided with full-length mirrors, a speaker system, and a control system for record players and microphones. There should also be practice bars on one wall at heights of 34 and 42 inches. The floor is an important consideration and it is recommended it be of sealed and buffed hard northern maple.

SPECIAL ACTIVITY AND OTHER AREAS

Where possible, special activity and other areas, such as a *gymnastic area* of 120 by 90 feet with a minimum ceiling height of 23 feet, should be provided. A *weight training area* will receive considerable use if provided. It is recommended that such a room contain a minimum of 2500 square feet. A *wrestling and martial arts area* of a minimum 50 by 100 feet will provide for two square mats 42 by 42 feet each. *Racquetball and handball courts* are common, particularly in colleges. Each four-wall court is 40 feet long and 20 feet wide with a ceiling height of 20 feet.

Other areas that may be considered are squash courts, multipurpose activity area, fencing area, indoor tennis facilities, indoor archery range, indoor rifle range, and golf practice area.

Research and teaching areas to be considered include laboratories for human performance projects, motor learning, biomechanics, the sociology of sport, and instructional media.

New features in the construction of physical education facilities

There are many new trends in facilities and materials for physical education programs, including new paving materials, new types of equipment, improved landscapes, new construction materials, new shapes for swimming pools, partial shelters, and synthetic grass. Combination indoor-outdoor pools, physical fitness equipment for outdoor use, all-weather tennis courts, and lines that now come in multicolors for various games and activities are other new developments.

In gymnasium construction some of the new features include using modern engineering techniques and materials, which has resulted in welded steel and laminated wood modular frames; arched and gabled roofs; domes that provide areas completely free from internal supports; exterior surfaces of aluminum, steel, fiberglass, and plastics; different window patterns and styles; several kinds of floor surfaces of nonslip material; prefabricated wall surfaces; better lighting systems with improved quality and quantity and less glare. Facilities are moving from using regular glass to either a plastic and fiberglass panel or to an overhead skydome. Lightweight fiberglass, sandwich panels, or fabricated sheets of translucent fiberglass laminated over an aluminum framework are proving popular. They require no painting, the cost of labor and materials is lower, there is no need for shades or blinds to eliminate glare, and the breakage problem is reduced or eliminated.

Locker rooms and service areas are including built-in locks with combination changers that permit staff members to change combinations when needed. There

Fig. 12-23. A, Graceland Fieldhouse, Lamoni, Iowa. **B,** Forman School, Litchfield, Conn.

A, Courtesy Shaver & Co., Salina, Kan.; **B,** courtesy Educational facilities Laboratories, New York.

is more extensive use of ceramic tile because of its durability and low-cost maintenance. Wallhung toilet compartment features permit easier maintenance and sanitation with no chance for rust to start from the floor. Odor control is being effectively handled by new dispensers. New thin-profile heating, ventilating, and air-conditioning fan coil units are now being used.

The athletic training and health suite is being modernized by making it more attractive and serviceable. There is also a trend toward better ventilation, heating, and lighting and more easily cleaned materials on walls and floors to guarantee improved sanitation.

New developments concerning indoor swimming pools include automatic control boards, where one person can have direct control over all filters, chlorinators, chemical pumps, and lever controllers; much larger deck space area constructed of nonslip ceramic tile; greater use of diatomaceous earth rather than sand filters to filter out small particles of matter including some bacteria; underwater lighting; water-level deck pools (where the overflow gutters are placed in the deck surrounding the pool instead of in the pool's side walls and provision is made for grating designed so the water that overflows is drained to a trench under the deck without the possibility of debris returning to the pool); air-supported roofs that can serve as removable tops in a combination indoor-outdoor pool; and movable bulkheads.

Fig. 12-24. Graceland Fieldhouse, Lamoni, Iowa.

Courtesy Shaver & Co., Salina, Kan.

New developments concerning outdoor swimming pools involve new shapes—including oval, wedge, kidney, figure-8, cloverleaf, and bean shaped—as well as modern accessories, including wave-making machines, gas heaters, automatic water levelers, and retractable roofs and sides. More supplmental recreational facilities, such as shuffleboard courts, volleyball, and horseshoes, and more deck equipment, including guard rails, slides, and pool covers, are being included around larger pools.

New concepts have been put to good use in the physical plants of the following schools:

Oak Grove High School, San Jose, California. This school has a movable interior partitioning system with adjustable lighting, acoustics, and air conditioning that can accommodate different types of activities on short notice.

Nova High School, Fort Lauderdale, Florida. This school spent 10% of the school's total cost on teaching aids so all types of audiovisual materials could be utilized or piped into most classrooms and teaching stations in the school.

Andrews Senior High School, Andrews, Texas. Here the open court has a windowless exterior and faces inward to a concourse and a domed rotunda. Along the concourse are a swimming pool and gymnasium, and under the rotunda is an assembly area.

Holland High School, Holland, Michigan. This school built its plant on the compass plan with four small schools. Physical education facilities are shared by all schools.

New Haven, Connecticut Public Schools. This city adapted its facilities to the community school concept with each school including community facilities involving the city's social and welfare agencies where such problems as health, family relations, and unemployment are major concerns.

Portland State University, Oregon. Here the roof of the physical education building was covered with artificial surfacing to provide tennis courts and a general sports area.

Brooklyn Polytech, New York City. A bubble was erected on top of the physics building for a gymnasium.

University of Texas at El Paso. This university covered its outdoor swimming pool with prefabricated material to have an all-weather, year-round facility.

Fig. 12-25. Super tent at LaVerne College, Calif.

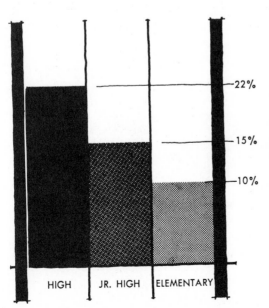

SCHOOL YEAR, ± 250 CALENDAR DAYS						
	D A Y S L O S T					
85	34	14	24	15	62	16
Good days - outdoor play without need of any protective devices	Precipitation - rain, snow, sleet -	Poor ground conditions	High winds - (Temp. O.K.)	Extreme cold - (no wind)	"Windchill" effects - (high winds + low temperatures)	High temp. + high humidity

Fig. 12-26. Charts showing amount of space devoted to physical activities in schools, the implications of weather conditions for the physical education program, and some ideas for partial shelters for physical education programs.

From Shelter for physical education; a study of the feasibility of the use of limited shelters for physical education, College Station, Texas, Texas Engineering Experiment Station, Texas A & M University.

22%

15%

10%

HIGH   JR. HIGH   ELEMENTARY

BUILDING SPACE DEVOTED TO PHYSICAL ACTIVITIES

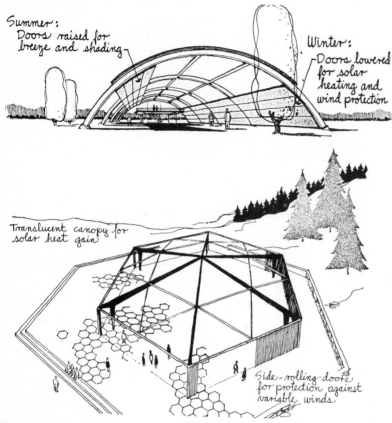

Summer:
Doors raised for
breeze and shading

Winter:
Doors lowered
for solar
heating and
wind protection

Translucent canopy for
solar heat gain

Side-rolling doors
for protection against
variable winds

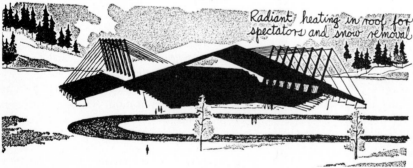

Radiant heating in roof for
spectators and snow removal

Fig. 12-27. Partial shelters for physical education.

LaVerne College, California. Here what some persons call a super tent, involving a cable-supported fabric roof structure made of fiber glass and Teflon, houses theater, gymnasium, cafeteria, bookstore, and health clinic.

Cuyahoga Falls, Ohio. Here a roof was installed over the swimming pool so it could be used during the winter and the summer months. In the summer months the roof is removed.

Thomas Jefferson Junior High School, Arlington, Virginia. This school has implemented the shared facilities concept by housing together performing arts, recreation, and physical education.

Harvard University, Massachusetts. Here the largest air-supported structure for a new track facility has been erected; it is 250 feet wide, 300 feet long, and 60 feet high.

Lewis and Clark Elementary School, St. Louis, Missouri. A physical education partial shelter has been erected with the sides of the open structure protected by banks of shrubbery.

Boston College, Massachusetts. A roof design of hyperbolic parabaloids is utilized. This efficient structure spans a large area—42,000 square feet of floor space.

LIMITED SHELTERS FOR PHYSICAL EDUCATION

The shelter or limited shelter provides protection from extremes of climate, uses the desirable elements of the natural environment, and creates an interesting background for physical education activities. See Fig. 12-27 for use of limited shelters.

The actual design of the shelter is determined by climate, use, and the activity program. Methods of controlling air movement may be developed by using natural elements (trees and plantings), architectural elements (wall, roofs, and screens), and mechanical devices (fan, moving walls, and screens). Solar radiation may be controlled with natural shading and moving walls. These shelters cost about half as much as the traditional gymnasium.

AIR-SUPPORTED STRUCTURES

An air-supported structure consists of a large plastic bubble that is inflated and supported by continuous

air pressure. It is the least expensive building one can erect, costing from one fifth to one half of what a solid structure would cost. These facilities have served for housing military equipment, theaters, factories, swimming pools, tennis courts, and gymnasiums.

The outside construction is usually made of vinyl-coated or Dacron plyester, which is lightweight, strong, and flexible. The fabric is flame-retardant, waterproof, tear-resistant, mildew-resistant, and sunlight-resistant. Installation is simple and may be completed in a few hours by a minimum crew. The installation process includes placement of vinyl envelope and inflation. The bubble is supported by a blower that provides a constant flow of air pressure. The bubble may be easily dismantled by stopping the blower, opening the door, unhitching the attachments, and folding the bubble compactly.

MINIGYMS AND FITNESS CORNERS

Most schoolchildren must confine their physical activities to the physical education class, which may not meet every day. Even in gym classes, students are often required to participate amid an atmosphere of formality when time is taken up in attendance lineups, exercises, testing, and other planned activities. How can this be changed?

The answer may be found in minigyms, which can be operated in the halls and alcoves of the school building. They may consist of climbing, pulling, and hanging apparatus that the students use between classes, at study hours, lunch, and recess. This idea is to distribute the gymnasium throughout the school. Some other suggestion include mats, chinning bars, inclines, walls to throw balls against, and carpeted corridors for stunts and tumbling.

Classrooms can also be turned into minigyms with fitness corners for exercise and equipment such as stationary bicycles, rowing machines, and stand-up desks to promote activity.

TENNIS COURTS AND OTHER FACILITIES

Rubber-cushioned tennis courts are being used in some places. They consist of tough durable material about 4 inches thick, which has the individual ad-

Fig. 12-28. Special tennis structure, Brigham Young University, Provo, Utah.

Fig. 12-29. Tennis courts at Sinclair Community College, Dayton, Ohio.

vantages of clay, turf, and composition courts combined in one surface.

Other new developments in physical education facilities are numerous. Sculptured play apparatus has been produced by a number of firms. It is designed to be more conducive to imaginative movements and creativity than conventional equipment. Hard-surfaced, rubberized, all-weather running tracks, radiant heating of decks on swimming pools, floating roofs that eliminate non-load-bearing walls, interior climate control, better indoor and outdoor lighting, rubber padding for use under apparatus, the park-school concept with land being used for school and recreational purposes, outdoor skating rinks, translucent plastic materials for swimming pool canopies and other uses, electrically operated machinery to move equipment and partitions and bleachers, and auxiliary gymnasiums for both activity and classroom use are more of the new developments in facilities for physical education programs.

Park-school facilities

In the park-school complex the school is erected near a park, and the park facilities are used by both the school and the community. This has implications particularly for physical education and recreation programs, for the school usually uses the park facilities during school hours and the recreation department uses them after school hours, on weekends, and during vacation periods.

The T. Wendall Williams Community Education Center in Flint, Michigan, is situated on a two-block site that adjoins a 72-acre park. The area consists of 30 classrooms, a lower elementary group activity area, a large sunken learning resources center, five team-teaching rooms, and a large gymnasium. The recreation area is located on park property and administered by the Flint Recreation and Park Department. Baseball, softball, soccer, football, basketball, and picnicking are provided for. There are swimming areas, tennis courts, and activity areas for small children. In the winter the pool is covered for all-year swimming, and the tennis courts are converted into a large artificial ice-skating rink. The park also provides natural areas for learning and recreation for all.

Maintenance of facilities

Planning and constructing facilities are important administrative functions. An equally important responsibility is maintaining facilities. With proper maintenance a facility will last longer, provide a healthier environment, be less costly, and provide a more satisfying experience for participants. Just as planning and constructing facilities in physical education and athletics are team efforts, so is maintaining these facilities. The custodial staff, the participants, and the physical education and athletic staffs must all work together in taking pride in their facility and putting forth a special effort to see that it is maintained in perfect condition.

Community use of school and college facilities

Schools and colleges continually receive requests to open their facilities to various community groups. It is therefore imperative for the administration to establish guidelines ensuring that appropriate precautions are taken and such facilities are used properly when approval is given.

First, the administration should see that a written policy is established and approved by proper authorities regarding community use of facilities (who can use, at what times, under what conditions). Second, the administrative procedure regarding community use should be established. This usually includes such things as making a proper application, obtaining the liability insurance coverage necessary, setting the fee payment, and making stipulations regarding maintenance and security. Third, administrative controls should be established to see that administrative policies and procedures are carried out as specified.

SCHOOLS USING COMMUNITY RESOURCES

Such facilities as parks, bowling alleys, swimming pools, ski slopes, and skating arenas can extend the school physical education program and related sports activities. Most community facilities can be used during off-hours and after school, and the charge is frequently nominal.

COPY DISTRIBUTION:
White: *Applicant*
Pink: *Univ. Bus. Ofc.*
Blue: *O&M*
White: *Men's Eq. Rm.*
Yellow: *P.E. Dept.*

USE AGREEMENT

MCDERMOTT PHYSICAL EDUCATION CENTER

The undersigned representing: ______________________________

(name of organization)

____

requests permission to use a part of the P.E. Center designated as ______________________________

____

____

for the period ______________________________

____

under the following conditions and terms:

Service or Equipment	Furnished by Applicant	Furnished by UNLV	Charge

You will be billed for any clean up or set charges, if necessary.

In addition to the above charges a basic fee in the amount of $ ______________

will be paid resulting in a total charge of $ ______________ of which one-half or

$ ______________ is paid with this application with the other half to be paid within five days after the last use covered by this agreement.

The applicant assumes responsibility for following University regulations with respect to the whole pattern of usage authorized by this agreement and agrees to indemnify and hold harmless the University from any loss or damage caused by the negligence of the applicant or its agents or employees.

SIGNED: ______________________________ ______________
Date

______________________________ ______________
Address — Phone Number

______________________________ ______________
Facility Coordinator, Department of PED — Date

______________________________ ______________
Business Office Representative — Date

(needed only when usage is for more than 7 days or charges total more than $1,000)

CLASSIFICATION OF ORGANIZATION

- ☐ A business enterprise organized for profit
- ☐ A non-profit educational, scientific, cultural organization
- ☐ A governmental entity
- ☐ A religious group
- ☐ Other ______________

Fig. 12-30. Use agreement for organizations using facilities.

UNIVERSITY OF NEVADA, LAS VEGAS

REQUEST FOR BUILDING USE

NOTE: This form must be prepared in quadruplicate
and approved and filed ONE WEEK prior to
use of the facility.

_____
Date

PLEASE TYPE

BUILDING requested _____ ROOM OR AREA _____

DATE & HOURS requested _____ FROM _____ TO _____
                  Date   Time (Specify A.M. or P.M.)

DATE & HOURS requested _____ FROM _____ TO _____
                  Date   Time (Specify A.M. or P.M.)

DATE & HOURS requested _____ FROM _____ TO _____
                  Date   Time (Specify A.M. or P.M.)

NATURE of function _____

NUMBER expected to attend _____

FURNITURE needed and special room arrangements (Diagram may be attached if desired):

_____

_____

_____

_____

_____ We will need to use UNLV audio-visual equipment and will be responsible for making the
arrangements with the UNLV Audio-Visual Services.

_____ We will need food and/or beverages and will be responsible for making the arrangements
with the campus food catering service.

SPONSORING ORGANIZATION _____

APPROVED _____ SIGNATURE _____
        UNLV Sponsor - Dept. Head   Applicant

APPROVALS:

CHARGES: $ _____

DISTRIBUTION:
  BUILDINGS & GROUNDS - WHITE
  SECURITY   - PINK
  APPLICANT   - GOLDENROD
  PHYSICAL EDUCATION - YELLOW

_____
FACILITY COORDINATOR   DATE

_____
BUILDINGS & GROUNDS   DATE

_____
SECURITY   DATE

Fig. 12-31. Request for building use by outside organizations.

CHECKLIST FOR FACILITY PLANNERS*

General	Yes	No

1. A clear-cut statement has been prepared on the nature and scope of the program, and the special requirements for space, equipment, fixtures, and facilities dictated by the activities to be conducted.
2. The facility has been planned to meet the total requirements of the program as well as the special needs of those who are to be served.
3. The plans and specifications have been checked by all governmental agencies (city, county, and state) whose approval is required by law.
4. Plans for areas and facilities conform to state and local regulations and to accepted standards and practices.
5. The areas and facilities planned make possible the programs that serve the interests and needs of all people.
6. Every available source of property or funds has been explored, evaluated, and utilized whenever appropriate.
7. All interested persons and organizations concerned with the facility have had an opportunity to share in its planning (professional educators, users, consultants, administrators, engineers, architects, program specialists, building managers, and builder—a team approach).
8. The facility and its appurtenances will fulfill the maximum demands of the program. The program has not been curtailed to fit the facility.
9. The facility has been functionally planned to meet the present and anticipated needs of specific programs, situations, and publics.
10. Future additions are included in present plans to permit economy of construction.
11. Lecture classrooms are isolated from distracting noises.
12. Storage areas for indoor and outdoor equipment are adequately sized. They are located adjacent to the gymnasiums.
13. Shelves in storage rooms are slanted toward the wall.
14. All passageways are free of obstructions; fixtures are recessed.
15. Facilities for health services, athletic training, health testing, health instruction, and the first aid and emergency-isolation rooms are suitably interrelated.
16. Buildings, specific areas, and facilities are clearly identified.
17. Locker rooms are arranged for ease of supervision.
18. Offices, teaching stations, and service facilities are properly interrelated.
19. Special needs of the physically handicapped are met, including a ramp into the building at a major entrance.
20. All "dead space" is used.
21. The building is compatible in design and comparable in quality and accommodation to other organizational structures.
22. Storage rooms are accessible to the play area.
23. Workrooms, conference rooms, and staff and administrative offices are interrelated.
24. Shower and dressing facilities are provided for professional staff members and are conveniently located.

*Adapted from Participants in National Facilities Conference, op. cit., pp. 256-260, updated by the author, 1979.

CHECKLIST FOR FACILITY PLANNERS—cont'd

General—cont'd   *Yes*   *No*

25. Thought and attention have been given to making facilities and equipment as durable and vandalproof as possible. _____ _____
26. Low-cost maintenance features have been adequately considered. _____ _____
27. This facility is a part of a well-integrated master plan. _____ _____
28. All areas, courts, facilities, equipment, climate control, security, etc. conform rigidly to detailed standards and specifications. _____ _____
29. Shelves are recessed and mirrors are supplied in appropriate places in rest rooms and dressing rooms. Mirrors are not placed above lavatories. _____ _____
30. Dressing space between locker rows is adjusted to the size and age level of participants. _____ _____
31. Drinking fountains are conveniently placed in locker room areas or immediately adjacent thereto. _____ _____
32. Special attention is given to provision for the locking of service windows and counters, supply bins, carts, shelves, and racks. _____ _____
33. Provision is made for the repair, maintenance, replacement, and off-season storage of equipment and uniforms. _____ _____
34. A well-defined program for laundering and cleaning of towels, uniforms, and equipment is included in the plan. _____ _____
35. Noncorrosive metal is used in dressing, drying, and shower areas except for enameled lockers. _____ _____
36. Antipanic hardware is used where required by fire regulations. _____ _____
37. Properly placed hose bibbs and drains are sufficient in size and quantity to permit flushing the entire area with a water hose. _____ _____
38. A water-resistant, coved base is used under the locker base and floor mat, and where floor and wall join. _____ _____
39. Chalkboards and/or tackboards with map tracks are located in appropriate places in dressing rooms, hallways, and classrooms. _____ _____
40. Book shelves are provided in toilet areas. _____ _____
41. Space and equipment are planned in accordance with the types and number of participants. _____ _____
42. Basement rooms, being undesirable for dressing, drying, and showering, are not planned for those purposes. _____ _____
43. Spectator seating (permanent) in areas that are basically instructional is kept at a minimum. Rollaway bleachers are used primarily. Balcony seating is considered as a possibility. _____ _____
44. Well-lighted and effectively displayed trophy cases enhance the interest and beauty of the lobby. _____ _____
45. The space under the stairs is used for storage. _____ _____
46. Department heads' offices are located near the central administrative office, which includes a well-planned conference room. _____ _____
47. Workrooms are located near the central office and serve as a repository for department materials and records. _____ _____

Continued.

CHECKLIST FOR FACILITY PLANNERS—cont'd

General—cont'd	*Yes*	*No*
48. The conference area includes a cloak room, lavatory, and toilet.	_____	_____
49. In addition to regular secretarial offices established in the central and department chairperson's offices, a special room to house a secretarial pool for staff members is provided.	_____	_____
50. Staff dressing facilities are provided. These facilities may also serve game officials.	_____	_____
51. The community and/or neighborhood has a "round table"—planning round table.	_____	_____
52. All those (persons and agencies) who should be a party to planning and development are invited and actively engaged in the planning process.	_____	_____
53. Space and area relationships are important. They have been carefully considered.	_____	_____
54. Both long-range plans and immediate plans have been made.	_____	_____
55. The body comfort of the student and other participants, a major factor in securing maximum learning, has been considered in the plans.	_____	_____
56. Plans for quiet areas have been made.	_____	_____
57. In the planning, consideration has been given to the need for adequate recreation areas and facilities, both near and distant from the homes of people.	_____	_____
58. Plans recognize the primary function of recreation as being enrichment of learning through creative self-expression, self-enhancement, and the achievement of self-potential.	_____	_____
59. Every effort has been exercised to eliminate hazards.	_____	_____
60. The installation of low-hanging door closers, light fixtures, signs, and other objects in traffic areas has been avoided.	_____	_____
61. Warning signals—both visible and audible—are included in the plans.	_____	_____
62. Ramps have a slope equal to or less than a 1-foot rise in 12 feet.	_____	_____
63. Minimum landings for ramps are 5 feet × 5 feet, they extend at least 1 foot beyond the swinging arc of a door, have at least a 6-foot clearance at the bottom, and have level platforms at 30-foot intervals on every turn.	_____	_____
64. Adequate locker and dressing spaces are provided.	_____	_____
65. The design of dressing, drying, and shower areas reduces foot traffic to a minimum and establishes clean, dry aisles for bare feet.	_____	_____
66. Teaching stations are properly related to service facilities.	_____	_____
67. Toilet facilities are adequate in number. They are located to serve all groups for which provisions are made.	_____	_____
68. Mail services, outgoing and incoming, are included in the plans.	_____	_____
69. Hallways, ramps, doorways, and elevators are designed to permit equipment to be moved easily and quickly.	_____	_____
70. A keying design suited to administrative and instructional needs is planned.	_____	_____
71. Toilets used by large groups have circulating (in and out) entrances and exists.	_____	_____

Climate control

	Yes	*No*
1. Provision is made throughout the building for climate control—heating, ventilating, and refrigerated cooling.	_____	_____

CHECKLIST FOR FACILITY PLANNERS—cont'd

	Yes	No
Climate control—cont'd		

2. Special ventilation is provided for locker, dressing, shower, drying, and toilet rooms. _____ _____
3. Heating plans permit both area and individual room control. _____ _____
4. Research areas where small animals are kept and where chemicals are used have been provided with special ventilating equipment. _____ _____
5. The heating and ventilating of the wrestling gymnasium have been given special attention. _____ _____

Electrical

1. Shielded, vaporproof lights are used in moisture-prevalent areas. _____ _____
2. Lights in strategic areas are key controlled. _____ _____
3. Lighting intensity conforms to approved standards. _____ _____
4. An adequate number of electrical outlets are strategically placed. _____ _____
5. Gymnasium lights are controlled by dimmer units. _____ _____
6. Locker room lights are mounted above the space between lockers. _____ _____
7. Natural light is controlled properly for purposes of visual aids and other avoidance of glare. _____ _____
8. Electrical outlet plates are installed 3 feet above the floor unless special use dictates other locations. _____ _____
9. Controls for light switches and projection equipment are suitably located and interrelated. _____ _____
10. All lights are shielded. Special protection is provided in gymnasiums, court areas, and shower rooms. _____ _____
11. Lights are placed to shine between rows of lockers. _____ _____

Walls

1. Movable and folding partitions are power-operated and controlled by keyed switches. _____ _____
2. Wall places are located where needed and are firmly attached. _____ _____
3. Hooks and rings for nets are placed (and recessed in walls) according to court locations and net heights. _____ _____
4. Materials that clean easily and are impervious to moisture are used where moisture is prevalent. _____ _____
5. Shower heads are placed at different heights—4 feet (elementary) to 7 feet (university)—for each school level. _____ _____
6. Protective matting is placed permanently on the walls in the wrestling room, at the ends of basketball courts, and in other areas where such protection is needed. _____ _____
7. An adequate number of drinking fountains is provided. They are properly placed (recessed in wall). _____ _____
8. One wall (at least) of the dance studio has full-length mirrors. _____ _____
9. All corners in locker rooms are rounded. _____ _____

Continued.

CHECKLIST FOR FACILITY PLANNERS—cont'd

Ceilings   Yes   No

1. Overhead-supported apparatus is secured to beams engineered to withstand stress. _____   _____
2. The ceiling height is adequate for the activities to be housed. _____   _____
3. Acoustical materials impervious to moisture are used in moisture-prevalent areas. _____   _____
4. Skylights, being impractical, are seldom used because of problems in waterproof- _____   _____
   ing roofs and the controlling of sun rays (gyms).
5. All ceilings except those in storage areas are acoustically treated with sound-ab- _____   _____
   sorbent materials.

Floors

1. Floor plates are placed where needed and are flush-mounted. _____   _____
2. Floor design and materials conform to recommended standards and specifications. _____   _____
3. Lines and markings are painted on floors before sealing is completed (when syn- _____   _____
   thetic tape is not used).
4. A coved base (around lockers and where wall and floor meet) or the same water- _____   _____
   resistant material used on floors is found in all dressing and shower rooms.
5. Abrasive, nonskid, slip-resistant flooring that is impervious to moisture is pro- _____   _____
   vided on all areas where water is used—laundry, swimming pool, shower, dressing, and drying rooms.
6. Floor drains are properly located, and the slope of the floor is adequate for rapid _____   _____
   drainage.

Gymnasiums and special rooms

1. Gymnasiums are planned so as to provide for safety zones (between courts, end _____   _____
   lines, and walls) and for best utilization of space.
2. One gymnasium wall is free of obstructions and is finished with a smooth, hard _____   _____
   surface for ball-rebounding activities.
3. The elementary school gymnasium has one wall free of obstructions, a minimum _____   _____
   ceiling height of 18 feet, a minimum of 4000 square feet of teaching area, and a
   recessed area for housing a piano.
4. Secondary school gymnasiums have a minimum ceiling height of 22 feet; a score- _____   _____
   board; electrical outlets placed to fit with bleacher installation; wall attachments
   for apparatus and nets; and a power-operated, sound-insulated, and movable partition with a small pass-through door at one end.
5. A small spectator alcove adjoins the wrestling room and contains a drinking foun- _____   _____
   tain (recessed in the walls).
6. Cabinets, storage closets, supply windows, and service areas have locks. _____   _____
7. Provisions have been made for the cleaning, storing, and issuing of physical edu- _____   _____
   cation and athletic uniforms.
8. Shower heads are placed at varying heights in the shower rooms on each school _____   _____
   level.
9. Equipment is provided for the use of the physically handicapped. _____   _____
10. Special provision has been made for audio and visual aids, including intercom- _____   _____
    munication systems, radio, and television.

CHECKLIST FOR FACILITY PLANNERS—cont'd

Gymnasiums and special rooms—cont'd   *Yes*   *No*

11. Team dressing rooms have provisions for:
    a. Hosing down room
    b. Floors pitched to drain easily
    c. Hot- and cold-water hose bibbs
    d. Windows located above locker heights
    e. Chalk, tack, and bulletin boards, and movie projection
    f. Lockers for each team member
    g. Drying facility for uniforms
12. The indoor rifle range includes:
    a. Targets located 54 inches apart and 50 feet from the firing line
    b. 3 feet to 8 feet space behind targets
    c. 12 feet of space behind firing line
    d. Ceilings 8 feet high
    e. Width adjusted to number of firing lines needed (1 line for each 3 students)
    f. A pulley device for target placement and return
    g. Storage and repair space
13. Dance facilities include:
    a. 100 square feet per student
    b. A minimum length of 60 linear feet for modern dance
    c. Full-height viewing mirrors on one wall (at least) of 30 feet; also a 20-foot mirror on an additional wall if possible
    d. Acoustical drapery to cover mirrors when not used and for protection if other activities are permitted
    e. Dispersed microphone jacks and speaker installation for music and instruction
    f. Built-in cabinets for record players, microphones, and amplifiers, with space for equipment carts
    g. Electrical outlets and microphone connections around perimeter of room
    h. An exercise bar (34 inches to 42 inches above floor) on one wall
    i. Drapes, surface colors, floors (maple preferred), and other room appointments to enhance the room's attractiveness
    j. Location near dressing rooms and outside entrances
14. Training rooms include:
    a. Rooms large enough to administer adequately proper health services
    b. Sanitary storage cabinets for medical supplies
    c. Installation of drains for whirlpool, tubs, etc.
    d. Installation of electrical outlets with proper capacities and voltage
    e. High stools for use of equipment such as whirlpool, ice tubs, etc.
    f. Water closet, hand lavatory, and shower
    g. Extra hand lavatory in the trainer's room proper
    h. Adjoining dressing rooms
    i. Installation and use of hydrotherapy and diathermy equipment is separate areas
    j. Space for the trainer, the physician, and the various services of this function
    k. Corrective exercise laboratories located conveniently and adapted to the needs of the handicapped

Continued.

CHECKLIST FOR FACILITY PLANNERS—cont'd

Gymnasiums and special rooms—cont'd   Yes   No

15. Coaches' room should provide:
    a. A sufficient number of dressing lockers for coaching staff and officials
    b. A security closet or cabinet for athletic equipment such as timing devices
    c. A sufficient number of showers and toilet facilities
    d. Drains and faucets for hosing down the rooms where this method of cleaning is desirable and possible
    e. A small chalkboard and tackboard
    f. A small movie screen and projection table for use of coaches to review films

Handicapped and disabled

Have you included those considerations that would make the facility accessible to, and usable by, the disabled? These considerations include:

1. The knowledge that the disabled will be participants in almost all activities, not merely spectators, if the facility is properly planned.
2. Ground-level entrance(s) or stair-free entrance(s) using inclined walk(s) or inclined ramp(s).
3. Uninterrupted walk surface; no abrupt changes in levels leading the facility.
4. Approach walks and connecting walks no less than 4 feet wide.
5. Walks with gradient no greater than 5%.
6. A ramp, when used, with rise no greater than 1 foot in 12 feet.
7. Flat or level surface inside and outside of all exterior doors, extending 5 feet from the door in the direction that the door swings, and extending 1 foot to each side of the door.
8. Flush thresholds at all doors.
9. Appropriate door widths, heights, and mechanical features.
10. At least 6 feet between vestibule doors in series, i.e., inside and outside doors.
11. Access and proximity to parking areas.
12. No obstructions by curbs at crosswalks, parking areas, etc.
13. Proper precautions (handrails, etc.) at basement-window areaways, open stairways, porches, ledges, and platforms.
14. Handrails on all steps and ramps.
15. Precautions against the placement of manholes in principal or major sidewalks.
16. Corridors that are at least 60 inches wide and without abrupt pillars or protrusions.
17. Floors that are nonskid and have no abrupt changes or interruptions in level.
18. Proper design of steps.
19. Access to rest rooms, water coolers, telephones, food-service areas, lounges, dressing rooms, play areas, and auxiliary services and areas.
20. Elevators in multiple-story buildings.
21. Appropriate placement of controls to permit and to prohibit use as desired.
22. Sound signals for the blind, and visual signals for the deaf as counterparts to regular sound and sight signals.
23. Proper placement, concealment, or insulation of radiators, heat pipes, hotwater pipes, drain pipes, etc.

CHECKLIST FOR FACILITY PLANNERS—cont'd

Swimming pools   Yes   No

1. Has a clear-cut statement been prepared on the nature and scope of the design program and the special requirements for space, equipment, and facilities dictated by the activities to be conducted?

2. Has the swimming pool been planned to meet the total requirements of the program to be conducted as well as any special needs of the clientele to be serviced?

3. Have all plans and specifications been checked and approved by the local board of health?

4. Is the pool the proper depth to accommodate the various age groups and types of activities it is intended to serve?

5. Does the design of the pool incorporate the most current knowledge and best experience available regarding swimming pools?

6. If a local architect or engineer who is inexperienced in pool construction is employed, has an experienced pool consultant, architect, or engineer been called in to advise on design and equipment?

7. Is there adequate deep water for diving (minimum of 9 feet for 1-meter boards, 12 feet for 3-meter boards, and 15 feet for 10-meter towers)?

8. Have the requirements for competitive swimming been met (7-foot lanes; 12-inch black or brown lines on the bottom; pool 1 inch longer than official measurement; depth and distance markings)?

9. Is there adequate deck space around the pool? Has more space been provided than that indicated by the minimum recommended deck/pool ratio?

10. Does the swimming instructor's office face the pool? And is there a window through which the instructor may view all the pool area? Is there a toilet-shower-dressing area next to the office for instructors?

11. Are recessed steps or removable ladders located on the walls so as not to interfere with competitive swimming turns?

12. Does a properly constructed overflow gutter extend around the pool perimeter?

13. Where skimmers are used, have they been properly located so that they are not on walls where competitive swimming is to be conducted?

14. Have separate storage spaces been allocated for maintenance and instructional equipment?

15. Has the area for spectators been properly separated from the pool area?

16. Have all diving standards and lifeguard chairs been properly anchored?

17. Does the pool layout provide the most efficient control of swimmers from showers and locker rooms to the pool? Are toilet facilities provided for wet swimmers separate from the dry area?

18. Is the recirculation pump located below the water level?

19. Is there easy vertical access to the filter room for both people and material (stairway if required)?

20. Has the proper pitch to drains been allowed in the pool, on the pool deck, in the overflow gutter, and on the floor of shower and dressing rooms?

21. Has adequate space been allowed between diving boards and between the diving boards and sidewalls?

22. Is there adequate provision for lifesaving equipment? Pool-cleaning equipment?

Continued.

CHECKLIST FOR FACILITY PLANNERS—cont'd

	Yes	No
Swimming pools—cont'd		

23. Are inlets and outlets adequate in number and located so as to ensure effective circulation of water in the pool?

24. Has consideration been given to underwater lights, underwater observation windows, and underwater speakers?

25. Is there a coping around the edge of the pool?

26. Has a pool heater been considered in northern climates in order to raise the temperature of the water?

27. Have underwater lights in end racing walls been located deep enough and directly below surface lane anchors, and are they on a separate circuit?

28. Has the plan been considered from the standpoint of handicapped persons (e.g., is there a gate adjacent to the turnstiles)?

29. Is seating for swimmers provided on the deck?

30. Has the recirculation-filtration system been designed to meet the anticipated future bathing load?

31. Has the gas chlorinator (if used) been placed in a separate room accessible from and vented to the outside?

32. Has the gutter waste water been valved to return to the filters, and also for direct waste?

Indoor pools

1. Is there proper mechanical ventilation?

2. Is there adequate acoustical treatment of walls and ceilings?

3. Is there adequate overhead clearance for diving (15 feet above low springboards, 15 feet for 3-meter boards, and 10 feet for 10-meter platforms)?

4. Is there adequate lighting (50 footcandles minimum)?

5. Has reflection of light from the outside been kept to the minimum by proper location of windows of skylights (windows on side walls are not desirable)?

6. Are all wall bases coved to facilitate cleaning?

7. Is there provision for proper temperature control in the pool room for both water and air?

8. Can the humidity of the pool room be controlled?

9. Is the wall and ceiling insulation adequate to prevent "sweating"?

10. Are all metal fittings of noncorrosive material?

11. Is there a tunnel around the outside of the pool, or a trench on the deck that permits ready access to pipes?

Outdoor pools

1. Is the site for the pool in the best possible location (away from railroad tracks, heavy industry, trees, and dusty open fields)?

2. Have sand and grass been kept the proper distance away from the pool to prevent them from being transmitted to the pool?

3. Has a fence been placed around the pool to assure safety when not in use?

4. Has proper subsurface drainage been provided?

5. Is there adequate deck space for sunbathing?

CHECKLIST FOR FACILITY PLANNERS—cont'd

Outdoor pools—cont'd

		Yes	*No*
6.	Are the outdoor lights placed far enough from the pool to prevent insects from dropping into the pool?		
7.	Is the deck of nonslip material?		
8.	Is there an area set aside for eating, separated from the pool deck?		
9.	Is the bathhouse properly located, with the entrance to the pool leading to the shallow end?		
10.	If the pool shell contains a concrete finish, has the length of the pool been increased by 3 inches over the "official" size in order to permit eventual tiling of the basin without making the pool "too short"?		
11.	Are there other recreational facilities nearby for the convenience and enjoyment of swimmers?		
12.	Do diving boards or platforms face north or east?		
13.	Are lifeguard stands provided and properly located?		
14.	Has adequate parking space been provided and properly located?		
15.	Is the pool oriented correctly in relation to the sun?		
16.	Have windshields been provided in situations where heavy winds prevail?		

SELF-ASSESSMENT TESTS

These tests are to assist students in determining if material and competencies presented in this chapter have been mastered.

1. State 10 basic considerations that should be followed by administrators in planning physical education and athletic facilities.

2. As an administrator of a physical education and athletic program, what steps would you follow in working with an architect in the construction of a gymnasium?

3. Prepare a sketch of what you consider to be an ideal indoor physical education plant.

4. Develop a list of standards for outdoor areas in physical education and athletics, including play areas and swimming pools, for an elementary school and for a high school.

5. You are a director of physical education in a secondary school with 500 students. There are five class periods a day with an average class size of 30 students, and physical education is required daily. What is the minimum number of teaching stations you will need?

6. Describe some new features being used in the construction of physical education and athletic facilities. What are the advantages of these new features?

7. Prepare a checklist for a physical education and athletic plant that will ensure that it is safe and healthful for all participants.

SELECTED REFERENCES

Aase, K.: The corner gym, Journal of Physical Education and Recreation 47:19, 1976.

American Association for Health, Physical Education, and Recreation: Planning areas and facilities for health, physical education, and recreation, Washington, D.C., 1965, The Association.

Architectural Research Group: Shelter for physical education, College Station, Texas, 1961, Publications Department, Texas Engineering Experiment Station, A & M College of Texas.

The Athletic Institute and American Alliance for Health, Physical Education, Recreation and Dance: Planning facilities for athletics, physical education, and recreation, Reston, Va., 1979, The Alliance.

Bannon, J.J.: Leisure resources—its comprehensive planning, Englewood Cliffs, N.J., 1976, Prentice-Hall, Inc.

Bingham, J.H.: A multipurpose court for all seasons, Parks and Recreation Trends, May, 1973.

Bronzan, R.T.: New concepts in planning and funding athletic, physical education, and recreation facilities, St. Paul, 1974, Phoenix Intermedia.

Broyles, J.F., and Hay, R.D.: Administration of athletic programs—a managerial approach, Englewood Cliffs, N.J., 1979, Prentice-Hall, Inc.

Buikema, K.A.: Centennial education park, Journal of Physical Education and Recreation 47:20, 1976.

California State Department of Education: Brief statement of principles involving the construction of school unit, State Health Committee Bulletin, Sacramento, The Department.

California State Joint Committee on School Health: Guide and check list for healthful and safe school environment, Sacramento, The Committee.

Carlson, J.: Sharing facilities, Journal of Physical Education and Recreation **49:**34-36, June 1978.

Coates, E.: Modular design for activity spaces in the physical education–intramural complex, Journal of Physical Education nd Recreation **46:**30, 1975.

Crowe, W.C., Auxter, D., and Pyfer, J.: Principles and methods of adapted physical education and recreation, ed. 4, St. Louis, 1981, The C.V. Mosby Co.

Environmental education facility resources: A report from the Educational Facilities Laboratory, New York, 1972, The Laboratories.

Ezersky, E.M.: Mini-gyms and fitness courts, Journal of Health, Physical Education, and Recreation **43:**38, 1972.

Ezersky, E.M., and Theibert, P.R.: Facilities in sports and physical education, St. Louis, 1976, The C.V. Mosby Co.

Finci, D.L.: Planning new facilities? don't forget the old, Athletic Purchasing and Facilities **4:**36-40, December 1980.

Flynn, R.B.: The team approach to facility planning, Athletic Purchasing and Facilities **5:**12-24, June 1981.

Fuoss, D.E., and Troppmenn, R.J.: Creative management techniques in interscholastic athletics, New York, 1977, John Wiley & Sons.

Gans, M.: Providing for low cost, multiple use, community college facilities for physical activity, Journal of Physical Education and Recreation **46:**27, 1975.

Kidder, W.: A rebuilt playground, Journal of Physical Education and Recreation **47:**17, 1976.

Kraft, G., and Mason, J.: An activity center that generates revenue, Journal of Physical Education, Recreation and Dance **52:**11-14, May 1981.

Kraus, R.G., and Curtis, J.E.: Creative administration in recreation and parks, ed. 3, St. Louis, 1982, The C.V. Mosby Co.

Penman, K.A.: Planning physical education and athletic facilities in schools, New York, 1977, John Wiley & Sons, Inc.

Pettine, A.M.: Planning a gymnasium, Journal of Health, Physical Education, and Recreation **44:**58, 1972.

Pettine, A.M., and Nettleton, J.D.: No money for new construction, Journal of Physical Education and Recreation **51:**26-27, June 1980.

Puckett, J.: Two promising innovations in physical education facilities, Journal of Health, Physical Education, and Recreation **43:**40, 1972.

Sharman, J.E.: A physical education plan concept to provide greater flexibility at minimum cost, Journal of Physical Education and Recreation **46:**25, 1975.

Theunissen, W.: Planning facilities—the role of the program specialist, Journal of Physical Education and Recreation **49:**27-29, June 1978.

Thiebert, P.R.: On facilities for lifetime sports, American School & University, November 1971.

Thomas, N., and Robbins, L.: An elementary school physical education complex, Journal of Physical Education and Recreation **47:**16, 1976.

Van Horn, E., and Seils, L.G.: Equality in the use of athletic facilities, Journal of Physical Education and Recreation **51:**22-23, May 1980.

Watkins, W.: Administrative guidelines for community use of physical education and recreation facilities, Journal of Physical Education and Recreation **49:**32, October 1978.

13

Fiscal management

Instructional objectives and competencies to be achieved

After reading this chapter the student should be able to

- Support the need for sound fiscal management in physical education and athletic programs.
- Explain the budgeting process and formulate a physical education and athletic budget.
- Apply a planning-programming-budgeting system (PPBS) in the administration of physical education and athletic programs.
- Understand the role of school and college business managers or administrators in fiscal management.
- Outline the principles necessary for administrators to follow to ensure financial accountability in a physical education and athletic program.

Fiscal management has become an increasingly important responsibility for administrators in light of current financial problems. In recent years these financial problems have made it much more difficult to fund physical education and athletic programs. Some of the reasons for this difficulty include the high price of supplies and equipment; the need to finance an increasing number of girls and women who are participating in sports; crowd control costs at athletic events as a result of violence; expensive product liability and lawyer contingency funds; and an inflation rate that is resulting in rising costs for labor, teachers, coaches, officials, and other personnel.

An analysis of the responses of directors of physical education and athletics in New York (more than 1000 questionnaires were sent), regarding the effect of budget cuts and austerity budgets on their programs, highlights the difficulties administrators of physical education and athletic programs are having today. The survey resulted in the following findings:

67% of the directors said they had to cut supplies, transportation, specific sports, and levels of sports to balance the budget.

29 athletic programs were conducted with private funds during the time they were on austerity budgets.

40% of the directors conducted athletic programs using volunteer coaches in parts of their programs.

Fund-raising activities for athletics included booster club memberships, participation fees, sales, student work projects, and promotional activities such as lotteries.

Regarding support for their athletic programs, the teachers' association was the least supportive and the students the most supportive. The school administration and the community were also highly supportive of their programs.

Efficient fiscal management is an essential administrative function that ensures proper money management. As a result, the administrator must understand thoroughly the fiscal needs and objectives of all the departments under his or her supervision. Budgeting must consider departmental requests. The fiscal management of an institution or department is a difficult, challenging responsibility.

Importance and function of fiscal management

The services a program provides, whether personnel, facilities, or other items, usually involve the disbursement of funds. This money must be secured from proper sources, be expended for proper purposes, and be accounted for item by item. The budget, the master financial plan for the organization, is constructed with this purpose in mind.

Policies for raising and spending money must be well reasoned. Persons responsible should know the procedures for handling such funds with integrity, the basic purposes for which the program exists, the laws, and the codes and regulations concerning fiscal management. Only as the funds are used wisely and in the best interests of all people concerned can the outlay of monies be justfied.

PLACE OF FISCAL MANAGEMENT IN PHYSICAL EDUCATION AND ATHLETIC PROGRAMS

Of all areas in school, college, or other organizations, physical education and athletics have a major outlay of funds. Personnel, health services, facilities, and supplies and equipment are only a few of the items that amount to large sums of money. As much as 25% of many school and college plants is devoted to these programs. There are probably as many as 250,000 physical educators and coaches collectively paid millions of dollars annually in salaries. More than 60 million students are the focus of attention in school physical education and athletic programs.

Gymnasiums, swimming pools, athletic training rooms, playgrounds, and other facilities are being constructed at the cost of astronomical sums to taxpayers.

What is true of schools and colleges regarding fiscal management is also true of recreation, industrial, and other settings where physical education and athletic programs exist.

The great outlay of funds for physical education and athletic programs makes sound financial management mandatory, to see that the monies are used in the best way possible. This is one of the most important responsibilities that educators, and particularly administrators have.

PURPOSES OF FISCAL MANAGEMENT

Some of the principal purposes of financial management in physical education and athletic programs are the following:

1. To prevent misuse and waste of funds that have been allocated to these special fields.
2. To help coordinate and relate the objectives of physical education and athletic programs with the money appropriated for achieving such outcomes.
3. To ensure that monies allocated to physical education will be based on research, study, and a careful analysis of the pertinent conditions that influence such a process.
4. To involve the entire staff in formulating policies and procedures and in preparing budgetary items that will help ensure that the right program directions are taken.
5. To use funds to develop the best physical education programs possible.
6. To exercise control over the process of fiscal management to guarantee that the entire financial process has integrity and purpose.
7. To make the greatest use of personnel, facilities, supplies, equipment, and other factors involved in accomplishing organizational objectives.

RESPONSIBILITY

The responsibility for fiscal management although falling largely on the shoulders of the administration, involves every member of the staff.

Formulating and preparing the budget, for example, are cooperative enterprises. They are based on information and reports that have been forwarded by staff members through the various departments and subdivisions of the organization. These reports must contain information on programs, projects, obligations that exist, funds that have been spent, and monies that have been received from various sources. Staff members help in this process. Administrators must have an overall picture of the entire enterprise at their fingertips. They must be cognizant of the work being done throughout the establishment, functions that should be carried out, needs of every facet of the organization, and other items that must be considered in preparing the budget. The larger the organization, the larger should be the budget organization under the administrator. The efficiency of the enterprise depends on expert judgment in fiscal matters. In schools and colleges, students themselves play a part. For example, through general organizations, budgets are prepared and outlays of funds relating to many activities, such as plays and ath-

Fig. 13-1. A soccer player in action at the State University College, Potsdam, N.Y.

Fig. 13-2. Dance class at Florida A & M University, Tallahasee, Fla.

UNIVERSITY OF NEVADA, LAS VEGAS
Las Vegas, Nevada

Office of the Controller

REQUEST FOR CHECK

TO THE OFFICE OF THE CONTROLLER: DATE _____

PLEASE ISSUE AND MAIL CHECK TO   **SOCIAL SECURITY OR IDENTIFICATION NO.**

NAME _____

ADDRESS _____   _____

_____

DISPOSITION OF CHECK IF NOT TO BE MAILED   **NOTE:** In all cases of payment for personal services or other payments subject to reporting for income tax purposes, the payee's Social Security or Employer Identification number must be shown before payment can be made.

_____   **WHEN IN DOUBT, SHOW THE NUMBER.**

AMOUNT OF CHECK: _____

ACCOUNT TO BE CHARGED: _____

IN PAYMENT OF THE FOLLOWING:	AMOUNT	
Requested by	Approved by	

INSTRUCTION: Submit two copies of this form to the Office of the Controller at least 48 hours before check is needed. If payment is for reimbursement of cash paid items attach receipts or sales slips. Nevada sales tax cannot be reimbursed.

UNLV 220   12/73/5,000

Fig. 13-3. Request for check form.

letics, are approved, amended, or rejected. Fiscal management involves many people, but the job of leadership and direction falls on the administration.

Budgeting

Budgeting is the formulation of a financial plan in terms of work to be accomplished and services to be performed. All expenditures should be closely related to the objectives the organization is trying to achieve. In this aspect the administration plays an important part in budgeting.

Budgets should be planned and prepared with a thought to the future. They are an important part of the administration's 3-year, 5-year, or 7-year plan and the program of accomplishment outlined for a fiscal period. Projects of any size should be integrated progressively over many years. Thus the outlay of monies to realize such aims requires long-term planning.

According to the strict interpretation of the word, a budget is merely a record of receipts and expenditures. As used here, however, it reflects the long-term planning of the organization, pointing up the needs with their estimated costs, and then ensuring that a realistic program is planned that will fit into the estimated income.

The budget forecasts revenues and expenses for a period of 1 year, known as the fiscal year.

PURPOSES OF BUDGETS

The purposes of budgets follow:

1. They express the plan and program for physical education and athletics. They determine such things as (a) size of classes, (b) supplies, equipment, and facilities, (c) methods used, (d) results and educational values sought, and (e) personnel available.
2. They reflect the philosophy and policies of the professions of physical education and athletics. They provide an overview of these specialized areas.
3. They determine what phases of the program are to be emphasized and help analyze all aspects of physical education and athletic programs.
4. They interpret the need and the funds necessary for physical education and athletics.
5. In a school program they help determine, together with the budgets of other subdivisions, the tax levy for the school district.

6. They make it possible to administer the physical education and athletic programs economically by improving accounting procedures.
7. They make it possible, on approval by the recognized officials, to authorize expenditures for the program of physical education and athletics.

TYPES OF BUDGETS

There are short-term and long-term budgets. The short-term is usually the annual budget. The long-term budget represents long-term fiscal planning, possibly for a 10-year period. Most physical education and athletic personnel will be concerned with short-term or annual budgets whereby they plan their financial needs for a period covering the school year.

RESPONSIBILITY FOR BUDGETS

The responsibility for the preparation of the budget may vary from one locality to another. In most school systems the superintendent of schools is responsible. In colleges it is the responsibility of the president and the dean. In other organizations the department head plays a key role. It is often possible for school administrators, department heads, teachers, professors, and members of the organization to participate in preparing the budget by submitting various requests for budget items. In other situations a comprehensive budget may first be prepared and then submitted to the subdivisions for consideration.

In some large school systems the superintendent of schools frequently delegates much of the budget responsibility to a business administrator, a clerk, or an assistant or associate superintendent.

The final official school authority concerned with school budgets is the board of education. In some organizations other than schools it is the controller. This agent or person can approve, reject, or amend. Beyond the board of education rests the authority of the people, who in most communities have the right to approve or reject the budget.

In colleges the budget may be handled in the dean's office, or the director or chairperson of the physical education department may have the responsibility. In some cases the director of athletics is responsible for the athletic budget.

Within school departments of physical education and athletics the chairperson, supervisor, or director

Fig. 13-4. A gymnast performing on the rings.

Courtesy Cramer Products, Inc., Gardner, Kan.

is the person responsible for the budget. However, he or she will usually consult with members of the department and receive their suggestions.

CRITERIA FOR A GOOD BUDGET

A budget for physical education and athletics should meet the following criteria:

1. The budget will clearly present the financial needs of the entire program in relation to the objectives sought.
2. Key persons in the organization have been consulted.
3. The budget will provide a realistic estimate of income to balance the expenditures anticipated.
4. The budget should reflect equitable allocations to boys' and girls' athletic programs and conform to Title IX regulations.

5. The possibility of emergencies is recognized through flexibility in the financial plan.
6. The budget will be prepared well in advance of the fiscal year to leave ample time for analysis, thought, criticism, and review.
7. Budget requests are realistic, not padded.
8. The budget meets the essential requirements of students, faculty, staff members, and administrators.

BUDGET PREPARATION AND PLANNING

The budget process is continuous. One authority on business management indicates the following are seven basic steps to this process*:

Planning: Administration uses the brain power of the staff members and community in creative planning.

Coordinating: Administration coordinates and integrates staff member and community suggestions and recommendations into a unified whole.

Interpreting: To have support for the budget, proper interpretation of plans and actions are a continual part of the budgetary process.

Presenting: The administration presents the budget in a simplified version so it can be readily understood. Pictures, diagrams, graphs, and other materials make such a presentation more interesting and informative.

Approving: Adoption of the budget is but the formal approval of many projects and much thinking that have been studied and considered throughout the year. The administration is continually planning, researching, and studying various budgetary items.

Administering: The budget, when approved, serves as an administrative guide throughout the year as to how monies will be spent and what activities will be conducted.

Appraising: Appraisal is a continuous process indicating how the budget is functioning. Methods used include daily observation, cost accounting records and reports, surveys, audits, checklists, and staff studies.

Four general procedures in budget planning that physical education and athletic personnel might consider include the following:

1. Actual preparation of the budget by the chairperson of the department with his or her staff, listing the various estimated receipts, expenditures, and any other information that needs to be included.

---

*Roe, W.H.: School business management, New York, 1961, McGraw-Hill Book Co.

Fig. 13-5. Rehearsing abstract designs from a modern dance titled Modern Math—Base 12 at the University of Mississippi.

Photograph by Nelson Neal.

2. Presentation of the budget to the principal, superintendent, dean, board of education, or other person or group that represents the proper authority and has the responsibility for reviewing it.
3. After formal approval of the budget, its use as a guide for the financial management and administration of the department or organization.
4. Critical evaluation of the budget periodically to determine its effectiveness in meeting organizational needs, with notations being made for the next year's budget.

The preparation of the budget, representing the first step, is a long-term endeavor that cannot be accomplished in 1 or 2 days. The budget can be prepared well only after a careful review of program effectiveness and extensive appraisal. However, the actual completion of the budget usually is accomplished in the early spring after a detailed inventory of program needs has been taken. The director of physical education or athletics, after close consultation with staff members and the principal, dean, superintendent of schools, or other responsible administrative officer, should formulate the budget.

INVOLVEMENT OF STAFF MEMBERS

Involving staff members in the budget-making process is very important. Klappholz* provides some

suggestions in this regard, presented here in the following adapted form:

- Teachers and coaches should maintain inventory forms indicating supplies and equipment on hand.
- Teachers, coaches, and directors should keep accurate records of all costs for each activity or sport.
- Teaching staff members and coaches should determine the items that were not a part of this year's budget but that should be included in the budget for the coming year.
- Accurate records should be kept by staff members regarding funds allocated and spent each year. Then it should be determined if funds were spent for purposes that were initially listed.
- When all pertinent information has been collected and analyzed, the administration should meet with all staff members and go over requests.
- The administration should prepare total physical education or athletic budgets including all valid requests. The budget should not be padded, but provision should be made for emergencies.

Klappholz stresses that administrators and staff members should do their homework by having the following:

- Latest prices for supplies and equipment
- Number of students or other personnel in the program
- Cost of such items as officials
- Cost of travel, meals, lodging, insurance, and medical supervision

---

*Klappholz, L.A.: Physical Education Newsletter, November 1980.

UNIVERSITY OF NEVADA SYSTEM
BUSINESS CENTER SOUTH
Las Vegas, Nevada 89154

OUT-OF-STATE TRAVEL REQUEST

Controller's Office

1. Date_____, 19____   2. Dept. Req. No. _____

INSTRUCTIONS FOR USE: Reimbursement for traveling expenses for trips outside the State of Nevada may not be secured without the prior authorization indicated on this form. Five copies of this form should be forwarded by the department, through the proper Dean, Director, or Administrative Office, to the Controller's Office. The fifth copy will be returned to the department with indication of the action taken.

3. Name _____   4. Title _____

5. **Department and campus**_____requests permission for out-of-state

travel, as follows: 6. Date leave _____   7. Date return _____

8. Trip (Include contemplated side trips): Mode of travel _____

9. From _____   10. To _____

11. Purpose of trip. If a conference or meeting is involved, give: name of organization, location and time of meeting, registration fees (if paid by **UNS**), , value of trip to university.

_____

_____

_____

_____

_____

_____

I (do/do not) expect to receive travel allowance or honorarium from sources other than the University.

12. Transportation . . . . _____   18. Requested _____
                                                            Traveller

13. Per Diem . . . . . . _____   19. Recommended _____
                                                            Head of Department

14. Estimated Total Cost . _____   20. Recommended _____
                                                            Dean or Administrative Officer

15. Requested in Advance . _____   21. Approved _____
                                                            Vice-President - Academic Affairs

16. Amount Advanced . . . _____   22. Approved _____
                                                            President

17. **Account(s) charged**   23. Approved as to funds available _____
                                                            Controller - Bus. Ctr. South

_____

_____

White—A/P Controllers Office
Blue—A/P Controllers Office (File)
Gold—A/P Controllers Office (Advances)
Yellow—A/P Controllers Office (Encumbrances)
Pink—Department (File)

BCS 200

Fig. 13-6. Out-of-state travel request.

A SCHOOL BUDGET

Proposed budget classification by major function

	Salaries, fees, and benefits	Equipment and supplies	Services and other expenses	Totals
Board of education and district administration				
Board/district administration	$183,400	$ 11,400	$ 45,900	$ 240,700
District insurance			74,600	74,600
Claims, property tax, BOCES* administration costs			78,300	78,300
Category total				$ 393,600
Instruction				
Building administration	302,600	19,700	8,600	330,900
Salaries and materials	3,178,300	169,000	439,700	3,787,000
Guidance and health	264,200	2,900	14,600	281,700
Student activities	57,300	22,900	6,700	86,900
Category total				$4,486,500
Support services				
Transportation	287,600	106,500	36,300	430,400
Operation and maintenance	362,000	42,900	378,400	783,300
School lunch			5,000	5,000
Category total				$1,218,700
Employees benefits	1,293,400			$1,293,400
Total operating expenses	$5,928,800	$375,300	$1,088,100	$7,392,200
Debt service			765,600	765,600
TOTAL BUDGET				$8,157,800

*Board of Cooperative Educational Services.

- Money needed for teaching aids and other materials
- Cost of attending professional meetings

Many records and reports are essential to budget preparation. The inventory of equipment and supplies on hand will be useful, and copies of inventories and budgets from previous years will provide good references. Comparison of budgetary items with those in other organizations of similar size may be of help. Accounting records will be valuable.

The preparation of the budget should allow flexibility for readjustments, if necessary. It is difficult to accurately and specifically list each detail in the way it will be needed and executed.

The budget should represent a schedule that can be justified. This means that each budgetary item must satisfy the needs and interests of all concerned. Furthermore, each item that constitutes an expenditure should be reflected in budget specifications.

Mitchell lists the following five important considerations in budget preparation:

1. What was planned last year? This constitutes the tying together of the proposed budget with the one ap-

UNIVERSITY OF NEVADA, LAS VEGAS
4505 Maryland Parkway   Las Vegas, Nevada 89154

Controller's Office (702) 739-3517

REFUND VOUCHER

To: The Office of the Controller   Date _____

Please issue and mail check to: Remarks:

Name _____

Address _____

City & State _____

Student S.S. # _____

Account Charged _____

Amount _____

Refund Authorized by: _____

INSTRUCTIONS: *Submit original & two copies to the Office of the Controller.*   UNLV Form 222

Fig. 13-7. Refund voucher.

proved last year to check on long-term planning goals.

2. What was accomplished last year? This step relates last year's accomplishments to the achievement of the department's long-term objectives.
3. What can realistically be accomplished this year? In light of past years, future trends, and the master plan, what can be accomplished this year?
4. What needs to be done? This constitutes the minimum essentials that must be accomplished this year. These items have priority.
5. How is it to be done? Such items as staff, equipment, supplies, and other requirements for accomplishment and meeting of needs would be outlined.*

BUDGET ORGANIZATION

Budgets can be organized in many ways. One pattern comprising four sections that might prove useful

*Mitchell, R.G.: Administrative planning—its effective use, Recreation **44**:426, 1961.

for a physical education and athletic administrator is described here:

1. An introductory message enables the administration to present the financial proposals in terms a person outside the specialized fields might readily understand. This section offers to physical education specialists an opportunity to discuss some aspects of the program in lay terms and some of the directions that need to be taken to provide for the physical fitness of the students.
2. The second section presents an overall view of the budget, with expenditures and anticipated revenues arranged clearly and systematically so any person can compare the two.
3. A third section, with an estimate of receipts and expenditures in much more detail, should enable a principal, superintendent of schools, board of education, or other interested person or group to understand the budget specifically and to follow up any item of cost.

THE ROLE OF THE ADMINISTRATOR
IN BUDGETING

A. Preliminary considerations in preparing the budget
  1. Program additions or deletions
  2. Staff changes
  3. Inventory of equipment on hand
B. Budget preparation: additional considerations
  1. Athletic gate receipts and expenditures—athletic association fund
  2. Board of education budget—allocations for physical education, including athletics
  3. Coaches' requests and requests of teachers and department heads
  4. Comparison of requests with inventories
  5. Itemizing and coding requests
  6. Budget conferences with administration
  7. Justification of requests
C. Athletic association funds: considerations
  1. Estimated income
    a. Gate receipts
    b. Student activities tickets
    c. Tournament receipts
  2. Estimated expenditures
    a. Awards
    b. Tournament fees
    c. Films
    d. Miscellaneous
    e. Surplus
D. General budget: considerations
  1. Breakdown
    a. By sport or activity
    b. Transportation
    c. Salaries of personnel
    d. Insurance
    e. Reconditioning of equipment
    f. Supervision
    g. General and miscellaneous
    h. Equipment
    i. Officials
  2. Codes
    a. Advertising
    b. Travel
    c. Conferences
    d. Others
E. Postbudget procedures
  1. Selection of equipment and supplies
  2. Preparation of list of dealers to bid
  3. Request for price quotations
  4. Requisitions
  5. Care of equipment

6. Notification of teachers and coaches of amounts approved
F. Ordering procedures
  1. Study the quality of various products
  2. Accept no substitutes for items ordered
  3. Submit request for price quotations
  4. Select low quotes or justify higher quotes
  5. Submit purchase orders
  6. Check and count all shipments
  7. Record items received on inventory cards
  8. Provide for equipment and supply accountability
G. Relationships with administration
  1. Consultation—program plans with building principal and/or superintendent
  2. Make budget recommendations to administration
  3. Advise business manager of procedures followed
  4. Discuss items approved and deleted with business manager
  5. Advise teachers and coaches of amounts available and adjust requests
H. Suggestions for prospective directors of physical education programs
  1. Develop a philosophy and approach to budgeting
  2. Consult with staff for their suggestions
  3. Select quality merchandise
  4. Provide proper care and maintenance of equipment and supplies
  5. Provide for all programs on an equitable basis
  6. Budget adequately but not elaborately
  7. Provide a sound, well-rounded program of physical education
  8. Emphasize equality for girls and boys
  9. Provide for basic instructional, adapted, intramural and extramural, and interscholastic parts of the program.
  10. Conduct a year-round public relations program
  11. Try to overcome these possible shortcomings:
    a. Board of education not oriented to needs of physical education
    b. Program not achieving established goals
    c. Staff not adequately informed and involved in administrative process

BREAKDOWN OF BUDGETARY ALLOCATIONS FOR REGULAR INSTRUCTIONAL PROGRAMS

The programs listed below describe the funding for regular classroom instruction. The costs of general classroom teachers in grades one through five are divided among the language arts, mathematics, and environment programs, according to the estimated percentage of instructional time each subject receives in the classroom curriculum.

Program costs in grades six through twelve are based on the division of staff members by academic specialization.

The unclassified code contains those general supply and equipment items that support the entire program and cannot be allocated by program.

	Salaries	Benefits	Equipment	Supplies	Services	Total
Art	$ 136,761	$ 38,434	$ 522	$ 10,401	$ 677	$ 186,795
Business education	66,465	18,681	2,150	1,638	1,350	90,284
Driver education	4,410	1,239	550	10,850	—	17,049
Environment	151,747	42,650	—	1,999	300	196,696
Health education	2,290	627	—	400	420	3,737
Home economics	39,609	11,313	—	3,341	447	54,528
Industrial arts	70,837	19,910	471	5,335	675	97,228
Kindergarten	47,203	13,267	—	1,255	—	61,725
Language arts	613,255	172,365	—	14,375	2,900	802,895
Foreign languages	158,078	44,430	—	5,361	1,715	209,584
Mathematics	452,918	127,291	710	7,489	560	588,968
Music	141,035	39,635	516	2,439	850	184,485
Physical education	233,176	65,552	2,147	6,069	2,590	309,534
Reading (special)	83,162	23,372	—	915	400	107,849
Science	333,804	87,083	3,124	11,140	1,850	437,001
Speech	10,751	3,018	—	261	—	14,030
Social studies	283,827	79,774		4,509	3,500	371,610
Unclassified	146,898	41,286	1,737	22,009	9,080	221,010
TOTAL	$2,976,226	$829,745	$11,927	$109,786	$27,314	$3,954,998

4. A fourth section might include supporting schedules to provide additional evidence for the requests outlined in the budget. Many times a budget will have a better chance of approval if there is sufficient documentation to support some items. For example, extra pay for coaching may be thought to be desirable. Salary schedules for coaches in other school systems could be included to support such a proposition.

Another type of budget organization might be one that consists of the following three parts: (1) an introductory statement of the objectives, policies, and program of the physical education department; (2) a résumé of the objectives, policies, and program interpreted in terms of proposed expenditures; and (3) a financial plan for meeting the needs during the fiscal period.

Not all budgets are broken down into these four or three divisions. All budgets do, however, give an itemized account of receipts and expenditures.

In a physical education budget common inclusions are items concerning instruction, such as extra compensation for coaches; matters of capital outlay, such as a new swimming pool or handball court; replacement of expendable equipment, such as basketballs and baseball bats; and provision for maintenance and repair, such as refurbishing football uniforms or doing some grading on the playground. It is difficult to

Table 13-1. General organization athletic account—financial report (September-December)

Expenses		
Football		
Officials (four home games)	$ 480.00	
Equipment and supplies	2364.02	
Transportation	175.00	
Supervision (police, ticket sellers and takers)	952.00	
Reconditioning and cleaning equipment	1313.20	
Medical supplies	125.40	
Scouting	60.00	
Film	31.36	
Guarantees	520.00	
Football dinner	231.00	
Miscellaneous (printing tickets, meetings)	172.00	
Total football expense		$6423.98
Cross country		
State and county entry fees	$ 10.00	
Transportation	64.00	
Total cross country expense		$ 74.00
Basketball		
Supervision (three games)	$ 36.00	
Custodian (three games)	26.00	
Police (one game)	12.00	
Total basketball expense		$ 74.00
Cheerleaders		
Transportation	$ 52.20	
Sixteen sweaters	320.00	
Cleaning sweaters	96.00	
Total cheerleader expense		$ 468.20
TOTAL EXPENSES		$7040.18
Receipts		
Football		
Newburgh game	$1311.70	
Norwalk game	1819.60	
Yonkers game	1129.50	
Bridgeport game	1100.00	
Guarantee (New Haven)	120.00	
TOTAL RECEIPTS		$5480.80

estimate many of these items without making a careful inventory and analysis of the condition of the facilities and equipment.

SOURCES OF INCOME

The sources of income for physical education and athletic programs depend on the organization sponsoring such a program. In community recreation programs the funds frequently come from the taxpayers. In industry the funds frequently emanate from the general treasury or employee contributions. In some youth-serving agencies some help may come from the United Fund, member contributions, or both.

New methods of raising revenues. The budget

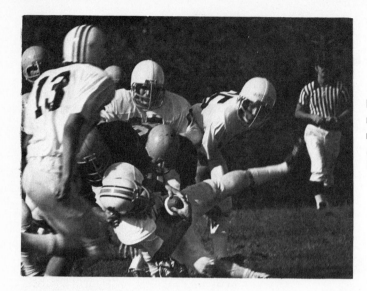

Fig. 13-8. Football requires large outlays of money.

Courtesy Cramer Products, Inc., Gardner, Kan.

crunch caused by Proposition 2½ in Massachusetts* has caused physical education and athletic directors to find new ways of raising revenues. Some methods they are using include the following:

- Getting business organizations to provide matching funds for specific programs
- Conducting fund raising campaigns among alumni of organization
- Establishing ways by which local citizens can make tax-free donations, including making a provision in their wills for leaving money to the program
- Selling passes to the public

The sources of income for most school and college physical education and athletic programs include the general school or college fund, gate receipts, general organization and activity fees, and some other revenues.

General school or college fund. In elementary and secondary schools, the physical education and athletic program would be financed through the general fund to a large extent. At colleges and universities, the general fund of the institution would also represent a major source of income.

Gate receipts. Gate receipts play an important part in some schools in financing at least part of the physical education and athletic program. Although there is usually less stress on gate receipts at lower educational levels, colleges and universities sometimes finance their entire athletic, intramural, and physical education programs through such a method. At a few high schools throughout the country, gate receipts have been abolished because of the feeling that if athletics represent an important part of the education program, they should be paid for in the same way that science and mathematics programs, for example, are financed.

General organization and activity fees. Some high schools either require or make available to students separate general organization or activity fees and tickets or some other inducement that enables them to attend athletic, dramatic, and musical events. In colleges and universities a similar plan is generally used, thus providing students with reduced rates to the various out-of-class activities offered by the institution. Table 13-1 shows a general organization financial statement.

Other sources of income. Some other sources of income, not so common to all educational levels, are (1) *special foundation, governmental, or individual grants or gifts* intended to promote physical fitness, athletics, or some phase of health and physical education programs; (2) the sale of *radio and television rights* at the college level, especially for those institutions with nationally ranking teams and where the athletic contests have great public appeal; (3) *conces-*

---

*What happens when the money runs out? Athletic Purchasing and Facilities 5:44-48, July 1981.

sions at athletic contests and other activity events; and (4) *special fund-raising events* such as a faculty-varsity basketball game or a gymnastic circus.

Some steps that might be followed for estimating receipts in the general school budget and that also have application to the physical education budget include the following:

1. Gathering and analyzing all pertinent data, including past and current information
2. Estimating all income based on comprehensive view of income sources
3. Organizing and classifying receipts in appropriate categories
4. Estimating revenue from all gathered data
5. Comparing estimates with previous years and drawing up final draft of receipts

EXPENDITURES

In physical education and athletic budgets, typical examples of expenditures are items of *capital outlay,* such as a swimming pool; *expendable equipment,* such as basketballs: and a *maintenance and repair provision,* such as towel and laundry service and the refurbishing of football uniforms. See Table 13-3 for a sample list of expenditures for athletics.

Some expenditures are easy to estimate but others are more difficult, requiring keeping accurate inventories, examining past records, and carefully analyzing the condition of the equipment. Some items and services will need to be figured by averaging costs over a period of years, such as cleaning and mending athletic equipment. Awards, new equipment needed, guarantees to visiting teams, and medical services for emergencies are other expenditures that must be included.

Some sound procedures to follow in estimating expenditures follow:

1. Determine objectives and goals of program.
2. Analyze expenditures in terms of program objectives.
3. Prepare a budgetary calendar that states what accomplishments are expected and by what date.
4. Estimate expenditures by also considering past, present, and future needs.
5. Compare estimates with expenditures for previous years.
6. Thoroughly evaluate estimates before preparing final draft.

Cost-cutting procedures. In light of current economic problems some administrators are cutting costs, according to the survey of directors of physical education and athletics in New York. This is being accomplished by such means as the following:

- Cutting referees' pay
- Eliminating insurance
- Having fewer athletic contests
- Doing away with low participation sports
- Using voluntary coaches
- Discontinuing the purchase of personally used items
- Reducing the number of coaches
- Lowering coaches' salaries
- Eliminating sports where rental facilities are used
- Scheduling different teams on the same day and combining transportation for these teams
- Sharing uniforms by several teams

BUDGET PRESENTATION AND ADOPTION

In a school, physical education budgets after being prepared should usually be submitted to the superintendent through the principal's office. The principal is the person in charge of his or her particular building; therefore subdivision budgets should be presented to him or her for approval. Good administration means, furthermore, that the budgetary items have been reviewed with the principal during their preparation, so that approval is usually routine.

In colleges and universities, the proper channels should be followed. This might mean clearance through a dean or other administrative officer. Each person, of course, who is responsible for budget preparation and presentation should be familiar with the proper working channels.

In other organizations budgets are presented to the proper officer.

For successful presentation and adoption, the budget should be prepared in final form only after careful consideration so that little change will be needed. Requests for funds should be justifiable, and ample preliminary discussion of the budget with persons and groups most directly concerned should be held so needless difficulty will be avoided.

BUDGET ADMINISTRATION

After the presentation and approval of the budget, the next step is to see that it is administered properly.

UNIVERSITY OF NEVADA SYSTEM
BUSINESS CENTER SOUTH

CLAIM FOR TRAVEL EXPENSE

(See State Administrative Manual 0600 for Travel Regulations)

Original: Filed with check
Duplicate: Travel file BCS

Office of the Controller

Name and Title _____

Official Station _____

Method of Travel

P	Plane	AV	Agency Vehicle	L	Limousine
B	Bus	PC	Private Car	T	Taxi
RR	Rail	X	Passenger in Car	MP	Motor Pool

I declare under penalties for perjury that this claim (including any accompanying evidence) has been examined by me and to the best of my knowledge and belief is a true and correct claim in conformance with the governing statutes and the rules and regulations as promulgated by the Board of Examiners. ( ) I do ( ) I do not have a travel advance.

_____
Claimant Must Sign Here

Date	Detail / List Purpose of Each Trip	Method of Travel	Time		Trip Mileage	Trans- portation Cost	Daily Expense Reimbursement						Total Claimed
			Depart	Return			Meals				Lodging	Total for Day	
							B	L	D	Total			

_____   _____   _____
Approved By   Date   Approved By   Date   Approved By   Date

ACCOUNT NUMBER(S) CHARGED							CLAIM SUMMARY	
Yr	Area	Fund	Department	Proj	Object	Amount	Total of this Claim	
							Charged by Travel Agency	
							Charged by Auto Rental Agency	
							Balance of Claim	
							Advance Received	
							Balance Due Traveler	
BCS 215							Balance Due University	

Fig. 13-9. Claim for travel expense.

This means it should be followed closely with periodic checks on expenditures to see that they fall within the budget appropriations provided. The budget should guide economical and efficient administration.

BUDGET APPRAISAL

Periodic appraisal calls for an audit of the accounts and an evaluation of the school program resulting from the administration of the current budget. Such appraisal should be done honestly and with a view to eliminating weaknesses in current budgets and strengthening future ones. It should also be remembered that the budget will be only as good as the administration makes it and that the budget will improve only as the administration improves.

PPBS—planning-programming-budgeting system

PPBS came about as a solution to problems of fiscal accountability and optimal use of limited resources.

PPBS—A HISTORY

PPBS started in 1949 when the Hoover Commission report on the organization of the Executive Branch recommended that the government adopt a budget based on function, activities, and objectives. In 1954 the Rand Corporation developed a performance budget for use in military spending. Planning-Programming-Budgeting System (PPBS) was the title given to this system. The Du Pont Corporation and the Ford Motor Company were among the first to use PPBS. In the early 1960s Robert McNamara introduced the system to the Defense Department. The results of the system were so impressive that President Johnson ordered all federal departments and agencies to adopt PPBS by August 1965. Presently, many schools, colleges and other organizations are using this system, and many more are researching the feasibility of using it in their particular cases.

DEFINITION OF PPBS

PPBS may be defined as a long-range plan to accomplish an organization's objectives, using contin-

ual feedback and updating of information to allow for greater efficiency of the decision-making process. The three elements of PPBS are explained by Katzenbach, as follows:

1. Planning—establishing objectives
2. Programming—combining activities and events to produce distinguishable results
3. Budgeting—allocating resources, the financial plan for meeting program needs*

First, the objectives of the organization must be clearly defined. All activities that contribute to the same objective, regardless of placement in the organization, are grouped together. A financial plan designed to reach these objectives is formulated for a particular time period. An analysis document discusses long-range needs and evaluates the adequacy and effectiveness, costs, benefits, and difficulties inherent in the proposed program. Under PPBS, funds must be used with definitive goals in mind. In this way accountability for expenditures is stressed. In using PPBS, each activity and educational program is considered, not only by itself but also with respect to other educational programs that the whole system comprises. In this way the needs of the entire school system rather than just one part are considered.

THE PPBS CYCLE

The steps necessary to apply PPBS follow:

1. *Goals and objectives must be determined.* Goals and objectives should be stated in terms of behavior and performance. The deserved results of the program should also be determined in relation to knowledges, skills, and attitudes.
2. *Statement of needs and problems.* Needs and problems of the particular organization must be adequately defined.
3. *A determination of expected satisfaction of needs is essential.* Numbers of persons and skills needed must also be determined.
4. *Constraints and feasibility.* Both of these items must be evaluated to determine whether the system can

---

*Katzenbach, E.: Planning, Programming Budgeting Systems; PPBS and Education, Cambridge, Mass., 1968, New England School Development Council.

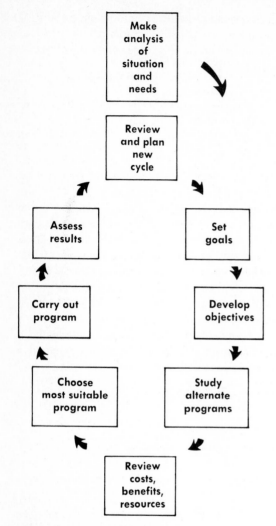

Fig. 13-10. The PPBS cycle.

From Clegg, A.A., Jr.: The teacher and manager of the curriculum, Educational Leadership, January 1973, p. 308.

overcome certain limitations (personnel, materials, facilities). The system may need modification in terms of needs or objectives to overcome the existing limitations.

5. *Alternative programs.* These programs outline the different ways the organization can reach its goals. Alternative programs should be evaluated in terms of needs, goals, and constraints of the system.

6. *Resource requirements must be estimated.* The resource needs of each alternative must be computed.

The easiest way to do this is to derive the faculty teaching cost per student credit hour and then add department costs, counseling, administration, equipment, and clerical costs.

7. *Estimate benefits to be gained from each alternative.* The benefits of the program must be determined in relationship to student accomplishment presently and in the future.

8. *Develop an operating plan.* From the data collected, all alternatives should be weighed against such fixed criteria as: cost of implementation and risk involved, estimated benefits, and future budget allocations.

9. *Pilot implementation of best alternative.* A pilot program should be conducted at a level where it could be modified or changed without involved or costly effort.

10. *Evaluation.* The data from the pilot program should be used in determining whether it is meeting the objectives of the organization. It should be modified accordingly.

11. *Feedback and further modification.* Once PPBS is in process, it should be continually reevaluated and modified to ensure the goals and objectives agreed on are being met.

ADVANTAGES AND DISADVANTAGES OF PPBS

Before implementing PPBS into an institution, the administrator must be thoroughly familiar with the advantages and disadvantages of such a system. Each situation differs, and careful analysis before implementation is essential.

Some of the advantages of PPBS follow.

1. The system aids in formulating goals, objectives, and skills.

2. Curriculum can be designed to meet the objectives formulated.

3. Staff members can be provided with prior planning and resource material.

4. Alternative plans can be more systematically analyzed.

5. Costs and accomplishments may be compared.

6. Staff members are more involved in decision making.

7. Instructional costs may be easily identified.

8. Innovation can be promoted in programs.

9. Evaluating criteria is continually applied to the system.

10. Public awareness and understanding are increased.

The disadvantages of such a system can be seen in the following:

1. Staff time is limited, and staff members with sufficient technical skills in these areas are also limited.
2. Implementation may lead to conflict and resistance from community members.
3. Cost-benefit analysis is a difficult example to quantitate; some benefits from education are not easily measurable.
4. Communication among staff members may be limited as a result of centralization of system planning.
5. PPBS is a method of indicating the best use of funds; however, in doing so, funds are also expended, and limited budgets may not be able to implement such a system.
6. The vocabulary is vague to those who are not directly involved in using such a system.
7. PPBS may be mistakenly seen as a substitute for management rather than a tool of management.
8. Alternatives with great potential are passed up because of their high chance of failure according to PPBS criteria.
9. Some persons may feel that they are answerable to the "system" for their program; however, the "system" should be an aid, not a deterrent.

USING PPBS

Surveys indicate that more than 1000 schools in the United States use PPBS with their budgets. Michigan and California are two examples where PPBS is used.

The Michigan program. Michigan has adopted PPBS in its publicly funded institutions of higher learning. Although the system costs more money, it enables administrators to have greater information for decision making and gives taxpayers a better indication of where their money is being spent.

The California program. Under the director of the Advisory Commission on School District Budgeting and Accounting, 15 pilot school districts used PPBS. They simplified plans so they were readily understandable to voters in the hope that the public's understanding would help the passage of school bond issues. When explained in terms of objectives and expected accomplishments, the voters supported budgets and approved programs.

It is obvious from the California and Michigan examples that PPBS is a process that can help use available funds wisely, point up problem areas, and improve program defects. In addition, the public is given clear and understandable data to aid in deciding on budgets.

HOW CAN PPBS BE APPLIED TO PHYSICAL EDUCATION AND ATHLETIC PROGRAMS?

Physical education has much to gain by implementing PPBS. If this system is used, physical education programs and budget requests cannot be arbitrarily dropped or refused because of inadequate funding. Each segment of the curriculum must be given equal emphasis according to objectives and benefits derived from meeting these objectives.

Physical education and athletic budgets before PPBS were considered in terms of bats and balls rather than total program needs and benefits. PPBS is now used by physical education departments to comprehensively present needed information required by administrators. PPBS provides administrators with a detailed list of goals and objectives, an analysis of problems, alternatives, solutions, and recommendations. The most important accomplishment of PPBS is the way it relates program costs to expected accomplishments.

Cost analysis

Cost analysis of materials used in a program is a derivative of cost accounting. Cost analysis is needed to help the administrator evaluate present operations, as well as project future planning. Cost analysis is limited to the types of accounting systems being used, as well as designating the unit to be compared. It is particularly applicable to schools and colleges. For example, some schools operate on grades one to eight, kindergarten to grade twelve, or some other educational pattern. Naturally, there would be a great difference in expenditures per pupil in the various patterns of organization.

Various units are used in cost analysis for the general education fund. The number of pupils in attendance, the census, average daily attendance, and average daily membership are some of those used. There are advantages and disadvantages to each of the various units.

Knezevich and Fowlkes point out that as a raw measure of educational burden, the average daily membership is a better measure than the average daily attendance. Teachers' salaries must be paid whether pupils are in 90% or 100% attendance, and desks and school books must be available whether pupils are in attendance or not. With respect to raw per capita units, the average daily membership is a better unit to measure the educational burden than the more commonly used average daily attendance unit. Tradition, however, has favored the average daily attendance unit over average daily membership.*

Cost analysis as it relates to equipment and supplies for physical education and athletics may be simply handled by allowing a certain number of dollars per pupil or per participant, depending on whether one is concerned with a school or another organizational program.

Some experts in fiscal management feel a per capita expenditure allocation for physical education and athletics represents a good foundation program. However, they recommend, in addition, (1) an extra percentage allocation for program enrichment, (2) an extra percentage allocation for variation in enrollment, and (3) a reference to a commodity index (current prices of equipment and supplies) that may indicate need for changes in the per capita expenditure because of current increase or decrease in the value of the items being purchased.

COST ANALYSIS IN PRACTICE IN SCHOOL PHYSICAL EDUCATION AND ATHLETIC PROGRAMS

To provide the reader with an understanding of the amount of money allocated to physical education programs throughout the United States and how it is determined, a survey of selected school systems was accomplished.

California. A large city system in California reports that physical education supplies are included in each school's allocation for instructional supplies, with the amount being based on the number of pupils enrolled—elementary schools, $4.25 per pupil; junior high schools, $3.44 per pupil; and senior high schools, $3.15 per pupil.

Physical education equipment was included in the budget for the year at $38,000. The maintenance of

physical education equipment was provided for, as needed, by the board of education, which also provided the towels and laundry service. Regarding the athletic program, the board of education provided extra pay for coaches and intramural directors, all the necessary athletic uniforms, the cleaning and repair of these uniforms and equipment, officials, and accident insurance for all boys and girls participating in the extramural and interschool athletic programs.

Illinois. A high school in Illinois reported that no set figure or set formula was used to arrive at the allocation for physical education and athletic programs. The board of education subsidized the program of physical education beyond the gate receipts. At the time of the survey, there was an equipment budget of $1000 and a supplies budget of $1300. The board of education reviews the anticipated budget each year for approval. The director of health and physical education submits a list of anticipated expenditures for such items as equipment, supplies, transportation, and officials. Gate receipts are also estimated. The difference between the two figures is the amount the board must approve or adjust before approval.

Indiana. One medium-sized school system in Indiana reported that each school (elementary, junior high, senior high) is allocated so much money for each student enrolled, and then the principal assigns the amount for each phase of the school program.

A large city school system in Indiana does not have a formula for determining the amount of money allocated for physical education. Budget requests are prepared by the high school department heads for grades nine to twelve and by the supervisor of health and physical education for grades one to eight. The amount requested is based on inventory, program needs of individual schools, and requirements for supplying new schools and additions to present plants.

Another Indiana school system finances the entire interscholastic athletic program from gate receipts. Extra pay for coaches and maintenance of athletic facilities is financed through the general fund. Concerning the physical education program, each department is given an allocation of funds based on the number of students served.

New Jersey. One large school system in New Jersey reported an allocation of 50 cents per student for

---

*Knezevich, S.J., and Fowlkes, J.G.: Business management of local school systems, New York, 1960, Harper & Row, Publishers.

Fig. 13-11. A swimmer in action at the State University College, Potsdam, N.Y.

physical education supplies, and a smaller school system reported an allocation of $3000 to $6000 for supplies and coaches' salaries for athletics. Most school districts in New Jersey, it was reported, do not seem to have difficulty in getting reasonable physical education supplies based on needs. For athletics, most schools in New Jersey are subsidized in whole or part by board of education funds.

New York. Twenty-five New York schools were surveyed to determine the amount of money allocated to their physical education programs. The amounts allocated were then changed into a per pupil allotment to provide a means of comparison. The items for which the money was allocated included athletic and gymnasium supplies and equipment, various athletic fees, officials, transportation, police, reconditioning of equipment, supplies and equipment needed in physical education classes, and intramurals and extramurals for men and women. In those schools in which the administrative pattern grouped grades seven to twelve, the highest allocation per pupil was $33.86 and the lowest was $10.07. In those schools in which budgets were figured on a kindergarten to grade twelve school administrative pattern, the highest per capita allocation was $13.22 and the lowest was $5.30. In those schools in which the administrative pattern included grades nine to twelve, the highest per capita allocation was $35.24 and the lowest was $13.68.

Each school surveyed was asked how the amount allocated per student was determined. The general practice was that the director of health and physical education submitted and substantiated the following:

1. Needs—for the coming school year
2. Increased expenditures—a sound estimate of projected increases regarding pupil program participation based on increased enrollments, pupil interest, program changes, and the anticipated cost of equipment and supplies to be used
3. Inventory—present equipment and supplies on hand and the condition of these items
4. Previous year's budget—amounts allocated in previous year or years

These four items represent the basis on which most allocations of funds to physical education and athletic programs were determined.

Directors of physical education and athletic programs surveyed felt that when they were granted increases in per capita allocations it was the result of such factors as increase in the number of participants, a careful evaluation of the number of participants and the time they spent using the equipment and supplies, the cost per hour (for example, it was determined in one community that it cost less than 50 cents per hour per student to participate in football), and an excellent working rapport with the board of education.

The survey also disclosed that most schools have a contingency fund to meet emergency needs, that many schools used the money saved when the proposed budget allocation was in excess of the actual bid price on certain supplies and equipment, that some schools used part of the money received from gate receipts, and that some other schools used part of the money from the sale of general organization tickets.

Oklahoma. A city school system in Oklahoma reported that budget allocations for physical education programs for boys and girls vary according to pupil enrollment. The superintendent of schools and the board of education decide the amount to be allocated to each of the special programs. Athletics are self-supporting and the board of education does not allocate money directly to them.

Texas. An independent school district in Texas pointed out it does not have a formula for physical education. The board of education and school administration decide the total budget.

The business administrator and fiscal management in schools and colleges*

Schools and colleges today are in the business of education. The size of the physical plant and the large expenditures require the talents of a qualified business administrator. The school or college business administrator is an integral part of the entire administrative team and ideally should have experience in both business administration and education. He or she is primarily responsible for the efficient and economic management of business matters concerning the educational institution.

Physical education and athletic directors must understand and appreciate the vital role of the business administrator. Many administrative functions of physical educators fall within the responsibility of the business administration. These functions include fiscal management. The business administrator is a specialist in this area, and educators should work closely with this individual in reference to business-related matters.

*Thanks are due H.J. Stevens of Nanuet, N.Y. Public Schools for his help in writing this section.

The school or college business administrator is an important member of the administrative team who has a significant contribution to make in the decision-making process, as well as in executing business functions. He or she is well versed in educational matters, as well as in business management. He or she is in a position to participate under the superintendent's or president's leadership in making decisions concerned with fiscal matters.

The college business manager, or the vice president for business affairs, as he or she is sometimes called, is responsible for budget preparation and fiscal accounting, investment of endowment and other monies, planning and construction of buildings, data processing, management of research and other contracts, business aspects of student loans, and intercollegiate activities.

Most key business officers have earned a master's or a doctor's degree, usually in business administration. However, some are certified public accountants and some have taken courses in management institutes. Most college business managers are recruited outside the academic world.

For the purposes of this text, the term *business administrator* is used, and the duties of such an educational officer are discussed in terms of schools and the school district. However, the functions outlined for the business administrator, the problems discussed, and the working relationship with physical education personnel are similar to or have implications for physical educators in colleges and other organizations.

FUNCTION

The business administrator's function is strictly limited by the size of the educational triangle—program, receipts, expenditures. The greater the perimeter of the triangle, the larger the sphere of operations. This applies to all departments in the system. Likewise, in times of inflation, the expenditures and receipts may increase, and as a result, the program side may also increase, but the actual program could remain the same. Hence, it is obvious that the business administrator must project both expenditures and receipts if a constant program is going to be maintained.

Receipts

Expenditures

Program

Fig. 13-12. The business administrator's isosceles triangle.

The business office represents a means to an end, and it can be evaluated in terms of how well it contributes to the realization of the objectives of education.

OBJECTIVES

In serving schools and colleges, the business administrator constantly has the goal of helping them obtain the greatest educational service possible from each tax or aid dollar spent. He or she should take a democratic approach on decisions affecting others. A decision will then be reached that will be for the best, with the assurance that the educational benefits are worth the cost.

The business administrator is part of the team of administrators—along with presidents, principals, superintendents, and board members—who may be expected to look into the years ahead and have some ideas regarding the future plans of the school or college.

RESPONSIBILITIES

The business administrator's responsibilities are varied. He or she is as familiar with employee health insurance problems as with state and federal allocations for education. In the smaller school district, the business responsibilities are incorporated into the duties of the chief school administrator. As districts enlarge, there is a need to hire a person to oversee all the nonteaching areas of the district so the chief school administrator is free to devote more time to the educational program of the district. No two districts are alike in handling business responsibilities.

Following are some of the administrator's duties as listed by Frederick W. Hill, a past president of the Association of School Business Officials:

1. *Budget and financial planning.* This is an area in which the business official has to be sensitive to the needs of staff members to carry out a program. One also must have a sixth sense to understand how much the community can expend on the program. This can be related to the accompanying isosceles triangle. There has to be a direct relationship among all the components that make up the three sides of the triangle.

2. *Purchasing and supply management.* The business official must use the best purchasing techniques to obtain maximum value for every dollar spent. After purchases are made and goods received, he or she is responsible for warehousing, storage, and inventory control. An article offered at the cheapest price is not always the most economical to purchase.

3. *Plans.* The business official works with administrators, teachers, architects, attorneys, and citizens of the community in developing plans for expansion of building facilities.

4. *Personnel.* The business official's duties vary in relation to the size of the district. In a large district he or she may be in charge of the nonteaching personnel, and in a small district he or she may be in charge of all personnel. In this capacity this official has to maintain records, pay schedules, retirement reports, and other personnel records.

5. *Staff improvement.* The business official is always interested in upgrading the people under his or her jurisdiction by providing workshops and in-service courses concerning latest developments in the field.

6. *Community relations.* Without community support the school would not operate. Some administrators tend to forget this when they become too far removed from the community. There is always a need to interpret the business area to the public.

7. *Transportation.* It has often been said that boards of education find themselves spending too much time on the three Bs—buses, buildings, and bonds. When this occurs, it is time to look into hiring a business official.

8. *Food services.* The business official is responsible for the efficient management of food services.

9. *Accounting and reporting.* The business official establishes and supervises the financial records and accounting procedures.

Table 13-2. Sample sports program, general organization, and board of education report of expenditures and receipts

Sports	Board of education	General organization	Total
Total expenditures			
Baseball	$ 765.75		$ 765.75
Basketball	890.70	$ 106.34	997.04
Football	847.68	3943.09	4340.77
Cross country	129.00	37.00	166.00
Cheerleaders	126.58	249.10	375.68
Golf	91.50		91.50
Hockey	842.25	48.95	891.20
Soccer	343.20		343.20
Swimming	456.10	41.10	497.20
Tennis	40.00	4.00	44.00
Track	516.27	15.03	531.30
TOTAL	$5049.03	$3994.61	$9043.64
Total general organization receipts			
Football		$2740.40	
Basketball		381.30	
TOTAL			$3121.70

10. *Debt service.* The business official is involved with various capital developments and financial planning through short-term and long-term programs. Part of the financial rating of a school or a college district is judged on the way its debt service is handled.

11. *Insurance.* The business official must be familiar with a large schedule of insurance provisions ranging from fire and liability to health insurance. He or she must maintain records for proof in case of loss.

12. *Legal matters.* The business official has to be familiar with education law, and he or she must know when to consult with attorneys.

13. *System analysis.* The business official must constantly question existing systems to see if they can be changed so the job can be done more efficiently. New methods are being introduced using data processing that will be a challenge, as well as an aid, to the business official.

14. *Money raising.* The business administrator is frequently called on to lead money-raising drives for colleges and universities.

15. *Grants and financial aid.* The business official must be aware of money available for programs through private, state, and federal grants and money available for scholarship candidates from private and public sources.

Financial accountability

The great amount of money involved in physical education and athletic programs makes strict accountability mandatory. This includes the maintenance of accurate records, proper distribution of materials, and adequate appraisal and evaluation of procedures. Financial accounting should provide the following:

1. A record of receipts and expenditures for all departmental transactions
2. A permanent record of all financial transactions for future reference
3. A pattern for expenditures closely related to the approved budget
4. A tangible documentation of compliance with mandates and requests either imposed by law or by administrative action

Table 13-3. A sample list of expenditures for athletics

	Baseball	Basket-ball	Football	Cross country	Golf	Hockey	Soccer	Swim-ming	Tennis	Track	Total
Equipment and supplies	$369.55	$158.30	$279.68	$ 45.80	$36.01	$251.65	$ 70.40	$ 80.05	$27.20	$231.77	$1549.50
Transportation	208.50	248.70	39.60	83.20	48.40	495.00	63.70	108.80	93.78	120.90	1510.48
Officials	122.00	391.35	50.00				52.00				615.35
Cleaning	65.70	30.95	129.40			95.60	57.20			141.10	519.95
Supervision		66.00									66.00
Custodian		37.00									37.00
Additional coaching			350.00				100.00				450.00
Entry fees					7.00			17.21	4.00	22.50	50.75
Rental, club pool								250.00			250.00
TOTALS	$765.75	$932.30	$847.68	$129.00	$91.50	$842.25	$343.20	$456.10	$124.78	$516.27	$5049.03

5. An evaluation procedure to ensure that funds are dealt with honestly, and proper management with respect to control, analysis of costs, and reporting

REASONS FOR FINANCIAL ACCOUNTING

Financial accounting is needed in physical education and athletic programs for the following reasons:

1. To provide a method of authorizing expenditures for items that have been included and approved in the budget. This means proper accounting records are being used.
2. To provide authorized procedures for making purchases of equipment, supplies, and other materials and to let contracts for various services.
3. To provide authorized procedures for paying the proper amounts (a) for purchases of equipment, supplies, and other materials, which have been checked upon receipt, (b) for actual labor, and (c) for other services rendered.
4. To provide a record of each payment made, including the date, to whom, for what purpose, and other pertinent material.
5. To provide authorized procedures for handling various receipts and sources of income.
6. To provide the detailed information essential for properly auditing accounts, such as confirmation that money has been spent for accurately specified items.
7. To provide material and information for the preparation of future budgets.
8. To provide a tangible base for developing future policies relating to financial planning.

ADMINISTRATIVE PRINCIPLES AND POLICIES FOR FINANCIAL ACCOUNTING

The Athletic Institute* has prepared some excellent material on accountability, which brings out such important principles and policies as the following:

1. The administrative head has the final responsibility for accountability for all equipment and supplies in his or her organization.
2. Departments should establish and enforce policies covering loss, damage, theft, misappropriation, or destruction of equipment and supplies or other materials.
3. A system of accurate record keeping should be established and be uniform throughout the department.
4. Accountability should demonstrate the close relationship that exists between equipment and supplies and the program objectives.
5. A system of policies should be developed that will guarantee the proper use and protection of all equipment and supplies within the department.
6. The person to whom equipment and supplies are issued should be held accountable for these materials.
7. Accurate inventories are essential to proper financial acounting.
8. A system of making equipment and supplies as proof of ownership should be instituted.

*The Athletic Institute: Equipment and supplies for athletics, physical education and recreation. Chicago, 1960, The Institute, Chapter 5.

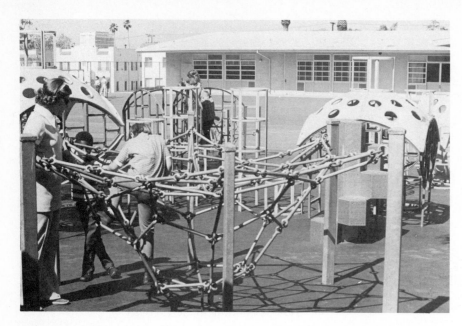

Fig. 13-13. The business administrator has the responsibility of purchasing playground equipment, such as this special equipment used on playground in Los Angeles City Schools.

Courtesy Playground Corporation of America.

9. A meaningful procedure should be established for properly distributing all equipment and supplies.
10. Discarding equipment and supplies should take place only in accordance with established procedures and by authorized persons.

ACCOUNTING FOR RECEIPTS AND EXPENDITURES

A centralized accounting system is advantageous, with all funds being deposited with the treasurer, business manager, or other responsible person. Purchase orders and other procedures are usually then countersigned or certified by the proper official, thus better guaranteeing integrity in the use of funds. A system of bookkeeping wherein books are housed in the central office by the finance officer helps ensure better control of finances and allows all subdivisions or departments in a system to be financially controlled in the same manner. Such a procedure also provides better and more centralized record keeping. The central accounting system fund accounts, in which are located the physical education and athletic funds, should be audited annually by qualified persons. Finally, an annual financial report should be made

and publicized to indicate receipts, expenditures, and other pertinent data associated with the enterprise.

All receipts and expenditures should be recorded in the ledger properly, providing such important information as the fund in which it has been deposited, or from which it was withdrawn; and the money received from such sources as athletics and organization dues should be shown with sufficient cross references and detailed information. Supporting vouchers should also be at hand. Tickets to athletic and other events should be numbered consecutively and checked to get an accurate record of ticket sales. Students should not be permitted to handle funds except under the supervision of some member of the administrative staff or faculty. All accounts should be properly audited at appropriate intervals.

Purchase orders on regular authorized forms issued by the organization should be used, so accurate records may be kept. To order verbally is a questionable policy. Preparing written purchase orders, on regular forms and according to good accountability procedure, better ensures legality of contract together with prompt delivery and payment. For more information see Chapter 14.

CHECKLIST FOR BUDGETING AND FINANCIAL ACCOUNTING

Yes   No

1. Has a complete inventory been taken and itemized on proper forms as a guide in estimating equipment needs?

2. Does the equipment inventory include a detailed account of the number of items on hand, size and quantity, type, condition, etc.?

3. Is the inventory complete, current, and up-to-date?

4. Are budgetary estimates as accurate and realistic as possible without padding?

5. Are provisions made in the budget for increases expected in enrollments, increased pupil participation, and changes in the cost of equipment and supplies?

6. Have supply house and the business administrator been consulted on the cost of new equipment?

7. Has the Director of Physical Education and Athletics consulted with the staff on various budget items?

8. Has the Director of Physical Education and Athletics consulted with the school business administrator in respect to the total budget for the department?

9. Are new equipment and supply needs for physical education and athletics determined and budgeted at least one year in advance?

10. Was the budget prepared according to the standards desired by the chief school administrator?

11. Are statistics and information for previous years indicated as a means of comparison?

12. Is there a summary of receipts and expenditures listed concisely on one page so that the total budget can be quickly seen?

13. If receipts from athletics or other funds are to be added to the budget, is this shown?

14. Are there alternate program plans with budgetary changes in the event the budget is not approved?

15. Has a statement of objectives of the program been included that reflects the overall educational philosophy and program of the total school and community?

16. Has the budget been prepared so that the major aspects may be viewed readily by those persons desiring a quick review and also in more detail for those persons desiring a further delineation of the budgetary items?

17. Is the period of time for which the budget has been prepared clearly indicated?

18. Is the physical education and athletics budget based on an educational plan developed to attain the goals and purposes agreed on by the director and his staff within the framework of the total school's philosophy?

19. Is the physical education and athletics plan a comprehensive one reflecting a healthful environment, physical education class, adapted, intramural and extramural, and interscholastic program?

20. Does the plan include a statement of the objectives of the physical education and athletic programs and are these reflected in the budget?

21. Are both long-range and short-range plans for achieving the purposes of the program provided?

22. Have provisions been made in the budget for emergencies?

23. Are accurate records kept on such activities involving expenditures of money as transportation, insurance, officials, laundry and dry cleaning, awards, guarantees, repairs, new equipment, medical expenses, and publicity?

Continued.

CHECKLIST FOR BUDGETING AND FINANCIAL ACCOUNTING—cont'd

	Yes	No
24. Are accurate records kept on the receipt of monies from such sources as gate receipts and advertising revenue?		
25. Once the budget has been approved, is there a specific plan provided for authorizing expenditures?		
26. Are specific forms used for recording purchase transactions?		
27. Are purchases on all major items based on competitive bidding?		
28. Are requisitions used in obtaining supplies and equipment?		
29. Are requisitions numbered and do they include such information as the name of the person originating the requisition, when the item to be purchased will be needed, where to ship the item, the description and/or code number, quantity, unit price, and amount?		
30. With the exception of petty cash accounts, is a central purchasing system in effect?		
31. Is the policy of quantity purchasing followed whever possible and desirable in the interests of economy?		
32. If quantity purchasing is used, are advanced thought and planning given to storage and maintenance facilities and procedures?		
33. Are performance tests made of items purchased? Are state, regional, or national testing bureaus or laboratories utilized where feasible?		
34. Are receipts of equipment and supplies checked carefully?		
35. Is an audit made of all expenditures?		
36. Are specific procedures in effect to safeguard money, property, and employees?		
37. Is there a check to determine that established standards, policies, and procedures have been followed?		
38. Are procedures in operation to check condition and use of equipment and supplies?		
39. Is a financial report made periodically?		
40. Are there proper procedures for the care and maintenance and accountability of all equipment and supplies?		
41. Are accurate records kept on all equipment and supplies, including condition, site, and age?		
42. Have established procedures been developed and are they followed in regard to the issuance, use, and return of equipment?		
43. Have provisions been made for making regular notations of future needs?		

SELF-ASSESSMENT TESTS

These tests are to assist students in determining if material and competencies presented in this chapter have been mastered.

1. What are five reasons for fiscal management in physical education and athletic programs?

2. Outline the procedure you would follow in preparing a budget if you were the chairperson of a department of physical education and athletics for a city educational system.

3. Develop a detailed PPBS plan for a department of physical education and athletics.

4. As a business administrator in a school system, what aspects of fiscal management would involve you with the administration of a physical education and athletic program?

5. Formulate 10 policies to ensure sound financial accounting.

SELECTED REFERENCES

Andrew, L., and Robertson, L.: PPBS in higher education: a case study, Educational Record **54:**61, 1973.

Avedisian, C.: Planning, programming, budgeting systems, Journal of Health, Physical Education, and Recreation **43:**37, 1972.

Bannon, J.J.: Leisure resources—its comprehensive planning, Englewood Cliffs, N.J., 1976, Prentice-Hall, Inc.

Boston, R.E.: Management by objectives: a management system for education, Educational Technology **12:**49, 1972.

Bronzan, R.T.: New concepts in planning and funding athletic, physical education, and recreation facilities, St. Paul, 1974, Phoenix Intermedia.

Bronzan, R.T.: Public relations, promotions and fund raising—for athletic and physical education programs, New York, 1977, John Wiley & Sons, Inc.

Broyles, J.F., and Hay, R.D.: Administration of athletic programs—a managerial approach, Englewood Cliffs, N.J., 1979, Prentice-Hall, Inc.

Fuoss, D.E., and Troppmann, R.J.: Creative management techniques in interscholastic athletics, New York, 1977, John Wiley & Sons, Inc.

Hall, J.T., et al.: Administration: principles, theory and practice, Pacific Palisades, Calif., 1973, Goodyear Publishing Co., Inc.

Hartley, H.J.: Educational planning-programming-budgeting, a systems approach, Englewood Cliffs, N.J., 1968, Prentice-Hall, Inc.

Hartley, H.J.: PPBS: a status report with operational suggestions, Educational Technology **12:**21, 1972.

Hitchcock, C.: An analysis of the responses of directors to a survey on the effect of budget cuts and austerity budgets on athletic programs, New York State Association for Health Physical Education and Recreation Journal, June 1978.

Jenkins, W.A., and Lehman, G.O.: Nine pitfalls of PPBS, School Management **16:**2, 1972.

Klappholz, L.A.: Involving the staff in the budget-making process, Physical Education Newsletter, November 1980.

Klappholz, L.A.: The presentation: a key to securing approval of the physical education and athletic budgets, Physical Education Newsletter, November 1980.

Knezevich, S.J., and Fowlkes, J.G.: Business management of local school systems, New York, 1960, Harper & Row, Publishers.

Murphy, H.B.: Coping with financial problems in high school athletics, The Athletic Educator's Report, August 1980.

Sisson, R.L., and others: An introduction to the educational planning, programming, budgeting system, Educational Technology **12:**54, 1972.

What happens when the money runs out? Athletic Purchasing and Facilities **5:**44-48, July 1981.

Zeigler, E.F., and Spaeth, M.J.: Administrative theory and practice in physical education and athletics, Englewood Cliffs, N.J., 1975, Prentice-Hall, Inc.

14

The purchase and care of supplies and equipment

Instructional objectives and competencies to be achieved

After reading this chapter the student should be able to

■ Show why sound supply and equipment management is important and explain the basis on which supplies and equipment should be selected for physical education and athletic programs.
■ Discuss the various procedures and principles that should be followed in purchasing supplies and equipment.
■ List guidelines for the selection of an equipment manager and for the administration of the equipment room.
■ Establish a system for checking, issuing, and maintaining supplies and equipment.
■ Justify the need for various types of audiovisual supplies and equipment for the physical education and athletic program.

Physical education and athletic programs use many supplies and equipment that cost thousands of dollars. *Supplies* are those materials that are expendable and that need to be replaced at frequent intervals, such as shuttlecocks and adhesive tape. *Equipment* refers to those items that are not considered expendable but are used for a period of years, such as parallel bars and audiometers.

Because so much money is spent on supplies and equipment and such materials are vital to the health and safety of participants, to good playing conditions, and to values derived from the programs, it is important that this administrative phase of the specialized fields of physical education and athletics be considered carefully. The purchase of supplies and equipment should also be related to achieving the objectives designated by PPBS. Physical educators should express their need for equipment and other materials in terms of the goals these aids represent.

Many different sources for purchasing equipment exist, many grades and qualities of materials are available, and many methods of storing and maintaining such merchandise are prevalent. Some of these sources, grades, and methods are good and some are

questionable. To obtain the greatest values for the money, basic principles of selecting, purchasing, and maintaining need to be understood.

Determining supply and equipment needs

Supplies and equipment needs vary according to certain influencing factors. These include, first, the programs themselves and the activities offered. Other factors are the facilities, the training rooms, and playing space available. Some organizations have only limited physical education facilities. Under such conditions the supplies and equipment needed differ from those required in settings where spacious accommodations exist. Other factors to consider are the nature of the clientele (age, sex, and number), the money available, the length of playing seasons, and health and safety provisions. Those responsible for purchasing supplies and equipment should carefully study their own particular situations and estimate their own needs objectively and realistically.

In the athletic training area, first aid supplies, scales, examining table, beds, towels, and sheets will be needed. In the physical education skill area, all types of balls, apparatus, uniforms, timers, and racks will be needed for individual, team, formal, aquatic, dance, and other activities. Different types of materials will be required for interschool and intercollegiate athletic programs, intramural and extramural programs, programs for the handicapped, and class programs.

Many decisions in purchasing equipment and supplies depend on the objectives of the administration. In general, however, the administration is interested in the following:

1. Trying to standardize supplies and equipment as much as possible
2. Supervising the entire process of selection, purchase, storage, and maintenance
3. Maintaining a list of sources of materials
4. Preparing specifications for items to be purchased
5. Securing bids for large purchases and those required by law
6. Deciding on or recommending organizations where materials are to be purchased
7. Testing products to see that specifications are satisfactorily met
8. Checking supplies and equipment to determine if all that were ordered have been delivered
9. Expediting the delivery of purchases so materials are available as needed
10. Continually seeking new products that meet the needs of the program
11. Providing overall supervision of purchase, care, and use of supplies and equipment

Guidelines for selecting supplies and equipment

Selection should be based on local needs. Supplies and equipment should be selected because they are needed in a particular situation and by a particular group. Items should be selected that represent materials needed to carry out the program as outlined and that represent essentials to fulfilling program objectives.

Selection should be based on quality. In the long run, the item of good quality is the cheapest and the safest. Bargains too often represent inferior materials that wear out much earlier. Only the best grade of

football equipment should be purchased. I did a study of football deaths that occurred during a 25-year period and found that many of these deaths had resulted from the use of inferior helmets and other poor equipment. What is true of football is also true of other activities.

Selection should be made by competent personnel. The persons selecting the supplies and equipment needed in physical education and athletic programs should be competent. To perform this responsibility efficiently means examining many types and makes of products, conducting experiments to determine economy and durability, listing and weighing the advantages and disadvantages of different items, and knowing how each item is going to be used. The person selecting supplies and equipment should be interested in this responsibility, have the time to do the job, and be able to perform the function efficiently. Some organizations have purchasing agents who are specially trained in these matters. In small organizations the chairperson, director, or coach frequently performs this responsibility. One other point is important: regardless of who the responsible person may be, the staff member who uses these supplies and equipment in his or her particular facet of the total program should have a great deal to say about the specific items chosen. He or she is the one who understands the functional use of the merchandise.

Selecting should be continuous. A product that ranks as the best available this year may not necessarily be the best next year. Manufacturers are constantly conducting research to produce something better. There is keen competition among them. The administration, therefore, cannot be complacent and apathetic, thinking that because a certain product has served them well in the past, it is the best buy for the future. Instead, there must be a continuous search for the best product available.

Selection should consider service and replacement needs. Items of supplies and equipment may be difficult to obtain in volume. On receipt of merchandise, sizes of uniforms may be wrong, and colors may be mixed up. Additional materials may be needed on short notice. Therefore one should select items that will be available in volume, if needed, and deal with business firms that will service and replace materials

A

KEY TO FIGURES

1. CHEST. Be sure the tape is snug under the arms and over the shoulder blades.

2. WAIST. Place the tape above the hips around waist like a belt to determine waist measurements.

3. HIPS. Measure hips around the widest part.

4. INSEAM. Measure inseam from close up the crotch to top of the heel of the shoe when full-length pants are ordered. For shorter pants, like baseball and football pants, check on the measurement recommendations of the manufacturer of the clothing you select.

5. OUTSEAM. Measure from the waistline to top of heel of shoe for full-length pants. For baseball, football, and shorter pants check the measurement recommendations of the particular manufacturer involved.

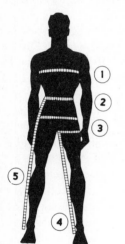

6. SLEEVE. Take measurments from center of back over elbow to wrist. Keep elbow bent, straight out from shoulder.

HEAD. (Not shown in diagram). The tape should run across forehead about 1½ inches above eyebrows and back around the large part of the head.

B

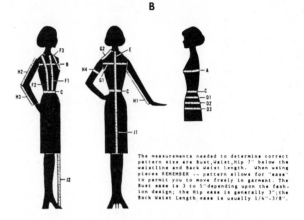

The measurements needed to determine correct pattern size are Bust, Waist, Hip 7" below the waistline and Back Waist Length. When using pieces REMEMBER -- pattern allows for "ease" to permit you to move freely in garment. The Bust ease is 3 to 5" depending upon the fashion design; the Hip ease is generally 3"; the Back Waist Length ease is usually 1/4"-3/8".

NAME		DATE	
A. BUST................................	in.	— Measure around fullest part — a little higher in back	
B. CHEST................................	in.	— Measure straight across front from seam to seam	
C. WAIST................................	in.	— Put string or elastic around waist to locate natural waistline.	
D. HIP 1................................	in.	— Measure 3" below natural waistline	
2................................	in.	— Measure 7" below natural waistline	
3................................	in.	— Measure 9" below natural waistline	
E. BACK WAIST LENGTH..............	in.	— Nape of neck to waistline	
F. FRONT WAIST LENGTH 1............	in.	— Neck to waistline at Center Front	
2............	in.	— Mid-shoulder to waist over bust	
3............	in.	— Base of neck at shoulder seamline to tip of bust	
G. SHOULDERS 1......................	in.	— Seam to seam across back 4" below neckline	
2......................	in.	— One shoulder from base of neck to seamline	
H. SLEEVE 1............................	in.	— Underarm to wrist	
2............................	in.	— Shoulder to elbow	
3............................	in.	— Elbow to wrist	
4............................	in.	— Around upper arm	
J. LENGTH 1............................	in.	— Waist to hemline at Center Back	
2............................	in.	— From floor to hemline	
		printed in u.s.a.	

Fig. 14-1. A, How to measure for athletic equipment. Correct measurement is essential for proper sizing of athletic equipment to ensure the comfort of the wearer, durability of equipment, proper protection, and appearance on the field. This illustration may be used as a measuring guide to ensure the proper fit of uniforms, jerseys, protective equipment, and warmup suits. This is a basic measuring guide for most types of athletic equipment. For a perfect fit it is also recommended that you state height, weight, and any special irregularities of build. **B,** How to take a woman's measurements.

A from How to budget, select, and order athletic equipment, Chicago, 1962, The Athletic Institute; **B** courtesy McCall's Patterns.

and take care of emergencies without delay and controversy.

Selection should consider the handicapped. The handicapped need special types of equipment to implement many of the activities that are a part of the physical education program. Equipment is needed for such aspects of the program to perform perceptual-motor activities, to stretch and strengthen certain muscle groups, to correct postural faults, to develop balance, and to develop physical fitness. Some of this equipment is illustrated in Fig. 14-2.

Selection should consider acceptable standards for athletic equipment. The stamp of approval of the National Operating Committee on Standards for Athletic Equipment (NOCSAE), for example, should be on football helmets. This will ensure that the helmet has been properly constructed and injury will be less likely to occur. The NOCSAE researches athletic equipment and encourages acceptable standards in manufacturing athletic equipment. They also distribute this information to various organizations and individuals in the interests of safety, utility, and legal considerations. Furthermore, they provide an opportunity for individuals and organizations to consider problems regarding various aspects of athletic equipment and how they can be solved.

Selection should consider trends in athletic uniforms. The emerging trends in athletic uniforms should also be taken into consideration. According to Derleth,* some of the most recent significant changes in uniforms include the following:

- Using ventilated mesh fabric
- Coaches and staff members dressing in school colors and in conformance with team uniforms
- Basketball uniforms becoming more casual; for example, shirts are worn outside pants
- Screen-printed lettering has become popular on uniforms; it is light, inexpensive, durable, and will stretch
- Wrestling uniforms are now one-piece instead of two-piece
- In baseball, pullover tops are being used instead of button-front or zipper-front shirts

Text continued on p. 477.

*Derleth, H.: Medalist sand knit, how important is the appearance of your team, Medalist Sports News **1**:5, March 1976.

Fig. 14-2. Inexpensive equipment for perceptual-motor activities: **A,** Rope or string; **B,** chalk. *Continued.*

A and **B** courtesy California State University, Audio Visual Center, Long Beach, Calif.

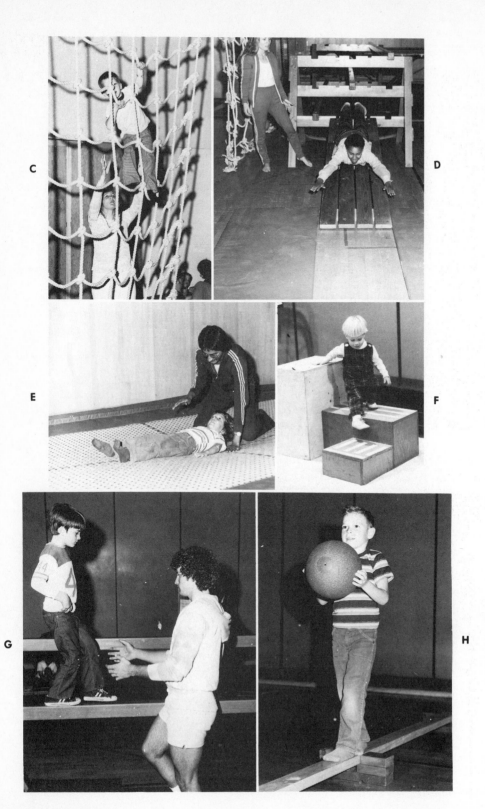

C

D

E

F

G

H

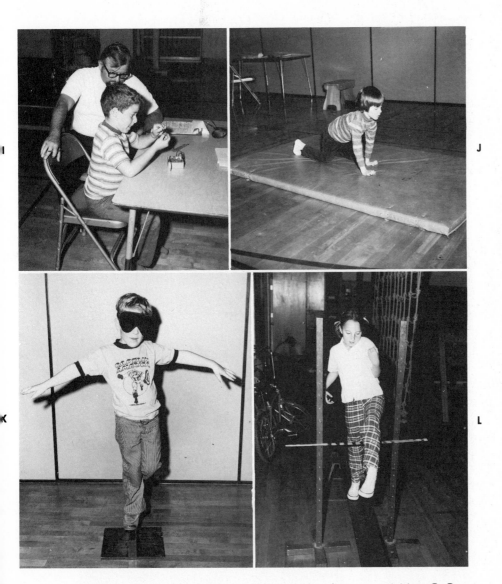

Fig. 14-2, cont'd. More elaborate equipment for perceptual-motor activities: **C,** Cargo net; **D,** scooter on incline; **E,** trampoline; **F,** wooden boxes; **G,** Stegel; **H,** balance beam. Activities using perceptual-motor testing equipment: **I,** Bead stringing; **J,** creeping; **K,** static balance; **L,** dynamic balance;   *Continued.*

C through **L,** courtesy California State University, Audio Visual Center, Long Beach, Calif.

M

N

O

Fig. 14-2, cont'd. M and **N,** towel and wood block used to stretch anterior shoulder muscles; **O** and **P,** three-way mirror (note use of vertical and horizontal lines to aid student with alignment problems); **Q,** stall bars and wall weights (installation of wall weights can be made behind stall bars if space is limited—note asymmetrical scoliosis exercise);

P, courtesy California State University, Audio Visual Center, Long Beach, Calif.; **M** through **O, Q** from Crowe, W.C., Auxter, D., and Pyfer, J.: Principles and methods of adapted physical education and recreation, ed. 4, St. Louis, 1981, The C.V. Mosby Co.

P

Q

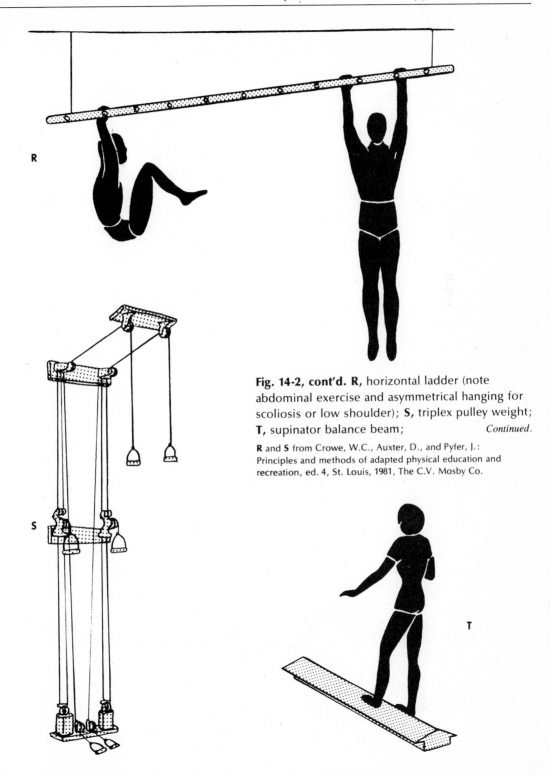

Fig. 14-2, cont'd. R, horizontal ladder (note abdominal exercise and asymmetrical hanging for scoliosis or low shoulder); **S,** triplex pulley weight; **T,** supinator balance beam; *Continued.*

R and **S** from Crowe, W.C., Auxter, D., and Pyfer, J.: Principles and methods of adapted physical education and recreation, ed. 4, St. Louis, 1981, The C.V. Mosby Co.

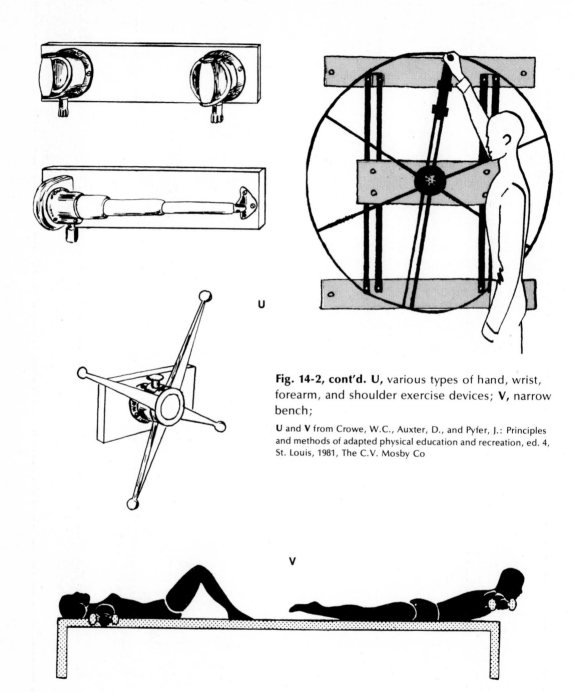

Fig. 14-2, cont'd. U, various types of hand, wrist, forearm, and shoulder exercise devices; **V,** narrow bench;

U and **V** from Crowe, W.C., Auxter, D., and Pyfer, J.: Principles and methods of adapted physical education and recreation, ed. 4, St. Louis, 1981, The C.V. Mosby Co

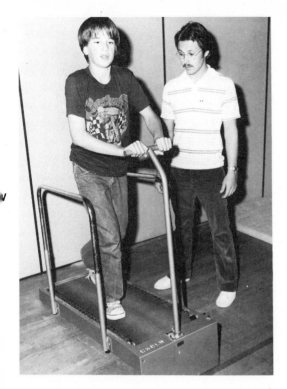

Fig. 14-2, cont'd. W, portable treadmill for development of cardiovascular fitness.

W courtesy California State University, Audio Visual Center, Long Beach, Calif.

Guidelines for purchasing supplies and equipment

Purchases should meet the organization's requirements and have administrative approval. Each organization has its own policy providing for the purchase of supplies and equipment. It is essential that the prescribed pattern be followed and that proper administrative approval be obtained. Requisition forms that contain descriptions of items, amounts, and costs; purchase orders that place the buying procedure on a written or contract basis; and voucher forms that show receipt of materials should all be used as prescribed by regulations. The physical education administrator and staff members should be familiar with and follow local purchasing policies.

Below are listed the steps one organization uses in purchasing equipment:

1. *Initiation.* A request is made for equipment to fulfill, augment, supplement, or improve the program.
2. *Review of request.* The proper administrative personnel approve or disapprove request after careful consideration of need.
3. *Review of budget allocation.* A budget code number is assigned after availability of funds in that category has been determined.
4. *Preparation of specifications.* Specifications are prepared in detail, giving exact quality requirements, and made available to prospective contractors or vendors.
5. *Receipt of bids.* Contractors or vendors submit price quotations.
6. *Comparison of bids to specifications.* Careful evaluation is made to determine exact fulfillment of quality requirements.
7. *Recommendations are made.* The business administrator prepares specific recommendations for approval.
8. *Purchase order to supplier.* After approval, a purchase is made that fulfills the requirements at a competitive price.

Purchasing should be done in advance of need. The main and bulk purchases of supplies and equipment for physical education and athletic programs should be completed well in advance of the time the materials will be used. Late orders, rushed through at the last moment, may mean mistakes or substitutions on the part of the manufacturer. When purchase orders are placed early, manufacturers have more time to carry out their responsibilities efficiently. Goods that do not meet specifications can be returned and replaced, and many other advantages result. Items needed in the fall should be ordered not later than the preceeding spring, and items desired for spring use should be ordered not later than the preceding fall.

Supplies and equipment should be standardized. Ease of ordering is accomplished and larger quantities of materials can be purchased at a saving

VP-F 27 (R-1/75)

IDR No.

UNIVERSITY OF NEVADA, LAS VEGAS

INTER-DEPARTMENTAL REQUISITION

....
Ordering Dep't

To .... Date ....
(Dep't from which services requested)

Account Charged...

Account Credited ....

Deliver to ....
Person   Building and Room   Phone

Quantity	Stock No.	Item	Amount
		Total	

Signed...   Approved ....
Head of Department   Dean or Administrative Officer

INSTRUCTIONS – This form is to be used for all inter-departmental orders; for example, to order supplies or services from Central Stores, Audio-Visual Department, Dining Commons and Motor Pool for vehicle requests. Submit original and 3 copies to vendor department, retain blue copy. When transaction has been completed a priced copy will be returned to the requisitioning department.

Fig. 14-3. Interdepartmental requisition.

UNIVERSITY OF NEVADA, LAS VEGAS
CENTRAL SERVICES WORK REQUEST

CENTRAL SERVICES

Dept: _____

Date _____

Job Submitted By _____

Account Charged_____

Account Credited   **8 - 2 - 221 - 4014 - 500 - 9404**

_____
Administrator

Deliver to _____
        Person   Building and Room

Today's date:

Needed no later than:

    (Use actual date needed please. Do not
    use *As soon as possible.*)

Number of copies _____

    INCLUDE SAMPLE WITH ORDER

_____

To be printed:

  Offset □   (Allow 15 working days)
    (Letterhead,
    Envelopes,
    Brochures,
    Form Letters,
    Forms,
    and
    ALL QUALITY WORK)

_____

Assemble □ Staple □ Pad □

Other _____

SPECIAL INSTRUCTIONS:

FOR CENTRAL SERVICES USE ONLY

     10 x 15   12 x 18   14 x 20   18 x 25
Plates □   □   □   □

             Amount   Stock No.

Film _____

Phototypesetting _____

PMT's _____

Copywhite _____

Letterhead _____

Sulphite Bond _____

Book Paper _____

Cover Stock _____

Envelopes _____

IBM Cards _____

Carbonless Paper _____

Index Stock _____

Stock Forms _____

Labor_____hr.

Misc. _____

No. _____   TOTAL: _____

By _____   Date of Completion:

           Date Received:

Received by _____   Date _____

NOTE: Send all but pink copy with order.

Fig. 14-4. Central services work request.

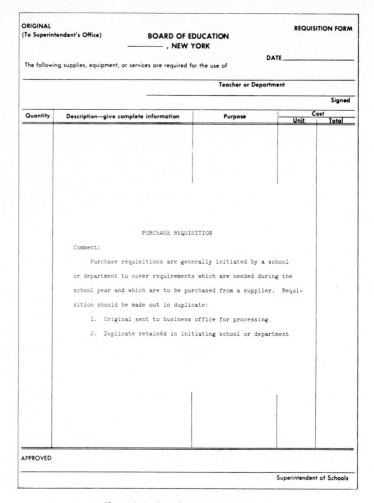

ORIGINAL
(To Superintendent's Office)

BOARD OF EDUCATION

———————— , NEW YORK

REQUISITION FORM

DATE_____

The following supplies, equipment, or services are required for the use of

_____

Teacher or Department

Signed

Quantity	Description—give complete information	Purpose	Cost	
			Unit	Total

PURCHASE REQUISITION

Comment:

    Purchase requisitions are generally initiated by a school or department to cover requirements which are needed during the school year and which are to be purchased from a supplier. Requisition should be made out in duplicate:

    1. Original sent to business office for processing

    2. Duplicate retained in initiating school or department

APPROVED

_____

Superintendent of Schools

Fig. 14-5. Purchase requisition.

when standardized items of supplies and equipment are used. Standardization means that certain colors, styles, and types of material are ordered consistently. This procedure can be followed after careful research to determine what is the best, most reliable, and most serviceable product for the money. However, standardization of supplies and equipment should never mean that further study and research to find the best materials to meet program objectives are terminated.

Specifications should be clearly set forth. The trademark, item number, catalog number, type of material, and other important specifications should be clearly stated when purchasing material to avoid any misunderstanding of what is being ordered. This procedure ensures that quality merchandise will be received when it is ordered. It also makes it possible to objectively compare bids of competing business firms.

Cost should be kept as low as possible without loss of quality. Quality of materials is a major consideration. However, among various manufacturers and business concerns, prices vary for products of equal quality. Because supplies and equipment are usually purchased in considerable volume, a few cents per unit could represent a saving of many hundreds of dollars to taxpayers. Therefore, if quality can

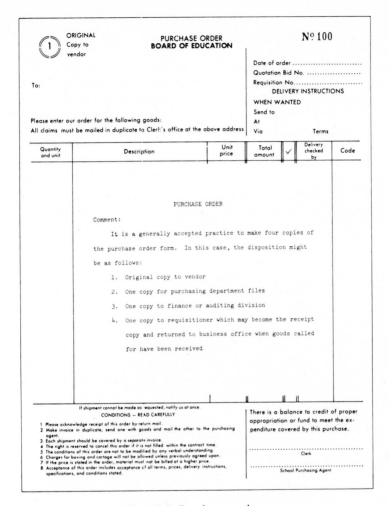

Fig. 14-6. Purchase order.

be maintained, materials should be purchased at the lowest cost figure.

Purchases should be made from reputable business firms. In some cases higher administrative authorities decide the firm from which supplies and equipment are to be purchased. In the event of such a procedure, this principle is academic. However, where the business firm from which purchases will be made is determined by physical education personnel, it is wise to deal with established, reputable businesses that are known to have reasonable prices, reliable materials, and good service. In the long run this is the best and safest procedure to follow.

Central purchasing can result in greater economy. Some school districts and other organizations purchase supplies and equipment for several schools or other groups. In this way they can buy larger amounts at a reduced price per unit. In some cases large school districts standardize their uniforms' colors, thus enabling them to purchase uniforms at lower prices. If desired, this system also makes it possible to have a central warehouse and a common location for orders, contracts, and other records.

Local firms should be considered. The administration's main concern is to obtain good value for money expended. If local firms can offer equal values, render equal or better service for the same money, and are reliable, then preference should probably be given to local dealers. If such conditions cannot be met, however, a question can be raised about the wisdom of such a procedure. In some cases it is advantageous to use local dealers, because they are more readily accessible and can provide quicker and better service than firms located farther away.

Bids should be obtained. A sound administrative procedure that helps eliminate any accusation of favoritism and obtain the best price available is competitive bidding. This procedure requires that special forms be distributed to many dealers who handle the supplies and equipment desired. In such cases, the specifics regarding the kind, amount, and quality of articles desired should be clearly stated. After bids

A FLOW CHART SHOWING STEPS OR MECHANICS OF PURCHASING

1. The idea	Teacher gets an idea for equipment to help her.
2. Consultation	Teacher goes to colleagues, consultants, and administration for advice on feasibility of idea and how it can be implemented.
3. Requisition	Principal approves and sends through requisition to purchasing agent.
4. Coordination	Purchasing agent sees that this is not a routine request, so he sends it to the audio-visual director and assistant superintendent for instruction.
5. Staff action	Audio-visual director and assistant superintendent agree that the idea is good, check on budget, fix responsibility for control, set up experimental procedures, and approve requisition.
6. Investigation	Purchasing agent uses his knowledge and contacts to determine the experience of other users and of suppliers; he sets up possible specifications.
7. Standardization	Meet with teachers to see if certain specifications can be agreed on and if standardization is possible; here he serves as consultant.
8. Specifications	Sets up specifications in line with meetings.
9. Bids or quotations	Checks with all possible sources to get the best buy.
10. Purchase order	Purchasing officer and designated cosigners sign purchase order in quadruplicate. One copy each goes to vendor, warehouse, purchasing agent, and accounting office.
11. Follow-up	Purchasing agent makes a follow-up if equipment is not received when due.
12. Receipt of goods	Warehouse receives goods, checks according to specifications, and returns purchase order with OK.
13. Payment	Purchasing agent and board of education approve purchase for payment, and accounting office pays.
14. Accountability	Goods are sent to the department which is held accountable for equipment.
15. User receives	Teacher picks up equipment at designated place.
16. Quality control	Equipment is used experimentally and tested under different conditions.

From Roe, W.H.: School business management, New York, 1961, McGraw-Hill Book Co., p. 133.

have been obtained, the choice can be made. Low bids do not have to be accepted. However, a decision not to honor one must be justified.

Gifts or favors should not be accepted from dealers. Some dealers and salesmen are happy to present an administrator or staff member with a new rifle, set of golf clubs, tennis racquet, or other gift if, in so doing, they believe it is possible to get an account. It is poor policy to accept such gifts or favors. This places a person under obligation to an individual or firm and can only result in difficulties and harm to the program. An administrator or staff member should never profit personally from any materials purchased for use in his or her programs.

A complete inventory analysis is essential before purchasing. Before purchases are made, the amount of supplies and equipment on hand and the condition of these items should be available. This knowledge prevents overbuying and large stockpiles of materials that may be outdated when they become needed.

Guidelines for the equipment and supply manager and equipment room

The equipment and supply manager's position is very important. The money spent on uniforms and other supplies and equipment amounts to a large part of an organization's budget. Therefore the person in charge of the equipment and supply room, whether a student or a paid employee, should be selected with care. A qualified person will be able to help make equipment and supplies last longer through proper storage, cleaning, and care. Accountability for equipment will be better assured because a system of good record keeping will be established and less equipment will be lost. Also, a qualified manager will be able to make sound recommendations regarding the purchasing of athletic equipment. In light of such important responsibilities an equipment manager should be selected who has such qualifications as

---

UNIVERSITY OF NEVADA, LAS VEGAS
CENTRAL SERVICES WORK REQUEST

CENTRAL SERVICES

— QUICK PRINT ONLY —

Dept: _____

Account Charged_____

Account Credited **8 - 2 - 221 - 4014 - 500 - 9404**

Deliver to _____
　　　　　　Person　　　　　Building and Room

Today's Date:

Needed no later than:

(Use actual date needed please.)

Number of Copies: _____
Special Instructions:

Color of Paper:　　　Watermark (white only) ☐
　☐ Buff　☐ Yellow　☐ Goldenrod　☐ White
　☐ Pink　☐ Green　☐ Blue

Received by _____

Job Submitted By

_____
Administrator

Your Code # _____

Prepare your copy on **PLAIN WHITE** paper.
(*Please* do not use erasable bond.)

Assemble ☐　Staple ☐　Pad ☐

Other _____

For Central Services Billing Use ONLY.

Print Both Sides (white only) ____　_____
8½ x 14 (white only) _____　_____
8½ x 11 _____　_____
Other _____　_____
　　　　　　　　　　　　　　Total　_____

Date _____

NOTE: Send all but Pink Copy With Order.

Fig. 14-7. Central services work request.

creative organizational ability, an understanding of athletic equipment and supplies and what is needed to maintain them, a willingness to learn, the ability to get along well with people, trustworthiness, the ability to supervise other people effectively, and a willingness to make minor repairs in equipment to make it more serviceable.

The equipment and supply room is an important facility in physical education and athletic programs. It is important to have sufficient space to take care of the various purposes for which such a room exists. There should be ample space to store, label, and identify the equipment and supplies needed in the program. An adequate number of bins and racks for equipment will be needed. Also, proper air circulation is important. There should be ample space to permit movement for handling the routine functions of issuing equipment and supplies. People working in the room should be able to move with ease throughout the facility. There should be ample space for drying equipment, such as football uniforms that have become wet when practice or games are held in the rain. The equipment and supply room should be well organized and be a model of efficiency and sound organization.

Guidelines for checking, storing, issuing, and maintaining supplies and equipment

All supplies and equipment should be carefully checked on receipt. Equipment and supplies that have been ordered should not be paid for until they have been checked for amount, type, quality, size, and other specifications listed on the purchase order. If any discrepancies are noted, they should be corrected before payment is made. This is an important responsibility and should be carefully followed. It represents a good business practice in a matter requiring good business sense.

Supplies and equipment requiring organization identification should be labeled. Equipment and supplies are often moved from location to location and also are issued to participants and staff members on a temporary basis. It is a good procedure to stencil or stamp everything with the organization's identification to check on such material, help trace missing articles, discourage misappropriation of such items, and know what is and what is not departmental property.

Procedures should be established for issuing and checking in supplies and equipment. There can be considerable loss of material if poor accounting procedures are followed. Procedures should be established so items are issued as prescribed, proper forms are completed, records are maintained, and all material can be located. Articles should be listed on the records according to various specifications of amount, size, or color, together with the name of the person to whom the item is issued. The individual's record should be classified according to name, street address, telephone, locker number, or other information important for identification. In all cases the person or persons to whom the supplies and equipment are issued should be held accountable.

Equipment should be in constant repair. Equipment should always be maintained in a serviceable condition. Procedures for caring for equipment should be routinized so repairs are provided as needed. All used equipment should be checked and then repaired, replaced, or serviced as needed. Repair can be justified, however, only when the cost for such is within reason. Supplies should be replaced when they have been expended.

Equipment and supplies should be stored properly. Supplies and equipment should be handled efficiently so space has been properly organized for storing, a procedure has been established for ease of location, and proper safeguards have been taken against fire and theft. Proper shovels, bins, hangers, and other accessories should be available. Temperature, humidity, and ventilation are also important considerations. Items going into the storeroom should be properly checked for quality and quantity. An inventory should be constantly available for all items on hand in the storeroom. Every precaution should be taken to provide for the adequate care of the material so that a wise investment has been made.

Garments should be cleaned and cared for properly. According to the *Rawlings Athletic Handbook,* the care of garments can be considered under four headings. First is *new garments;* they should be kept

UNIVERSITY OF NEVADA, LAS VEGAS
PROPERTY MOVEMENT REQUEST

Date: _____

From: _____
      (Department Chairperson)

Via: Purchasing Administrator

Via: Inventory Control, Purchasing Department

To: Operations and Maintenance

_____
(Signature)

_____
(Signature)

_____
(Signature)

     It is requested that the following item(s) of University property be moved on
_____: (Allow 5 days for scheduling.)
  (Date)

It is essential that all columns be accurately and completely accomplished.

Inventory decal number	Description of item to be transferred	Check one From		Check one To	
		Furn. pool		Furn. pool	
		Bldg.	Room	Bldg.	Room

Move completed:	Master inventory update
_____ _____	_____ _____
(Signature) (Date) Operations and Maintenance)	(Computer batch (Date) number)

Fig. 14-8. Property movement request.

Fig. 14-9. Equipment room.

Courtesy Sinclair Community College, Dayton, Ohio.

NOTICE TO BIDDERS

(For use in advertising)

The board of education of ___(legal name)___ School District

No. ___ of the Town(s) of _____ popularly known

as _____ , (in accordance with Section 103 of

Article 5-A of the General Municipal Law) hereby invites the sub-

mission of sealed bids on _____ for use in the

schools of the district. Bids will be received until _____ on the
                                                      (hour)

_____ day of _____, 19 ___, at _____
(date)   (month)   (place of bid

_____, at which time and place all bids will be publicly opened.
opening)

Specifications and bid form may be obtained at the same office. The

board of education reserves the right to reject all bids. Any bid

submitted will be binding for _____ days subsequent to the date of

bid opening.

                              Board of Education

                    _____ School District No. ___

                    of the Town(s) of _____

                    County(ies) of _____

                    _____
                              (Address)
                    By _____
                              (Purchasing Agent)

_____
(Date)

Note: The hour should indicate whether it is Eastern Standard or
       Eastern Daylight Saving Time.

Fig. 14-10. Sample notice to bidders form.

From School Business Management Handbook Number 5. The University of the State of New York, Albany, N.Y.

EQUIPMENT ISSUE

Date..

I .... have

accepted school property ....

.... (write in article and its number)

and agree to return it clean and in good condition or pay for said uniform.

Signed ....

H. R. #

Home Phone #   Home Address..

Fig. 14-11. Form for checking out physical education and athletic equipment.

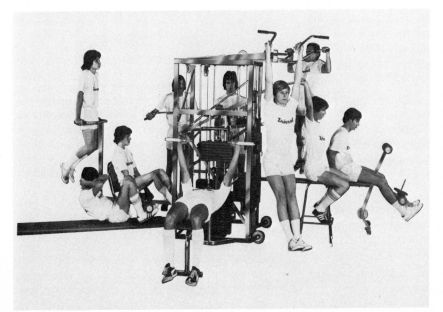

Fig. 14-12. Some organizations purchase Universal exercise equipment for their physical education program, such as the equipment shown here.

Courtesy Universal Gym Equipment, Irvine, Calif.

Fig. 14-13. Playground equipment.

Courtesy Playground Corporation of America.

in original packing boxes and stored in a cool, dry area where there is low humidity. Second, *during the season* garments should be cared for immediately following a game. Before sending them to the cleaner they should be inspected for tears or other defects and repaired as soon as possible. Third, *on a trip* the garments should be packed for the trip home and then hung up as soon as one returns. If an extended trip is being made, or if the trip home will not take place until the next day, the garments should be hung up for drying after each game is completed. Fourth, *between seasons* the most important procedure is to take care of the final cleaning, repair, and storage of the garments as soon as the last game has been played and the season is over. By following these procedures the garments will last longer and look better and there will be a resultant savings of time and money.

The Rawlings Sporting Goods Company has also set forth the following suggestions concerning the cleaning of athletic equipment:

- The cleaner should be informed concerning the need for special handling of the garments.
- Dry cleaning usually will remove dirt and stains but

normally will not remove perspiration. (Some people are stressing that garments should be purchased that can be cleaned by soap and water rather than by dry cleaning, because dry cleaning will not remove perspiration.)
- Garments of different colors should not be laundered together.
- Strong chemicals or alkalies should not be used because they will fade colors and may damage the material.
- A chlorine bleach should not be used.
- Water level in washing equipment should be kept high if lower mechanical action is desired, but kept low if uniforms are badly soiled, to increase mechanical action. Do not overload washing equipment.
- When using commercial steam press, it is recommended that garments should be stretched back to original size.
- Uniforms and other garments should be dry before being stored.
- Water temperatures above 120° F may fade colors and cause shrinkage.
- Specialized all-automatic athletic laundry facilities that are owned by the organization are recommended as a means of protecting garments against shrinkage, color fading, snags, and bleeding.

```
              EQUIPMENT CHECKOUT RECORD

Player_____    Home Room_____

Address_____     Phone_____

Class_____ Height_____ Weight_____ Age_____

Parents Waiver_____ Examination_____ Insurance_____
-----------------------------------------------------------------
Football    Cross Country    Basketball    Swimming    Wrestling

Baseball    Track            Tennis        Golf
-----------------------------------------------------------------
```

	Out	In	Game Equipment	Out	In
Blocking pads			White jersey		
Shoulder pads			Maroon jersey		
Hip pads			White pants		
Thigh pads			Maroon pants		
Knee pads			Warm-up pants		
Helmet			Warm-up jacket		
Shoes			Stockings		
Practice pants					
Practice jersey					

```
I hereby certify that I have received the above-listed athletic equipment
and will return same not later than the day following the last game of
the season for the sport checked.

                    Signature_____
```

Fig. 14-14. Equipment checkout record.

From Bucher, C.A., and Koenig, C.R.: Methods and materials
in secondary school physical education,
ed. 6, St. Louis, 1983, The C.V. Mosby Co.

MONTH	TYPE OF ATHLETIC EQUIPMENT			
	FOOTBALL	**BASEBALL**	**BASKETBALL**	**TRACK**
JANUARY	ORDER NEW EQUIPMENT	ORDER NEW EQUIPMENT	PRACTICE FREE THROWS DURING STUDY HALL	ORDER NEW EQUIPMENT
FEBRUARY	ORDER NEW EQUIPMENT	TIME IS RUNNING OUT		TIME IS RUNNING OUT
MARCH	ORDER NEW EQUIPMENT	DELIVERY	TAKE INVENTORY	MAKE PLANS FOR VACATION
APRIL	TIME IS RUNNING OUT	MARK EQUIPMENT	ORDER NEW EQUIPMENT	GO FISHING
MAY	MOW PRINCIPAL'S LAWN		ORDER NEW EQUIPMENT	
JUNE	GO TO SCHOOL BOARD PICNIC	TAKE INVENTORY	ORDER NEW EQUIPMENT	TAKE INVENTORY
JULY	DELIVERY		ORDER NEW EQUIPMENT	
AUGUST	MARK EQUIPMENT	ATTEND COUNTY FAIR	TIME IS RUNNING OUT	
SEPTEMBER			DELIVERY	DELIVERY
OCTOBER		ORDER NEW EQUIPMENT	MARK EQUIPMENT	MARK EQUIPMENT
NOVEMBER	TAKE INVENTORY	ORDER NEW EQUIPMENT		ORDER NEW EQUIPMENT
DECEMBER	ORDER NEW EQUIPMENT	ORDER NEW EQUIPMENT		ORDER NEW EQUIPMENT

ORDER NEW EQUIPMENT   TIME IS RUNNING OUT   YOU MAY BE TOO LATE

Fig. 14-15. Athletic equipment buyers' almanac.

From How to budget, select, and order athletic equipment, Chicago, 1962, The Athletic Institute.

Fig. 14-17. Laundry for washable supplies.
University of California at Irvine.

Fig. 14-16. Gymnastic room with equipment.
University of California at Irvine.

Fig. 14-18. Some organizations purchase Nautilus exercise equipment for their physical education program, such as the equipment demonstrated here.

Courtesy Nautilus Sports/ Medical Industries, DeLand, Fla.

Audiovisual supplies and equipment

Audiovisual aids and materials have become an important part of physical education and athletics programs.

A survey among 100 schools, colleges, and many other organizations found that more than one half of them used some form of audiovisual aid in their programs. All of the persons surveyed felt that audiovisual media are valuable supplements to instruction in learning motor skills and in encouraging persons to be physically fit. The survey also found that videotaping is on the increase as an instructional tool. The audiovisual media used most frequently by those persons surveyed included cartridge films, loop films, 16- and 8-mm films, wall charts, slide films, film strips, and instructional television.

REASONS FOR INCREASED USE OF AUDIOVISUAL MATERIALS IN PHYSICAL EDUCATION AND ATHLETIC PROGRAMS

1. *They enable the viewer to better understand concepts and the performance of a skill, events, and other experiences.* Using a film, pictures, or other materials gives a clearer idea of the subject being taught, whether it is how a heart functions or how to perfect a golf swing.

2. *They help provide variety to teaching.* There is increased motivation, the attention span of students and others is prolonged, and the subject matter is more exciting when audiovisual aids are used in addition to other teaching techniques.

3. *They increase motivation on the part of the viewer.* To see a game played, a skill performed, or an experiment conducted in clear, understandable, illustrated form helps motivate a person to engage in a game, perform a skill more effectively, or want to know more about the relation of exercise to health. This is particularly true in video replay, for example, where a person can actually see how he or she performs a skill and then can compare the performance to what should be done.

4. *They provide an extension of what can normally be taught in a classroom, gymnasium, or playground.*

Audiovisual aids enable the viewer to be taken to other countries, and to experience sporting events in other parts of the United States and the rest of the world. All of these are important to physical education and athletic programs.

5. *They provide a historical reference for physical education and athletics.* Outstanding events in sports, physical education, and health that have occurred in past years can be brought to life before viewers' eyes. In this way the person obtains a better understanding of these fields and the important role they play in our society and other cultures of the world.

SELECTED TYPES OF AUDIOVISUAL AIDS

Audiovisual materials commonly used today by physical educators and athletic personnel follow:

VISUAL AIDS (AUDIOVISUAL IN SOME CASES)

Chalkboards—for recording plays, thoughts, and ideas

Wall charts—of self-explanatory terms

Flat pictures, cartoons, posters, photographs

Graphs—bar, circle, line, and other types

Maps and globes

Bulletin boards—for posting program materials

Models and specimens—the human body, skeleton, animals, insects, and others

Opaque projector—used to display on a screen an enlarged picture too small in the original for all students readily see and understand its message

Overhead projector—a compact, lightweight machine that can be operated with ease and used to project materials on a screen; the material projected is a transparency, made of film that can either be purchased or made

Stereoscopes—machines that project a picture in three dimensions and thus give a better understanding of space relationships

Silent films

Slides—generally three types: 35-mm individual slide encased in a cardboard holder; the larger lantern slide usually 3¼ by 4 inches; and the lantern slide that may be prepared for immediate use by a Polaroid transparency film

Filmstrips

Loop films—available in cartridges that can be inserted into a projector and shown with comparative ease; there are three types: a free 8-mm loop film that can

Fig. 14-19. Rolling equipment cart, one of several designed for specific classes of the physical education program. These are stored in the equipment room and transported to activity areas by student helpers.

University of California at Irvine.

be shown in an 8-mm projector; an 8-mm cartridge film encased in a plastic cartridge that requires a special projector; and the super–8-mm film encased in a plastic cartridge that requires a still different type of projection

Motion pictures —usually in 8-, 16-, and 35-mm sizes

Television —educational and closed circuit television and the kinescope recorder; videotape recording that enables a person to actually see how he or she performs a particular skill, for example, has proved effective as an instructional medium

AUDIO AIDS

Radio —educational and commercial programs

Records and transcriptions —of important events, speeches, musical productions, and music for dances

Tape recordings —special events recorded and used to appraise student progress in conduct, skills, concepts, and appreciation and to cover current happenings pertinent to health and physical education

GUIDELINES FOR SELECTING AND USING AUDIOVISUAL AIDS

1. *Audiovisual materials should be carefully selected and screened before using.* Appropriateness for age and grade level of students and others, adequacy of subject matter, technical qualities, inclusion of current information, cost, and other factors are important to know when selecting audiovisual materials.

2. *The presentation of materials should be carefully planned to provide continuity in the subject being taught.* Materials should be selected and used that amplify and illustrate some important part of the material being covered in a particular course. Furthermore, they should be used at a time that logically fits into the presentation of certain material and concepts.

3. *The materials should be carefully evaluated after they have been used.* Whether or not materials are used a second time should be determined on the

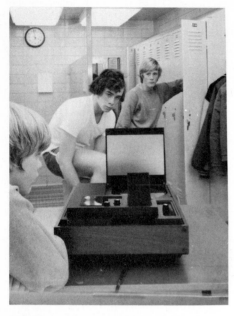

Fig. 14-20. Visual teaching aids.

Courtesy Eastman Kodak Co.

basis of their worth the first time they were used. Therefore they should be evaluated carefully after their use. Records of evaluation should be maintained.

4. *Slow-motion and stop-action projections are best when a pattern of coordination of movements in a skill is to be taught.* When teaching a skill, the physical educator usually likes to analyze the various parts of the whole and also to stop and discuss various aspects of the skill with the students.

5. *Equipment should be properly maintained and prepared.* Projectors, record players, television equipment, and other materials need to be kept in good operating condition and operated by qualified personnel to have an effective audiovisual program.

NEW DEVELOPMENTS IN AUDIOVISUAL AIDS

Dial access systems, satellite television, cable television, videotape systems, and media centers are being used more and more in physical education and athletic programs.

Dial access systems. The Dial Access Information Retrieval System provides immediate, automatic access to a wide variety of audiovisual materials. A coaxial television cable is connected to a centralized distribution center, industrial plant, gymnasium, school libraries, selected classrooms, and other settings. The physical educator can consult a catalog of available audiovisual materials and can request material, which is then directed through an electronic switching system to one of the television terminals in the organization. The primary objective of the Dial Access program is to provide individuals access to all audiovisual materials.

Satellite television. When satellite television is used, certain factors have to be considered: (1) adequate ground facilities that can send and transmit radio and television signals must be available, (2) adequate programs must be developed, (3) physical educators must be trained in its use, and (4) scheduling of programs may be added by the use of videotape recorders to play back programs that were viewed at an earlier time.

ADMINISTRATOR'S CODE OF ETHICS FOR PERSONNEL INVOLVED IN PURCHASING*

1. To consider first the interests of the organization and the betterment of the program.
2. To be receptive to advice and suggestions of colleagues, both in the department and in business administration, and others insofar as advice is compatible with legal and moral requirements.
3. To endeavor to obtain the greatest value for every dollar spent.
4. To strive to develop an expertise and knowledge of supplies and equipment that ensure recommendations for purchases of greatest value.
5. To insist on honesty in the sales representation of every product submitted for consideration for purchase.
6. To give all responsible bidders equal consideration in determining whether their produce meets specifications and the educational needs of your program.
7. To discourage and to decline gifts that in any way might influence a purchase.
8. To provide a courteous reception for all persons who may call on legitimate business missions regarding supplies and equipment.
9. To counsel and help others involved in purchasing.
10. To cooperate with governmental or other organizations or persons and help in developing sound business methods in the procurement of equipment and supplies.

*Adapted from the New York State Association of School Business officials: Code of ethics for school purchasing officials.

Cable television. Cable television's possibilities for educational use are tremendous. Educators, administrators, and curriculum specialists can collaborate in producing instructional programming. Students can also produce programs to be aired over cable television. For example, on Long Island, New York, an area educational service center has worked with cable television to produce programs concerning school budgets, drug abuse, and field trips.

Videotape systems. Videotape systems have already made a significant contribution to education and can make further contributions in many areas. This magnetic recording device makes it possible to record film and sound programs on tape and play them back for immediate use (as used in sporting events), or they can be stored for future presentation.

Videotaping can make a valuable contribution to physical education, as shown by the videotape laboratory at the State University of New York. The project was designed to complement laboratory experiences for physical education major students. A prototype videotape was produced to allow students to participate with motor skills shown on the tape. The tape was accompanied by a booklet that included immediate-response questions and in-depth analyses. The program was evaluated by students and teachers and found to be both interesting and educational.

Pretaping instructional classes by the physical educator can be a great time-saver for the teacher and provide a view of how he or she is teaching and whether modification of methods is necessary.

Media centers. Media resource centers are being developed by various professional organizations, as well as by schools and colleges. These centers are concerned with the collection, storage, and dissemination of various audiovisual materials, such as videotapes to organizations and persons who desire them. For example, the National Center on Education Media and Material for the Handicapped has been developed. Also, the AAHPERD has established a resource center on media in physical education where videotapes and audiotapes are duplicated and distributed, teachers' guides are collected, and tapes of speeches and conference proceedings are stored.

CHECKLIST OF SELECTIVE ITEMS TO CONSIDER IN THE PURCHASE AND CARE OF SUPPLIES AND EQUIPMENT

	Yes	No
1. Selection of equipment and supplies is related to the achievement of the goals of physical education and athletics.		
2. Equipment and supplies are selected in accordance with the needs and capacities of the participants, including consideration for age, sex, skill, and interest.		
3. A manual or written policies have been prepared regarding the procedure for purchasing and care of all supplies and equipment.		
4. Such mechanics of purchasing as the following are used: requisitions, specifications, bids, and quotations, contracts and purchase orders, delivery data, receipt of merchandise, vendor invoices, and payment.		
5. The relationship of such functions as the following to purchasing is considered: programming, budgeting and financing, auditing and accounting, property maintenance, legal regulations, ethics, and philosophy of education.		
6. Such principles of purchasing as the following are adhered to: quality, quantity, storage, inventory, and salvage value.		
7. A close working relationship exists between the department chairperson and school or college business administrator.		
8. Both girls and boys have their own equipment and supplies when needed.		
9. Merchandise is purchased only from reputable manufacturers and distributors, and consideration is also given to their replacement and the services provided.		
10. The greatest value is achieved for each dollar expended.		
11. Administration possesses current knowledge of equipment and supplies.		
12. Administration is receptive to advice and suggestions from colleagues who know, use, and purchase equipment and supplies.		
13. The coach of a sport is contacted when ordering merchandise for his or her activity, and specifications and other matters are checked.		
14. The director of physical education and athletics consults with the business administration when equipment and supplies are needed and ordered.		
15. Local regulations for competitive purchasing are followed.		
16. Equipment and supply purchases are standardized wherever possible to make replacement easier.		
17. Administration is alert to improvements and advantages and disadvantages of various types of equipment and supplies.		
18. Brand, trademark, and catalog specifications are clearly defined in the purchase requisitions.		
19. Purchase orders are made on regular school forms.		
20. Functional quality of merchandise and the safety it affords are major considerations.		
21. The inventory is to plan for replacements and additions.		
22. Complete and accurate records are kept on all merchandise purchased.		
23. New equipment and supply needs are determined well in advance.		
24. New materials and equipment are tested are evaluated before being purchased in quantity lots.		
25. New equipment complies with minimum safety requirements.		

CHECKLIST OF SELECTIVE ITEMS TO CONSIDER IN THE PURCHASE AND CARE OF SUPPLIES AND EQUIPMENT—cont'd

	Yes	No
26. Honesty is expected in all sales representation.		
27. State contracts are used when they are available.		
28. Administration is prompt and courteous in receiving legitimate salespeople and businesspeople.		
29. All competitors who sell merchandise are given fair and equal consideration.		
30. Gifts or favors offered by sales people or manufacturers are refused.		
31. Materials received are checked with respect to quality and quantity and whether they meet specifications that have been indicated in school requisitions.		
32. Prompt payment is assured on contracts that have been made.		
33. All orders are checked carefully for damaged merchandise, shortages, and errors in shipment.		
34. Policies have been established for designating procedure to be followed when there is theft, loss, or destruction of merchandise.		
35. People who are issued equipment and supplies are held accountable for them.		
36. Inventories are taken periodically to account for all materials.		
37. A uniform plan is established for marking equipment and supplies.		
38. A written procedure has been established for borrowing and returning equipment and supplies.		
39. A procedure has been established for holding students accountable for merchandise that is not returned.		
40. Proper storage facilities have been provided.		
41. Equipment is cleaned and repaired where necessary before it is stored.		

SELF-ASSESSMENT TESTS

These tests are to assist students in determining if material and competencies presented in this chapter have been mastered:

1. Why is supply and equipment management important, and what factors need to be considered regarding this administrative responsibility?

2. List and discuss five principles that should be followed when purchasing supplies and equipment. Apply these procedures and principles to selecting a diving board for a swimming pool.

3. Establish a set of guidelines for the position of equipment manager and the conduct of the equipment room.

4. Prepare an administrative plan that you as chair person of a physical education and athletic department would recommend for checking, issuing, and maintaining physical education supplies and equipment.

5. Prepare a report on the various types of audiovisual aids that could be used effectively in teaching volleyball.

SELECTED REFERENCES

American Association for Health, Physical Education, and Recreation: Equipment and supplies for athletics, physical education and recreation, Washington, D.C., The Association. (Published Periodically in the Journal of Health, Physical Education, and Recreation.)

Avedisian, C.T.: PPBS; planning, programming, budgeting systems, Journal of Health, Physical Education, and Recreation **43**:37, 1972.

Bannon, J.J.: Leisure resources—its comprehensive planning, Englewood Cliffs, N.J., 1976, Prentice-Hall, Inc.

Bronzan, R.T.: New concepts in planning and funding athletic, physical education and recreation facilities, St. Paul, 1974, Phoenix Intermedia.

Bronzan, R.T.: Public relations, promotions and fund raising—for athletic and physical education programs, New York, 1977, John Wiley & Sons, Inc.

Broyles, J.F., and Hay, R.D.: Administration of athletic programs—a managerial approach, Englewood Cliffs, N.J., 1979, Prentice-Hall, Inc.

Care of athletic equipment, River Grove, Ill., Wilson Sporting Goods Co.

Deatherage, D., and Reid, C.P.: Administration of women's competitive sports, Dubuque, Iowa, 1977, William C. Brown Co., Publishers.

Fuoss, D.E., and Troppmann, R.J.: Creative management techniques in interscholastic athletics, New York, 1977, John Wiley & Sons, Inc.

Greenberg, J.L.: How videotaping improves teaching behavior, Journal of Health, Physical Education, and Recreation **44:**36, 1973.

How to budget, select, and order athletic equipment. Available from Athletic Goods Manufacturers Association, Merchandise Mart, Chicago, Ill.; also through MacGregor & Rawlings Sporting Goods.

Koerner, J.: Educational technology, Saturday Review of Education **1:**43, 1973.

Piscopo, J.: Videotape laborating; a programmed instructional sequence, Journal of Health, Physical Education, and Recreation **44:**32, 1973.

Suppes, P.: computer confrontation, Saturday Review of Education **1:**48, 1973.

15

Athletic training, safety, and health service

Instructional objectives and competencies to be achieved

After reading this chapter the student should be able to

■ Summarize the incidence of injuries among athletes.
■ Understand the role of the prevention and care of injuries in the athletic program.
■ Discuss the qualifications, duties, and responsibilities of team physicians and athletic trainers.
■ Discuss some administrative procedures that should be taken to emphasize safety in a school or other organization.
■ Outline the nature and scope of health services in school and college programs.
■ Draw implications for the administration of school and college physical education programs regarding health appraisal, health counseling, correction of remediable defects, and emergency care of students.

The number of athletes injured increases every year. An estimated 42,000 team sport injuries requiring hospital treatment occur each year, and many more go unreported. More than 1 million boys participate in high school football annually, another 70,000 at college, and still another 200,000 in other organizations. There are an estimated 200,000 to 600,000 football injuries alone—injuries caused by such things as poor football helmets, pads, and other equipment; hazardous playing surfaces; and players returning to action before fully recovering from injuries. Many basketball players suffer sprained ankles, broken bones, and other injuries to the head, elbows, knees and Achilles tendons. In baseball, most injuries occur in arms, legs, feet, heads, and necks, some of which are caused by improper sliding techniques, poor playing surfaces, collisions, and being hit with balls. In track and field, muscle pulls, abrasions, and knee and ankle injuries are common. Sprains and fractures plague skiers, and hockey players are injured from body checks and being hit with a puck or stick.

John Marshall, orthopedic surgeon at the Hospital for Special Services in New York City, states that less than 10 out of every 100 of the nation's 22,000

high schools have proper medical care for their athletes. A professor of biomechanics in Michigan says that the majority of high schools in his state do not provide adequately for athletic injuries. A survey by the federal Department of Health, Education, and Welfare reported at least 111,000 serious sports-related injuries each year that cause students to miss at least 3 weeks of school.

Klafs and Arnheim* indicate that as a result of the ever-increasing participation of girls and women in sports there has been a decided upswing in both the number and severity of injuries among female participants.

The most common types of injures were ankle sprains, knee injuries, and contusions (Table 15-5). The least common injuries were those to the breast, head, and neck. When the same data were organized into type of major injuries by sport, the most serious injuries, including major fractures, head injuries, and dislocations, were in basketball, field hockey, softball, and gymnastics (Tables 15-6 and 15-7).

---

*Klafs, C.E., and Arnheim, D.D.: Modern principles of athletic training, ed. 5, St. Louis, 1981, The C.V. Mosby Co.

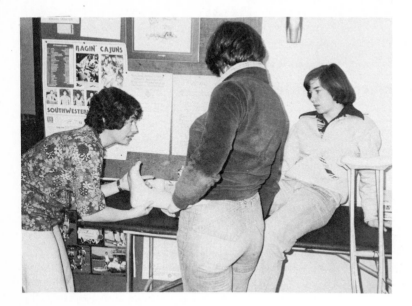

Fig. 15-1. Athletic trainer at work.
Courtesy Cramer Products, Inc.,
Gardner, Kan.

Table 15-1. Survey of sports injuries and fatalities, total number of major injuries, by type of institution, sex, activity group, and sports category (United States, (1975-1976)*

| | Secondary schools | | | | Colleges/universities | | | |
| | Public | | Private | | 2-year | | 4-year | |
	Male	Female	Male	Female	Male	Female	Male	Female
TOTAL	65,196	13,072	8,201	1,605	3,637	553	15,744	3.090
Athletic competition	34,536	6,626	4,143	828	1,737	288	6,289	1,125
Tackle football	21,107	0	2,455	0	652	0	2,738	0
Other contact sports	10,122	4,299	1,289	606	903	211	2,899	736
Noncontact sports	3,307	2,327	398	222	182	77	632	389
Athletic practice	28,620	5,207	3,226	557	1,511	49	6,480	1,263
Tackle football	16,144	0	1,926	0	728	0	3,165	0
Other contact sports	8,669	2,120	1,058	375	653	90	2,395	605
Noncontact sports	3,807	3,087	241	182	130	59	920	658
Intramurals	2,040	1,233	833	220	387	116	2,993	702
Tackle football	57	0	88	0	0	1	111	0
Other contact sports	1,388	505	636	112	310	51	2,259	476
Noncontact sports	595	728	109	109	77	64	623	226

*Courtesy Calvert, R.C., Jr.: Athletic injuries and deaths in secondary schools and colleges, 1975-76, Washington, D.C., National Center for Education Statistics.

The estimated injury rate of boys and girls up to 15 years of age who play sports is 1 in 3. Winter sports take their toll with an estimated 400,000 injuries per year.

Medical supervision is essential for all sports participants. Unfortunately, many athletic contests are not adequately supervised medically. Dr. Allan J. Ryan cites his experiences at the University of Wisconsin concerning the lack of medical supervision in high school athletics. In one semester Dr. Ryan encountered 27 male freshmen enrolled in an adaptive physical education program who were suffering from musculoskeletal system defects. Eighteen of these students incurred the defects as a result of athletic competition in football, basketball, and ice hockey.

Football fatalities caused by neck and brain injuries and deaths from heat stroke because of inadequate preventive measures have been reported. Numerous injuries also occur in wrestling. Many reports are cited where boys on wrestling teams endure dramatic weight losses to qualify for lower weight class matches. In many cases there is a lack of communication between physicians and coaches.

Sports medicine

Sports medicine is a rapidly expanding area of health services for athletes. The fact that more than an estimated 17 million persons are injured each year in this country in physical activities and sports has accented this new field. Sports medicine is particularly concerned with how sports injuries occur, how they can be prevented, and the long-range impact they have on a person's performance.

Sports medicine is the medical relationship between physical activity and the human body. It is concerned with the scientific study of the effects of physical activity on the human body and of the influence of such elements as the environment, drugs, emotions, intellect, age, and growth on human physical activity. It also is concerned with the prevention of disease and injury and with therapy and rehabilitation.

An institute of sports medicine and athletic trauma has been founded by Dr. James Nicholas, orthopedic surgeon at Lenox Hill Hospital in New York City. The center is concerned with a study of "the mechanics, diagnosis, treatment and rehabilitation of

Table 15-2. Actual number of fatalities in sample schools (1975-76)*†

	Secondary school		College or university	
	Male	*Female*	*Male*	*Female*
TOTAL	6	1	7	0
Tackle football				
Athletic competition	2	0	1	0
Athletic practice	1	0	0	0
Intramurals	0	0	0	0
Other contact sports				
Athletic competition	0	0	2	0
Athletic practice	1	0	1	0
Intramurals	0	0	0	0
Noncontact sports				
Athletic competition	0	0	0	0
Athletic practice	2	0	1	0
Intramurals	0	0	0	0
Physical education classes	0	1	2	0

*Courtesy Calvert, op. cit.
†This table presents the actual fatalities that were reported by the 1510 secondary schools and 980 colleges and universities responding to the survey. Of the deaths, four of the eight secondary school and six of the seven college or university deaths occurred where an athletic trainer or other health person was available.

physical injuries sustained in organized and unorganized athletics and recreational activities.''

Sports medicine has provided new knowledge of sports injuries. For example, Dr. Nicholas has found a relationship between joint flexibility and injury; tight-jointed players are more likely to have muscle and tendon strains than loose-jointed players. On the other hand, loose-jointed players more frequently suffer dislocations. These findings indicate that tight-jointed players should exercise to increase flexibility and loose-jointed players should exercise to firm up the joints. Dr. Nicholas has also found a relationship between flexibility and power. He points out that one who is extremely flexible will have less strength.

Dr. John L. Marshall, another physician concerned with sports medicine in New York City, has found that high arches in the foot and tight heel cords are conducive to ankle sprains.

The health of the athlete

Although this chapter has implications for all persons who participate in physical education programs, essential health services are especially important for athletes. The growth of sports and athletic programs supports this emphasis.

Health services for athletes involve continuous medical attention, sound policies and procedures, and the availability of qualified personnel. A close working relationship should exist among physicians, coaches, trainers, athletic directors, administrators, and medical society representatives to protect athletes adequately from injury and harm.

The American Medical Association, through its Committee on the Medical Aspects of Sports, the National Trainers' Association, and such athletic organizations as the National Collegiate Athletic Association, and the National Federation of State High School Athletic Associations, have done an outstanding job in preparing materials, making recommendations to safeguard the health of the athlete, and outlining first aid procedures for athletic injuries.

Medical supervision of athletes can be improved if the administration, physical educators, physicians, coaches, and trainers make this a priority. Frequently,

Table 15-3. Common injuries among high school female athletes*

Sport	Most frequent type of injury	Site of injury
Basketball	Sprains	Ankle
Golf	Blisters	Hands, feet
Gymnastics	Contusions	Hip
	Dislocations	Elbow
	Blisters	Hands
Swimming	Strains	Shoulder
	Cramps	Legs
Tennis	Strains	Upper body
	Blisters	Feet
Track and field	Strains	Quadriceps
		Hamstrings
		Groin
	Abrasions	Extremities
	Shin splints	Leg
	Sprains	Ankle
Volleyball	Contusions	Knee, elbows
	Sprains	Fingers
	Abrasions	Knee, elbow

*Reprinted by permission from Albohm, Marge: The Physician and Sportsmedicine **4:**46, Feb. 1976.

coaches lack medical training, and they feel that too much supervision from doctors and nurses will hurt their team's won-lost record. A philosophy of medical supervision must be adopted that places the individual athlete first and enables him or her to have the best possible medical attention.

Adequate health supervision of sports is essential because of (1) the physical, physiological, and psychological demands of competition; (2) the problem of treatment and rehabilitation involved in athletic injuries; (3) the increased possibility of infectious diseases caused by lowered resistance; and (4) the close relationship between physical activity and disease and injury.

A survey by Rolnick conducted as part of his doctoral study at New York University to determine the standards of health supervision and how they were implemented in 2-year college intercollegiate sports concluded there was a need for improvement. The survey recommended the following:

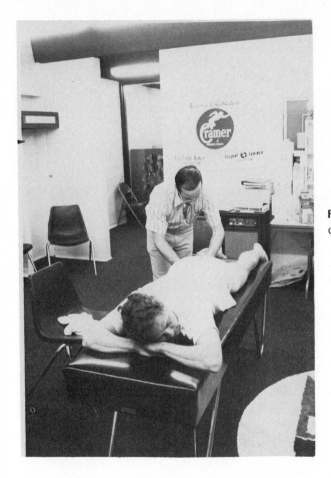

Fig. 15-2. Athletic trainer at work.

Courtesy Cramer Products, Inc., Gardner, Kan.

1. Centralization of medical control of intercollegiate athletics in the college health service.
2. Implementation of nationally and regionally adopted standards governing health aspects of intercollegiate sports, including: (a) a physical examination and medical history for each athlete, (b) medical supervision at all contact sports, (c) ambulance at all contact sports, (d) availability of communication for emergency purposes, (e) athletic facilities that are safe and meet size requirements, (f) use of noncaustic materials for marking athletic fields.
3. Certification by National Junior College Athletic Association that health standards have been implemented.
4. Stipulation of medical standards in contracts with competing colleges, with failure to comply resulting in forfeiture.

These suggestions for adequate medical supervision should also apply to all schools and colleges with interscholastic and intercollegiate activity programs.

The team physician

A team physician must be selected with care. He or she must not neglect team responsibilities because of a growing practice or other commitments. The physician should remain objective and avoid being influenced by students, parents, and coaches. If a physician is needed and none is available, the local medical society should be consulted for a recommendation of one or perhaps two physicians who will jointly care for the team. An injured athlete

Fig. 15-3. Athletic trainer preparing a player for competition.

Courtesy Cramer Products, Inc., Gardner, Kan.

should not return to play until authorized by the team physician.

According to Parkhouse and Lapin* the team physician's duties include the following:

1. Preparing and compiling medical histories of students, noting injuries and other health conditions.
2. Examining athletes, reporting to coaches the results of such examinations, and making recommendations regarding whether or not player can participate, or under what conditions he or she can play.
3. Supervising and counseling athletic trainers and working with coaches, athletes, and parents in determining the best course of action to follow.

4. Attending home games and also practices, if at all possible.
5. Working cooperatively with the athletic trainer and the athletic director in preparing emergency procedures.
6. Examining all injuries and making recommendations about the future play of the athlete. The player must receive the physician's approval to play.
7. Providing time for students' queries regarding such matters as nutrition, conditioning, and injuries.
8. Engaging in in-service self-education to keep abreast of the latest in sports medicine and injuries.
9. Making recommendations to the athletic director and coaches regarding injury prevention.
10. Vertifying injuries when required for insurance settlements.
11. Making recommendations regarding and helping to select proper protective equipment.

---

*Modified from Parkhouse, B.L., and Lapin, J.: The woman in athletic administration, Santa Monica, Calif., 1980, Goodyear Publishing Co., Inc.

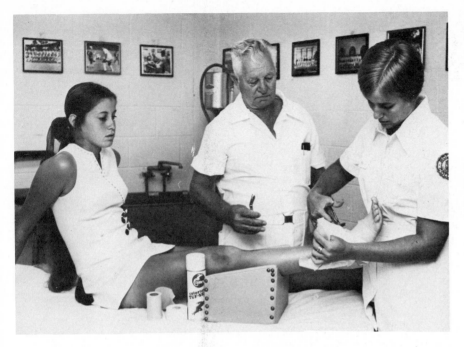

Fig. 15-4. Athletic training has no sex barriers.

Courtesy Cramer Products, Inc., Gardner, Kan.

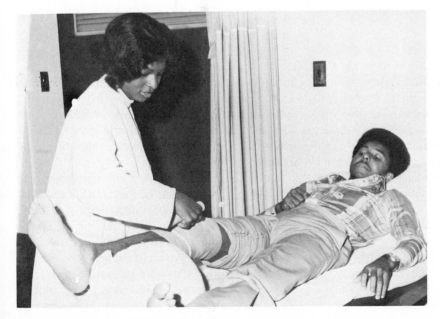

Fig. 15-5. Athletic trainer in training as part of professional preparation program at Tuskegee Institute, Ala.

Table 15-4. Injuries to women in 19 intercollegiate sports (1974-1974)*

Activity or sport	Number of injuries	Number of colleges participating	Average number of injuries per college
Basketball	1178	186	4.12
Volleyball	691	251	2.75
Field hockey	668	148	4.51
Gymnastics	453	122	3.71
Track and field	306	105	2.91
Tennis	275	259	1.06
Softball	240	157	1.53
Lacrosse	192	38	5.05
Competitive swimming	128	119	1.08
Badminton	50	70	0.71
Snow skiing	37	33	1.12
Cross-country	36	28	1.29
Fencing	24	44	0.55
Bowling	10	46	0.22
Soccer	8	10	0.08
Synchronized swimming	8	39	0.21
Archery	8	29	0.28
Squash	7	9	0.78
Golf	7	72	0.10

*Reprinted by permission from Gillette, J.: The Physician and Sportsmedicine **3:**61, May 1975.

Athletic trainers

The importance of athletic trainers in sports injury prevention and treatment cannot be overlooked. Unfortunately, in the secondary schools where athletic trainers are most needed, they are poorly represented; only about 100 schools have a full-time teacher-athletic trainer. Compounding this situation is the inadequate medical and injury prevention training of most coaches. Even if the coach has been well prepared in these areas, he or she does not have sufficient time to carry out both coaching duties and the responsibilities of the athletic trainer.

Traditionally the athletic trainer simply applied ankle wraps and administered first aid to athletes. He or she usually had no special preparation for this role but had learned through on-the-job training. Often, such as individual had little scientific knowledge concerning the prevention and care of athletic injuries.

Today, considerable scientific information, such as awareness of biomechanics, that is, how and why certain injuries occur in human motion, is available to help the athletic trainer reduce sports injuries, modify equipment, and care for athletes. Furthermore, knowledge of rehabilitation procedures and ways to prescribe exercise is expanding. As a result of the training needed, a trend today is to hire trainers who have an undergraduate major in physical education with graduate work in physical therapy or athletic training.

The qualifications for an athletic trainer are both personal and professional. Personal qualifications include poise, good health, intelligence, maturity, emotional stability, compassion, cleanliness, ethics, and fairness. Professional qualifications include a knowledge of anatomy and physiology, conditioning, nutrition, taping, methods for preventing injury, and protective equipment. Furthermore, the athletic trainer should have qualities that provide a harmonious and productive rapport with the team physician, coaches, athletic administrators, and the public in

Table 15-5. Most common injuries to female athletes*

Injury	Number of responses	Percent of responses
Sprained ankles	312	86
Knee injuries	236	65
Contusions	154	43
Low back injuries	50	14
Muscle pulls and strains	26	7
Shin splints	25	7
Hand and finger	13	4
Wrist	6	2
Blisters	3	1

*Reprinted by permission from Gillette, J.: The Physician and Sportsmedicine **3:**61, May 1975.

general. The trainer must be able to practice good human relations, as well as protect the athletes' well-being.

The National Athletic Trainers Association's (NATA) basic minimum requirements for the professional preparation of athletic trainers are recommended by most experts in the field. These standards include graduating from an approved undergraduate or graduate program that meets specific criteria set forth by the NATA, being a physical therapy degree graduate (such preparation meeting the specific requirements set forth by the NATA), or serving an apprenticeship that meets NATA specifications. Persons preparing for positions in athletic training should also be certified as such by the NATA. To do this, they must have proper training and pass the NATA certification examination. Important courses in preparing to be an athletic trainer include anatomy and physiology, physiology of activity, kinesiology, psychology, first aid and safety, nutrition, remedial exercises, health, techniques of athletic training, and advanced techniques of athletic training.

The duties of the athletic trainer include the following:

1. To prevent and care for injuries associated with competitive athletics
2. To prepare and use an athletic conditioning program
3. To administer first aid as needed
4. To apply devices such as strapping or bandaging to prevent injury
5. To administer therapeutic techniques under the direction of physician
6. To develop and supervise rehabilitation programs for injured athletes under supervision of team physician
7. To select, care, and fit equipment
8. To supervise training menus and diets
9. To supervise safety factors involved in facilities and use of equipment

The entry of more women into the field is long overdue. Athletic competition among women has greatly increased, and female athletic trainers are needed. Administrators and physical educators must be made aware of the need for women trainers, and students interested in physical education should be told about the profession of athletic training. With the acceptance of the fact that girls and women can play and compete against men in certain sports, such as swimming, volleyball, and tennis, as well as engage in highly competitive programs of their own, there is a vital need for women who have the knowledge and training to handle and prevent sports injuries.

The training room

Elaborate training rooms and equipment are not always essential in athletic programs. A private examining room with an examining table, a desk, and a few chairs is a minimum requirement. However, a training room should be provided if possible, for it will serve both physical education and athletic programs as a multipurpose place for first aid, physical examinations, bandaging and taping, reconditioning, treating athletes, keeping records, and other functions concerned with the health of students, athletes, and staff members. The training room should be near the dressing, shower, and athletic areas. A telephone, proper lights, and equipment for thermal and mechanical therapy, electrotherapy, and hydrotherapy are essential. There should also be a place for the trainer's office.

If the athletic program involves a great number of sports and participants, it is recommended that special service sections be arranged with low walls or partitions provided if possible. Separate sections would include those for taping, bandaging, and orthotics;

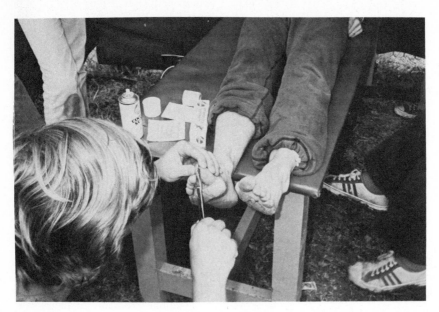

Fig. 15-6. Proper conditioning of athletes helps prevent sports injuries. Here an athletic trainer helps athlete with foot problems.
Courtesy Cramer Products Inc., Gardner, Kan.

Table 15-6. Type of major injuries by sport*

	Fractures	Dislocations	Severe sprains and strains	Extensive lacerations	Concussion or skull fracture	Eye injuries	Dental injuries	Tendon tears	Heat exhaustion	Cervical neck injury	Total
Basketball	X	X	X	X	X	X			X		7
Volleyball	X	X	X			X					4
Field hockey	X	X	X	X	X		X				6
Gymnastics	X	X	X		X					X	5
Track and field	X	X						X			3
Tennis		X				X		X			3
Softball	X	X	X	X	X						5
Lacrosse	X	X	X	X							4
Competition swimming			X								1
Badminton			X								1
Snow skiing			X								1
Cross-country skiing			X								1
Fencing				X							1
Bowling			X								1
Soccer			X								1
Synchronized swimming			X								1
Archery											0
Squash			X								1
Golf			X								1

*From Haycock, C.E., and Gillette, J.V.: JAMA **236:**163, July 1976.

Fig. 15-7. Adequate training room facilities contribute to the prevention and care of athletic injuries. Training room at the University of Notre Dame.

thermal and mechanical therapy; electrotherapy; hydrotherapy; and a reconditioning section with such equipment as knee exercisers and bicycle exercisers. Of course, there should be a section for storage so adequate training supplies would always be available.

Administrator's responsibility

What is the administrator's responsibility in preventing sports injuries? His or her first responsibility is to hire physicians, coaches, and trainers who understand sports injuries and how to treat them. These persons should also be aware of preventive measures necessary for sports safety. This may not be a simple job for the administrator, because trained personnel are difficult to find. The administrator may also run into budget difficulties, proliferation of sports, and established regulations. In addition, schedules may prohibit proper training before athletic competition, because sports seasons tend to overlap more and more.

To prevent injuries, complete medical examinations must be given to each athlete, including blood tests. Athletes who are immature physically, who have sustained previous athletic injuries, or who are inadequately conditioned are all prone to sports injuries. Crash diets and dehydration are injurious to an athlete's health. Training practices based on sound physiological principles are the best way to avoid sports injuries. Of course, proper protective equipment must be used in appropriate sports.

In general, governmental agencies, nonprofit public service organizations, voluntary associations, and educational institutions must intensify efforts toward safety in sports. Facilities and equipment must be developed with safety in mind, and sports safety regulations must be reviewed. Research also must be conducted to improve sports safety.

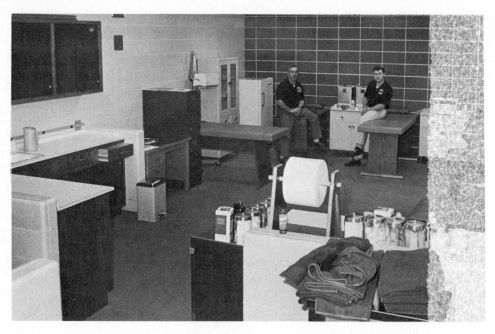

Fig. 15-8. Training room for athletes.
Trinity College, Hartford, Conn.

Proper conditioning of athletes. Conditioning athletes helps prevent sports injuries. It requires preseason training, as well as proper maintenance during the season, careful selection and fitting of equipment, protective strapping, counseling athletes about nutrition and rest, proper playing surfaces and facilities, and educators who know correct athletic training procedures and how to coach sports fundamentals.

Conditioning exercises for athletics should be compatible with the athlete's capacity and include a warmup, a progressive exercise routine both in-season and out-of-season, and special exercises to increase strength, flexibility, and relaxation.

Protective sports equipment. Sports equipment that protects vulnerable parts of the athlete's body from injury is important, particularly in such contact sports as football, hockey, and lacrosse. For example, football helmets should be purchased in accordance with standards established by the NOCSAE. The NOCSAE seal on a football helmet indicates that the manufacturer has complied with the best standards available for protection of the head. Increasingly, as basketball and soccer become more aggressive, prop-

er equipment is also vital in these sports.

Sports protective equipment must be tested for adequacy, kept in good repair, and able to prevent injury. Excellent equipment is needed to protect the head in such activities as football and hockey and to protect the face of the baseball catcher and the goalie in ice hockey and lacrosse. Also, mouth guards, ear guards, and guards to protect the athletes who wear glasses are often necessary. Furthermore, proper equipment to protect the chest, ribs, elbows, knees, and shins is required in certain sports. Shoes should always be carefully selected to ensure maximum comfort and protection.

Taping, bandaging, and padding. Protective taping, bandaging, and padding can help prevent, as well as care for, athletic injuries. Bandaging is needed at times to protect wounds from infection, to immobilize an injured area, to protect an injury, to support an injured part, to hold protective equipment in place, and to make arm slings and eye bandages. Padding and orthoses are needed to cushion against injury, to restrict the athlete's range of joint motion, and as foot pads. Orthoses can help in knee

Fig. 15-9. Adequate storage facilities are essential to a good training program.

From Klafs, C.E., and Arnheim, D.D.: Modern principles of athletic training, ed. 5, St. Louis, 1981, The C.V. Mosby Co.

supports and shoulder braces. Taping, bandaging, padding, and orthoses require special skill and knowledge. They should not be attempted by the untrained.

Nutrition. Proper nutrition is important to the health of the athlete for physical fitness, recuperation from fatigue, energy, and the repair of damaged tissues. The athlete should include proper amounts of carbohydrates, fats, proteins, minerals, vitamins, and water in his or her diet.

Ergogenic aids. Ergogenic aids are supplements or agents that supposedly enhance athletic performance. In other words, they are work-producing aids and are supposed to improve physical effort and perfor-

mance. They include drugs, food, physical stimulants such as thermal packs or electrical devices, and hypnosis. Some are questionable and unethical.

Coaches, athletic trainers, and physical educators should not use any substance that may be harmful to the participant. They should endorse only ethically and morally sound training practices. Some athletic associations and sports medicine leaders have taken a strong stand against the use of agents or drugs that enhance performance through artificial means. For example, the use of amphetamines such as Benzedrine to reduce fatigue, and of anabolic steroids to gain weight and strength, is not approved or condoned.

Table 15-7. Probable causes of injury*

Cause	Number of responses	Percent of responses†
Improper training methods	214	59
Inadequate facilities	81	22
Poor coaching techniques	75	21
Inadequate equipment	50	14
Improper use of equipment	40	11
Other‡	120	33

*Reprinted by permission from Gillette, J.: The Physician and Sportsmedicine **3**:61, May 1975.
†Total is greater than 100% because respondents often indicate more than one cause.
‡Includes responses related to the above causes but generally of an ambivalent nature.

Also, the use of dimethyl sulfoxide, better known as DMSO, is frowned on by most administrators as a means of alleviating injuries.

Safety in athletics and physical education

In light of the great increase in participation in athletics and physical education, attention must be given to providing for the safety of those persons who engage in these activities. Injuries not only are related to actual participation in these activities but also to such things as the equipment provided and the surfacing of athletic and playfields.

Accidents are an important consideration in our way of life. The National Safety Council indicates that over 100,000 people die annually as a result of accidents. Another 10 million experience disabling injuries. Accidents are the main cause of death in the range of people 1 to 38 years old, and in the 15 to 24 age range more young people die from accidents than from all other causes combined.

Sports participation results in many accidents and injuries. In soccer, for example, there is a high incidence of such injuries as skin abrasions or blisters, contusions, strains and sprains, fractures, knee ligament damage, cartilage tears, and brain concussion. In racquetball there are an estimated 7.5 million players and over 850 registered racquetball court clubs. There has been a dramatic increase in injuries

to the eyes and the facial area. In swimming there are approximately 8000 drownings a year.

Given the large number of participants and accidents, it is recommended that as a first administrative step a policy statement should be prepared by each organization involved in these activities. Written policy has been a valuable tool in enforcing safety regulations.

A second administrative recommendation is to appoint an individual who will be responsible for the safety program of the organization. This professional would have such responsibilities as developing policies and procedures, inspecting facilities and equipment, reporting accidents, and conducting safety research. In large organizations, in particular, such a position would pay for itself in cutting down on the accident rate, the loss of production, and other costs related to accidents and injuries. If a full-time professional cannot be employed, this responsibility should be assigned to a staff member.

A third administrative recommendation is to develop a proper accident reporting system. According to the National Safety Council, a well-organized accident report is essential to a safety program. The council points out that accident reports help to prevent further accidents by getting at the causes of unsafe acts and unsafe conditions and by developing a program that results in the removal of such unsafe acts and conditions.

In schools a school safety handbook is recommended, which can contain specific guidelines for maintaining a safe environment, can identify individual responsibilities, and can call attention to safe work practices.

Another administrative recommendation is to establish a safety committee. Safety committees have proved helpful in gaining organizational support for sound safety practices. According to *Safety in Industry*, a publication of the U.S. Department of Labor and Industry, the functions of such a committee are as follows: to develop procedures and implement safety suggestions, to hold regular meetings to discuss safety promotion, to conduct periodic inspections, to conduct accident investigations, to recommend changes in equipment or eliminate hazards, and to promote safety and first aid training.

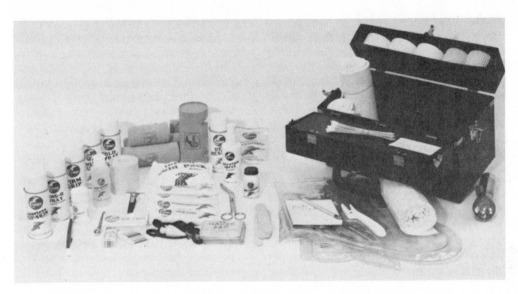

Fig. 15-10. A well-outfitted trainer's kit contains carefully selected pharmaceuticals.

Courtesy Cramer Products, Inc., Gardner, Kan.

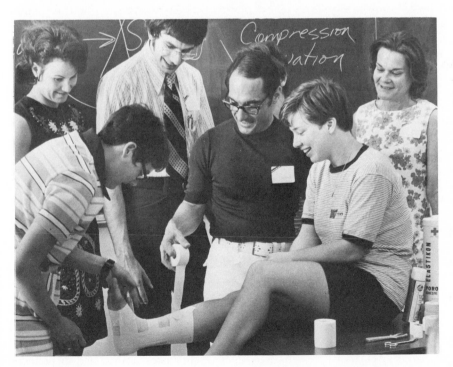

Fig. 15-11. Athletic trainers also need to be evaluated. College of DuPage, Glen Ellyn, Ill., held special 2-day athletic team trainer seminar showing techniques and methods to current and prospective team trainers.

first aid chart for athletic injuries

FIRST AID, the immediate and temporary care offered to the stricken athlete until the services of a physician can be obtained, minimizes the aggravation of injury and enhances the earliest possible return of the athlete to peak performance. To this end, it is strongly recommended that:

ALL ATHLETIC PROGRAMS include prearranged procedures for obtaining emergency first aid, transportation, and medical care.

ALL COACHES AND TRAINERS be competent in first aid techniques and procedures.

ALL ATHLETES be properly immunized as medically recommended, especially against tetanus and polio.

> Committee on the
> Medical Aspects of Sports
> AMERICAN MEDICAL ASSOCIATION

to protect the athlete at time of injury, FOLLOW THESE FIRST STEPS FOR FIRST AID

STOP play immediately at first indication of possible injury or illness.

LOOK for obvious deformity or other deviation from the athlete's normal structure or motion.

LISTEN to the athlete's description of his complaint and how the injury occurred.

ACT, but move the athlete *only* after serious injury is ruled out.

BONES AND JOINTS

fracture Never move athlete if fracture of back, neck, or skull is suspected. If athlete *can* be moved, carefully splint any possible fracture. Obtain medical care at once.

dislocation Support joint. Apply ice bag or cold cloths to reduce swelling, and refer to physician at once.

bone bruise Apply ice bag or cold cloths and protect from further injury. If severe, refer to physician.

broken nose Apply cold cloths and refer to physician.

HEAT ILLNESSES

heat stroke Collapse—with dry warm skin—indicates sweating mechanism failure and rising body temperature. THIS IS AN EMERGENCY; DELAY COULD BE FATAL. Immediately cool athlete by the most expedient means (immersion in cool water is best method). Obtain medical care at once.

heat exhaustion Weakness—with profuse sweating—indicates state of shock due to depletion of salt and water. Place in shade with head level or lower than body. Give sips of dilute salt water. Obtain medical care at once.

sunburn If severe, apply sterile gauze dressing and refer to physician.

IMPACT BLOWS

head If any period of dizziness, headache, incoordination or unconsciousness occurs, disallow any further activity and obtain medical care at once. Keep athlete lying down; if unconscious, give nothing by mouth.

teeth Save teeth, if completely removed from socket. If loosened, do not disturb; cover with sterile gauze and refer to dentist at once.

solar plexus Rest athlete on back and moisten face with cool water. Loosen clothing around waist and chest. Do nothing else except obtain medical care if needed.

testicle Rest athlete on back and apply ice bag or cold cloths. Obtain medical care if pain persists.

eye If vision is impaired, refer to physician at once. With soft tissue injury, apply ice bag or cold cloths to reduce swelling.

MUSCLES AND LIGAMENTS

bruise Apply ice bag or cold cloths and rest injured muscle. Protect from further aggravation. If severe, refer to physician.

cramp Have opposite muscles contracted forcefully, using firm hand pressure on cramped muscle. If during hot day, give sips of dilute salt water. If recurring, refer to physician.

strain and sprain Elevate injured part and apply ice bag or cold cloths. Apply pressure bandage to reduce swelling. Avoid weight bearing and obtain medical care.

OPEN WOUNDS

heavy bleeding Apply sterile pressure bandage using hand pressure if necessary. Refer to physician at once.

cut and abrasion Hold briefly under cold water. Then cleanse with mild soap and water. Apply sterile pad firmly until bleeding stops, then protect with more loosely applied sterile bandage. If extensive, refer to physician.

puncture wound Handle same as cuts; refer to physician.

nosebleed Keep athlete sitting or standing; cover nose with cold cloths. If bleeding is heavy, pinch nose and place *small* cotton pack in nostrils. If bleeding continues, refer to physician.

OTHER CONCERNS

blisters Keep clean with mild soap and water and protect from aggravation. If already broken, trim ragged edges with sterilized equipment. If extensive or infected, refer to physician.

foreign body in eye Do not rub. Gently touch particle with point of clean, moist cloth and wash with cold water. If unsuccessful or if pain persists, refer to physician.

lime burns Wash thoroughly with water. Apply sterile gauze dressing and refer to physician.

EMERGENCY PHONE NUMBERS

Physician		Phone:	
Physician		Phone:	
Hospital		Ambulance	
Police	Fire		Other

Fig. 15-12. First aid chart for athletic injuries.

Health services in schools and colleges

The health services program must be well publicized so educators, coaches, and the general public will understand why such services are essential. Only then will there be adequate planning and provision for such services.

The Joint Committee of the American Medical Association and the National Education Association has listed the following reasons for health services programs:

1. They contribute to the learning experience and the realization of other educational aims.
2. They facilitate adaptation of school and college programs to individual needs.
3. They help maintain a healthful environment.
4. They help individuals secure the medical or dental care they need.
5. They possess inherent values for increasing students' understanding of health and health problems.

Health services contribute to the realization of educational aims. Educational committees, conferences, and other important groups have continually listed health as one of the objectives of education. Health services are necessary to attain this objective.

Health services minimize the hazards of school and college attendance. They make it possible for the student to attend school and college under safe conditions. Qualified emergency care greatly reduces the harmful effects of accidental injuries. Adequate precautions are taken against the spread of communicable disease. Medical examinations identify health defects, making participation in athletics and other school activities safer. These are only a few of the many hazards that can be removed or minimized through effective health services.

Health services help youths adapt better to school and college programs. Careful and regular vision, hearing, and physical checks and correction of defects, will help students assume their responsibilities. Prevalent deficiencies, defects, and weaknesses will be noted and provided for.

Health services have potential for educating the parents, as well as the students, for developing proper attitudes toward health and physical fitness, for developing proper habits, and for imparting scientific information. The medical examination, for example, gives the teacher, nurse, physician, coach, and others an opportunity to educate students and parents about various aspects of health.

Health services with which the physical educator should be familiar include (1) health appraisal, (2) health counseling, (3) correction of remediable defects, (4) communicable disease control, (5) emergency care, and (6) health of organizational personnel. Other health services, such as the provision for the handicapped, are considered in other chapters of this text.

HEALTH APPRAISAL

Health appraisal is concerned with evaluating the health of an individual as objectively as possible through examinations, observations, and records.

Health appraisal techniques include medical, psychological, and dental examinations, vision and hearing screening, teacher observations, and health records.

Examinations

Medical examinations. The administrator must keep in mind the following important considerations if medical examinations are to fulfill their objective.

Types. Both periodic and referral examinations should be given. *Periodic* medical examinations are given at stated intervals. *Referral* examinations are given to persons with health problems who need special attention and have been referred to the proper professional source. The *examination of athletes* is a type of medical examination.

Planning. Medical examinations require planning to ensure that facilities are adequate and that necessary health records are available at the time of the examination.

Frequency. Each person should have a medical examination each year. Referral examinations should be given any time health problems are detected. Frequent medical examinations are needed for athletes and for those with health conditions the physician wants to examine often.

Examiner. It is recommended that the family physi-

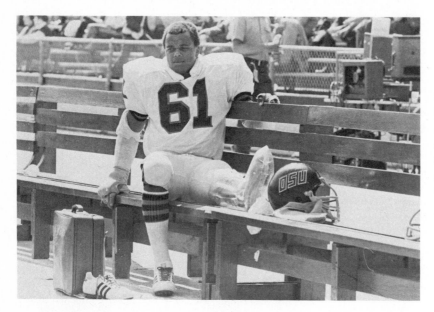

Fig. 15-13. Injured players should receive prompt medical attention and proper treatment.

Courtesy Cramer Products, Inc., Gardner, Kan.

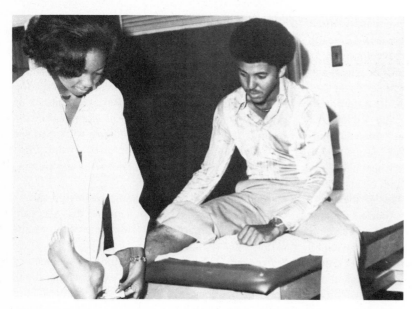

Fig. 15-14. Athletic trainer at Tuskegee Institute, Ala.

Fig. 15-15. The nurse is a key person in school and college health services. Nursing program at College of DuPage, Glen Ellyn, Ill., has provided Chicago area with qualified nurses since 1971.

cian, a medical center, team physician, company physician, or other qualified physician conduct the medical examination. Some families do not have their own physicians because of the expense. For this and other reasons, many schools must rely on a school physician to administer the examination. The procedure used should be a local and personal prerogative and one that will produce the best results.

Setting. The physical and the emotional atmosphere of the examining room should be conducive to good results. There should be privacy for disrobing so interruptions will not occur, and quiet so distractions will be reduced to a minimum. The examination room should also provide ample space for personnel, equipment, and supplies. Tension, hurry, and excitement should be minimized. The entire setting should be friendly, informal, and attractive.

Records available. Essential health records should be up to date and available at the time of the examination, including the person's health history, vision and hearing records, height-weight statistics, accident reports, and any other information that will help the physician interpret the results of the examination.

Examination of athletes. Administrative guides for athletic examinations are as follows:

1. Medical examinations should be administered to all athletes before actual participation and as they are needed during the time the sport is in progress. This refers to all forms of strenuous athletics.

2. Medical service must be provided at all athletic contests.

3. A physician's recommendation should accompany any athlete returning to competition after a period of illness.

Psychological examinations. With the increased emphasis on mental health, various psychological examinations are being used more extensively. These examinations, however, represent only a small part of the mental health services that should be available. Mental health programs are concerned with helping students adjust satisfactorily to the school or college environment; detecting individual behavior problems; helping the teacher, parent, and others better understand human behavior; and appraising personality to discover mental handicaps, emotional difficulties, and maladjustments.

Psychological examinations and tests that appraise such factors as a person's abilities, attitudes, personalities, intelligence, and social adjustment offer techniques for obtaining much information. The administration and interpretation of the findings of such techniques should be handled by qualified individuals.

Vision and hearing screening

Screening for vision defects. Physical educators are frequently asked to help screen students for vision defects, which requires a consideration of many factors.

Table 15-8. Checklist for trainer's kit*†

Item	Amount	Football-rugby	Basketball-volleyball-soccer	Wrestling	Baseball	Track and cross country	Water polo and swimming	Gymnastics	Tennis
Adhesive tape									
½-inch	1 roll	X	X	X	X	X		X	X
1-inch	2 rolls	X	X	X	X	X		X	X
1½-inch	3 rolls	X	X	X	X	X		X	X
2-inch	1 roll	X	X	X	X	X		X	X
Alcohol (isopropyl)	4 ounces	X	X	X	X	X	X	X	X
Ammonia ampules	10	X	X	X	X	X	X	X	X
Analgesic balm	½ pound	X	X	X	X	X	X	X	X
Ankle wraps	2	X	X		X	X			X
Antacid tablets or liquid	100	X	X	X	X	X	X	X	X
Antiglare salve	4 ounces	X				X			
Antiseptic powder	4 ounces	X	X	X	X	X	X	X	X
Antiseptic soap (liquid)	4 ounces	X	X	X	X	X	X	X	X
Aspirin tablets	100	X	X	X	X	X	X	X	X
Band-Aids (assorted sizes)	2 dozen	X	X	X	X	X	X	X	X
Butterfly bandages (sterile strip)									
Medium	6 dozen	X	X	X	X	X		X	
Small	6 dozen	X	X	X	X	X		X	
Cotton (sterile)	1 ounce	X	X	X	X	X	X	X	X
Cotton-tipped applicators	2 dozen	X	X	X	X	X	X	X	X
Elastic bandages									
3-inch	2 rolls	X	X	X	X	X		X	X
4-inch	2 rolls	X	X	X	X	X		X	X
6-inch	2 rolls	X	X	X	X	X	X	X	X
Elastic tape roll (3-inch)	2 rolls	X	X	X	X	X		X	X
Eyewash	2 ounces	X	X	X	X	X	X	X	X
Felt									
¼-inch	6 by 6 sheet	X	X	X	X	X		X	X
½-inch	6 by 6 sheet	X							
Flexible collodion	2 ounces	X	X	X	X	X		X	
Foot antifungus powder	2 ounces	X	X	X	X	X	X	X	X
Forceps (tweezers)	1	X	X	X	X	X	X	X	X
Fungicide (salve)	2 ounces	X	X	X	X	X	X	X	X
Germicide (solution)	2 ounces	X	X	X	X	X	X	X	X
Grease (lubrication)	2 ounces	X	X	X	X	X			X
Gum rosin (adherent)	1 ounce	X	X		X	X			X

*From Klafs, C.E., and Arnheim, D.D.: Modern principles of athletic training, ed. 5, St. Louis, 1981, The C.V. Mosby Co.
†Extra amounts of items such as tape and protective padding are carried in other bags.

Table 15-8. Checklist for trainer's kit—cont'd

Item	Amount	Football-rugby	Basketball-volleyball-soccer	Wrestling	Baseball	Track and cross country	Water polo and swimming	Gymnastics	Tennis
Heel cups	2			X		X		X	
Instant cold pack	2	X	X	X	X	X	X	X	X
Liniment	2 ounces	X	X	X	X	X	X	X	X
Medicated salve	2 ounces	X	X	X	X	X	X	X	X
Mirror (hand)	1	X	X	X	X	X		X	X
Moleskin	6 by 6 sheet	X	X	X	X	X		X	X
Nonadhering sterile pad (3 by 3)	12	X	X	X	X	X		X	X
Oral screw	1	X	X	X	X	X	X	X	X
Oral thermometer	1	X	X	X	X	X	X	X	X
Peroxide	2 ounces	X	X	X	X	X	X	X	X
Salt tablets	50	X	X	X	X	X		X	X
Shoehorn	1	X	X	X	X	X			X
Sponge rubber									
⅛-inch	6 by 6 sheet	X	X	X	X	X		X	X
¼-inch	6 by 6 sheet	X	X	X	X	X		X	X
½-inch	6 by 6 sheet	X							
Sterile gauze pads (3 by 3)	6	X	X	X	X	X		X	X
Sun lotion	2 ounces	X	X	X	X	X	X	X	X
Surgical scissors	1	X	X	X	X	X	X	X	X
Tape adherent	6-ounce spray can	X	X	X	X	X		X	X
Tape remover	2 ounces	X	X	X	X	X	X	X	X
Tape scissors (pointed)	1	X	X	X	X	X	X	X	X
Tongue depressors	5	X	X	X	X	X	X	X	X
Triangular bandages	2	X	X	X	X	X	X	X	X
Waterproof tape (1-inch)	1 roll						X		

Vision health services. The vision health services program in the school is concerned with the physician's examination and appraisal of visual acuity, which is accomplished through continuous observations and screening examinations. Both are necessary for the continual and satisfactory appraisal of the vision of school children.

Frequency of screening tests. Vision tests should be given annually immediately after the opening of school in the fall.

Administration of screening tests. After proper instruction and training, the physical educator is qualified to administer various screening devices for vision. These devices, however, are only for detecting individuals who need special vision care; their use is not diagnostic.

Selection of screening devices. The particular device used for checking visual acuity, together with the plans for appraisal, should be selected and arranged through conferences of school administrators, physical educators, nurses, physicians, ophthalmologists, and optometrists.

Referrals. The results of the screening examinations should be recorded and studied. These results and the physical educator's observations will determine which students should be referred for eye examinations.

Observations. The physical educator, as well as the parent, should be alert to visual difficulties and problems among children. By being aware of certain actions and manifestations of the child from day to day under varying situations, one can detect many eye difficulties that should be referred for examinations. Many of these eye difficulties go unnoticed unless the alert physical educator or parent is aware of certain characterictics that indicate vision problems.

Screening for hearing defects. Following are administrative guides for conducting hearing health services.

Scope. The main responsibility of the schools regarding auditory health services is to detect pupils with hearing difficulties as early as possible. This can be accomplished through observations and screening tests. A counseling and follow-through program that aims at remedying the defect should also be a part of the total plan.

Frequency. Continuous observations should be a part of the school routine. Annual screening tests during the elementary years and biennial ones at the secondary level are recommended. A preschool hearing test should be given wherever possible.

Technique. The pure-tone audiometer is one of the most effective techniques for all ages. This is a reliable instrument for checking either or both ears.

Referrals. Students with a hearing loss in one or both ears should be rechecked to determine the accuracy of screening. If results are consistent, parents should be informed and encouraged to follow through with more complete examination.

Physical educators who observe mouth breathing, ear discharge, or other abnormalities or characteristics that might arouse suspicion of hearing loss should refer the case to the proper authorities.

Observations. The physical educator can play an important part in continually observing the student for indications of hearing loss and in administering screening techniques. He or she should be watchful for such mannerisms as speech difficulties, requests for repetition of questions, turning of head to better hear what is said, and inattention, together with such noticeable characteristics as ear discharge, earaches, and other departures from the normal makeup of the student. Such observations will detect individuals who need to be referred for more careful study and examination.

Physical educator's observations

Observations are important in detecting the health needs of students. Furthermore, they increase in importance in the absence of nurses and physicians. Through observations of the appearance and behavior of pupils from day to day, any deviations from normal appearance and action will be detected quickly by the alert physical educator.

Such observations, after careful examination by nurses and physicians, may disclose various deficiencies. They may show that some students are maladjusted socially and emotionally, are undernourished, are in the early stages of a communicable or other disease, have some neurological difficulties or other physical defects, or have developed poor health habits. If a student is referred to a nurse or physician, the parents should also be informed of such discoveries. In no case does the physical educator diagnose. Instead, he or she refers the matter to the nurse, physician, and parent for further action.

There are many physical, social, and behavioral conditions that the physical educator should be alert to in the classroom and the gymnasium.

General physical condition. The physical educator should notice such conditions as malnutrition, distended abdomen, excessive obesity or underweight, paleness, drawn look, tiredness or apathy, and rapid loss or gain of weight.

Eyes. Any of the following eye conditions should be noted and referred to proper medical supervision: tearing, sties, crusted eyelids, inflammation, squinting, protrusion, excessive blinking or rubbing, and twitching eyelids.

Ears. Medical referral should take place if any of the following conditions exist: difficulty hearing teacher or other students, earache or discharge from ear, excessive noisiness, or ear picking.

Nose and throat. Any of the following conditions require medical attention: mouth breathing, persistent coughing, sore throat, recurrent cold, nose bleeds, and nasal speech pattern.

Teeth and mouth. Dental supervision may be needed in the following conditions: visible or painful cavities, gum inflammation, bleeding gums, lack of cleanliness, mouth odor, tooth irregularities, and habits such as thumb sucking or nail biting.

Skin and scalp. Special attention should be paid to any of the following conditions: hair infestation, skin rashes, excessive dandruff or other scalp condition, and general lack of cleanliness.

Heart and glands. Any swelling of the neck glands or thyroid should be referred for medical treatment. Indications of possible heart defects include excessive tiredness or listlessness, blue lip coloring, pallor, and breathlessness.

Behavioral problems. Any of the following conditions should be referred to school or private counseling services: withdrawal, overaggressive behavior, inability to adapt to group situations, rapid change of moods, uncontrollable behavior patterns, lack of self-confidence, chronic lying, stealing, constant antagonism, or sexual problems.

Health records

The following are some administrative guides in connection with health records:

1. A health record that contains a complete appraisal of the student's health should be a part of the overall school or college record.

2. The records should be cumulative, pointing out the complete health history of the student, together with a continuous appraisal of his or her health.

3. The health record should be made available to medical and other personnel who are concerned with and who work toward the maintenance and improvement of a student's health. Professional ethics should govern the handling of such information.

4. An up-to-date, accurate health record will prove a useful and effective device to further the health of all students.

Accident records.* Accident records, as a means of health appraisal, provide information about reasons for physical abnormalities and emotional maladjustment that may occur in students. They should be carefully kept and contain complete information.

HEALTH COUNSELING

Health counseling is an important phase of the total health services program. As health needs and problems are revealed through medical examinations and other techniques, defects must be corrected, advice given, and a planned procedure established to provide for these needs and eliminate the problems. Health counseling can help achieve these goals.

Purposes. One general objective of health counseling is to provide individuals with a better understanding of their health needs and the procedures to follow to satisfy these needs. Conferences and discussions regarding health problems can develop sound health attitudes. Facts are presented that indicate the need for following acceptable health practices. In addition, health counseling can help develop a feeling of responsibility in persons for the correction of health defects and for promoting school and community health programs.

Using counseling as part of the health services program has limitations. Counselors cannot always change individuals. This has been true, for example, of some handicapped individuals who may be subjected to pity or ridicule. Counselors can help individuals understand themselves, realize their potential,

---

*For further discussion of accident records see Chapter 16.

H-6 3M 9-36

LONG BEACH CITY SCHOOLS
HEALTH SERVICE DEPARTMENT
ATHLETIC PHYSICAL EXAMINATION REPORT

Name_____ School_____ Class_____

Age_____

Type of Athletic Activity   F. B., Basket Ball, Track, B. B., Class A. B. C.

Height_____Weight_____Standard_____Chest Circum.

In_____   Ex_____

Standing, Posture_____ Musculature_____ Nutrition_____

Skin_____ Superficial Glands_____

Hands_____ Arms _____ Abdomen_____

Hernia_____ Genitalia_____ Leg_____

Feet_____

Sitting: Hair_____ Teeth_____ Eyes, Reflexes_____

R._____   R._____

Vision—   Corrected—

L._____   L._____

R._____

Hearing—   Nose_____ Gums_____

L._____

Tongue_____ Tonsils_____ Pharynx_____

Ears_____ Chest_____ Heart_____

Pulse, sitting_____ After exercise_____

2 min. later_____ Temp._____ Lungs_____

Blood Pressure Systolic_____ Diastolic_____

Knee Reflexes_____

Urine Analysis: Sp. Grav._____ Alb._____ Sugar_____

Summary

Advice   Date_____

Fig. 15-16. Athletic physical examination report.

Long Beach, Calif., Public Schools.

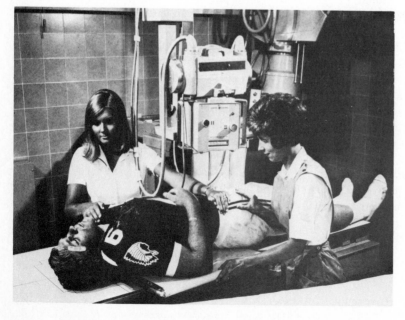

Fig. 15-17. Proper health service techniques provide that athletes are transferred with care. Here is the Spenco Roll-Aid, a lightweight patient transfer device that can easily be manipulated by one person. Length is designed to support properly the shoulders and hips of the patient for easy transfer.

Courtesy Spenco Medical Corporation, Waco, Tex.

SUGGESTED HEALTH EXAMINATION FORM

(Cooperatively prepared by the National Federation of State High School Athletic Associations and the Committee on Medical Aspects of Sports of the American Medical Association.) Health examination for athletes should be rendered after August 1 preceding school year concerned.

(Please Print) Name of Student_____   City and School_____

Grade_____Age_____Height_____Weight_____Blood Pressure_____

Significant Past Illness or Injury_____

Eyes_____ R 20/   ; L20   /; Ears_____ Hearing R /15; L /15

Respiratory_____

Cardiovascular_____

Liver_____Spleen_____Hernia_____

Musculoskeletal_____Skin_____

Neurological_____Genitalia_____

Laboratory: Urinalysis_____Other:_____

Comments_____

Completed Immunizations: Polio_____ Tetanus_____
                                              Date   Date

| Instructions for use of card | Other_____

I certify that I have on this date examined this pupil and find him (her) physically able to compete in supervised activities NOT CROSSED OUT BELOW.

BASEBALL   FOOTBALL   ROWING   SOFTBALL   TRACK
BASKETBALL   HOCKEY   SKATING   SPEEDBALL   VOLLEYBALL
CROSS COUNTRY GOLF   SKIING   SWIMMING   *WRESTLING
FIELD HOCKEY GYMNASTICS   SOCCER   TENNIS   OTHERS_____

*Weight loss permitted to make lower weight class: Yes_____ No_____; if "Yes" may lose _____pounds.

Date of Examination:_____Signed:_____
                                                        Examining Physician

Physician's Address_____Telephone_____

- -

STUDENT PARTICIPATION AND PARENTAL APPROVAL FORM

Name of student:_____ Name of School:_____
                     First   Last   Middle Initial

Date:_____Date of Birth:_____Place of Birth:_____

This application to compete in interscholastic athletics for the above high school is entirely voluntary on my part and is made with the understanding that I have not violated any of the eligibility rules and regulations of the State Association.

| Instructions for use of card | Signature of Student:_____

PARENT'S OR GUARDIAN'S PERMISSION

I hereby give my consent for the above high school student to engage in State Association approved athletic activities as a representative of his high school, except those crossed out on reverse side of this form by the examining physician, and I also give my consent for the above student to accompany the team as a member on its out-of-town trips.

Signature of Parent or Guardian:_____

Date:_____Address:_____
                                           (Street)   (City or Town)

NOTE: This form is to be filled out completely and filed in the office of the high school principal or superintendent of schools before student is allowed to practice and/or compete.

Fig. 15-18. Suggested health examination form.

From Committee on the Medical Aspects of Sports, American Medical Association: A guide for medical evaluation of candidates for school sports, 1966, The Association. Reprinted with permission of the American Medical Association.

and live their lives happily and productively. In some individuals, however, the social and physical environments have left their stamp so indelibly that counseling can do only a limited amount of good.

The counselor. The physical educator has potential as a counselor. To be effective, a counselor must be interested in serving people. The desire to help others live healthy, happy, and successful lives and to help eliminate problems that handicap the achievement of such goals must predominate in the counselor's mind. A second basic requirement is the counselor's personality, which must be friendly and inspire trust. A third requirement is competency in counseling skills.

CORRECTION OF REMEDIABLE DEFECTS

Two phases of school health services have been discussed. The individual's health must first be appraised. Second, there must be a counseling procedure so the necessary action can be taken. After health appraisal and health counseling have been completed, and work is not yet accomplished, a follow-through is essential to see that remediable defects are corrected in malnutrition, hearing, speech, postural defects, diseased tonsils and adenoids, vision, dental caries, and emotional disorders. Planning, conferences, and adequate record keeping ensure the best results in the correction of remediable defects.

COMMUNICABLE DISEASE CONTROL

Whenever students congregate, the possibility of spreading disease exists. Because school attendance is compulsory, certain protective measures and precautions must be taken to ensure that everything is done to guard the health of the student. This includes the necessary procedures for controlling communicable disease. Although students are not required to go to college, higher education institutions also have the responsibility to control communicable disease.

Responsibility. The legal responsibility for communicable disease control rests with state and local departments of health. Public health officials have control over school and college personnel in this matter. In most cases, however, this is a case of cooperation rather than compulsion. School and college officials should work closely with public health officials so cases of communicable disease are reported and proper measures taken to prevent others from contracting the disease.

Control measures. Every school or college should follow certain control measures to prevent the spread of disease.

Healthful environment. Provisions for a healthful environment necessary to control communicable disease including sufficient space to avoid undue crowding, adequate toilet and washroom facilities, proper ventilation and heating, safe running water, properly installed drinking fountains, use of pasteurized milk, a system of exclusions and control of admissions for students who may have communicable diseases, and policies toward absences that do not require students and teachers to be in school when they may be ill and capable of spreading communicable disease germs.

Isolation of students. The student who is suspected of having a communicable disease should immediately be isolated from the group. Isolating a student does not constitute diagnosis. The details and procedures followed in each school or college regarding isolation should be in writing and clearly understood by all concerned. The adopted plan should have the approval of the health service staff.

The physical educator should be continually on the lookout for the following indications of communicable disease:

Unusual pallor or flushed face
Unusual listlessness or quietness
Red or watery eyes
Eyes sensitive to light
Skin rash
Cough
Need for frequent use of toilet
Nausea or vomiting
Running nose or sniffles
Excessive irritability
Jaundice

Readmitting students to school or college. After having a communicable disease, a student should not be readmitted to school or college until it is certain that his or her return is in the best interests of the health of both the student concerned and the other students.

HEALTH RECORD

Parents or Guardians—Mr. and Mrs.

Occupation of Father — Session Teacher

Occupation of Mother — Family Doctor — Family Dentist

Last Name — First Name — Address — Telephone

MEDICAL EXAMINATION		1	2	3	4
1. Date of Examination					
2. Age					
3. Weight					
4. Height					
5. Hearing	Rt.				
	Lt.				
6. Eyes	Rt.				
	Lt.				
7. Test with glasses		Yes No	Yes No	Yes No	Yes No
8. Ring Worm					
9. Plantar Warts					
10. Hair					
11. Personal Hygiene					
12. Pulse before exercise					
13. Pulse after exercise					
14. Heart					
15. Lungs					
16. Tremor					
17. Abdomen					
18. Hernia					
19. Ears					
20. Nose					
21. Tonsils					
22. Adenoids					
23. Teeth					
24. Thyroid					
25. Glands					
26. Nutrition					
27. Skin					
28. P. E. Classification					
Unrestricted (A or B)					
Partially Restricted (C)					
Rest Only (D)					
Permanent Excuse					
Temporary Excuse					
29. Swimming					
Permanent Excuse					
Temporary Excuse					
Doctor's Initials					

HISTORY OF DISEASE

Chicken Pox	St. Vitus Dance	Diphtheria	Measles	Mumps	Pneumonia	Scarlet Fever	Rheumatic Fever	Whooping Cough	Tonsillitis	Hay Fever	Asthma	Date of Vaccination for Small Pox	T. B. in Family?	Date of Skin Test

Headaches:	Menstruation
Never	Regular
Occasionally	Irregular
Frequently	Dysmenorrhea
Operations:	Injuries
Tonsils	
Others:	

Postural Findings	L	R	L	R	L	R	L	R
Scoliosis								
Shoulder High								
Hip High								
Feet:								
Pronation								
Long. Arch								
Transverse Arch								
Head Forward								
Round Shoulders								
Hollow Back								
Abdomen								
Body Balance								
Posture Grade								
Corrective Gym								

COMMENTS:

Explanation of Terms: "O"—Normal; "X"—Slight Defect; "XX"—Moderate; "XXX"—Marked.

Fig. 15-19. Health record for girls. (Highland Park High School, Highland Park, Ill.)

Immunization. Every student should be immunized against tetanus, poliomyelitis, diphtheria, whooping cough, measles, mumps, and rubella. Most of this should be done in the preschool years when danger from such diseases is prevalent.

Attendance. Perfect attendance for school children should not be overemphasized. This often results in children coming to school regardless of the condition of their health and the danger to others. Furthermore, state aid should be based on some method other than attendance.

EMERGENCY CARE

Elementary and secondary schools, as well as other organizations where physical education programs exist, are responsible for providing the necessary protection and care for each person in their organization. The school acts in loco parentis, and the child should receive the same care and protection during the hours of school that he or she receives at home. Children often become sick or injured during school hours. Therefore, the school must provide the necessary attention until this can be undertaken by the parents.

According to the Joint Committee on Health Problems, the school has four responsibilities for emergency care procedures: ''(1) giving immediate care, (2) notifying the pupil's parents, (3) arranging for the pupil to get home, and (4) guiding parents, when necessary, to sources of treatment.''

Some administrative guides for emergency care are as follows:

1. Every school, college, and other organization where physical education programs exist should have a written plan for emergency care, carefully prepared by the school administration and with the help of the school or college physician, parents, medical and dental professions, hospitals, nurses, teachers, and others interested and responsible in this area. The time to plan and decide on procedure is before an accident occurs. This should be one of the first administrative responsibilities accomplished.

The written plan should contain such essentials as first aid instructions; procedures for getting medical help, transportation, and notifying parents; staff responsibilities; supplies, equipment, and facilities available; and any other information to clarify exact procedures in time of emergency.

The plan should be reviewed periodically, revised so it is continually up to date, posted in conspicuous places, and discussed with school staff members and community groups.

2. As many staff members as possible should be trained in first aid procedures. Special knowledge and training are essential in emergency care procedures for broken bones, use of artificial respiration, cardiopulmonary resuscitation (CPR), control of hemorrhage, and patients suffering from shock. The more staff members trained in these specific first aid procedures, the better the coverage for accidents that may occur at any time when school activities are in progress.

Some organizations have the American Red Cross give inservice courses in first aid procedures to ensure that the staff is competent in first aid.

When a nurse is on duty, his or her responsibility includes seeing that proper first aid procedures are carried out.

3. A large, clean, well-lighted health room with necessary equipment and supplies for first aid and emergency care should always be available for emergency cases.

4. Proper emergency equipment and supplies, in addition to being located in the health room, should also be available in strategic school or college locations that are accident-prone because of activity courses and in places remote from the health room, including the gymnasium, laboratories, shops, school busses, annexes, and buildings housing school activities apart from the central unit.

5. School, college, and other organizational records should contain complete information on each person, including his or her address; parent's name, address, and phone number; business address of parent and phone number; family physician, address, and phone number; family dentist, address, and phone number; parent instruction in case of emergency; choice of hospital; and any other pertinent information.

6. There should be a complete record of every emergency, including first aid given and emergency

SAN FRANCISCO DEPARTMENT OF PUBLIC HEALTH
IMMUNIZATION AND TEST CONSENT

Date_____

Name_____ Address_____ Phone No._____

School_____ Grade_____ Room_____ Phy. Ed. Period_____ P. E. Teacher_____ Birth-date_____

In looking over your child's health record, it is recommended that the following immunizations and/or tests be given. Please sign your name opposite the recommended procedure if you wish your child to have the benefit of the test or immunization.

If your child has had a positive Tuberculin Test in the past, it will probably remain positive and should not be repeated. If your child's test was ever positive, please indicate when or approximately when

_____

Negative Tuberculin Tests may be repeated yearly.

F 1515 1-56

Immunizations and Tests	Recommended	Parent's Signature
Smallpox Vaccination		
Diphtheria Pertussis Tetanus } D.P.T.		
Polio Vaccination		
Tuberculin Test		

PLEASE RETURN TO PUBLIC HEALTH NURSE

Fig. 15-20. Immunization and test consent form.

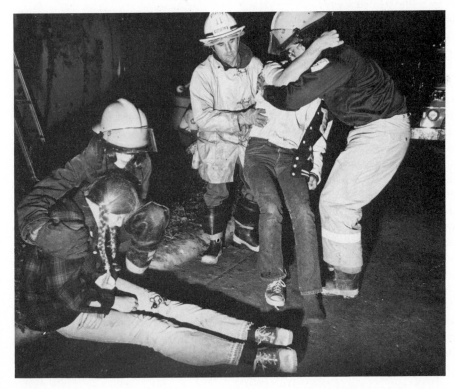

Fig. 15-21. Schools and colleges have responsibility for emergency care. Students at College of DuPage, Glen Ellyn, Ill., participate in local emergency drill.

Fig. 15-22. The incidence of injuries among athletes is growing. A common sight on football gridirons is an injured player.

Courtesy Cramer Products Inc., Gardner, Kan.

care administered in the event of illness. This record is important if questions arise in the future. Such information preserves for future reference the procedures followed in each case and prevents forgetfulness, misinterpretation, misunderstanding, and inaccurate conclusions from being drawn. Records can also be used to disclose hazards that should be eliminated and weak spots in procedures for emergency care that should be improved. Finally, such records aid in impressing on students, staff members, parents, and other concerned individuals the importance of good procedures for safe and healthful living.

7. The legal aspects of emergency care should be discussed and understood so staff members will be aware of the laws of the state and locality and know the importance of avoiding negligence in duty.

8. Insurance plans for staff members, athletes, and students should be made clear. They should be in writing and well publicized so each individual will know the extent to which expenses, claims, and other items will be paid in event of accident, or the extent to which he or she can or should procure additional coverage.

HEALTH OF ORGANIZATIONAL PERSONNEL

Organizations need to be aware of the health of their personnel to ensure efficiency and to promote the most healthful and pleasant environment possible. Boards of education, boards of trustees, and other administrators, therefore, need to concern themselves with sick leave, health insurance, sabbatical leaves, retirement provisions, maternity leaves, medical examinations, exclusion of teachers with health conditions that have implications for students' health and well-being, and other matters that concern the health of all employees.

SAFEGUARDING THE HEALTH OF THE ATHLETE*

A joint statement of the Committee on the Medical Aspects of the American Medical Association and the National Federation of State High School Athletic Associations

A checklist to help evaluate five major factors in health supervision of athletics

Participation in athletics is a privilege involving both responsibilities and rights. The athletes' responsibilities are to play fair, to keep in training, and to conduct themselves with credit to their sport and their school. In turn they have the right to optimal protection against injury as this may be assured through good conditioning and technical instruction, proper regulations and conditions of play, and adequate health supervision.

Periodic evaluation of each of the factors will help assure a safe and healthful experience for players. The checklist below contains the kinds of questions to be answered in such an appraisal.

PROPER CONDITIONING helps prevent injuries by hardening the body and increasing resistance to fatigue.

1. Are prospective players given directions and activities for preseason conditioning?
2. Is there a minimum of 3 weeks of practice before the first game or contest?
3. Are precautions taken to prevent heat exhaustion and heat stroke?
4. Is each player required to warm up thoroughly before participation?
5. Are substitutions made without hesitation when players evidence disability?

CAREFUL COACHING leads to skillful performance, which lowers the incidence of injuries.

1. Is emphasis given to safety in teaching techniques and elements of play?
2. Are injuries analyzed to determine causes and to suggest preventive programs?
3. Are tactics discouraged that may increase the hazards and thus the incidence of injuries?
4. Are practice periods carefully planned and of reasonable duration?

GOOD OFFICIATING promotes enjoyment of the game and the protection of players.

1. Are players as well as coaches thoroughly schooled in the rules of the game?
2. Are rules and regulations strictly enforced in practice periods as well as in games?
3. Are officials qualified both emotionally and technically for their responsibilities?
4. Do players and coaches respect the decisions of officials?

RIGHT EQUIPMENT AND FACILITIES serve a unique purpose in protection of players.

1. Is the best protective equipment provided for contact sports?
2. Is careful attention given to proper fitting and adjustment of equipment?
3. Is equipment properly maintained, and are worn and outmoded items discarded?
4. Are proper areas for play provided and carefully maintained?

ADEQUATE MEDICAL CARE is a necessity in the prevention and control of injuries.

1. Is there a thorough preseason health history and medical examination?
2. Is a physician present at contests and readily available during practice sessions?
3. Does the physician make the decision as to whether an athlete should return to play following injury during games?
4. Is authority from a physician required before an athlete can return to practice after being out of play because of disabling injury?
5. Is the care given athletes by coach or trainer limited to first aid and medically prescribed services?

*Adapted from Committee on the Medical Aspects of Sports of the American Medical Association and the National Federation of State High School Athletic Associations: Tips on athletic training, XI, Chicago, Illinois, 1969, The American Medical Association.

DISQUALIFYING CONDITIONS FOR SPORTS PARTICIPATION*

Conditions	Contact†	Noncontact endurance‡	Others§
General			
Acute infections:			
Respiratory, genitourinary, infectious mononucleosis, hepatitis, active rheumatic fever, active tuberculosis, boils, furuncles, impetigo	X	X	X
Obvious physical immaturity in comparison with other competitors	X	X	
Obvious growth retardation	X		
Hemorrhagic disease:			
Hemophilia, purpura, and other bleeding tendencies	X		
Diabetes, inadequately controlled	X	X	X
Jaundice, whatever cause	X	X	X
Eyes			
Absence or loss of function of one eye	X		
Severe myopia, even if correctable	X		
Ears			
Significant impairment	X		
Respiratory			
Tuberculosis (active or under treatment)	X	X	X
Severe pulmonary insufficiency	X	X	X
Cardiovascular			
Mitral stenosis, aortic stenosis, aortic insufficiency, coarctation of aorta, cyanotic heart disease, recent carditis of any kind	X	X	X
Hypertension of organic basis	X	X	X
Previous heart surgery for congenital or acquired heart disease	X	X	
Liver			
Enlarged liver	X		
Spleen			
Enlarged spleen	X		
Hernia			
Inguinal or femoral hernia	X	X	
Musculoskeletal			
Symptomatic abnormalities or inflammations	X	X	X
Functional inadequacy of the musculoskeletal system, congenital or acquired, incompatible with the contact or skill demands of the sport	X	X	
Neurological			
History of symptoms of previous serious head trauma or repeated concussions	X		
Convulsive disorder not completely controlled by medication	X	X	
Previous surgery on head or spine	X	X	
Renal			
Absence of one kidney	X		
Renal disease	X	X	X
Genitalia			
Absence of one testicle	X		
Undescended testicle	X		

*From Committee on the Medical Aspects of Sports, American Medical Association: A guide for medical evaluation of candidates for school sports, Chicago, Illinois, 1966, The Association, pp. 4-5.
†Lacrosse, baseball, soccer, basketball, football, wrestling, hockey, rugby, etc.
‡Cross country, track, tennis, crew, swimming, etc.
§Bowling, golf, archery, field events, etc.

SUGGESTED SPORTS CANDIDATES' QUESTIONNAIRE*

(To be completed by parents or family physician)

Name _____ Birth date _____

Home address _____

Parents' name _____ Tel. no. _____

1. Has had injuries requiring medical attention   Yes No
2. Has had illness lasting more than a week   Yes No
3. Is under a physician's care now   Yes No
4. Takes medication now   Yes No
5. Wears glasses   Yes No
             contact lenses   Yes No
6. Has had a surgical operation   Yes No
7. Has been in hospital (except for tonsillectomy)   Yes No
8. Do you know of any reason why this individual should not participate in all sports? Yes No

Please explain any "yes" answers to above questions:

_____

_____

9. Has had complete poliomyelitis immunization by inoculations (Salk) or oral vaccine (Sabin) Yes No
10. Has had tetanus toxoid and booster inoculation within past 3 years   Yes No
11. Has seen a dentist within the past 6 months   Yes No

_____

                                          Parent or Physician

*From Committee on the Medical Aspects of Sports, American Medical Association: A guide for medical evaluation of candidates for school sports, 1966, The Association, p. 2. Reprinted with permission of the American Medical Association.

SELF-ASSESSMENT TESTS

These tests are to assist students in determining if material and competencies presented in this chapter have been mastered.

1. Prepare a report on the nature and scope of injuries that occur to athletes each year in various sports.

2. As a coach of a football or basketball team, what steps should you take in preventing injuries to your players? Describe the procedures you would follow if a player broke a leg in practice.

3. What are the duties of a team physician?

4. Prepare a list of arguments to present to the board of education to justify the addition of an athletic trainer to the school staff. Also indicate the qualifications and responsibilities of the athletic trainer.

5. As an administrator, what would you recommend regarding a safety program in your organization?

6. What are the component parts of a school or college health service program? State the importance of each for the student.

7. Prepare a mock health counseling conference with a student and the parents after the school medical examination has revealed several defects needing correction.

SELECTED REFERENCES

Agre, J.C., and Krotee, M.L.: Soccer safety—prevention and cure, Journal of Physical Education and Recreation **52:**52-54, May 1981.

American School and Community Safety Association: Administration and supervision for safety in sports, Reston, Va., 1977, AAHPERD.

Bucher, C.A.: Foundations of physical education, ed. 9, St. Louis, 1983, The C.V. Mosby Co.

Bucher, C.A., and Koenig, C.: Methods and materials for secondary school physical education, ed. 6, St. Louis, 1983, The C.V. Mosby Co.

Bucher, C.A., and Thaxton, N.: Physical education and sport: change and challenge, St. Louis, 1981, The C.V. Mosby Co.

Committee on the Medical Aspects of Sports of the American Medical Association: The team physician, The Journal of School Health **37:**497, 1967.

Delforge, G., and Klein, R.: High school athletic trainers internship, Journal of Health, Physical Education, and Recreation **44:** 42, 1973.

Della-Giustina, D.E.: Why use eyeguards in racquetball? Journal of Physical Education and Recreation **51:**41, June 1980.

Fuoss, D.E., and Troppmann, R.J.: Creative management techniques in interscholastic athletics, New York, 1977, John Wiley & Sons, Inc.

Frederick, A.B.: Safety on the trampoline, Journal of Physical Education and Recreation **50:**24-27, April 1979.

Gabrielsen, M.A., and Johnson, R.L.: Swimming pool safety, Journal of Physical Education and Recreation **50:**43-46, June 1979.

Haering, F.C.: Safety is big business, Journal of Physical Education and Recreation **50:**41-43, June 1979.

Hutton, L., and Silkin, J.: Needed; women athletic trainers, Journal of Health, Physical Education, and Recreation **43:**77, 1972.

Hyatt, R.W.: Intramural sports: organization and administration, St. Louis, 1977, The C.V. Mosby Co.

Johnson, W.R., and Buskirk, E.R.: Science and medicine of exercise and sport, New York, 1974, Harper & Row, Publishers.

Joint Committee on Health Problems in Education of National Education Association and American Medical Association: School health services, ed. 2, Washington, D.C., 1964, National Education Association.

Joint Committee on Health Problems in Education of National Education Association and American Medical Association: School health services, ed. 2, Washington, D.C., 1964, National Education Association.

Joint Committee on Health Problems in Education of National Education Association and American Medical Association: Health appraisal of school children, Washington, D.C., 1969, National Education Association.

Kegerreis, S.: An economic alternative, Journal of Physical Education and Recreation **50:**70-71, September 1979.

Klafs, C.E., and Arnheim, D.D.: Modern principles of athletic training, ed. 5, St. Louis, 1981, The C.V. Mosby Co.

Lerner, J.W.: Learning disabilities: a school health problem, The Journal of School Health **42:**320, 1972.

Morehouse, C.A.: Exercise in the 70s—implications for safer practices, Journal of Physical Education and Recreation **52:** 63-66, January 1981.

Moskowitz, M.: Safety hints for the administrator; Journal of Physical Education and Recreation **52:**62, January 1981.

National Association for Physical Education for College Women and The National College Physical Education Association for Men: Careers in physical education, Briefings 3, The Associations.

Oyeda, F.: The detection of learning disabilities in the early school-age child, The Journal of School Health **42:**214, 1972.

Parkhouse, B.L., and Lapin, J.: The woman in athletic administration, Santa Monica, Calif., 1980, Goodyear Publishing Co., Inc.

Reed, J.D.: A miracle! or is it a mirage? Sports Illustrated, April 20, 1981.

Resick, M.C., and Erickson, C.E.: Intercollegiate and interscholastic athletics for men and women, Reading, Mass. 1975, Addison-Wesley Publishing Co.

Rolnick, M.: Health supervision of intercollegiate sports in junior and community colleges, JUCO Review **24:**20, 1972.

Ryan, A.J.: Prevention of sports injury; a problem solving approach, Journal of Health, Physical Education, and Recreation **42:**24, 1971.

Ryan, A.J.: Providing medical services for athletes, School Activities, November 1967.

Schwank, W.C., and Miller, S.S.: New dimensions for the athletic training profession, Journal of Health, Physical Education, and Recreation **42:**41, 1971.

Shared responsibility for sports safety, The Athletic Educator's Report, August 1980.

Spiker, J.C.: Athletic trainer education, Journal of Physical Education and Recreation **50:**72, September 1979.

Vannier, M.: Physical activities for the handicapped, Englewood Cliffs, N.J., 1977, Prentice-Hall, Inc.

Wilson, H., and Albohn, M.: Women athletic trainers, Journal of Health, Physical Education, and Recreation **44:**57, 1973.

16

Legal liability and insurance management

Instructional objectives and competencies to be achieved

After reading this chapter the student should be able to

■ Define each of the following terms: *legal liability, tort, negligence, in loco parentis, save harmless, assumption of risk, attractive nuisance, immunity,* and *insurance management.*

■ Indicate the legal basis for physical education programs throughout the United States and the implications this has for making physical education a requirement for all students.

■ Discuss recent court interpretations regarding sports product liability, violence, and physical education activities held off-campus.

■ Illustrate what constitutes negligent behavior on the part of physical educators and coaches and what constitutes defenses against negligence.

■ Identify common areas of negligence in the conduct of physical education and athletic programs, and explain what can be done to eliminate such negligence.

■ Appreciate the relationship of Title IX to legal liability in the conduct of physical education and athletic programs.

■ Discuss precautions that physical educators can take to prevent accidents and provide for the safety of students and other individuals who participate in their programs.

■ Recommend a sound insurance management plan for a physical education and athletic program.

Legal liability and insurance management are important responsibilities of administrators. They involve some highly specialized areas, many of which will be discussed in this chapter.

According to Bouvier's *Law Dictionary,* liability is "the responsibility, the state of one who is bound in law and justice to do something which may be enforced by action." Another definition states: "Liability is the condition of affairs that gives rise to an obligation to do a particular thing to be enforced by court action."

Leaders in physical education and athletics should know how far they can go with various aspects of their programs and what precautions are necessary so they will not be held legally liable in the event of an accident. The fact that approximately 67% of all school jurisdiction accidents involving boys and 59% involving girls occur in physical education and recreation programs has implications for these specialized fields. Furthermore, the fact that millions of boys and girls and adults participate in athletic programs indicates a further administrative concern for physical education programs. It is estimated that every year one out of every 33 students attending school will be injured. It is alarming to note that physical educators are involved in more than 50% of the injuries sustained by students each year.* Furthermore, industrial

---

*Chambless, J.R., and Mangin, C.: Legal liability and the physical educator, Journal of Health, Physical Education, and Recreation **44:**42, 1973.

fitness programs, health spas, and other areas where physical educators are employed involve millions of people where accidents and injuries occur.

When an accident resulting in personal injury occurs, the question often arises about whether damages can be recovered. All employees run the risk of suit by injured persons on the basis of alleged negligence that causes bodily injury. Such injuries occur on playgrounds, on athletic fields, in fitness laboratories, in classes, or in any place where physical education and athletic programs take place.

The legal rights of the individuals involved in such cases are worthy of study. Although the law varies from state to state, it is possible to discuss liability in a general way that has implications for all sections of the country and for any setting in which physical educators work. First, it is important to understand the legal basis for physical education, athletics, and allied areas.

The legal basis for physical education, athletics, and allied areas

Surveys concerning physical education requirements by law in elementary, junior, and senior high schools indicate certain interesting facts. One survey showed that all but five states had physical education requirements. Some degree of physical education instruction was required in grades nine through twelve in 46 states. The range was from 1 to 4 years. Forty-four states had some degree of required programs in grades seven and eight. Forty-four states also required some type of physical education program at the elementary level. Physical education was required in all grades (one through twelve) to some degree in 14 states.*

LEGAL IMPLICATIONS FOR REQUIRING PHYSICAL EDUCATION

Shroyer† made a study of the legal implications of requiring pupils to enroll in physical education classes

---

*Grieve, A.: State legal requirements for physical education, Journal of Health, Physical Education, and Recreation **42:**19, 1971.
†Shroyer, G.F.: Legal implications of requiring pupils to enroll in physical education, Journal of Health, Physical Education, and Recreation **35:**51, 1964.

and found that the courts have handed down decisions from which the following conclusions may be drawn:

1. Students may be required to take physical education. However, there should be some flexibility to provide for those cases where an individual's constitutional rights might be violated if such activities are against his or her principles, for example, dancing.
2. Where reasonable parental demands for deviation from the physical education requirement are called for, every effort should be made to comply with the parent's wishes. However, unreasonable demands should not result in acquiescence.
3. Where rules and regulations may be questioned, the board of education should provide for a review of the rationale behind the rule or regulation and why the policy is needed.
4. A student may be denied the right to graduate and receive a diploma when a required course such as physical education is not taken.

Legal liability

Some years ago the courts recognized the hazards involved in the play activities that are a part of the educational program. An injury occurred to a boy while he was playing tag. The court recognized the possibility and risk of some injury in physical education programs and would not award damages. However, it pointed out that care must be taken by both the participant and the authorities in charge. It further implied that the benefits derived from participating in physical education activities such as tag offset the occasional injury that might occur.

The cited decision regarding the benefits derived from participating in physical education programs was handed down at a time when the attitude of the law was that no government agency, which would include the school, could be held liable for the acts of its employees unless it so consented. Since that time a changing attitude in the courts has been evident. As more accidents occurred, the courts frequently decided in favor of the injured party when negligence could be shown. The immunity derived from the old common-law rule that a government agency cannot be sued without its consent is slowly changing in the eyes of the courts so that both federal and state governments may be sued.

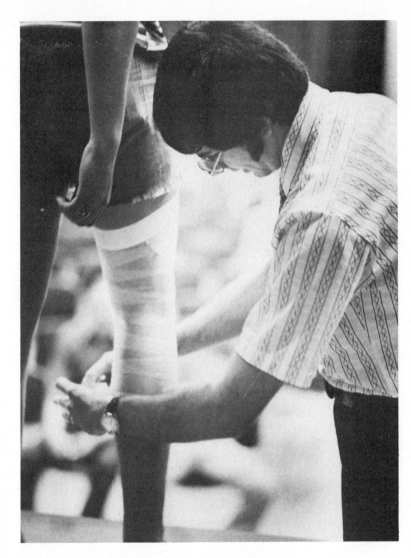

Fig. 16-1. College of DuPage, Glen Ellyn, Ill., held special 2-day seminar for athletic team trainers, showing techniques and methods to current and prospective team trainers.

Elements of a school curriculum that are compulsory, such as physical education, prompt courts to decide on the basis of what is in the best interests of the public. Instead of being merely a moral responsibility, safety has become a legal responsibility. Those who uphold the doctrine that a government agency should be immune from liability maintain that payments for injury to constituents are misapplications of public funds. On the other hand, some persons feel it is wrong for the cost of injuries to fall on one or a few persons and, instead, should be shared by all. To further their case, these persons cite the constitutional provision that compensation must be given for taking or damaging private property. They argue it is inconsistent that the government cannot take or damage private property without just compensation on the one hand, yet on the other hand can injure or destroy the life of a person without liability for compensation. This position is held more and more by the courts.

The role of immunity (because school districts are instrumentalities of the state, and the state is

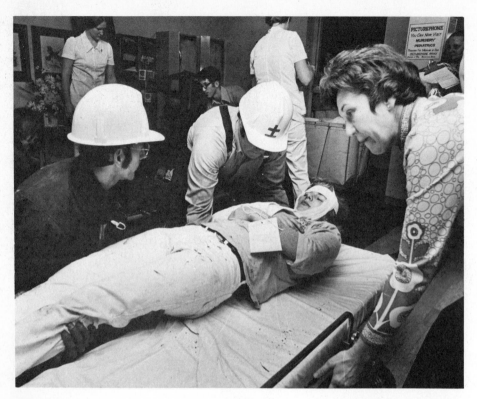

Fig. 16-2. Liability may be involved when injuries occur. Students from College of DuPage, Glen Ellyn, Ill., are participating in a local emergency drill to be prepared in the event of emergency and injuries.

immune from suit unless it consents, the state's immunity extends to the districts) is the law in some states. Some exceptions are California, Washington, and New York. However, as has been pointed out previously, the doctrine of immunity is starting to crumble. *Bingham v. Board of Education of Oregon City,* 223 P2d 432, handed down by the Supreme Court in Utah in October 1950, involved a 3-year-old child who, while riding her tricycle on the school grounds, fell into some burning embers left on the grounds and suffered severe burns. The school maintained an incinerator adjacent to the playground area in which rubbish was burned. From time to time embers and ashes were removed and scattered around the adjoining area. The parents sued to recover damages, and the court held that the dis-

trict was not liable. Judge Latimer, who wrote the court's opinion, said: "While the law writers, editors, and judges have criticized and disapproved the foregoing doctrine of government immunity as illogical and unjust, the weight of precedent of decided cases supports the general rule and we prefer not to disregard a principle so well established without statutory authority. We, therefore, adopt the rule of the majority and hold that school boards cannot be held liable for ordinary negligent acts."

The importance of this case is that two judges dissented. The dissenting judges pointed out: "I prefer to regard said principle for the purpose of overruling it. I would not wait for the dim distant future in never-never land when the legislature may act." It was also pointed out that the rule rests on the "im-

Fig. 16-3. Many accidents occur on athletic fields.

Courtesy Cramer Products Inc., Gardner, Kan.

mortal and indefensible doctrine'' that ''the king (sovereign) can do no wrong'' and that a state should not be allowed to use this as a shield.

There has been considerable court activity regarding the principle of governmental immunity. In 1959 the Illinois Supreme Court (*Molitor v. Kaneland Community Unit,* District No. 302, 163 N. E. 2d 89) overruled the immunity doctrine. The supreme courts of Wisconsin, Arizona, and Minnesota legislature followed suit, but in 1963 the Minnesota legislature restored the rule but provided that where school districts had liability insurance they were responsible for damages up to the coverage. The principle of governmental immunity has also been put to the test in courts in such states as Colorado, Iowa, Kansas, Oregon, Pennsylvania, and Utah. However, the courts in some of these states are hesitant to depart from the precedent and furthermore insist that it is the legislature of the state rather than the courts that should waive the rule.*

In many of the 50 states school districts have governmental immunity, which means that as long as they are engaging in a governmental function they

cannot be sued, even though negligence has been determined. In a few states governmental immunity has been annulled either by legislation or judicial decision. In some states schools may legally purchase liability insurance (California requires and several other states expressly authorize school districts to carry liability insurance) protecting school districts that may become involved in lawsuits, although this does not necessarily mean governmental immunity has been waived. Of course, in the absence of insurance and ''save harmless'' laws (laws requiring that school districts assume the liability of the teacher, whether negligence is proved or not), any judgment rendered against a school district must be met out of personal funds. School districts in such states as Connecticut, Massachusetts, New Jersey, and New York have ''save harmless'' laws. Wyoming permits school districts to indemnify employees.

School districts still enjoying governmental immunity usually are either required or permitted to carry liability insurance that specifically covers the operation of school buses.

There is a strong feeling among educators and many in the legal profession that the doctrine of sovereign immunity should be abandoned. In some states students injured as a result of negligence are assured

---

*Shapiro, F.S.: Your liability for student accidents, National Education Association Journal **54:**46, 1965.

recompense for damages directly or indirectly, either because governmental immunity has been abrogated or because school districts are legally required to indemnify school employees against financial loss. In other states, if liability insurance has been secured, there is a possibility that students may recover damages incurred.

Although school districts have been granted immunity in many states, teachers do not have such immunity. A decision of an Iowa court in 1938 provides some of the thinking regarding the teacher's responsibility for his or her own actions (*Montanick v. McMillin,* 225 Iowa 442, 452-453, 458, 280 N. W. 608, 1938).

[The employee's liability] is not predicated upon any relationship growing out of his [her] employment, but is based upon the fundamental and underlying law of torts, that he [she] who does injury to the person or property of another is civilly liable in damages for the injuries inflicted. . . . The doctrine of *respondeat superior,* literally, "let the principle answer," is an extension of the fundamental principle of torts, and an added remedy to the injured party, under which a party injured by some act of misfeasance may hold both the servant and the master. The exemption of governmental bodies and their officers from liability under the doctrine of *respondeat superior* is a limitation of exception to the rule of *respondeat superior* and in no way affects the fundamental principle of torts that one who wrongfully inflicts injury upon another is liable to the injured person for damages. . . . An act of misfeasance is a positive wrong, and every employee, whether employed by a private person or a municipal corporation owes a duty not to injure another by a negligent act of commission.

NEW INTERPRETATIONS OF LEGAL LIABILITY BY THE COURTS

In recent years the courts have had cases involving physical education and athletics that have resulted in a new look at such areas as sports product liability, violence and legal liability, and physical education classes held off-campus and legal liability.

Sports product liability*

The sale of sporting goods is a multibillion dollar industry today. The desire on the part of many people

to engage in physical fitness and sports activities is one reason for this growth in sales. In turn, recent years have seen the subject of sports product liability arise. The term *sports product liability,* according to Arnold, refers to the liability of the manufacturer to the person who uses his or her manufactured product and who sustains injury or damage as a result of using the product. What is most important to physical educators, athletic directors, and coaches is that they are being named as codefendents in approximately one third of all liability suits involving sports product liability.

Years ago the buyer was responsible for inspecting the product before making the purchase. He or she assumed the risk of injury or damage to property. Today, however, the courts are placing more and more responsibility on the manufacturer to discover weaknesses and defects in the product. The manufacturer is required to exercise due care in designing, manufacturing, and packaging the product. The manufacturer guarantees the product to be safe for consumer use.

According to Arnold, within the last 25 years an estimated 42 states have used the *strict liability doctrine* for some products. Under this doctrine the plaintiff must establish proof that the product contained a defect causing the injury or damage. In addition to this doctrine, a breach of the manufacturer's warranty can also be just cause for awarding damages.

The number of suits involving product liability has increased dramatically in the last few years. One reason is the large amounts of money involved in the settlements. Persons involved feel it is possible to get a large award from the courts if an injury has occurred. Also as a result of these large awards, insurance rates have skyrocketed.

Arnold has listed 10 ways that the risks associated with sports product liability may be reduced and that will help in being successful in product liability litigation. They are presented here in the following adapted form:

1. Become involved in collecting pertinent facts and information associated with illness and injury. This procedure can result in discouraging unwarranted claims.
2. Purchase the best quality equipment available. Equipment should be carefully evaluated and tested.

*Arnold, D.E.: Sports product liability, Journal of Physical Education and Recreation **49**:25-28, November/December 1978.

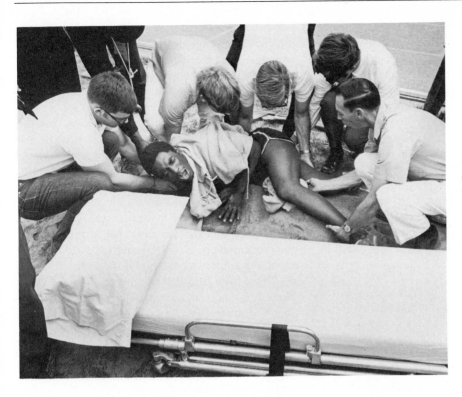

Fig. 16-4. In some cases of injuries and accidents there are questions of legal liability.

Courtesy Cramer Products, Inc., Gardner, Kan.

When purchased, records should be kept regarding such items as date of purchase. Also, reconditioned and repaired items should be recorded.

3. Purchase only from reputable dealers. Reputable dealers stand behind their products and provide replacements when called for.

4. Use only reputable reconditioning equipment companies that have high standards. For example, the NOCSAE stamp of approval should apply to reconditioned football helmets.

5. Follow manufacturer's instructions regarding fitting, adjusting, and repairing equipment, particularly protective equipment. Also, urge participants to wear protective equipment regularly.

6. Be careful not to blame someone or something for the injury without just cause. Furthermore, it is best to confine such remarks to the accident report.

7. Good teaching and supervising are important. Do not use any drills or techniques frowned on by professional associations and respected leaders in the field.

8. An emergency care plan should be prepared and be ready to be implemented when needed.

9. Insurance coverage for accident and general liability should be purchased or be available to all parties

concerned, including athletes, staff members, and schools.

10. When and if serious injuries occur, preserve items of evidence associated with the injury, such as pieces of equipment.

Violence and legal liability*

An increasing number of injuries involved in sports contests are not accidental but intentional. When such an act occurs, it is referred to as battery and "involves the harmful, unpermitted contact of one person by another." Carpenter and Acosta point out that courts are making large awards for violence in sports cases. They cite the 1979 case of the professional basketball player who was hit in the face with a powerful punch and was awarded in excess of $3 million in damages. The authors also indicate that the courts are attempting to curb violence in sports.

Carpenter and Acosta also point out that the coach is not necessarily free from liability in such cases of

*Carpenter, L.J., and Acosta, R.V.: Violence in sport—is it part of the game or the intentional tort of battery?, Journal of Physical Education and Recreation 51:18, September 1980.

violence. They cite two theoretical situations when the coach may be held liable. The first situation is when a coach knows a player is likely to commit a violent act in a sports situation but yet puts the player into the lineup. In this case the coach is not taking the necessary precautions to protect opponents from harm and injury, and in the event injury occurs, the coach may be found negligent. The second situation is when a coach may instruct a player "to take X out of the game." In this case the player who follows such an instruction is acting as an agent of the coach; as a result, a person who causes battery to be committed (in this case the coach) is just as negligent as the person who commits the act. In both of these cases the coach should exercise leadership and see that he or she and the team conduct themselves in accordance with proper standards of conduct.

Physical education classes held off-campus and legal liability*

Off-campus physical education activities have become popular in many communities, schools, and colleges. In such cases instruction in the activity may be provided by faculty members, or faculty members may only provide supervision, with the activity being instructed by a specialist not associated with the school or university, or no faculty member may be present on a regular basis.

Although instruction may take place in off-campus settings and by nonfaculty members, considerable responsibility and control still rest on the administration and staff members of the organization sponsoring these activities. Arnold cites the case of a college that had a person not affiliated with the college teach a course at an off-campus equestrian center. The plaintiff was injured in a fall from a horse while receiving instruction. The plaintiff's attorney argued that the college was vicariously liable for the negligence of the riding academy. The court's ruling went in favor of the college, which did not have to pay damages on the grounds that a master-servant relationship did not exist between the plaintiff and the college. To show such a relationship the plaintiff would have had to

prove that among other things the college could control the instruction taking place. Furthermore, the court ruled that the agency relationship did not result in the college authorizing the fall leading to the injury and that no complaints had been supplied regarding the instruction given.

Where off-campus physical education activities are conducted, a primary consideration of whether *due care* is provided. The type of activity offered would indicate the amount of care that should be provided. For example, according to Arnold, bowling in a town bowling alley would not need as much care in most cases as a skiing class. It is the responsibility of the organization and the administration to exercise care and prudence in selecting the sites to be used for off-campus activities, the quality of the instruction, and the supervision provided. Failure to observe proper care can result in negligence on the part of the organization. The administration should also look into other aspects of off-campus activities such as transportation.

Tort

A tort is a legal wrong resulting in direct or indirect injury to another individual or to property. A tortious act is a wrongful act, and damages can be collected through court action. Tort can be committed through an act of *omission* or *commission*. An act of omission results when the accident occurs during failure to perform a legal duty, such as when a teacher fails to obey a fire alarm after he or she has been informed of the procedure to be followed. An act of commission results when the accident occurs while an unlawful act is being performed, such as assault.

The National Education Association points out that

A tort may arise out of the following acts: (a) an act which without lawful justification or excuse is intended by a person to cause harm and does cause the harm complained of; (b) an act in itself contrary to law or an omission of specific legal duty, which causes harm not intended by the person so acting or omitting; (c) an act or omission causing harm which the person so acting or omitting did not intend to cause, but which might and should, with due diligence, have been foreseen and prevented.*

---

*Arnold, D.E.: Legal aspects of off-campus physical education programs, Journal of Physical Education and Recreation **50**:21-23, April 1979.

*National Education Research Division for the National Commission on Safety Education: Who is liable for pupil injuries? Washington, D.C., 1950, National Education Association, p. 5.

Fig. 16-5. Equipment and supplies must be in good repair at all times to avoid charges of negligence. Some playground equipment in the elementary school.

Courtesy Playground Corporation of America.

Fig. 16-6. Physical education personnel are responsible in off-campus activities such as horseback riding.

Courtesy State University College, Potsdam, N.Y.

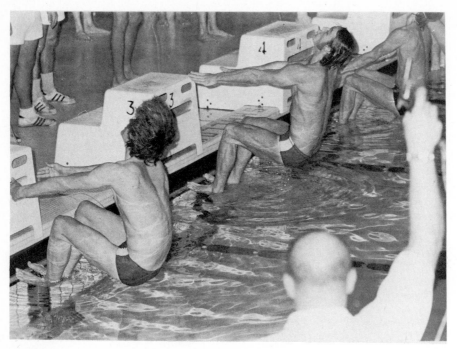

Fig. 16-7. Good supervision is required for swimming.

Courtesy State University College, Potsdam, N.Y.

The teacher, leader, or other individual not only has a legal responsibility as described by law but also has a responsibility to prevent injury. This means that in addition to complying with certain legal regulations, such as proper facilities, the teacher must comply with the principle that children should be taught without injury to them and that prudent care, such as a parent would give, must be exercised. The term *legal duty* does not mean only those duties imposed by law but also the duty owed to society to prevent injury to others. A duty imposed by law would be one such as complying with housing regulations and traffic regulations. A duty that teachers owe to society in general consists of teaching children without injury to them. For example, it was stated in one case (*Hoose v. Drumm,* 281 N.Y. 54):

Teachers have watched over the play of their pupils time out of mind. At recess periods, not less than in the classroom, a teacher owes it to his charges to exercise such care of them as a parent of ordinary prudence would observe in comparable circumstances.

It is important to understand the legal meaning of the word *accident* in relation to the topic under discussion. According to the Black's *Law Dictionary:*

An accident is an unforeseen event occurring without the will or design of the person whose mere act causes it. In its proper use the term excludes negligence. It is an event which occurs without fault, carelessness, or want of proper circumspection for the person affected, or which could not have been avoided by the use of that kind and degree of care necessary to the exigency and in the circumstance in which he was placed.

Lee v. Board of Education of City of New York in 1941, for example, showed that prudent care was not exercised, and the defendant was liable for negligence. A boy was hit by a car while playing football in the street as a part of the physical education program. The street had not been completely closed off to traffic. The board of education and the teacher were found negligent.

Negligence

Questions of liability and negligence occupy a prominent position in connection with the actions of teachers and leaders in physical education and athletic programs.

The law in America pertaining to negligence is based on common law, previous judicial rulings, or established legal procedure. This type of law differs from statutory law, which has been written into the statutes by lawmaking bodies.

Negligence implies that someone has not fulfilled his or her legal duty or has failed to do something that according to common-sense reasoning should have been done. Negligence can be avoided with common knowledge of basic legal principles and proper vigilance. One of the first things that must be determined in event of accident is whether there has been negligence.

Rosenfield* defines negligence as follows: ''Negligence consists of the failure to act as a reasonably prudent and careful person would under the circumstances involved.'' The National Education Association's report elaborates further:

Negligence is any conduct which falls below the standard established by law for the protection of others against unreasonable risk of harm. In general, such conduct may be of two types: (a) an act which a reasonable man would have realized involved an unreasonable risk of injury to others, and (b) failure to do an act which is necessary for the protection or assistance of another and which one is under a duty to do.†

According to Garber, a school employee may be negligent because of the following reasons:

1. He did not take appropriate care.
2. Although he used due care, he acted in circumstances which created risks.
3. His acts created an unreasonable risk of direct and immediate injury to others.⁴
4. He set in motion a force which was unreasonably hazardous to others.

5. He created a situation in which third persons, such as pupils, or inanimate forces, such as shop machinery, may reasonably have been expected to injure others.
6. He allowed pupils to use dangerous devices although they were incompetent to use them.
7. He did not control a third person, such as an abnormal pupil, whom he knew to be likely to inflict intended injury on others because of some incapacity or abnormality.
8. He did not give adequate warning.
9. He did not look out for persons, such as pupils, who were in danger.
10. He acted without sufficient skill.
11. He did not make sufficient preparation to avoid an injury to pupils before beginning an activity where such preparation is reasonably necessary.
12. He failed to inspect and repair mechanical devices to be used by pupils.
13. He prevented someone, such as another teacher, from assisting a pupil who was endangered, although the pupil's peril was not caused by his negligence.*

The National Education Association report includes the following additional comment:

The law prohibits careless action; whatever is done must be done well and with reasonable caution. Failure to employ care not to harm others is a misfeasance. For example, an Oregon school bus driver who parked the bus across a driveway when he knew the pupils were coasting down the hill was held liable for injuries sustained by a pupil who coasted into the bus. (*Fahlstrom v. Denk,* 1933.)†

Negligence may be claimed when the plaintiff has suffered injury either to self or to property, when the defendant has not performed his or her legal duty and has been negligent, and when the plaintiff has constitutional rights and is not guilty of contributory negligence. The teacher or leader for children in such cases is regarded as *in loco parentis,* that is, acting in the place of the parent in relation to the child.

Because negligence implies failure to act as a reasonably prudent and careful person, necessary pre-

---

*Rosenfield, H.N.: Liability for school accident, New York, 1940, Harper & Row, Publishers.
†National Education Research Division for the National Commission on Safety Education, op. cit., p. 6.

*Garber, L.O.: Law and the school business manager, Danville, Ill., 1957, Interstate Printers & Publishers, Inc., pp. 205-206. (Note: These stipulations also apply to women.)
†National Education Research Division for the National Commission on Safety Education, op. cit., p. 6.

cautions should be taken, danger should be anticipated, and common sense be used. For example, if a teacher permits a group of very young children to go up a high slide alone and without supervision, he or she is not acting as a prudent person would act. In *Lee v. Board of Education of City of New York,* when the physical education class was held in a street where cars were also allowed to pass, negligence existed.

Four factors of negligence must be proved before a lawsuit can be won. First, there must be conformance to a standard of behavior that avoids subjecting a person to reasonable risk or injury. Second, a breach of duty must be shown. Third, the breach of duty must be the cause of injury to the victim. The final factor that must be proved is that injury did occur.

A verdict by the jury in a California district court points up negligence in football. Press dispatches indicated that the high school athlete who suffered a disabling football injury was brought into court on a stretcher. The award was $325,000 (against the school district) in a suit in which the parent charged the coach "was negligent in having the boy moved to the sidelines *too soon* after he was injured." The newspaper report seemed to imply that the negligence was involved not in the *method* of moving the boy from the field, but rather in the *time* at which he was moved.

An interesting case where the court ruled negligence occurred in New Jersey. In 1962 a student in the Chatham Junior High School was severely injured in an accident while participating in physical education. The testimony brought out that the physical education teacher was not present when the accident occurred but was treating another child for a rope burn. However, he had continually warned his class not to use the springboard at any time he was out of the room. (The student was trying to perform the exercise where he would dive from a springboard over an obstacle and finish with a forward roll.) The prosecution argued that the warning had not been stressed sufficiently and that the teacher's absence from the gymnasium, leaving student aides in charge, was an act of negligence. The court ruled negligence and awarded the boy $1.2 million dollars for injuries.

His parents were awarded $35,140. On appeal, the award to the boy was reduced to $300,000, but the award to the parents remained the same.

Concerning negligence, considerable weight is given in the law to the *foreseeability of danger.* One authority points out that "if a danger is obvious and a reasonably prudent person could have foreseen it and could have avoided the resulting harm by care and caution, the person who did not foresee or failed to prevent a foreseeable injury is liable for a tort on account of negligence."[*] If a person fails to take the needed precautions and care, he or she is negligent. However, it must be established on the basis of facts in the case. It cannot be based on mere conjecture.

Physical educators must realize that children will behave in certain ways, that certain juvenile acts will cause injuries unless properly supervised, and that hazards must be anticipated, reported, and eliminated. The question raised by most courts of law is: "Should the physical educators have had prudence enough to foresee the possible dangers or occurrence of an act?"

Two court actions point up legal reasoning on negligence as interpreted in one state. In *Lane v. City of Buffalo* in 1931, the board of education was found not liable. In this case a child fell from a piece of apparatus in the schoolyard. It was found that the apparatus was in good condition and that proper supervision was present. In *Cambareri v. Board of Albany,* the defendant was found liable. The City of Buffalo owned a park supervised by the park department. While skating on the lake in the park, a boy playing crack the whip hit a 12-year-old boy who was also skating. Workers and a policeman had been assigned to supervise activity and had been instructed not to allow rough or dangerous games.

Although there are no absolute, factual standards for determining negligence, certain guides have been established that should be familiar to teachers and others engaged in physical education. Attorney Cymrot, in discussing negligence at a conference in New York City, suggested the following:

*National Education Research Division for National Commission on Safety Education, op. cit., p. 6.

Fig. 16-8. Performance objectives can be used in physical education classes such as this one at Florissant Valley Community College in St. Louis to determine how students can perform various routines that have been taught.

Photograph by LeMoyne Coates.

1. The person must be acting within the scope of his or her employment and in the discharge of his or her duties in order to obtain the benefits of the statute.
2. There must be a breach of a recognized duty owed to the participant.
3. There must be a negligent breach of such duty.
4. The accident and resulting injuries must be the natural and foreseeable consequence of the person's negligence arising from a negligent breach of duty.
5. The person must be a participant in an activity under the control of the instructor, or, put in another way, the accident must have occurred under circumstances where the instructor owes a duty of care to the participant.
6. A person's contributory negligence, however modified, will bar his or her recovery for damages.

7. The plaintiff must establish the negligence of the instructor and his or her own freedom from contributory negligence by a fair preponderance of evidence. The burden of proof on both issues is on the plaintiff.
8. Generally speaking, in a school situation, the board of education alone is responsible for accidents caused by the faulty maintenance of plants and equipment.*

Some states have a "save harmless" law. For example in New Jersey the law reads:

---

*Proceedings of the City Wide Conference with Principal's Representatives and Men and Women Chairmen of Health Education, City of New York Board of Education, Brooklyn, N.Y., 1953, Bureau of Health Education.

Chapter 311, P.L. 1938. Boards assume liability of teachers. It shall be the duty of each board of education in any school district to save harmless and protect all teachers and members of supervisory and administrative staff from financial loss arising out of any claim, demand, suit or judgment by reason of alleged negligence or other act resulting in accidental bodily injury to any person within or without the school building; provided, such teacher or member of the supervisory or administrative staff at the time of the accident or injury was acting in the discharge of his duties within the scope of his employment and/or under the direction of said board of education; and said board of education may arrange for and maintain appropriate insurance with any company created by or under the laws of this state, or in any insurance company authorized by law to transact business in this state, or such board may elect to act as self-insurers to maintain the aforesaid protection.

NEGLIGENCE CONCERNING EQUIPMENT AND FACILITIES

Defective or otherwise hazardous equipment or inadequate facilities are often the cause of injuries that lead to court action. If a physical educator has noted the equipment is defective, he or she should put this observation in writing for personal future protection. A letter should be written to the principal and superintendent of schools or other responsible person stating that danger exists and the areas of such danger. The physical educator should keep a copy for evidence in a possible lawsuit. In these cases the courts tend to agree with the student, even if dangerous conditions had been noted. Conditions cannot only be recognized but must also be corrected.

NEGLIGENCE CONCERNING INSTRUCTION

Many cases result from situations concerning instruction in an activity. For example, if a child is injured in a fall from a trampoline, a case might ensue where the child and his or her parents may try to show that instruction had been inadequate. These cases are often found in favor of the student because of the inherent danger of the activity. Other students and their families have sued teachers because they did not follow a class syllabus that many states require of their teachers. Such a syllabus outlines the course content, and if injury occurs in an unlisted activity, then a basis for suit is apparent.

NEGLIGENCE IN ATHLETIC PARTICIPATION

Many injuries are related to participation in athletics. Unequal competition is often the cause of athletic accidents. Physical educators should consider sex, age, size, and skill of students in grouping players for an activity.

The Coaches Handbook of the AAHPERD has listed some ways by which a reasonable and prudent coach can avoid charges of negligence and a law suit. In adapted form these include the following:

- Be familiar with the health status of players.
- Require medical clearance of players who have been seriously injured or ill.
- Render services only in those areas where fully qualified.
- Follow proper procedures in the case of injuries.
- See that medical personnel are available at all games and on call for practice sessions.
- See that all activities are conducted in safe areas.
- Be careful not to diagnose or treat players' injuries.
- See that protective equipment is properly fitted and worn by players who need such equipment.
- See that coaching methods and procedures provide for the safety of players.
- See that only qualified personnel are assigned responsibilities.
- See that proper instruction is given before players are permitted to engage in contests.
- See that a careful and accurate record is kept of injuries and procedures followed.
- Act as a prudent, careful, and discerning coach whose players are the first consideration.

DEFENSES AGAINST NEGLIGENCE

Despite the fact that an individual is negligent, to collect damages one must show the negligence resulted in or was closely connected with the injury. The legal question in such a case is whether or not the negligence was the ''proximate cause'' (legal cause) of the injury. Furthermore, even though it be determined that negligence is the proximate cause of the injury, there are still certain defenses on which a defendant may base his or her case.

Proximate cause. The negligence of the defendant may not have been the proximate cause of the plaintiff's injury.

Example: in *Ohmon v. Board of Education of the City of New York,* 99 N.Y.S. 2d 273 (1949), it was declared that when a 13-year-old pupil in public school was struck in the eye by a pencil thrown in classroom by another pupil to a third pupil, who stepped aside, the proximate cause of injury was an unforeseen act of the pupil who threw the pencil and that absence of the teacher (who was stacking supplies in a closet nearby the classroom) was not proximate cause of injury so as to impose liability for the injury on the board of education.

Act of God. An act of God is a situation that exists because of certain conditions beyond the control of human beings. For example, a flash of lightning, a gust of wind, a cloudburst, and other such factors may result in injury. However, this assumption applies only in cases where injury would not have occurred had prudent action been taken.

Assumption of risk. Assumption of risk is especially pertinent to games, sports, and other phases of the physical education and athletic program. It is assumed that an individual takes a certain risk when engaging in various games and sports where bodies are coming in contact with each other and where balls and apparatus are used. Participation in such activity indicates that the person assumes a normal risk.

Example: In *Scala v. City of New York,* 102 N.Y.S. 2d 709, the plaintiff when playing softball on a public playground was aware of the risks caused by curbing and concrete benches near the playing fields. It was decided that the plaintiff must be held to have voluntarily and fully assumed the dangers and, having done so, must abide by the consequences.

Example: In an action by Maltz (*Maltz v. Board of Education of New York City,* 114 N.Y.S. 2d 856, 1952) against the Board of Education of the City of New York for injuries, the court held that a 19-year-old (who was injured when he collided with a doorjamb in a brick wall 2 feet from the backboard and basket in a public school basketball court and who had played on that same court several times before the accident) knew the basket and backboard were but 2 feet from the wall, had previously hit the wall or gone through the door without injury, was not a student at the school but a voluntary member of a team that engaged in basketball tournaments with other clubs, knew or should have known the danger, and thus assumed the risk of injury.

Contributory negligence. Another legal defense is contributory negligence. A person who does not act as would a normal individual of similar age and nature thereby contributes to the injury. In such cases negligence on the part of the defendant might be ruled out. Individuals are subject to contributory negligence if they expose themselves unnecessarily to dangers. The main consideration that seems to turn the tide in such cases is the age of the individual and the nature of the activity in which he engaged.

The National Education Association's report makes the following statement regarding contributory negligence:

Contributory negligence is defined in law as conduct on the part of the injured person which falls below the standard to which he should conform for his own protection and which is legally contributing cause, cooperating with the negligence of the defendant in bringing about the plaintiff's harm. Reasonable self-protection is to be expected of all sane adults. With some few exceptions, contributory negligence bars recovery against the defendant whose negligent conduct would otherwise make him liable to the plaintiff for the harm sustained by him. Both parties being in fault, neither can recover from the other for resulting harm. When there is mutual wrong and negligence on both sides, the law will not attempt to apportion the wrong between them.

Contributory negligence is usually a matter of defense, and the burden of proof is put upon the defendant to convince the jury of the plaintiff's fault and of its causal connection with the harm sustained. Minors are not held to the same degree of care as is demanded of adults.*

Contributory negligence has implications for a difference in the responsibility of elementary school teachers as contrasted with high school teachers. The elementary school teacher, because the children are immature, has to assume greater responsibility for the safety of the child. That is, accidents in which an elementary school child is injured are not held in the same light from the standpoint of negligence as those involving high school students who are more mature. The courts might say that a high school student was mature enough to avoid doing the thing causing him or her to be injured, whereas if the same thing oc-

---

*National Education Research Division for the National Commission on Safety Education, op. cit., p. 9.

curred with an elementary school child the courts could say the child was too immature and that the teacher should have prevented or protected the child from doing the act that caused the injury.

Sudden emergency. Sudden emergency is pertinent in cases where the exigencies of the situation require immediate action on the part of a teacher and, as a result, an accident occurs. For example, an instructor in a swimming pool is suddenly alerted to a child drowning in the water. The teacher's immediate objective is to save the child. He or she runs to help the drowning person and in doing so knocks down another student who is watching from the side of the pool. The student who is knocked down hits his head on the tile floor and is injured. This would be a case of sudden emergency and, if legal action is taken, the defense could be based on this premise.

Law suits

Law suits only need a complaint to exist. The NCAA Committee on Competitive Safeguards and Medical Aspects of Sports* assumes that those who sponsor and govern athletic programs have accepted the responsibility of attempting to keep the risk of injury to a minimum. Because law suits are apt to occur in the cases of injury, despite the efforts of athletic educators, attempts should be made to be protected legally. The Committee contends that the principal defense against an unwarranted complaint is documentation that adequate measures have been taken and programs have been established to minimize the risk inherent in sports. No checklist is ever complete, but the checklist that follows should serve as a review of safety considerations for those responsible for the administration of interscholastic and intercollegiate sports programs.

CHECKLIST

Preparticipation medical examination. Before an athlete is permitted to participate in organized sports at the high school or college level, he or she should have his or her health status evaluated. When the

*From Coping with the "sue syndrome," The Athletic Educator's Report, August 1980, Physical Education Publications.

athlete first enters the school or college athletic program, he or she should have a thorough medical examination. Subsequently, an annual update of a student's health history with the use of referral exams when warranted is sufficient. The NCAA Committee on Competitive Safeguards and Medicals Aspects of Sports has developed a health questionnaire to assist in conducting a preparticipation medical examination.

Health insurance. Each student-athlete should have or secure, by parental coverage or institutional plan, access to customary hospitalization and physician benefits for defraying the cost of a significant injury or illness.

Preseason preparation. Particular practices and controls should protect the candidate for the team from premature exposure to the full rigors of the sport. Preseason conditioning recommendations from the coaching staff will help the candidate arrive at the first practice in good condition. Attention to heat stress and cautious matching of candidates during the first weeks are additional considerations.

Acceptance of risk. "Informed consent" or "waiver of responsibility" by athletes, or their parents if the athlete is a minor, should be based on an informed awareness of the risk of injury being accepted as a result of the student-athlete's participation in the sport involved. Not only does the individual share responsibility in preventive measures, but he or she should appreciate the nature and significance of these measures.

Planning and supervision. Competent attention to a sizable group of energetic and highly motivated student-athletes can only be attained by appropriate planning. Such planning should ensure both general supervision and organized instruction. Instruction should provide individualized attention to the refinement of skills and conditioning. First aid evaluation should also be included with the instruction. Such planning for particular and specific health and safety concerns should take into consideration conditions encountered during travel for competitive purposes.

Equipment. As a result of the increase in product liability litigation, purchasers of equipment should be aware of impending, as well as current, safety standards being recommended by authoritative groups and purchase materials only from reputable dealers.

In addition, attention should be directed to the proper repair and fitting of equipment.

In accordance with the above paragraph, one should know that NOCSAE has established a voluntary football helmet standard that has been adopted by the NCAA, the National Association for Intercollegiate Athletics (NAIA), the National Junior College Athletic Association (NJCAA), and the National Federation of State High School Associations. All new helmets purchased by high schools and colleges must bear the NOCSE seal. According to NCAA football rules, if a helmet is in need of repair, it must be reconditioned according to the NOCSAE Football Helmet Standard recertification procedures.

Facilities. The adequacy and condition of the facilities used for all sports should not be overlooked. The facilities should be examined regularly. Inspection should include warm-up and adjacent areas, as well as the actual competitive area.

Emergency care. The NCAA guidelines state that attention to all possible preventive measures will help to eliminate sports injuries. At each practice session or game, the following should be available:

- The presence or immediate availability of a person qualified and delegated to render emergency care to an injured participant.
- Planned access to a physician by phone or nearby presence for prompt medical evaluation of the situation when warranted.
- Planned access to a medical facility—including a plan for communication and transportation between the athletic site and medical facility—for prompt medical services when needed.
- A thorough understanding by all affected persons, including the leadership of visiting teams, of the personnel and procedures involved.

Records. Documentation is fundamental to administration. Authoritative sports safety regulations, standards, and guidelines kept current and on file provide ready reference and understanding. Waiver forms may not prevent law suits, but they help reflect organized attention to injury control.

PRECAUTIONS

Certain precautions must be taken by the physical educator to avoid possible legal liability. Some of the precautions include the following:

1. Be familiar with the health status of each person in the program.
2. Consider the individuals' skills when teaching new activities.
3. Group participants together on equal competitive levels.
4. Be sure equipment and facilities are safe.
5. Organize and carefully supervise the class. Never leave the class unattended—even in emergencies. If an emergency occurs, get a replacement before leaving the room.
6. Administer only first aid—never prescribe or diagnose.
7. Use only qualified personnel to aid in classrooms
8. Keep accurate accident records.
9. Provide adequate instruction especially in potentially dangerous activities.
10. Make sure any injured person receives a medical examination.

Nuisance

Action can be instituted for nuisance when the circumstances surrounding the act are dangerous to life or health, result in offense to the senses, are in violation of the laws of decency, or cause an obstruction to the reasonable use of property.

An authentic source states the following regarding a nuisance:

There are some conditions which are naturally dangerous and the danger is a continuing one. An inherent danger of this sort is called at law a "nuisance"; the one responsible is liable for maintaining a nuisance. His liability may be predicated upon negligence in permitting the continuing danger to exist, but even without a showing of negligence the mere fact that a nuisance does exist is usually sufficient to justify a determination of liability. For example, a junk pile in the corner of the grounds of a country school was considered a nuisance for which the district was liable when a pupil stumbled over a piece of junk and fell while playing at recess (*Popow v. Central School District No. 1, Towns of Hillsdale et al., New York,* 1938). Dangerous playground equipment available for use by pupils of all ages and degrees of skills has also been determined to be a nuisance (*Bush v. City of Norwalk, Connecticut,* 1937).

On the other hand, allegations that the district has maintained a nuisance have been denied in some cases; for example, when a small child fell into a natural ditch near the schoolyard not guarded by a fence, the ditch was held

Fig. 16-9. Women in track activity at Aledo, Ill.

Courtesy Barbara Ann Chiles.

not to be a nuisance for which the district would be liable (*Whitfield v. East Baton Rouge Parish School Board, Louisiana,* 1949). The court said this ditch did not constitute a nuisance; nor did the principle of *res ipsa loquitur* apply. Under this principle the thing which causes the injury is under the management of the defendant and the accident is such that in the ordinary course of events, it would not have happened if the defendant had used proper care.*

Mr. Cymrot, attorney at law, in addressing the Health Education Division of the New York City Schools had the following to say about an "attractive nuisance:"

Teachers need to be aware of decisions of the courts pertaining to "attractive nuisance," . . . an attractive contrivance which is maintained, alluring to children but inherently dangerous to them. This constitutes neglect. But it is not every contrivance or apparatus that a jury may treat as an "attractice nuisance." Before liability may be

imposed, there must always be something in the evidence tending to show that the device was something of a new or uncommon nature with which children might be supposed to be unfamiliar or not know of its danger. Many courts have held, however, that for children above the age of 10 years the doctrine of "attractive nuisance" does not hold. Other children are expected to exercise such prudence as those of their age may be expected to possess*

The following cases point up some court rulings concerning nuisance.

In *Texas v. Reinhardt* in 1913, it was ruled that ball games with their noises and conduct were not a nuisance in the particular case in question and an injunction should not be issued stopping such activity.

In *Iacono v. Fitzpatrick* in Rhode Island in 1938, a 17-year-old boy, while playing touch football on a

---

*National Education Research Division for the National Commission on Safety Education, op. cit., p. 6.

*Proceedings of the City Wide Conference with Principals' Representatives and Men and Women Chairmen of Health Education, City of New York Board of Education, Brooklyn, N.Y., March, 1953, Bureau of Health Education.

Fig. 16-10. The community and the school ensure a safe bicycling program.

Courtesy AAHPERD and The Bicycle Institute of America.

playground, received an injury that later resulted in his death. He was attempting to catch a pass and crashed into a piece of apparatus. The court held the apparatus was in evidence and the deceased knew of its presence. It further stated the city had not created or maintained a nuisance.

In *Schwarz v. City of Cincinnati, Ohio,* the city had permitted an organization to have fireworks in one of its public parks. The next day a 12-year-old boy was injured after lighting an unexploded bomb he found. The court ruled the permit granted the association was "not authority to create a nuisance . . . not authority to leave an unexploded bomb in the park." The city, which was the defendant in the case, was not held liable.

Governmental versus proprietary functions

The government in a legal sense is engaged in two types of activity: (1) governmental and (2) proprietary.

The *governmental function* refers to particular activities of a sovereign nature. This theory dates back to the time when kings ruled under the divine right theory, were absolute in their power, and could do no wrong. As such the sovereign was granted immunity and could not be sued without his consent for failing to exercise governmental powers or for negligence. Furthermore, a subordinate agency of the sovereign could not be sued. The municipality, according to this interpretation, acts as an agent of the state in a governmental capacity. The logic behind this reasoning is that the municipality is helping the state govern the people who live within its geographic limits.

Many activities are classified under the governmental function. Such functions as education, police protection, and public health fall in this category.

Regarding public education, the courts hold this is a governmental function and therefore is entitled to state's immunity from liability for its own negligence. As has previously been pointed out, however, the attitude of the courts has changed and has taken on a broader social outlook that allows in some cases reimbursement of the injured.

Proprietary function pertains to government functions similar to those of a business enterprise. Such functions are for the benefit of the constituents within the corporate limits of the governmental agency. An example of this would be the manufacture, distribution, and sale of some product to the public. A cafeteria conducted for profit in a school is a proprietary function. In proprietary functions, a governmental agency is held liable in the same manner as an individual or a private corporation would be held liable.

In *Watson v. School District of Bay City,* 324 Mich. 1, 36 N.W. 2d 195, a decision was handed down by the supreme court of Michigan in February 1949. In this case a 15-year-old girl attended a high school night football game. In going to her car she was required to walk around a concrete wall. As she attempted to do this, she fell over the wall and onto a ramp. She suffered paralysis and died 8 months later. The parking area was very poorly lighted. The supreme court held that staging a high school football game was a governmental function and refused to impose liability on the district.

From this discussion it can be seen that education, recreation, and health are governmental functions. Whereas this distinction between governmental and proprietary functions precludes a recovery from the governmental agency if the function was governmental, the federal government and some of the states by legislation have eliminated this distinction.

FEES

Most public recreation activities, facilities, and the like are offered free to the public. However, certain activities, because of the expenses involved, necessitate a fee to continue. For example, golf courses are expensive, and charges are usually made so they may be maintained. This is sometimes true also of such facilities as camps, bathing beaches, and swimming pools.

The fees charged have a bearing on whether recreation is a governmental or a proprietary function. The courts in most states have upheld recreation as a governmental function, because of its contribution to public health and welfare and also because its programs are free to the public at large. When fees are charged, however, the whole picture takes on a different aspect.

The attitude of the courts has been that the amount of the fee and whether or not the activity was profit making are considerations in determining whether recreation is a governmental or a priprietary function. Incidental fees used in the conduct of the enterprise do not usually change the nature of the enterprise. If the enterprise is run for profit, however, such as a health spa, the function changes from governmental to proprietary.

Liability of the municipality

It has been previously noted that a municipality as a governmental agency performs both governmental and proprietary functions.

When the municipality is performing a governmental function, it is acting in the interests of the state, receives no profit or advantage, and is not liable for negligence on the part of its employees or for failure to perform these functions. However, this would not hold if there were a specific statute imposing liability for negligence. When the municipality is performing a proprietary function—some function for profit or advantage of the agency or people it comprises—rather than the public in general, it is liable for negligence of those carrying out the function.

This discussion readily shows the importance of conducting recreation as a governmental function.

Liability of the school district

As a general rule the school district is not held liable for acts of negligence on the part of its officers or employees, provided a state statute does not exist to the contrary. The reasoning behind this is that the school district or district school board in maintaining public schools acts as an agent of the state. It performs a purely public or governmental duty imposed on it by law for the benefit of the public; and in so doing, it receives no profit or advantage.

Some state laws, however, provide that the state may be sued in cases of negligence in the performance of certain duties, such as providing for a safe environment and competent leadership. Furthermore, the school district's immunity in many cases does not cover acts that bring damage or injury through trespass of another's premises or where a nuisance exists on a school district's property, resulting in damage to other property.

Liability of school, park, and recreation board members

Generally speaking, members are not personally liable for any duties in their corporate capacities as board members that they perform negligently. Furthermore, they cannot be held personally liable for acts of employees of the district or organization over which they have jurisdiction on the theory of *respondeat superior* (let the master pay for the servant). Board members act in a corporate capacity and do not act for themselves. For example, in the state of Oregon the general rule about the personal liability of members of district schools boards is stated in 56C.J., page 348, section 223, as follows:

> School officers, or members of the board of education, or directors, trustees, or the like, of a school district or other local school organization are not personally liable for the negligence of persons rightfully employed by them in behalf of the district, and not under the direct personal supervision or control of such officer or member in doing the negligent act, since such employee is a servant of the district and not of the officer or board members, and the doctrine of *respondeat superior* accordingly has no application; and members of a district board are not personally

liable for the negligence or other wrong of the board as such. A school officer or member of a district board is, however, personally liable for his own negligence or other tort, or that of an agent or employee of the district when acting directly under his supervision or by his direction.

However, a board member can be held liable for a *ministerial* act even though he or she cannot be held for the exercise of discretion as a member of the board. If the board acts in bad faith and with unworthy motives, and if this can be shown, it can also be held liable.

Liability of teacher, leaders, and instructors

The individual is responsible for negligence of his or her own acts. With the exception of certain specific immunity, the teacher or leader in programs of physical education, athletics, and recreation is responsible for what he or she does. The Supreme Court has reaffirmed this principle, and all should recognize its important implications. Immunity of the governmental agency such as a state, school district, or board does not release the teacher or leader from liability for his or her own negligent acts.

In New York a physical education teacher was held personally liable when he sat in the bleachers while two strong boys, untrained in boxing, were permitted by the instructor to fight through nearly two rounds. The plaintiff was hit in the temple and suffered a cerebral hemorrhage. The court said: "It is the duty of a teacher to exercise reasonable care to prevent injuries. Pupils should be warned before being permitted to engage in a dangerous and hazardous exercise. Skilled boxers at times are injured, and . . . these young men should have been taught the principles of defense if indeed it was a reasonable thing to permit a slugging match of the kind which the testimony shows this contest was. The testimony indicates that the teacher failed in his duties in this regard and that he was negligent, and the plaintiff is entitled to recover." (*LaValley v. Stanford*, 272 App. Div. 183, 70 N.Y.S. 2d 460.)

In New York (*Keesee v. Board of Education of City of New York*, 5 N.Y.S. 2d 300, 1962) a junior high school girl was injured while playing line soccer. She was kicked by another player. The board of education syllabus listed line soccer as a game for boys and stated that "after sufficient skill has been aquired two or more forwards may be selected from each team." The syllabus called for ten to twenty players on each team and required a space of 30 to 40 feet. The physical education teacher divided into two teams some 40 to 45 girls who had not had any experience in soccer. A witness who was an expert in such matters testified that to avoid accidents no more than two people should be on the ball at any time and criticized the board syllabus for permitting the use of more than two forwards. The expert also testified that pupils should have experience in kicking, dribbling, and passing before being permitted to play line soccer. The evidence showed the teacher permitted six to eight inexperienced girls to be on the ball at one time. The court held that possible injury was at least reasonably foreseeable under such conditions, the teacher had been negligent, and the teacher's negligence was the cause of the pupil being injured.*

Teachers and leaders are expected to conduct their various activities carefully and prudently. If this is not done, they are exposing themselves to lawsuits for their own negligence. The National Education Association's report has the following to say regarding administrators:

The fact that administrators (speaking mainly of principals and superintendents) are rarely made defendants in pupil-injury cases seems unjust to the teachers who are found negligent because of inadequate supervision, and unjust also to the school boards who are required to defend themselves in such suits. When the injury is caused by defective equipment, it is the building principal who should have actual or constructive notice of the defect; when the injury is caused by inadequate playground supervision, the inadequacy of the supervision frequently exists because of arrangements made by the building principal. For example, a teacher in charge of one playground was required to stay in the building to teach a make-up class; another teacher was required to supervise large grounds

on which 150 pupils were playing; another teacher neglected the playground to answer the telephone. All of these inadequacies in playground supervision were morally chargeable to administrators; in none of these instances did the court action direct a charge of responsibility to the administrator. Whether the administrator in such cases would have been held liable, if charged with negligence, is problematical. The issue has not been decided, since the administrator's legal responsibility for pupil injuries has never been discussed by the courts to an extent that would make possible the elucidation of general principles; the administrator's moral responsibilities must be conceded.*

Accident-prone settings

Because many accidents occur on the playground, during recess periods, in physical education classes, and at sports events, some pertinent remarks are included here from the National Education Association's report:

PLAYGROUND AND RECESS GAMES

. . . [T]he unorganized games during recess and noon intermissions are more likely to result in pupil injuries than the organized games of physical education classes. Playground injuries may be pure accidents, such as when a pupil ran against the flagpole while playing (*Hough v. Orleans Elementary School District of Humboldt County, California*, 1943), or when a pupil was hit by a ball (*Graff v. Board of Education of New York City, New York*, 1940), or by a stone batted by another pupil (*Wilbur v. City of Binghamton, New York*, 1946). The courts have said in connection with this type of injury that every act of every pupil cannot be anticipated. However, the school district should make rules and regulations for pupils' conduct on playgounds so as to minimize dangers. For example, it was held to be negligence to permit pupils to ride bicycles on the playground while other pupils were playing. (*Buzzard v. East Lake School District of Lake County, California*, 1939.)

Playgrounds should be supervised during unorganized play and such supervision should be adequate. One teacher cannot supervise a large playground with over a hundred pupils playing (*Charonnat v. San Francisco Unified School District, California*, 1943), and when the supervision is

---

*School Law Series: The pupil's day in court; review of 1963, Washington, D.C., 1964, Research Division, National Education Association, p. 43.

*National Education Research Division for the National Commission on Safety Education, op. cit., p. 14.

either lacking or inadequate districts which are not immune are liable for negligence in not providing adequate supervision (*Forgnone v. Slavadore Union Elementary School District, California*, 1940). Pupils are known to engage in fights and may be expected to be injured in fights; it is the responsibility of the school authorities to attempt to prevent such injuries. The misconduct of other pupils could be an intervening cause to break the chain of causation if the supervision is adequate; but when the supervision is not adequate, misconduct of other pupils is not an intervening superseding cause of the injury.

If a pupil wanders from the group during playground games and is injured by a dangerous condition into which he places himself, the teacher in charge of the playground may be liable for negligence in pupil supervision (*Miller v. Board of Education, Union Free School District, New York*, 1943), although the district would not be liable in common-law state because of its immunity (*Whitfield v. East Baton Rouge Parish School Board, Louisiana*, 1949).

Supervision of unorganized play at recess or noon intermission should be by competent personnel. A school janitor is not qualified to supervise play. (*Garber v. Central School District No. 1 of Town of Sharon, New York*, 1937.)

All injuries sustained by pupils on playground equipment are excluded in the Washington statute imposing liability for certain other kinds of accidents. Injuries may occur because playground equipment is in a defective condition. The New York courts have not been consistent in their rulings on this point. In one New York case the district was not liable for injury caused by a defect in a slide because there was no evidence that the defect had existed a sufficient length of time for the school authorities to have knowledge of it (*Handy v. Haldey-Luzerne Union Free School District No. 1, New York*, 1938), but another district in New York was held liable for a defect in a slide (*Howell v. Union Free School District No. 1, New York*, 1937).

Nor have the New York courts been consistent in fixing liability when the injury was sustained on playground equipment which was not defective but was dangerous for the individual pupil who played on it. One pupil who fell off a monkey bar was unable to collect damages because the court held specific supervision of each game and each piece of playground equipment would be an unreasonable requirement. The pupil merely met with an accident which was not the fault of the playground supervisor. (*Miller v. Board of Education of Union Free School District No. 1, Town of Oyster Bay, New York*, 1936.) However, another district was declared liable for injuries sustained by a pupil who fell from a ramp during recess, the court holding that liability rested upon the maintenance of a dangerous piece of playground equipment. This ramp had been constructed for the use of older boys and even they were to use it only under supervision; the injured pupil was a small child. (*Sullivan v. City of Binghamton, New York*, 1946.)

Where children of all ages share a playground, extra precautions should be taken to prevent accidents, since some children are more adept in using equipment than others and some playground equipment is dangerous to the unskilled.

PHYSICAL EDUCATION AND SPORTS EVENTS

Pupil injuries in this area occur when playground or gymnasium equipment is defective, when pupils attempt an exercise or sport for which they have not been sufficiently trained, when there is inadequate supervision of the exercise, when other pupils conduct themselves in a negligent manner, and even when the pupils are mere spectators at sports events.

It has been held that physical education teachers, or the school district in States where the district is subject to liability, are responsible for injuries caused by defective equipment. For example, there was liability for the injury to a pupil who was injured in a tumbling race when the mat, not firmly fixed, slipped on the slippery floor. (*Cambareri v. Board of Education of Albany, New York*, 1940.)

Defects in equipment should be known to the physical education instructor. There may be what is called actual or constructive notice of the defect. Actual knowledge is understandable; constructive notice means that the defect has existed for a sufficient time so that the instructor should have known of its existence, whether he did or not. Teachers of physical education should make periodic examination of all equipment at rather frequent intervals; otherwise they may be charged with negligence in not having corrected defects in equipment which have existed for a sufficient time that ignorance of the defect is a presumption of negligence.

Physical education teachers may be liable also for injuries which occur to pupils who attempt to do an exercise which is beyond their skills. A running-jump somersault is one such instance (*Govel v. Board of Education of Albany, New Yor*, 1944); boxing is another (*LaValley v. Stanford, New York*, 1947); and a headstand exercise is another (*Gardner v. State of New York, New York*, 1939). All of these exercises were found to be inherently dangerous by the courts, and the evidence showed that previous instruction had been inadequate and the pupils had not been warned of the dangers. However, where the previous instruction and the supervision during the exercise are both adequate, there is no liability so long as it cannot be proved that the teacher is generally incompetent. (*Kolar v. Union Free School District No. 9, Town of Lenox, New York,* 1939). These cases suggest that teachers should not permit pupils to attempt exercises for which they have not been fully prepared by warnings of the dangers and preliminary exercises to develop the required skills.

As in other types of pupil injuries, the physical education teacher is not liable if the injury occurred without his negligence. If caused by the negligence of another pupil, the teacher will likely be relieved of liability if the other pupil's misconduct was not foreseeable. Pure accidents occur in sport also, and if there is no negligence there is no liability (*Mauer v. Board of Education of New York City, New York,* 1945).

Sports events to which nonparticipating pupils and even the public are invited raise other problems of liability for the district or the physical education teacher in charge. If the locality is in a common-law State where the district is immune, the charge of an admission fee does not nullify the district's immunity or make the activity a proprietary function as an exception to the immunity rule (*Watson v. School District of Bay City, Michigan,* 1949). If the accident occurs in a State where the district is liable for at least certain kinds of injuries, such as California, the invitation to attend a sports event includes an invitation to the nearby grounds and equipment, imposing liability for injury from hidden glass or other dangers (*Brown v. City of Oakland, California,* 1942). If a spectator is accidentally hit by a ball, however, there is no liability; even when a pupil was injured by being hit by a bottle at a game there was no liability because the misconduct of the other spectator was not foreseeable (*Weldy v. Oakland High School District of Alameda County, California,* 1937.)*

Common areas of negligence

Common areas of negligence in physical education and athletic activities listed by Begley† in a New York University publication are situations involving poor selection of activities, failure to take protective procedures, hazardous conditions of buildings or grounds, faulty equipment, inadequate supervi-

sion, and poor selection of play area. Cases involving each of these common areas of negligence follow.

Poor selection of activities. The activity must be suitable to the child or youth. In *Rook v. New York* 4 N.Y.S. 2d 116 (1930), the court ruled that tossing a child in a blanket constituted a dangerous activity.

Failure to take protective measures. The element of foreseeability enters here, and proper protective measures must be taken to provide a safe place for children and youth to play. In *Roth v. New York,* 262 App. Div. 370, 29 N.Y.S. 2d 442 (1942), inadequate provisions were made to prevent bathers from stepping into deep water. When a bather drowned, the court held the state was liable.

Hazardous conditions of buildings or grounds. Buildings and grounds must be safe. Construction of facilities and their continual repair must have as one objective the elimination of hazards. In *Novak et al. v. Borough of Ford City,* 141 Atl. 496 (Pa., 1928), unsafe conditions were caused by an electric wire over the play area. In *Honaman v. City of Philadelphia,* 185 Atl. 750 (Pa., 1936), unsafe conditions were caused by failure to erect a backstop.

Faulty equipment. All play and other equipment must be in good condition at all times. In *Van Dyke v. Utica,* 203 App. Div. 26, 196 N.Y. Supp. 277 (1922), concerning a slide that fell over on a child and killed him, the court ruled that the slide was defective.

Inadequate supervision. There must be qualified supervision in charge of all play activities. In *Garber v. Central School District No. 1, Town of Sharon, N.Y.,* 251, App. Div. 214, 295 N.Y. Supp. 850, the court held a school janitor was not qualified to supervise school children playing in a gymnasium during lunch hour.

Poor selection of play area. The setting for games and sports should be selected with a view to the safety of the participants. In *Morse v. New York,* 262 App. Div. 324, 29 N.Y.S. 2d 34 (1941), when sledding and skiing were permitted on the same hill without adequate barriers to prevent participants in each activity from colliding with each other, the court held that state was liable for negligence.

---

*National Education Research Division for the National Commission on Safety Education, op. cit., pp. 18-20.

†Begley, R.F.: Legal liability in organized recreational playground areas, Safety Education Digest, 1955.

```
Gen. No. 1 100M-1-54-3181          WAIVER FORM              Long Beach, California
                          LONG BEACH PUBLIC SCHOOLS   Date_____

     We,_____, are the parents or guardians
of_____, and in consideration of the special benefits
of the extracurricular activity being afforded the student by the Long Beach Board of Education and
the school districts whose school the aforementioned child attends, hereby permit_____
_____to participate in_____
_____
_____
and we hereby release and discharge the said Long Beach Board of Education, the said school district,
and each and all their agents and employees from any liability whatever to the undersigned re-
sulting from or in any manner arising out of any injury or damage which may be sustained by
the said_____, on account of his participation in
_____or in the transportation in connection therewith.
     We further agree that in case of any action being brought for, or on behalf of the aforemen-
tioned child on account of any injury received during his participation in the above mentioned
events, or in the transportation connected therewith, that we will be personally responsible to the
school district, the Board of Education, and any of its officials or agents concerned, and will repay
to them and hold them harmless against any judgment recovered in any such action against them
or either of them.
     Signed this_____day of_____, 195____

_____          _____
    Signature of Parent or Guardian                    Address

_____          _____
    Signature of Parent or Guardian                    Address
NOTE: Parents or Guardians, read the reverse side of this form.
```

Fig. 16-11. Waiver form.

Supervision

Children are entrusted by parents to recreation, physical education, and athletic programs, and parents expect adequate supervision will be provided to minimize the possibility of accidents.

Questions of liability regarding supervision pertain to two points: (1) the extent of the supervision and (2) the quality of the supervision.

Regarding the first point, the question is raised about whether adequate supervision was provided. This is difficult to answer because it varies from situation to situation. However, the answers to these questions help determine this: "Would additional supervision have eliminated the accident?" and "Is it reasonable to expect that additional supervision should have been provided?"

Regarding the quality of the supervision, it is expected that competent personnel will handle spe-cialized programs in physical education, athletics, and recreation. If the supervisors of such activities do not possess proper training in such work, the question of negligence can be raised.

Waivers and consent slips

Waivers and consent slips are not synonymous. A waiver is an agreement whereby one party waives a particular right. A consent slip is an authorization, usually signed by the parent, permitting a child to take part in some activity.

Regarding a waiver, a parent cannot waive the rights of a child who is under 21 years of age. When a parent signs such a slip, he or she is merely waiving his or her right to sue for damages. A parent can sue in two ways, from the standpoint of his or her rights as the parent and from the standpoint of the child's own rights that he or she has as an individual, irrespective of the parent. A parent cannot waive the right of the child to sue as an individual.

Consent slips offer protection from the standpoint of showing the child has the parent's permission to engage in an activity.

The courts and eligibility rules

Traditionally, when eligibility regulations have been challenged, courts have been reluctant to substitute their judgment for the judgments of school athletic associations. In recent years, however, federal judges have been finding eligibility rules unconstitutional, and administrators and physical educators should note this change in court rulings.

Court decisions where eligibility rules have been found to be segregationist have been consistently found unconstitutional. A ruling found that the common practice in Alabama of having racially based athletic associations was unconstitutional, and a specific ruling of the United States Circuit Court ordered the Louisiana High School Athletic Association to admit a private black high school.

Other significant rulings concerning eligibility include a recent federal court order voiding the Indiana High School Athletic Association rule that prohibited married students from athletic participation. Another significant decision involved the Iowa High School Athletic Association and their suspension of a student athlete because he was riding in a car that was transporting beer. The student was not drinking, athletic training was not taking place, and the event occurred in the summer when school was not in session. In addition, no state or federal law was broken. The eligibility law was found to be unreasonable, and the student was reinstated.

Title IX and the courts

Recent years have found the media reporting on numerous cases involving discrimination against women in sports. In 1978 a federal judge in Dayton, Ohio ruled that girls may not be barred from playing on boys' school athletic teams, even in contact sports such as football and wrestling. In his decision the judge pointed out there might be many reasons why

girls would not want to play on boys' teams, such as "reasons of stature or weight or reasons of temperament, motivation, or interest. This is a matter of choice. But a prohibition without exception based on sex is not." The judge also indicated his ruling would have national implications. The Ohio High School Athletic Association had barred girls from contact sports.

A ruling by the State Division on Civil Rights of New Jersey requires Little League baseball teams to permit girls to play. New Jersey was the first state to have such a ruling. The order also requires that both boys and girls be notified of team tryouts and that both sexes be treated equally.

An amendment to the Education Law of New York State provides that no one may be disqualified from school athletic teams because of sex, except by certain regulations of the state commissioner of education.

Another case involved two women coaches who were denied admittance to the North Carolina Coaching Clinic because of their sex. A lawsuit was instituted by the women against the all-male coaching association.

In Indiana, the Indiana Supreme Court ruled that it was discriminatory for a high school to sponsor a boys' team and not a girls' team.

Title IX has legislated that there should be no discrimination by sex. Although it is a federal law, it still is necessary for many girls and women to go to court to ensure their rights under the law.

A Michigan judge's court ruling in 1981, if allowed to stand, may have serious implications for the implementation of Title IX. Federal District Court Judge Joiner ruled that Title IX can only apply to programs that directly receive federal funds. In the case in question, the judge ruled the U.S. Department of Education could not enforce Title IX in the Ann Arbor School District's interscholastic sports program because the program did not itself receive any federal funding. If the precedent is established, it will have a far-reaching effect not only on athletics but also on other areas.

The United States Court of Appeals for the First Circuit has also ruled Title IX is programmatic, and not institutional, in scope. The Court of Appeals ruled that "the only meaningful interpretation of (Title IX) is that it prohibits sex discrimination in a Federally funded education program offered by an educational institution." In support of its decision, the court relied on the language of the statute (including its definition of the term *educational institution*), the legislative history of Title IX, and previous court rulings that have addressed the question.

The fall 1978 issue of *In The Running* gave the following advice to girls and women regarding filing a Title IX complaint. The advantages are that the person filing the complaint may win, may encourage other women to consider similar action, may result in the elimination of discriminatory practices, may help many girls and women, and may result in an investigation into the organization; therefore the organization will probably be in better compliance with the law. The disadvantages are that the person filing the complaint can lose, may lose her job or scholarship, may experience frustrations, may be involved with a process that could take months and years to resolve, may reap no personal or professional reward, and may be branded a troublemaker.

Safety

It is important to take every precaution possible to prevent accidents by providing for the safety of students and other individuals who participate in programs of physical education, athletics, and recreation. If such precautions are taken, the likelihood of a lawsuit will diminish and the question of negligence will be eliminated. Precautions the leader or teacher should take follow:

1. Instructor should be properly trained and qualified to perform specialized work.

2. Instructor should be present at all organized activities in the program.

3. Classes should be organized properly according to size, activity, physical condition, and other factors that have a bearing on safety and health of the individual.

4. Health examinations should be given to all pupils.

5. A planned, written program for proper disposi-

tion of participants who are injured or become sick should be followed.

6. Regular inspections should be made of such items as equipment, apparatus, ropes, or chains, placing extra pressure on them, and taking other precautions to make sure they are safe. They should also be checked for deterioration, looseness, fraying, and splinters.

7. Overcrowding athletic and other events should be avoided, building codes and fire regulations should be adhered to, and adequate lighting for all facilities should be provided.

8. Protective equipment such as mats should be used wherever possible. Any hazards such as projections or obstacles in an area where activity is taking place should be eliminated. Floors should not be slippery. Shower rooms should have surfaces conducive to secure footing.

9. Sneakers should be worn on gymnasium floors and adequate space provided for each activity.

10. Activities should be adapted to the age and maturity of the participants, proper and competent supervision should be provided, and spotters should be used in gymnastics and other similar activities.

11. Students and other participants should be instructed in correctly using apparatus and performing in physical activities. Any misuse of equipment should be prohibited.

12. The buildings and other facilities used should be inspected regularly for safety hazards, such as loose tiles, broken fences, cracked glass, and uneven pavement. Defects should be reported immediately to responsible persons and necessary precautions taken.

13. In planning play and other instructional areas the following precautions should be taken:

a. There should be sufficient space for all games.
b. Games using balls and other equipment that can cause damage should be conducted in areas where there is minimum danger of injuring someone.
c. Quiet games and activities requiring working at benches, such as arts and crafts, should be in places that are well protected.

14. Truesdale lists certain questionable practices in which teachers, coaches, nurses, and trainers sometimes engage:

a. Supply "pills" for headaches or as laxatives or for menstrual discomfort.

b. Examine and diagnose by the stethoscope.

c. Prescribe anticold pills or capsules.

d. Strap joint injuries under supposition of sprain without expert assessment for possible fracture.

e. Permit return to play of a player with a head injury.

f. Play injured players not medically certified.

g. Permit return of students without medical certification to class, or particularly to activity, after illness.

h. Prescribe gargles or swabs for sore throats.

i. Use cutting tools (knives or razor blades) on calluses, corns, blisters, ingrown nails, etc.

j. Administer local anaesthesia to permit play after injury.

k. Employ physical forces such as heat or electric current to produce tissue change and decongestion and repair without medical order, or by unqualified persons.

l. Possibly further damage unconscious players by dashing water in the face, by slapping the face or by unwarranted use or aromatic spirits of ammonia to "bring them to."*

Truesdale also points out that "it is the duty of adults engaged in education not only to know of and be skillful in the proper techniques for protecting persons against injury, or protecting injured persons against aggravation, but also to know the limits beyond which the untrained or the partially trained person may not go."

15. In the event of accident the following or a similar procedure should be followed:

a. The nearest teacher or leader should proceed to the scene of the accident immediately, notifying the person in charge and nurse, if available, by messenger. Also, a physician should be called at once if one is necessary.

b. A hurried examination of the injured person will give some idea of the nature and extent of the injury and the emergency of the situation.

c. If the teacher or leader is well versed in first aid, assistance should be given (a qualified first aid certificate will usually absolve the teacher of negligence). Every teacher or leader who works in these specialized areas should and is expected to know first

aid procedures. In any event everything should be done to make the injured person comfortable and reassure the injured until the services of a physician can be secured.

d. If the injury is serious, an ambulance should be called.

e. After the injured person has been provided for, the person in charge should fill out the accident forms and take the statements of witnesses and file for future reference. Reports of accidents should be prepared promptly and sent to proper persons. They should be accurate and complete. Among other things they should contain information about:

Name and address of injured person
Activity engaged in
Date, hour, and place
Person in charge
Witnesses
Cause and extent of injury
Medical attention given
Circumstances surrounding incident

f. There should be a complete followup of the accident, an analysis of the situation, and an eradication of any existing hazards.

Herman Rosenthal, Assistant to the Law Secretary, City of New York, in addressing a health education conference in New York City, made the following remarks concerning reporting accidents:

Reports should be complete, full and in detail. He advised that where a case does go into litigation, there is a delay in the court calendar of 2 to 3 years before the case is tried. A complete and detailed report is always better than a teacher's or a child's memory. He pointed out that the completion of accident reports was the function and duty of the teacher and in no case should a child be expected to prepare the report. Reports in the handwriting of children, he said, should be limited only to the statements and signatures of the injured and of the witnesses to the accident. He emphasized that should an injured child at the time of the accident be unable to prepare a written statement or affix his signature to a report, the teacher should prepare the necessary statement and signature and indicate the reasons for so doing. He further focused attention on the fact that teachers should not attempt to color or distort facts in order to protect the school of the child, because such a practice does more harm than good. An extremely important point, he said, was the need to report where the teacher was at the time of the accident, the extent of the supervision, and the teacher control of the activ-

---

*Truesdale, J.C.: So you're a good samaritan! Journal of the American Association for Health, Physical Education, and Recreation **25**:25, 1954.

Fig. 16-12. Every precaution must be taken to prevent accidents. Students learn to handle a canoe in water safety course at Cuyahoga Community College in Cleveland.

ity at the time of the accident. Also, he said that with few exceptions reports should be submitted within 24 hours of the time of the accident. He explained that in some cases this might not be possible, but in such cases no report need be delayed more than 48 hours.*

Thelma Reed, Chairman of Standard Student Accident Report Committee of the National Safety Council, listed the following reasons why detailed injury reports are important for school authorities:

1. Aid in protecting the school personnel and district from unfortunate publicity and from liability suits growing out of student injury cases;
2. Aid in evaluating the relative importance of the various safety areas and the time each merits in the total school safety effort;
3. Suggest modification in the structure, use, and maintenance of buildings, grounds, and equipment;

4. Suggest curriculum adjustments to meet immediate student needs;
5. Provide significant data for individual student guidance;
6. Give substance to the school administrators' appeal for community support of the school safety program;
7. Aid the school administration in guiding the school safety activities of individual patrons and patrons' groups.

SAFETY CODE FOR THE PHYSICAL EDUCATION INSTRUCTOR

The following safety code should be followed by the physical education instructor:

1. Have a proper teacher's certificate in full force and effect.
2. Operate and teach at all times, within the scope of his or her employment as delimited and defined by the rules and regulations of the employing board of education and within the statutory limitations imposed by the state.

---

*Proceedings of the City Wide Conference with Principals' Representatives and Men and Women Chairmen of Health Education, City of New York Board of Education, Brooklyn, N.Y., 1953, Bureau of Health Education.

3. Provide the safeguards designed to minimize the dangers inherent in a particular activity.

4. Provide the amount of supervision for each activity required to ensure the maximum safety of all the pupils.

5. Inspect equipment and facilites periodically to determine whether or not they are safe for use.

6. Notify the proper authorities forthwith concerning the existence of any dangerous condition as it continues to exist.

7. Provide sufficient instruction in the performance of any activity before exposing pupils to its hazards.

8. Be certain the task is one approved by the employing board of education for the age and attainments of the pupils involved.

9. Do not force a pupil to perform a physical feat the pupil obviously feels incapable of performing.

10. Act promptly and use discretion in giving first aid to an injured pupil, but nothing more.

11. Exercise due care in practicing his or her profession.

12. Act as a reasonably prudent person would under the given circumstances.

13. Anticipate the dangers that should be apparent to a trained, intelligent person (foreseeability).*

Insurance management

There are three major types of insurance management that schools and other organizations use to protect themselves against loss. The first is insurance for *property*. The second is insurance for *liability protection* when there might be financial loss arising from personal injury or property damage for which the school district or organization is liable. The third is insurance for *crime protection* against a financial loss that might be incurred as a result of theft or other illegal act. This section on insurance management is primarily concerned with liability protection.

A definite trend can be seen in school districts toward having some form of school accident insurance to protect students against injury. The same is true wherever physical education programs are conducted. Along with this trend can be seen the impact on casualty and life insurance companies that offer

insurance policies. The premium costs of accident policies vary from community to community and also in accordance with the age of the insured and type of plan offered. Interscholastic athletics have been responsible for the development of many state athletic protection plans, as well as the issuance of special policies by commercial insurance companies. When it is realized that accidents are the chief cause of death among students between the ages of 5 and 18, it can readily be seen that some protection is needed.

COMMON FEATURES OF SCHOOL INSURANCE MANAGEMENT PLANS

Some common features of insurance management plans across the United States follow:

1. Premiums are paid for by the school, by the parent, or jointly by the school and parent.

2. Schools obtain their money for payment of premiums from the board of education, general organization fund, or a pooling of funds for many schools taken from gate receipts in league games.

3. Schools place the responsibility on the parents to pay for any injuries incurred.

4. Blanket coverage is a very common policy for insurance companies to offer.

5. Insurance companies frequently offer insurance coverage for athletic injuries as part of a package plan that also includes an accident plan for all students.

6. Most schools have insurance plans for the protection of athletes.

7. Most schools seek insurance coverage that provides for benefits whether x-ray films are positive or negative.

8. Hospitalization, x-ray films, and medical fees and dental fees are increasingly becoming part of the insurance coverage in schools.

Some school boards have found it a good policy to pay the premium on insurance policies because the full coverage of students provides peace of mind for both parents and teachers. Furthermore, many liability suits have been avoided in this manner.

Other school officials investigate the various insurance plans available and then recommend a particular plan, and the parents deal directly with the company. Such parent-paid plans are frequently divided into two options: (1) they provide coverage for the

---

*Munize, A.J.: The teacher, pupil injury, and legal liability, Journal of Health, Physical Education, and Recreation **33:**28, 1962.

student on a door-to-door basis (to and from school, while at school, and in school-sponsored activities) and (2) they provide 24-hour accident coverage with premiums usually running to four times higher than the "school only" policy. The school only policy rates are based on age, with rates for children in the elementary grades lower than those in the higher grades. These policies also usually run only for the school year.

Student accident insurance provides coverage for all accidents regardless of whether the insured is hospitalized or treated in a doctor's office. Such medical plans as Blue Cross and Blue Shield are limited in the payments they make. Student accident insurance policies, as a general rule, offer reasonable rates and are a good investment for all concerned. Parents should be encouraged, however, to examine their existing family policies before taking out such policies to avoid overlapping coverage.

A survey of nine school districts in Ohio disclosed the following practices and problems concerned with selecting an insurance policy for athletics:

1. The chief school administrator was the person who usually selected the insurance company from whom the policy would be purchased.
2. Medical coverage on policies purchased ranged from $30 to $5000 and dental coverage from nothing to $500.
3. The claims collected for one particular type of injury ranged from nothing to $792.30.
4. Companies did not follow through at all times in paying the amount for which the claim was made.
5. Most insurance companies writing athletic policies have scheduled benefit plans.
6. Catastrophe clauses were absent from all policies.
7. Athletes covered ranged from 80% to 100%.
8. In most cases part of each athlete's premium was paid for from a school athletic fund.
9. Football was covered in separate policies.

As a result of this survey the following recommendations were made:

1. Some person or group of persons should be delegated to explore insurance policies and, after developing a set of criteria, to purchase the best one possible.
2. Where feasible, cooperative plans with other schools on a county or other basis should be encouraged to obtain less expensive group rates.

3. Criteria for selecting an insurance policy should, in addition to cost, relate to such important benefits as maximum medical, excluded benefits, maximum dental, hospital, dental or dismemberment, surgical, and x-ray films.
4. The greatest possible coverage for cost involved should be an important basis for selecting a policy.
5. In light of football programs especially, the catastrophe clause should be investigated as possible additional coverage.
6. Deductible clause policies should not be purchased.
7. Dental injury benefits are an important consideration.
8. Determine what claims the insurance company will and will not pay.
9. The school should insist on 100% enrollment in the athletic insurance program.
10. Schools should have a central location for keeping insurance records, and there should be an annual survey to ascertain all the pertinent facts about the cost and effectiveness of such coverage.

PROCEDURE FOR INSURANCE MANAGEMENT

Every school should be covered by insurance. There are five types of accident insurance that can be used: "(1) commercial insurance policies written on an individual basis, (2) student medical benefit plans written on a group basis by commercial insurers, (3) state high school athletic association benefit plans, (4) medical benefit plans operated by specific city school systems, and (5) self-insurance."* Before adoption by any school, each type of insurance should be carefully weighed so the best coverage is obtained for the type of program sponsored.

A suggested procedure for the administration of an insurance program follows:

(1) the entire school should be organized to study the insurance problems and needs, (2) a survey should be made to ascertain the need for insurance before it is purchased, (3) after the need has been established, specifications should be constructed indicating the kind and amount of insurance needed, (4) the specifications should be presented to several insurers to obtain estimates of coverage and costs, (5) the plans presented to the school by the several insurers

---

*Joint Committee: Administrative problems in health education, physical education and recreation, Washington, D.C., 1953, American Association for Health, Physical Education, and Recreation, p. 105.

should be studied, and the one best suited to that particular situation should be selected, (6) parents should be given full information about the insurance, (7) workable and harmonious relations should be established with the insurer selected, (8) continuous evaluation of the insurance program should be carried out, and (9) records should be carefully kept of costs, accidents, claims payments, and other pertinent data.

School administrators should insist upon the following conditions and requirements when purchasing accident insurance: (1) the coverage should include all school activities and provide up to $500 [more today] for each injury to each pupil, (2) the medical services should include (a) cost of professional services of physician or surgeon, (b) cost of hospital care and service, (c) cost of a trained nurse, (d) cost of ambulance, surgical appliances, dressings, x-rays, etc., and (e) cost of repair and care of natural teeth, (3) the policy should be tailor-made to fit the needs of the school, (4) the coverage should be maximum for minimum cost, (5) all pupils as well as all teachers, should be included, (6) a deductible clause should be avoided unless it reduces the premium substantially and the policy still fulfills its purpose, (7) blanket rather than schedule type coverage should be selected, and (8) claims payment must be simple, certain, and fast.*

ATHLETICS AND INSURANCE COVERAGE

Some schools and colleges do not provide an athletic insurance program. If a student is injured in an athletic event, the family is then responsible for all medical expenditures. There is no provision for the school or college to reimburse the family for its expense. Of course, the school or college is always open to a lawsuit by the parents in an effort to reclaim expenses. This is expensive for the school or college, for if the claim is settled in favor of the parents, the school's or college's insurance premiums for the next few years are increased. If the lawsuit is settled in favor of the school or college, the insurance company has already placed a sum of money in reserve until the final decision is reached. This is also costly because the premium is increased during the time the money is in reserve. An intangible effect is the damage to the school's or college's public relations.

An alternative is to provide an opportunity for

students to purchase athletic insurance or, better yet, for the school or college to purchase a policy for students participating in sports. Of course, the latter is the best method because all students are covered, regardless of their economic status, and the students' liability policy is not subject to suit. Most parents are only interested in recovering monies actually spent, and they are satisfied accordingly. Usually a blanket policy purchased by the school or college can be obtained at a lower unit cost than a policy purchased by individuals. The athletic insurance program can be administered by a local or regional broker, relieving the school or college of going into the insurance business.

It is the responsibility of the director of physical education to supply accurate lists of participating students to the business office before the beginning of sports seasons. It is imperative for the various coaches to become aware of the insurance coverage so when accidents happen, they can inform the athletes of the proper procedure to follow in filing reports and claims. Usually the business office will supply policies for every participant in a covered athletic team. The coach should not only be knowledgeable, but he or she should also show concern for accident victims. This is not only a form of good public relations, but it may also make the difference in the parents' minds concerning a lawsuit. The coaches then must be instructed in the proper attitude to take when such mishaps occur.

SCHOOL ATHLETIC INSURANCE

Athletic protection funds usually have these characteristics: they are a nonprofit venture, they are not compulsory, a specific fee is charged for each person registered with the plan, and there is provision for recovery for specific injuries. Generally the money is not paid out of tax funds but instead is paid either by the participants themselves or by the school or other agency.

In connection with such plans, an individual, after receiving benefits, could in most states still bring action against the coach or other leader whose negligence contributed to the injury.

In respect to paying for liability and accident insurance out of public tax funds, the states vary in

---

*Joint Committee, ibid., p. 106.

(check one)
☐ School Jurisdictional
☐ Non-School Jurisdictional

RECOMMENDED
STANDARD STUDENT ACCIDENT REPORT
(See instructions on reverse side)

(check one)
Recordable ☐
Reportable Only ☐

School District:
City, State:

General

| 1. Name | 2. Address |

| 3. School | 4. Sex | Male ☐ Female ☐ | 5. Age | 6. Grade/Special Program |

7. Time Accident Occurred
Date: Day of Week: Exact Time: AM ☐ PM ☐

Injury

8. Nature of Injury

9. Part of Body Injured

10. Degree of Injury (check one)
Death ☐   Permanent ☐   Temporary (lost time) ☐   Non-Disabling (no lost time) ☐

11. Days Lost
From School: From Activities Other Than School: Total:

12. Cause of Injury

Accident

13. Accident Jurisdiction (check one)
School: Grounds ☐   Building ☐   To and From ☐   Other Activities Not on School Property ☐
Non-School: Home ☐   Other ☐

14. Location of Accident (be specific)

15. Activity of Person (be specific)

16. Status of Activity

17. Supervision (if yes, give title & name of supervisor)
Yes ☐
No ☐

18. Agency Involved

19. Unsafe Act

20. Unsafe Mechanical/Physical Condition

21. Unsafe Personal Factor

22. Corrective Action Taken or Recommended

23. Property Damage
School $ Non-School $ Total $

24. Description (Give a word picture of the accident, explaining who, what, when, why and how)

Signature

25. Date of Report

26. Report Prepared by (signature & title)

27. Principal's Signature

This form is recommended for securing data for accident prevention and safety education. School districts may reproduce this form adding space for optional data. Reference: *Student Accident Reporting Guidebook*, National Safety Council, 425 N. Michigan Avenue, Chicago, Illinois 60611. 1966. 34 pages.

(over)

Fig. 16-13. Accident report form recommended by National Safety Council.

their practices. Some states do not permit tax money to be used for liability or accident insurance to cover students in physical education activities. On the other hand, the state legislature of Oregon permits school districts to carry liability insurance. This section is stated as follows in the revised code, O.R.S.:

332.180 Liability insurance; medical and hospital benefits insurance. Any district school board may enter into contracts of insurance for liability coverage of all activities engaged in by the district, for medical and hospital benefits for students engaging in athletic contests and for public liability and property damage covering motor vehicles operated by the district, and may pay the necessary premiums thereon. Failure to procure such insurance shall in no case be construed as negligence or lack of diligence on the part of the district school board or the members thereof.

Some athletic insurance plans in use in the schools today are entirely inadequate. These plans indicate a certain amount of money as the maximum that can be collected. For example, a boy may lose the sight of an eye. According to the athletic protection fund, the loss of an eye will draw, say, $1,500. This amount does not come even remotely close to paying for such a serious injury. In this case a hypothetical example could be taken by saying that the parents sue the athletic protection fund and the teacher for $30,000. In some states, if the case is lost, the athletic fund will pay the $1,500 and the teacher the other $28,500. It can be seen that some of these insurance plans do not give complete and adequate coverage.

In many states physical educators need additional protection against being sued for accidental injury to students. Legislation is needed permitting school funds to be used as protection against student injuries. In this way a school would be legally permitted and could be required to purchase liability insurance to cover all pupils.

Table 16-1. A sample of insurance rates for athletes as well as cheerleaders*

Football and sports plan $10,000 Basic medical expense benefit $250,000 Catastrophe supplemental benefit $7,500 Dismemberment benefit $2,000 Accidental death benefit	No deductible $260,000 maximum			$50 deductible $260,000 maximum		
	Non- excess basis	Partial excess basis	Full excess basis	Non- excess basis	Partial excess basis	Full excess basis
Football Full season rate per player	$55.80	$22.75	$17.75	$45.80	$18.75	$15.75
All other sports Premium per athlete (regardless of the number of sports in which an athlete may participate)	$10.70	$ 6.20	$ 5.20	$ 8.20	$ 4.20	$ 3.20
Associated activities Premium per band member, cheerleader, etc.	$ 3.05	$ 2.30	$ 2.05	$ 2.55	$ 1.80	$ 1.55
$30,000 Disability Benefit Per football player	$2.95					
Per athlete	$ .80					
Per band member, cheerleader, etc.	$ .20					

*Note: on a Partial Excess Clause only a portion of hospital expenses and/or surgery expenses are covered. On a Full Excess Clause benefits will be payable only for that portion of all medical expenses not covered by other insurance. (Courtesy C.W. Bollinger Co. Insurance, Montclair, N.J.)

GROVER CLEVELAND HIGH SCHOOL
HIMROD & GRANDVIEW AVE.
Ridgewood, New York
STATEMENT BY WITNESS
(Write in Ink)

Witness..Address...

Age..Rank...Class..

Name of one injured.............................Injured's Official Class...............Age of Injured.................

Date of accident.............................Time.........................Day of week......................

A. Circumstances of Accident

1. Locate the position from which you witnessed the accident, using such phrases as, in front of, as I entered, standing on the, in back of, etc...

....

....

2. Locate the position where the accident occurred, using such phrases as, on the landing, exit 8 up, on the horizontal bar, etc..

....

....

3. Tell what you saw...

....

....

....

B. Additional remarks, if any...

....

....

C. Signature of Witness..

Fig. 16-14. Statement by witness to accident.
Grover Cleveland High School, Ridgewood, N.Y.

CLAIM NO. ....
To be filled in by School

REQUEST FOR ACCIDENT BENEFIT
INTERSCHOLASTIC

SPORT ____________

Dr. ____________
X-Ray ____________
Total ____________
DO NOT WRITE IN ABOVE SPACE

1. School ____________ 4. Grade ____________
2. Name ____________ 5. Age ____________
3. Date and Time of Injury ____________ 6. No. of years of competition ____________

7. Game ______	8. Type of play at time of injury		9. Boy activity at time of injury
Practice ______	Offense ______	Run ______	Block ______
Scrimmage ______	Defense ______	Pass ______	Tackle ______
Skills ______	Rebound ______	Kick ______	Shooting ______
Night Football Game ______	Etc. ______		Etc. ______

10. Explain exactly where and how the injury occurred ____________

11. Name of the doctor who first attended or examined your injury ____________
Date and hour? ____________ STATE DATES of treatment ____________
12. After the injury I returned to the squad on ____________ (date), was not in school for ____________ days.
13. Does the parent have other insurance to cover this expense ____________

I, Principal of ____________ High School, have examined the above statements, and the statements of the Doctor or Dentist who attended this student. The statements are true to the best of my knowledge and I believe this claim to be just.

____________ (Date) ____________ (Principal)

____________ (Signature of Claimant)

This boy was given a Physical Examination on (DATE) ____________ at the beginning of THIS SPORTS SEASON, which was recorded on the regulation Physical Examination Card which is on file in the school.

____________ (Signature of Coach present at time of injury)

AFFIDAVIT OF ATTENDING PHYSICIAN

1. Date of first treatment ____________ 2. Diagnosis ____________
(Here state the nature, character and extent of injury to claimant)

3. **X-RAY READING REPORT MUST ACCOMPANY ALL CLAIMS FOR INDEMNITY FOR FRACTURE OR DISLOCATION.**

4. In your opinion was there any predisposing factor contributory to the injury? ____________
5. Give name of any consulting or assistant physician ____________
6. Describe your treatment and **State Dates** of examination or treatment ____________
7. Prognosis and General Remarks ____________

Facsimile of Physician's Fees

( ) Office Calls @ $3.00 ...... $______
( ) Home Calls @ $4.00 ...... $______
( ) Operation ...... $______
( ) X-ray ...... $______
...... $______
Total ...... $______

X-RAY not taken by you — attach official copy of report and statement for charge.

SINCE THE PROTECTION PLAN IS A NON-PROFIT ORGANIZATION ESTABLISHED TO SERVE THE SCHOOLS, THE MAXIMUM SCHEDULED INDEMNITY IS NOT TO BE CLAIMED UNLESS ITEMIZED PROFESSIONAL SERVICES JUSTIFY THAT AMOUNT AS LISTED ON REVERSE SIDE.

8. The above named student is again able to PARTICIPATE in athletics and physical education on ____________ date
9. Patient discharged from my care on ____________ date

I, a Duly Licensed Physician, personally performed the above services.
Signature of Physician: ____________ M. D.
Address ____________

Form No. 3
25M—5-62

PHYSICIAN: RETURN FORM TO SCHOOL WITH STUDENT ON LAST VISIT
All Bills Must Be Presented Within 90 Days of Accident If Claims Are To Be Paid

Fig. 16-15. Request for accident benefit form

New York State High School Athletic Protection Plan, Inc.

The following exercise should provide personal guidance for the administrator as to the establishment of an appropriate degree of prudence commensurate with the professional, as well as legal, responsibility of the contemporary administrator in physical education and athletics.*

Degree of compliance

The prudent administrator:

	Always	Frequently	Rarely	Never
1. Seeks to prohibit the situation which may lead to litigation through constant foresight and care inherent in the professional role he/she holds.	___	___	___	___
2. Assigns instructional and supervisory duties concerning an activity to only those people who are qualified for that particular activity.	___	___	___	___
3. Conducts regular inspections of all equipment used and insists on full repair of faulty items prior to use.	___	___	___	___
4. Establishes procedures and enforces rules concerning safe use of equipment and proper fitting of all uniforms and protective gear.	___	___	___	___
5. Has written plans with adequate review procedures to assure that participants do not progress too rapidly into areas of skill performance beyond their present skill level.	___	___	___	___
6. Selects opponents for each participant/team with care to avoid potentially dangerous mismatching.	___	___	___	___
7. Establishes and scrupulously enforces rules regarding reporting of illness or injury, to include compilation of written records and names and addresses of witnesses.	___	___	___	___
8. Does not treat injuries unless professionally prepared and certified to do so.	___	___	___	___
9. Regularly updates first aid and emergency medical care credentials.	___	___	___	___
10. Does not permit participation in any activity without medical approval following serious illness or injury.	___	___	___	___
11. Readily recognizes the presence of any attractive nuisance, and initiates firm control measures.	___	___	___	___
12. Posts safety rules for use of facilities, then orients students and colleagues to danger areas in activities, facilities, and personal conduct.	___	___	___	___
13. Does not place the activity area in the control of nonqualified personnel for *any* reason.	___	___	___	___
14. Relies on waiver forms not as a negation for responsibility for injury only as a means of assuring that parents/guardians recognize students' intent to participate.	___	___	___	___
15. Does not permit zeal for accomplishment or emotion of the moment to suppress rationale behavior.	___	___	___	___

*From Parsons, T.W.: What price prudence? Journal of Physical Education and Recreation **50:**45, January 1979. Courtesy American Alliance for Health, Physical Education, Recreation, and Dance, 1900 Association Dr., Reston, Va. *Continued.*

	Degree of complaince—cont'd			
	Always	*Frequently*	*Rarely*	*Never*
16. Provides in letter and spirit nondiscriminatory programs for all students.	___	___	___	___
17. Cancels transportation plans if unable to be thoroughly convinced of the personal and prudent reliability of drivers, means of transportation and adequacy of insurance coverage.	___	___	___	___
18. Does not conduct a class/or practice/or contest without a plan for medical assistance in the event of injury regardless of the setting.	___	___	___	___
19. Holds professional liability insurance of significant dollar dimensions and pertinent applicability to professional pursuits involving physical activity.	___	___	___	___
20. Does not permit excessive concern about legal liability to prohibit the development of a challenging and accountable physical education experience for each participant.	___	___	___	___

SELF-ASSESSMENT TESTS

These tests are to assist students in determining if material and competencies presented in this chapter have been mastered.

1. Without consulting your text, write out a one-sentence definition of each of the following terms: *legal liability, tort, negligence, in loco parentis, save harmless law, assumption of risk, attractive nuisance, immunity,* and *insurance management.* Check your definitions with those in the text.

2. Prepare a legal brief for a case in your state that justifies a rule that requires all students in grades 1 to 12 be required to attend physical education classes.

3. Outline recent court interpretations of sports product liability, violence, and physical education activities that are held off-campus.

4. Arrange a mock trial in your class. Have a jury, prosecutor, defendant, witnesses, and other features characteristic of a regular court trial. The case before the court is that the coach of a high school football team used a player in the final minutes of a game who had incurred a brain concussion in the first quarter. The player later died from the injury.

5. Survey the physical education and athletic programs at your college and identify any areas of negligence that might exist in the conduct of the programs. If any are found, recommend how they can be eliminated.

6. Discuss some of the legal aspects of women in sports and also of coeducational physical education classes as a result of the passage of Title IX.

7. Prepare a list of safety procedures that should be followed by every physical education teacher and coach to provide for the welfare of all students and players.

8. Prepare a sound insurance management plan for a high school physical education and athletic program. After preparing the plan, check with an insurance broker to get his or her reaction to your plan. Discuss the results with your class.

SELECTED REFERENCES

Appenzeller, H.: Bench and bar, Kendal Sports Trial **28**:12, 1973.

Arnold, D.E.: Legal aspects of off-campus physical education programs, Journal of Physical Education and Recreation **50**:21-23, April 1979.

Arnold, D.E.: Sports product liability, Journal of Physical Education and Recreation **49**:25-28, November/December 1978.

Bird, P.J.: Tort liability, Journal of Health, Physical Education, and Recreation **41**:38, 1970.

Bucher. C.A.: Football can be made safer, New York World-Telegram and Sun. Saturday Feature Magazine, September 1956.

Carpenter, L.J., and Acosta, R.V.: Violence in sport—is it part of the game or the intentional tort of battery?, Journal of Physical Education and Recreation **51**:18, September 1980.

Chambless, J.R., and Mangin, C.: Legal liability and the physical educator, Journal of Health, Physical Education, and Recreation **44**:42, 1973.

Coping with the "sue syndrome," The Athletic Educator's Report, August 1980.

Deatherage, D., and Reid, C.P.: Administration of women's competitive athletics, Dubuque, Iowa, 1977, William C. Brown Co., Publishers.

Foraker, T., et al.: School insurance, School and Community, p. 28, October 1967.

Fuoss, D.E., and Troppmann, R.J.: Creative management techniques in interscholastic athletics, New York, 1977, John Wiley & Sons, Inc.

Garber, L.O.: Yearbook of school law, Danville, Ill., 1963, The Interstate Printers & Publishers, Inc.

Gauerke, W.E.: School Law, New York, 1965, The Center for Applied Research in Education, Inc. (The Library of Education).

Grieve, A.: Legal aspects of spectator injuries, The Athletic Journal **47**:74, 1967.

Grieve, A.: State requirements for physical education, Journal of Health, Physical Education, and Recreation **42**:19, 1971.

Guenther, D.: Problems involving legal liability in schools, Journal of the American Association for Health, Physical Education, and Recreation **20**:511, 1949.

Hall, J.T., et al.: Administration; principles, theory and practice—with applications to physical education, Pacific Palisades, Calif., 1973, Goodyear Publishing Co. Inc.

Hamilton, R.R.: School liability, Chicago, 1952, National Safety Council.

Jensen, G.O.: State requirements in health and physical education, The Society of State of Health, Physical Education, and Recreation, July, 1973.

Johnson, T.P.: The court's and eligibility rules; is a new attitude emerging? Journal of Health, Physical Education, and Recreation **44**:34, 1973.

Kurtzman, J.: Legal liability and physical education, The Physical Educator **24**:20, 1967.

National Education Association, Research Division: School laws and teacher negligence; summary of who is responsible for pupil injuries, National Education Association Research Bulletin **40**: 75, 1962.

National Education Association: The pupil's day in court; review of 1968, Washington, D.C., 1969. The Association.

National Education Association: Tort liability and liability insurance, School Law Summaries. NEA Research Division, March, 1969.

Parsons, T.W.: What price prudence?, Journal of Physical Education and Recreation, **50**:45, January 1979.

Proceedings of the City Wide Conference with Principals' Representatives and Men and Women Chairmen of Health Education, City of New York Board of Education, Bureau of Health Education, 1953.

Rosenfield, H.N.: Liability for school accidents, New York, 1940, Harper & Row, Publishers.

Rosenwieg, M.: Want to file a title IX complaint?, In the Running **1**:2, Fall 1978.

Shroyer, G.F.: Coach's legal liability for athletic injuries, Scholastic Coach **34**:18, 1964.

State school laws and regulations for health, safety, driver, outdoor, and physical education, Washington, D.C., 1964, Department of Health, Education, and Welfare.

The coaches and the courts: Journal of Health, Physical Education and Recreation **41**:10, 1970.

Truesdale, J.C.: So you're a good samaritan! Journal of the American Association for Health, Physical Education, and Recreation **25**:25, 1954.

Van Der Smissen, B.: Legal liability of cities and schools for injuries in recreation and parks, including physical education and athletics, Cincinnati, 1968, suppl. 1973, W.H. Anderson Co., Legal Publishers.

Van Der Smissen, B.: Legal aspects of adult fitness programs, Journal of Health, Physical Education, and Recreation **45**: 54, 1974.

Zeigler, E.F., and Spaeth, M.J.: Administrative theory and practice in physical education and athletics, Englewood Cliffs, N.J., 1975, Prentice-Hall, Inc.

17

Winning community and professional support

Instructional objectives and competencies to be achieved

After reading this chapter the student should be able to

■ Recognize the importance of community relations to the profession in ensuring the success of physical education and athletic programs.
■ Plan a community relations program for physical education and athletics.
■ Draw implications for physical education and athletics regarding the use of such community relations media as television, radio, newspapers, magazines, and films.
■ Prepare a public relations program for each of several publics where support for physical education and athletics is needed.
■ Understand and identify basic principles that should be observed in developing and implementing a community relations program.

According to many leaders in physical education and athletics, most department, school, college, and other organization physical education programs do not have a sound and well-organized program of community and professional relations. Because of this, The Council of the City-County Director's theme for 1980-81 was "Community Awareness and Involvement." This theme was given high priority to determine community needs and interests, provide new program ideas, reemphasize physical education, and enhance the participant's experience. As part of their special feature in the *Journal of Physical Education, Recreation, and Dance,* they provided a description of several programs that had excellent community and professional relations with many benefits accruing to these programs. Two of these programs are discussed here with a description of how they were able to involve the community and bring professional recognition and prestige to their programs.

Willet* relates how physical education is alive,

well, and growing in the Oklahoma City Public Schools.

Physical education programs in Oklahoma City, despite tight budgets and staff reductions, have gained outstanding support, both financial and moral, in the last few years. For example, there were no physical education specialists in the Oklahoma School System in 1972. However, in the 1979-80 school year, 31 new physical education specialists for elementary schools were hired. Three more were added in 1980-81. In addition, 80 minutes of physical education instruction were provided each week by a specialist, the maximum size of a class was set at 35 students, and the administration stated that a system-wide physical education curriculum should be developed and implemented. In addition, financial support was provided to purchase hundreds of balls, ropes, maps, and other equipment. Monthly in-service sessions were held for the new instructors.

Physical education teachers accepted the responsibility for developing positive public relations with the faculty, administration, students, and public in general. The public in Oklahoma City responded with enthusiasm. They have given physical education excellent support and devised many money-making projects in order to do such things as install creative playgrounds.

---

*Modified from Willet, L.: Physical education—alive, well, and growing, Journal of Physical Education, Recreation, and Dance, **52**:18, 1981.

Fig. 17-1. Varsity basketball usually attracts great community interest.

Courtesy State University College at Postdam, N.Y.

In order to reach the public, the media were involved and special events were planned. One of these events was a *Physical Education Exposition*, planned and implemented by the physical education staff to demonstrate skills and activities that had been learned in the program. Another event was utilizing 5000 fifth grade students in a *Fitness Festival* to demonstrate various activities. There was extensive media coverage for each of these events.

As Willet points out, the Oklahoma City physical education program shows what can be accomplished when a team effort of administrators, teachers, parents, and community work together.

Clay,* in an article on the Norfolk, Virginia phys-

*Clay, W.B.: First class and getting better, Journal of Physical Education and Recreation, **52**:19, 1981.

ical education, health, and safety program, indicates how community awareness and involvement in this city have resulted in an outstanding physical education program. The public is involved in planning, implementing, and evaluating the program.

Clay indicates the vehicle that is most important for gaining community support is the instructional physical education program. He also relates the following successful methods that have been used over the years to interpret the program to the public.

School-parent communication. School-parent communication is carried on using several techniques. First a *Handbook for Pupils and Parents* is given to each student in the school system at the beginning of each year. It discusses the nature and scope of the program. The handbook is taken home by the students, and parents are briefed by them. Second, a *Student-Parent Interest Survey* is conducted by the physical education and research departments. This survey is designed to determine the interest and leisure-time needs of both parents and students and whether the physical education program is meeting these needs and interests.

Government and agency cooperation. The number of agencies and businesses in Norfolk that cooperate with the physical education department is outstanding. The Norfolk Chamber of Commerce has developed an "Adopt-a-School" program whereby a business or corporation adopts a school nearby or in which it is interested and helps to contribute to its physical education program by building facilities or helping in other ways. As a result of this project the Chesapeake and Potomac Telephone Company adopted Granby High School and constructed the Granby Community Track, officially dedicated on June 5, 1980. This $100,000 facility was built through volunteer effort at little cost to the public.

The United Virginia Bank adopted Maury High in the spring of 1980. It had a new gymnasium, swimming, and tennis courts, but it did not have a track. As a result, friends and alumni of the school raised $15,000 and construction companies contributed the rest.

Many other agencies and community organizations contribute to the physical education program. The Norfolk Parks and Recreation Department helps by providing six instructors annually to teach pupils swimming. The Norfolk police department and Tidewater rape crisis center conduct a crime-resistance program. The Norfolk Public Works Department installed walkways and ramps at an outdoor education facility. The Norfolk Mayor's Youth Commission provided the physical education department with two outdoor swimming pools.

Community sponsors. Several community organizations in Norfolk sponsor activities for the school program. For example, the Northside Norfolk Rotary Club sponsors an Annual Leisure Time Track and Field Demonstration; the Khedive Shrine Temple sponsors Sportscope, the Annual Physical Education Demonstration; the Cosmopolitan Club of Norfolk and 36 cooperating organizations sponsor a Health Education Fair; the Tidewater Heart Association and the Norfolk Paramedics train health and physical education teachers to teach cardiopulmonary resuscitation to all eighth, tenth, and eleventh grade students; the Tidewater Virginia Lung Association and other organizations provide instruction in smoking and alcohol; and more than 75 agencies provide instructional materials, financial aid, or other assistance to the physical education, health, and safety department.

The Norfolk physical education program is an excellent example of how community involvement can enhance its offerings, offer service to the community, and provide for the interests and needs, not only of students but also of adults.

Today, when budget cutbacks are affecting physical education and athletic programs, a sound community relations program is needed to interpret to the public the worth of physical education and athletics. For example, it has been estimated that over half of all school bond issues were defeated in recent years. Such defeats produce revenue losses that frequently result in smaller budgets for physical education and athletic programs. A sound community relations program is needed to prevent such cutbacks.

Sometimes the terms *community relations* and *professional relations* are interpreted by physical educators to mean radio and television. However, they should not forget that the most effective avenues of community and professional relations include relations with students and adult participants, the leadership role exerted by physical educators in their communities, the personal contacts established with various groups in the community, and communications media such as correspondence, records, and telephone conversations.

Community relations defined

Community relations is a much-defined term. Some of the common definitions for this term as given by experts in this specialized field follow. Philip Lesly speaks of it as comprising the activities and attitudes used to influence, judge, and control the opinion of any individual, group, or groups of persons in the interest of some other individuals. Professor Harwood L. Childs defines it as a name for those activities and relations with others that are public and that have significance socially. J. Handly Wright and Byron H. Christian, experts in public relations, refer to it as a program that has the characteristics of careful planning and proper conduct, which in turn will result in public understanding and confidence. Edward L. Bernays, who has written widely on the subject of public relations, lists three items in his definition: first, information for public

Fig. 17-2. College basketball is highly competitive and has become a very popular activity.

Courtesy Cramer Products, Inc., Gardner, Kan.

Fig. 17-3. Kindergarten children performing Chinese ribbon dance at physical education demonstration at Oak View Elementary School in Fiarfax, Va.

Fig. 17-4. Wisconsin State College at LaCrosse uses a physical education demonstration to inform the public about its work.

consumption; second, an attempt to modify the attitudes and actions of the public through persuasion; and third, the objective of attempting to integrate the attitudes and actions of the public and of the organization or people who are conducting the public relations program. Benjamin Fine, a former specialist in educational community relations defines community relations as the entire body of relationships that make up our impressions of an individual, an organization, or an idea.

These selected definitions of community relations help clarify its importance for any organization, institution, or group of individuals trying to develop an enterprise, profession, or business. Community relations considers such important factors as consumers' interests, human relationships, public understanding, and good will. In business, it attempts to show the important place that specialized enterprises have in society and how they exist and operate in the public interest. In education, it is concerned with public opinion, the needs of the school or college,

and acquainting constituents with what is being done in the public interest. It also concerns itself with acquainting the community with the educational problems that must be considered to render a greater service.

Some of the purposes of school community relations include: (1) serving as a public information source concerning school activities, (2) aiding the promotion of confidence in the schools or other organizations, (3) gathering support for school or organizational funding and programs, (4) stressing the value of education of all individuals, (5) improving communication between students, teachers, parents, and community members, (6) evaluating school and organization programs, and (7) correcting misunderstandings and misinformation concerning the aims and objectives of the school or other organizations.

Community relations means the opinions of the populace must be considered. Public opinion is powerful, and individuals, organizations, and institutions succeed or fail in terms of its influence. Therefore, to have good community relations, the interests of human beings and what is good for people in general must be considered.

The practice of community relations is pertinent to all areas of human activity: religion, education, business, politics, military, government, labor, and other affairs. A sound community relations program is not hit-or-miss. It is planned with considerable care, and great amounts of time and effort are necessary to produce results. Furthermore, it is not something in which only the top management, executives, or administrative officers should be interested. For any organization to have a good program, all members must be community relations–conscious.

The extent to which interest has grown in community relations is indicated by the number of individuals specializing in it. The *Public Relations Directory and Yearbook* lists personnel who specialize in this work. A recent edition of this publication listed nearly 1000 individuals who are working independently, approximately 5000 who were directors of public relations with business firms, approximately 2000 who were associated with trade and professional groups, and nearly 1000 who were with social organizations. In a recent Manhattan telephone directory there were over 500 names listed under the heading of ''Public Relations.'' In contrast, in 1935, there were only 10 names.

The importance of community relations is being increasingly recognized for the part it can play in educational, business, or social advancement. All need public support and understanding to survive. Community relations helps obtain these essentials.

Planning the community relations program

Community relations programs are more effective when they are planned by many interested and informed individuals and groups. Such individuals and groups as school boards, management personnel, teachers, administrators, and citizens' committees can provide valuable assistance in certain areas of the community relations program. These people, serving in an advisory capacity to physical education and athletic departments, can help immeasurably in planning a community relations program by following the following specific steps, which have been identified by one expert in community relations:

1. Establish a sound public communications policy.
2. Determine what services will yield the greatest dividends.
3. Obtain facts about what citizens do and do not know and believe about educational values and needs.
4. Decide what facts and ideas will best enable citizens to understand the benefits obtained from good programs and what improvements will increase these benefits.
5. Make full use of effective planning techniques to generate understanding and appreciation.
6. Relate cost to opportunity for participants to achieve.
7. Decide who is going to perform specific communication tasks at particular times.

After the community relations plan is put into operation, it is important to test and evaluate its results and then improve the educational program accordingly.

Community relations media

Many media can be employed in a community relations program. Some have more significance in certain localities than others. Some are more readily accessible than others. Physical educators, athletic directors, and coaches should survey their communities to determine media that can be used and will be most effective.

PROGRAM AND STAFF

The program and the staff represent the best media for an effective community relations program. Through the activities and experiences provided and the leadership given, much good will may be built for any school, college, department, or profession.

Another important consideration is that the most effective community relations is carried on person-to-person. This might be teacher to student, student to parent, teacher to citizen, or physical educator to participant. In all cases the participant is an important consideration, indeed the most important means of communication.

Fig. 17-5. Gymnastic display at Renfrew Community Center in Vancouver.

Courtesy Board of Parks and Public Recreation, Vancouver, B.C.

NEWSPAPERS

The newspaper is one of the most common and useful media for disseminating information. It reaches a large audience and can be helpful in interpreting physical education and athletics to the public at large. Some questions that might be asked to determine what makes a good news story are: Is the news of interest to the public? Are the facts correct? Is the style direct? Is it written in the third person in a layperson's vocabulary, and is it well organized? Does it include news on individuals who are closely related to the schools, colleges, or other organization? Does the article have a plan of action, and does it play a significant part in interpreting the program?

When a story is submitted to a newspaper, the following standard rules apply to copy preparation:

1. Prepare all copy in typewritten form as neatly as possible, double-spaced, and on one side of the paper only.

2. The name, address, and telephone number of your organization should be on page one, in the upper left-hand corner. Also at the top of page one, but below the address, should be the headline and release date for the story.

3. Paragraphs should be short, and if the story necessitates more than one page, write the word "more" at the end of each page. At the top of each additional page, list the name of the story in the upper left-hand corner. The symbols # # # should be placed at the end of the article.

One expert on newspapers has pointed out that the most common reasons for rejecting material include limited reader interest, poor writing, inaccuracies, and insufficient information.

PICTURES AND GRAPHICS

Pictures represent an effective medium for public relations. Two words should be kept in mind by the persons who take and select the pictures for pub-

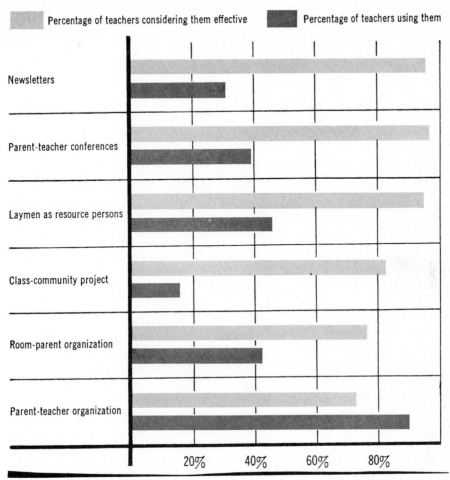

Fig. 17-6. Community relations techniques and their use.

From NEA Research Bulletin **37:**39, 1959.

lication: "action" and "people." Pictures that reflect action are more interesting and appealing than still pictures. Furthermore, pictures with people in them are more effective than ones that do not. Usually a few people are better than many. Finally, such considerations as good background, accuracy in details, clearness, and educational significance should not be forgotten.

Educational problems, such as budgets, statistical information regarding growth of school population, information about participation in various school or college activities, and many other items relating to schools and other organizations can be made more

interesting, intelligible, and appealing if presented through colorful and artistic charts, graphs, and diagrams.

MAGAZINES

Thousands of popular magazines, professional journals, trade publications, and other periodicals are published today.

Such national magazines as *Newsweek, U.S. News and World Report, McCall's,* and *Reader's Digest* are excellent for publicity purposes. It is, however, difficult to get stories in such publications because of their rigid requirements and because the editors like to cover the stories with their own staff writers. Many times it is better to suggest ideas to them rather than to submit a manuscript. Other methods may be used. One can attempt to interest the editors in some particular work being done and have them send a staff writer to cover the story. It might be possible to get a free-lance writer interested in the organization and have him or her develop a story. Someone on the department staff with writing skill can be assigned to write a piece for magazine consumption and then submit it to various periodicals for consideration.

PUBLIC SPEAKING

Public speaking can be an effective medium for community relations. Public addresses to civic and social groups in the community, at public affairs, gatherings, and professional meetings afford good opportunities for interpreting one's profession to the public. However, it is important to do a commendable job, or the result can be poor rather than good community relations.

To make an effective speech, one should observe many fundamentals, including mastery of the subject, sincere interest and enthusiasm, interest in putting thoughts rather than the speaker across to the public, directness, straightforwardness, preparation, brevity, and clear and distinct enunciation.

If the organization is large enough and there are several qualified speakers within it, a speaker's bureau may be an asset. Various civic, school, college, church, and other leaders within a community can be informed of the services the organization has to offer. Then, when the requests come in, speakers can be assigned on the basis of qualifications and availability. The entire department or organization should set up facilities and make information and material available for the preparation of such speeches. If desired by the members of the organization, inservice training courses could even be worked out in conjunction with the English department or some experienced person in developing this particular phase of the community relations program.

DISCUSSION GROUPS

Discussion groups, forums, and similar meetings are frequently held in communities. At such gather-

ings, representatives from the community, including educators, industrialists, businesspeople, physicians, laywers, clergy, union leaders, and others, discuss topics of general interest. This is an excellent setting to clarify issues, clear up misunderstandings, enlighten civic leaders and discuss the pros and cons of community projects. Physical educators should play a larger role in such meetings than in the past. Much good could be done for these specialized fields through this medium.

RADIO AND TELEVISION

Radio and television are powerful communication media because of their universal appeal. These media are well worth the money spent for public relations, if this is the only way they are available. First, however, the possibilities of obtaining free time should be thoroughly examined. The idea of public service will influence some radio and television station managers to grant free time to an organization. This may be in the nature of an item included in a newscast program, a spot announcement, or a public service program that uses a quarter, half, or even a full hour.

Some radio and television stations are reserved for educational purposes. This possibility should be investigated. Many schools and colleges have stations of their own that may be used.

Sometimes one must take advantage of these media on short notice; therefore, it is important for an organization to be prepared with written plans that can be put into operation immediately. This might make the difference between being accepted or rejected for such an assignment. The organization must also be prepared to assume the work involved in rehearsals, preparation of scenery, or other items essential in presenting such a program.

Radio and television offer some of the best means of reaching a large number of people at one time. As such, organizations concerned with physical education and athletics should continually use their imaginations to translate the story of their professions into material that can be used effectively by these media.

FILMS

Films can present dramatically and informatively such stories as an organization's services to the pub-

Fig. 17-7. Community involvement in cross-country run in Vancouver, B.C.
Courtesy Board of Parks and Public Recreation.

Fig. 17-8. Omaha
Public Schools use
television in physical
education classes.

lic and highlights in the training of its leaders. They constitute an effective medium for presenting a story briefly. A series of visual impressions will remain long in the minds of the audience.

Because such a great majority of the American people enjoy movies today, it is important to consider them in any community relations program. Movies are not only a form of entertainment but also an effective medium of information and education. Films stimulate attention, create interest, and provide a way of getting across information not inherent in printed matter.

Movies, slides, slide film, educational television, and other phases of these visual aids have been used by a number of departments of physical education and athletics to present their programs to the public and to interest individuals in their work. Voluntary associations, professional associations, and official agencies in these fields have also used them to advantage.

POSTERS, EXHIBITS, BROCHURES, DEMONSTRATIONS, MISCELLANEOUS MEDIA

Posters, exhibits, and brochures are important in any public relations program concerned with physical education and athletics. Well-illustrated, brief, and attractive brochures can visually and informatively depict activities, facilities, projects, and services that a department or organization has as part of its total program.

Drawings, paintings, charts, graphs, pictures, and other aids, when placed on posters and given proper distribution, will illustrate activities, show progress, and present information visually. These media will attract and interest public thinking.

Exhibits, when properly prepared, interestingly presented, and properly located, such as in store window or some other prominent spot, can do much to demonstrate work being done by an organization.

Demonstrations that present the total program of an organization or profession entertainingly and informatively have a place in any community relations program. The main objectives for a physical education demonstration are to: (1) inform the public and provide an outlet for interest in physical education

programs by community members, (2) provide an opportunity for members of an organization to work together toward a common goal, (3) demonstrate the need and benefit of physical education to all participants, (4) provide opportunities for the general public to see the physical education program in action, (5) contribute to the objectives of the organization, (6) include all participants in the activities, (7) reflect the needs of the consumer in the present and in the future, and (8) contribute to the health, social, and emotional well-being of participants and spectators.

Other miscellaneous media, such as correspondence in the forms of letters and messages to parents, student publications, and reports, offer opportunities to develop good relations and favorable understanding concerning schools, colleges, and other organizations and the work they are doing. Every opportunity must be used to build good community relations.

PBBS and community relations

School systems using PPBS have found it easier to take their budget problems to the public and gain positive support. Where taxpayers are given a clear picture of the budget in terms of overall educational objectives, they can see the need for funding requirements and therefore will be more likely to support bond issues and other funding programs. PPBS budgets can be expressed in terms the layperson can easily understand. Areas of the program suffering from funding inadequacies can more easily be appreciated in terms of PPBS.

The PEPI Project

The Physical Education Public Information (PEPI) Project is designed to educate the public regarding the vital contribution of physical education to children, youths, and adults. Through the project, the use of local media—press, radio, and television—is emphasized as a means of gaining greater public understanding.

In its initial phase the project identified a local PEPI coordinator for each of the nation's 100 largest metropolitan (listening and viewing) areas. (There are now more than 600 PEPI coordinators.) The PEPI coordinator's responsibility is to organize and report PEPI activity in his or her area. This means such things as arranging with local radio and television stations for programming.

PEPI was developed by the Physical Education Division of the AAHPERD and funded by the AAHPERD. The President's Council on Physical Fitness and Sports also provides both technical and material support for PEPI.

The basic concepts of the PEPI program include: (1) physical education is a form of health insurance, (2) physical education contributes to academic achievement, (3) physical education contributes to lifetime sports skills, and (4) physical education helps develop a positive self-concept and an ability to both compete and cooperate with others.

The PEPI Action Corps (PAC) was organized to aid PEPI coordinators with public information and media contact. PAC consultants were selected on the basis of their enthusiasm and outstanding achievements in behalf of physical education. Some of the consultants have their own television and radio programs, and all act in an advisory position to further the objective of publicizing the benefits of physical education.

The many publics

For any community relations program to be successful, accurate facts must be presented. To establish what facts are to be given to the public, the particular public at which the program is directed must be known.

A public is a group of people drawn together by common interests who are in a specific geographic area, or characterized by some other common feature. The people in the United States comprise hundreds of different publics—farmers, organized laborers, unorganized workers, students, professional people, and veterans. The various publics may be national, regional, and local. They can be classified according to race or nationality, age, religion, occupation, politics, sex, income, profession, economic level, or business, fraternal, and educational backgrounds. Each organization or group with a special interest

is a public. The community relations–minded person must always think in terms of the publics with which he or she desires to promote understanding and how they can best be reached.

To have a meaningful and purposeful community relations program, it is essential to obtain some facts about these various publics, to know their understanding of the professions, their needs and interests, their health practices and hobbies, and other essential information.

Public opinion decides whether a profession is important or not, whether it meets an essential need, and whether it is making a contribution to enriched living. It determines the success or failure of a department, school, institution, business, or profession. Public opinion is dynamic and continually changing. Public opinion results from the interaction of people. Public opinion has great impact, and any group or organization that wants to survive should know as much about it as possible.

To get information on what the public thinks, why it thinks as it does, and how it reaches its conclusions, various techniques may be used. Surveys, questionnaires, opinion polls, interviews, expert opinion, discussions, and other techniques have proved valuable. Anyone interested in community relations should be acquainted with these various techniques.

Public opinion is formed to a great degree as a result of influences in early life, such as the effect of parents, home, and environment; on the basis of people's own experiences in everyday living, what they see, hear, and experience in other ways; and finally by communication media such as newspapers, radio, and television. It is important not only to be aware of these facts but also to remember that one is dealing with many different publics, each requiring a special source of research and study to know the most effective way to plan, organize, and administer the community relations program.

Community relations in practice

A survey was conducted among eleven school systems to determine the nature and scope of their professional and community relations programs. Several questions were asked of physical education personnel through personal interviews. The information gained from these interviews is highlighted in the following paragraphs.

POLICIES

1. The director of physical education and athletics was directly responsible for all public relations releases to the press.
2. All printed matter needed the approval of the director and the superintendent of schools before being released.
3. The coaches of interscholastic athletics were responsible for preparing all releases regarding their programs.
4. Each physical educator was urged to recognize that his or her activities were part of the professional and community relations programs of the school.

COMMUNICATION

The following communications media were used:

Total physical education program
Newspaper
Posters
Films
Public speaking
School publications
Newsletter
Letters to parents
Demonstrations and exhibits
Personal contact
Pictures
Radio
Television
Window displays
Brochures
Sports days
Bulletin boards

The five media found to be the most effective in their professional and public relations programs were (1) the total physical education program, (2) personal contact, (3) newspapers, (4) public speaking, and (5) demonstrations and exhibits.

All the directors of physical education and athletics indicated that athletics received more publicity than any other phase of the physical education program. When asked why they thought this was so, some typical comments were: "The public demands it,"

"It is required because of public interest," and "The newspapers will only accept and print releases on athletics."

THE DESIRED MESSAGE TO COMMUNICATE TO THE PUBLIC

When the directors were asked, "What message are you trying to convey to the public?" the following were typical answers:

1. The value of the total physical education and athletic programs.
2. The importance of the programs to the student.
3. Recognition and achievement of all students in all areas of physical education and athletics.
4. Efforts and energies being expended to give each person a worthwhile experience in physical education and athletics.
5. The role of the physical education and athletic programs in enhancing the health and welfare of the participant.
6. The aims and objectives of the total physical education and athletic programs.

GUIDING PRINCIPLES

In summary, the professional and community relations programs in the eleven school districts were conducted in light of the following principles:

1. Each physical education and athletic department recognized the importance of an active community relations program.
2. Definite policies guided the program.
3. Responsibility for community relations was shared by all members of the department, with the central authority residing with the director.
4. Many different communications media were used to interpret the program to the numerous publics.
5. The total physical education and athletic program was recognized as being the most effective medium of professional and community relations.
6. Efforts were made to interpret accurate facts about physical education to the public.
7. Considerable planning was needed for the effective utilization of public relations media.

LIMITATIONS OF COMMUNITY RELATIONS PROGRAMS

Some obvious limitations of the professional and community relations programs surveyed follow:

Fig. 17-9.
Demonstrations as
part of a public relations
program. Gamma Phi
gym circus.

Illinois State University,
Normal, Ill.

1. Information had not been gained through research on how various publics thought and felt about physical education and athletics—what they did and did not know concerning these special fields.
2. There was a lack of budgetary allocations to carry on a professional and community relations program.
3. No specific plans had been established to evaluate the professional and community relations programs in the various schools.
4. Communications media emphasized mainly the role of athletics in the total physical education program.
5. Information had not been gained through research on what services most benefited pupils and what facts best enabled the public to understand the benefits derived from such programs.
6. There was a lack of effective pupil-teacher planning techniques.

Principles of community relations

Principles to observe in developing a community relations program follow:

1. Community relations should be considered internally before being developed externally. The support of everyone within the organization, from the top administrator down to the last worker, should be procured. Furthermore, such items as purpose of program, person or persons responsible, funds available, media to use, and tools to carry on the program should be primary considerations.
2. A community relations program should be outlined and put in writing, and every member of the organization should become familiar with it. The better it is

known and understood, the better chance it has of succeeding.

3. The persons directly in charge of the community relations program must have complete knowledge of the professional services being rendered; the attitudes of those who are members of the profession and of the organization represented; and the nature, background, and reaction of the consumers and of all the publics directly or indirectly related to the job being performed.

4. After all the information has been gathered, a program should be developed that meets the needs as shown by research.

5. Adequate funds should be available to do the job. Furthermore, the person or persons in charge of the community relations program should be given freedom to spend this money in whatever ways they feel will be most helpful and productive for the organization.

6. The formation of a community relations staff will be determined by the needs of the organization, the amount of money available, the attitude of the administration, and the size of the organization. If additional staff members are available, special talents should be sought to provide effectively for a well-rounded program.

7. Individuals assigned community relations work should stay in the background instead of seeking the limelight, keep abreast of the factors that affect the program, develop a wide acquaintance, and make contacts that will be helpful.

8. As a community relations program is developed, the following items should be checked: Is there a handbook or a newsletter to keep members of the organization informed? Is there a system for dispensing information to local radio and press outlets? Is there a booklet, flyer, or printed matter that tells the story of the organization? Do members of the organization participate regularly in community affairs? Is there provision for a speakers' bureau where civic clubs and other organizations may procure speakers on various topics? Does the organization hold open house for interested persons? Does the organization have a film or other visual material that can be shown to interested groups and that explains and interprets the work?

9. A good community relations program will employ all available resources and machinery to disseminate information to the public to ensure adequate coverage.

SELF-ASSESSMENT TESTS

These tests are to assist students in determining if material and competencies presented in this chapter have been mastered:

1. As an administrator you are conducting a staff meeting in your organization. Explain to your staff why you feel that an inservice program in professional and community relations would be valuable to staff members and administrators alike.

2. Outline what you consider to be an effective professional and community relations plan for a program of physical education and athletics.

3. Prepare a news release or a story on some event or phase of a physical education or athletic program to be published or broadcast to the public at large. Have the class evaluate your release or story.

4. What is meant by the fact that physical education and athletics are dealing with not just one but many publics? Identify two different publics and indicate what type of community relations program you would use with each and how they differ from each other.

5. List some principles that should be observed in professional and community relations. How would you apply some of these principles to communicate the importance of a strong physical education program in your school?

SELECTED REFERENCES

American Association for Health, Physical Education, and Recreation: PEPI-GRAMS, a series of communications on the Physical Education Public Information Project, 1972.

American Association for Health, Physical Education, and Recreation: Physical education—an interpretation, Washington, D.C., The Association.

Bronzan, R.T.: Public relations, promotions and fund raising for athletic and physical education programs, New York, 1977, John Wiley & Sons, Inc.

Bucher, C.A.: Play and your child's report card (syndicated newspaper column), Washington, D.C., May, 1972, President's Council on Physical Fitness and Sports.

Bucher, C.A.: Back to school—what kind of education is relevant? (syndicated newspaper column), Washington, D.C., September, 1972, President's Council on Physical Fitness and Sports.

Bucher, C.A.: Foundations of physical education, ed. 9, St. Louis, 1983, The C.V. Mosby Co.

Bucher, C.A., and Koenig, C.: Methods and materials for secondary school physical education, ed. 6, St. Louis, 1983, The C.V. Mosby Co.

Bucher, C.A., and Thaxton, N.: Physical education and sport: change and challenge, St. Louis, 1981, The C.V. Mosby Co.

Caldwell, S.F.: Toward a humanistic physical education, Journal of Health, Physical Education, and Recreation **43:**31, 1972.

Clay, W.B.: First class and getting better, Journal of Physical Education, Recreation, and Dance **52:**19-21, June 1981.

Deatherage, D., and Reid, C.P.: Administration of women's competitive sports, Dubuque, Iowa, 1977, William C. Brown Co., Publishers.

Fuoss, D.E., and Troppmann, R.J.: Creative management techniques in interscholastic athletics, New York, 1977, John Wiley & Sons, Inc.

Geyer, C.: Physical education for the electronic age, Journal of Health, Physical Education, and Recreation **43:**32, 1972.

Healey, W.: Physical education demonstrations, Journal of Health, Physical Education, and Recreation **42:**43, 1971.

Lepke, P.: PR for PE, Journal of Health, Physical Education, and Recreation **44:**10, 1973.

Marsh, D.B.: Program promotion, Journal of Physical Education, Recreation, and Dance **52:**24-25, June 1981.

McCloskey, G.: Planning the public relations program, National Education Association Journal **59:**17, 1970.

McLaughlin, R.D.: "Chip-n-block" for parental involvement, Journal of Physical Education, Recreation, and Dance **52:**22-23, June 1981.

Muller, P., et al.: Intramural-recreational sports: programming and administration, New York, 1979, John Wiley & Sons, Inc.

Parkhouse, B.L., and Lapin, J.: The woman in athletic administration, Santa Monica, Calif., 1980, Goodyear Publishing Co., Inc.

PEPI-GRAM #9: A report of progress, Journal of Health, Physical Education, and Recreation **44:**10, 1973.

Smith, N.W.: Community involvement through a curriculum study project, Journal of Physical Education, Recreation, and Dance **52:**16-17, June 1981.

Wagenhals, J.G.: Involving parents in after school activity programs, Journal of Physical Education and Recreation **51:**13 October 1980.

Willet, L.: Physical education—alive, well, and growing, Journal of Physical Education, Recreation, and Dance **52:**18, June 1981.

18

Office management

Instructional objectives and competencies to be achieved

After reading this chapter the student should be able to

■ Appreciate the importance of efficient office management in the administration of a physical education and athletic program.
■ Justify the need for office personnel in the administration of a physical education and athletic program.
■ Identify basic office administrative procedures that should be observed in conducting the affairs of a physical education and athletic program.
■ List the records that should be maintained in a physical education and athletic administrator's office.

Office management has often been neglected by physical educators and administrators. Efficient office management often indicates a well-run department. The office is the place for first impressions, communication between student and teacher and consumer and business executive, the focus of administrative duties, and a point of contact for the administration and staff members.

Office management tasks

Office management is responsible for many important tasks, including the following:

1. Communication. The office is the nerve center of the organization whereby information is transmitted to various staff members and other members via such means as face-to-face conferences, telephone, correspondence, and intercom systems.

2. Correspondence. The office is the setting for preparing and filing letters for administrators and staff members and for handling their incoming and outgoing mail.

3. Supplies and equipment. The office is the place for requesting, receiving, and disbursing supplies and equipment needed in conducting the organization's various activities.

4. Processing materials. The office is a central point for duplicating and typing materials pertinent to the administration of the program.

5. Record keeping. The office is the place where pertinent records involving matters concerned with staff members, students, athletes, and materials are kept.

6. Report preparation. The office is a place for preparing reports for various staff members, as well as for officers and personnel to whom the administration is required to report.

7. Budget preparation and implementation. The office is where budget information is centralized, where revenues and expenditures are recorded, and where financial reports and summaries are compiled.

8. Community and public relations. The office is a key communications center for the conduct, planning, and administration of community and professional projects that are closely related and important to the achievement of the goals and functions of the organization.

9. Emergencies. The office is a focal point for

meeting day-to-day emergency situations that arise and call for immediate action.

Importance of office management

Colleagues, business prospects, new members, pupils, and visitors frequently have their initial contacts with physical education departments in the central office. Their reception, the courtesies they are shown, the efficiency with which the office work is carried out, and other operational details leave lasting impressions. Friends are often made or lost at this strategic point.

CENTER FOR COMMUNICATIONS

'Office work, broadly conceived, is the handling and management of information. The office is usually the place where schedules are arranged and distributed, telephone calls made and received, reports typed and mimeographed, bulletins prepared and issued, conferences arranged and held, appointments made and confirmed, and greetings voiced and exchanged. The office represents the hub of activity around which revolves the efficient functioning of the physical education personnel. Unless these communications are carried out with dispatch, accurately and courteously, the entire administrative process breaks down.

FOCUS OF ADMINISTRATIVE DUTIES

The chief administrative personnel, secretarial assistants, and clerical help constitutes the office staff. The filing system, key records, and reports are usually housed in the office. When inventories need to be examined, letters pulled from files, or the chairperson of the department consulted on important matters, the office is frequently the point of contact. Administrative responsibilities are carried out in the office, making this space a point of focus for the entire organization.

POINT OF CONTACT FOR ADMINISTRATION AND STAFF MEMBERS

Staff members visit the office regularly. Mailboxes are located there, and telephone calls may be taken in the office. Conferences and appointments with pupils and visitors often bring staff members to the office. Constant communication takes place between the administration and staff members in this setting. The atmosphere in the office can create high staff morale, efficiency, a friendly climate, and a feeling of working toward common goals.

Relation of administration to office staff members

The administration should establish effective human relations with office staff members. Secretaries and other personnel should have a feeling of belonging and a recognition that they are an important part of the organization. The work each one performs is essential to the achievement of the organization's goals.

Most administrators depend heavily on their office staff members to carry out day-to-day duties and routines efficiently and productively. Furthermore, administrators are frequently away from their desks on organization assignments. In their absence the office needs to function in the same efficient manner as though the administrator was present. These goals cannot be achieved unless there is an excellent working relationship between the administration and office staff members.

In-service education of office staff members. The administration should encourage office staff members to engage in in-service education and also be alert to the improvement of office procedures. Some areas where improvement might take place include typing and shorthand skills, answering telephones, personal appearance, office housekeeping, updating the filing system, simplifying record keeping, and human relations skills.

Sexual harassment of office staff members. Sexual harassment of office staff members is a problem that has been revealed in recent years. Newspaper stories and court cases have described how sexual harassment in business and corporate affairs has been used against women who desire to get promotions, salary raises, and stay on the job. Administrators must recognize that such methods cannot be tolerated. The administrator who uses sexual harassment to achieve personal erotic desires and to ease his passions is asking for trouble. This trouble may take the form of litigation, public censure, reprimand, or dismissal.

There have been a few cases where men administrators have been unjustly accused of sexual harassment by women and vice versa, seeking to achieve their own personal goals. The best advice to administrators is to behave in such a way that their behavior does not suggest thay are making advances toward members of the opposite sex.

Office space

The central office for the physical education and athletic department, in accordance with its clearinghouse activities, should be readily accessible. This office should be near health service and athletic training offices, gymnasiums, exercise rooms, locker rooms, athletic fields, and other facilities of the department.

Most central offices for physical education and athletics should consist of at least three divisions: general reception area, clerical space, and private offices. Other desirable features to be considered are a bathroom, storage room, and conference room for staff and other meetings.

GENERAL RECEPTION AREA

The general reception office is used by visitors as a waiting room or information center, for staff members who desire to get their mail, have appointments, or wish information, and for office services in general. It should be attractive, with some pictures on the wall, comfortable chairs, bulletin boards, and other items essential to carrying out the necessary administrative routines and creating a warm, friendly climate. A counter or railing should separate the general waiting room from the rest of the office facilities. This helps ensure greater privacy and more efficient conduct of office responsibilities.

CLERICAL SPACE

The clerical space should be separated from the general waiting and reception room. It should be equipped with typewriters, files, tables, and telephones. It is often desirable to have a private alcove

or office for one or more of the secretaries, depending on the size of the department and office. Privacy is often needed for typing, preparing reports, or for the convenience of visitors and other personnel. There should be ample lighting, freedom of movement, and sufficient space for the various administrative duties to be carried out with a minimum of confusion and difficulty.

PRIVATE OFFICES

The chairperson of the department and possibly other personnel, depending on the size of the department, should have private offices. The offices should be such that the persons in charge of administration can concentrate on their work without interruptions, have private conferences with students, staff members, or visitors, and in general carry out their duties as efficiently as possible. The offices should be decorated and equipped appropriately. Desks should be neat and large enough, with calendars, schedule pads for appointments and conferences, and other essential materials. Filing cases, storage cabinets, and other equipment should be provided as needed. The staff should also be provided with offices whenever possible.

Office personnel

The number of office personnel depends on the size of the department. The staff can consist of secretaries, stenographers, transcribing machine operators, a receptionist, switchboard operator, and typists in a large department. However, the office usually consists of one secretary. In some small schools, student help may be all the personnel available.

The *secretary* should be a good right arm to the chairperson and to the department as a whole. To be most helpful, he or she will be a typist, a stenographer, and a public relations representative, will operate a dictaphone, photocopier, and mimeograph machine, and will see that the office runs smoothly. The secretary will help the chairperson and other staff members remember facts, appointments, and other important information. He or she should know where materials are filed and be able to obtain them quickly, relieve the supervisor of minor details, and

Fig. 18-1. The secretary should be a good right arm to the administrator. Office in senior high school, Mamaroneck, N.Y.

see that reports are sent out on time and that accurate records are kept.

A *stenographer* is a typist who can also take shorthand. A stenographer, however, differs from a secretary. The stenographer usually takes dictation and types letters and other material but does not have the personal relationship and confidential duties a secretary has. Large departments frequently have stenographic pools wherein individuals are on call to do work for any staff member having work to be done.

A *transcribing operator* takes correspondence and other material that has been dictated and listens to a dictaphone or other playback mechanism on which such information has been recorded. Using earphones, he or she sits at a typewriter and listens and types in accordance with the instructions given.

A *receptionist's* position will vary with the department. In some departments a receptionist is a greeter who presents an attractive appearance and is polite, courteous, and helpful to callers. Some departments also assign to this person certain typing, filing, and telephone duties, in addition to the reception of callers.

Large departments frequently have *switchboard operators* who cover the phones for many staff members and other personnel. Frequently staff members are not in, and messages are then relayed by the switchboard operator through the prescribed channels.

Office personnel should be selected very carefully. Experience, character, personality, appearance, and ability should play important roles in the selection process. The secretary should have, as a minimum, a high school diploma. An individual who has been through the commerical course and who has a good background in typewriting, bookkeeping, English, and secretarial practice is valuable to the department.

The chairperson of the department and other staff members should treat a secretary and other office personnel with respect. Staff members should be patient and see that clerical help know the details of their jobs, recognize the importance of each, and appreciate the responsibilities of their positions.

In small high schools, elementary schools, and colleges, the administrator may have to rely partially or entirely on *students* to get some of the clerical work accomplished. Inservice education should take place for these students to see that acceptable procedures are followed in filing, typing, mimeographing, maintaining records, and performing other office duties.

Equipment and supplies

Whether or not an office is efficient depends on the equipment and supplies available. The materials needed vary with the size of the organization. In smaller organizations such equipment as adding machines might readily be available in the central office but not in departmental offices. Following are some of the items that should be considered:

Adding machine	Paste
Bookcases	Pencil sharpeners
Bulletin boards	Pencils and pens
Buzzers	Photocopier
Calendars	Reproducing machines
Chairs	Rulers
Clips	Safe
Cloak racks	Scissors
Clock	Scrapbooks
Desk baskets	Stamps
Desk lights	Stapling machine
Desk pads	Stationery and paper
Desks	Tables
Dictionaries	Telephone
Ditto machine	Typewriters
First aid cabinet	Umbrella rack
Letter trays	Wardrobe cabinets
Magazine racks	Wastebaskets
Paper cutter	

In some large offices where many details are handled, data processing equipment should be available.

Office work and automation

Whether or not new automated equipment should be installed in the office depends on such factors as the extent of the program the office serves, the amount of clerical work that needs to be done, and the size of the budget.

When considering whether or not more mechanized equipment should be added to the office, five important questions should be asked: (1) *How much labor will it save?* In other words, can it result in the elimination of office personnel or can it result in not having to hire another office worker? (2) *How much time will it save?* Is time a major consideration so as to provide office personnel with more time to perform other essential tasks? (3) *Will it ensure more accuracy?* Will the machine help to eliminate human errors such as those involved in computation tasks? (4) *Will it provide for a more efficient operation?* Will the office run more efficiently as a result of purchasing the machine? (5) *Is the cost of the machine a sound investment?* Will the machine pay for itself

in the work it performs? (6) *Will the machine contribute to the morale of office staff members?* Will the machine eliminate some tasks office staff members find difficult to do or that are tedious and take an inordinate amount of time?

Automation as used here refers to processing data by some mechanical device or system other than typewriters, adding machines, calculators, and photocopiers. Automation can be used in handling such items as accounts payable, cumulative records, health records, inventories, personnel records, schedules, work requests, and transcripts.

Automation can be used by an organization either by installing its own machines or by working through some business organization that processes educational data for a fee. Also, the procedure of joining with several other departments or organizations for such a service works well in some situations. Depending on the size of the operation, it may be that a job can be done better, hiring additional personnel can be eliminated, and the cost is less with automation.

Reference materials

Reference materials should not be overlooked. Organizations find it valuable to develop professional libraries that contain some of the outstanding professional books, periodicals, and standard references for their professional fields, along with bulletins of the state department of education, state department of health, state and national professional organizations; facility references; and catalogs of athletic equipment and supplies.

Although there may be such material in other libraries, it is valuable to have such references in the central office. In this way staff members use them to a greater extent and thus keep up to date with their professional fields.

Administrative routine

The administrative routine or manner in which the day-to-day business of the department is carried out by the office represents the basic reason why such a facility exists. Therefore this matter should receive careful consideration.

OFFICE HOURS

The office should be open during regular hours. This usually means from 8 or 9 AM to 4 or 5 PM. During this time there should always be someone present to answer the telephone, greet visitors, and answer questions. There may be some exceptions to these hours, but even in these cases regular office hours that have been publicized as widely as possible are essential.

Staff members should also have regular office hours when they will be accessible to colleagues and others who would like to see them. These office hours should be posted, office personnel informed, and the schedule carefully observed so requests for information and assistance can be properly handled.

ASSIGNMENTS

All assignments, whether for office personnel or staff members, should be clear, in writing, and properly publicized. Office personnel may be required to set clocks, take messages, mimeograph daily or weekly bulletins, distribute minor supplies, check the calendar of events, provide messenger service, or assist in health examinations. These details should be clearly understood and carried out at the proper time. Specific responsibilities should be fixed and a schedule of duties prepared to prevent any misunderstanding.

CORRESPONDENCE

Correspondence represents a most effective public relations medium. Letters can be written in a cold, impersonal manner, or they can carry warmth and help interpret what a program expects and is trying to do for a student or other person. Letters should be prepared carefully, using proper grammar and a neat manner that meets the highest standards of secretarial practice. If a physical educator must do his or her own letters, these same standards should be met. Letters should convey the feeling that the department is anxious to help wherever possible. Letters should be answered promptly, not placed in a drawer and left for weeks or months. Carbon copies of letters should be made and filed for future reference.

FILES AND FILING

The office should contain steel filing cases for vertical filing. The filing system used depends on the number of personnel involved and the person doing the filing, but in any case it should be simple and practical. Files usually consist of correspondence and informational material. For ease of finding material, some form of alphabetical filing should usually be used, although numerical filing may at times be practical. The alphabetical files can be done on a name or subject basis, such as "Brown, Charles A.," or "Health Examinations," using a manila folder for all the material to be filed under the name or subject. Cross references should be included to facilitate finding material. Guide cards can be used to show which divisions of the file pertain to each letter of the alphabet, thus facilitating the search for material.

A visible filing system for any current records and reports that are used constantly proves helpful. These records are usually prepared on cards, and the visible filing case contains flat drawers that show the names or index numbers when pulled outward.

Office files should be kept accurately. The person filing should be careful to see that the letter or other material gets into the proper folder and that folder into its correct location. Filing should also be kept up to date. A periodic review of the files should be made to weed out material that is no longer pertinent to the department. Files that for any reason are removed from the cabinet should be returned. If one is kept out for any length of time, an "out" sign should be substituted, showing where it is.

TELEPHONE

The use of the office telephone is a major consideration for good departmental public relations. A few simple rules that should be observed follow.

Promptness. The telephone should be answered as promptly as possible. Answering promptly reflects efficient office practice and consideration for the person calling.

Professional purposes. The telephone is installed in an office for professional purposes. Secretaries or other office personnel should not be permitted to talk for long about personal matters that have no relation-

X denotes records kept	School 1	School 2	School 3	School 4	School 5	School 6	School 7	School 8	School 9	School 10	School 11	School 12	School 13	School 14	School 15	School 16	School 17	School 18	School 19	School 20	School 21
Physical fitness	×	×	×	×	×	×	×	×		×		×		×			×		×	×	×
Parental permission sports		×	×	×	×	×		×		×	×		×		×		×	×		×	
Medical form for physical education				×							×					×			×		
Medical form for inter-scholastic sports			×	×	×						×									×	×
Inventory		×		×			×	×			×	×	×					×			
Intramurals	×	×				×		×		×	×	×	×								×
Interscholastic sports	×		×		×			×			×	×		×							×
Health	×		×					×							×	×		×			×
Game reports			×			×									×						
Extracurricular activities								×						×							×
Equipment				×								×	×			×					×
Cumulative class record	×	×			×	×			×								×				×
Attendance	×		×	×		×	×	×	×	×	×	×	×	×	×	×			×	×	×
Application for participation in interscholastic sports								×			×						×				×
Adapted program			×			×						×		×	×						
Accident	×		×	×			×	×		×	×		×		×	×				×	×

Fig. 18-2. Physical education records used in 21 schools.

ship to departmental affairs. The telephone should be kept clear for business important to the achievement of professional objectives.

Courtesy, friendliness, and helpfulness. The person answering the phone should be pleasant and courteous and should desire to be of assistance to the caller. This should be the procedure not only when one is feeling his or her best but at all times. Such a telephone manner represents a professional responsibility that should be carried out with regularity.

Messages. At times staff members who are being called will not be available. A pencil and telephone pad should be kept at hand for recording calls in such cases, and a definite procedure should be established for relaying these messages to the proper person.

APPOINTMENTS

Appointments should not be made unless it is believed they can be kept. Furthermore, all appointments should be kept as nearly at the time scheduled as possible. Many times the person making an appointment has arranged his or her day with the understanding that the conference will be at a certain time. If this time is not adhered to, it means the schedule has to be altered, and complications frequently arise as a result. The secretary should keep an accurate list of appointments. If no secretary is available, the staff member should keep his or her own schedule of appointments and check it regularly to see that it is met.

Records and reports

At times, records and reports are not prepared and maintained accurately because the directions given by the chairperson of the department or the staff members are not clear and definite. When complicated reports are to be prepared, oral instructions, by themselves, will usually not be sufficient. Instead, directions should be written, typed, and distributed. The preparation of a sample will also help ensure better results.

Administrators are often responsible for poorly kept records, inaccurate reports, and late submissions. Directions should be clear, with announce-

ments at regular intervals, reminders of when reports are due, and a prompt checking of reports to see if they are all in and whether there are omissions or other inaccuracies.

A survey was conducted of 21 school systems to determine the types of records that were kept in departmental files for physical education personnel (see p. 594). The results of this survey showed that some of the schools were conscientious in record keeping; others were not. In general, most of the department heads and teachers admitted they should put more time and effort into this phase of physical education administration.

The survey showed that in some schools records were kept in the physical education department, whereas in other schools these same records were kept in another department. For example, in some schools attendance records were kept by the physical education department, whereas in other schools an attendance officer had complete control. In some schools the physical education department kept records on health, whereas in other schools these records were kept by the school nurse. The same was true regarding budgetary and inventory records. Some heads of physical education departments kept these records, whereas the business administrator and principles kept them in other schools.

Examples of reports and records maintained by the physical education departments include the following:

HEALTH RECORDS AND REPORTS
Health consultation request
Medical examination record
Health history
Growth records
Excuse forms
Exercise card
Height and weight card
Body mechanics inspection form
Films and visual aids list
Health habits record form
Accident records

PHYSICAL EDUCATION ACTIVITY, SKILL, AND SQUAD RECORDS AND REPORTS
Basket card
Physical education record
Field event report card

CHECKLIST OF SOME IMPORTANT CONSIDERATIONS FOR OFFICE MANAGEMENT

Space and working conditions   Yes   No

1. Does the reception room provide ample space for waiting guests? _____ _____
2. Is the clerical space separated from the reception room so office work is not interrupted by the arrival of guests? _____ _____
3. Are there private offices for the director of physical education and athletics and as many staff members as possible? _____ _____
4. Is there an up-to-date health suite that provides an office and other essential facilities for the school nurse? _____ _____
5. Are there adequate space and equipment for filing? _____ _____
6. Are file drawers arranged so papers can be inserted and removed easily and with space for future expansion? _____ _____
7. Is the office arranged so as many workers as possible get the best natural light, with glare from sunlight or reflected sunlight avoided? _____ _____
8. Has the office space been painted in accordance with the best in color dynamics? _____ _____
9. Have provisions been made so unnecessary noise is eliminated, distractions are kept to a minimum, and cleanliness prevails? _____ _____
10. Is there good ventilation, appropriate artificial lighting, and satisfactory heating conditions? _____ _____

Personnel

11. Is a receptionist available to greet guests and answer queries? _____ _____
12. Is there a recorded analysis of the duties of each secretarial position? _____ _____
13. Are channels available for ascertaining causes of dissatisfaction among secretarial help? _____ _____
14. Do secretaries dress neatly and conservatively? _____ _____
15. Do secretaries maintain a desk that has an orderly appearance and clear their desks of working papers each day? _____ _____
16. Do secretaries concern themselves with the efficiency of the office? _____ _____
17. Are secretaries loyal to the department and staff members? _____ _____
18. Do staff members have regular office hours? _____ _____
19. Are appointments kept promptly? _____ _____

PHYSICAL EDUCATION TEST AND ACHIEVEMENT FORMS

Physical fitness record
Report to parents
Résumé of personality traits
Citizenship guide sheet
Athletic report

PHYSICAL EDUCATION ATTENDANCE AND EXCUSE RECORDS AND REPORTS

Squad card attendance record
Appointment slip

Absence report
Change of program

PHYSICAL EDUCATION EQUIPMENT FORMS

Padlock record
Equipment record
Equipment inventory and condition report
Lost property report

CHECKLIST OF SOME IMPORTANT CONSIDERATIONS FOR OFFICE MANAGEMENT—cont'd

Procedures	*Yes*	*No*
20. Is up-to-date reading material furnished for waiting guests?		
21. Does the office help continually pay attention to maintaining offices that are neat, with papers, books, and other materials arranged in an orderly manner?		
22. Are the secretaries knowledgeable about departmental activities so that they can answer intelligently queries about staff members and activities?		
23. Do secretaries wait on guests promptly and courteously?		
24. Are letters typed neatly, well placed on the sheet, properly spaced, free from erasures, smudge, and typographic errors?		
25. Is correspondence handled promptly?		
26. Is the filing system easily learned and is the filing done promptly so the work does not pile up?		
27. Does the office routine use human time and energy efficiently eliminating duplicate operations or forms?		
28. Are the most effective and efficient office methods used?		
29. Is the clerical output satisfactory, with work starting promptly in the morning and after lunch, breaks taken according to schedule, and work stoppage taking place as scheduled?		
30. Has a streamlined procedure been developed so telephones are answered promptly, guests are courteously treated, and personal argument and gossiping eliminated?		
31. Are essential records properly maintained and kept up to date?		
32. Have procedures for typing and duplicating course outlines, committee reports, examinations, bulletins, fliers, letters, and announcements been developed to eliminate uncertainty or confusion on the part of staff members?		
33. Are regular office hours for staff posted and known so office staff members can make appointments as needed?		
34. Are secretaries acquainted with such details as securing films and other visual aids, obtaining reference material, helping in registration, duplicating material, and obtaining additional forms and records?		
35. Is the office covered continuously during working hours?		

SELF-ASSESSMENT TESTS

These tests are to assist students in determining if material and competencies presented in this chapter have been mastered.

1. Why is sound office management essential to effective public relations? What are some important reasons why office management is important to a department of physical education and athletics?

2. As an administrator of a large high school physical education and athletic program, describe the office personnel you would need and then justify your request.

3. Establish a set of rules for an effective administrative routine in respect to (a) office hours, (b) assignments, (c) correspondence, (d) files and filing, (e) telephone, and (f) appointments.

4. Prepare a set of sample records you would want to maintain as part of a small elementary, junior high school, and senior high school physical education and athletic program.

SELECTED REFERENCES

American Association of School Administrators: Profiles of the administrative team, Washington, D.C., 1971, The Association.

Avedisian, C.T.: PPBS: Planning, programming, budgeting systems, Journal of Health, Physical Education, and Recreation **43:**37, 1972.

Bannon, J.J.: Leisure resources—its comprehensive planning, Englewood Cliffs, N.J., 1976, Prentice-Hall, Inc.

Bronzan, R.T.: Public relations, promotions and fund raising—for athletic and physical education programs, New York, 1977, John Wiley & Sons, Inc.

Castetter, W.B.: The personnel function in educational administration, New York, 1971, Macmillan, Inc.

Courtesy in correspondence, The Royal Bank of Canada Monthly Letter **46:**1, 1965.

Deatherage, D., and Reid, C.P.: Administration of women's competitive sports, Dubuque, Iowa, 1977, William C. Brown Co., Publishers.

Duryea, E.D., and others: Faculty unions and collective bargaining, San Francisco, 1973, Jossey-Bass, Inc., Publishers.

Ford, K.: The development of our office copying processes, The Office, June, 1973, p. 18.

Fuoss, D.E., and Troppmann, R.J.: Creative management techniques in interscholastic athletics, Athletics, New York, 1977, John Wiley & Sons, Inc.

Pittman, J.: Office may become a leader of management, The Office **67:**110, 1968.

19

Evaluating individual achievement of physical education objectives*

Instructional objectives and competencies to be achieved

After reading this chapter the student should be able to

- Understand why evaluation of individual achievement in terms of the objectives of physical education and athletics is important.
- Identify several techniques and instruments available for obtaining desired information about individual achievement in terms of the objectives of physical education and athletics.
- Define the term *physical fitness,* and explain how its various components may be objectively measured.
- Plan a measurement program for physical education concerned with any age group of participants.
- Outline a basis for giving grades in physical education in school programs, based on such factors as objectives and performance.

Measurement techniques and evaluation procedures have seen many changes in recent years. The progress of participants in such areas as physical fitness, social development, cognitive achievement, and skill improvement are some of the areas where change has taken place.

The term *measurement* is used here to refer to the use of techniques to determine the degree to which a trait, ability, or characteristic exists in an individual.

During the last 40 years many measurement techniques have been developed in physical education. Some of these have been carefully and scientifically constructed, but many fall below acceptable standards. The administration should focus its attention on the materials that give valid and reliable results. Measurement techniques other than tests include

rating scales, checklists, photographic devices, controlled observation, and various measuring instruments.

Purposes of measurement

Measurement helps determine the progress being made in meeting objectives. It aids in discovering the needs of the participants. It identifies strengths and weaknesses of participants and instructors, aids in curriculum planning, and shows where emphasis should be placed. It also gives direction and helps supply information for guidance purposes.

Measurement helps determine where instructional emphasis should be placed and which procedures are effective and ineffective. It also is used to help persons determine their own progress in physical education practices, as a basis for giving grades, and as a means of interpreting programs to administrators and the public in general.

The information provided by measurement tech-

*Program evaluation is discussed as part of those chapters concerned with the various components of the physical education program. Teacher and coach evaluation is discussed in Chapter 10.

niques can also be used in other ways. Findings can be used for determining a person's exercise tolerance and for grouping individuals according to similar mental, physical, and other traits that will ensure better instruction. Measurement yields information that can be used as an indication of a person's achievement in various skills and activities. It provides information that can be used to predict future performance and development. It affords data on attitudes that determine whether or not the participant has proper motivation, and it focuses attention on future action that should be taken in the program.

Verducci* states that measurement and evaluation in physical education has student-related uses, teacher-related uses, and administrator-related uses. *Student-related uses* involve determining student objectives, predicting future performance, directing student programs, classifying students, individualizing student learning situations, motivating students, developing student skills, determining student improvement, determining student achievement, and grading. *Teacher-related uses* involve determining teaching effectiveness and adjusting course content. *Administrator-related uses* involve evaluating the curriculum, justifying the physical education program, and developing community interest.

The computer and measurement

The computer has many implications for the management of data concerned with achievement in physical education programs. It enables the administration to reduce the amount of time devoted to the data analysis. The computer permits the analysis of test scores for thousands of persons with comparative ease. It enables the physical educator to identify differentiating characteristics of participants, such as scores that are high or low. The computer enables a battery of test items on such characteristics as speed, strength, or power to be analyzed item by item. It is an aid in scheduling in light of the results of measurement, for example, for purposes of grouping persons

---

*Verducci, F.M.: Measurement concepts in physical education, St. Louis, 1980, The C.V. Mosby Co.

with similar deficiencies into the same class. The computer makes it possible to prepare a profile of each person on the various physical education tests administered. Test scores of one class of students can be compared with other classes within the same school or with other schools where national norms are available.

The uses of the computer for the imaginative and creative administrator are limitless. The nation and world are rapidly being run on an electronic basis. Physical education and athletics, if they desire to make their measurement programs most effective and meaningful, should examine the possibilities of the computer for their programs.

Criteria for test construction and selection

Criteria refer to those particular standards that may be used to evaluate measurement and evaluation materials. Such criteria as validity, reliability, objectivity, norms, and administrative economy provide the scientific basis for the selection and construction of tests. Administrators should be particularly concerned that the tests they use meet these criteria. If they do, properly interpreted results should aid considerably in developing adequate physical education programs.

Validity. Validity may be defined as how well a test measures what it claims to measure. To determine validity, an instructor should ask some of the following questions:

1. Does the test cover the content area for which it was designed?
2. Is it applicable to the participants for whom it was designed?
3. Is the criterion with which the material was correlated acceptable, and is the correlation coefficient also acceptable?
4. Does the test give insight into program objectives?
5. Is the sampling sufficiently representative and random?
6. Does evidence support whether the test is a classification, achievement, diagnostic, or prognostic technique?
7. Has the technique been tested in the appropriate area?

Fig. 19-1. Courtesy Youth Services Section, Student Auxilliary Services Branch, Los Angeles Unified School District, and Gwen R. Waters.

Reliability. Reliability may be defined as the consistency of measurement on the same individual or group, under the same conditions, and by the same person. Some questions relating to reliability include the following:

1. What are conditions under which reliability has been determined?
2. Is the size of the coefficient correlation acceptable?
3. What are the means of the two tests?
4. What is the method used for determining reliability? Is it valid?
5. Is the sample sufficient, random, and representative?
6. Has realiability been determined by using a group similar to the group for which the technique has been designed?

Objectivity. Objectivity is the degree to which the test or technique can be given by different individuals and obtain the same results. Questions that may be asked include the following:

1. Are the instructions simple and complete?
2. Is objectivity determination valid?
3. Is the sample sufficient, representative, and random?
4. Are the means indicated? Is there a difference in mean scores?
5. Are the procedures easily understood by examiner and subject?
6. Are alternate test forms available if needed?

Norms. The level of group performance or a statistical average may be defined as a norm for a group. Some questions concerning norms include the following:

1. What basis is used for norm construction—chronological age, grade level, skill achievement?
2. Is the sample sufficient, random, and representative?
3. Are the norms based on local or national statistics?
4. Are the norms tentative, arbitrary, or experimental?
5. Are all important extraneous factors eliminated?
6. Are the statistics sufficiently refined?
7. Is the appropriate statistical tool used?

Fig. 19-2. Physical education class using Geocubes at Oak View Elementary School in Fairfax, Va. One purpose of measurement is to determine outcomes that occur as result of such activities.

Administrative economy. The procedures involved with conducting the program may be defined as administrative economy. Questions concerning this area of testing criteria include the following:

1. What is the time allotment for the administration of the test or other technique?
2. What are the costs involved in administering the technique?
3. Is the technique easy to administer, and does it require much training on the part of the examiner?
4. Are the objectives of the technique and the program compatible?
5. How many examiners are necessary, and is the technique within the scope of the physical educator's training?

Techniques and instruments for obtaining desired information about people

Many techniques and instruments can be used to obtain the various types of classification, achievement, diagnostic, and prognostic information about participants.

Classification information. An example of an instrument that yields classification information is Mc-

Cloy's Classification Index I.* This classification index considers such items as age, height, weight, and athletic skill, with a simple formula developed for calculating the index.

Another example of an instrument helpful for classification purposes is the Wetzel Grid.† This is valuable in either health or physical education programs, because it considers such elements as physique, developmental level, and nutritional progress with respect to weight, age, and height.

Achievement information. An example of an instrument that reflects achievement information is the Indiana Physical Fitness Test.‡ This instrument involves such test items as straddle chins, squatthrusts, pushups, and vertical jumps. Norms have been developed for boys and girls.

There are many achievement tests available that can be used by physical education programs.

---

*McCloy, C.H., and Young, N.D.: Tests and measurements in health and physical education, ed. 3, New York 1954, Appleton-Century-Crofts, pp. 59-60.

†Wetzel, N.C.: Grid for evaluating physical fitness, Cleveland, 1948, National Education Association Service, Inc.

‡State of Indiana Department of Public Instruction: High school physical education course of study, Bulletin 222, Indianapolis, 1958, The Department.

Diagnostic information. An example of a diagnostic instrument in physical education is the Dyer Backboard Test* for tennis. This test evaluates general tennis ability. It does not analyze the various strokes and elements of the game. It merely consists of volleying a tennis ball as rapidly as possible against a backboard.

Prognostic information. An example of a prognostic instrument is a sociometric test, which reflects a person's ability to get along with others. A test of mental capacity to forecast academic achievement and a test of general motor ability to forecast achievement in specific skills are two other prognostic instruments.

Techniques and instruments for obtaining information about objectives

In addition to gaining classification, achievement, diagnostic, and prognostic information about persons, it also is necessary to identify particular instruments, materials, resources, and methods for evaluating a person's status in respect to organic, neuromuscular, cognitive, and social development.

ORGANIC DEVELOPMENT OBJECTIVE

A medical examination is a valuable technique for obtaining information about the organic development of an individual. Such an examination should be given at least once a year by a competent physician.

Other tests that should be reviewed as possible instruments for determining organic development status follow.†

CIRCULATORY-RESPIRATORY TESTS‡

Stress tests
Cureton All-Out Treadmill Test
Henry Tests of Vasomotor Weakness
MacCurdy-Larson Organic Efficiency Test

Schneider Cardiovascular Test
Turner Test of Circulatory Reaction to Prolonged Standing
Tuttle Pulse-Ratio Test

ANTHROPOMETRIC, POSTURE, AND BODY MECHANICS MEASUREMENTS

Cureton Technique for Scaling Postural Photographs and Silhouettes
Cureton Tissue Symmetry test
Cureton-Grover Fat Test
Cureton-Gunby Conformateur Test of Antero-Posterior Posture
Cureton-Holmes Tests for Functional Fitness of the Feet
Cureton-Nordstrom Skeletal Build Index
Cureton-Wickens Center of Gravity Tests

MUSCULAR STRENGTH, POWER, AND ENDURANCE TESTS

Anderson Strength Index for High School Girls
Carpenter Strength Test for Women
Cureton Muscular Endurance Tests
Larson Dynamic Strength Test for Men
MacCurdy Test of Physical Capacity
McCloy Athletic Strength Index
Rogers Physical Capacity Test and Physical Fitness Index
Wendler Strength Index

FLEXIBILITY TESTS

Cureton Flexibility Tests
Leighton Flexometer Tests

MOTOR DEVELOPMENT OBJECTIVE

Physical skills represent a major part of the physical education program; therefore, appropriate valid tests of physical skills should be used. Such qualities as *motor educability, motor capacity, physical capacity, motor ability,* and *motor efficiency* are terms frequently used in connection with neuromuscular development.

Tests have been developed for skills in sports such as archery, badminton, soccer, basketball, bowling, football, golf, handball, field hockey, and ice hockey. Descriptions of these tests are given in some of the source books listed at the end of this chapter. These suggested tests should be studied carefully to determine their suitability or adaptability to a particular situation. Some of the instruments that should be explored in measuring this objective follow:

---

*Dyer, J.T.: The backboard test of tennis ability, Supplement to the Research Quarterly **6:**63, 1935; Revision of backboard test of tennis ability, Research Quarterly **9:**25, 1938.
†Also see AAHPERD Health-Related Physical Fitness and other physical fitness tests on pp. 612-613.
‡These tests may be found in copies of Research Quarterly, American Alliance of Health, Physical Education, and Recreation, or in one of the measurement and evaluation texts listed in the selected references at the end of this chapter.

MOTOR FITNESS TESTS

Bookwalter Motor Fitness Tests
Cureton-Illinois Motor Fitness Tests
O'Connor-Cureton Motor Tests for High School Girls
Latchaw Motor Achievement Test

GENERAL MOTOR SKILLS TESTS

Brace Test of Motor Ability
Carpenter Test of Motor Educability for Primary Grade
   Children
Cozens Test of General Athletic Ability
Humiston Test of Motor Ability for Women
Iowa Revision of the Brace Motor Ability Test
Johnson Test of Motor Educability
Larson Test of Motor Ability for Men
Metheny Revision of the Johnson Test
Powell-Howe Motor Ability Tests for High School Girls
Scott Test of Motor Ability for Women

SPORTS SKILLS TESTS

AAHPERD Sports Skills Tests
Borleske Touch Football Test for Men
Cureton Swimming Endurance Tests
Cureton Swimming Tests
Dyer Backboard Test of Tennis Ability
Johnson Basketball Test for Men
Lehsten Basketball Test for Men
Rodgers-Health Soccer Skills Tests for Elementary
   Schools
Russell-Lange Volleyball Test for Girls
Schmithals-French Field Hockey Tests for Women
Young-Moser Basketball Test for Women

COGNITIVE DEVELOPMENT OBJECTIVE

In physical education, several standardized tests are available for written tests in various sports. Also, some tests may be found in rule books and source books. Some knowledge and understanding tests in physical education that should be explored are the French Tests for Professional Courses in Knowledge and Sports, Hewitt Comprehensive Tennis Knowledge Tests, Scott Badminton Knowledge Text, Scott Swimming Knowledge Test, and Scott Tennis Knowledge Test.

Physical educators may devise their own tests appropriate to the subject and age level being taught. When tests are developed, however, the following principles of test construction should be kept in mind:

1. The items selected should stress the most important aspects of the material.
2. The length of the test should be determined in relation to the time available for testing.
3. The test should be appropriately worded and geared for the age level to be tested.
4. Questions or test items should be worded to avoid ambiguity.
5. Statements should be simple and direct, not tricky or involved.

AFFECTIVE DOMAIN—SOCIAL DEVELOPMENT OBJECTIVE*

The affective domain is concerned with such concepts as attitudes, appreciation, and values of students as they relate to the students themselves, to others, and to physical education. The development of a meaningful social experience is also listed as one of the objectives of physical education. Social development refers to such aspects of behavior as cooperation, leadership and followership, courtesy, honesty, and respect for rules and authority. Social interaction within a group is also a part of social development.

Affective measures and social development components are difficult to measure. However, there are some objective instruments and techniques for measuring aspects of each area. Selected testing instruments and techniques for both affective and social development areas are described. Complete directions for administering the tests, along with other pertinent information, are contained in the source included after each test description.

Testing instruments for the affective domain

Testing instruments described for the affective domain include (1) Coopersmith's Self-Esteem Inventory, (2) How I See Myself Scale, (3) Kim-Anderson-Bradshaw Child Behavior Scale, (4) Martinek-Zaichokowsky Self-Concept Scales (MZSCS), and (5) The Piers-Harris Children's Self-Concept Scale.

---

*Parts of this section were adapted from Bucher, C.A., and Thaxton, N.: Physical education for children—movement foundations and experiences, New York, 1979, Macmillan, Inc.

YORKTOWN HEIGHTS ELEMENTARY SCHOOLS

PHYSICAL EDUCATION Progress Record	Grade Weight Height	3				4				5				6			
Name		Dec. 196...	Grade Average	June 196...	Grade Average	Dec. 196...	Grade Average	June 196...	Grade Average	Dec. 196...	Grade Average	June 196...	Grade Average	Dec. 196...	Grade Average	June 196...	Grade Average
CHIN-UPS (Arm strength)																	
JUMPING ROPE - number of jumps completed in 30 seconds (Endurance, leg strength, coordination)																	
STANDING BROAD JUMP (Body movement forward) (feet)																	
JUMPING FOR HEIGHT (Jump - Reach - Body movement upward) (inches)																	
CLIMBING 20-FOOT ROPE (General strength & coordination) (feet)																	
TRAVEL HORIZONTAL LADDER (Arm strength & coordination) (feet)																	
SIT-UPS* (Abdominal strength)																	
50-YARD DASH (Speed) (seconds)																	
SOFTBALL THROW 30 FEET, **10 THROWS** (Accuracy)																	
* Maximum sit-ups: 3rd - 20 4th - 30 5th - 50 6th - 50																	

FOUR YEAR FITNESS REPORT CARD

Fig. 19-3. Fitness report card reflects growth and progress. Parents in Yorktown Heights, N.Y., know just how their children did in every phase of the semiannual physical fitness test because they receive fitness report cards each year and can check progress and growth.

From Klappholz, L., editor: Successful practices in teaching physical fitness, New London, Conn., 1964, Croft Educational Services. Reprinted by permission.

Fig. 19-4. The consumer is important in program development; his or her opinion is valuable.

Fig. 19-5. With the individualized approach to learning in Omaha Public Schools, each student meets with the teacher for evaluation of the prescribed task.

Courtesy Omaha Public Schools.

COMPARISON OF ESSAY AND OBJECTIVE TESTS*

Characteristic	Essay test	Objective test
Preparation of test item	Items are relatively easy to construct	Items are relatively difficult to construct
Sampling of the subject matter	Sampling is often limited	Sampling is usually extensive
Measurement of knowledges and understandings	Items can measure both; measurement of understanding is recommended	Items can measure both; measurement of knowledges is emphasized
Preparation by pupil	Emphasis is primarily on larger units of material	Emphasis is primarily on factual details
Nature of response by pupil	Pupil organizes original response	Except for supply test items, pupil selects response
Guessing of correct response by pupil	Successful guessing is minor problem	Successful guessing is major problem
Scoring of pupil responses	Scoring is difficult, time-consuming, and somewhat unreliable	Scoring is simple, rapid, and highly reliable

*From Ahmann, J.S.: Testing student achievements and aptitudes, New York, 1962, The Center for Applied Research in Education, Inc. (The Library of Education), p. 35.

Coopersmith's Self-Esteem Inventory.* A 58-item test battery designed to measure self-esteem in preadolescent boys and girls. The test items cover different areas of experience, that is, as a student, athlete, and person.

How I See Myself Scale.† This test consists of 40 items and is designed to measure self-concept with regard to body, peers, teachers, school, and emotional control in children in grades three through six.

Kim-Anderson-Bradshaw Child Behavior Scale.‡ A behavior scale to measure maturity development in young children. The 18-item scale consists of 6 items in each of the three identified factors of maturity: academic, interpersonal, and emotional. The scale is developed for use with second-grade children but interpersonal and emotional factors in the test are appropriate to administer to 4- and 5-year-olds.

Martinek-Zaichokowsky Self-Concept Scale (MZSCS).* A nonverbal scale consisting of 25 items. It is designed to measure global self-concept of elementary and middle school children. The scale measures such attributes as appropriate behavior, intellectual, social, and physical aspects of a child's self-concept.

The Piers-Harris Children's Self-Concept Scale (CSCS).† The CSCS is a test that can be used for

*Self-esteem was defined by Coopersmith as a relatively stable assessment that an individual makes of himself or herself, Coopersmith, S.: The antecedents of self-esteem, San Francisco, 1967, W.H. Freeman and Co., pp. 4-5.

†Gordon, I.J.: Studying the Child in the School, New York, 1966, John Wiley & Sons, Inc., pp. 55-59; and Gordon, I.J.: A Test Manual for How I See Myself Scale, Gainsville, Fla., 1968, The Florida Educational and Research and Development Council.

‡Kim, Y., et al.: The simple structure of social maturity at the second grade level. Educational and Psychological Measurement 28:145-153, 1968; and Anderson, H.E., et al.: Normative and partial validity data for the KAB-CBS, Educational and Psychological Measurement 29:927-933, 1969.

*Martinek, T.J., and Zaichokowsky, L.D.: Manual for the Martinek-Zaichokowsky Self-Concept Scale for Children, Jacksonville, Ill., 1977, Psychologists and Educators, Inc.

†Buros, O.K., editor: The seventh mental measurements yearbook, vol. 1, Highland Park, N.J., 1972, The Gryphon Press, pp. 124-126; and Piers, E.V.: Manual for the Piers-Harris Children's Self-Concept Scale (the way I feel about myself), Nashville, Tenn., 1969, Counselor Recordings and Tests.

students in grades three to twelve. The test consists of 80 first-person declarative statements to which a child responds by answering "Yes" or "No," according to the way he or she feels. Half of the sentences are worded to indicate a positive self-concept and half to indicate a negative self-concept. The internal consistency of the scale ranges from 0.78 to 0.93 and retest reliability from 0.71 to 0.77.

Other measurement devices. The teacher can use observation to note affective behavior in students but the observation should be systematic and should be recorded objectively in some manner; for example, by use of checklists and anecdotal records.

In observing students for evaluation the teacher should have specific questions in mind. In the affective domain, for example, the following questions would be of interest:

1. Does the student participate enthusiastically in the activities?
2. Does the student demonstrate a positive self-concept in the way he or she interacts with the teacher? With classmates?
3. Does the student appear happy and confident?
4. Does the student change behavior as a result of evaluation feedback sessions?

Testing instruments for social development

Some of the more widely used measuring devices for social development are rating scales, checklists, sociograms, interviews, questionnaires, and anecdotal records. Rating scales and checklists were discussed under the area of motor skill evaluation and will not be discussed here. However, it should be emphasized that these techniques are extremely helpful in evaluating personal-social development. Sociograms, interviews, questionnaires, and anecdotal records are briefly discussed.

Before discussing instruments that may be used to record personal-social development, it should be pointed out that some of the instruments are impractical to use for classes of 200 or 300 students. When using several different techniques for large classes, however, they may be very effective. It should also be kept in mind that only a few students in a class of 100 might require the teacher to use the interview

technique, for example, which would be very impractical to use with all 100 students.

Sociograms. A sociogram is a special sociometric technique for evaluating the social status of individuals within a group. It indicates the people who are most liked in the group, among other things. By asking students in a class to list two classmates whom they would like to have as their friends, a chart could be made to show the preferences. As an example, a schematic is shown in Fig. 19-6.

This is a simplified version of a sociogram for illustrative purposes. Different kinds of group relations may be evaluated, using much larger groups of children. As one can see from the example, the teacher can easily determine the small, select groups of students in the class, as well as the children who are left out. In the present example, John is the most popular child, having been chosen by four of the other children. Charlie was the least popular since he was the only person not chosen by anyone.

Information such as that provided by the sociogram can be very useful in helping the teacher to better organize the physical education class. Those students who are very popular should be used to help the least popular children by acting as group leaders in social situations. Class organization should be designed to prevent negative results of small, select groups of students remaining together.

Interviews. In many instances the personal interview is one of the few settings in which the student will be completely honest with the teacher. Students should be listened to carefully when speaking with the teacher in an interview. During free hours, play periods in the gym, and after school activities, opportunities present themselves for instructive interviews.

Whatever information is discussed during personal interviews should be treated as confidential, and the student should be so informed. If the teacher feels that information revealed during the interview should be discussed with other people, the child should be asked to give his or her consent.

Questionnaires. Questionnaires are more impersonal than interviews and might be used when requesting information from large numbers of students about attitudes toward the program and about the instruction received. Specifically, a questionnaire

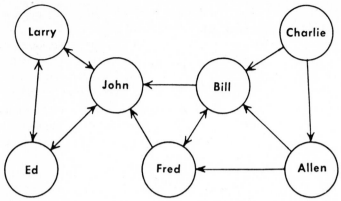

Fig. 19-6. Sociogram depicting social interactions.

might serve as an excellent device for obtaining the general reactions of the class regarding the activities being offered and the manner in which they are being taught.

Anecdotal records. A written description of special behavior patterns of all students is valuable but time consuming. In addition, teachers who use this method must be careful observers and must be objective in their analyses.

A systematic method of collecting and recording information must be developed when using the anecdotal record technique. A file card system might be used so that the cards can be retained for future reference. All cards should be dated and kept in chronological order. A record of both good and bad patterns of behavior should be included so as to get a complete picture of students.

Three other general suggestions to follow when using the anecdotal record and an example of an entry are included. The suggestions are as follows:

1. Record the behavior incident as soon as possible after it occurs. Be inconspicuous when recording "behavior logs"; the student's behavior should not be further influenced by the knowledge that the teacher is keeping records.
2. Be careful to report only the facts. This does not mean that the teacher should omit related events surrounding the behavior being recorded. Moreover, the teacher is encouraged to give an interpretation of the circumstances or events influencing the specific behavior being recorded.
3. Remember that physical education teachers are not

qualified to diagnose students with severe maladjustments in social development. Secure the help of the school psychologist or social worker in cases where the problems are too difficult for the teacher to handle.

Physical fitness testing

Physical fitness testing probably started as part of the physical education profession at the time when anthropometry was used. Anthropometry involved measuring the body and its parts, because size seemed to be related to strength. Then there was the emphasis on strength testing, often through use of dynamometers. The work of Dudley A. Sargent and his development of the Intercollegiate Strength Test are characteristic of this early era. It was soon realized, however, that strength testing alone could not measure the functional capacity of individuals. This realization led to cardiorespiratory testing. Schneider expressed this concept when he said:

Physical exertion overtaxes the circulatory mechanism long before it exhausts skeletal musculature; and while it is not easy to overwork the muscles, the heart can quite readily be overworked. The convalescent from infectious disease is limited in his exercise not by what his muscles can do but by the strength of his heart. Hence today the general opinion is that strength tests do not permit us to draw satisfactory conclusions regarding the efficiency of the entire body.*

*Schneider, E.C.: Physical efficiency and the limitations of efficiency tests, American Physical Education Review **28:**405, 1923.

GIRLS' PHYSICAL FITNESS TEST RECORD

Name				Grade		Period	
School		Age	Ht.	Wt.	Test 1 Classification		
		Age	Ht.	Wt.	Test 2 Classification		

Test No.	1		2	
Date				
Event	Score	Percentile	Score	Percentile
Modified Pull-Ups				
Sit-Ups (Max 50)				
Broad Jump				
50-yd. Dash				
Shuttle Run				
Modified Push-Ups				
600-yd. Run-Walk				
Softball Throw				
P.F.I.—Average percentile of 5 events				

Fig. 19-7. Girls' physical fitness test records.

As a result of this emphasis on functional capacity, many tests were developed, most of which involved changes in frequency of heart rate and blood pressure as a result of exercise. Examples of these are Tuttle's Pulse Ratio Test, McCurdy-Larson's Organic Efficiency Test, Carlson's Fatigue Test Curve, and Brouha's Step Test.

In 1925 strength testing was revived by Frederick Rand Rogers with his emphasis on physical capacity tests in physical education administration. Other developments in strength testing have been accomplished by Harrison Clarke, who developed the tensiometer for use with orthopedic disabilities and by Hans Kraus and Ruth P. Hirschland, who devised a six-item test of "minimum muscular fitness" that appraises flexibility as well as strength.

During World War II, when physical fitness was a major objective, several performance type tests were developed. Some of these were the Army Air Force Test, the Army Physical Efficiency Test, the Navy Standard Physical Fitness Test, and the Victory Corps Test.

Several tests with which to measure physical fitness are available today. Some of these have been scientifically validated, whereas others have been presented without objective evidence of validity. Validity and reliability are important criteria of a test, but administrative efficiency may place one test ahead of another. Validity, however, is the weak point in most physical fitness tests today.

Not all physical fitness tests measure the same kind of physical fitness. The evidence is that tests of physical fitness do not correlate very highly. Therefore it is necessary to select a fitness test that measures the kind of fitness the program is aiming to achieve.

It is difficult to identify the items desired to measure physical fitness. Many experts feel that it would be better to test component parts of physical fitness (posture, strength, balance, endurance) by means of several tests of each component. Then, through a partial correlation process it would be possible to determine the most valid test of each component. In turn, these most valid tests could be combined into a battery. Most physical fitness tests measure component factors that are not truly comprehensive. They

Table 19-1. Physical fitness components and tests*

Component	Selected tests
Arm and shoulder strength	Pull-ups, push-ups, parallel bar, dips, rope climb
Speed	50-yard dash, 100-yard dash
Agility	Shuttle run, agility run
Abdominal and hip strength	Sit-ups, sit-ups with knees flexed, 2-minute sit-ups
Flexibility	Trunk flexion standing, trunk flexion sitting, trunk extension (prone position)
Cardiorespiratory endurance	600-yard run, half-mile run, mile run, 5-minute step test
Explosive power	Standing broad jump, vertical jump
Static strength	Grip strength, back lift, leg lift
Balance	Bass test, Brace test, tests on balance beam
Muscular endurance	Push-ups, chest raisings (prone position, hands behind neck, legs held down), V-sit (against time)

*From Hunsicker, P.: Physical fitness—what research says to the teacher, Washington, D.C., 1963, National Education Association, p. 17.

stress primarily arm strength, leg strength, and endurance. However, there are other considerations. For example, a husky body requires more strength for one pull-up than does a slight one. In addition to body build, physiological age (when dealing with children) should also be considered. These and similar factors may account for the difficulty in validating tests.

The possibility of a universal battery of tests is remote because of disagreement among experts as to the nature of physical fitness. Many physical education leaders feel, however, it is important that the profession consider adopting a single tool of measurement.

Tables 19-1 and 19-2 list the physical fitness components and tests that measure these components, as well as the selected tests of physical fitness.

The four components of the AAHPERD *Health Related Physical Fitness Test* and the items used to measure each component are listed in the box on p. 613.

The AAHPERD* has also developed another physical fitness test for national use. It consists of the following six basic items:

1. Pull-ups (modified for girls to flexed arm hang): to test arm and shoulder girdle strength

2. Sit-ups: to test strength of abdominal muscles and hip flexors
3. Shuttle run: to test speed and change of direction
4. Standing broad jump: to test explosive power of leg extensors
5. 50-yard dash: to test speed
6. 600-yard walk or run: to test cardiovascular system

Norms have been established for girls and boys in grades five through twelve and for college students and may be obtained from the AAHPERD. A manual gives, in addition, complete directions for testing each item.

The State Department of Education of New York State* is an example of many state groups that have developed their own physical fitness tests for local use. The New York test consists of the following seven components that are measured to obtain a total physical fitness score:

1. Posture: evaluated by means of a posture rating chart
2. Accuracy: measured by means of a target throw, utilizing a softball and a circular target
3. Strength: evaluated by pull-ups for boys and modified pull-ups for girls
4. Agility: evaluated by means of the side step
5. Speed: evaluated by means of the 50-yard dash
6. Balance: evaluated by means of the squat-stand
7. Endurance: evaluated by means of the treadmill

*AAHPERD Youth fitness test manual, Washington, D.C., 1976, American Alliance for Health, Physical Education, Recreation and Dance.

*New York State physical fitness test. The University of the State of New York, The State Education Department, Albany, New York.

Norms have been established and are listed in a manual, together with a description of the test.

In recent years statements have been made that question the validity of fitness testing. One of the tests questioned is the AAHPERD Youth Fitness Test.* One may ask the question, "Is it really a fitness test

*Smith, C.O.: Fitness testing; questions about how, what, and with what, Journal of Health, Physical Education, and Recreation **43**:37, 1972; Plowman, S., and Falls, H.B.: AAHPERD Youth Fitness Test Revision, Journal of Physical Education and Recreation **49**:22, November-December 1978.

or a test of fitness-motor capability?" Should the 50-yard dash be used as a measure of fitness? The ability to run fast is not really a fitness component. Some "unfit" persons may run fast, whereas "fit" people may do poorly on such a test. In addition, the standing broad jump requires a high degree of body coordination but does not necessarily indicate fitness. The validity of most currently used physical fitness tests should be carefully researched, tested, and updated by experts in this field.

Table 19-2. Selected tests of physical fitness*

Test	Source
AAHPERD Youth Fitness Test	American Alliance for Health, Physical Education, Recreation, and Dance, 1900 Association Drive, Reston, Virginia.
AAHPERD-U.S. Office of Education Committee on Physical Fitness for Girls	Journal of HPER, pp. 308-311, 354-355, June 1945.
All-around Muscular Endurance	Anderson, John E.: Endurance of young men, Society for Research in Child Development, vol. X, serial No. 40, No. 1, Washington, D.C., 1958, American Association for Health, Physical Education, and Recreation.
Army Air Force Physical Fitness Test	AAHPER Research Quarterly **15**:12-15, March 1944.
Army Physical Fitness Test	War Department, FM 21-20, 1945.
California Physical Fitness Test	California State Department of Education, February 1948.
Harvard Step Test	AAHPER Research Quarterly **14**:31-36, March 1943.
Illinois Physical Fitness Test for High School Boys	Illinois State Department of Public Instruction, Bulletin No. 6, 1944.
Indiana High School Physical Condition Test	Indiana State Office of Public Instruction, Bulletin No. 136, September 1944.
The JCR Test	AAHPER Research Quarterly **18**:12-29, March 1947.
Kraus-Weber Test of Minimum Muscular Fitness	AAHPER Research Quarterly **25**:178-188, May 1954.
Larson Muscular Strength Test	AAHPER Research Quarterly **11**:82-96, December 1940.
McCloy Strength Test	McCloy, H.C., and Young, N.E.: Tests and measurements in health and physical education, ed. 3, New York, 1954, Appleton-Century-Crofts, pp. 128-152.
Navy Standard Physical Fitness	Bureau of Naval Personnel, Training Division, Physical Fitness Section, 1943.
New York State Physical Fitness Test	New York State Education Department, 1948.
Youth Physical Fitness	President's Council on Youth Fitness: Youth physical fitness, Washington, D.C., 1961, United States Government Printing Office.
Rogers Strength Test	Clarke, H. Harrison: Application of measurement to health and physical education, ed. 3, New York, 1959, Prentice-Hall, Inc. pp. 182-213.

*From Hunsicker, P.: Physical fitness—what research says to the teacher, Washington, D.C., 1963, National Education Association, p. 17.

AAHPERD HEALTH-RELATED PHYSICAL FITNESS TEST

Item A: Distance run

Fitness component: Cardiorespiratory fitness
Purpose: To measure the maximal function and endurance of the cardiorespiratory system.
Item description:

Procedures and norms are provided for two optional distance run tests: the mile run for time and the nine minute run for distance. The decision as to which of the two tests to administer should be based on facilities, equipment, time limitations, and personal preference of the teacher. For students 13 years of age and older, the 1.5 mile run for time or the 12 minute run for distance may be utilized as the distance run items.

Item B: Sum of skinfolds (triceps and subscapular)

Fitness component: Body composition
Purpose: To evaluate the level of body fatness
Item description:

In a number of regions of the body, the subcutaneous adipose tissue may be lifted with the fingers to form a skinfold. The skinfold consists of a double layer of subcutaneous fat and skin whose thickness may be measured with a skinfold caliper. The skinfold sites (triceps and subscapular) have been chosen for this test because they are easily measured and are highly correlated with total body fat.

Item C: Sit-ups

Fitness component: Muscular strength/endurance
Purpose: To test muscular strength and endurance of the abdominal muscles.

Item description:

The pupil lies on his back with knees flexed, feet on floor, with the heels between twelve and eighteen inches from buttocks. The pupil crosses arms on chest placing hands on the opposite shoulder. His feet are held by his partner to keep them in touch with the testing surface. The pupil, by tightening his abdominal muscles, curls to the sitting position. Arm contact with the chest must be maintained. The sit-up is completed when elbows tough the thighs. The pupil returns to down position until the midback makes contact with the testing surface.

Item D: Sit and reach

Fitness component: Flexibility
Purpose: To test the flexibility of the low back and posterior thigh
Item description:

The pupil removes his shoes and assumes the sitting position with the knees fully extended and the feet against the apparatus shoulder width apart. The arms are extended forward with the hands placed one on top of the other. The pupil reaches directly forward, palms down, along the measuring scale. In this position, the pupil slowly stretches forward four times and holds the position of maximum reach on the fourth count. The position of maximum reach must be held for one second with knees in full extension while the feet are in contact with the apparatus.

From American Alliance for Health, Physical Education, Recreation, and Dance: Test items in the AAHPERD Health-Related Physical Fitness Test described, AAHPERD Update, June 1980.

Measurement and evaluation for adapted physical education

In developing a measurement and evaluation program for the handicapped it is important to determine the physical status of the individual before preparing an outline of activities that will constitute the program. First, determine the individual's physical limitation. Second, the physical limitations imposed should be carefully analyzed, after which objectives should be established. Third, using the objectives indicated, a program of physical activities can be developed that fits the individual. One should be careful to select activities in which the individual can be successful. Fourth, after the activities have been engaged in for a period of time, progress should be determined for each participant. If progress has not been made, this should also be noted. Fifth, the progress made or not made should be evaluated and the activities engaged in studied and then suitable changes made, if necessary. Periodic testing and retesting are used throughout the program to assess the physical functioning of the handicapped person and then to make necessary modifications where needed to assure educational progress. It should, however, be noted that the rate of improvement is different for each individual. In some cases there may be a regression, and as a result objectives will need to be modified.

The beginning physical educator should examine several adapted physical education and special education texts to become more knowledgeable about handicapped individuals.

Minimum and desirable standards for testing students

A minimal program of measurement must include the following points:

1. A *health examination* should be conducted by a physician; as a minimum it would be given to all first-year students. It should be given at the start of every school year, if possible. A posture screening test should be given at the same time.
2. *Neuromuscular skills* should be tested after the final period of instruction for each new motor activity.

This provides the teacher and student with information concerning skill mastery and may also be used later for classification purposes.

3. *Cognitive testing* enables the teacher to ascertain knowledge and information gained from activity programs.
4. *Attitude testing* may be based on observation and evaluation techniques. Students asked to evaluate the activity program will also express their general attitudes concerning the content and instruction of the program. Observation of students on a daily basis can give the instructor a good idea of student attitudes toward the class.
5. *Physical fitness tests* should be conducted annually to determine the progress of the student.
6. *Self-evaluation* by the instructor is essential to the program, as well as to the professional, personal, and social growth of the teacher.

Principles to observe in evaluating adult exercise programs

Some principles that will help determine whether adult exercise programs are adapted to the participant follow:

1, *Does the participant check with his or her family physician to determine exercise tolerance and medical status?* Exercise tolerance refers to the person's ability to react favorably to exercise. Many physiologists and physicians indicate that 10 minutes after exercising a person's pulse rate should return to normal and there should not be breathlessness or pounding of the heart. Two hours after engaging in activity the person should not experience extreme fatigue. The next day the person should not have a feeling of extreme tiredness or have disturbed sleep at night as a result of the activity.

2. *Does the person who is obese, has a history of heart disease, or suffers from high blood pressure see his or her family physician before engaging in any strenuous activity?* Also, if one develops any of the following symptoms, he or she should see a physician: pains in chest, dizziness or faintness, nausea, or difficulty in breathing.

3. *Has the person had a stress test to determine exercise tolerance?*

4. *Does the person who is not in good physical*

Fig. 19-8. Measurement and evaluation are also important in adult physical education and fitness programs. Men playing basketball in indoor gymnasium at Fitness and Recreation Center, Xerox Corporation, Leesburg, Va.

condition get back into shape gradually? A little today and a little more tomorrow is a good rule to follow. The intensity and duration of the exercise should be gradually increased. Persons who have exercised for a long time need an extended period of activity to get into proper physical condition.

5. *Does the person warm up before engaging in exercise?* A warm-up prevents injury and helps get the most out of the physical workout. Light conditioning and stretching exercises help prepare the body for more vigorous exercise. In warming up, it is wise to being slowly and then gradually accelerate. The amount of warm-up needed will depend on the individual.

6. *Does the person cool down after engaging in exercise?* A participant should cool down by engaging in light exercise following strenuous exercise.

7. *Does the person initiate a general fitness routine that strengthens the muscles, increases flexibility, and develops cardiorespiratory endurance?*

8. *Does the person progressively overload his or her cardiorespiratory mechanism?* To increase heart

and respiratory rate, exercise physiologists advocate periodically skipping rope, bicycling, or running (jogging). To determine the degree of overload (that is, the target zone or training pulse rate) the person should gradually try to achieve, subtract his or her age from 220. Then, for about the first 6 to 8 weeks, 3 to 5 times a week, try to get the heart rate up to 60% of this figure for about 20 minutes each time (rests should be taken as needed). For the second 6 to 8 week period try to get the heart rate up to 70% of this figure, and for the third 6 to 8 week period and for maintenance, 80% of this figure. For example, for a person who is 40 years old, the formula is 220 minus 40, or 180. Sixty percent of this figure, the target zone for the first 6 to 8 week period, is 108. Therefore, this person should try to get his or her heart rate up to about 108 to 110 for about 20 minutes 3 to 5 times a week during this period.

A method that has proved successful for assessing heart rate is to count beats for 10 seconds and then multiply by 6, either at the carotid artery in the neck or by placing the palm of the hand over the apex of the heart. With practice this method has proved to be accurate. Pulse should be taken immediately after exercising.

In any exercise program an important principle to follow is that *exercise must be adapted to a person's individual physical needs*.

Keeping records and using test results

Many clerical duties are associated with the measurement program. For most effective use, records should be kept up to date and new test results constantly analyzed in terms of the participants' progress and program planning. Also, in today's automation era, some organizations have found it advantageous to use IBM cards to record test results. It may also be helpful to maintain a record file of measurement instruments used, adding comments concerning possible success or problems involved in their administration. This would prevent repetition of testing with unsuitable instruments.

The purpose of testing is to help the participant and to improve the program. Therefore, after the testing has been accomplished, the results should be used appropriately.

Grading in school physical education programs

Giving grades in most school physical education programs is an administrative necessity. The purposes for grading include the following:

1. It indicates student achievement in the areas for which the course or experience is offered.
2. It informs parents, employers, colleges and universities, honorary societies, and other groups of the quality of a pupil's work.
3. It is a motivational device for some students.
4. It is a guide to program planning and for grouping students (grades identify areas of strength and weakness in the curriculum and in the students).
5. It can be a basis for counseling students (abrupt changes in a student's grades might indicate problems).

Because grading is an established custom in the educational system of this country, physical education must conform and grant grades or use some other method of denoting the progress that has been achieved.

Grades have been issued in physical education in several ways, ranging from granting letter or numeral grades to ranking in a class. These grades have also

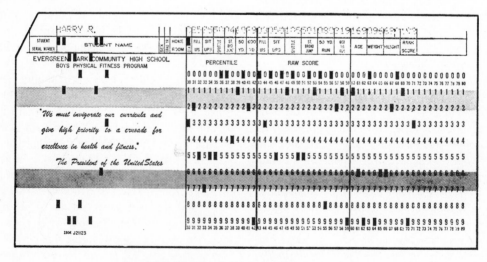

Fig. 19-9. IBM card for recording test results.

From Bucher, C.A., and Koenig, C.R.: Methods and materials for secondary school physical education, ed. 6, 1983, The C.V. Mosby Co.

been based on some factors that have questionable value. Some present practices base grades on such factors as attendance, punctuality, effort, dress, achievement, general attitude, initiative, hygiene, skill, knowledge of rules, and cooperation. Nationally, there seems to be no set formula or procedure. Each individual instructor establishes the basis on which grades should be granted.

The following recommendations represent some advanced thinking among educators in general. At the elementary level especially, the feeling is increasing that it is not wise to issue a single grade or numerical rating, that a descriptive paragraph telling in more detail what progress is being made by the pupil is much better. Discussing such items as a student's strengths and weaknesses and where he or she needs to improve is more meaningful and purposeful. This type of report and talks with parents achieve the purpose of showing to what degree educational objectives are being attained and what needs to be accomplished in the future. This method also has implications for grading above the elementary level.

When grades are given, they should be based on the achievement of objectives—the degree to which the student has achieved the desired outcomes. These objectives should be clear in the instructor's and students' minds at the outset of the course. The individuals receiving the best grades should be those students most nearly achieving the objectives for the course. In physical education the physical, motor, cognitive, and social objectives should all be kept in mind.

The degree to which desired objectives are achieved should be determined objectively rather than subjectively. This means that, wherever possible, scientific evaluation and measurement techniques should be employed. Because there is a dearth of such techniques, some subjective judgments will have to be made.

Grades should be understood by the student. He or she should know how they are arrived at and how the factors that go into the grades are weighed. The grades should also be easily understood by parents, particularly how they relate to the objectives of the course the student is taking. As far as possible, the grades should be expressed in the same manner as grades in other subject matter areas throughout the school. This not only facilitates record keeping and transfer of credits but also places physical education on the same level as other subjects.

Table 19-3 outlines a proposed plan by Dr. Lynn McCraw for grading as a means of assessing the various goals objectively.

CONTRACT GRADING

Contract grading permits the student to choose a standard of performance established by the instructor (sometimes with student participation) and work toward satisfying the contract to receive a certain specified grade. Different grades (A, B, C) require different contract items to be satisfied. To receive an A in a course, the student must complete all the A requirements, as well as satisfactorily complete an examination in that area.

Contract learning is an innovation some school teachers are applying in various subjects to individualize learning and provide for students who have different interests and motivations. These teachers have described the contract-for-grade system as a way in which they can interact with students and both students and teachers have the opportunity to indicate their expectations for the course.

To fulfill contract requirements, students frequently use as resources the school library, programmed texts and other supplemental materials, teacher-student discussions, visual aids, the community, and consultants who are familiar with the subject. The teacher is on call to advise students during and after school hours. The sources of information for the students are as unlimited as their imagination and ingenuity. Attendance in class is not always required. In some schools the students check in to class daily but thereafter are free to go where their resources are located.

Contract learning is an innovation school systems will want to consider as a possible method to personalize and motivate student learning.

PERFORMANCE OBJECTIVES

Performance objectives can also be used as a grading method. An Illinois high school uses this method. The performance objectives were written by a group

Fig. 19-10. Physical education report card, Nashville city schools.

From Bucher, C.A., and Koenig, C.R.: Methods and materials for secondary school physical education, ed. 6, St. Louis, 1983, The C.V. Mosby Co.

PHYSICAL EDUCATION REPORT CARD
NASHVILLE CITY SCHOOLS

Pupil_____ School_____

Homeroom_____Classroom _____Year 19_____ 19_____

GRADE LEVEL	FALL					SPRING					YEAR'S AVERAGE
	1	2	3	Ex	Av	4	5	6	Ex	Av	

Items checked (✔) below need improvement

	1	2	3	4	5	6
Develops co-ordination						
Shows knowledge of rules						
Develops physically						
Strength						
Endurance						
Weight						
Participates						
Dress						
Playing						
Shower						
Attendance (Days absent from class)						
Conduct						

CODE
(Teacher may add plus or minus if she wishes)

A=90 - 100—Consistently does excellent work
B =82 - 89—Does good work
C=75 - 81—Does fair work
D=70 - 74—Low, but passing
F =Below 70—Failing

Comments enclosed Date_____ Date_____ Date_____
Date_____ Date_____ Date_____

Teacher_____

of physical educators and were based on organic, motor, emotional, social, and cognitive goals. For example, a performance objective unit in gymnastics for freshmen was divided into a 10-day introductory unit and a 3-week advanced unit. A lecture and a demonstration of the 40 selected gymnastic stunts were presented to the students, followed by the introductory unit of instruction and practice. The grading system was as follows, based on satisfactory performance as predetermined by the instructor:

16 to 28 stunts—A
10 to 15 stunts—B
6 to 9 stunts—C
3 to 5 stunts—D
0 to 2 stunts—F*

The advanced unit required a 3-week instruction-demonstration period with the students continuing

*Sherman, W.: Performance objectives, Journal of Health, Physical Education, and Recreation **42:**37, 1971.

ATTITUDES AND PRACTICES	Items checked (✓) below need improvement					
	1	2	3	4	5	6
SOCIAL						
Uses self-control						
Is courteous in speech and action						
Co-operates						
Cares for property (incl. textbooks)						
Is considerate toward others						
Respects and obeys school rules						
WORK						
Makes good use of abilities						
Follows directions promptly						
Completes each task						
Works independently						
Uses initiative						
HEALTH						
Maintains personal cleanliness						
Maintains correct posture						
Obeys safety precautions						

Fig. 19-10. cont'd. For legend see opposite page.

PARENT'S SIGNATURE

1. _____
2. _____
3. _____
4. _____
5. _____
6. _____

from the introductory unit. A student who satisfactorily completed 29 to 40 stunts received an A, 16 to 27 stunts a B, and 10 to 15 stunts a C. A performance objective unit was also prepared for sophomores who were required to take a 3-week unit in soccer.

The committee wrote performance objectives for all activities in the 4-year high school curriculum. The freshman and sophomores started in the program with those teachers who desired to work with the performance objective concept. The initial evaluation was positive for both students and teachers involved in the performance-objective units.

INDIVIDUALIZED LEARNING

Individualized learning has had a great impact on education in recent years. Grading concepts have also changed in schools that have adopted the concept of individualized learning. In student-centered learning the following processes are included:

1. Performance objectives are based on psychomotor and cognitive tasks.
2. The individual is allowed to regulate his or her own progress.
3. The teacher is an aid in learning rather than a demonstrator.
4. The gymnasium becomes a resource center that includes areas for audiovisual aids, discussions, practice, and evaluation.
5. Students help in directing each other, as well as themselves.
6. Grading is eliminated and replaced by a progress reporting system.

According to this system, the teacher is an evaluator and determines each student's success in meeting the established educational objectives. The student consults with the teacher concerning his or her progress and comes to the teacher when prepared for the final evaluation, which consists of satisfactory completion of tasks, acknowledgment by other students, teacher approval, and recording progress on a record card. If a student has not completed the tasks successfully, alternative approaches are suggested by the teacher. This one-to-one contact has had positive results in schools that have adopted the individualized learning concept.

Table 19-3. Proposed plan for grading*

Components	Weightings	Instruments
Attitude in terms of Attendance Punctuality Suiting out Participation	5% to 25%	Attendance and other records Teacher observation
Skills in terms of Form in execution of skill Standard of performance Application in game situation	20% to 35%	Objective tests Teacher observation Student evaluation
Physical fitness with emphasis on Muscular strength and endurance Cardiovascular-respiratory endurance Agility Flexibility	20% to 35%	Objective tests Teacher observation
Knowledge and appreciation of Skills Strategy Rules History and terms	5% to 25%	Written tests Teacher observation
Behavior in terms of Social conduct Health and safety practices	5% to 25%	Teacher observation Student evaluation

*From McCraw, L.W.: Principles and practices for assigning grades in physical education, Journal of Health, Physical Education, and Recreation **35**:2, 1964.

Student ....

....   19 .... - 19 ......
Grade
RICHWOODS COMMUNITY HIGH SCHOOL

Progress Report in Physical Education

....
Teacher   Counselor

1st pd.	2nd pd.	3rd pd.	Sem. exam	Sem. avg.	4th pd.	5th pd.	6th pd.	Sem. exam	Sem. avg.	Units crdt.

EXPLANATION OF MARKING SYSTEM

Achievement—Grading for actual work done by the student

A—94-100—Excellent   D—70-77—Below Average
B—86- 93—Above Avg.   F—Below 70—Failure
C—78- 85—Average   E—Conditional
                            Inc.—Incomplete

ACTIVITIES INCLUDED IN GRADING PERIODS

ACTIVITIES	PERIOD					
	1	2	3	4	5	6
Flicker Ball						
Flag Football						
Soccer						
*Field Hockey						
*Speed Ball						
*Campcraft						
Basketball (beginning) (advanced)						
Volleyball (beginning) (advanced)						
Tumbling (beginning) (advanced)						
Apparatus (beginning) (advanced)						
Wrestling (beginning) (advanced)						
Handball						
Badminton						
Recreational Games						
*Fundamental Rhythms—Modern Dance						
Track and Field						
Softball						
Archery						
Golf						
Co. P.E. Social Dance						
Co. P.E. Square Dance						
Co. P.E. Volleyball & Rec. Games						
Driver Training (Classroom)						
Health Education (Classroom)						
*Indicates Girls' Activity Only						

GRADING PROCEDURE

The six week grade is evaluated in the following areas:
1. Performance of Skills
2. Knowledge of Skills and Physical Fitness
3. Social Attitudes including cooperation, sportsmanship, and leadership
4. Hygiene conditions (uniforms, showers), and attendance.

PHYSICAL FITNESS TESTS
(Based on National Norms)

	Trial 1 (Fall)		Trial 2 (Spring)	
	Score	% ile	Score	% ile
Pull-Ups (Boys) (shoulder strength)				
Modified Pull-Ups (Girls) (shoulder strength)				
Sit-Ups (abdominal strength)				
Shuttle Run (agility)				
Standing Broad Jump (leg power)				
50-Yard Dash (speed)				
Softball Throw (arm power)				
600-Yard Run-Walk (endurance)				

The National Norms and Scores are based on Age, Weight, and Height.

PARENT'S SIGNATURE

Your signature means only that you have seen this report.

1st Period..

2nd Period..

3rd Period..

4th Period..

5th Period..

Each absence, however short, interferes with the student's progress.

Fig. 19-11. Progress report in physical education, Richwoods Community High School, Peoria Heights, Ill.

From Bucher, C.A., and Koenig, C.R.: Methods and materials for secondary school physical education, ed. 6, St. Louis, 1983, The C.V. Mosby Co.

Fig. 19-12. Teacher of physical education discussing physical education contract with student in Omaha Public Schools.

Fig. 19-13. Grading based on performance objectives in Omaha Public Schools.

PASSING OR FAILING IN PHYSICAL EDUCATION*

In response to numerous inquiries from school officials, the following is intended to clarify the statement that boards of education may not refuse graduation or promotion because of failure in physical education.

Physical education is required for all pupils by Education Law and Regulations of the Commissioner of Education. It is expected that each pupil will participate in such classes and that he will exert sufficient effort to enable him to achieve his optimal progress toward all program objectives. If a pupil refuses to attend physical education classes and otherwise does not fulfill course requirements approved by the board of education, and prompt and appropriate notification is given to all concerned, a failing mark may be given and graduation withheld until such time as the deficiency has been removed.

On the other hand, a pupil who fulfills all the requirements and has exhibited acceptable evidence of satisfactory progress in terms of his abilities but who has been unable to meet minimal standards of physical performance may not be given a failing mark in physical education.

Pupils who act in ways deemed undesirable as good school citizens while participating in physical education classes, such as disobeying the teacher, refusing to exert reasonable effort or deliberately violating stated policies and procedures, should be treated as disciplinary cases.

Physical education is an integral part of the school curriculum. It is recognized that achievement of the program's major goals including physical fitness, skills, knowledge, social qualities and attitudes will help provide valuable assets for each pupil. Therefore, every effort should be made to insure that physical education is a meaningful and profitable experience for each boy and girl, particularly for those who possess lower levels of physical ability. One of the most valuable outcomes of a physical education program is the inculcation of a strong appreciation of, desire for and interest in participation in physical activities which will endure throughout life. Would failing in physical education help to reach this goal?

Reviewed and Approved by Division of Law,
State Education Department,
January, 1969

*From New York State Education Department: Curriculum guide; physical education in the secondary school.

SELF-ASSESSMENT TESTS

These tests are to assist students in determining if material and competencies presented in this chapter have been mastered.

1. Define the term *measurement* and indicate why it is important to the successful administration of any physical education and athletic program. What is the relationship of measurement to objectives?

2. List as many measurement techniques as possible used in schools and in programs for adults. Take three of these techniques and describe their use in detail.

3. Develop what you consider to be a satisfactory and practical measurement program for determining the physical fitness of students in a high school and in an adult physical education program.

4. As an administrator of a physical education and athletic program, prepare a list of *minimum* and *desirable* standards for a school physical education program and for an adult program.

5. Explain how performance objectives can be used as a basis for grading. Develop a performance-based grading plan for a unit of a physical education track and field program.

SELECTED REFERENCES

American Alliance for Health, Physical Education, and Recreation: Completed research in health, physical education, and recreation, Washington, D.C., 1975, The Alliance.

American Alliance for Health, Physical Education, and Recreation: AAHPER youth fitness manual, Washington, D.C., 1976, The Alliance.

American Association of Health, Physical Education, and Recreation: Sports skills test manuals (archery, basketball, football, softball), 1966, The Association.

American Association for Health, Physical Education, and Recreation: Grading in physical education, Journal of Health, Physical Education, and Recreation 38:34, 1967.

Aten, R.: Formative and summative evaluation in the instructional process, Journal of Physical Education and Recreation 51:68-69, September 1980.

Bucher, C.A.: Foundations of physical education, St. Louis, 1983, The C.V. Mosby Co.

Bucher, C.A., and Koenig, C.: Methods and materials for secondary school physical education, St. Louis, 1983, The C.V. Mosby Co.

Clarke, H.H.: Application of measurement to health and physical education, ed. 5, Englewood Cliffs, N.J., 1976, Prentice-Hall, Inc.

Dotson, C.O., and Kirkendall, D.R.: Statistics for physical education, health and recreation. New York, 1974, Harper & Row, Publishers.

Fabricius, H., and others: Grading in physical education, Journal of Health, Physical Education, and Recreation 38:5, 1967.

Fast, B.: Contracting, Journal of Health, Physical Education, and Recreation 42:31, 1971.

Hall, J.T., and others: Administration; principles, theory and practice—with applications to physical education, Pacific Palisades, Calif., 1973, Goodyear Publishing Co., Inc.

Lawrence, T.: Appraisal of emotional health at the secondary school level, The Research Quarterly 37:2, 1966.

Liba, M.R., and Loy, J.W.: Some comments on grading, The Physical Educator 22:4, 1965.

Mathews, D.K.: Measurement in physical education, ed. 2, Philadelphia, 1963, W.B. Saunders Co.

McDonald, E.D., and Yeates, M.E.: Measuring improvement in physical education, Journal of Physical Education and Recreation 50:79-80, Feburary 1979.

National Education Association: Reports to parents, National Association Research Bulletin 45:2, 1967.

Oxendine, J.B.: Social development—the forgotten objective? Journal of Health, Physical Education, and Recreation 37:5, 1966.

Plowman, S., and Falls, H.B.: AAHPERD Youth Fitness Test Revision, Journal of Physical Education and Recreation 49:22, November-December 1978.

President's Council on Physical Fitness and Sports: National adult physical fitness survey, Washington, D.C., 1973, The Council.

Proctor, A.J.: Computers in tests and measurements courses, Journal of Physical Education and Recreation 51:73, 75, October 1980.

Sherman, W.: Performance objectives, Journal of Health, Physical Education, and Recreation 42:37, 1971.

Shrader, R.: Individualized approach to learning, Journal of Health, Physical Education, and Recreation 42:33, 1971.

Smith, C.D.: Fitness testing questions about how, why, and with what, Journal of Health, Physical Education, and Recreation 43:37, 1972.

Smith, B., and Lerch, H.: Contract grading, The Physical Educator 29:80, 1972.

Solleder, M.K.: Evaluation instruments in health education, Washington, D.C., 1965, American Association for Health, Physical Education, and Recreation.

Trump, C.: Meaningful grading. Scholastic Coach 35:44, 1966.

Verducci, F.M.: Measurement concepts in physical education, St. Louis, 1980, The C.V. Mosby Co.

Weber, L., and Paul, T.: Approaches to grading in physical education. The Physical Educator 28:59, 1972.

Zeigler, E.F., and Spaeth, M.J.: Administrative theory and practice in physical education and athletics, Englewood Cliffs, N.J., 1975, Prentice-Hall, Inc.

Index